CONSUMER BEHAVIOR

Concepts and Strategies

Harold W. Berkman
School of Business Administration
University of Miami

Christopher C. Gilson
Rapp & Collins/Doyle Dane Bernbach
New York

Kent Publishing Company
Boston, Massachusetts
A Division of Wadsworth, Inc.

To Greta and Jerry
—HWB

To Edda Nell and Christopher
—CCG

Printed in the United States of America
Printing (last digit): 9   8   7   6   5   4   3

Library of Congress Cataloging in Publication Data

Berkman, Harold W.
Consumer behavior.

Bibliography: p.
Includes index.
1. Consumers.   2. Consumers—United States.
I. Gilson, Christopher C., joint author.   II. Title.
HF5415.3.B42   658.8′34   77-8959
ISBN 0-8221-0199-8

Interior design: Kadi Tint
Cover: Preston J. Mitchell

CONTENTS

TO THE STUDENT

We wrote this book to help you get what nobody gave us when we were in school, just a few years ago, namely, the chance to apply an insider's knowledge of consumer behavior to real-world marketing strategies. This is training that will make you more marketable, because you will learn how to solve the kind of un-textbook problems you'll find in business—no matter what your major or specialty might be.

You're allowed to ask why, if this information is so valuable, we aren't practicing it instead of preaching to you. The fact is, we do practice what we preach, every day, as a retail-chain owner turned professor and a marketing executive. We can offer you more than theoretical concepts.

Specifically, we can offer you:

1. Sound theory of why consumers behave as they do, which will give you a depth that many business people lack (and admire in others).

2. An understanding of consumer research operations and jargon, so you will recognize the often-exotic techniques that are enjoying great popularity in today's marketing arena.

3. Selected applications of theory and research to business problems you will encounter.

4. The opportunity to assume "jobs" like product manager for a large packaged goods company, advertising creative director, political campaign manager, department store executive, feature film researcher, and many other positions that will let you apply what you learn to actual (and often sticky) marketing situations.

So, why not take a few minutes to look through the book. Note the overview at the beginning of each chapter telling you what you'll find; the objectives telling you what to remember to succeed in the course; and the applications and assignments.

We think you'll see for yourself what you can expect to do for a Consumer Behavior course.

And what a Consumer Behavior course can do for you.

TO THE INSTRUCTOR

Aimed directly at the business student, this text concentrates on two objectives: (1) to build a working knowledge of consumer behavior concepts, research procedure, and key findings from all relevant disciplines; (2) to show exactly how that knowledge is used to solve real-world marketing problems.

The dual focus reflects our shared philosophy about the consumer behavior course. As a marketing professor with business experience and a marketing practitioner with teaching experience, we feel that each student should recognize what he or she is learning as valuable "insider" information. And that any professor who uses this text should be able to adapt the material without difficulty to his or her own perspective and style.

During the past ten years, many consumer behavior texts have surfaced to match the growing popularity of the course. We are introducing this book in response to comments from professors, students, and marketing practitioners that certain improvements might be made—especially in readability, increased emphasis on the business of marketing, and teaching flexibility.

Readability Every text preface mentions that the authors have taken pains to offer an exciting treatment of their subject matter. Yet students and professors alike still pose this criticism of existing texts above all others.

A quick look at Chapter 1 will reveal a style that is closer to conversation than "textbook-ese." In the initial sections, scholarly concepts unfold at a measured pace, so the readers develop a feeling for the material before plunging into thorny questions of research, methodology, and interpretation of findings. At the same time, sophistication in the behavioral sciences and marketing is established early, through careful definition of important terms and a liberal sprinkling of the marketing vocabulary which students will rapidly encounter in today's business world.

For a smooth transition between topics, an introductory overview appears at the beginning of each chapter, set off in italics. On the facing page of the chapter opening is a statement of chapter objectives and the page numbers referring to the corresponding text material.

Marketing Applications and Activities At the end of each chapter, theoretical material is made "actionable" through Marketing Applications—clear statements that indicate exactly how the information can be profitably used. Finally, three types of student activities called Research, Creative, and Managerial Assignments conclude each chapter. There are sixty in all. Each activity places the student in a position of decision-making responsibility. Many involve contact with consumers and members of the local business community; others may be solved through individual creativity or multiple-source research. But all of the projects build marketable skills for tackling business and public policy decisions.

Research Assignments place the student in positions such as research consultant to a new magazine, owner of a cable TV franchise, and director of a "stop-smoking" clinic. In assuming these "jobs," the student designs questionnaires, interviews respondents, organizes data for presentations, and performs some of the simpler statistical operations used in consumer research.

Creative Assignments offer experience in completing the tasks faced by advertising and promotion people, graphics consultants, public relations counselors, and other professionals who use consumer information in creative problem solving. Because the advertising industry remains the most voracious user of consumer research, many of the projects require developing strategies and concepts for advertising communications. Others entail naming new brands, making packaging and sales promotion decisions, and evaluating other marketers' ads for effectiveness.

Managerial Assignments may usually be performed by studying a problem, synthesizing available information, and making effective presentations with recommendations for action. These range from product management duties in a large corporation to deciding whether to legalize gambling in a cash-poor city.

Because the text is designed to adapt to the needs of instructors, rather than vice versa, no substantial revisions in existing lecture material should be necessary. Individual chapters may be emphasized or de-emphasized according to the instructor's own teaching philosophy. Instructors who choose to emphasize a cognitive or information process approach to the course, for example, may wish to introduce individual variables before sociocultural variables in the following sequence of chapter number and title:

 1 Consumer Behavior: An Overview
 2 Theories and Models
 3 Research and Measurement Techniques
 9 Learning
10 Perception
11 Motivation and Personality
12 Attitudes
13 Attitude Change
 4 Culture and Consumption
 5 Subcultures in the United States
 6 Social Organization
 7 Social Class
 8 The Family
14 Media Communications
15 Interpersonal Communications
16 Consumer Choice Behavior
17 Purchasing and Postpurchase Behavior
18 Diffusion of Innovation

19 Life Style and Psychographics
20 Consumerism and Social Responsibility

The social science approach features contributions from anthropology, sociology, and psychology. Consumer decision making and market research are de-emphasized. The sequence of chapters is as follows: 1, 4, 5, 6, 7, 8, 9, 10, 12, 13, 11, 18. An optional group of chapters is: 14, 15, 16, 17.

The life-style approach introduces the life-style concept early in the course as an organizational structure and discusses current life style and psychographic research. This orientation will be especially useful for students developing competencies in market research. The sequence of chapters is as follows: 1, 3, 19, 2, 4, 5, 6, 7, 8, 18, 9, 10, 12, 13, 11, 14, 15, 16, 17, 20.

Additional plans to accommodate courses of varying lengths may be found in the Professional Supplement.

We wish to thank the many people who have made significant contributions to this text. For their valuable insights, suggestions, improvements, we are grateful to our reviewers, Daniel R Allen, Foothill College; Kenneth A. Coney, Arizona State University; Mike Harvey, Southern Methodist University; David Kurtz, Eastern Michigan University; John B. McFall, California State University, San Diego; and William G. Zikmund, Oklahoma State University; and our talented editors, Elaine Linden and Bernice Lifton. For research assistance, we are greatly indebted to Professors Sylvia Malamud and Ruth Macy of the B. Davis Schwartz Memorial Library, C. W. Post Center, Long Island University, to Karen Berkman for psychological research, and we wish to express our special appreciation to Muriel Berkman for tracking down citations long missing and feared lost. For their contributions to the field of consumer behavior, we gratefully acknowledge the scholars, practitioners, and consumers whose work we have cited here. For her uncanny ability to decipher and type the manuscript, we thank Bernice Adler. Finally, for creative assistance and inspiration, we thank Rosemary Samuels; Sara Chase; Eugene Powers, Bechtel Corporation; Dean Kenneth L. Meinke, University of Hartford; and Donald Turner, Doubleday Advertising Company.

Harold W. Berkman
Christopher C. Gilson

I
INTRODUCTION TO CONSUMER BEHAVIOR

Consumer Behavior: An Overview
Theories and Models
Research and Measurement Techniques

OBJECTIVES

ONE

Consumer Behavior: An Overview

Scratch the surface of any consumer and you will find an intricate web of complex, often conflicting needs: a restless craving for frequent stimulation in the form of new products and services, but a growing skepticism toward the advertising messages that promise to gratify those cravings; a set of established preferences for some products, but a willingness to switch to new ones under the right conditions. What influences create these needs and, most important, how can marketers recognize and serve them? These are the subject matter of the study of consumer behavior.

Most business students are familiar with the marketing concept—the focusing of all marketing activity to satisfying consumer needs. Implicit in this concept is the central role of the consumer, because meeting these needs requires some accurate knowledge of who the consumer really is and what he or she really wants. This text is designed to help you develop that understanding for today's competitive market place. It combines the social scientist's perspective of influences on consumption—a perspective which many practicing marketers unfortunately lack—with a view of current behavioral research findings and the many opportunities to apply them in real-world marketing activities.

The following chapter introduces the nature of consumer behavior, offers an overview of the text, and discusses the ways consumer behavioral information may be used for more effective marketing decisions and more responsive public policy. Some specific topics include:

• Why the reasons you chose your last tube of toothpaste are more complex than you might imagine.

• What marketers learn about consumers from cultural anthropologists, sociologists, and psychologists.

• How your values compare with those of the "typical American" consumer.

3

• How a knowledge of consumer behavior can enhance your own marketability.

Like any specialized field, the study of consumer behavior has given birth to its own vocabulary, derived from both the social sciences and marketing. Because they are frequently encountered when dealing with researchers and practitioners in marketing applications, these are the terms used, with appropriate explanation, throughout the text.

Consumer Decision Making

Think back for a moment and recall the last time you bought a tube of toothpaste. Unless it was quite recently, your recollection of such a minor purchase is probably vague. But a number of high-salaried people would relish the opportunity to find out why you chose the brand you brought home, where you purchased it, and how soon you will be back for your next tube. They include marketing managers, product development scientists, advertising men and women, market researchers, distributing and retail executives. All share a deep concern (which may extend to keeping their jobs) over why, how, and where consumers obtain products and services. And you, in this instance as a consumer of toothpaste, have been a target of their collective efforts since you first learned to wield a toothbrush.

What undoubtedly seemed at the toothpaste counter to be an instant, unthinking decision was in reality a highly complex process fraught with variables. Consider the *cultural* framework of your buying decision. Most people in the United States learn early in life that toothbrushing is an important ritual. First we hear that it is good for our teeth. Later we recognize that toothbrushing affords two culturally prized features—a gleaming smile and pristine breath. All three reasons for consuming relatively large quan-

tities of toothpaste are cultural values transmitted from generation to generation.

Perhaps you always buy the same brand of toothpaste. *Sociologically,* your buying decision may have been influenced by your family. You may have purchased the brand your parents are inclined to use, or chosen some other brand because your parents do *not* use it. Seeing the brands your friends prefer may have affected your decision. Even the social class to which you belong may have determined to some degree the toothpaste you purchased, the size of the tube, and the amount of attention you devoted to its price.

Your decision also took place in a *psychological* context. For purely individual reasons, you may be more intrigued with toothpaste as a whitening cosmetic than as a decay-preventive dentifrice. You may remember a television commercial for the brand you purchased. Perhaps the advertising appeal used to persuade you to buy that brand coincided with a desire on your part for sparkling white teeth. Or possibly a design genius created a startling package which virtually stole your attention away from all other brands on the shelf.

Product attributes and the *buying environment* may have affected your decision as well. Maybe the brand you chose was on sale, or was in the most convenient spot on the shelf when you were pressed for time. Perhaps your usual brand was out of stock and you were forced into a second choice. If so, you might have bought a smaller tube of the latter rather than continuing your search at another store. You may not have intended to buy toothpaste that day at all, but a point-of-purchase display offering a contest or give-away compelled you to buy anyway.

These are only a few of the variables that could explain your last toothpaste choice. And this example concerns a *packaged goods* purchase—one of the simplest consumer decision processes. When the product is a *considered* purchase such as a stereo system, automobile, European vacation, or condominium apartment, the considerations multiply. Because we are beginning to recognize the processes and determinants of consumer decision making in their full complexity, the study of consumer behavior has become vitally important to anyone who plans to pursue a career in marketing.

Scope of the Consumer Behavior Field

In the United States, people devote a considerable portion of their time to consumption. Few products and services in our economy are free for the asking; most of us must purchase our own food, transportation, homes, furnishings, higher education, the means for enjoying leisure, health care, and so on. The field of consumer behavior explores *why* people make certain purchasing decisions, *what* products and services they buy, *where* they buy them, *how* they use them, the *frequency* with which they purchase them, and the consumer *decision process* in action.

Consumer Behavior Defined

In the above context, consumer behavior may be defined as *the activities of people engaged in actual or potential use of market items—whether products, services, retail environments, or ideas.*

From the toothpaste example alone, it follows that the analysis of consumer behavior should draw its findings from a variety of disciplines. And so it does. *Anthropology* contributes an understanding of the cultural setting in which decisions are made. In addition to the mainstream cultural values that may be characterized as American, subcultural influences—whether ethnic, regional, or based on other factors—affect buying decisions. *Sociology* and *social psychology* bolster our knowledge of how consumers behave by pointing out the effects of group behavior on individual decision-making. Family, peer group, and social class differences emerge as particularly influential in purchasing decisions. *Psychology*, the study of individual behavior, offers insights about consumers' personal characteristics such as learning experiences, perception, attitudes, motivation, and personality. *Marketing research* provides information about consumer responses to product attributes (such as, pricing and packaging) and to the environment surrounding purchasing decisions. *Economics,* the study of how a society distributes its resources, sets the larger context in which all consumer behavior occurs.

Consumer Terminology

Because consumers and their activities are referred to in a number of ways, some distinctions will be made here.

Consumers versus Buyers   Although the term "buyer" often serves to describe a specialized retailing executive, "consumer" and "buyer" are used interchangeably here. This, however, leads to a second differentiation, that between ultimate consumers on the one hand and industrial and institutional consumers on the other.

Ultimate Consumers versus Industrial and Institutional Consumers   The final, or ultimate, consumer takes market items from channels of distribution and uses them at the household level. Most marketing activity is geared to the ultimate consumer, who will be our focus of discussion unless otherwise noted. Industrial and institutional consumers are generally those buying items for resale or for use in making some product or service avail-

able to ultimate consumers. The purchasing executive who buys pipe systems for a beverage factory is an industrial consumer. The instructor who ordered this book from the publisher for you to read ultimately is an institutional consumer. Because industrial and institutional markets have attracted much attention recently in consumer behavior, examples from both occur throughout the text.

Consuming versus Purchasing   As may be inferred from the definition of consumer behavior, purchasing represents only one aspect of consumer decisions and activities. It refers to obtaining any market item from some channel of distribution, such as buying a can of soda at the delicatessen. But purchasing is not confined to the retail environment, as descriptions of catalog and other nonretail shopping will indicate. At the industrial and institutional levels, purchasing is often the term applied to the consumption process.

Consumers versus Customers   Marketing people usually refer to the consumers who use, or might use, their specific products and services as their customers. These are the individuals who collectively form target markets for different items. But everyone who buys and uses *any* item is a consumer.

An Overview of Consumer Behavior

The approach taken in this text begins with a multidisciplinary introduction to theory and research (Section I). Because cultural and social influences form the boundaries of consumer behavior, these variables are con-

sidered next (Section II). Then individual determinants of consumer buying patterns are analyzed (Section III). Consumer decision making is then examined against this background of environmental and individual factors (Section IV). And, finally, current directions of study are explored, with some discussion of consumerism and the recent emergence of the socially-responsible consumer (Section V). An initial, sweeping picture of each of these facets of consumer behavior will make it easier for the reader to grasp their fine points as they are presented in subsequent chapters.

The consumption process described here may thus be viewed as:

| Macro-perspective (cultural influences) | → | Group perspective (social influences) | → | Individual perspective (psychological influences) |

Emergence of Consumer Behavior Field

The field of consumer behavior is relatively new. Even the earliest formal studies may be traced back no further than the late 1940s, and most of the research now available has been generated only in the past fifteen to twenty years. But, for a young discipline, consumer behavior studies have proliferated at an almost dazzling rate. This is due primarily to three factors: (1) the centrality of the consumer in contemporary marketing practice; (2) the interdisciplinary nature of the field, which permits borrowing from many older disciplines; and (3) the growth of computer technology, which has enabled researchers to "simulate" consumer behavior electronically. Increasingly, research studies are developing along rigorous lines, highly quantitative and objective rather than subjective and difficult to repeat. An impressive body of literature grows monthly in publications such as the *Journal of Marketing,* the *Journal of Marketing Research* and the *Journal of Consumer Research.* And investigations into consumer behavior patterns are continually sponsored by business, academic, and government resources.

Theory and Measurement

The role of scientific *theory* in consumer behavior and the development of *research models* to test various theories (chapter 2) have come to overshadow more traditional approaches to explaining what makes consumers behave as they do. The traditional theories usually were a marketer's own opinions or expressed the view of economic philosophers that a consumer was a purely rational creature who responded mechanistically to economic laws. The newer approaches are theory-based in psychology, sociology, and related fields and are often accompanied by "models." A model is essentially a representation of some behavioral system which is used to explain behavior in that system. One simple model developed by Allport to depict the relationship of sociocultural, social and individual factors in consumer behavior is shown in Figure 1-1.

Like many theories of consumer behavior, the research and measurement techniques of this field (chapter 3) have been adapted from other disciplines, particularly psychology. These include attitude scaling techniques (asking consumers to vote or compare brands,

Figure 1-1   Allport consumer behavior model.

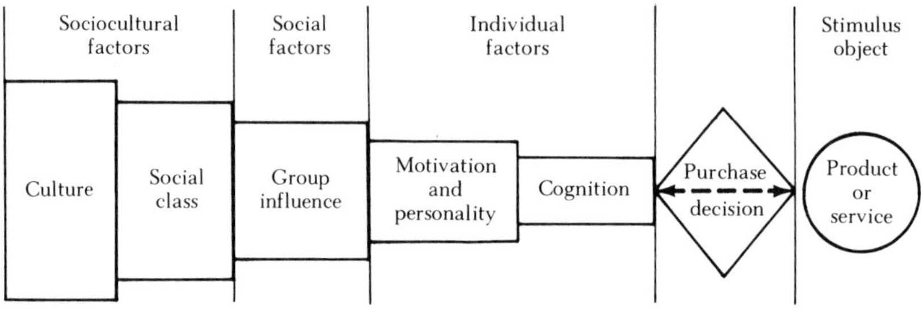

Source: Gordon W. Allport, The Nature of Prejudice, *(Reading, Mass.,: Addison-Wesley Publishing Co., Inc. 1954), p. 207.*

advertisements, or some other item along a continuum), and occasionally projective techniques (attempting to uncover "latent" reasons for consumer buying behavior through methods originally developed for psychiatric interviews).

Another familiar staple of consumer research is *demographic* data, which is information about the age, sex, marital status, income, occupation, education, and geographic location of consumers for use in market segmentation.

Cultural-Social Influences

The cultural setting in which any consumer behavior occurs (chapter 4) will affect the products and services we want (or are allowed to have), the ways in which we use them, and the methods we employ to get them.[1] Because marketing is increasingly a multinational activity, marketers are becoming as concerned with consumer behavior in other cultures as in our own. Some cultural traits are universal. Others vary considerably from one

culture to the next, and many international marketing efforts have failed because these differences were ignored.

Consumer activity in the United States is strongly influenced by the values and artifacts we call the American cultural system.[2] This system has always been characterized by rapid technological changes and value shifts, but some values seem to be more enduring than others. In the twentieth century, American culture has reflected a distinct "consumption ethic" based upon affluence and gratification of desires through material acquisition.[3] And our acquisitiveness is well integrated within a system of traditional American values such as self-reliance, orderliness, and optimism about the future.[4]

In view of social and economic developments during the past few years, we might question whether this spirit still prevails. Certainly there has been a movement away from material possessions on the part of many young people. But most not-so-young individuals and the majority of people who make up our "Youth Markets" continue to exhibit life styles based on abundance. The products and services desired have been modified somewhat; where young people once coveted sports cars, for example, they now appear to place more emphasis on foreign travel. And despite the infusion of new cultural values—relaxed sexual mores, permissiveness in education, and so on—most Americans are still seen as unshaken from traditional values.

William Wells offers some insights into typical American values today. Through a methodology known as *life-style research,* Wells investigated the hypothesis that forces of social and economic change have turned conventional attitudes toward the good life into a pattern of anxiety, alienation, and apathy. He concludes that, on the contrary, the majority of people in the United States portray themselves as "happy, homeloving, clean, and square."[5]

Selected questions from Wells's survey are reproduced in Table 1-1, and your own responses may be gauged against a value profile of the "typical American." Indicate your degree of agreement with each of the following statements by scoring *A* for strong agreement, *D* for strong disagreement, and *M* for a middle-value response. Results obtained from the survey are indicated in the footnote.*

Still, many traditional American values are changing, due to influences such as the counterculture movement of the late 1960s, economic changes, depleted natural resources, and various other factors. Thus both traditional and emergent values will be analyzed in some detail in chapter 4.

While many aspects of American culture are homogenized by national marketing and media, great diversity may be found in *subcultures* throughout the United States (chapter 5). Whether an individual belongs to

a black, Jewish, or Mexican-American subculture helps to determine the products and services he or she will use. Other subcultures with distinct consumer profiles include the young, upper socioeconomic "singles" market; the aging; and an ever-present subculture of the urban and rural poor. As well as defining certain buying patterns for their members, subcultures tend to introduce their own artifacts to mainstream American culture.

Societal influences upon consumer behavior (chapter 6) are just as pervasive as cultural influences. For example, consumer buying patterns are affected by how people "learn" acceptable life styles in American society; how reference groups such as family, peer groups, and other types of human relationships determine individual consumption; and how social changes such as the emancipation of women are influencing product and service use.

Despite changes in relative income among white- and blue-collar groups, social classes are alive and well in the United States (chapter 7). This particular kind of reference group remains a popular focus of consumer research, and may be a better predictor of buying behavior than income alone.[6] Two standard classification schemes for identifying social class membership are presented, along with some indications that these class structures are changing. Because social class provides a principal indicator of consumer preferences, the relationship between an individual's social class and that person's buying behavior are outlined.

The *family* as a social unit (chapter 8) wields a major and continuing influence over individual consumer behavior.[7] Additionally, a tremendous number of consumer decisions are made not individually, but together with other family members. And the relative weight which each family member will bring

*Survey results: Questions 1–15: M; Questions 16–25: A; Questions 26–30: D.

Table 1-1   "Typical American" Values Questionnaire

_____ 1. A house should be dusted and polished at least three times a week.

_____ 2. My choice of brands for many products is influenced by advertising.

_____ 3. Classical music is more interesting than popular music.

_____ 4. I buy many things with a credit card or a charge card.

_____ 5. The government in Washington is too big and powerful.

_____ 6. I often try new brands before my friends and neighbors do.

_____ 7. I usually look for the lowest possible prices when I shop.

_____ 8. Most big companies are just out for themselves.

_____ 9. Magazines are more interesting than television.

_____ 10. Every family should own a dog.

_____ 11. The television set should not be in the living room.

_____ 12. I exercise regularly.

_____ 13. I hate to get up in the morning.

_____ 14. A good mother will not serve her family TV dinners.

_____ 15. I sometimes influence what my friends buy.

_____ 16. It is important to have a well-stocked first-aid kit in the home.

_____ 17. There is too much advertising on television.

_____ 18. My family's health is excellent.

_____ 19. When buying appliances, it pays to get the best model even though it is more expensive.

_____ 20. You get what you pay for most of the time.

_____ 21. Once I find a brand I like, I stick to it.

_____ 22. Our home is furnished for comfort, not for style.

_____ 23. I like television news programs.

_____ 24. Air pollution is one of our biggest problems today.

_____ 25. Everyone should take walks, bicycle, garden, or otherwise exercise several times a week.

_____ 26. I spend too much time talking on the telephone.

_____ 27. Grocery shopping is a waste of time.

_____ 28. I have used Metrecal or other diet foods at least one meal a day.

_____ 29. In the last ten years, we have lived in at least three different cities.

_____ 30. I spend money on myself that I should spend on the family.

Source: William D. Wells, "It's a Wyeth, not a Warhol, World," Harvard Business Review, No. 48 (January-February, 1970).

to bear on any decision depends on the type of product or service considered. Husbands tend to maintain final authority over some decisions while other choices are dominated by wives or, sometimes, children. How families behave as consumer units, how consumption needs change over the family "life cycle," and how children themselves behave as consumers point up some considerations often neglected by marketers.

Individual Influences

Beyond the environmental influences, cultural and social, that affect consumer decisions, each consumer behaves as a unique individual in adopting a personal life style and buying the products and services which augment that style. Most of our current knowledge about consumer behavior comes from the discipline of psychology, which directs itself to the study of individual behavior.

Like virtually all other human activities, consumer behavioral patterns are *learned* (chapter 9). No one is born with certain purchasing predispositions (just as there are no born athletes or musicians). Buying habits or "loyalties" are learned through experience. Because a major marketing goal is to build consistent consumer preferences for a given brand or store over all others, marketers attempt to create *brand loyalties* by studying and applying principles of habit formation from learning theory. Provided with information about a consumer's past choice behavior, we may predict future purchasing behavior with reasonable accuracy through *probability models*.[8] Learning theory offers specific information about how advertising may be made more effective by explaining how consumers discriminate among ads, learn and retain information from media, and why they may easily forget that information if it is not constantly repeated.

The role of *perception* in consumer decisions (chapter 10) draws upon another broad set of findings from psychology. Different consumers perceive the same products and services quite differently. These variations are due to physiological traits such as the acuity of one's senses; to individual percep-

tions of a brand's *image* (which has been created primarily through packaging, advertising, and other marketing techniques); to the fact that consumers cannot possibly notice all that goes on around them, but must perceive *selectively*; and to the individual personality characteristics of any one consumer. Also, perceptions of product qualities such as *price* will determine whether a consumer accepts or rejects most items. Finally, *risk* perception enters into many consumer decisions—even those that seem as spontaneous or trivial as which brand of antiperspirant to buy.[9]

Questions of consumer motivation and personality (chapter 11) generate much interest but few universally accepted conclusions. During the 1950s, a technique known as *motivation research* was used to probe "hidden" consumer needs for buying various items. This approach yielded exotic findings such as "A woman is very serious when she bakes a cake because unconsciously she is going through the symbolic act of giving birth" and "A man buys a convertible as a substitute mistress."[10] The popularity of this technique has waned considerably, but *personality* research remains a device for relating psychological characteristics of different consumers to their patterns of product use. For instance, personality traits such as "aggressiveness" and "compliance" have been applied to distinguish the consumers likely to buy certain brands of packaged goods from those less apt to buy those brands.[11] And other researchers contend that "achievement" needs may determine whether an automobile buyer will choose a Ford versus a Chevrolet.[12]

Attitudes (chapter 12) are considered to be the single most critical influence affecting consumer decision making. A consumer's attitude toward some market item is a predisposition to buy or not to buy. If you love a particular singer's style, your positive attitude will probably make you a likely candidate for any new album of that artist's, even if you haven't heard the particular songs. Negative attitudes are just as influential. When an airline loses your luggage the first time you fly with them, your soured attitude will predispose you to plan future flights with another carrier. Thus attitudes can be pursued as one of the few reasonably accurate predictors of actual buying behavior. This is why marketers, as well as politicians, religious leaders, and others concerned with popular acceptance of what they have to offer, devote much energy to finding out how people feel about things—and spend money on advertising and public relations campaigns which attempt to nurture favorable consumer attitudes.

Once formed, attitudes are stubbornly resistant to change (chapter 13). Yet the prospect of persuading consumers to change their attitudes is both interesting to academic researchers and attractive to marketers. Is attitude change ever a realistic marketing goal? Sometimes. The most successful strategy involves designing persuasive communications to change the cognitive structure of attitudes.[13] But even the most sophisticated approach to modifying consumer attitudes will, in most cases, be a risky proposition at best.

Consumer Information Processing and Decision Making

The consumer thus enters into each buying situation with a unique set of environmental and individual variables influencing his or her behavior. These factors will be active throughout the process of receiving and using information to make decisions.

Buying decisions are affected by *media communications* (chapter 14), because media serve the consumer with two distinct information functions. As entertainment vehicles, the media provide behavioral cues about what people are wearing, how they interact with each other, the kinds of cars they are driving, and other opportunities for consumer "identification" with well-known users of various products and services. As marketing vehicles, the media carry advertising messages designed to prod consumers into buying specific brands, shopping at particular stores, clipping coupons for "cents-off," or giving to the United Fund. The degree of media influence is determined by factors such as exposure, advertising effectiveness, and consumer characteristics regulating an individual's susceptibility to influence.

Interpersonal communications (chapter 15), also enter into consumer buying decisions. In our search for the products and services that will provide us with the greatest satisfaction, we communicate with other consumers who can help us. Certain individuals who are authoritative in the areas where we require information, say, in buying a car or choosing an educational program, are known as "opinion leaders." Opinion leaders, of course, are desirable targets for marketing efforts, so these individuals have been the subjects of considerable research. Some consumers are more susceptible to personal influence than others.[14] Similarly, some product purchases are more likely to involve interpersonal communication, such as those highly visible ones that tend to define the personalities or life styles of consumers who buy them.

Consumer *choice* behavior (chapter 16) entails the critical selection of one product, store, or brand over another and the pre- and post-choice attitudes and activities contributing to that selection.[15] Some of the components of choice behavior include need recognition, search, brand comprehension, and evaluation.[16] As a somewhat oversimplified example, if you lose your wristwatch but still have to know the time regularly, this is called "need recognition." You could decide to replace the watch with the same brand and model and end the choice sequence by just deciding where to buy it, or you could search for information about other brands and develop a "brand comprehension"[17] as to the product category of watch brands with which you are familiar. Then you could evaluate the alternatives available to you and choose the brand, model, and store according to a number of product and personal variables.

Purchasing behavior (chapter 17) summarizes what occurs when a consumer enters a retail establishment and makes an actual purchase. This behavior will depend on factors such as whether the purchase was planned or the result of an unplanned "impulse," the physical attributes of the store and the sales situation including product displays and pricing, the interaction between consumer and salesperson, the influence of special sales, and the ability of the consumer to "bargain" successfully.[18] The dimension of post-purchase satisfaction (or dissatisfaction) is an important final outcome of purchase behavior that may or may not affect subsequent purchasing.

Current Topics in Consumer Behavior

Every year a vast number of new products and services greet consumers; some are accepted and popularized almost immediately (like the skimobile) while others simply flop (like striped toothpaste). In marketing research parlance, a new product is known as an "innovation" and the process through which consumers adopt and continue using a new product over time is called *diffusion of innovation* (chapter 18).[19] Whether consumers will accept or reject a new product involves several factors: the characteristics of the product itself (is it really an innovation or just a dressed-up version of some existing product?), the communication processes accompanying the innovation (both media and interpersonal varieties), and the characteristics of the consumers who are expected to adopt it (some consumers are much more likely to accept innovations than others).[20] The diffusion process is a topic of critical interest to marketers, and is discussed in this text with examples from the areas of fashion, packaged goods marketing, and adoptions at the retail distribution and industrial buying levels.

One increasingly popular technique in consumer study is *life-style and psychographic* research (chapter 19), which combines demographic data about consumers with information about their activities, interests, opinions, and their use patterns for different products, services, and media.[21]

Profiles of "heavy" users of certain products and media may be drawn to distinguish them from "light" or "nonusers." This methodology offers the most intriguing uses for market segmentation purposes to date. By going beyond conventional demographics to draw personality and life-style portraits of target consumers, it appeals to most marketers who want to see their markets as made up of real people rather than as a collection of statistics.

A life-style portrait of the eye makeup user, for example, shows us a woman who is young, well educated, living in metropolitan areas, tending to be a working wife if married, a heavy user of the telephone and gasoline, preferring movies and talk shows to Westerns on television, and a reader of fashion and news magazines rather than *True Confessions.* She is interested in fashion, likes to be attractive to others, enjoys foreign travel and concerts given the opportunity, goes to parties, is style conscious rather than utilitarian at home, is not a compulsive housekeeper (although personally meticulous), and accepts contemporary rather than traditional values.[22]

Life-style and psychographic research is currently used in a variety of ways, including media selection, developing advertising strategy, and other applications which require sophisticated market segmentation.

Consumerism and social responsibility (chapter 20), are two topics that have appeared quite prominently in consumer research. Consumerism refers to activism on the part of consumers in seeking elimination of product or service frustrations. Generally, consumerist goals may be classified as truth in marketing, product quality and safety, and redress of grievances. Recently, the profile of a socially responsible consumer has emerged from marketing research, a consumer who identifies with (and feels strongly about solving) social problems. Most studies focusing on the socially responsible consumer have uncovered the recurrent problem of concern about the environment versus market choice. In the wake of current controversy, a redefinition of the marketing concept is suggested to include considerations such as responsible consumption, strategies for buyers as well as sellers, and marketing of services for society's benefit.[23]

Marketing Applications of Consumer Behavior Theory

The study of consumer behavior offers vast potential for real-world application. And the possibilities open to people trained in this field range from positions in market research firms to jobs in government regulatory agencies investigating consumer fraud.

Micromarketing Problems

The most common uses of consumer behavior theory and research remain in the realm of *micromarketing*, better known as the business of marketing. Here the implications are managerial, research-oriented, and creative—to manage marketing operations effectively, provide research input for meeting consumer demands, and devise strategies for persuasive communications.

Anticipating New Markets   This aspect of the marketing concept challenges business people to regard every nuance of social change as a potential market development. In a rapidly changing economy such as that of the United States, the challenge becomes particularly acute. Improved educational opportunities, some say, have helped to create a new breed of consumers, more aware, more demanding, and more skeptical of advertising claims than their predecessors. Widespread affluence has prompted a demand for new and different leisure products, expanded travel services, and increased production of items once considered luxuries. A nationwide orientation towards youthfulness, born during the 1960s, keeps marketers frantically turning to each innovation originating in the under-twenty-five group. And growing consciousness among blacks and other ethnic groups opens a huge, largely untapped market for properly aimed products and services. These developments alone may be accountable for juggernaut growth in the industries turning out blue jeans, leisure homes, packaged travel, rock music, motorcycles, and pleasure boats.

Market Segmentation   No marketer could hope to interest every existing consumer in the specific product or service offered. Thus, markets are *segmented*. Segmentation involves selecting groups of consumers who would probably be most receptive to a given product and directing the marketing effort specifically to those groups. One might concentrate on as small a segment as people likely to buy private planes or as large a group as potential users of hand soap. A wide range of variables has been investigated for the purpose of segmenting consumer markets: for example, age, social class, family size, leisure pursuits, income, and geographic region. Magazines provide advertisers with *demographic* profiles of their readers which may indicate that people who read a publication are under thirty-five, enjoy annual incomes over $20,000, and have attained an average educational level of 4.2 years beyond high school. On this basis, the magazine hopes to attract advertisers who feel that this segment of the population will be especially prone to buy their products. Research in consumer behavior most often focuses on areas that would *facilitate* segmentation, for instance, evaluating membership in an ethnic group as a determinant of buying behavior or differen-

tiating heavy users of various products on the basis of life style.

Developing Strategies   Contemporary business relies increasingly on strategy formation at all levels of the marketing effort, from product development to retailing. This phenomenon becomes readily apparent in persuasive communications: advertising, promotion, and selling. One impetus for the careful planning of strategy is the sheer volume of products on the market. Another is the fact that many are "parity" products, with different brand names and packaging but no real product differences. Gasoline, detergent, and aspirin are examples. Consider the clutter of television commercials and it is understandable why viewers can recall so few advertising messages. Here it becomes necessary to "position"* products in the consumer's frame of reference. And this requires an understanding of what the consumer's frame of reference actually is. Avis successfully positioned itself as Number Two in car rental services, "trying harder"; this appeal struck a responsive chord with most consumers, who like to root for the underdog. Positioning and other strategic topics are discussed at point-of-use throughout the text.

Macromarketing Problems

The applications of an understanding of consumer behavior are not restricted to the realm of business and profit. Practitioners concerned with urban planning, administer-

---

*Positioning is usually described as finding a "niche" for one's product in the consumer's need system. When a specific need arises, the successfully positioned producer will come to the purchaser's mind.

ing social services, and economic policy require information about consumers to perform their roles effectively. These individuals wrestle with *macromarketing* problems, that is, determining how society in general may best serve the needs of its members.

Public Policy Decisions   Government agencies have recently taken a more activist role in regulating business practices. Some of their efforts are generally accepted by consumers; virtually everyone stands against deceptive advertising, for example. Other questions cannot be resolved without considerable research into consumer attitudes and desires. To alleviate atmospheric pollution, for instance, drastic measures like gasoline rationing and even outright automobile bans in urban areas seem called for. But Americans have grown accustomed to easy mobility and attached to the concept of private automobiles. The process of drawing people gradually away from their cars to mass urban transit must be a well-researched and thoughtfully planned effort to succeed. Convenience packaging such as beer and soft drink cans are highly visible sources of visual pollution, and many environmentalists propose banning them. But consumers may be less than willing to expend the energy to return bottles when

the prospect of a ban on nonreturnable packages arises. Such policy-making dilemmas are examined in chapter 20 on Consumerism and Social Responsibility.

Contributions to the Behavioral Sciences
Because so much time and energy are devoted to consumption in the United States, consumer behavior forms a surprisingly large component of American behavior. Research into consumer learning, attitudes, and influences upon decision-making often overlaps with psychological and sociological investigation. However, while the field of consumer behavior draws heavily on these disciplines for information, the relationship is at least mutually rewarding. Findings concerning consumer perception, motivation, and conditioning add to the body of knowledge about individual behavior. Studies exploring the relationship between reference groups and consumer decision-making contribute to sociological theory and practice.

So the study of consumer behavior is useful to anyone who will deal with the interests, activities, and purchasing patterns of consumers in business, government, or academic pursuits. The particular emphasis of this text, however, is directed to micromarketing applications that will best serve consumer needs.

Summary

Consumer behavior refers to the activities of people engaged in actual or potential use of market items: products, services, retail environments, and ideas. The study of how consumers behave draws its findings from a variety of disciplines such as anthropology, sociology, psychology, social psychology, economics, and marketing research. The field of consumer behavior is currently most useful to the business community in solving *micromarketing* problems—segmenting markets, opening new markets, and devising strategy. But increasingly sophisticated techniques and broader investigations promise to assist those concerned with *macromarketing* problems, including public policy formation and general enrichment of the behavioral sciences.

NOTES

1. Thomas P. Hustad, Charles S. Mayer, and Thomas W. Whipple, "Consideration of Context Differences in Product Evaluation and Market Segmentation," *Journal of the Academy of Marketing Science*, Vol. 3, No. 1 (Winter 1975), p. 34.

2. Walter A. Henry, "Cultural Values Do Correlate with Consumer Behavior," *Journal of Marketing Research* (May 1976), p. 121.

3. David Reisman, "Some Questions about the Study of American Character in the Twentieth Century," *Annals of the American Academy of Political and Social Science*, No. 370 (March 1967), pp. 36–47.

4. Robin M. Williams, Jr., *American Society: A Sociological Interpretation* (New York: Alfred A. Knopf Inc., 1960).

5. William D. Wells, "It's a Wyeth, not a Warhol World," *Harvard Business Review*, No. 48, January-February 1970.

6. H. Lee Mathews and John W. Slocum, "Social Class and Income as Indicators of Consumer Credit Behavior," *Journal of Marketing*, Vol. 34 (Apr. 1970), pp. 69–74.

7. Harry L. Davis, "Decision Making within the Household," *Journal of Consumer Research*, Vol. 2, No. 4 (March 1976), p. 241.

8. Tanniru R. Rao, "Validation of Stochastic Models: Some Perspectives," *Journal of the Academy of Marketing Science*, Vol. 3, No. 2 (Spring 1975), p. 192.

9. J. Paul Peter and Michael J. Ryan, "An Investigation of Perceived Risk at the Brand Level," *Journal of Marketing Research*, Vol. 13 (May 1976), p. 184.

10. Philip Kotler, "Behavioral Models for Analyzing Buyers," *Journal of Marketing*, Vol. 21 (October 1965), pp. 39–40.

11. Joel B. Cohen, "Toward an Interpersonal Theory of Consumer Behavior," in *Perspectives in Consumer Behavior*, Harold H. Kassarjian and Thomas S. Robertson, eds. (Glenview, Ill.: Scott, Foresman and Co., 1968).

12. Franklin B. Evans, "Psychological and Objective Factors in the Prediction of Brand Choice," *Journal of Business*, Vol. 32 (October 1959).

13. Richard J. Lutz, "Changing Brand Attitudes through Modification of Cognitive Structure," *Journal of Consumer Research*, Vol. 1, No. 4 (March 1975), p. 49.

14. Yoram Wind, "Preference of Relevant Others and Individual Choice Models," *Journal of Consumer Research*, Vol. 3, No. 1 (June 1976), p. 50.

15. Flemming Hansen, *Consumer Choice Behavior: A Cognitive Theory* (New York: Free Press, 1972).

16. William J. McGuire, "Some Internal Factors Influencing Consumer Choice," *Journal of Consumer Research*, Vol. 2, No. 4 (March 1976).

17. John A. Howard and Lyman E. Ostlund (Eds.), *Buyer Behavior* (New York: Random House, Inc., 1973), p. 241.

18. Joseph F. Dash, Leon G. Schiffman, and Conrad Berenson, "Risk and Personality Related Dimensions of Store Choice," *Journal of Marketing*, Vol. 40, No. 1 (January 1976), p. 32.

19. Everett M. Rogers, "New Product Adoption and Diffusion," *Journal of Consumer Research*, Vol. 2, No. 4 (March 1976), p. 290.

20. Robert T. Green and Eric Langeard, "A Cross-National Comparison of Consumer Habits and Innovator Characteristics," *Journal of Marketing*, Vol. 39, No. 3 (July 1975), p. 34.

21. William D. Wells, ed., *Life Style and Psychographic Research* (Chicago, Ill.: American Marketing Association, 1974).

22. William D. Wells and Douglas J. Tigert, "Activities, Interests and Opinions," *Journal of Advertising Research*, Vol. 11, (1971) p. 29.

23. Normal Kangun et. al., "Consumerism and Marketing Management," *Journal of Marketing*, Vol. 39, No. 2 (April 1975), p. 3.

MARKETING APPLICATIONS

Conclusion 1 *Information about how different people behave as consumers indicates what market items they will be most likely to use.*
Application Markets may be *segmented* by isolating groups of consumers who share certain behavioral traits—age, sex, income, education, social class, psychological variables, and so on. These groups form *target* segments for marketers of products and services, who will design and promote their items according to the needs, interests, and media preferences of the segments they hope to reach.

Conclusion 2 *Consumers are exposed to a huge variety of market items and communications. It becomes necessary to establish any given product in the consumer's frame of reference to gain awareness and sales in the market place.*
Application Products may be "positioned" in the consumer's frame of reference through understanding the behavioral needs of consumers who use that product and designing communications which give the product a "niche" in consumers' need systems. With astute positioning, the product should appear to be the only one in the marketplace that meets the specific needs of the target consumers.

ASSIGNMENTS

Research Assignment

You are hired for the summer as a Research Assistant by the market research firm of Turner and Wolfe. This firm conducts consumer research projects for a number of marketers, advertising agencies, public service organizations, and government regulatory agencies. But its specialty lies in the area of *market segmentation* studies for leading marketers.

Your first assignment is to prepare a bibliography of market segmentation studies from the current literature in consumer research, beginning with a review of the most recent studies in the field. Your sources are the last twelve issues of these four publications:

• *The Journal of Marketing*
• *The Journal of Marketing Research*

• *The Journal of Consumer Research*
• *The Journal of the Academy of Marketing Science*

From this review, you should select articles that relate directly to cases or problems of market segmentation based on *consumer* variables. These include characteristics such as:

• Demographic data—age, sex, occupation, income, geographic region
• Social class membership
• Family variables
• Psychological variables—attitude, perception, personality
• Life style variables—activities, interests, opinions

List as many studies as possible under each of the preceding categories. Keep your list for reference in future research.

Creative Assignment

You feel that it's time to trade your four-year-old MG convertible for a new model. But shopping around for the last few days as a shrewd consumer, you aren't satisfied with the low "book" price dealers are offering for the cream puff you've maintained so lovingly all these years. The alternative is to sell privately through an ad on your school's bulletin board. And because you're already sophisticated enough to know that you must direct your selling appeal to people's needs, you decide to write an ad that is more than a simple description of the car. Fortunately, your MG holds two distinct advantages for people looking in the price range you'll set:

• It gets very good gas mileage.
• Even though it's a sports car, a few insurance companies are willing to underwrite that model as an "economy" car because of the small engine size.

Stating your main selling proposition in an arresting and meaningful way, write an ad that will generate more than the usual interest in your car.

Managerial Assignment

In recent years, much attention has focused on "positioning" as a marketing strategy. This concept has been introduced briefly on page 15. Intelligent positioning depends heavily on our knowledge of how consumers perceive different products and services in the marketplace.

As a new Brand Manager for the Valley Brewing Company of Colorado, you find it necessary to brush up on your own knowledge of positioning for an upcoming sales conference. You will be asked to discuss positioning generally as a concept. You will also be expected to relate the concept to suggesting kinds of consumer research that should be conducted for your particular brand—a new regional beer called Coldstream, which is bottled from Colorado spring water.

For background, refer to positioning articles in the *Journal of Marketing* and *Advertising Age*, especially Jack Trout and Al Ries, "The Positioning Era Cometh," *Advertising Age* reprint of a three-part series, (Chicago: Crain Publications, 1972).

From your readings, discuss positioning briefly and offer a few suggestions for applying the concept to your Coldstream brand through appropriate consumer research.

SELECTED READINGS

Hise, Richard T., John K. Ryans, Jr. and Willem Van't Spijker. "Theory in Consumer Behavior: A Status Report," *The Journal of the Academy of Marketing Science*, Vol. 3, No. 2 (Spring 1975), pp. 182–91.

Maggard, John P. "Positioning Revisited." *Journal of Marketing*, Vol. 40, No. 1 (January 1976), pp. 63–66.

Warwick, Kenneth M. and Saul Sands. "Product Positioning: Problems and Promise." *University of Michigan Business Review* (November 1975), pp. 17–20.

OBJECTIVES

TWO

Theories and Models

At one time consumers were believed to be rational creatures who behaved in compliance with the laws of economics. Feed them greater income and they would automatically make more purchases. Reduce the supply of a market item and sit back to enjoy the inevitable rise in demand for that product.

Today, consumer study draws its theoretical basis primarily from the social and behavioral sciences. While the "laws" may be less precise, they have proven considerably more useful in explaining the erratic, capricious, and generally "irrational" behavior that can be expected from consumers in the real world.

This chapter concerns itself with how consumer behavior theory has been derived through a long standing practice of "eclectic borrowing" from other disciplines and the ways in which contemporary researchers use pure theory to build models of decision making and buying activity. Developing models which attempt to simulate how people behave serves investigators in several ways. A model can organize many variables in a comprehensive way. It can reveal subtle relationships among different variables. And, to the extent that it represents an accurate synthesis of all the factors which may influence or confound behavior, it may also be used for predicting such behavior. But there are some noteworthy disadvantages to using models as well, and these will be analyzed as specific models are presented.

Some of the topics which follow include:
- Why sound theories are difficult to come by.
- The differences between inner-directed and other-directed consumers.
- Why consumers with high achievement needs may shy away from mouthwash and deodorant.
- Twenty-eight "small" models useful to consumer behaviorists.
- How a computer can be programmed to "behave" like a consumer on a supermarket shopping trip.

This book touts no single theory or model as "the" explanation of consumer behavior. But mainstream consumer theory today leans toward a cognitive approach based in psy-chology—focusing on the individual consumer as an information processor and decision maker.

Theory Building

Virtually everyone involved in marketing has formed some conclusions about why people behave as they do and how their behavior might be shaped toward specific buying patterns. An experienced appliance salesperson uses techniques polished over the years to turn "just looking" customers into buyers. The advertising copywriter working on an airline account applies creative judgment to the problem of making one airline more appealing to consumers than all the rest, possibly arriving at a theme such as "Fly Me!" or "Fly the friendly skies of United" that will prove highly successful in persuading people to try that particular airline.

But investigators probing consumer behavior in a scientific way are concerned with a more formal kind of theory building. In chapter 1, the field of consumer behavior was described as an interdisciplinary study, drawing theory and findings from anthropology, sociology, social psychology, individual psychology, economics, and marketing. Yet there is no one accepted viewpoint as to which influences are most important or how the various cultural, sociological, and psychological determinants of buying behavior fit together. Rather, there are several broad comprehensive theories for consumer decision processes, as well as a number of other theories designed to explain more specific behavioral situations such as brand choice, personal influence, or household budgeting. This chapter discusses several of these theories and presents *models* of consumer behavior which have been developed by different theorists.

Theoretical Origins of Consumer Behavior

Consumer behavior research is moving increasingly in the direction of scientific method and empirical (observable and measurable) results.[1] So theory building to explain and predict consumer decisions closely resembles theoretical approaches of the physical sciences.

The Role of Theory in Science

To researchers, theory implies a relationship among observable facts, and an integration of these facts in some meaningful way.

Facts are only useful to science when they are ordered. Without some organizational principle, scientists would collect facts at random, using a different approach to each data collection and obtaining no predictive generalizations from one situation to the next. Theory, therefore, is useful to science in five ways:[2]

1. It defines the principal orientation of a science by indicating the kinds of data that will be sought.

2. It provides a conceptual scheme for systematizing and classifying data.

3. It summarizes facts into empirical generalizations.

4. It predicts facts.

5. It points out gaps in our knowledge.

Theory offers an *orientation* for scientific inquiry by defining which facts are relevant, narrowly focusing on them while disregarding others. As a means of *classification* and *conceptualization*, theory imposes an observable system of categories and a structure of concepts upon each set of facts. Theory also enables scientists to *summarize* empirical generalizations and relationships among propositions. Through summary and uniformity of method, theory *predicts* facts that might be observed under identical or similar circumstances. And because theory summarizes known facts and predicts those which have not been observed, it suggests research into areas not yet explored.

The Role of Theory in Consumer Behavior

John A. Howard, whose own theoretical model of consumer decision making will be discussed later in this chapter, offers four criteria for a sound theory of buyer behavior:[3]

1. *Theory must aid significantly in explaining buyer behavior, not merely describe it.* Unlike their role in market segmentation, buyers are not just divided into subgroups in theory building. A theory must trace consumer processes from awareness of a buying stimulus through processes of cognition which are not easily measured and sometimes must be assumed.

2. *Theory must incorporate mainstream thinking from principal avenues of research to explain behavior effectively.* The study of consumer behavior must necessarily draw upon the findings of all behavioral disciplines. But such borrowing must be limited to carefully substantiated and well-supported findings which truly represent the mainstream of those disciplines.

3. *Theory should have the property of suggesting clear avenues for fruitful research.* Sound theory in this sense would serve to channel research which would otherwise be dispersed in different, unrelated directions. For this reason, the *relevance* of a buyer behavioral theory should be readily apparent to researchers.

4. *Theory should include measures and definitions of its elements to meet the criteria established above.* This remains the most difficult criterion to meet, given the problems of measurement that have traditionally hampered the behavioral sciences.

In addition to these considerations, Mittelstaedt has pointed to even more basic criteria of sound theory in consumer behavior:[4]

1. *A theory must incorporate known regularities.*

2. *A theory must be able to suggest new regularities to be observed.*

3. *A single, unified theory is preferred to eclectic borrowing.*

With these guidelines in mind, we may examine some of the theoretical origins of consumer behavior from other disciplines.

Economic Theory

As early as Adam Smith, economists were constructing theories of buyer behavior. The classical position holds that consumers make choices and purchasing decisions solely on the basis of *rational self-interest* and carefully considered economic motivations. This concept rests on an assumption that a consumer possesses a finite system of resources (such as income), but maintains an infinite body of desires and needs. Thus, all consumer behavior involves the element of *choice*.

Utility Theory   In the nineteenth century, the philosopher Jeremy Bentham proposed a theory of consumer behavior based on his view of human beings as creatures who attempt to acquire the greatest satisfaction (known as utility) and avoid dissatisfaction (disutility) at all costs. The consumer, then, strives to *maximize the total utility* from all the products and services he or she consumes. Kotler has updated this concept to what is called *modern utility theory,* the idea that consumers will attempt to maximize their utility through calculating the consequences of their purchases.

Consumer choice is influenced by the utility concept that, the more one uses a certain product or service, the less satisfying it becomes. This is known as the *law of diminishing marginal utility*, which states formally that, as the quantity of an item consumed in-

creases, the *marginal* utility of the item increases at a decreasing rate. Marginal utility is defined as the increase in utility obtained from using an additional unit of some item. At some point, the addition of one more unit of that item will have no effect whatsoever upon total utility. For example, many people drink coffee because they enjoy the slight "up" feeling derived from that small dose of caffeine. So, the first cup of coffee on any given day shakes us out of our sleepy lethargy and stimulates us enough to accomplish whatever is at hand. This represents an increase in utility. But the serious coffee drinker will not stop with one cup. The second will bring about another increase in degree of stimulation, but not as much as the first. The marginal utility is beginning to increase, but at a drooping rate. This pattern will continue through the third and fourth cups until finally, by the seventh perhaps, the individual's nerves are jangled and consuming any more coffee fails to offer any satisfaction whatsoever.

How does utility theory explain consumer spending? Through the principle that a consumer will attempt to spend his or her finite resources so that equal marginal utility is received with each dollar spent for every item wanted. This is known as the law of *equal marginal utility per dollar.* Calculations are made on the basis that utility can be measured in units termed *utiles.* These calculations also assume that a measure known as *weighted marginal utility* enables us to compare different kinds of consumer items in terms of the satisfaction (utility) each one provides. This leads to an equation which states that weighted marginal utility for all goods should be equal when resources are properly allocated,

$$\frac{MU_a}{P_a} = \frac{MU_b}{P_b}$$

where MU_a (marginal utility divided by P_a price) is the weighted marginal utility for product A, and MU_b is the weighted marginal utility for product B.

Indifference Theory If it seems somewhat difficult to measure a vague construct like utility (really a term for satisfaction, which is highly individual and felt rather than observed), so it seemed even to many economists. Thus, some advocates of the utility theory who found the measurement problem insurmountable devised their own explanation—*indifference theory.*

This states, basically, that consumers form preferences for some combinations of products over others and view some combinations with complete indifference. All of the combinations of products to which a consumer is indifferent form what is known as an *indifference curve.* Above the curved indifference line are combinations of products the consumer tends to prefer. Below the line are combinations he or she is inclined to sidestep. A graphic representation of the indifference curve also contains a budget line, representing the notion that a consumer only has so much money to spend on a combination of products.

The consumer's objective in indifference theory is to maximize utility by choosing the most preferred combinations available within the constraint of a budget.

An *indifference map* for beer and cigarettes devised by Solomon (Figure 2-1) plots four different curves and a budget line. Each indifference curve shows all the combinations of beer and cigarettes that give a particular consumer (whom we'll call Pat) the same amount of satisfaction; thus Pat is indifferent to which

combination of the two he or she chooses. Moving to the right, the curves represent greater magnitudes of combinations. We assume that Pat will prefer to be located on the curve farthest to the right, under the economic assumption that more is better than less.

This map of curves reveals the range of Pat's preferences; the budget line (in black) indicates which of the combinations Pat can afford. These are A, B, D, and E. Theoretically, Pat will receive the greatest satisfaction by selecting the combination offering the most, which is the point farthest to the right—E.

Figure 2-1   Indifference map for beer and cigarettes.

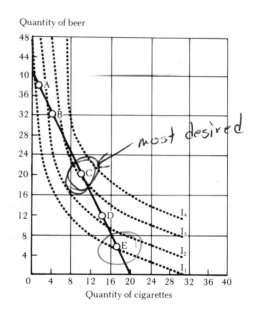

Source: Lewis C. Solomon, Economics, *Second Edition, (Reading, Mass.: Addison-Wesley Publishing Co., 1976) p. 490.*

Rising-Income Theory   It is generally accepted that consumer behavioral patterns change as income rises. Ernst Engel, the nineteenth century German statistician, formalized this relationship with the original Engel's Law, stating that the percentage of income spent on food tends to decrease as income increases. This has been extended into a series of laws (still referred to as Engel's Laws), which are summarized as follows:

As income rises, family expenditures tend to increase in all categories. The percentage spent on food, however, tends to decline. The percentage spent on housing and furniture tends to stay constant. And the percentage allotted to both luxuries and savings tends to increase.

These laws have been validated over the years by numerous researchers and comprise one of the few series of conclusions in consumer behavior study that are not subject to controversy.

Evaluation of Economic Theories   The marketing implications of economic principles expounded here have been synthesized into four general market "laws":

1. Lowering the price of an item will increase its sales.

2. When prices of substitute products are lowered, sales of the original item will decrease; and when prices of complementary products are lowered, sales of the original item will increase.

3. The higher the real income of consumers in general, the higher the sales of an individual product.

4. The greater the promotional effort, the higher the sales.[5]

However, these "laws" are not always evident in marketing practice. Consumers might view a price decrease in a negative way, as an indication of an inferior product that will not budge off the shelves except by drastic discounting. Extra promotion may make no difference whatsoever in sales if the promotion is not viewed as trustworthy. And the sales of a given product may not be stimulated at all by an increase in consumer income if there was no significant interest in the product to begin with, regardless of price or availability.

Economic theories have generally been credited with two contributions to consumer behavior study:

• Maximization of satisfaction is the *rational* goal of consumer behavior.

• The importance of *buying power* is stressed in economic theory.

However, they have also been faulted on a number of points and have lost conceptual ground to the behavioral sciences. The arguments against economic theories as broad, comprehensive explanations of buying include:

• *The consumer is portrayed as rational at all times.* This concept is not true, as will be demonstrated in chapters on learning, perception, attitudes, motivation, and decision making. The consumer's judgment is, in fact, clouded with a number of "irrational" influences.

• *The consumer is presented as unsusceptible to interpersonal influence.* Again, this view is severely challenged by all that is known today about social and cultural effects on consumption.

• *The consumer is described as acutely aware of all factors in his or her market domain.* Actually, consumers see what's around them very selectively and make market decisions accordingly.

In short, the criticisms directed at these theories see their rational, utilitarian consumer as a rather robotlike picture of human behavior, one which fails to account for individual learning, attitudes, motivation, personality, and interpersonal influences. Thus, the conclusions of the economic theorists should be regarded as generalizations to serve as a foundation for findings from the behavioral sciences.

This should not be taken to mean that nothing useful has appeared from the economic sector since Engel's time. Contemporary theorists such as Lancaster and Rosen have contributed new models of economic influence. The developments attributed to those theorists are, respectively, (1) an economic theory of brand preference based on the assumption that consumers value not just goods per se but the *attributes* that goods possess, and that different products are really different packages of attributes; and (2) a theory of consumers as *producers* in many activities, combining their own time and labor with their products to obtain satisfaction.[6] Both theories, while still in the testing stage, should prove useful in bridging the gap between the approaches of economics and the behavioral sciences to consumer behavior.

Psychological Theory

Three distinct theoretical orientations from the field of psychology have been applied to consumer behavior: cognitive theory, learning theory, and psychoanalytic theory.

Cognitive Theory Cognitive theory has been mentioned as the most popular current approach to understanding individual consumer behavior. Basically, cognitive theory explains buying activities as *problem solving* through (1) information processing and (2) decision making.[7] Chapter 9 on learning and Section IV analyze this problem-solving process in great detail.

Learning Theory Learning theory is also discussed in some detail in chapter 9. John B. Watson, generally regarded as the father of learning theory, postulated that buying behavior occurs as a simple stimulus-response relationship and that responses which are reinforced most positively and frequently will become relatively permanent behaviors. Watson applied this view to problems of advertising effectiveness, pointing out that constant *repetition* is the key to building consumer awareness and brand preference.[8]

Psychoanalytic Theory Psychoanalytic theory, pioneered by Sigmund Freud, offers a quite different view of human behavior, one based upon innate needs. While the learning theorists held that virtually all behaviors are acquired through experience, Freud maintained that the human organism must contend with a bundle of instinctual needs, most of which are too antisocial to be gratified through normal interaction with others. As an explanation for a human being's ability to overcome strong sexual and aggressive needs, Freud postulated a *psyche* divided into three components: first, the *id*, repository for the basic drives and motivations; secondly, the *super-ego*, which struggles with the id to repress these drives; and third, the *ego*, which presides over this conflict and attempts to find socially approved expression for the powerful reprehensible drives brewing within the id.[9]

How are the instinctual needs such as libido (commonly translated as sex drive) gratified in the course of social relationships? Freud believed that they are either forced back into the unconscious or *sublimated* into culturally accepted activities through cognitive processes known as *defense mechanisms*. These include such popular concepts as *rationalization* and *projection* (attributing our own "shameful" desires to others). Psychoanalytic theory became firmly established in consumer behavior studies through the advent of *motivational research* in the 1950s. This technique, discussed in chapter 11, produced exotic findings such as these about the "symbolic" needs behind product choice and preference:[10]

Many a businessman doesn't fly because of a fear of posthumous guilt—if he crashed, his wife would think of him as stupid for not taking a train.

Men want their cigars to be odoriferous in order to prove that they (the men) are masculine.

Consumers prefer vegetable shortening because animal fats stimulate a sense of sin.

Men who wear suspenders are reacting to an unresolved castration complex.

As might be expected, the problems encountered in proving and replicating these findings are considerable. Because the study of human behavior has veered toward empirical methods of research, models of consumer behavior today reflect cognitive learning theories rather than a psychoanalytic orientation.

Social Psychological Theory

Because individual behavior must be seen in the context of interaction with others, social psychological theories have been applied in the study of consumers. Perhaps the earliest contributor in this area was Thorstein Veblen,

an economist influenced at the turn of the century by the popularity of social anthropology. Veblen hypothesized that the human being was a *social animal* whose behavior was very much affected by peer groups, subcultures, and other reference groups. His best-recognized study is his analysis of the so-called leisure class, a description of consumers motivated not by rational needs but by status considerations. This study noted the phenomenon of purchasing goods and services for the impression they make upon others, a phenomenon Veblen characterized as *conspicuous consumption*.[11]

Achievement Motivation   In the tradition of Veblen, McClelland has investigated the theory of *achievement motivation* as a determinant of buying behavior. The need to achieve, and to make others aware of those achievements, is a two-sided process. On one hand, there is the challenge of having one's behavior judged against a performance standard so that a measure of achievement may result. But on the other there is also the threat of failure, of not meeting the desired standard, and these two components of achievement motivation exist in conflict. Researchers who have attempted to link achievement motivation with buying behavior report these findings:[12]

1. Men scoring high on need achievement (using self-report rechniques) were inclined to favor products thought of as virile and masculine—boating equipment, skis, and straight razors. Men with low achievement scores tended to favor products which were deemed "meticulous or fastidious" such as mouthwash, deodorant, and automatic dishwashers.

2. High achievement needs have been found in a large sample of people who prefer active outdoor sports.

3. Individuals high in achievement needs were light television viewers and heavier users of magazines and radio.

Cognitive Dissonance Theory Cognitive dissonance theory is discussed in chapters 12 and 13 as a social psychological contribution to the understanding of the role of attitudes in consumer behavior. In brief, dissonance occurs when an individual consumer's behavior is inconsistent with the person's internal attitudes, as when a natural foods advocate sneaks a Big Mac. The principles of dissonance theory have been applied to problems of brand and store selection, advertising effectiveness, pricing, and brand loyalty.

Sociological Theory

Inner versus Other-Direction Sociologist David Reisman contends that societies and people may be characterized as three sociological "types": tradition-directed, inner-directed, and other-directed.[13] *Tradition-directed* refers to slow changing, family oriented societies in which people are wholly dependent on extended family ties and experience little social mobility. There are few tradition oriented individuals in American society, except in small subcultures such as the Amish of Pennsylvania. *Inner-direction* describes a society characterized by greater mobility, rapid industrialization, and the accumulation of capital. Individuals who are inner-directed tend to feel substantial control over their behavior and set well-defined goals for achievement. *Other-directed* societies have surpassed the need for industrialization and socialize their individuals as consumers rather than producers. Other-directed people are concerned not so much with personal achievement and inner satisfaction as with the expectations of their peer groups. Applications of Reisman's theory to consumer research have generally contrasted inner-direction with other-direction as intervening variables:[14]

• Studies probing diffusion of innovations have concluded that innovators tend to be inner-directed persons.

• In advertising preferences, inner-directed individuals favor inner-directed appeals while other-directed people prefer appeals which promise peer group acceptance.

Role Theory As presented by Erving Goffman, *role theory* characterizes individuals as "actors" who play roles in the presence of others to convey certain impressions. This process is termed *role enactment*. It includes *expectations* that define the rights and privileges of participants in a given social situation; *location* of the actor at the appropriate place in the social structure (determined by expectation); *demands* that may be imposed on the choice of role; *skills*, both physical and psychological, which enable the "actor" to play a given role; and an *audience* composed of the people for whom the role enactment is staged. The audience and actor interact in each role enactment, which may be successful or unsuccessful.[15] The concept of role theory is most often used in discussions of a product's image, which an actor may use to create a desired effect with an audience. The kind of automobile we drive, the clothes we wear, and the kind of haircut we prefer may all be used as props in conveying some desired image to an audience.

Many of these theoretical orientations—economic, psychological, social psychological, and sociological—have been integrated in the most comprehensive *models* devised for consumer behavior research.

Using Models in Consumer Behavior Research

A research model may be thought of as a *representation of some larger system*[16] *which is used to identify, explain, or predict behavior within that system.*

In chapter 1, a model developed by Allport was introduced to show, in a simplified way, how consumer behavior is influenced by cultural, social, and individual factors (see Fig. 1-1, p. 8). After the foregoing comprehensive discussions of these influences, the model serves as a simple means of viewing the interrelationships of many factors. All models of consumer behavior, although most are not so simplified, attempt to organize many variables and relationships in a meaningful way.

Models are useful to both consumer behavior students and researchers in five ways: For one, they set a *context* for research by carefully integrating all the components of a system under scrutiny. Secondly, models *identify* elements of a system and the relationships among them. Third, they *explain* how given systems operate by representing the flow of variables in a logical way. Fourth, they enable researchers to *predict* behavior that will emanate from a system. And finally, they aid researchers in *theory-building* by providing a framework for new hypotheses.

How Models Are Constructed

Consumer behavior models may be developed through two different approaches identified by Lazer.[17] One process is termed *abstraction,* in which an actual situation is represented (or abstracted) by a model as shown in Figure 2-2. The model builder starts by observing a specific consumer situation and drawing conclusions about the variable relationships in that situation—a consumer choice process, for example—which the builder then tests empirically. If testing indicates that this perception is accurate, a general model may be constructed on this basis to identify, explain, or predict similar choice process, for example—which the to other situations, "feedback" will enable the model builder to verify the original perceptions once again and rework the model if necessary.

The second approach is referred to as *realization.* In this process, the model builder formulates a general theory which might apply to some consumer behavior situation and constructs a model representing that theory. Research findings are assembled that will establish the existing consumer relationships of that situation and the information is fed into the model. Then the model is applied to an actual situation to determine whether the theory "works." Again, feedback enables the builder to revise the model until it proves consistent with observable findings. Figure 2-3 illustrates this method.

Other factors in model building depend on what the model will be used to represent:[18]

1. In each model there is a relationship between *independent* variables* and *dependent* variables, and the structure of the model will be described in terms of the specific relationship.

2. Models may deal with *different kinds of consumer situations,* such as exposure, de-

*Used to describe, explain, or predict a movement or variation in another variable called the dependent variable.

Figure 2-2 Model development by abstraction.

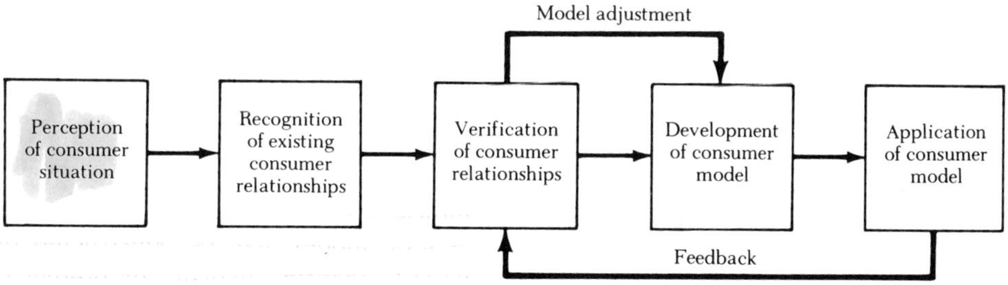

Model adjustment

| Perception of consumer situation | → | Recognition of existing consumer relationships | → | Verification of consumer relationships | → | Development of consumer model | → | Application of consumer model |

Feedback

Source: William Lazer, "The Role of Models in Marketing", Journal of Marketing, Vol. 26, No. 2 (April 1962) p. 9. Reprinted by permission of the American Marketing Association.

liberation, and response choice and may be oriented toward, say, communication rather than consumption.

3. Models may be constructed at an *individual* or a *household* level to represent consumer decision and choice processes.

4. Models may be more or less *aggregated* (applicable to larger groups). The least aggregated models concern individual choices.

5. Models may be *dynamic* or *static*: A dynamic model emphasizes the force of change or movement while a static model is concerned with a single point in time.

The models presented in this chapter will illustrate the great diversity in model construction, representing consumer behavioral systems from specific choice behaviors to large patterns of integrated behaviors.

Figure 2-3 Model development by realization.

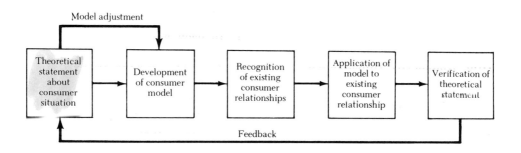

Model adjustment

| Theoretical statement about consumer situation | → | Development of consumer model | → | Recognition of existing consumer relationships | → | Application of model to existing consumer relationship | → | Verification of theoretical statement |

Feedback

Source: William Lazer, "The Role of Models in Marketing," Journal of Marketing, Vol. 26, No. 2 (April 1962) p. 9. Reprinted by permission of the American Marketing Association.

Classification of Consumer Behavior Models

Formal consumer behavior models have been classified by Bettman and Jones into four types: *stochastic, linear-experimental, information processing,* and *large system* models.

Stochastic Models   Stochastic, or *probability,* models are based on the learning assumption that a consumer's previous, and especially last, purchasing behavior will determine future behavior. A stochastic model involves two components: (1) a model which identifies individual behavior and (2) a methodology for aggregating these individual models. The individual model is concerned with some specific aspect of an individual consumer's purchase behavior such as brand choice or brand loyalty. In models of brand choice behavior, for example, the probability of the consumer's purchasing a given brand is viewed as an outcome of determinants such as the brand last purchased, time effects, purchasing history, or some combination of these. The aggregation element (extending the individual behavior to explain similar behavior by large groups) may be accomplished by assuming that all individuals are the same in all aspects of behavior or by assuming that different individuals will respond differently to the same stimuli, which makes the aggregation problem more complex.[20]

One popular example of a stochastic model is the *Brand Loyalty Model* developed by Morrison. This model postulates brand choice probabilities (which are conditional upon the most recent brand purchase) of the form

$$P (A_t +1 / A_t) = P$$

In this instance, A is the consumer's preferred brand and $P(A_t +1)$ refers to the probability that the consumer will purchase brand A at purchase occasion $+ 1$, depending on the brand the consumer bought at purchase occasion t.[21]

Applications of stochastic models to brand loyalty, brand switching, and new product forecasting may be found in chapter 9.

Linear-Experimental Models   Models in this category are generally used to represent a *market* rather than the individual consumer. They are characterized by a formal mathematical structure and usually describe product aspects of consumer behavior such as one brand's share of market. Bettman and Jones describe the basic linear model as

$$f(y) = \sum_i g_i(x_i) + \epsilon,$$

where y is the dependent variable (aspect being modeled) x_i is the independent variables, and ϵ is a random element.[22] Because the linear models are usually descriptive and represent an entire market or population, a thorough analysis of this classification may best be found in other sources.*

Information-Processing Models of Consumer Choice   Formal information-processing models are an important development in consumer behavior research. They are founded on the hypothesis that a consumer is constantly receiving communications from the

---

*Linear models are systematically presented in Martin Fishbein, "Attitude and the Prediction of Behavior," in *Readings in Attitude Theory and Measurement,* ed. M. Fishbein (New York: John Wiley and Sons, 1967). See also Peter Simpson and Paul Harris, "A User's Guide to Fishbein," *Journal of the Market Research Society,* Vol. 12, No. 3 (July 1970), pp. 145–64.

environment and processes these communications as information for decision making and choice behavior. In this category of model building, the focus is on individual choice behavior. The models are developed through a technique in which subjects think out loud while their behavior is being modeled. The researcher instructs his consumers to "think" verbally while they go about their actual shopping behavior.[23] Then the verbal record obtained from each subject is taken as an indication of how he or she processes information during choice and purchase situations.

This approach has been applied to situations such as women's fashion choices,[24] grocery product choice,[25] and stock purchases.[26] The model employed in the study of women's clothing purchases is shown in Figure 2-4.

Because of the individual nature of this modeling approach, very small numbers of subjects are used in building information-processing models. Similarly, this approach is characterized by the fact that every subject virtually requires his or her own model. Thus, such models are presently limited to small groups and markets.

Large Systems Models The comprehensive models of consumer behavior with which most researchers familiarize themselves fall into this category. These models are broad, general designs including many variables and relationships. Each is based on a major conceptual scheme of consumer behavior. A sampling of these models will be introduced here.

Figure 2-4   Overview of shopping process decision.

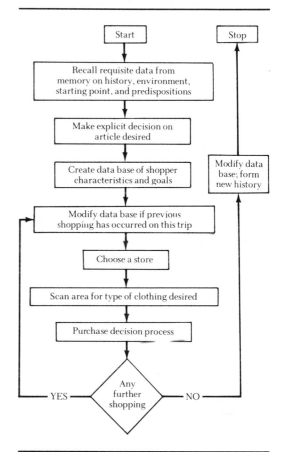

Source: Leonard Simon, et al, "Consumer Information Processing—the Case of Women's Clothing," Proceedings of the American Marketing Association *(September 28, 1968), p. 199. Reprinted by permission of the American Marketing Association.*

Systems Models of Consumer Behavior

Three major models of consumer behavior have attracted considerable interest from researchers and marketers: (1) the Howard-Sheth Model, (2) the Nicosia Model, and (3) gel, Kollat, and Blackwell Model. In ibsections following, each model is ipanied by a brief overview of its purpose, components, utility, and possible shortcomings. But each summary serves merely as an introduction to the model rather than a definitive statement of its contribution to the field.

The Howard-Sheth Model

This was one of the first large systems models and remains one of the most elaborate and comprehensive. Presented in its original form by John A. Howard in 1963,[27] it was later refined by Howard and Jagdish N. Sheth.[28]

Their model, depicted in Figure 2-5, is based on *learning theory* in its systematic use of the stimulus-response relationship to explain consumer *choice* behavior. Additionally, this model emphasizes the process of *repeat* buying through consideration of a time dimension, a dynamic rather than static model of buying behavior. So it has emerged as particularly useful for explanation of frequent, repetitive purchases such as packaged goods, which involve brand preference and loyalties.

The essential theory represented states that, faced with a given drive, a consumer will perceive relevant cues and make a certain response. If this response is reinforced, learning will occur.

Design   Stimuli (or inputs) are described as *significative, symbolic,* and *social*—in other words, physical things, representative things, and communication from others.[29]

When the senses are exposed to one of the three kinds of stimulus inputs, the attention that will be paid to any one of them is a func-

tion of *stimulus ambiguity*. Ambiguity will, in turn, create a need for more information. Once information is obtained, it is filtered through the variable of *perceptual bias* caused by the intervention of *attitudes* and *motives*. However, the new information might very well change the present attitudes and motives and will affect brand *comprehension, intention* to purchase, and the *purchasing behavior* itself. If the purchase is concluded and the individual is reinforced by *satisfaction* with the choice, confidence will be strengthened, and the buying process is likely to be repeated.

Advantages   The Howard-Sheth model has enjoyed considerable popularity for its systematic presentation of a great number of variables. A test of the model based upon the instant breakfast market has demonstrated "consistent but modest" overall predictive merit,[30] and the model is continually being updated in its theory elements and operational definitions.[31]

Disadvantages   Through applications of the model in behavioral research, certain methodological problems have been identified. These include:[32]

1. Difficulties in measurement due to the elaborate nature of the model and its great number of variables.

2. Difficulties in defining certain operations and discrepancies between theoretical definitions of some variables and their operational definitions.

3. Discontinuity of certain variables, which appear at the beginning of the system but are not continued throughout the model.

But, as noted, the model is undergoing continuous refinement to make adjustments for some of those methodological difficulties.

1300 messages/day

Figure 2-5 The Howard-Sheth model.

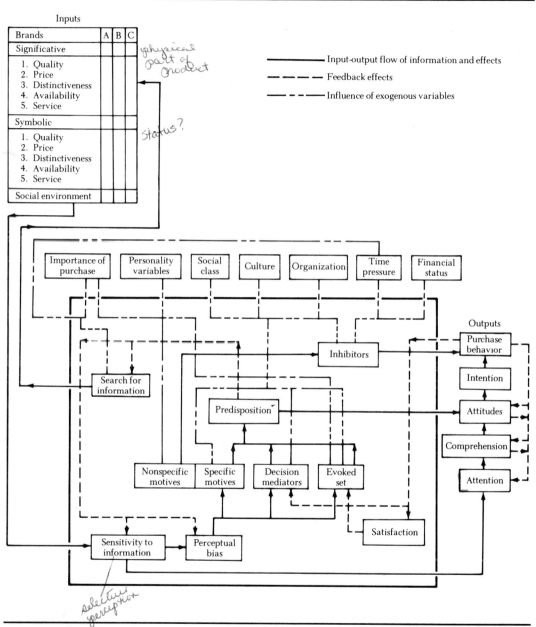

physical part of product

status?

selective perception

Source: John A. Howard and Jagdish N. Sheth, The Theory of Buyer Behavior *(New York: John Wiley and Sons, 1969).*

Figure 2-6   The Nicosia computer simulation model.

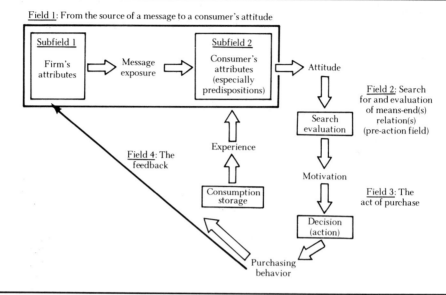

Source: Francesco M. Nicosia, "Advertising Management, Consumer Behavior and Simulation," Journal of Advertising Research, *Vol. 8 (March 1968) pp. 29–37. Copyright © 1968, by the Advertising Research Foundation.*

The Nicosia Model

Another early model of a comprehensive system is the *computer simulation* of the consumer decision process developed by Francesco M. Nicosia. This model, seen in Figure 2-6, assumes that decision behavior can best be represented as a flow-chart diagram. Beginning with a marketing firm's introduction of a new product, the flow consists of an advertisement, the consumer's possible exposure to it, the interaction between the advertisement and the consumer's given predispositions at the time of the exposure, the possibility of an attitude formation concerning the new product, the transformation of this motivation into a pur-

chase process, and a return to both the consumer's predisposition and the firm.[33]

Design[34]   *Field 1* encompasses the flow of a message from its original source (a firm) to the consumer's internalization of the message. *Subfield 1* includes the various attributes of the firm and the way these attributes interact to focus on a certain type of consumer (the market segment). If the consumer is exposed to the message, that message enters *Subfield 2*, the consumer's space, where perception and cognition are brought into action. The result of these operations is the output of Subfield 2, which may or may not add up to an attitude formation toward the new product. The input which enters *Field 2* is the new attitude formation, which brings about search (internal or external) and evaluation processes that relate the new attitude to the advertised product and available brands. The motivation which may emerge from Field 2 is the input entering *Field 3*, where the motivation may be directed toward actual purchase depending on brand availability, in-store factors such as point-of-purchase material and pricing, and other variables. The output may or may not be the purchase of the advertised brand. The purchase that may emerge from Field 3 is the input into *Field 4*, which consists of operations such as storage and consumption that lead to experience with the brand. The experiential output then becomes the input for *Field 1*, closing the consumer's loop.

Advantages Nicosia's model is an excellent example of computer simulation techniques, one methodology which has contributed a new dimension to theory building. It is a relatively complete model that remains both logical and understandable.

Disadvantages Generally, the criticisms leveled at this model have emphasized the oversimplification of processes such as motivation and attitude formation, which seldom occur in such a logical and mechanistic fashion. In addition, the model seems to have no immediate application to real-world marketing problems.

The Engel, Kollat, and Blackwell Model

One of the most comprehensive research models in the field of consumer behavior is that developed by James F. Engel, David T. Kollat, and Roger D. Blackwell. It is referred to by its authors as a "multimediation" model because many processes mediate (or intervene) between exposure to an initial stimulus

and ultimate behavioral outcomes, measurably affecting these outcomes.[35] Figure 2-7 portrays this model.

Design[36] Basically, this model is constructed around three major components: the central control unit, information processing, and the decision process.

The *central control unit* contains individual consumer variables such as stored information and experiences, perceptual attributes, attitudes toward alternatives, and personality characteristics. All of these variables interact to filter incoming stimuli, retaining some and discarding others.

In the *information processing* component, incoming stimuli are similarly processed through exposure, attention, comprehension, and retention in continuous interaction with the central control unit.

The *decision process* component involves the operations of problem recognition, internal search and alternative evaluation, purchasing processes, and their outcomes. The two possible outcomes of purchase are "post purchase evaluation" and "further behavior."

Advantages This model has attracted widespread interest for a variety of reasons. It is both comprehensive and comprehensible, it delineates cause-effect relationships better than most models, and it focuses on the decision process perhaps more effectively than other models. The authors have applied their system to buying situations as diverse as the purchase of small automobiles and laundry detergents, with impressive results for marketing decisions.

Disadvantages Bass points out that systems models such as the one developed by Engel, Kollat, and Blackwell, however valuable they may have been in providing structure and

Figure 2-7   The Engel, Kollat, and Blackwell multimediation model.

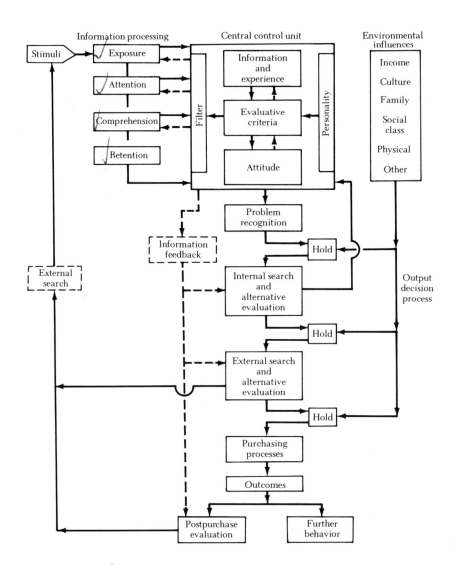

Source: Consumer Behavior, *Second Edition, by James F. Engel, David T. Kollat, and Roger D. Blackwell. Copyright © 1968, 1973 by Holt, Rinehart, and Winston Inc. Reprinted by permission of The Dryden Press.*

framework for empirical scrutiny, may have misdirected research by overemphasizing deterministic ("every event has a cause") models of behavior.[37]

Evaluation of Large Systems Models

Generally, these models may be characterized as representations of *broad* theories about consumer choice processes, which account for considerably more variables than other types of models. Their strengths are, understandably, in the areas of describing complex decision making processes that may occur in consumer choice and purchasing situations.

The problems with large scale models fall within the realm of measurement and estimation, mainly because they are highly abstracted and generalized in presentation of variables. Many of the difficulties with the Howard-Sheth model, for instance, are encountered in specifying operational definitions and in measuring the variables. Similarly, Nicosia's model appears to depict a very generalized consumer, and his model has not been applied, as yet, to real data.[38] The Engel, Kollat, and Blackwell model seems to enjoy greater success against the test of real-world situations.

Basic Consumer Behavior Models

Most models designed to identify, explain, or predict how consumers will behave are not the large conceptualizations identified so far. The great majority of models are used instead to represent *specific* areas of interest to researchers.

Hansen has compiled a total of twenty-eight basic consumer behavior models (see Table 2-1) with respect to (1) dependent variables, (2) independent variables and (3) the products to which they are most frequently applied.

Two basic models which are used to represent specific consumer situations are discussed briefly here, personal influence models and household budgeting models.[39]

Personal Influence

Formally, this model may be stated as:

$$Ei = f \, (\text{PC}i)$$
$$Ei = \text{maximum}$$

where the dependent variable (Ei) is the evaluation of brands and products and the independent variable (PCi), the personal communication received about these brands. The hypothesis states that the alternative for which the difference between positive and negative communication is the *greatest* will be the alternative selected. (Figure 2-8.)

Table 2-1   Twenty-eight Basic Models

BASIC MODEL	DEPENDENT VARIABLES	INDEPENDENT VARIABLES	PRODUCTS MOST FREQUENTLY APPLIED TO
1. Utility models	Purchases	Utility of alternatives	All
2. Perceived-risk models	Purchases, information acquisition	Perceived risk	All products brands with some importance and uncertainty (often first purchases)
3. Dissonance models	Purchases, information acquisition, and post-choice attitudes	Dissonance	All (conflict products of some importance)
4. Attitude and preference models I	Brand, product and store choices, occasionally information sources	Preferences and attitudes towards brands, products, etc.	All (with a tendency towards nondurables)
5. Attitudes and preference models II	Discretionary spending	Attitudes towards price and income changes and income	Major durables
6. Interest and value models	Purchases (consumption)	Values, interests	All
7. Image models	Brand choices	Perception of brands	Frequently used nondurable products
8. Perceptual preference models	Brand choices	Perception of brands	Not known
9. Lewinfield models	Purchases	Approaching and avoiding forces	All (mostly applied to product level choices)
10. Hierarchy of effects models	Purchases	Mass communication	Frequently used nondurable brands
11. Situational-learning models	Response choice	Situational aspects	All (most frequently brand choices)
12. Personality and motivational models	Purchases and choices of information sources	Motives and personality traits	All (mostly applied at brand level)

Table 2-1 (Continued)

BASIC MODEL	DEPENDENT VARIABLES	INDEPENDENT VARIABLES	PRODUCTS MOST FREQUENTLY APPLIED TO
13. Personal influence models	Purchases, preferences	Personal communication	All (conspicuous products and brands which arouse some interest)
14. Media exposure models	Exposure (purchases)	Descriptive content, media, and message variables	Frequently advertised products and brands
15. Decision process models	Steps from problem identification to purchase	Information, previous experiences	All (most frequently major durables)
16. Satisficing models	Purchases and information acquisition	Satisfaction levels (goals) and information	All
17. Innovation models	Awareness to adoption	Individual and mass communication	First purchases
18. Fashion models	Fashion adoption (purchase and use)	Previous adoption, personal communication	Fashion products
19. Household budgeting models	Income allocation	Income, household characteristics, preferences	Larger single purchases and major product classes
20. Plans and intentions	Purchases	Plans, intentions	Major durable products
21. Simple probability models	Purchases	Purchasing probabilities	All
22. Brand share models	Brand choices	Preferences (loyalty), previous purchases, and distribution	Frequently purchased nondurables
23. Segmentation models	Purchases	Socioeconomic, purchase and personality variables	All brands
24. Life cycle models	Major purchases and saving	Stages in family life cycle	Major durable products

Table 2-1   (Continued)

BASIC MODEL	DEPENDENT VARIABLES	INDEPENDENT VARIABLES	PRODUCTS MOST FREQUENTLY APPLIED TO
25. Social class models	Purchases, store choices, choice of information sources, consumption	Social class	Store, brand, and product choices
26. Income hypotheses models	Total spending and saving	Income	Total spending
27. Demand function models	Product (and brand) purchases	Price, quality, promotion, etc.	Product class choices (less applicable to brand choices)
28. Cultural-anthropological models	Exposure, consumption, and purchases	Cultural variables	All

Source: Adapted from Consumer Choice Behavior: A Cognitive Theory, *by Flemming Hansen, 1972, pp. 436–438. Copyright © 1972 by the Free Press, a Division of Macmillan Publishing Co., Inc. Reprinted by permission.*

Figure 2-8   The structure of personal communication models.

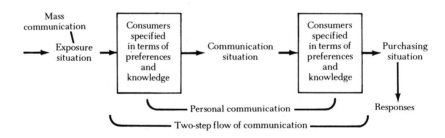

Source: Consumer Choice Behavior: A Cognitive Theory *by Flemming Hansen, 1972, p. 450. Copyright © 1972 by the Free Press, a Division of Macmillan Publishing Co., Inc. Reprinted by permission.*

Household Budgeting

The formal statement of this model is:

(purchases of   = *f* (budgeted spending
product class *j*)   for *j*)
(budgeted   = *f* (income, preferences,
spending for *j*)   family structure)

where the dependent variable is the amount of money spent on products and major purchases and the independent variables are family income, consumption preferences, and interaction within the household.[39] The model is structured in Figure 2-9.

Figure 2-9 **The structure of household budgeting models.**

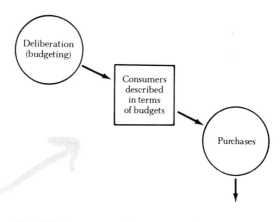

Source: Consumer Choice Behavior: A Cognitive Theory *by Flemming Hansen, 1972, p. 454. Copyright © 1972 by the Free Press, a Division of Macmillan Publishing Co., Inc. Reprinted by permission.*

Marketing Applications of a Consumer Behavior Model

Won't concentrate on this for Exams, et.

One of the most intriguing models to emerge in recent years is the computer simulation known as *Consumenoid I*, developed by Moran, Light, Starr, and Longman. The model is so named as the first operational "Consumenoid," a computer creation which behaves like a human consumer.

Consumenoid I is based on a concept of maximization of *entropy change* (termed "Delta," or Δ). Entropy refers to a measure of variety, choice, surprise, and similar factors. Maximization of entropy change rests on the behavioral assumption that the single motive force producing behavior is the desire to maximize change in the perceptual universe.[40]

Structure of Consumenoid I

Figure 2-10 illustrates the components of Consumenoid I as it makes a purchasing decision. The central core is labeled *memory,* which is both dynamic and fallible, subject to the effects of selective distortion and retention. All events in the decision process are moderated by the state of memory, and its characteristics are changed with new input. The model requires constant *stimulus input,* which is always perceived by Consumenoid I in the context of the perceived *environmental*

Figure 2-10 How Consumenoid I makes a purchase decision.

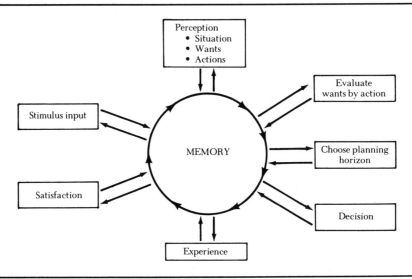

Source: Lawrence Light, "Consumenoid I: An Explanation and an Illustration." Batten, Barton, Durstine and Osborne.

situation, perceived *wants,* and perceived *action alternatives.* Each want is assigned a level, affected by such influences as mass communications, biological states, and social pressures. If a current want level is high, new information is likely to have a small effect. To establish wants, Consumenoid I must perceive *action alternatives,* which are filtered through a *selective screening* process so that (like a human consumer) it is never actually perceiving all the available alternatives.[41]

Consumenoid I in Action

Assume that Consumenoid I is a housewife in a supermarket, confronting a shelf full of different brands of toothpaste. When the model begins to define a situation, a *stimulus set* is formed from the memory unit. Stimuli in this set have different probabilities of being perceived, which are termed *predispositions.* In addition, environmental factors provide different action alternatives with different levels of *visibility.* The action alternatives are now brands of toothpaste. Thus, predispositions are affected by advertising recall, brand preference, and other factors; while brand visibility is affected by factors like pricing and in-store promotion. Because Consumenoid I can not examine all the available alternatives, the concept of *perceptual threshold* is included in the model: for a brand to be perceived in the current set of action alternatives, its perception probability must exceed this threshold.

Next, Consumenoid I makes a *forecast* of the effect of a given selection from the alternatives on the basis of a *planning horizon.* A long planning horizon means looking into the distant future while a short planning horizon implies immediate gratification.

Now Consumenoid I is ready to make a decision, to select the alternative that maximizes entropy change over a planning horizon. The equation for this situation is:[42]

$$\Delta H^k = {}^r\Sigma\, H^k_{t+r} \quad - \quad H_{t-1}$$

H_{t-1} = the entropy level in period *t*-1

ΔH^k = entropy level produced by selecting alternative *K*

r = planning horizon = number of periods over which ΔH^k is to be computed

$H_{t-1} = -\Sigma W^q_{t-1} \qquad \log W^q_{t-1}$

W^q_{t-1} = want level in period *t*-1 for want *q*

And Consumenoid I chooses the action alternative producing the largest Π^k.

Taking this model through fifteen consecutive purchasing cycles, a pattern of brand loyalty with occasional brand switching is observed. But unlike most research into brand loyalty, Consumenoid I offers an explanation of brand switching. Although satisfaction with a brand may be high and logically a consumer should never switch, the occasional *exploratory* behavior may be viewed as a maximization of entropy. Thus, Consumenoid I, patterned as closely as possible after a human consumer and subject to the very same influences, provides an explanation which has not been obtained from conventional research.

Consumenoid Applications

Because this model is dynamic in explaining why a consumer will buy brand *A* today, brand *B* tomorrow, and so on, the implications for consumer behavioral predictions are many.[43]

Brand Switching and Loyalty The most obvious application is in determining whether an individual brand change is a change of general preference or merely exploratory behavior. Thus, marketers may trace the influences of advertising messages in leading to brand perceptions and then to *changed* brand perceptions. The length and frequency of the effect of a change in brand preference on purchasing might also be measured.

Automatic Brand Choice Consumenoid I identifies two sources of brand habituation: (1) received satisfaction as a factor in forecasting and (2) the effect of the planning horizon on the consumer's confidence about perceiving long-term outcomes. These sources together lead to such habituations as getting used to cigarettes low in tar and nicotine. In effect, a consumer is "trading off" the long-term benefit of expected health with perceptions of taste. The Consumenoid model makes possible assessments of how a preferred brand may reinforce an accustomed pattern or how another brand might break the pattern.

Increasing Market Size In the context of this model, nonusers of a product may be seen in either of two ways: (1) They may not associate the product with specific needs and so fail to consider it an action alternative, or (2) they may always find another brand preferable, even though other items in the product category are viewed as action alternatives. Marketers who wish to expand their share of market might, on this basis, simply change the context in which the brand is presented. Or they may recognize that a real problem exists in how their product goes about satisfying consumer needs.

Heavy Users In packaged goods marketing, heavy users do not always remain heavy users.

In Consumenoid terms, this problem might be viewed as the need to change "compulsive" behavior to maximize entropy.

Fads and Fatigue Purchases   When a marketer attempts to increase sales of a product that most people use occasionally but which competes with a brand consumed regularly, the objective is to get people to use the product longer and more frequently. In other words, the marketer tries to induce longer "fads" more often, for example, drinking 7-Up, "The Uncola," instead of Coca Cola. This model is particularly useful in analyzing how action alternatives are defined, how perceptions change with our communications, and how frequently these changes might lead to the purchase of a given brand.

Empathic Product Use   This theory maintains that the choice of a product at any given time may be highly situational. Eating ravioli for dinner instead of steak does not indicate a general preference for ravioli over steak. These alternatives are instead based on perception of options for a particular situation. In this way, a marketer can evaluate perceptions of brand switching and determine how sales might be increased by repositioning, finding a new "niche" in the consumer's mind.

Consumenoid I, a modeling innovation, offers some indication of how a model may be designed for a specific task and how a model of consumer behavior may be applied to marketing decision making.

Other situational models constructed in recent years have focused on specific marketing areas. These are:

1. NEWPROD—a model designed to help the marketing manager decide whether or not to continue the introduction of a new product.[44]

2. A model marketers can use to communicate with their target consumers when need arousal is highest for certain products.[45]

3. ADMOD—an advertising decision model for testing different ads, media, and budget levels simultaneously on the basis of specific consumer decisions that advertising is attempting to precipitate.[46]

4. A model for collecting sensitive information from consumers. This was used to estimate the intensity of shoplifting in a Honolulu shopping center by drawing the information from shoplifters themselves.[47]

The role of consumer behavior models in general is also fairly new (most have been devised in the last decade or so) and promises to expand with improved measurement, operational definitions, and empirical rigor. Because discussion here has been necessarily limited to a brief overview, many of the concepts which entered into the actual development of each model have been omitted. Therefore, a variety of original sources may be found in the chapter bibliography, under different categories of consumer behavior models.

Summary

Research in consumer behavior utilizes formal theories and models derived from disciplines such as sociology, psychology and social psychology. *Models* of consumer behavior are representations of conceptual schemes used to identify, explain, and predict consumer decisions. Such models may be built through a process of *abstraction* or of *realization*. Formal models of consumer behavior have been classified into four types—*stochastic* models, *linear-experimental* models, *information-processing* models, and *large system* models. Large system models represent comprehensive schemes such as those developed by Howard and Sheth, Nicosia, and Engel, Kollat, and

Blackwell. Most consumer behavior models, however, are applied to specific consumer situations. Twenty-eight such models have been listed in this chapter. One interesting approach to model building is the Consumenoid I, a computer simulation which replicates individual choice behavior as a function of entropy change maximization. This model yields a number of applications to actual marketing decisions.

NOTES

1. Richard T. Hise, John K. Ryans, Jr., and Willem Van't Spijker, "Theory in Consumer Behavior: A Status Report," *Journal of the Academy of Marketing Science*, Vol. 3, No. 2 (Spring 1975), p. 182.

2. William J. Goode and Paul K. Hatt, *Methods in Social Research* (New York: McGraw-Hill Book Co., 1952).

3. John A. Howard and Lyman E. Ostlund, eds., "The Model: Current Status of Buyer Behavior Theory," in Howard and Ostlund *Buyer Behavior* (New York: Alfred A. Knopf), 1973.

4. Robert A. Mittelstaedt, "Criteria for a Theory of Consumer Behavior," in Holloway, Mittelstaedt, and Ventkatesan, eds., *Consumer Behavior: Contemporary Research in Action* (Boston: Houghton-Mifflin Co., 1971), pp. 8–13.

5. Philip Kotler, "Behavioral Models for Analyzing Buyers," *Journal of Marketing*, Vol. 21 (October 1965), pp. 39–40.

6. Brian T. Ratchford, "The New Economic Theory of Consumer Behavior: An Interpretive Essay," *Journal of Consumer Research*, Vol. 2, No. 2 (September 1975), p. 65.

7. William J. McGuire, "Some Internal Psychological Factors Influencing Consumer Choice," *Journal of Consumer Research*, Vol. 2, No. 4 (March 1976), p. 302.

8. John B. Watson, *Behaviorism*, (New York: The People's Institute, 1925).

9. Daniel Yankelovich and William Barrett, *Ego and Instinct: The Psychoanalytic View of Human Nature* (New York: Random House, 1970).

10. Kotler, *Behavioral Models*, p. 41.

11. Thorstein Veblen, *The Theory of the Leisure Class* (New York: Viking Press, 1967).

12. Charles D. Schewe, "Selected Social Psychological Models for Analyzing Buyers," *Journal of Marketing*, Vol. 37 (July 1973), pp. 32–33.

13. David Reisman, Nathan Glazer, and Reuel Denney, *The Lonely Crowd* (New Haven: Yale University Press, 1961).

14. Schewe, 9 *Social Psychological Models*, p. 38.

15. Erving Goffman, *The Presentation of Self in Everyday Life* (Garden City: Doubleday & Co., 1959).

16. David B. Montgomery and Glenn L. Urban, *Management Science in Marketing* (Englewood Cliffs, N.J.: Prentice-Hall, 1969), p. 9.

17. William Lazer, "The Role of Models in Marketing," *Journal of Marketing*, Vol. 26, No. 2 (April 1962), pp. 9–14.

18. Flemming Hansen, *Consumer Choice Behavior: A Cognitive Theory* (New York: The Free Press, 1972), p. 433.

19. James R. Bettman and J. Morgan Jones, "Formal Models of Consumer Behavior: A Conceptual Overview," *Journal of Business*, Vol. 45 (October 1972), pp. 544–62.

20. Bettman and Jones, *Models of Consumer Behavior*, p. 545.

21. D. G. Morrison, "Testing Brand Switching Models," *Journal of Marketing Research*, Vol. 3 (November 1966), pp. 401–409.

22. Bettman and Jones, *Models of Consumer*

Behavior, p. 548.

23. Bettman and Jones, *Models of Consumer Behavior*, p. 546.

24. Marcus Alexis, George Haines, and Leonard Simon, "Consumer Information Processing: The Case of Women's Clothing," *Proceedings of the American Marketing Association*, September 28, 1968, pp. 197–205.

25. James R. Bettman, "Information Processing Models of Consumer Behavior," *Journal of Marketing Research*, August 1970, pp. 370–76.

26. Geoffrey Clarkson, *Portfolio Selection: A Simulation of Trust Investment* (Englewood Cliffs, N.J.: Prentice-Hall, 1962).

27. John A. Howard, *Marketing Management Analysis and Planning*, rev. ed. (Homewood, Ill.: Richard D. Irwin, 1963).

28. John A. Howard and Jagdish N. Sheth, *The Theory of Buyer Behavior*, (New York: John Wiley and Sons, 1969).

29. Howard and Sheth, *Buyer Behavior*, p. 416.

30. J. V. Farley and L. W. Ring, "An Empirical Test of the Howard-Sheth Model of Buyer Behavior," *Journal of Marketing Research*, Vol. 7, 1970, pp. 427–438.

31. John V. Farley, John A. Howard, and L. Winston Ring, *Consumer Behavior: Theory and Application* (Boston, Mass.: Allyn and Bacon, 1976).

32. D. R. Lehmann et al., "Empirical Contributions to Buyer Behavior Theory" (unpublished, New York: Columbia University, May 1971).

33. Francesco M. Nicosia, *Consumer Decisions* (Englewood Cliffs, N.J.: Prentice-Hall, 1966).

34. Francesco M. Nicosia, "Advertising Management, Consumer Behavior and Simulation," *Journal of Marketing Research*, Vol. 8 (March 1968), pp. 29–32.

35. James P. Engel, David T. Kollat, and Roger D. Blackwell, *Consumer Behavior*, 2nd ed. (New York: Holt, Rinehart and Winston, 1973), p. 49.

36. Engel et al., *Consumer Behavior*, pp. 50–59.

37. Frank M. Bass, "The Theory of Stochastic Preference and Brand Switching," *Journal of Marketing Research*, Vol. 11, (February 1974), pp. 1–20.

38. Bettman and Jones, *Models of Consumer Behavior*, pp. 549–560.

39. Flemming Hansen, *Consumer Choice Behavior: A Cognitive Theory* (New York: The Free Press, 1972).

40. William T. Moran, "Saints and Sinners: The Meaning of the Consumenoid Model of Human Behavior," Address to the 80th Annual Convention of the American Psychological Association, Honolulu, Hawaii, September 7, 1972.

41. M. Lawrence Light, *Consumenoid I: An Explanation and Illustration*," Batten, Barton, Durstine and Osborn, 1972.

42. Light, *Consumenoid I*, p. 40.

43. Kenneth A. Longman, *Applications of Consumenoid I*, Address to the 80th National Convention of the American Psychological Association, Honolulu, Hawaii, September 1972.

44. Gert Assmus, "NEWPROD: The Design and Implementation of a New Product Model," *Journal of Marketing*, Vol. 39, No. 1 (January 1975), p. 16.

45. Robert E. Burnkrant, "A Motivational Model of Information Processing Intensity," *Journal of Consumer Research*, Vol. 3, No. 1 (June 1976), p. 21.

46. David A. Aaker, "ADMOD: An Advertising Decision Model," *Journal of Marketing Research*, Vol. 12, No. 1 (February 1975), p. 37.

47. James E. Reinmuth and Michael D. Guerts, "The Collection of Sensitive Information Using a Two-Stage, Randomized Response Model." *Journal of Marketing Research*, Vol. 12, No. 4 (November 1975), p. 402.

MARKETING APPLICATIONS

Conclusion 1   *Theories from a variety of disciplines are used in consumer behavior research to explain why consumers behave as they do. By testing theories in a scientific way, we can establish observable patterns of behavior which will help marketers make decisions about product development, pricing, promotion, and distribution.*

Application   Two examples of theoretical contributions from the social sciences are useful to marketers:

1. Learning theory from psychology has established the need for repetition in marketing communications, particularly advertising.

2. Sociological theory points to the importance of self-enhancement through products which bestow social status. Many successful items such as the Lincoln Continental and Louis Vuitton luggage have been promoted almost exclusively on this basis.

Conclusion 2   *Models are devised to identify, explain, and predict consumer behavior. These may apply to specific activities such as household budgeting, choosing a packaged goods brand, and adopting new fashions.*

Application   The Consumenoid I Model, as one example, can simulate the consumer choice and purchasing process for a particular brand in a supermarket setting. It may be used by marketers to determine the reasons for brand change, to identify brand-choice habits over time, explain "fad" purchases, and to predict when "brand fatigue" may occur.

ASSIGNMENTS

Research Assignment

Background   As a Research Consultant to the Federal Consumer Agency in Washington, D.C., you are asked to make a presentation on using theoretical models to represent consumer behavior. Your explanation will be important in that it will help the government decide whether to allocate funds in this direction or spend the money in some other avenue of research.

Methodology   Prepare your presentation using Lazer's discussion of how models are constructed, found in this chapter. To offer a balanced view, discuss the advantages of using models and the disadvantages, in about three or four pages.

Extrapolation   Draw some tentative conclusions about the utility of model building, based on what you have written.

Creative Assignment

At U.S. Brands, a large food company, you are Brand Manager in charge of advertising for the Devil or Angel cake mixture. A memo has just crossed your desk from another Brand Manager (who secretly wants your job) criticizing the current TV commercials you have approved for Devil or Angel. The commercials, his memo states in stern, authoritative tones, are too "humorous" for the product. As substantiation for his critique, your colleague writes "motivation research has pointed out that women are very serious when they bake a cake because they are undergoing a symbolic act of birth." Since the memo has also gone to your Group-Marketing Director, you are now obliged to respond.

Write your own memo, putting that finding from motivation research in perspective and using the context of several different theories of consumer behavior to quiet your critic and reestablish your claim to knowledge of consumer theory.

Managerial Assignment

You have just accepted a position as Assistant Account Executive at the Maxwell and Mabbott ad agency. Because you are working on a packaged goods account—Fresh Antiperspirant—you would like to apply the computer model known as Consumenoid I in your agency's research. Make a recommendation to your Account Supervisor, briefly describing what the model does and discussing the kinds of information that can be obtained about how an individual consumer makes a purchasing decision for a product such as Fresh.

SELECTED READINGS

Bettman, James R., Noel Capon and Richard J. Lutz. "Multiattribute Measurement Models and Multiattribute Attitude Theory: A Test of Construct Validity." *Journal of Consumer Research*, Vol. 1, No. 4 (March 1975), pp. 1–15.

Lehmann, Donald R., et al. "Some Empirical Contributions To Buyer Behavior Theory." *Journal of Consumer Research*, Vol. 1, No. 3 (December 1974), pp. 43–55.

Ratchford, Brian T. "The New Economic Theory of Consumer Behavior: An Interpretive Essay." *Journal of Consumer Research,* Vol. 2, No. 2 (September 1975), pp. 65–75.

Ryan, Michael J. and E. H. Bonfield. "The Fishbein Extended Model and Consumer Behavior." *Journal of Consumer Research,* Vol. 2, No. 2 (September 1975), pp. 118–36.

Wilson, David T., H. Lee Mathews and James W. Harvey. "An Empirical Test of the Fishbein Behavioral Intention Model." *Journal of Consumer Research,* Vol. 1, No. 4 (March 1975), pp. 39–48.

OBJECTIVES

1. Discuss the *nine demographic* considerations used to segment consumer markets. *59*

2. Explain how sociocultural *values* may be quantified. *63*

3. Compare five *scaling procedures*. *66*

4. Summarize the *advantages* and *disadvantages* of projective techniques. *73*

THREE

Research and Measurement Techniques

Consumer research covers a wide range of activity, from pretesting television commercials to see, before they are aired, how they will affect viewers to government sponsored studies of how buyers have benefited from protective consumer legislation. But the great bulk of investigation is directed to discovering what consumers' needs are and how markets might be segmented accordingly.

Before marketers turned from a production to a consumer orientation, the concept of formal research into consumer behavior would have seemed laughable. Producers already "knew" their markets by the very nature of the products they manufactured. Their customers were everyone who could be sold a black Model T or a miracle hair-growing tonic. Then the forces of technological and social change, followed by increasingly fierce market competition, placed consumers squarely at the center of attention. And producers began seeking more empirical means of

scrutinizing them as the target of their vast resources.

The research which developed out of this need is generated by three principal sources. First, marketing firms, their advertising agencies, and consulting research firms produce a number of studies which are largely (and understandably) confidential. Second, the academic community—including sociologists, psychologists, and investigators specializing in marketing—contributes an ever-mounting body of consumer research available to anyone through scholarly and business publications. And, third, the federal government remains the most important source of free marketing data, in particular for publishing the $200-million population census every ten years.

This chapter explores several of the research and measurement methods adapted to the study of consumers, as well as innovative techniques considered promising for further de-

velopment. Sample topics from this discussion include:

• *How marketers use demographics to segment consumers.*

• *An empirical technique for gauging the effect of changing cultural values on consumption.*

• *How brand or store "images" may be measured and compared.*

• *What a cartoon test can indicate about*

attitudes which consumers can not (or will not) overtly express.

• *Why the size of a model's eyes may affect the appeal of an advertisement.*

Measurement techniques are described here for the purpose of building a general familiarity with current methods. For instructions on implementation of specific techniques, readers are referred to the bibliography at the end of this chapter.

Research Techniques Studied

Many individual research studies are cited throughout this text. There are two reasons for this. One is that consumer behavior theory has proceeded along the lines of scientific rigor, which subjects theories to constant testing by researchers. The second is that much of our knowledge of consumer behavior comes from marketing studies investigating specific product-use behavior, which is situational rather than suggestive of broad patterns of conduct. So each study of this kind is explained in its own context.

The most common research techniques are introduced here so they will be familiar to the reader in later discussions. The simplest methods, measuring aggregate *consumer purchases* and *demographics*, are analyzed first. Section II on cultural influences will discuss research probing cultural values, which are previewed in this chapter with a socioeconomic measure for quantifying values. *Scaling* techniques will be encountered in discussions of attitudes and consumer decision processes;

here, representative scaling operations such as the Likert, Thurstone, and Semantic Differential scales are presented in some detail. Research into consumer motivation has popularized the *projective* techniques once confined to practitioners of clinical and educational psychology; some of these are included in this discussion.

Finally, new techniques are constantly appearing in consumer study. As an example, the principles of eye pupil measurement are analyzed in this chapter, with evaluations of its likely role in future research.

As mentioned in the preceding chapter, consumer research strives to accomplish at least one of three objectives: to *describe*, *explain*, or *predict* behavior. Today, most studies generate findings at the descriptive and explanatory levels. It is in relatively restricted areas such as stochastic modeling of brand loyalty that predictive conclusions may be drawn.

How to Obtain *Primary* Consumer Behavior Data

There are three basic ways to collect primary, or first-hand, information directly from consumers.

1. *Observation Methods*   Actually watching consumers in the purchasing act is possible with in-store cameras. Subtle actions can be detected through this method that would not emerge from questioning a consumer away from the buying environment.

2. *Survey Methods*   Consumers may be questioned about their personal characteristics, attitudes, and product use or preferences by mail, telephone, or personal interview. *Mail* surveys may draw as little as 5 to 10 percent response levels; the best results, however, are reported when follow-up letters and money incentives are used.[1] *Telephone* surveying should be conducted with a well-tested question form to ferret out the most useful information in a short time.[2] *Personal interviews* are the most desirable (but also most expensive) means of collecting consumer data since they permit the greatest accuracy in both questions and answers, particularly when the information sought is personal or sensitive.[3]

3. *Experimental Methods*   Sometimes consumers participate in controlled experiments, and the findings for small *samples* of consumers are used to predict how larger populations can be expected to behave. This is the case when a new product is introduced in test markets, which are supposed to be representative of the rest of the country. If the product is successful in the test city, it should theoretically do well in the national market. If it bombs in testing, chances are it will fizzle nationally, too.[4]

Where to Find *Secondary* Consumer Behavior Data

Published information is readily available from a wide range of sources. A small sample is included here.

1. *Demographic Information:*
U.S. Census of Population
Marketing Information Guide
A Guide to Consumer Markets
State and city governments
Media (newspapers, magazines, television and radio stations) make demographic data about their readers or audiences available to advertisers

2. ***Consumer Research Findings:***
Journal of Consumer Research
Journal of Marketing
Journal of Marketing Research
Journal of Advertising Research
Journal of the Academy of Marketing Science
Journal of Psychology
Journal of Experimental Psychology
Harvard Business Review

3. ***Marketing Applications***
Advertising Age
Marketing Communications
Sales Management
Business Week
Nation's Business
Fortune
Forbes
Industry and trade magazines

Purchase and Demographic Measures

Measurement of aggregate consumer purchases and demographic data serve descriptive purposes. One keeps marketers informed as to how products are actually selling in the market place. The second provides information for segmentation purposes—the composition of consumer markets in terms of age, sex, income, and other objective characteristics of consumers who purchase (or might purchase) particular products and services.

Measuring Consumer Purchases

For the past thirty-five years or so, the Market Research Corporation of America has

reported every week on which consumer products are actually purchased across the country. The corporation uses a "panel" of 7,500 representative households, statistically selected, which provides some indication of the total purchasing behavior of the entire population or of that within geographic regions. The procedure is quite simple: Consumers on the panel carry a preprinted diary to record information about the brands or varieties of the products they buy, the amounts, prices paid, and the stores where they go to shop; they also note whether or not they are responding to a special sale or inducement such as a coupon for cents-off or a premium. Total sales of any product during a given time period are equal to the number of consumers, times purchase frequency, times the average purchase size.

Because data indicating consumers' ages, incomes, education, family size, and other demographic factors are weighed with purchase tabulations, marketers receive an evaluation of their particular market concentration, which includes the percentage of sales attributed to light, medium, and heavy users of a product and how one brand compares with its competitors in these variables. Such insights are particularly useful when a new product is introduced, permitting marketers to find out for certain exactly to whom the new item appeals.

Since Market Research Corporation launched this program, other consumer panels have been established to offer purchase data for specific test markets. Thus, a new product, packaging design, or other innovation may be introduced in just one or two sample cities from which inferences can be drawn about total market potential.

Demographic Measurement

The kind of data which describes where people live, how old they are, whether they went to college, and their ethnic group is known as *demographic information*, or "demographics" for short. The most comprehensive source of this knowledge is, of course, the huge collection of data obtained by the U.S. Census Bureau.

Consumer markets in the United States are segmented along demographic lines: by age, sex, marital status, family size, income, occupation, education, and geographical location.[5]

Age and Sex Considerations Most marketers consider age an important variable in

how consumers will respond to a product or service (see Figure 3-1). The brands of packaged goods an individual chooses, the kind of car he or she will buy, media preferences, and interest in specialty products all vary according to general age grouping. Some purchases such as toys and retirement condominiums, are purely a function of age.

Similarly, sex becomes a salient variable in many purchasing decisions. Some products are designed solely for men or women; others are much more likely to be purchased by members of one sex than the other.

Figure 3-1 Population by age and sex: estimates and projections.

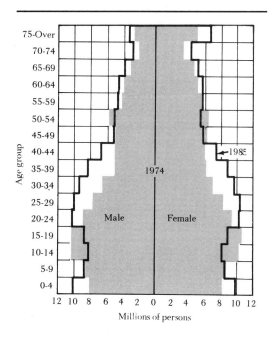

Source: Helen Axel, Editor, A Guide to Consumer Markets 1975/1976, *Conference Board Report No. 675, p. 19. © 1975 The Conference Board, Inc., New York, N.Y.*

Figure 3-1 segments the population of the United States from 1974 to 1985 by age and sex.

Marital Status and Family Size   Chapter 5 points out that the market of single people in the United States has swollen considerably over the past few years, creating a fractional subculture composed of mobile, upper-income singles with specialized consumer needs.

Similarly, family size wields great influence on how family budgets will be allocated and the usage of products such as foods, detergents, and Pampers.

Income, Occupation, and Education These variables are particularly useful to marketers of luxury-oriented products and services as well as to those who wish to reach individuals in specific occupations or better-educated consumers.

Table 3-1 segments the United States population by income group, major occupational status, and educational attainment.

Geographic Location   Where people live exerts certain influences upon purchasing behavior in clothing, local brand choices, and other patterns that may be a function of metropolitan, urban, rural, or suburban life styles. Geographic mobility has increased dramatically over the past couple of decades and varies according to age group, as shown in Figure 3-2.

Demographic data enjoys a widespread application across many different kinds of consumer behavior research. Market researchers assemble representative samples for study by means of demographics and draw correlations

Table 3-1   Characteristics of Families by Income Level, 1973

FAMILY CHARACTERISTIC	TOTAL FAMILIES (MILLIONS)	PER CENT DISTRIBUTION BY INCOME CLASS					
		UNDER $3,000	$3,000-5,000	$5,000-7,000	$7,000-10,000	$10,000-15,000	$15,000 & OVER
Total Families ..	55.1	6.0%	8.6%	9.4%	14.9%	25.5%	35.5%
Total Income	749.9[a]	.8	2.5	4.1	9.3	23.1	60.2
Race of Head							
White	48.9	4.9	7.6	8.8	14.6	26.3	37.6
Negro and other races	6.1	15.4	16.7	14.1	16.9	19.1	17.9
Negro	5.4	16.5	17.6	14.1	17.1	19.0	15.7
Age of Head							
Under 25	4.3	11.8	12.0	17.3	24.0	24.9	9.8
25–34	12.3	4.8	6.1	7.5	16.4	33.1	31.8
35–44	10.7	3.8	4.6	6.1	12.5	26.8	46.3
45–54	11.2	3.8	4.3	5.6	11.6	24.0	50.8
55–64	8.6	5.2	6.9	8.4	14.5	25.7	39.1
65 and over	7.9	11.9	23.7	19.4	16.4	14.3	14.3

Table 3-1 (Continued)

FAMILY CHARACTERISTIC	TOTAL FAMILIES (MILLIONS)	PER CENT DISTRIBUTION BY INCOME CLASS					
		UNDER $3,000	$3,000-5,000	$5,000-7,000	$7,000-10,000	$10,000-15,000	$15,000 & OVER
Education of Head[1]							
Elementary, 8 yrs.	5.6	7.8	13.9	15.5	18.3	23.0	21.5
High school graduate .	16.8	3.5	5.0	6.8	14.8	30.7	39.0
Some college	6.2	2.5	4.1	5.7	11.7	27.5	48.6
College graduate.....	8.0	1.6	2.2	2.7	6.8	19.5	67.3
Occupation of Head							
Professional, tech. ...	6.2	.9	2.0	2.6	8.2	22.7	63.5
Mgrs., administrators .	6.5	1.7	1.8	3.4	8.3	21.2	63.5
Clerical workers	3.4	3.4	4.5	8.8	17.6	32.4	33.4
Sales workers	2.5	2.4	3.2	5.1	10.2	26.9	52.1
Craft workers	9.0	1.4	2.3	5.5	14.7	35.0	41.1
Operatives	7.2	2.1	5.0	9.6	19.1	35.1	29.0
Service workers[2]	3.2	5.1	9.7	13.1	21.7	26.9	23.4
Type of Family							
Husband-wife	46.8	3.7	6.8	8.4	14.5	27.2	39.5
Wife working......	19.5	1.2	3.0	4.9	12.6	27.5	51.0
Wife not working ..	27.3	5.4	9.5	10.8	16.1	27.0	31.4
Other male head.....	1.4	9.9	9.4	11.2	15.7	24.3	29.6
Female head	6.8	22.1	21.0	16.5	17.4	14.1	8.9
Residence							
Nonfarm	52.5	5.8	8.4	9.3	14.8	25.7	35.8
Farm..............	2.5	10.0	11.6	12.4	15.8	22.0	28.3
Metropolitan	37.3	4.9	7.9	8.6	13.5	25.4	39.9
Central cities	16.0	6.9	10.4	10.5	15.0	24.3	32.9
Outside central cities	21.3	3.5	5.9	7.1	12.3	26.1	45.1
Nonmetropolitan.....	17.7	8.4	10.1	11.3	18.0	25.9	26.1
Region							
Northeast	12.8	4.6	8.3	8.5	13.9	26.1	38.8
North Central	14.9	4.7	7.2	7.8	14.6	27.2	38.6
South	17.6	8.8	10.1	11.6	16.2	24.2	29.2
West	9.8	5.3	8.5	9.1	14.7	24.7	37.7

[1]Family heads 25 years and over
[2]Except private household
[a]—Billions of dollars

Source: Helen Axel, *Editor,* A Guide to Consumer Markets 1975/1976, *Conference Board Report No. 675, p. 132.* © 1975 The Conference Board, Inc., New York, N.Y.

Figure 3-2   Geographic mobility.

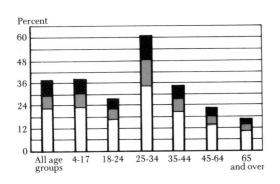

Source: Helen Axel, Editor, A Guide to Consumer Markets 1975/1976, *Conference Board Report No. 675, p. 39.* © *1975 The Conference Board, Inc., New York, N.Y.*

among demographic facts about consumers gauged against other cultural, social, attitudinal, perceptual, and personality variables.

Profiling Consumers by Demographics A demographic profile of the market for a product, service, or retail store summarizes the age, sex, income, and other characteristics of the consumers who are most likely to purchase a specific product or brand or to shop in a particular establishment. Data for research may also be highly organized in this way.

In addition, demographics are used by print and broadcast media to attract advertisers. Figure 3-3 depicts a demographic profile of *Cosmopolitan* readers designed to portray women who regularly enjoy *Cosmo* as prime prospects for a number of heavily advertised products and services.

Figure 3-3   Demographic profile of a *Cosmopolitan* reader.

	Cosmopolitan 1964 vs. 1977		U.S. Average 1977
SHE'S YOUNG: In 18-34 Age group	45.4%	60.0%	36.2%
SHE'S WELL EDUCATED: Attended or graduated college	33.2%	44.5%	22.5%
SHE WORKS: Employed	46.6%	61.3%	42.2%
SHE'S IN HIGH INCOME H H:	47.3% $8,000 & Over	70.5% $10,000 & Over	47.0%
SHE'S BIG CITY: Metro areas	66.8%	78.0%	68.7%
MARITAL STATUS: Not married	29.5%	38.8%	33.2%

Source: W. R. Simmons & Associates, New York, N.Y. Reprinted by permission.

A Sociocultural Measurement

Certain values* which come into play in consumer behavior may be quantified for research purposes, as in one study which investigated consumer purchases within a sociological model of changing values.[6] This investigation probed value shifts which occurred during 1929–1957, a period of accelerated change in both the American economy and culture. While economic change was moving the country from a production to a consumption orientation, values were shifting from traditional patterns to those emerging ones discussed in chapter 5.

Identification of Consumer Values

The prominent consumer values of that period were identified on the basis of a hierarchy of value criteria suggested by Robin Williams.[7]

Dominant and subordinate values for a group or social system as a whole can be roughly ordered according to these criteria:

1. *Extensiveness* of the value in the total activity of the system. What proportion of a population and its activities manifests the value?

2. *Duration* of the value. Has it been persistently important over a considerable period of time?

3. *Intensity* with which the value is sought or maintained, as shown by effort; crucial choices; verbal affirmation; and reactions to threats to the value—for example, the

*Values are cultural ideas about what is good or proper, by which people in a society conduct themselves.

promptness, certainty, and severity of sanctions.

4. *Prestige* of value carriers, that is, of persons, objects, or organizations considered to be bearers of the value.

Quantification of Consumer Values

The values which emerged were thrift, durability, innovation, and status enhancement, which were then quantified by means of economic data.

Thrift, defined as the economical management of financial resources, was measured through (1) comparisons of percentages of family income placed in savings accounts, (2) comparisons of the amount of installment buying of durable goods, (3) comparisons of percentage of income spent on luxuries, and (4) analysis of the basic appeals of advertising of durable goods in a major print medium.

Durability as a value orientation was measured by automobile ownership through (1) comparison of the average length of a car's serviceability, (2) analysis of automobile advertising, and (3) comparison of the amount of private expenditure for durable and nondurable goods.

Innovation was quantified through (1) comparison of the amounts of money spent for research and development by manufacturers, (2) comparison of the numbers of new products introduced to the market, and (3) an analysis of automobile advertising in its appeal to the value of innovation.

Status Enhancement, seen as a quality of symbolic application with a high status level, was measured by (1) a correlation between the

**Figure 3-4   Thrift: Relative growth rates of thrift and GNP
(in 1958 dollars measured in percent).**

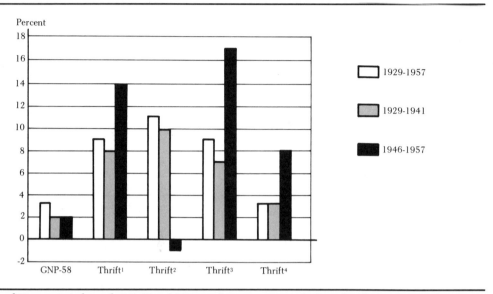

Source of Figures 3-4 through 3-7: Harold W. Berkman, A Quantified Study of Economic Behavior Interpreted Within a Model of Changing Value Orientations. *Unpublished doctoral dissertation, St. John's University, December 1970.*

purchase of household furnishings and the position of those furnishings on a status scale and (2) an analysis of automobile advertising for its appeal to status enhancement.

Through these measurement techniques, it was demonstrated that the values of thrift and durability both declined in their influence upon consumer behavior in that period, while the values of innovation and status enhance-ment increased in influence.

Figures 3-4 to 3-7 illustrate shifts in these American value orientations from 1929–1957.

Similar quantification methods might be applied to other American consumer values which have emerged in recent years; *ecological concern, youthfulness,* and *ethnic awareness* are only a few examples of "new" values that could be measured in a similar fashion.

Scaling Techniques

A growing amount of research in consumer behavior attempts to study *qualitative* rather than quantitative data. Particularly in the realm of attitude assessment—how consumers feel about brands, store images, and other subjective questions—some measure of

Figure 3-5   Thrift: A scatter diagram and trend analysis illustrating a shift in value orientation.

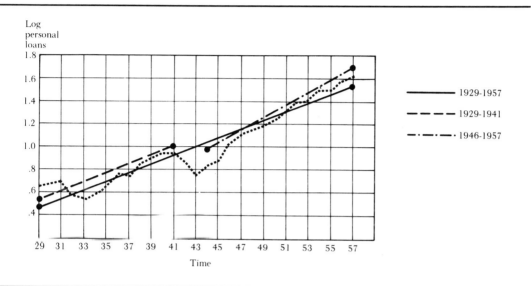

---

personal reactions becomes necessary. This problem is usually approached through the use of *scaling* operations.[8]

Types of Scaling Procedures

Qualitative attributes may be gauged through *nominal, ordinal,* and *interval* scales. A nominal scale is used when people are asked to rate something as equal to something else, but this case is rare in consumer research. Usually, a researcher's most basic scale involves ordinal values, asking consumers to say whether they prefer Heinz Ketchup to Hunt's Ketchup as one example. This is an *ordinal* measure. A more sophisticated technique uses subdivisions of equal intervals along a *linear* scale. In this approach, consumers may

Figure 3-6   Status enhancement: Relative growth rates of status-enhancement and GNP (in 1958 dollars measured in percent).

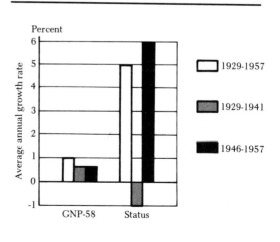

Figure 3-7   Status enhancement: A scatter diagram and trend analysis illustrating a shift in value orientation.

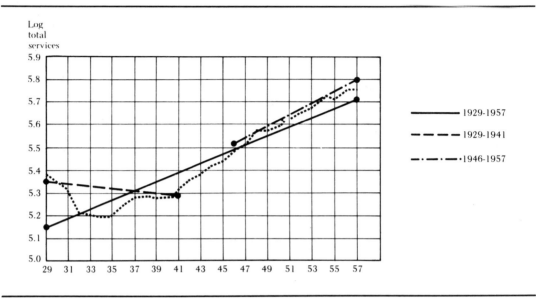

indicate that they find Hunt's Ketchup about three units superior to Heinz or vice versa. A number of different items may be included in both interval and ordinal techniques: subjects may rate a number of products in order of preference in an ordinal scale or make subtle judgments of differences in amount of preference through the interval approach.

Table 3-2 summarizes the three types of scales and the statistical operations applied to generate conclusions.

The most common type used in consumer research is the ordinal scale, which may also use equal units of difference to reveal subtle gradations in response. Although these units are represented as equal, the scale is still ordinal because there is no assurance that "respondents will be able to judge equal units or that the units conceived by one respondent

will be of the same magnitude as those conceived by any other respondent."[9]

Scaling procedures which will be analyzed here include the Thurstone, Likert, Guttman, Stapel, and Semantic Differential approaches.

Thurstone-type Scales

In Thurstone-type scales, a number of short opinion statements about the subject to be measured are collected, then categorized by judges (who are different from respondents) into a series of eleven piles. The piles are arranged in sequence from highly favorable to highly unfavorable statements, with a neutral set in the center. This sorting procedure is

Table 3-2   Nominal, Ordinal, and Interval Scales

SCALE	BASIC EMPIRICAL OPERATIONS	PERMISSIBLE STATISTICS	SIGNIFICANCE TESTS
Nominal	Determination of equality	Number of cases, mode	Chi square
Ordinal	Determination of greater or less	Median, percentiles, rank-order correlation	Sign test
Interval	Determination of equality of intervals or differences	Mean, standard deviation product moment correlation	*t* Test *must have equal* *F* Test *intervals*

Source: Lyndon O. Brown and Leland L. Beik, Marketing Research and Analysis, *Fourth Edition, p. 279. Copyright © 1969 The Ronald Press Company, New York.*

known as the method of "equal-appearing intervals."[10]

The percentage of judges who place each item in the different categories constitutes the

Figure 3-8   Determination of scale values for Thurstone-type attitude scale.

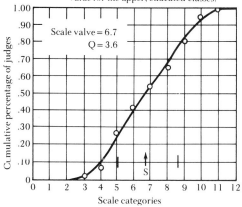

Statement No. 8: "I believe the church has a good influence on the lower and uneducated classes but has no value for the upper, educated classes."

Scale value = 6.7
Q = 3.6

Source: Anne Anastasi, Psychological Testing, *Third Edition. Copyright © 1968 Macmillan Publishing Co., Inc., New York.*

basic data for determining the scale value of the statements, as shown in Figure 3-8. On the baseline of the graph, the numbers 1 to 11 correspond to the categories. The vertical axis shows the percentage of judges placing the statement in or below each category. And the fiftieth percentile, or median position, is taken as the scale value of the statement in question. Here the statements are derived from a Thurstone study of attitudes toward the church.[11]

The respondent applying a Thurstone scale marks all the statements he or she agrees with, and the score for that individual is the median scale value of those statements. In a hypothetical study involving attitudes toward a retail store, sample statements might be scaled as follows:

I think that the Star store has the best sales-people in town. (10.5)

The Star store is no better and no worse than any of its competitors. (5.0)

I wouldn't shop at the Star store unless they carried something I couldn't find at another store. (.7)

One difficulty with Thurstone scales is the possibility that the judges' selections will be affected by their individual attitudes toward the subject. Evidence is generally inconclusive, however, as to how profoundly this bias may affect test results. And it is generally agreed that such influence does not invalidate the technique for construction of attitude scales.[12]

Likert Scales

nominal scale   *How strong is your attitude*

Where Thurstone scales require judges for initial classification of items, Likert scales, devised by Rensis Likert, allow subjects to select items purely on the basis of their responses.

First, a large number of statements about the phenomenon being measured are assembled. Then an item analysis sorts relevant statements and selects those which will be used in the scale. Internal consistency is usually the principal basis for item selection.

Test subjects indicate degree of agreement or disagreement with each statement by registering one of the following standard responses: strongly agree (SA), agree (A), undecided (U), disagree (D), and strongly disagree (SD). Scores are obtained by crediting the responses with 5, 4, 3, 2, and 1, respectively. The sum of the item credits is the individual's total score; thus the Likert technique is said to be *summated.* Finally, the position of an individual in the group applying the scale is compared with the distribution of the positions of the entire group.[13]

Statements which appear on Likert-type scales are of this variety:

Antiperspirants give a person confidence.
Antiperspirants have pleasant scents.
Antiperspirants are sticky and uncomfortable.
Antiperspirants are unnatural.

In consumer research, Likert scaling methods are used more often than Thurstone scales because subjects themselves (instead of judges) select the items. This technique is simpler as well as better designed to avoid the possibility of bias.

Guttman Scales

The Guttman approach to scaling is referred to as *cumulative.* Respondents agree or disagree with items as in the Likert scales, but Guttman statements are so arranged that agreement with, say, a strongly favorable statement will indicate agreement with similarly strong, favorable statements and disagreement with highly negative ones.[14]

If an individual were to agree vigorously with a statement such as "*Time* magazine is an authoritative source of news information," we would expect that person's hearty agreement with an item which states, "Articles in *Time* are written by persons with great expertise in their specialties," and marked disagreement with a statement that "*Time* articles represent irresponsible news reporting."

To test the accuracy of the cumulative approach, Guttman requires 90 percent of individual responses to fit this consistent pattern before an attitude may be said to exist toward the object measured by the procedure.[15]

Stapel Scales

 attribute

In Stapel scales, a ten-point nonverbal rating scale is used to measure both intensity and direction of attitudes. Usually adjectives are used to describe a product, brand, or store, and respondents indicate their agreement or disagreement with an adjective on a scale from +5 (strong agreement) to −5 (strong disagreement).[16] If a soap product is the object of a study, for example, consumers might be asked to respond to the adjective "fragrant" by indicating a numerical score on the plus or minus side. This technique is highly useful for its simplicity and economical means of data-gathering.

The Semantic Differential

how import. an attribute is.

The Semantic Differential, a popular technique in consumer research, also utilizes adjectives about brands, products, or retail establishments to draw portraits of consumer attitudes. It is used with particular frequency in studies of brand or store *image*.[17]

The procedure consists of a bipolar scale, usually segmented into seven equal units, with antithetical adjectives at each end of the scale. Thus, a single scale for rating an automobile might appear as:

Beautiful ___|___|___|___|___|___|___ Ugly

Most items are presented as positive versus negative choices, with the number four position designated as the median. Subjects then indicate the position on the scale which is most descriptive of their attitude toward the brand or store. A profile is drawn by connecting the points marked along all scale items. With this procedure, several products may be compared, as shown in Figure 3-9. This particular differential was designed to obtain attitudes toward the brand and company images of three competing beer brands.

A semantic differential may be constructed to probe attitudes toward any number of

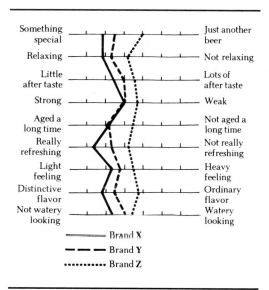

Figure 3-9   A semantic differential comparison of branded beers.

Source: William A. Mindak, "Fitting the Semantic Differential to the Marketing Problem," Journal of Marketing, Vol. 25 (April 1961). Reprinted by permission of the American Marketing Association.

relevant variables, as shown in Figure 3-10 for patronage of a retail establishment.

Like the Guttman method, the Semantic Differential is relatively easy to design and administer.

Monadic versus Comparative Scales

Clancy and Garson suggest that some types of scaling techniques may be better measures of consumers' actual attitudes than others. In this respect, they contrast *monadic preference* scales with *comparative preference* scales. The monadic variety attempts to mea-

Figure 3-10   A semantic differential for retail store patronage.

	Extremely	Quite	Slightly	Neither one nor the other	Slightly	Quite	Extremely	
well known generally	—	—	—	—	—	—	—	unknown generally
small number of stores operated by company	—	—	—	—	—	—	—	large number of stores operated by company
long time in community	—	—	—	—	—	—	—	short time in community

PHYSICAL CHARACTERISTICS OF THE STORE

	Extremely	Quite	Slightly	Neither one nor the other	Slightly	Quite	Extremely	
dirty	—	—	—	—	—	—	—	clean
unattractive decor	—	—	—	—	—	—	—	attractive decor
easy to find items you want	—	—	—	—	—	—	—	difficult to find items you want
easy to move through store	—	—	—	—	—	—	—	difficult to move through store
fast checkout	—	—	—	—	—	—	—	slow checkout

CONVENIENCE OF REACHING THE STORE FROM YOUR LOCATION

	Extremely	Quite	Slightly	Neither one nor the other	Slightly	Quite	Extremely	
near by	—	—	—	—	—	—	—	distant
short time required to reach store	—	—	—	—	—	—	—	long time required to reach store
difficult drive	—	—	—	—	—	—	—	easy drive
difficult to find parking place	—	—	—	—	—	—	—	easy to find parking place
convenient to other stores I shop	—	—	—	—	—	—	—	inconvenient to other stores I shop

PRODUCTS OFFERED

	Extremely	Quite	Slightly	Neither one nor the other	Slightly	Quite	Extremely	
wide selection of different kinds or products	—	—	—	—	—	—	—	limited selection of different kinds of products
fully stocked	—	—	—	—	—	—	—	understocked
undependable products	—	—	—	—	—	—	—	dependable products
high quality	—	—	—	—	—	—	—	low quality
numerous brands	—	—	—	—	—	—	—	few brands

PRICES CHARGED BY THE STORE

well known brands	—	—	—	—	—	—	unknown brands
high compared to other stores	—	—	—	—	—	—	low compared to other stores
high values for money spent	—	—	—	—	—	—	low values for money spent
small number of items specially priced	—	—	—	—	—	—	large number of items specially priced

STORE PERSONNEL

discourteous	—	—	—	—	—	—	courteous
friendly	—	—	—	—	—	—	cold
helpful	—	—	—	—	—	—	unhelpful
inadequate number	—	—	—	—	—	—	adequate number

ADVERTISING BY THE STORE

informative	—	—	—	—	—	—	uninformative
helpful in planning purchases	—	—	—	—	—	—	unhelpful in planning purchases
unappealing	—	—	—	—	—	—	appealing
misleading	—	—	—	—	—	—	believable
infrequently seen by you	—	—	—	—	—	—	frequently seen by you

YOUR FRIENDS AND THE STORE

well known to your friends	—	—	—	—	—	—	unknown to your friends
disliked by your friends	—	—	—	—	—	—	well liked by your friends
well recommended by your friends	—	—	—	—	—	—	poorly recommended by your friends
few friends shop there	—	—	—	—	—	—	numerous friends shop there

Source: Robert F. Kelly and Ronald Stephenson, "The Semantic Differential: An Information Source for Designing Retail Patronage Appeals", Journal of Marketing, Vol. 31 (October 1967), p. 45. Reprinted by permission of the American Marketing Association.

sure a consumer's interest in a brand or product on an absolute basis; it is the most widely used scaling technique in consumer research. Comparative scales, on the other hand, are designed to measure a consumer's interest in a brand or product relative to its competitors.[18] The differences between the two approaches may be seen in a comparison of instructions to respondents for both techniques, shown in Table 3-3.

Table 3-3 Monadic vs. Comparative Preference Scales

MONADIC REFERENCE SCALES

The +5 to −5 Rating Scale

I would like you to rate some brands of (product class) from +5 to −5. The more you think a brand is above average for all (product class) brands, the higher the plus number you should give it, up to +5. The more you think a brand is below average, the bigger the minus number you should give it, all the way down to −5: Remember, you can use every number between +5 and −5.

The Predisposition-to-Buy Scale

Now I would like you to tell me about your interest in purchasing various brands of (product class) by using this card. Tell me which statement describes your feelings about each brand as I name them.

I will definitely buy the brand next time.

I will probably buy the brand in the near future.

I might buy the brand in the future.

I don't know whether or not I will buy the brand.

I will probably not buy the brand.

I will certainly not buy the brand.

I would not use this brand under any circumstances.

COMPARATIVE PREFERENCE SCALES

The Constant Sum Scale

Here's a sheet on which I have listed several brands of (product class). Next to each brand is a pocket. Here are 11 cards. I would like you to put these cards in the pockets next to the brands to indicate how likely it is that you would buy each brand. You can put as many cards as you want in front of a brand.

Paired Comparisons

I'm going to name some pairs of brands (product class). I'd like you to tell me which of each pair you would be more likely to purchase.

Source: *Kevin J. Clancy and Robert Garson, "Why Some Scales Predict Better,"* Journal of Advertising Research, *Vol. 10, No. 5 (1970), p. 34. Copyright © 1970, by the Advertising Research Foundation and reprinted by permission.*

Clancy and Garson conclude that the monadic scales tend to suffer from what is termed "response style"—a tendency to agree or disagree with items regardless of content. These styles are commonly referred to as "yea saying" and "nay saying." Studies which are most invalidated by these respondent quirks are those of the monadic type, which try to assess *absolute* appeals of some marketing stimulus. And the difficulty appears to be related to socioeconomic variables:

• Lower socioeconomic consumers want to "please" researchers by rating everything positively or "high."

• Upper socioeconomic respondents may express their feelings of suspicion and greater sophistication by rating artificially "low".

Thus, comparative scaling to measure the relative appeal on two or more variables may prove more valid.[19]

Projective Techniques

The use of "projective" tests to uncover "subconscious" motivations became popular during the 1950s, coinciding with a widespread fascination with the Freudian psychoanalytic concepts on which they were based. Today, the popularity of those concepts has waned considerably.

But projective testing retains certain inherent advantages for interview procedures where it seems necessary to get beyond subjects' "defensive" reactions. In the typical interview procedure, people may not always share their innermost feelings about, say, the use of personal products with a researcher who is, after all, a stranger. Also, individuals are not always aware of their underlying motives for buying a product or choosing one brand over another. In such situations it may be useful to have the techniques at hand to ferret out motives based on barely recognized needs or associations. Then, too, consumers in interview situations exhibit a very human tendency to shade their responses for the interviewer. Most people would rather have us believe that they drink Chivas Regal scotch for its quality than for the status-enhancement of the brand name. Similarly, a few individuals would prefer to have an interviewer think that they purchase only Chivas Regal when in fact they buy only an inexpensive scotch and, before guests are about to arrive, transfer that scotch to an empty Chivas bottle!

For these reasons, projective techniques serve as a useful complement to mainstream research methods. Four types of projective procedures will be described here: word association, sentence completion, cartoon completion, and thematic apperception tests.

Word-Association Techniques

In this protocol, subjects are asked to read a list of words and, after each, to say the first word that comes to mind. The list is carefully organized beforehand, with some test words interspersed among a number of "neutral" words to elicit some response about the item under consideration. Some reactions are classified as relatively common, while unexpected responses may point to attitude patterns of the subject. Information obtained from responses is usually evaluated for (1) frequency of any response word, (2) hesitation before responding, and (3) blocking.[20]

Frequency Surprisingly enough, there are greater similarities than differences among consumers in their responses to items on a typical word-association test. When the same word occurs frequently as a response, it is usually indicative of an attitude set toward the test word, as when many subjects reply to the stimulus word "margarine" with the response word "imitation." Additionally, responses can be categorized in terms of positive-negative, traditional-contemporary, or other groupings.

Hesitation A pause of, usually, more than three seconds before responding to the stimulus word is defined as "hesitation." This is believed to reveal that the subject is somehow emotionally involved with the test word or is substituting what he or she feels is an "acceptable" response for one which might be considered "unacceptable."

Blocking Sometimes a respondent is unable to come out with any response at all after a reasonable length of time. This is referred to as "blocking," and suggests that the stimulus word is not getting any significant message across or that the subject wants to give an unacceptable response and is inhibited about doing so. The rate of blocking is usually taken into account with the rate of hesitation. When a word becomes associated with low blocking and hesitation rates, it is thought to convey a meaningful message. But when the hesitation and blocking rates are high for a word, it is believed to be less than useful for communication with a consumer audience.

Thus word-association methods may prove useful in determining brand names, advertising copy headlines, and other expressions which are crucial to a product or brand's acceptance.[21]

Sentence-Completion Techniques

This approach represents an extension of the word-association technique, since subjects are given a series of incomplete statements which guide their responses.[22]

A hypothetical set of sentences for use in hair product marketing might begin with:

Most people think blondes are _____ .
People who color their hair blonde are _____ .
Blonde coloring makes a woman _____ .
Blondes are more likely than brunettes
    to _____ .

Sentences to be completed are usually varied in content so that respondents do not figure out the interviewer's objectives. And open-ended statements are designed to be sufficiently ambiguous that people may complete them in a way that truly reflects their own attitudes.

Sentence-completion gives subjects considerably more latitude than word-association to qualify their responses and take greater care in organizing their opinions. However, this removes some of the spontaneity obtained in single-word responses.

Cartoon Techniques

The use of cartoons is a purely projective technique in that through it subjects can project their own feelings onto others. In the standard format, a situation appears in cartoon form with a blank cartoon "bubble" over one or more of the characters. Both stimuli words and the space for responses are restricted so that the subject may give a relatively unqualified response. Characters are necessarily portrayed in a rather vague way that offers no cues to personality, attitudes, social class, or other factors that might affect the response.

Cartoons may be especially useful for eliciting a certain kind of response. In Rosensweig's Picture-Frustration Test, characters who are to be provided with responses by those being tested are deliberately placed in frustrating circumstances to draw out subjects' frustration reactions, which usually take the form of aggression.[23]

The cartoon protocol seems intriguing to most consumers and for this reason may produce a higher level of motivation in test-taking.[24] Figure 3-11 illustrates one classic cartoon example in which a husband and wife are portrayed in a retail establishment. The researcher's instructions for interpreting responses accompanies the cartoon.

Figure 3-11   An extended cartoon procedure.

Role-Playing To Reveal Buying Attitudes

The drawing of a husband and wife in an appliance store was shown to women. The husband is shown as saying, "Oh, here comes the salesman." On display is a range of major appliances.

From this one situation are extracted 3 areas:

1. What the woman is actually saying *out loud* to her husband.
2. What she is thinking to herself, but probably would not say out loud.
3. What she feels he is thinking, which gives an indication of anxieties developed by the husband's attitudes as she interprets them.

Through the device of a role-playing situation, respondents are actually revealing their own attitudes while feeling they are interpreting those of others.

Source: The Chicago Tribune, "The Consumer Speaks About Appliances," Tribune Company, 1959. Reprinted by permission.

The Thematic Apperception Test

The Murray Thematic Apperception Test, usually referred to as the TAT, originally used with psychiatric patients, has achieved some degree of acceptance in personality research.

The test consists of twenty ambiguous pictures of people in situations which are tailored to a given subject's age and sex. Introduction to the subject's task usually takes the form of "I am going to show you some pictures. I want you to tell me a story about what is going on in each picture. What led up to it and what will the outcome be?"[25]

The TAT is designed to provide considerable information on a subject's personality, motivation, and attitudes as this technique permits the subject to attribute his or her own self-image, feelings, and frustrations to vague characters and situations.

Through the use of new pictures—similarly ambiguous—designed to suggest scenes of consumers in product-use situations, the TAT has been applied to:[26]

• *Launching a new food product*. In this case, subjects were shown a series of five pictures portraying a mother preparing and serving food to her family and were asked to describe the kind of person this woman might be who is using the new product.

• *Changing a standard product*. Here a picture of two women conversing served as the basis for a series of questions about a modified food product.

• *Studying attitudes toward brands, retail stores, and media*. Because much of the TAT protocol is verbal, the subject may be asked relevant questions about specific or generic brands while responding to the picture stimuli.

Evaluation of Projective Techniques

Some of the major criticisms of projective techniques in consumer research point to problems in reliability and validity, questions about the theoretical bases for the tests, the fact that they were developed to study deviant personalities under the observation of a trained clinical therapist, and other substantial drawbacks.

In a more positive vein, Thorndike notes several advantages of projective tests which may render them exceedingly useful in certain situations:[27]

1. *The tasks presented to the individual are usually both somewhat novel and quite unstructured.* The subject cannot depend upon established, conventional, and stereotyped patterns of response. Rather, the respondent is thrown back upon his or her psyche and must delve within it, for the test situation demands creation of a new response.

2. *The nature of the appraisals being made is usually well disguised.* The subject is ordinarily not aware of the true purpose of the test and, even if the general nature of the appraisal is clear, does not know what aspects of the response are significant or what significance they have. The individual is not called upon to verbalize anxieties or emotions or to reveal his or her personality directly and consciously to the tester. Thus, inhibitions and conscious controls may be bypassed, and intentional distortion of the picture presented is difficult for any but the most sophisticated subject.

3. *Most of the tests make little or no demand on literacy or academic skills.* They are nonreading, largely independent of any particular language, and in some cases do not involve speech at all. Thus, their scope is much wider

than that of self-report or rating procedures.

4. *They provide a view of the total functioning individual.* They do not slice off one piece or trait for analysis. They preserve, it is alleged, the unity and integration of the total personality.

These features suggest that projective tests may complement other testing procedures in drawing meaningful, whole portraits of consumers.

Innovative Measurement Techniques

In the burgeoning field of consumer behavior research, new techniques are always welcome to be scrutinized, replicated, and possibly included in the mainstream of theory and research. Consider, for instance, the measurement of *pupil size* and *eye location* in advertising creation and testing. In recent years, we have become more sophisticated about the nonverbal communication of "body language" and the impact of our facial expressions upon people with whom we interact. In this context, King has studied the intriguing proposition that the presentation of a *model's eyes* in advertisements—in both print and television media—may generate positive or negative responses to the ad.[28]

His hypothesis is based upon two sets of findings from physiological psychology. One is that subjects tend to respond to appealing stimuli with dilation (enlargement) of their pupils; pupil diameter has been shown to increase by more than 50 percent when subjects are startled by a pleasant stimulus. Conversely, constriction of the pupils occurs when disagreeable, unappealing stimuli are shown. The second set of findings suggests that the joint movement of one's eyes to the right or the left (technically known as conjunctive lateral eye movement, or CLEM) may be associated with personality characteristics. People whose predominant eye direction is to the *left* tend to be more re-

laxed, sociable, imaginative, open to suggestion, and more affectionate than right lookers. In short, they may be described as having greater emotionality. And while *left* lookers are inclined to exhibit greater interest in philosophy, music, art, and the humanities, individuals who look predominantly to the *right* tend to reveal more scientific inclinations.[29]

Applying these generalizations to subjects' responses to advertisements, King found that:[30]

1. Enlarged pupil size is indicative of favorable attitudes toward others and covertly influences consumers' interests and attitudes toward the communicator. All subjects in this study responded to a model with pupils expanded as prettier and more appealing than the same model with pupils held at normal size; yet none of the subjects could explain why.

2. When eye direction is to the right, rational and objective thoughts are reinforced; eyes focused to the left reinforce emotional and subjective expressions. "Right-lookers" in the study found the model more appealing when her eyes were directed to the right, while "left-lookers" believed her to be more attractive when looking to the left. Again, none of the subjects could specify their reasons for these choices.

The implications of eye measurement are quite significant for many forms of advertising research, including test situations where subjects evaluate ads by means of pupillograph measurement. Additionally, these findings may prove beneficial to personality researchers in interview situations.

The overview of measurement techniques in this chapter has been necessarily brisk—many questions of methodology, as well as other research techniques, have not been introduced. The vast amount of current information on consumer research measurement fills many volumes, some of which are included in the bibliography for readers seeking additional information.

Similarly, a number of research techniques utilize more than one form of measurement. Chapter 19, on *psychographics and life-style research*, introduces a methodology which combines demographics, attitude and personality data, and behavioral information to develop meaningful profiles of consumers.[31]

Summary

Measurement in consumer behavior may take the form of purchasing data, demographics, scaling techniques, and projective approaches. Purchasing information is collected to determine what consumers are actually buying in the market place, as well as to provide *demographic* information—age, sex, marital status, income, occupation, education, and geographical location. This data is generally used to create demographic profiles of target markets. *Scaling* techniques are often applied to the study of attitudes and other qualitative problems. They include the Thurstone, Likert, Guttman, and Stapel scales and the Semantic Differential technique. *Projective* tests are generally used in motivation and personality research. The familiar techniques in this category are word-association, sentence-completion, cartoons, and the Thematic Apperception Test. New approaches to measurement are constantly being developed, such as using eye movement measures in personality and advertising research.

NOTES

1. Leslie Kanuk and Conrad Berenson, "Mail Surveys and Response Rates: A Literature Review," *Journal of Marketing Research*, Vol. 12, No. 4 (November 1975), p. 440.

2. William B. Locander and John P. Burton, "The Effect of Question Form on Gathering Income Data by Telephone," *Journal of Marketing Research*, Vol. 13, No. 2 (May 1976), p. 189.

3. James E. Reinmuth and Michael D. Geurts, "The Collection of Sensitive Information Using a Two-Stage, Randomized Response Model," *Journal of Marketing Research*, Vol. 12, No. 4 (November 1975), p. 402.

4. Christopher C. Gilson, Jr., "Test Market Consumers Are Different from You and Me," *Doubleday Advertising Newsletter* (September 1976).

5. Helen Axel, *A Guide to Consumer Markets*

1975/1976, (New York: The Conference Board, 1975).

6. Harold W. Berkman, *A Quantified Study of Economic Behavior Interpreted within a Sociological Model of Changing Value Orientations* Unpublished doctoral dissertation (New York: St. John's University, 1970).

7. Robin Williams, *American Society: A Sociological Interpretation* (New York: Alfred A. Knopf, Inc., 1960), p. 410.

8. Lyndon O. Brown and Leland L. Beik, *Marketing Research and Analysis* (New York: Ronald Press, 1969), p. 277.

9. Brown and Beik, *Marketing Research*, p. 278.

10. L. L. Thurstone, *The Measurement of Values* (Chicago, Ill.: University of Chicago Press, 1959).

11. Anne Anastasi, *Psychological Testing*, 3rd ed. (New York: The Macmillan Co., 1968).

12. H. S. Upshaw, "The Effects of Variable Perspectives on Judgements of Opinion Statements for Thurstone Scales: Equal Appearing Intervals,"*Journal of Personality and Social Psychology*, Vol. 2 (1965).

13. Rensis Likert, "A Technique for the Measurement of Attitudes," *Psychology Archives*, Vol. 22 (June 1932).

14 Louis Guttman, "A Basis for Selecting Qualitative Data," *American Sociological Review*, Vol. 9 (April 1944).

15. Elizabeth Richards, "A Commercial Application of Guttman Attitude Scaling Techniques," *Journal of Marketing*, Vol. 22, (October 1957).

16. Irving Crespi, "Use of a Scaling Technique in Surveys," *Journal of Marketing*, Vol. 25 (July 1961), pp. 69–72.

17. William A. Mindak, "Fitting The Semantic Differential to the Marketing Problem," *Journal of Marketing*, Vol. 25 (April 1961).

18. Kevin J. Clancy and Robert Garson, "Why Some Scales Predict Better," *Journal of Advertising Research*,Vol. 10, No. 5 (1970) pp. 33–38.

19. Clancy and Garson, "Some Scales Predict," p. 38.

20. Harold H. Anderson and Gladys L. Anderson, eds., *An Introduction to Projective Techniques* (Englewood Cliffs, N.J.: Prentice-Hall, 1951).

21. Pierre Martineau, *Motivation in Advertising* (New York: McGraw-Hill Book Co., 1957).

22. George H. Smith, *Motivation Research in Advertising and Marketing* (New York: McGraw-Hill Book Co., 1954).

23. Smith, *Motivation Research*, p. 115.

24. Chester R. Wasson, *Research Analysis for Marketing Decisions* (New York: Appleton-Century-Crofts, 1965), pp. 74–77.

25. Robert L. Thorndike and Elizabeth Hagan, *Measurement and Evaluation in Psychology and Education* (New York: John Wiley and Sons, 1966).

26. Leonard Dietz, *The Human Equation in Marketing Research* (New York: American Management Association, 1967).

27. Thorndike and Hagan, *Measurement and Evaluation*, p. 832.

28. Albert S. King, "Pupil Size, Eye Direction, and Message Appeal: Some Preliminary Findings," *Journal of Marketing*, Vol. 36, No. 3 (July 1972).

29. Merle E. Day, "Eye Movement Phenomenon Relating to Attention, Thought, and Anxiety," *Perceptual and Motor Skills*, Vol. 19, No. 2 (1964).

30. King, "Pupil Size," pp. 56–57.

31. William D. Wells, "Psychographics: A Critical Review," *Journal of Marketing Research*, Vol. 12, No. 2 (May 1975).

MARKETING APPLICATIONS

Conclusion 1   *Demographic measures are used to segment markets on the basis of age, sex, family size, income, education, and geographic location.*
Application   In promoting market items, it is important to choose the right medium for communicating with a target segment. When the demographic profile of a target segment is known, this profile may be matched against the demographic data that the various media—print, radio, and TV—provide advertisers about their readers, listeners, and viewers. The media which are most heavily used by the consumers one wishes to reach may then be selected for advertising.

Conclusion 2   *Consumer attitudes can be measured with some accuracy through scaling techniques, such as the Thurstone, Likert, and Semantic Differential tests.*
Application   Attitude measures enable marketers to identify consumers' preferences for certain products over others (for example, which of two soap products they prefer). These scales also gauge subjective attitudes ("I like this ketchup because it pours easily"). Finally, they offer empirical yardsticks of such vague concepts as store "image" (in this case, based on responses to a semantic differential for store patronage). Marketers apply their findings to isolating consumer problems which can be solved by changing or repositioning the product, discovering why a product may be in trouble, and evaluating the image of a product, brand, service or store.

Conclusion 3   *Projective tests may be used to uncover consumer attitudes and motivations for buying which are not divulged in standard interview procedures. They are valuable in research where 1) actual buying motives may not be fully realized by consumers, or 2) responses to questions may be altered for the interviewer's benefit.*
Application   Interviews using projective testing are indicated where discussion of the market item may touch on questions of the consumer's self-esteem, attractiveness to the opposite sex, status-enhancement, or other sensitive areas. For example, asking people direct questions about which books they prefer to read may draw responses that portray their favorite books as prestige best sellers, autobiographies, and important reference books. Yet projective testing with the same consumers may indicate that they actually prefer light escape entertainment and books with romantic and sexual interest. Other product categories where projective testing may prove useful include hair color, cosmetics, and personal care items.

ASSIGNMENTS

Research Assignment

Background   Samurai House restaurants are a chain of fast food enterprises serving Japanese specialties such as teriyaki and sukiyaki. The operation has expanded into your area with the objective of opening two or three franchises. As a new Media Analyst for the Samurai chain, you wish to advertise on television as well as in local newspapers to reach your target market. Your prime customers have already been identified as young (21 to 34), single people and married couples who enjoy fairly high incomes ($15,000-$25,000), and are generally college-educated. Now you must determine whether the local television station (or which ones, if there are several) can deliver the kind of viewers you want to justify a recommendation for buying heavy television time.

Methodology   Contact the television stations in your area and ask for demographic profiles of their viewers. Compare this information with the demographic data you already have about your prime market.

Extrapolation   From your comparison, decide

1. Whether the local station's viewers represent a reasonable "fit" with the characteristics of the people you want to reach, or

2. Which of the stations (if there are several) best reflects your market's demographic profile.

On this basis, make a recommendation about buying a television schedule to advertise Samurai House.

Creative Assignment

You are a partner in Creative Management, Inc., a consulting firm specializing in improving your retail clients' performance by establishing a positive store image and developing that image through advertising and public relations. In your search for new clients, you have focused on a department store in your area (your choice) which could benefit from your expertise. As part of your presentation to the store to obtain their business, you decide to show their management how they now stand with consumers.

Duplicate the Semantic Differential for Retail Store Patronage (Figure 3-10) on page 70. Give one copy each to five friends or classmates and ask them to fill out the scale after patronizing that store. On the basis of their responses, determine the most significant problems the store faces in how their consumers see them. Then make a creative recommendation on ways to improve those customer perceptions, including:

1. What the store could do to counteract *negative* attitudes. A New York City men's store, for example, discovered that its customers believed the salespeople to be too "pushy." Thereafter, customers were issued buttons enscribed "Just Looking" to wear if they wanted to be left alone.

2. How *positive* attitudes toward the store could best be developed in future communications. For example, a general rating of "dependable products" could be translated into the slogan, "If they don't guarantee it, we don't sell it."

Summarize your recommendations in a presentation of two to three pages.

Managerial Assignment

As a Group Marketing Director for The Record Guild, a mail order record club advertised in popular magazines and on television, you are confronted with a high incidence of members who accept the first ten records for $1 but fail to live up to their commitment to purchase the required number of additional records. Furthermore, an equally high percentage of members are accepting the additional records but are not paying for them. Collecting bad debts is a thorny problem in mail order marketing, so you look for a more plausible solution—identifying bad credit risks on the applications you receive before the Club has gifted them with records for which no money will be received.

Now you are faced with the task of devising some way consumer attitudes towards paying their bills might be measured through research. Make some suggestions for this project.

SELECTED READINGS

Fry, Joseph N., and John D. Claxton. "Semantic Differentials and Nonmetric Multidimensional Scaling Descriptions of Brand Images." *Journal of Marketing Research*, May 1971, pp. 238–40.

Gamble, Kenneth R. "The Holtzman Inkblot Technique: A Review." *Psychological Bulletin*, Vol. 77, No. 3 (August 1974), pp. 471–97.

Kaplan, Kalman J. "On the Ambivalence-Indifference Problem in Attitude Theory and Measurement: A Suggested Modification of the Semantic Differential Technique." *Psychological Bulletin*, Vol. 75, No. 5 (May 1972), pp. 361–72.

MacCallum, Robert C. "Relations Between Factor Analysis and Multidimensional Scaling." *Psychological Bulletin*, Vol. 81, No. 8 (August 1974), pp. 505–16.

MacKenzie, Brian D. "Measuring the Strength, Structure, and Reliability of Free Associations." *Psychological Bulletin*, Vol. 77, No. 6 (June 1972), pp. 438–45.

II
ENVIRONMENTAL INFLUENCES

Culture and the Consumer
Subcultures in the United States
Social Organization and Reference Groups
Social Class
The Family

OBJECTIVES

1. Define *culture* as applied to consumer study. *87*

2. Discuss the *three components of culture*—particularly the *normative system.* *88*

3. Describe *ethnocentrism* and *cultural relativism.* *91*

4. Explain how *cultural change* can affect consumption. *92*

5. Discuss four *market expansion strategies* for international marketing. *95*

6. Describe the relation between *traditional American values* and consumer behavior. *100*

7. Describe the *emergent American values.* *102*

FOUR

Culture and the Consumer

For many years now anthropologists have studied the ways in which people from different cultures consume, using the same principles to explain why Americans buy vinyl roofs for their cars as they do to understand why certain island tribesmen value red seashells but not coral ones.

Yet it is just recently that marketers have turned a keen ear to the ways in which culture affects consumer preferences. One reason is that a brisk growth in multinational marketing over the past few years has created a problem-ridden, competitive world market. So people engaged in international business become cultural experts out of necessity. A second reason is that researchers analyzing consumer behavior now recognize that cultural values affect the way Americans look at, say, soft drinks as much as they influence the way the Chinese regard them. In fact, no culture in the world is so closely related to consumption patterns as our own. But because we are now

investigating the norms, or rules of conduct, on which most of us have been nurtured, a note on objectivity seems in order.

Practically everyone tends toward ethnocentrism—feeling that one's own cultural norms and values are the only reasonable ones, while other cultural behaviors are somehow aberrant or strange. The most successful international marketers are those who have overcome this tendency. By the same token, we must be especially careful to adopt the role of social scientist when scrutinizing our own culture to avoid ethnocentric thinking ("American values are inherently correct") or the more recent negative ethnocentric position ("American values are inherently corrupt").

A close look at our own culture will help us recognize why Americans consume as freely as we do, even to the point of straining our natural resources and upsetting our ecological well-being. It can also help us see why basic cultural preferences ensure the continued success of certain market items and condemn other products and services to marginal acceptance or outright failure.

Some of the specific topics raised in this chapter include:

• Why cultural symbols are important to consumers.

• How cross-cultural research can prevent some of the costliest mistakes in international marketing.

• Eight traditional cultural traits Americans reveal that influence their behavior as consumers.

• How the "counterculture" born during the 1960s has shaped American values and buying patterns.

• How consumer demand will change by 1990.

Adopting the cultural perspectives outlined here will enable the reader to scrutinize both mass American culture and the subcultures in the United States discussed in chapter 5.

Cultural Setting

At a supermarket checkout counter, a television interviewer waits with hidden cameras to ask mothers why they purchased his sponsor's brand of prepared baby food. When a young mother, whose shopping cart groans under many jars of the product, appears, she is steered to the microphone and replies: "Why did I buy this baby food? I guess because in our culture we think babies are so special, we have to feed them this scientifically flavored, purified, vitamin fortified stuff in vacuum sealed jars instead of the same food we eat."

Although her answer may have been unexpected, it was also fundamentally correct. Our culture is such a basic factor in what we think, say, and do that we rarely even consider it a factor. Yet it influences the clothes we wear (not to mention the fact that we wear clothing at all), the foods we will eat, all the products and services we use, and the ways in which we use them.[1]

This chapter introduces the *cultural setting* in which all buying behavior takes place. First, culture is defined and basic *concepts of culture* useful to marketers are presented. An overview of *cross-cultural research* next establishes some guidelines for studying consumers in our own cultural setting and in international markets where other cultural perspectives apply. Then the *characteristics of American culture* which influence buying behavior come under scrutiny.

Defining Culture

Because few anthropologists see culture in exactly the same way and the concept is applied to different contexts, there are almost as many definitions of culture as there are anthropologists. For our purposes, culture may be defined in a descriptive way, as pat-

terns of learned behavior which are held in common and transmitted by the members of any given society.[2]

Cultural Patterning

Culture first of all refers to *patterns* of behavior which are held in common by members of a society. Different cultures reveal a tremendous spectrum of diversity in what a society expects of its members. But all cultures exist for the *gratification of groups of people.*[3] They are designed to satisfy *biological* needs such as food and shelter and to provide for *secondary* needs such as esteem and companionship.

Individual behavior which is perceived as meeting the needs of the societal group will be rewarded in any culture; for example, people who heal the sick are granted deferential treatment and prestige whether they are graduates of Yale Medical School or Nyoro witch doctors. A consumption oriented society such as our own rewards its most productive members with money and social esteem. By the same token, *group* behavior must somehow contribute to the general well-being to be rewarded. Young, striving societies like the United States during the 1800s placed high cultural values on childbearing to build a population and a labor force, among other reasons. Now our cultural values have shifted somewhat to de-emphasize the value of raising many children because our population centers are overcrowded and our environment steadily deteriorating.

Briefly, a cultural setting determines the generalized behavior patterns that virtually everyone in the culture will adopt and encourages such patterns because they gratify people's needs. These are functions of culture important to marketers who hope to encourage certain patterns of consumption behavior themselves.

Learning Culture

Secondly, culture is *learned* rather than programmed genetically. Many anthropologists now contend that our learning is the result of our cognition—the ways in which we think about things. They see culture as a *cognitive map* which people use to relate to their environment and to other people within it. Downs points out that each culture provides its own map and offers an illustration of different "mappings":[4]

Persons from different cultural backgrounds see the same objects and situations differently. This should not be taken to mean that cultural differences are simply a matter of taste—a "one man's meat is another's poison" sort of thing. An American lumber baron and an American conservationist are in complete agreement as to what a tree is; they disagree on how it should be used. Both would be surprised and a bit baffled to learn that an Indian villager may view a tree as a living thing with needs, perceptions, and values of its own.

Learning culturally approved behaviors involves feedback from others, who selectively reward, tolerate, or censure different attitudes and activities. Through early observation of others, we see how consumer products and services are used by our parents and others who influence us. Food is not just a biological necessity; it also serves as a focal point of social contact at the family dinner table, in other homes, and in restaurants. "Meet me for lunch" covers a number of different meanings, none of them suggesting that both parties will eat together in stony silence. Because eating is a ritual with several cultural connotations, we are more concerned with the preparation and serving of food than some other cultures, and will buy items such as French gourmet cookbooks and electric pepper mills to prove it.

Cultural Transmission

Through learning, cultural elements are *transmitted* from one generation to the next and survive the life span of any one person or group. This process is known as *enculturation.*

According to Margaret Mead, cultural transmission is an on-going *communication* process which begins with a child's first con-tact with its surroundings.[5] Parents transmit the primary set of messages during infancy and childhood. This largely nonverbal communication establishes a basis for later transmission of the same messages conveyed in more diverse and sophisticated ways as the child achieves more contact with the adult culture.

As a consumer, the individual in the United States receives pressures at all levels to accept culturally approved patterns of decision making and buying behavior. Not the least important transmitter of American culture by any means, the *entertainment media* such as television teach individuals that people in our society wear business suits, live in apartments and houses that are decorated in much the same way, enjoy themselves by going to football games, use laundry detergents, and sometimes carry guns.

Components of Culture

Culture may be analyzed according to its *cognitive, material,* and *normative* aspects.

Cognitive Components

Each culture sustains its own explanation of reality—how the world exists according to the interpretations of that culture. The principal cognitive aspect of a culture is *knowledge,*[6] ideas that have some basis in observable, factual evidence. In a primitive culture these are likely to include ideas about gods, supernatural phenomena, and concepts of an after-life. In American culture, knowledge has become highly refined through systematic testing and observation (*science*), and the practical application of science to the physical and social environment (*technology*).

Material Components

Closely tied to the technology a society possesses are the material features of its culture known as *artifacts.* These vary among cultures from the broken pieces of pottery anthropologists discover in New Guinea to our own packaged pantyhose, supersonic jets, computer systems, reels of movie film, and high-rise apartment complexes.

Normative Components

Every culture maintains a *normative system* consisting of values and rules of conduct, known as "norms," which guide and regulate behavior.

Values are ideas about what is good or correct by which people conduct themselves. They refer less to what people actually say or do than to the principles underlying those actions. In our own culture, one principal value is the acceptance of change—a desire for the innovative or "new" reflected in our buying patterns.

Norms are standards of behavior which govern how people think or act in specific situations. In all cultures, some norms are more important than others. Norms that regulate behavior considered very significant to a society are called *mores* (moor-rays). A person in our culture who is caught breaking such norms by, say, stealing another person's credit cards to go shopping will run afoul of laws laid down to enforce these important standards. Other norms are generally accepted but the consequences for breaking them are less severe. One could appear at a friend's wedding in a T-shirt and golf shoes without the risk of being arrested, but such behavior would probably cause some embarrassment. This sort of norm is known as a *folkway.* [7]

Both values and norms indicate to marketers why certain modes of consumption are appropriate to a particular culture and others are not. In the United States, individual ownership of property reflects our tradition of hard work rewarded by material gain. Thus, people are encouraged to use a considerable range of products and services. In a communist country, which discourages personal wealth, the citizen who flaunts expensive clothing and an array of luxury goods will become the object of resentment, suspicion, and possibly worse sanctions against such ostentatious display.

Useful Concepts of Cultural Analysis

Analyzing a total, unified cultural system means identifying its values and norms, observing how these normative aspects are translated into group and individual behavior, and examining the material aspects of the culture. [8]

The most popular form of cultural study today is known as the *participant-observer* technique and was developed by Malinowski. [9] This is a traditional field study approach of entering a culture, observing and recording data, and asking questions. But the scientist is more than an observer—he or she is also a participant expected to plunge into the cultural milieu, learn to speak the language, and interact socially with the people being studied. One intriguing use of this method was the recent filming of a television series called "An American Family," where the director and camera crew moved in with a Southern California family to record its day-to-day activities. Members of the family report that initially they behaved with an eye toward the television cameras, but eventually came to accept the filming crew and equipment as though they were a part of the family and furniture.

Formal studies utilizing the participant-observer method, however, are not commonly used by marketers to analyze American culture. Such studies are more often found in consumer research literature comparing *different* cultures. This form of analysis is known as *cross-cultural* research and will be explored later in this chapter.

Three concepts that have emerged from anthropological research prove useful in identifying cultural influences on consumption. These are cultural *symbolism, relativism,* and *change.*

Cultural Symbolism

The feature that distinguishes human culture from other forms of animal behavior is our ability to create *symbols*. A symbol is anything that stands for or suggests something else by association such as words, illustrations, or numbers.[10]

There are two types of symbols that people use in cognition, *referential* and *expressive*.[11] Referential symbols are words or items that refer to specific objects. The word "telephone" used as a noun means only the class of things we recognize as telephones, whether we are talking about the push-button or French decorator variety. It is simply a culturally accepted, convenient way of referring to the item. Expressive symbols, on the other hand, carry connotative meanings which are subject to interpretation rather than limited. And it is to analyze and utilize this form of symbolism that many marketing dollars have been spent.

Virtually all product packaging and advertising use some form of expressive symbolism to get a desired message across and elicit a specific kind of response from consumers. Symbols may be used in this sense to make a product seem prestigious, inexpensive, exotic, practical, or to persuade the consumer that the product can bestow some culturally defined advantage. Cosmetics advertising employs a different set of symbols than breakfast food advertising, and thus offers a different type of cultural appeal. One says "Look how glamorous (or natural) you will be." The other says "Look what a hero or heroine you will be to your children." And symbolism plays an important role in marketing to any culture. The success of a frozen seafood line introduced in Mexico could be traced directly to the colors chosen for its packaging, which happened to be the red, white, and green of the Mexican flag.[13]

Clothing represents a highly visible form of expressive symbolism in any cultural system. Marshall McLuhan has noted a pattern in which styles of dress may reflect cultural change in the United States. Americans, he contends, are shedding "visual" style for a more "tactile" style; clothing is becoming as important for its feel as its appearance. And he offers a parallel example of fashion's relatedness to cultural change from European history:[14]

The Europeans . . . underwent a sort of consumer revolution at the end of the eighteenth century. When industrialism was a novelty, it became fashionable for upper classes to abandon rich, courtly attire in favor of simpler materials. That was the time when men first donned the trousers of the common foot soldier (or pioneer—the original French usage) but it was done at the time as a kind of brash gesture of social "integration." Up until then, the feudal system had inclined the upper classes to dress as they spoke, in a

The High Cost of Cultural Symbolism: Chevrolet versus Cadillac

Although the production cost difference between a Chevrolet Caprice and a Cadillac de Ville with comparable equipment is only about $300, the selling price differs by $2,700. This gives General Motors a $2,400 extra gross profit on the Cadillac.[12]

Why are Cadillac buyers willing to pay so much more?

For years General Motors has promoted the word "Cadillac" as an expressive symbol of prestige, a "standard of excellence." To a large segment of our society, "Cadillac" conjures up images of country estates, yacht clubs, and other visible symbols of affluence and social esteem.

The marketing of this symbolism has been so widely successful that other products and services—from local dry cleaners to a dog food brand—have borrowed the name "Cadillac" in hopes of creating the same lofty associations.

courtly style quite removed from that of ordinary people. Dress and speech were accorded a degree of splendor and richness of texture that universal literacy and mass production were eventually to eliminate completely. The sewing machine, for example, created the long straight-line clothes, as much as the linotype flattened the human vocal style.

In our culture, differences in clothing style do not have to be gross to be noticeable; extremely subtle gradations of color, fabric, and fit comprise what we refer to as "fashion" or "taste." The well-tailored business suit at any point in fashion acceptance may have lapels merely an inch wider and trousers a fraction of an inch lower than the suit considered hopelessly out-of-date. Yet such small distinctions matter in our perceptions of a person based on what he or she is wearing. Today, we accept considerable diversity in clothing as expressive symbolism. Long sideburns are now worn by many of those males who were scandalized by the same hair styles ten years ago. Women enjoy cultural approval

today for wearing pants in business situations where they could have evoked raised eyebrows and perhaps scolding memos only a few years back.

Cultural Relativism

People have always been inclined to view their own cultural milieu as superior to others, exemplified by the stereotypical American tourist who complains about the drinking water, service, and generally "backward" behavior encountered away from home. Downs notes that this attitude is hardly restricted to members of technologically advanced societies, citing the Navajo Indian who told him "'. . . You white men are not hospitable. Any time a man comes to my hogan he is welcome to my food. But if I go into Winslow or Flagstaff (Arizona) I go into a restaurant, I gotta pay for food.' By his cultural standards, expecting a man to pay for food was heartless and cold. On the other hand, a Navajo will often expect payment for 'helpful' behavior, thus appearing greedy in the eyes of white Americans."[15]

This human trait is known as *ethnocentrism*, a tendency to view and judge other cultures by the standards of one's own cultural system. It inevitably leads to the conclusion that the way we do things is somehow "right" and the way others behave is "wrong," or at least substandard. Ethnocentrism serves a useful function in that people who see their own normative system as fundamentally correct will be motivated to abide by it. However, it is a dangerous attitude for marketers to adopt if they hope to understand consumer behavior that is based upon different values. And this holds true in marketing to American subcultural entities such as an ethnic urban ghetto as well as to international markets.

Anthropologists, who can hardly afford to be ethnocentric in outlook, use the term *cultural relativism* as the opposite viewpoint of ethnocentrism. Cultural relativism is simply the principle of judging any behavior in its own societal and cultural context.

Cultural Change

Because a culture must be adaptive to survive, cultural change is an on-going (if sometimes uneven) process. Two factors responsible for cultural flux are technological change and cultural diffusion.

Technological Change   As technological breakthroughs occur, cultural norms and values must change to accommodate them; but very often technological developments happen because values are already changing. Frozen foods were introduced and quickly became popular because housewives were quite ready to place more emphasis on convenience and less on the merits of home cooking. "Fast food" franchises became a national institution as a result of our society's increasing mobility and dedication to the automobile. As a prime example of technology reflecting but also speeding up changes in our normative system, the birth control pill drew instant acceptance because our sexual attitudes were moving in a more permissive direction. The pill simply precipitated a faster rate of behavioral change, change that might have occurred anyway. It is important to bear in mind that a material innovation never arrives too far ahead of changes in values. Society develops its technology because there is a use for it—a cultural extension of the marketing concept.

Cultural Diffusion   Change that occurs because one culture becomes exposed to another, is known as *cultural diffusion*. Some classic examples include trade agreements between the United States and China, the introduction of a new subculture to a mass culture through migration (such as the Puerto Rican influence in New York), and the effect of the English Beatles on the rest of the world's youth.

Ralph Linton illustrates how diffusion has influenced our own culture with a few minutes in the typical morning of a middle-class American commuter:[16]

Breakfast over, he places on his head a molded piece of felt, invented by the nomads of Eastern India, and, if it looks like rain, puts on outer shoes of rubber, discovered by the ancient Mexicans, and takes an umbrella invented in India. . . . At the station, he pauses for a moment to buy a newspaper, paying for it with coins invented in ancient Lydia . . . he reads the news of the day, imprinted in characters invented by the ancient

Semites, by a process invented in Germany, upon a material invented in China. As he scans the latest editorial pointing out the dire results to our institutions of accepting foreign ideas, he will not fail to thank a Hebrew God in an Indo-European language that he is a one hundred percent (decimal system invented by the Greeks) American (from Americus Vespucci, Italian geographer).

The technologies of jet travel and satellite communications have produced snowballing demand for products and services from different cultures. Perhaps the most significant example of diffusion between our culture and another's during recent years has been that between East and West. Since World War II, Japan has emerged as a model of Western technology and marketing expertise. In turn, the United States has for the first time experienced Chinese ballet and the martial arts craze.

Cross-Cultural Research and Multinational Marketing

One motivating force for the new interest marketers find in cultural study is sheer survival. Marketing is becoming increasingly an international venture, with new far-flung markets developing at a dizzying rate. It was no accident that International Marketing became a burgeoning specialty in graduate schools during the late 1960s; a real need had appeared for marketing strategists with multinational expertise.

It is easy to make huge mistakes in international markets simply by applying formulas proven successful in the American experience. Many astute companies have made such tactical errors because they did not fully understand the cultural settings they entered and failed to make appropriate adaptations in product, promotion, pricing, and distribution in approaching their new customers. Anthropology contributes a useful technique for exploring consumer behavior in virtually any market. This is known as *cross-cultural research*, a methodology for comparing cultures on the basis of similarities and differences as well as studying small segments of a total culture. Comparisons are usually made by analyzing the *statistical, typological,* and *content* aspects of cultures—in other words, what the demographics of a population are, what cultural "types" may be identified, and what kinds of values and norms people accept and live by.

Traditionally, anthropologists have used cross-cultural research to explore a wide variety of topics. These include comparing love and courtship patterns[17] and political power.[18] Some studies on general phenomena have provided information of interest to market researchers. Knowledge about the cultural meanings of color, for example, gives marketers some cues to effective product design, advertising, and packaging for specific societies. It may also point out some cultural universals. Adams and Osgood discovered that in twenty-three different cultures, black and grey are considered "bad" while white, blue, and green are perceived as "good." Yellow, white, and grey are universally seen as weak but red and black are strong. And where black and grey are described as passive colors, red is definitely active.[19]

Approaching World Markets

Recently, cross-cultural methodology has been applied to marketing research, closely aligned with developments in multinational marketing.[20] But a controversy has emerged over the best means to approach world markets; one argument maintains that markets should be *segmented* along national boundaries and another contends that markets are sufficiently alike to standardize marketing initiatives.

Segmentation versus Standardization   The more traditional technique has been to treat markets as *local* entities; each society, or part of a society, is regarded as a unique and well-defined cultural milieu.

Ernest Dichter conceptualized six different types of countries based on the degree of *middle class development*.[21] In this context, he related each type to characteristics of automobile consumption. One group of countries was defined as *almost classless* and contented. In what are primarily Scandinavian countries, the middle class predominates and few people are either very rich or very poor. Attitudes toward products are rational rather than status oriented, and automobiles are regarded as strictly utilitarian. This premise appears to be supported by the functional design of the Swedish Volvo and Saab. The second group was described as *affluent*, and includes the United States, Canada, and Holland. Few people go hungry and there is potential for upward mobility, especially at the top end of the upper middle class. Individualistic, high quality products are sought after, and automobiles tend to follow that pattern. In the United States, the new car buyer may choose from a dazzling array of optional accessories to customize even the lowest priced models. The third group is termed *countries in transition*, such as England, France, and Italy. All of these nations sustain a working class of the nineteenth century variety, but this class is really working at joining the middle class. Where upper class individuals still enjoy special privileges, automobiles may be opulent and expensive. We might note that England produces the ultra high-ticket Rolls Royce and Italy the exotic Ferrari and Maserati. In the United States, by contrast, no mass production cars appear in this $20,000-and-up category.

Group four consists of *revolutionary* countries; India and the Philippines are examples. Here there are extremely wealthy people, a small but growing middle class, and huge numbers of poor. Automobile consumption is limited to a very few, who tend to import their cars from other countries. The fifth group is made up of *primitive* countries such as the new nations of Africa. In these there is a small, wealthy class of political leaders and foreign businessmen, but a predominantly illiterate and economically depressed population. No real automobile market exists there as yet. Finally, the sixth group is called the *new class* society and is made up of Russia and its satellite countries. Here a newly established class of bureaucrats represents a kind of aristocracy while everyone else seems grouped into a low middle class existence. The automobiles available seem patterned closely after models of other countries.

Generally, the recent trend in international marketing has veered away from segmentation toward greater *standardization* of markets. Because a significant degree of cultural universality exists throughout the world, marketing experts urge the more economical approach of viewing several countries as one market. Erik Elinder notes that Europe has experienced a gradual breakdown of language and custom barriers due to mass media, migration, and tourism and suggests that advertising should be geared to "all-European" media rather than custom-fitted for specific localities.[22] Buzzell, citing the economic advantages of standardizing products, packaging, and promotion, cautions that segmentation may still be appropriate where income levels, shopping patterns, language, access to media, and other factors seem to warrant a more narrowly focused approach.[23]

Market Expansion Strategies In a cross-cultural analysis of English, United States, Canadian, and Australian markets, Sommers and Kernan offer four strategies for expanding existing products into new markets.[24] Their primary considerations are twofold: (1) the cultural values which will determine how a product is positioned and (2) cultural cues as to how a product may best be marketed. The strategies are:

1. *Same product–same promotion.* In this case, a new market's established way of life indicates that a given product will be accepted and the current promotion is sufficiently widespread to sell it. Coca-Cola represents a widely successful example.

2. *Same product–different promotion.* This method is appropriate where the new market reflects a way of life similar to that in the established market, but individual life styles are patterned differently. A standard Ford, no great luxury in the United States, would be an extravagant purchase for most New Zealanders.

3. *Different product–same promotion.* When a new market exhibits product-use styles quite different from the present market, some reworking of the product itself may be in order. A laundry detergent might be branded and packaged differently in Europe but would still be advertised with "brightness" claims.

4. *Different product–different promotion.* If both the cultural way of life and individual life styles are dramatically different in a new market, it may be most advisable to acquire existing firms there. Walgreen's, for instance, entered the Mexican market by acquiring a retail chain known as Sanborn's.

A Case Study: Advertising's Image in the United States and Yugoslavia*

Sheth and Smiljanic applied cross-cultural methodology to a study of how people feel about advertising in both the United States and Yugoslavia. Their research is summarized here as a model of this technique and an illustration of how two different cultures may place quite different values on a specific type of marketing.

Background In 1968, Bauer and Greyser conducted an intensive study of attitudes about advertising in the United States. They discovered that people did not think about advertising as much as they did about some other comparable issues. But a majority of the people who had something definitive to say about advertising judged it favorably (41 percent as opposed to 14 percent unfavorable), although a large segment of the population held mixed (34 percent) or indifferent (8 percent) feelings.

Sheth and Smiljanic decided to replicate this study in Yugoslavia to determine whether differences in attitude existed between the two cultures. They chose Yugoslavia because

*Adapted from Jagdish N. Sheth and Milan Smiljanic, "Advertising's Images in the United States and Yugoslavia," *Journal of the Academy of Marketing Science*, Vol. 1, No. 2 (Fall 1973), pp. 167–179, by permission of the Academy of Marketing Science, copyright 1973.

(1) Yugoslavia is one of the few Eastern European countries that has permitted trade with the West and private foreign investment; (2) Yugoslavia allows advertising of branded products on all the mass media, including radio and television; and (3) Yugoslavia as a Communist country adheres to different economic, social, and political values than the United States—particularly with respect to social ownership (ownership by employees) and self-management (management by workers) of business and industry.

Because of Yugoslavia's political and social structure, the researchers started with two hypotheses: (1) That advertising would be less important to Yugoslavs than to Americans, and (2) that Yugoslavs would be more inclined to respond negatively to advertising.

Cultural Adjustments in Methodology   In cross-cultural research, studies often must be adapted to the cultural milieu under observation. In Yugoslavia, these were some of the necessary adjustments:

1. Information on family income was not obtained, as it had been in the United States. The researchers felt that such questions might be viewed as too personal by the Yugoslavs and so might jeopardize cooperation from respondents.

2. Because the population of Yugoslavia is relatively homogeneous, questions about racial and ethnic background were also discarded.

3. Questions about some social and economic institutions were considered inappropriate in Yugoslavia. For example, attitudes about religion, government, labor unions, and big business were not investigated, but reactions to city transportation, housing, television, and movies as institutions were sought to gauge comparative importance.

Conclusions   Sheth and Smiljanic arrived at the following conclusions:

• As the authors expected, more people were indifferent to advertising in Yugoslavia than in the United States. More people are favorably disposed toward advertising in the United States sample.

• Where Americans who do like advertising see it as a source of information and education, Yugoslavs who enjoy it cite entertainment as an important reason. Americans do not like advertising because of its intrusiveness, but Yugoslavs tend to dislike it because it seems unnecessary. (See Tables 4-1 and 4-2.)

The researchers suggest that these differences are probably due to greater intensity, variety, and exaggeration of advertising in the United States. But while it has reached the point of becoming a salient irritant with a minority of American consumers, that does not seem to be the case in Yugoslavia. Sheth and Smiljanic also point to a need for improved creative quality in Yugoslav advertising. Many Yugoslavs seemed unable to understand the purpose of advertisements or relate ad messages to the products advertised.

Adopting a Cultural Perspective

In the same way that consumers tend to overlook the cultural influences that shape their buying behavior, marketers have often neglected the cultural dimension in formulating strategies. But the realities of multinational trade are beginning to encourage

Table 4-1   Reasons Why People Like Advertising

	U.S. STUDY (PERCENT)	YUGOSLAVIA STUDY (PERCENT)
1. Information-related Reasons	57	26
a. Informative, educational	35	18
b. Information on new products	17	—
c. Information on price	5	8
2. Invidious Reasons for Liking Advertising	22	—
3. Entertainment-related Reasons	13	21
a. Advertising is enjoyable, humorous and sometimes interesting	9	21
b. Advertising pays for entertainment	4	—
4. No Specific Reason	4	10
5. Miscellaneous Reasons	11	—
6. No Opinion, Don't Know	12	30
TOTAL RESPONSES	119%	87%

Table 4-2   Reasons Why People Don't Like Advertising

	U.S. STUDY (PERCENT)	YUGOSLAVIA STUDY (PERCENT)
1. Advertising's Intrusiveness	40	—
2. Untruthful or Exaggerated	26	12
3. Silly; Insults People's Intelligence	11	9
4. Offensive or Bad for Children	8	12
5. High-pressure Selling	6	—
6. Advertising Increases Prices	3	5
7. It Is Boring	—	13
8. People Not Interested in Advertising	—	17
9. Good Products Don't Need Advertising	—	4
10. Don't Understand Advertisements (sense and purpose)	—	10
11. Don't Know; No Opinion	15	13
12. Miscellaneous Reasons	11	—
13. No Specific Reason	9	—
TOTAL RESPONSES	129%	95%

Source: Tables 4-1 and 4-2 reprinted from the Journal of the Academy of Marketing Science, *Vol. 1, No. 2 (Fall, 1973), by permission of the Academy of Marketing Science, Copyright © 1973.*

sophisticated marketers to develop the cultural perspective,[25] both in overseas markets and in their own cultural milieu.

Obtaining and using cultural information effectively means asking a few pertinent questions about any social group under consideration:

1. How does the cultural setting influence or determine product and service needs?
2. How well does an existing product meet those needs or how could it be adapted to do so?
3. How can information about the product be communicated for optimal results?
4. How can the product best be distributed in this culture?

The answers usually lie in research findings about the normative, material, and cognitive aspects of that culture, findings that will provide the marketer with some knowledge as to what kinds of consumer behavior might be expected.

Characteristics of American Culture

"American culture" carries a variety of meanings for different interpreters. Some critics have argued, as they compared elements of contemporary Americana with some of the world's great civilizations, that there is *no* culture to speak of in the United States. While it may be true that Norman Rockwell and McDonald's Golden Arches suffer by comparison with Michelangelo and the Louvre, this is not all our culture is about.

Anthropologists see American culture in socio-scientific terms—as simply one system that may be analyzed and categorized with others. Through analysis of our collective *knowledge,* our *material output,* and our *norms and values,* they are able to draw conclusions about how American culture influences and reflects our behavior.

A Consumption Ethic

Consider how profoundly marketing has influenced American technology, education, and values. The bulk of our technological know-how is employed in developing goods and services that people will want to buy. Our educational system is geared toward preparing individuals to be productive members of an affluent society—as citizens, workers, and consumers. And the cultural values we learn are most often aligned with the goals of a marketing economy, such as rewarding performance with material payoffs and defining life styles through patterns of consumption. Television, our most important communications medium, exists almost solely through commercial sponsorship. Therefore, its function to entertain and inform might be perceived as secondary to its marketing purpose, which is to sell the products, services, and life styles advertised.

The spirit of affluent consumption surrounds such American cultural rites as weddings, funerals, and bar mitzvahs, creating industries to cater and costume the participants lavishly. Organized religious groups in the United States employ advertising agencies to prepare media campaigns for fund-raising, and political candidates have used market segmentation with other marketplace strategies with varying degrees of success.[26] Thus the consumption ethic enters many aspects of life in the United States. Some observers maintain that it has replaced the older Protestant ethic of hard work as a basis for the American value system.

Cultural Uniformity versus Cultural Diversity

In a number of ways, American culture is relatively standardized and homogeneous.

We are all exposed to the same communications media, use the same standard brands, and note great similarities in such artifacts as suburban architecture throughout the country. But American society is also characterized by considerable diversity; behavior, values, and norms differ from one region to another, among ethnic and religious groups, and are affected by factors such as age, marital status, occupation, and income. These *subcultural* influences in life styles and consumption are treated at length in chapter 5.

Components of American Culture

As discussed previously, a culture may be broken down into three components: cognitive, material, and normative.

Cognitive Aspects

In the United States, *technology* and *scientific method* are highly sophisticated and generally serve as our sources of knowledge about what is real and why. Americans express a high level of confidence in the ability of technology to make life continually more comfortable. They are inclined to believe that medical science will find a cure for cancer in their lifetimes (particularly if they are anxiety-ridden about smoking cigarettes). They feel that our demonstrated technical proficiency in putting a man on the moon means that we will also be able to produce new sources of energy if our present resources

dry up, or find copious supplies of something or other that may be technologically converted to food, thus preventing the world from starving.

Material Aspects

Anthropologists can draw important conclusions about a culture from its artifacts, and American culture is no exception. If we were to bury a time capsule for archeologists of the year 5,000, it might consist of such diverse elements as a taped recording of the CBS Evening News; the latest model Ford; complex technical devices developed by space scientists; copies of *The Encyclopedia Brittanica*, *Saturday Review*, *Ladies Home Journal*, and *Playboy*; a bucket of Kentucky Fried Chicken; a cassette of that week's Top Forty songs; a reel of films enjoying current success at the box office; current best-sellers, and a host of other items that reveal what today's Americans think about, how they spend their time, and what material items they use in everyday living. From these artifacts, our future anthropologists could make fairly accurate generalizations about our values and norms.

Normative Aspects

In every culture, a normative system establishes values and rules governing conduct which together are called norms. American values tend to thwart analysis by social scientists because they are too situational and contradictory. Coleman, for example, identifies such American traits as: democracy and faith in it; belief in the equality of all as a fact and a right; freedom of the individual in ideal and in fact; disregard of law and direct action; practicality; prosperity and material well-being; puritanism; uniformity and conformity.[27]

Further complicating American value analysis is the fact that our values are in a state of flux, since our normal rate of cultural change has accelerated wildly since the 1960s. For instance, "puritanism" as an American value seems to have been shed in the more permissive climate prevalent now. We appear to be at a point of transition between so-called "traditional" American values and the more contemporary "emergent" values which have been noted in both scientific literature and mass media. The traditional values will be discussed as one conceptual framework, and the emergent values will be outlined separately.

Traditional American Values and Consumption

Williams has summarized the values which are basic to American culture (and is the first to admit that there are exceptions in each case).[28]

1. American culture is organized around the attempt at *active mastery* rather than passive acceptance. Into this dimension fall the low tolerance of frustration; the refusal to accept ascetic renunciation; the positive encouragement of desire; the stress on power; the approval of ego-assertion, and so on.
2. It tends to be interested in the *external world* of things and events, of the palpable and immediate, rather than in the inner experience of meaning and affect. Its genius is manipulative rather than contemplative.
3. Its *world view tends to be open* rather than closed; it emphasizes change, flux, movement; its central personality types are adaptive, accessible, outgoing and assimilative.
4. In wide historical and comparative perspective, the culture places its primary faith in *rationalism* as opposed to traditionalism; it de-emphasizes the past, orients strongly to the future, does not accept things just because they have been done before.
5. Closely related to the above is the dimension of *orderliness* rather than unsystematic ad hoc acceptance of transitory experience. (This emphasis is most marked with the upper middle classes.)
6. With conspicuous deviations, a main theme is a *universalistic* rather than particu-

laristic ethic (rules of conduct should apply to all rather than to different people selectively).

7. In interpersonal relationships, the weight of the value system is on the side of *"horizontal"* rather than "vertical" emphasis: peer relations, not superordinate-subordinate relations; equality rather than hierarchy.

8. Subject to increased strains and modifications, the received culture emphasizes *individual personality* rather than group identity and responsibility.

So American culture may be viewed as an active, pluralistic system in which many people have the opportunity to achieve a number of goals.

Unfortunately, precious little consumer research has focused on the relationship between the traditional American normative system and actual consumption patterns. The generalities that may be posed (and are presented here) are based largely on hypotheses and findings from cross-cultural research where an American sample is considered.

1. *Americans are interested in the performance aspects of products and services.* What is the product for? What can it do? The product features they are concerned about include precision, ease of operation, safety and speed.[29] This orientation comes from the traditional value of *active* mastery, compelling Americans to find out how tasks can be accomplished with highly specialized products. Advertising appeals reflect this characteristic—"Drain clogged? Use Drano"; "Compute your income tax with the Bowmar Brain (electronic calculator)." In tests of advertising effectiveness, headlines which begin "How to . . ." perform better than the same headlines without this problem solving claim.[30]

2. *American consumers are more receptive to products that enable them to manipulate*

things than to those that involve contemplation or reflection. This tendency coincides with an American orientation to the *external world.* Most Americans would prefer reading a book entitled *How to Make Money with Your Credit Cards* than Proust's *Remembrance of Things Past.* For the same reason, more people subscribe to *Reader's Digest* than did to the late *Intellectual Digest.*

3. *Americans are willing to be innovative in trying new products and services.* This feature corresponds to Williams's description of an *open world view* emphasizing adaptability. Consumers in the United States are treated to a staggering variety of new products every year. These range from parity items such as new detergent brands (which are not really different from other detergents on the market) to true innovations like kitchen compactors for refuse. The novelty of a brand-new product is often enough to attract consumers; whether the item will become established depends on whether it lives up to its claims. Comet Cleanser, a long-standing brand, retains a large share of market through reintroducing a "New, Improved Comet" at regular intervals.

4. *Americans, especially those who identify with the upper middle class, express a need for products and services that bring order to their existence.* This trait has two manifestations. On the one hand, it is reflected in a preoccupation with neatness and cleanliness. American consumers buy huge amounts of deodorants, soaps, cleansers, detergents, shampoos, and other packaged goods to be fastidious in personal appearance and environment. Some critics maintain that such behavior, which might be considered rather bizarre in other cultures, results from "Madison Avenue brainwashing." But the fact that these products were developed in the first

place suggests that our enculturation process had already created some desire for them. Frontiersmen and their wives fabricated soap at home before Procter was even introduced to Gamble. The marketing system has simply produced such items for an increasingly larger population and has continued to promote the desirability of cleanliness accordingly.

A second expression of the desire for order falls under the heading of *security*. Americans want to be assured that the future will continue as predictably as the present; that they will be able to provide college for their children, income for their retirement, and a relatively comfortable income for family members who might be affected by the premature death of family breadwinners. To meet these needs, industries offering insurance, savings facilities, and long-term investment opportunities flourish in the United States.

5. *Americans use consumption to conform in varying degrees to the behavior of other Americans.* The tendency to conform may derive from two values noted by Williams. One is the *universalistic* feature of American culture, which dictates equal standards applied to all. The second is a *horizontal* system of interpersonal relationships, which orders people as peers rather than superiors and inferiors. Most people in the United States elect to live in housing which is relatively standardized, wear clothing styles that fall within generally accepted norms, and structure other features of their life styles according to standards adopted by their peers.

6. *While Americans strive for some measure of conformity, they also aspire to buy products which reflect a level of individual achievement.* Most consumers wish to assert themselves with symbols of position, status, and wealth, thus showing others that they are successful in competition. This may be seen as an expression of the "contest mobility" ethic, in which opportunity in the United States is available to all and superior performance earns material rewards. And Americans are quick to note small differences among products—in style, design, or packaging—which they may use to differentiate themselves.[31] In New York corporate circles, the type of wristwatch an individual wears has become an important status symbol. A simply designed face with no numerals is considered most desirable as this suggests that the executive delegates the prosaic responsibility of keeping time to his secretary and callers.

These consumption patterns are all reflections of *traditional* American values, long institutionalized by the norms which many consumers continue to accept. But American culture has undergone dramatic change since the mid-1960s and traditional patterns are being modified by insistent new values gaining gradual acceptance.

Emergent American Values

The basic origin of recent value shifts in our culture is economic, the fact that our economy has provided us with general well-being and freedom of choice. Once Americans began enjoying their great abundance of material comforts, consumption rose above work as an end in itself: "the glorification of plenty rather than bending to niggardly nature."[32] And new generations of Americans who were strangers to the hardships of war and depression began searching for meaningful new values—beyond just consuming.

Countercultural Influences

Early in 1967, the American media reported a major anthropological find: a subculture of young men and women who flaunted long hair, colorful dress, and life styles devoted to exotic drug use, open sex, and spiritualism, and who styled themselves as "hippies." Soon these "hippies" were joined by student radicals and young members of minority groups to form what has collectively been termed "the counterculture." Few observers predicted what a profound effect this development would have upon American culture and consumer behavior.

Values Spates and Levin have identified four principal value trends popularized by the counterculture[33]:

1. *Self Expression:* An individual should be allowed to live life as he or she saw fit rather than succumbing to societal customs and role demands.

2. *Concern for Others:* Expressed by the "love ethic," this value embraced altruistic desires to help others and ultimately developed into activism for the rights of "oppressed peoples" such as minority groups.

3. *Affective Affiliation:* The barriers between people were de-emphasized in favor of honest communication. This included experimentation with communal living.

4. *Religious-Philosophical Orientation.* This value trend was identified with Eastern mysticism, astrology, Tarot cards, meditation, and health foods.

These values and their widespread media coverage created new markets for products and services quite foreign to the dominant culture.

Influence on Consumption Supplying the counterculture began as a sort of cottage industry in cities such as San Francisco and New York, but as young and affluent market segments revealed interest in counterculture paraphernalia, products and services were mass merchandised. Some examples are noted.

Media In music, "hard rock" became a major force in both single recording and album sales. Films celebrating the counterculture, on the order of *Woodstock*, were produced, and an "underground" news network became established. Magazines such as *Rolling Stone* were introduced.

Clothing and Accessories Boutiques and head shops featured flamboyant, unisexual styles for men and women. Denim pants, sandals for men and women, and other innovative clothing were introduced to traditional stores, influencing fashions for all age groups.

Grooming "Unisex haircutters" appeared in many urban and suburban markets, to the dismay of conventional barbers and hairdressers. Cosmetics adopted a more "natural" look.

Miscellaneous An avalanche of astrology merchandise was quickly developed and marketed, as well as health foods; literature devoted to astrology, the occult and meditation; and such esoteric products and services as the waterbed and "sensitivity group" sessions.

While both hippiedom and student activism declined measurably during the early 1970s, both value orientations and product innovations continued to diffuse into the dominant American culture.

The Youth Culture

With the advent of the counterculture, American marketers became more fascinated with youthful values and behavior. Even antimaterialistic youth values were found to be quite profitable with some redirection of marketing efforts. One could look more closely, for example, at the teenager who appeared to be wearing clothes of little material value:[34]

The hair, for instance. It may look unshorn, but that young fellow just paid a razor-wielding tonsorial artist $7.50 to get every strand carefully whittled into the right degree of shagginess. You certainly wouldn't put greasy kid stuff on after that. No, that head has been sprayed with a $1.50 can of ungreasy stuff that's guaranteed to leave hair looking like nothing has been put on it. And the clothes? If you check the label, you'll find the "surplus" jacket came off the rack at a hip little boutique just last week. The T-shirt is new too; the tie-dyed version costs $2 more than the regular kind. The jeans are also brand-new; you have to pay extra to get them all faded and tattered like that. As for the sandals, they're the new "tire look" numbers. The knack of making them was picked up from impoverished South American Indians; you pay $10.

The success of these products tends to suggest that for every true nonmaterialist, there are many others who wish to adopt the outward styles of the counterculture without becoming committed to its fundamental values. So marketers, by keeping a close eye on

developments in the youth culture, may turn even an antimaterialistic orientation to a component of what has been called the "youth market."

Innovation and Youth Culture   The most salient feature of the youth culture is its orientation toward change, which finds expression in the continual adoption of new life styles and the products to complement them. Young people have become the avant-garde segment of society in setting new styles for two principal reasons. First, their affluence provides a wider choice in how to live. They may spend money on expensive clothing, cosmetics, motorcycles, trips to Europe, and other products and services which were unheard-of luxuries to most of their parents when they were adolescents. Second, the young consumers are less bound by tradition, having received much of their enculturation in the rational, skeptical, and scientific modes of thought which have been developing in American education. The mass media have effectively replaced tradition as a source of taste and style. But this also means that once a style has been adopted by the avant-garde youth culture, it will soon by diffused to the dominant culture, leaving the young in search of still newer styles.

Because the values of young Americans are intricately tied to their consumer desires, marketers who wish to approach them should have some knowledge of what the current values are. So with the reminder that *change* is the only constant factor, some generalizations about youthful values in the 1970s are discussed here.

Differences between Youth and Parent Values   There has been much controversy in recent years over the degree to which young Americans' values differ from those held by their parents. Some observers contend that a fundamental "generational distance" exists in America, with the youth culture viewed as a phenomenon totally distinct from the dominant culture.[36]

The celebration of youth culture as a complete answer to every human need undoubtedly seems bizarre to anyone over the age of thirty . . . younger generations in times past seem to have latched onto experiences they called their own . . . only to find more lasting satisfaction with the prevailing culture. The difference today is that the new experiences of the young are no longer confined to a response to new *fragments* of reality. For the first time, in recent history at least, youth culture is a response to a totally new environment [shaped by] mass communications . . . widespread affluence . . . The Bomb. The new environment makes us an experience-oriented generation; the prevailing culture makes us experience-starved.

But another current view maintains that young Americans differ significantly from their parents in some basic value orientations and not in others. One representative study concluded that a sample of college students and their parents displayed considerably divergent attitudes toward marijuana use and sexual behavior; reported distinguishable, but lesser, differences in their views on marriage; and revealed only slight variations in their feelings about work.[37]

Marijuana Students tended to see marijuana as a "fairly harmless drug, neither valuable nor harmful." A majority of their parents believed that the drug is "possibly harmful and its dangers outweigh its benefits." Additionally, 21 percent of the students described the drug as "beneficial" or felt its "benefits offset its risks," whereas no parents expressed either of these opinions. The degree of divergence can be seen in more detail in Table 4-3.

Sexual behavior The greatest discrepancy between students and their parents appears here. While 73.5 percent of the students found coitus acceptable for unmarried college females, only 18.5 percent of their parents believed it to be acceptable for males and 10 percent for females.

Marriage A smaller percentage of students (64 percent) reported that marriage was important to them than their parents indicated (88 percent). However, the relative importance of different qualities to look for in a marriage partner was remarkably similar between the two groups.

Work The work ethic seems to have declined only slightly, with 84 percent of the students endorsing it compared with 95.5 percent of their parents. Interestingly enough, students and their parents were in general agreement about the factors important to job satisfaction, indicating that parents were no more or less materialistic than their college-age offspring.

Values of College versus Noncollege Youth Yankelovich, Skelly and White, Incorporated, investigated differences in value orientations between college and noncollege youth in a more recent survey. Findings from this study suggest that college students may be more likely to express "emergent" American values than their more "traditional," noncollege peers (Table 4-4).

The "Young" Youth Culture While most studies of cultural values have focused on college students, there is a younger population in the youth culture roughly made up of 14- to 17-year-olds. *Seventeen* magazine has conducted research into the attitudes of this group compared with those of the 18- to

22-year-old population, and findings indicate that the two age groups are in accord on most issues.[38]

One intriguing conclusion from this study is the great reported concern over industrial pollution and attitudes toward using products that increase or reduce pollution. Although almost all the young people surveyed want stricter laws to punish polluters, there is some variance in their willingness to accept environmentally oriented products. For example, approximately 98 percent claim they would use returnable bottles but an average of only 30 percent would do without an automobile (Figure 4-1).

Consumer Implications of Youth Culture
Basically there are three implications of youth culture: (1) that markets may be segmented to reach specific age groups in the youth culture,

Table 4-3   Student versus Parent Values Regarding Marijuana

CRITERIA	STUDENTS			PARENTS		
	FEMALE N-100	MALE N-100	TOTAL	FEMALE N-100	MALE N-100	TOTAL
Judgment as to beneficial-harmful nature						
Beneficial, values outweigh harm	12%	12%	12 %	0%	0%	0 %
May be dangerous, but benefits offset risks	7	11	9	0	0	0
Fairly harmless, neither valuable nor harmful	40	45	42.5	5	3	4
Possibly harmful, dangers outweigh benefits	35	19	27	66	70	58
Extremely dangerous, with little benefit	6	3	4.5	29	26	27.5
No opinion	0	10	5	0	1	.5
Judgment as to legal controls						
No legal controls	16	14	15	0	1	.5
Controlling sale and distribution	39	35	37	19	29	24
Prohibiting sale and distribution	7	7	7	34	24	29
Prohibiting possession by anyone under 18 (or 21)	24	26	25	19	9	14
Prohibiting possession by anyone	12	11	11.5	28	37	32.5
No opinion	2	7	4.5	0	1	.5

Source: Harvey R. Freeman, "The Generation Gap: Attitudes of Students and Their Parents," Journal of Counseling Psychology, *Vol. 19, No. 5, 1972, pp. 441–447. Copyright © 1972 by the American Psychological Association. Reprinted by permission.*

(2) that the emerging values held by young consumers may become relatively permanent as they grow older, and (3) that youth culture innovations will tend to diffuse into the dominant culture.

Segmentation In reality there is not one youth market but several. A fifteen-year-old female high school student living in Burbank, California, patterns her consumption quite differently than does a twenty-two-year-old

Likert

Table 4-4 Personal and Social Values
(By Total Noncollege Youth versus Total College Youth)

	TOTAL NONCOLLEGE PERCENT	TOTAL COLLEGE PERCENT
Belief in Traditional American Values		
Doing any job well is important	89	84
Business is entitled to make a profit	85	85
People should save money regularly	80	71
Commitment to a meaningful career is very important	79	81
Private property is sacred	74	67
A "strong" person can control own life	70	65
Competition encourages excellence	66	62
Duty before pleasure	66	54
Hard work will always pay off	56	44
People are basically good, but society corrupts	50	46
People who "accept" things are better off	31	15
Activities Thought to Be Morally Wrong		
Destroying private property	88	78
Taking things without paying for them	88	84
Collecting welfare when you could work	83	77
Paying for college by selling dope	80	64
Interchanging partners among couples	72	57
Using violence to achieve worthwhile results	72	66
Cheating big companies	66	50
Extramarital sexual relations	65	60
Having children without formal marriage	58	40
Living with a spouse you don't love	52	41
Having an abortion	48	32
Relations between consenting homosexuals	47	25
Casual premarital sexual relations	34	22

Source: The Youth Study-1974. (JDR Third Fund) Yankelovich, Skelly and White, Inc., New York.

Figure 4-1   Young people's attitudes about product use and the environment.

male college student in Kansas, although both may enjoy the same records, wear the same type of blue denim shirt, and long for the same expensive stereo system. Thus youth is only one basis for segmentation; other factors include actual age, sex, region, ethnic affiliation if any, religion, and social class. These topics will be developed more fully in subsequent chapters.

Enduring Values Today's young consumers have been enculturated with certain common value patterns, ranging from their own family's influence through an educational system veering toward less authoritarianism and more participation, and the legacy of such unique influences as the Beatles phenomenon, the Vietnam war, and the counterculture. As middle-aged consumers now experience bittersweet nostalgia on hearing Peggy Lee, our middle-aged consumers of the year 2000 will recall the long-lost days of the Rolling Stones with fond memories. As consumers they have developed (and are developing) loyalties to products, retail stores, and other marketing institutions that will endure to varying degrees, subject to changes in our economic system and other intangibles. So it is important for marketers to win loyalties for the long term while catering to youthful needs.

Diffusion of Innovations As long as youthfulness remains a culturally prized trait, the innovations adopted by the youth culture will continue to seep into the dominant culture. Consider the long-term diffusion resulting from the original hippie counterculture. The so-called "Peacock Revolution" in men's clothing arose out of fascination with the flamboyant outfits worn by the young. Businessmen grew sideburns and read *The Greening of America*. Secretaries began arriving at the office in beads and carrying astrology

guides. Housewives bought organic foods. All of these behaviors became established norms without many Americans being fully aware of their origins. Thus the youth culture may be a weathervane for other markets where people want to appear youthful.

New American Cultural Patterns

In American culture, change occurs at a sometimes dizzying rate brought about by a highly sophisticated technology. Because changes in values are seldom too far behind changes in technology, our normative system is now straining to keep pace. What is happening at this stage of our cultural evolution may be viewed in the framework of a *need hierarchy* proposed by Abraham Maslow, one which is applicable to people in societies as well as to individuals.

Maslow's Need Hierarchy All men and women share basic needs in common, ranging from the simplest physiological needs to intricate yearnings for self-realization. And these needs may be arranged at five ascending levels:[39]

1. *Physiological.* These are the basic requirements for life such as food, shelter, sleep, and some form of clothing to protect one from the elements.

2. *Safety and Security.* Once the first set of needs is taken care of and people can remain alive, they begin looking out for their own safety and consider protecting what they have.

3. *Social Contact.* With security assured, human beings seek to associate with others, each person to belong with another person or to a group, and to give and receive affection.

4. *Ego Fulfillment.* Through association with others, people develop needs for self-esteem, power, status, and other ego enrichments.

5. *Self-Fulfillment.* Once all other needs have been fulfilled, men and women desire self-actualization, to realize their full potential as human beings. Moving up the hierarchy, each new need level creates the necessity for some form of consumption or expression. And one does not reach the next level until needs at the immediate level are gratified.

By 1990, economists predict, most Americans are expected to reach levels Four and Five, which are the two levels of greatest options and opportunities (assuming that prevailing social trends such as an income maintenance program, guaranteed health care, and other social benefit proposals are brought to fruition). This suggests that the United States in 1990 will be a society with greater diversification of human interests, subcultures, institutions, consumption patterns, and the arts.[40] And the elevation of most Americans to levels of ego fulfillment and self-expression will bring about changes in our basic value orientation, as indicated in Figure 4-2 and Table 4-5.

Figure 4-2   Need profile 1965–1990.

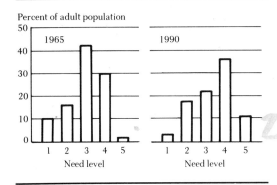

New Value Orientations   In the context of the traditional American values outlined earlier in this chapter, a number of new *directions* in value orientation have been proposed by Ian Wilson, Daniel Yankelovich, and others. Five such directions that are expected to affect consumer behavior patterns include movements from: (1) work to leisure, (2) puritanism to hedonism, (3) conformity to individuality, (4) independence to interdependence, and (5) materialism to an emphasis on the quality of life.

From Work to Leisure   Through a "hard work" ethic, America developed its technology; now that accomplishment has reduced the need for hard work. The nature and structure of work are expected to change as the work week grows shorter, sabbaticals become common in more occupations, and part-time jobs grow more popular.[41] This may lead to *modular* scheduling of work, in which employees may indicate the number of modules (time units) they wish to work.[42] Such developments will significantly increase leisure time, creating the need for new products and services with which people may occupy themselves.

Yet Lee Rainwater raises an intriguing point about American workers—with increasing affluence, many have been inclined to choose moonlighting rather than leisure. So even though people may have a great deal of money to spend on leisure products, their actual spare time for consumption may not change. The net effect of all this will be that the products offering the *least time expended per unit of satisfaction provided* will be most in demand.[43]

From Puritanism to Hedonism[44]   Everywhere there are indications that Americans no longer want to defer gratification; they are eager to pursue pleasure for its own sake and, furthermore, want to play now and pay

Table 4-5   Selected Value Trends to 1990

LESS EMPHASIS	MORE EMPHASIS
Status achievement	Self-expression achievement
Conformity	Individualism, autonomy
Racism	Equality
Mass art	Personal esthetics
Authoritarianism	Tolerance, participation
Puritanism	Sensualism, "metahedonism"
Moralism	Romanticism
Hard work a virtue	Rewarding work a virtue
Institutional leadership	Political and individual leadership
Desire for status quo	Acceptance of change
Group-control	Self-control, self-expression
Tradition	Experimentation

Source: Figure 4-2 and Table 4-5 from Arnold Mitchell and Mary K. Baird, American Values, (Menlo Park, Calif.: Stanford Research Institute, Long Range Planning Service Report No. 378, June 1969).

later. Thus American consumers have found a new way of life—debt—as they use credit to finance purchases. The already heavy use of consumer credit is predicted to increase as traditional inhibitions about indebtedness continue to be relaxed. The decline of puritanism also marks a trend toward greater sexual liberalism, clearly hastened by the development of the birth control pill. Products and services formerly taboo in advertising now appear in the media with great frequency. Finally, distinctions between male and female roles are beginning to blur as women seek careers and men assume the duties of "househusbands."[45] A large number of househusbands could dramatically affect the present "woman's market" for household products, changing the way that such products are positioned and promoted.

From Conformity to Individuality Americans are moving rapidly from the sameness and conformity that characterized their cul-

ture during the 1950s. Consumers are expressing desires to be individualistic in shaping their own life styles, a trend that could signal a shift from mass merchandising with its connotations of blandness toward highly individualized products and services. The direction toward personal creativity also embraces the realization that creating things is not the sole province of the artist. Everyone can be expressive through clothing, activities, and hobbies like painting or music. In this vein, educational courses are being advertised to offer people new life options. A poster for the School of Visual Arts in New York City reads, "Spend a few evenings with us. It may change the way you spend the rest of your days."

From Independence to Interdependence The competitive edge of American society is diminishing as a new *cooperative* orientation takes hold. At a personal level, this suggests a preference for a few deep friendships rather than general sociability.[46] In living relationships, there is a slight move from monogamy and the nuclear family toward experiments with communal living. Studies have already been conducted with upper middle class professionals who have chosen group marriage with other couples as their preferred mode of living.[47] If this new version of the extended family should gain popularity, then housing patterns, child-care products and

Figure 4-3   Profile of significant value-system changes: 1969–1980 (as seen by General Electric's Business Environment section).

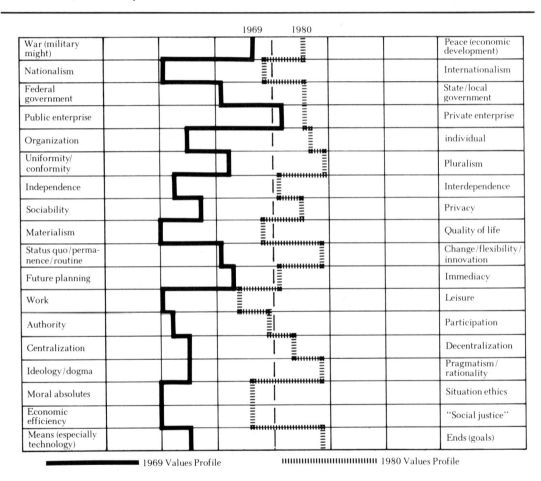

1969	1980		Peace (economic development)
War (military might)			Peace (economic development)
Nationalism			Internationalism
Federal government			State/local government
Public enterprise			Private enterprise
Organization			individual
Uniformity/conformity			Pluralism
Independence			Interdependence
Sociability			Privacy
Materialism			Quality of life
Status quo/permanence/routine			Change/flexibility/innovation
Future planning			Immediacy
Work			Leisure
Authority			Participation
Centralization			Decentralization
Ideology/dogma			Pragmatism/rationality
Moral absolutes			Situation ethics
Economic efficiency			"Social justice"
Means (especially technology)			Ends (goals)

━━━━━ 1969 Values Profile   ⅢⅢⅢⅢⅢⅢ 1980 Values Profile

Source: Ian H. Wilson, "How Our Values Are Changing," The Futurist, February 1970. Reprinted by permission of The Futurist, published by the World Future Society, P.O. Box 30369 (Bethesda), Washington, D.C. 20014.

services, and other necessities of family life will be modified to meet different needs. And marketing methods will change with them.[48]

From Materialism to Emphasizing Quality of Life As more Americans come to enjoy affluence and education, the pursuit of materialism as an end in itself will pale in contrast with the pleasures of self-actualization. Already the traditional status symbols of cars, diamonds, and fur coats are becoming less attractive. People are driving smaller cars than they can afford ("living below their means," as Volkswagen has expressed the concept), giving each other plain wedding bands, and thinking twice before wearing the pelt of a near-extinct species. Much of this concern about quality of life comes from the wretched excesses of pollution and exploitation of vanishing resources, which will increasingly restrict the boundaries of our life styles.

These are just a few of the directions emerging from within the American normative system; other examples appear in Figure 4-3. Considered in profile with traditional American values, patterns of cultural change can offer marketers useful guidelines for long-range planning.

Summary

Culture may be defined as patterns of learned behavior which are held in common and transmitted by the members of any given society. The components of a culture are three dimensional: cognitive, material, and normative. A normative system consists of values (or ideas about what is good or correct) by which people conduct themselves, and *norms,* meaning standards of behavior that govern how people think or act in specific situations. Relativism is the opposite of *ethnocentrism,* the view that other cultures can be judged by one's own cultural standards. Consumer behavior is influenced by cultural *symbols,* which may carry connotative meanings to consumers like the name "Cadillac" and by *change,* whether technological or by diffusion. *Cross-cultural* research compares features of different cultures, offering useful information for approaching world markets. But it is first of all necessary to adopt a cultural perspective when formulating strategies of multinational scope.

Observers of *American* culture may begin with two generalizations: (1) that our culture operates under an ethic of consumption and (2) that diversity in life styles is offset by homogeneity in mass production. The American normative system is best characterized by establishing a framework of *traditional values,* recognizing the forces of *cultural change,* and noting *new value directions* in which American culture seems to be headed.

NOTES

1. Walter A. Henry, "Cultural Values Do Correlate with Consumer Behavior," *Journal of Marketing Research*, Vol. 13, No. 2 (May 1976), p. 121.

2. Adapted from Ralph Linton, *The Cultural Background of Personality* (New York: Appleton–Century–Crofts, 1945).

3. George P. Murdock, "Uniformities in Culture," *American Sociological Review*, Vol. 5 (1940), pp. 361–67.

4. James F. Downs, *Culture in Crisis* (Beverly Hills: Glencoe Press, 1971), p. 35.

5. Margaret Mead and Martha Wolfenstein, eds., *Childhood in Contemporary Cultures* (Chicago: University of Chicago Press, 1955).

6. Peter Berger and Thomas Luckman, *The Social Construction of Reality*, (Garden City, New York: Doubleday and Co., 1966).

7. William Graham Sumner, *Folkways* (New York: Mentor Press, 1960).

8. Thomas P. Hustad, Charles S. Mayer, and Thomas W. Whipple, "Consideration of Context Differences in Product Evaluation and Market Segmentation," *Journal of the Academy of Marketing Science*, Vol. 3, No. 1 (Winter 1975), p. 34.

9. Bronislaw Malinowski, *Argonauts of the Western Pacific* (New York: E. P. Dutton and Co., 1922).

10. Lyman Bryson et al., eds., *Symbols and Values: An Initial Study* (New York: Cooper Square, 1964).

11. Edward Sapir, "Symbolism," *Encyclopedia of the Social Sciences* (1934), 14, as cited in Broome and Selznick, *Sociology* (New York: Harper & Row, publishers, 1968).

12. *Consumer Reports*, February 1975, p. 82.

13. James H. Myers and William Reynolds, *Consumer Behavior and Marketing Management* (Boston: Houghton Mifflin Co., 1967), p. 234.

14. Marshall McLuhan, *Understanding Media: The Extensions of Man* (New York: McGraw-Hill Book Co.), 1964.

15. Downs, *Culture in Crisis*, p. 15.

16. Ralph Linton, "One Hundred Percent American," *The American Mercury*, Vol. 40, April 1937.

17. Paul C. Rosenblatt and Paul C. Cozby, "Courtship Pattern Associated with Freedom of Spouse," *Journal of Marriage and the Family*, Vol. 34, No. 4 (November 1972), pp. 689–95.

18. Rolf Wirsig, "Political Power and Information," *American Anthropologist*, Vol. 75, No. 1 (February 1973), pp. 153–70.

19. Francis M. Adams and Charles E. Osgood, "A Cross-Cultural Study of the Affective Meanings of Color," *Journal of Cross-Cultural Psychology*, Vol. 4, No. 2 (June 1973).

20. Susan P. Douglas, "Cross-National Comparisons and Consumer Stereotypes: A Case Study of Working and Nonworking Wives in the U.S. and France," *Journal of Consumer Research*, Vol. 3, No. 1 (June 1976).

21. Ernest Dichter, "The World Customer," *Harvard Business Review*, Vol. 40 (July-August 1962), pp. 119–121.

22. Erik Elinder, "How International Can European Advertising Be?" *Journal of Marketing*, Vol. 29 (April 1965).

23. Robert D. Buzzell, "Can You Standardize Multinational Marketing?" *Harvard Business Review*, Vol. 46 (November-December 1968).

24. Montrose Sommers and Jerome Kernan, "Why Products Flourish Here, Fizzle There," *Columbia Journal of World Business*, Vol. 2, (March-April 1967), pp. 89–97.

25. G. Peter Lauter and Paul M. Dickie, "Multinational Corporations in Eastern European Socialist Countries," *Journal of Marketing*, Vol. 39, No. 4 (October 1975), p. 40.

26. Joe McGinniss, *The Selling of the President*, (New York: Trident Press, 1969).

27. Lee Coleman, "What is American: A Study of Alleged American Traits," *Social Forces*, Vol. 19, No. 4 (1941).

28. Robin M. Williams, Jr., *American Society: A Sociological Interpretation* (New York, Alfred A. Knopf, 1960), pp. 469–70.

29. Sommers and Kernan, "Why Products Flourish."

30. *A Split Test of Advertising Effectiveness*, New York: Doubleday Advertising Company, 1977.

31. Sommers and Kernan, "Why Products Flourish."

32. Daniel Bell as cited in Charles E. Silberman, "Identity Crisis in the Consumer Markets," *Fortune*, March, 1971.

33. James L. Spates and Jack Levin, "Beats, Hippies, the Hip Generation and the American Middle Class: An Analysis of Values," *International Social Science Journal*, Vol. 24, No. 2 (1972), pp. 326–53.

34. "Riches in Rags," *Wall Street Journal*, April 27, 1971.

35. Charles E. Silberman, "Identity Crisis in the Consumer Markets," *Fortune*, March 1971.

36. Sherman B. Chickering, "How We Got That Way," in *Natural Enemies?* ed. Alexander Klein (Philadelphia: J. B. Lippincott Co., 1969).

37. Harvey R. Freeman, "The Generation Gap: Attitudes of Students and Their Parents," *Journal of Counseling Psychology*, Vol. 19, No. 5 (1972), pp. 441–47.

38. *Seventeen*, "You Tell What's Right and Wrong with America," February 1971, p. 126.

39. A. H. Maslow, *Motivation and Personality* (New York: Harper and Row, Inc., 1954).

40. Arnold Mitchell and Mary K. Baird, *American Values* (Menlo Park, California: Stanford Research Institute, Report No. 378, June, 1969).

41. "Herman Kahn's Confident Look at the Future," *New York*, August 9, 1976, p. 34.

42. Ian H. Wilson, "How Our Values Are Changing," *The Futurist*, February 1970.

43. Lee Rainwater, "Post-1984 America," *Society*, February 1972, p. 26.

44. Daniel Yankelovich, Inc., "Thirty Social Trends that Alter Consumption,"*Marketing News*, May 1971, pp. 7–8.

45. Ahmed Belkaoui and Janice Belkaoui, "A Comparative Analysis of Roles Portrayed by Women in Print Advertisements: 1958, 1970, 1972," *Journal of Marketing Research*, Vol. 13, No. 2 (May 1976).

46. Wilson, "Values Are Changing," p. 7.

47. James S. Ramey, "Communes, Group Marriage, and the Upper Middle Class," *Journal of Marriage and the Family*, November 1972, pp. 647–655.

48. Nessim Hanna, A. H. Kizilbash, and Albert Smart, "Marketing Strategy under Conditions of Economic Scarcity," *Journal of Marketing*, Vol. 39, No. 1 (January 1975).

MARKETING APPLICATIONS

Conclusion 1 *Cultural symbolism plays an important role in how product packaging and advertising are received in any given culture.*
Application When entering international markets with a new package design or promotional campaign, the first step should be to test them with small groups of consumers to uncover any cultural biases likely to affect the product's success.

Conclusion 2 *Cultural relativism is the correct perspective to adopt when marketing to another culture—this is the principle of judging any behavior in its cultural context.*
Application Assuming that a product which is successful in the American market will automatically find favor in another market represents a costly form of ethnocentrism—the belief that our own cultural values should be the standards for everyone's behavior. For example, American marketers, who see innovation as a virtue in itself, express surprise when American products introduced in the English market are not gratefully accepted. Yet it has become apparent through cross-cultural research that the English feel many innovative American products are slightly ridiculous and prefer more traditional, time-proven products. Thus, while it might seem appropriate to launch a new salt which "doesn't roll off potato chips" in England (for the favorite "fish and chips"), the consumer reaction would probably be that it is just another frivolous new American invention hardly worth one's attention.

Conclusion 3 *Traditional American values stress cultural traits such as active mastery, innovativeness, and problem solving.*
Application In the United States, the most successful products and services remain those which promise new ways to solve consumer problems. The first consideration in developing a new product or service is to identify a source of consumer dissatisfaction with current market items in that category and design the new product to overcome that problem. The first "dandruff" shampoo was a success because, while existing shampoos on the market could eliminate dandruff, the idea that a new shampoo was specifically designed for that purpose appealed to the great number of consumers who viewed dandruff as a problem.

Conclusion 4 *Emergent American cultural values have been identified as shifts from work to leisure, puritanism to hedonism, conformity to individuality, independence to interdependence, and materialism to quality of life.*
Application Changing directions in cultural values can be projected and applied in long-range planning. This process is critical in a culture which emphasizes change such as the

116

United States. The current trends mentioned, for example, will affect marketing in a number of industries—recreational homes and vehicles, "self-realization" products and services, clothing, automobiles, entertainment, and so on. For this reason, marketers should actively sponsor predictive studies of cultural change—and listen to the findings—when making decisions that will be influenced by future consumer needs.

ASSIGNMENTS

Managerial Assignment

Traditionally, Canadian marketing has been dominated by United States corporations. Products which are offered to Canadians are very often U.S. merchandise with little variation other than differences in advertising to take cultural variables into account. But the current trend is toward Canadian ownership of companies doing business in that country and, particularly, to the internal development of Canadian products specifically for the Canadian market.

As Marketing Manager of a United States cosmetic company, you are developing a men's after-shave product to be launched in Canada and must choose one of two strategies: (1) to repackage an American after-shave formula and offer it to the Canadian markets by creating a Canadian-oriented advertising campaign. This would be the most effective route for short-term profits, or (2) to create an all-new product after conducting market research in Canada and deciding what scent might appeal to Canadian men—and especially women, who buy most of the after-shave sold as gifts for men. This would then become the first men's after-shave created in Canada. Advertising and promotion would focus on this theme.

Decide on one of the alternatives and be prepared to defend it.

Research Assignment

Background   Iraudi, a newly oil-rich (but apolitical) sheikdom in the Middle East, has just bought a fleet of Boeing 747s to launch its own airline—*Iraudi Air*. In addition to its air route from New York to Iraudi, the airline has secured a New York-to-London route and wishes to promote Iraudi Air service to London from within the United States. Melanie and Smith, a New York market research firm, is hired to study the possibilities for attracting New York-London travelers to Iraudi Air to compete with the more established airlines servicing that route. Fares are regulated; thus they are the same for all airlines. For this reason, appeals to consumers other than saving money must be developed.

Methodology Because the consumer research which individual airlines conduct is highly confidential, a competitive file of other airlines' advertising offers the best indication of the appeals they are currently testing or have already found most effective in filling their seats (since their advertising is largely based on their confidential research).

1. Establish a competitive file of ads for all major carriers which have routes to London, including:

> British Airways
> TWA
> Pan Am
> Air India
> Aeroflot (Russian airline)

(These ads are available from past media and, particularly, special interest publications for heavy travelers such as credit card magazines.)

2. List the most popular appeals that appear in competitive ads and analyze them from the standpoint of *Iraudi Air*. What can Iraudi offer that is different and compelling for the London traveler?

Extrapolation Make an informal recommendation (two or three pages) to the management of Iraudi Air which offers suggestions for establishing and positioning that airline as a New York-London carrier.

Is the best appeal a cultural one—to make the Iraudi airline different and distinctive? Or should the cultural differences be played down in this case?

Creative Assignment

The Powers, Reindorf and Copacino advertising agency has just acquired a new automobile account—the small, economical Bitsu imported from Japan. While hardly luxurious, the car has many features found on American cars, including accessories like automatic transmission, bucket seats with a center console, a vinyl roof option, and so on. Yet it still manages to average 30 mpg around town and 45 on the highways.

The consensus among agency creative people who will actually produce the advertising for the car is that it should be sold not only for its economy benefits. While economy is important, it is felt that the ads should convince consumers that buying a small car is more of a status symbol today than buying a medium-sized or large car, due to changes in American cultural values.

Create three rough ads—headline or visual or both—which will meet those objectives in appealing to the consumer. Evaluate and defend them from the standpoint of what we know about cultural change in the United States.

SELECTED READINGS

Banting, Peter M. and Randolph E. Ross. "Canada: Obstacles and Opportunities." *The Journal of the Academy of Marketing Science*, Vol. 3, No. 1 (Winter 1975), pp. 1–19.

Henry, Walter A. "Cultural Values Do Correlate With Consumer Behavior." *Journal of Marketing Research*, Vol. 13, No. 2 (May 1976), pp. 121–27.

Kerskhoff, Alan C. "Pattern of Marriage and Family Formation and Dissolution." *Journal of Consumer Research*, Vol. 2, No. 4 (March 1976), pp. 261–75.

OBJECTIVES

FIVE

Subcultures in the United States

Not everyone in the United States shares the norms and values of "mainstream" American culture. People who belong to a particular subculture—whether held together by ethnic, religious, or some other common bond—tend to behave differently as consumers than people who identify with the dominant culture.

Some subcultures maintain features of older cultures they have left behind (as many of the ethnic groups that have immigrated to our urban centers manage to do). Others adhere to religious practices that may prohibit certain kinds of consumption. And some consumers reflect the preferences of a given region, which may be based on nothing more complex than an ultra-hot or -cold climate.

This chapter concludes our analysis of cultural influences on consumption by analyzing seven different kinds of subcultures found in the United States. All tend to exhibit con-sumer preferences that veer from the prevailing culture, creating special markets for products and services.

Some representative topics include:

• Consumer traits of the emerging ethnic subcultures, and how they affect the dominant American culture.

• How black consumers distinguish themselves in attitudes toward products and brands, retail stores, and media.

• Why the elderly may be viewed as a consumer subculture.

• The urban "singles" market—affluent hedonists in the dating game.

• Why the poor still pay more than other consumers for the same products and services.

Some recommendations for gauging consumer needs of the different subcultures are presented, as well as suggestions on how to direct communications to subcultural groups.

The Subculture Concept

An American traveling in Europe may seem to be just another American to the natives. But the same person in the United States maintains a more complicated identity—as a black woman lawyer practicing in New York, an elderly retiree living in Fort Lauderdale, or a Mexican-American insurance salesman from Albuquerque. All adhere for the most part to fundamental norms, values, and behavior patterns of American culture; yet each person identifies with a segment of that culture that shares certain cultural traits unlike those of any other segment. These groupings may be based on any number of life-style variables including age, ethnicity, occupation, region, and religion.

To organize this behavioral diversity in America in some fashion, anthropologists use the term *subculture*. Like the larger concept of culture, "subculture" is ambiguous and lends itself to different interpretations. Some social scientists intend it to mean groups of real people. Others use it to refer to the values and norms held by those groups.[1] For marketing purposes, a subculture may be described as *any cultural patterning that preserves important features of the dominant society but provides values and life styles of its own.*

This suggests an infinite number of population segments that could be characterized as subcultures. Police and military organizations are examples, as are other occupations that require specific modes of behavior and imply values not necessarily those of the larger culture. But occupation has come to be associated with a special kind of subculture, social class, which will be treated thoroughly in another chapter. Also, the term subculture found early use and popularity in studies of juvenile delinquents and deviant or criminal groups. They are not included here because few marketers consciously direct their efforts to those segments. The subcultures covered in this chapter are those based on *ethnicity and religion, race, region, old age, poverty,* and the marital status known as *single*. Each grouping has unique product and service needs, calls for special considerations of pricing and distribution, and demands a thoughtful study to determine the media and types of persuasive communications most likely to be effective. Some have generated more interest from marketers than others, but most promise to grow more prominent over the next decade and beyond.

Researchers study subcultural patterns through the methods of cross-cultural research described in chapter 4. Some results of these studies appear where they offer insights into the group's consumption behavior.

Ethnic and Religious Subcultures

Because some of the first immigrants to settle successfully in the United States were European nationality groups and harassed religious sects, ethnic and religious subcultures were the first to become established here. They also became the most diversified as immigrants poured into the country during the nineteenth and early twentieth centuries.

But some controversy surrounds the nature of ethnic (nationality based) subcultures today. One argument, the theory of *assimilation,* maintains that ethnic groups lose their nationality traits over time and adopt the behaviors associated with their new culture.[2] Through the forces of occupational and regional mobility, the homogenizing media, and other influences, ethnic identities are slowly eroded. This has seemed to be the pattern for most immigrant groups in the United States, where foreign-born individuals have traditionally been regarded with a measure of disdain and suspicion. Some evidence suggests that members of the earlier ethnic groups, such as the Irish, have labored mightily to adopt "American" life styles. Another explanation, the theory of *mobilization,* states that ethnic identification is actually preserved from one generation to the next through the institutions of parochial schools, family traditions, and churches. According to some observers, there is now a decided movement away from assimilation toward increased ethnic consciousness among Poles, Italians, and other nationality groups.[3] Early indications of this trend are the formation of civil rights groups made up of Polish-Americans, Italian-Americans, and so on, as well as the appearance of ethnic characters in prime-time television shows.

Functions of Ethnic Subcultures

There are good reasons for ethnic groups to maintain "subsocieties" within the mass culture. Gordon points out that the ethnic subculture serves three important functions:[4]

1. *To provide a psychological source of group identification.* Members of an ethnic subculture gain a sense of identity from association with their "own" people. They also derive a strong feeling of intimacy.

2. *To offer a patterned network of groups and institutions.* If a member wishes to, he or she may maintain primary relationships with others in the ethnic subculture throughout life.

3. *To serve as a frame of reference for viewing the new culture.* The subculture member retains a cultural heritage through which to perceive the values and norms of the "host" society. This creates the cultural pluralism evident in the United States—a society composed of groups that have retained, to varying degrees, their own cultural heritage.

Emerging Ethnic Subcultures

Patterns of ethnic groupings are constantly changing. Some of the earlier immigrant groups have been assimilated to a large degree, as is the case with the Irish, Italians, Poles, and Jews. Immigration into this country from European nations continues to decline, while new immigrants from Central and South American countries are more in evidence. This trend should encourage marketers to study the characteristics of new subcultures—particularly Mexican-American, Puerto Rican, Cuban, and Vietnamese. Because Cuban and Vietnamese subcultures represent the most recent, and smallest, emerging subcultures, there is little published research about their demographic profiles or consumption patterns. But both groups will be of interest to marketers in the geographic regions of their highest concentration—Miami, Florida (Cuban), and California (Vietnamese).

The Mexican-American Subculture Most Mexican-Americans have settled in the Southwestern states, notably California and Texas. Historically, members of this subculture have suffered discrimination in housing, employment opportunities, voting, and other forms of participation in the dominant culture.[5] But there is a growing middle class among second- and third-generation Mexican-Americans—and evidence that those who have achieved educational success, higher status occupations, and other requirements of middle-class social acceptance experience little or no overt discrimination.[6]

The Puerto Rican Subculture New York City has received the largest migration of *puertorriquenos* in recent years, but the members of this subculture are hardly homogenous in degree of assimilation. Many have been born in the city; others only recently left the Caribbean island. As one of the last wave of immigrants to arrive upon the urban scene, a large number of poor Puerto Ricans come seeking employment opportunities but are forced to settle for the Spanish Harlem barrio and public assistance. In Spanish Harlem unemployment is three times as high as the national average. The problems of Puerto Ricans in Harlem are closely aligned with those of Mexican-Americans in the Southwest; language barriers and discrimination are the most profound. But the Puerto Rican population is young—more than half are under 21—and the possibilities for upward mobility increase with each generation. A study conducted among Puerto Rican families in Connecticut indicates that, although the parents interviewed had received a low level of education, their aspirations for their children reflected white middle-class norms.[7]

Religious Subcultures

Because the importance of strict, formalized religious practice has reportedly waned over the past few decades, religious influence on consumption behavior may have decreased accordingly. Yet there are still norms that restrict or dictate certain products and services for devout members of religious subcultures. Many Mormans abstain from liquor and tobacco in line with their beliefs. Christian Scientists, obeying religious precepts, may refrain from taking over-the-counter or prescription drugs and consult religious "practitioners" for physical and emotional problems rather than physicians. Orthodox Jews buy kosher foods. For mass marketing purposes, religious subcultures are not usually treated as important segments. But those who market *exclusively* to religious segments are often quite successful, thanks to an apparent resurgence of Evangelical-type religious activism.

The reported shift to Evangelicalism is illustrated by the success of religious books. For example:[8]
• Billy Graham's *Angels* had sold 1.4 million copies by 1976.
• Hal Lindsey, a former leader of the Jesus Movement, has sold over 15 million books since 1970.
• The Christian Booksellers Association's 2,100 stores reported total sales of over $375 million in 1976.
This has persuaded some secular book publishing houses to start divisions specializing in religious titles.

Marketing to Ethnic Subculture Segments

Ethnic subcultures are becoming increasingly popular with researchers investigating urban markets. (See Figure 5-1.)

Some Consumption Patterns From various

Figure 5-1 An ethnic subculture product successfully directed to the mass market.

ANNCR: Government regulations say we can make our Hebrew National Beef Hot Dogs from frozen beef.

We don't.

The government says we can use artificial coloring.

We don't.

They say we can add meat by-products.

We don't.

They say we can add non-meat fillers.

We can't. We're Kosher...

And have to answer to an even higher authority.

(SFX: WIND)

(SFX: WIND)

Courtesy Hebrew National Kosher Foods Inc.

studies of urban ethnic subcultures, behavior patterns associated with products, pricing, and store selection have emerged:

• In acceptance of convenience foods such as TV dinners and instant coffee, Puerto Rican shoppers were most likely to buy these "new" products to supplement their traditional diets. Italian-Americans were less likely to buy processed-packaged foods, preferring fresh meat and vegetables. Jewish consumers exhibited the highest resistance to frozen meats but were more favorable toward instant coffee. This could be attributed in part to their religious dietary laws. [9]

• A study comparing Japanese-Americans with black as well as white consumers at different income levels reported that Japanese-Americans chose their stores on the basis of economy, were least concerned with brands, and were more inclined to innovate in buying small appliances. Japanese-Americans also mentioned more total information sources (such as advertising) than either black or white consumers. [10]

Reaching Ethnic Subculture Consumers
Political writers have been known to refer to "the ethnic bloc" or "the Italian vote" in analyzing voting behavior. These are misnomers that marketers should recognize and avoid. All Italians do not vote the same way, nor do they consume the same products and services. Ethnic markets, like any large groups, must be further segmented by age, sex, income, social class, region, and other dimensions of life styles. Consider how little resemblance an affluent young Jewish doctor (female) living in Houston bears to the middle-aged Jewish policeman (male) struggling with a mortgage in a suburb of New York City. Also, the value of ethnic subcultural considerations lessens as a group becomes assimilated into the mass culture (the "new ethnic consciousness" notwithstanding). It is logically most fruitful to study the ethnic groups that cling most tenaciously to the culture left behind, for this is what distinguishes them from other groups.

In practice, ethnic considerations crop up most frequently in urban mass marketing. A New York savings bank offering new high-interest certificates attached coupons to advertisements and received numerous orders at all its branches but one—the office serving the Chinese community, where not a single coupon was received. Later the bank discovered that Chinese consumers do not especially like coupons and would never think to mail one for a purchase as important as a savings certificate.

Sometimes an advertising appeal targeted toward ethnic markets can backfire completely, as was the case with a brewery that ran television commercials depicting different ethnic groups enjoying its beer. When the brand's share of market declined, it developed that none of the ethnic groups liked to see other groups drinking the same beer that it preferred. The campaign was hastily withdrawn.

Black America

Of all the subcultures in the United States, blacks are studied the most frequently and thoroughly. One reason is the enormous size of the black population. A corollary reason is that blacks in the United States wield as much spending clout as all the citizens of

Canada. But some controversy surrounds the existence and significance of a distinct black market.

Investigators generally agree that the black subculture derives from a history of deprivation and adjustment to white prejudice and discrimination. Heavily concentrated geographically, blacks have long felt the existence of a "color caste" system in our culture. This system has produced shared psychological frustrations and needs stemming from inequities in education, employment, and income. Most studies of black consumers have reached the conclusion that, in spite of these frustrations, blacks have come to accept the values of white-middle-class society toward products and services.

Bauer and Cunningham point to increased black mobility in housing and travel as well as expanded employment opportunities in describing what they call the "black dilemma." This is reported to be a desire to share white values about consumption, a desire thwarted by lower income and other forms of deprivation that persist despite affirmative action programs. The problem is whether to struggle against formidable odds to achieve middle-class consumption patterns or simply to give up and settle for a lower-scale existence.[11]

Other researchers suggest that the black subculture embraces values quite different from mainstream America's reflected in life styles distinct from those of the white community.[12] Examples of consumption trends almost uniquely black include the African influence in clothing and hair styles and the appearance of black movies and television shows.

Some Dimensions of Black America

It is a common mistake to think of the "black market" as a monolithic, homogeneous group of consumers with like needs, desires, and resources.[13] But research has uncovered certain characteristics and patterns of consumption that deserve to be considered in any marketing decision affecting blacks. These are discussed here, with some prescriptions for positioning products and selecting media.

Geographic Concentration Blacks have established a pattern of migration from rural to urban areas, largely due to diminished employment opportunities in Southern agriculture. Today, blacks account for approximately 20 percent of large-city populations. Regionally, 50 percent of Black America continues to live in the South, 18 percent in the Northeast, 22 percent in the North Central states, and 10 percent in the West.[14]

Income Levels Although black median incomes are rising steadily each year, a great discrepancy remains between black and white earnings.[15] This holds true even for blacks who have attained the same educational levels as whites.[16] Naturally enough, income deprivation affects the consumption behavior of blacks both physically and psychologically. Yet, although a greater proportion of blacks than whites fall below the poverty level, improved educational opportunities and employment policies have created a significant black middle class, and even an upper class.

Family Structure Black America remains very young, with a median age of 21.4 years as against a 28.7 median age for whites. Practically one out of every two blacks in the United States is under 18. Black family life has been described by some researchers as predominately matriarchal. Studies have suggested a higher degree of instability in black homes, using criteria such as percentage of illegitimate births and children living with only one parent.[17] All of these characteristics are closely related to lower income levels.

Educational Patterns   Blacks are now going to school in greater numbers and staying longer than ever before. They are widening their curriculum choices as well, with more choosing careers in business and industry.[18] But these developments still fall short of outstanding progress. Studies of black learning at all educational levels indicate that many schools are failing to prepare black students adequately for the realities of business and society.[19] Open enrollment in community colleges and universities remains a controversial policy.

Attitudes and Behavior of Black Consumers

All of the conditions that plague Black America—income deprivation, educational limitations, and the effects of discrimination—influence how black consumers establish preferences for products and services. Blacks may buy differently from whites because they have less money to spend, but this is only a partial explanation of black purchasing behavior. There is the question of owning certain products for their esteem or status value. There are also differences in the kinds of persuasive communications that seem to appeal to blacks as against whites. Nor are the outlets where white consumers prefer to shop necessarily those favored by black consumers.

Some research findings on consumption patterns of Black America will be discussed here under four categories: attitudes toward the market place, brand preferences, shopping behavior, and receptiveness to communication.

Attitudes toward Products and Services
Blacks appear to spend less money on housing, medical care, education, and utilities than do comparable whites. But proportionately more is reportedly spent on clothing, personal care, alcohol, tobacco, and home furnishings.[20] Blacks are supposed to be more innovative in clothing selection and generally more fashion conscious than whites, with high-income blacks the most avant-garde of all in new fashion acceptance.[21] Comparisons of black vs. white women in terms of fashion consciousness show similar patterns at all income levels.[22] In home appliance buying, blacks are considerably less innovative than whites, although those in high-income brackets reveal a greater proximity to the pattern of whites than they do to low-income blacks.[23]

These differences have persuaded some researchers that blacks tend to be innovative where the products command high social visibility but are less concerned with new products that are, for example, hidden in the kitchen.[24]

In other research, blacks have emerged as heavier consumers than whites of milk, soft drinks, and liquor. They appear to use certain kinds of liquor in disproportionately huge quantities—over 50 percent of the scotch, about 50 percent of the rum, and more than 77 percent of the Canadian whiskey sold in 1962 were bought by black consumers[25]— more recently, scotch has become the most frequently purchased whiskey. Blacks spend *relatively* as much on recreation and leisure as whites. But they go to the movies more frequently and are less likely prospects for expensive leisure products such as boats and skis.[26] Although their dealings with savings banks, insurance companies, and other financial institutions may be less frequent, blacks appear to be thriftier than whites. A black family earning, say, $10,000 will be likely to save a larger portion annually than a white family with the same income.[27]

Brand Selection   Until recently, most researchers were convinced that blacks buy favorite brand names more than whites do, thus could be described as more "brand loyal."[28] But new evidence suggests a strong tendency toward "disloyalty" among black consumers.[29] Sexton points out that this may reflect less distrust of products offered in disadvantaged black neighborhoods and a desire to support black-owned enterprises.[30] Blacks are more concerned with pricing than white consumers are at all income levels, but also consider product status important; and status concern tends to increase with income.[31] Blacks are more *aware* of brands— both national and private than whites. A study of low-income blacks' and whites' attitudes toward food prices revealed that blacks knew more about private brands, stocked more of them in their kitchens, and were more familiar with the prices of all brands studied.[32] Blacks in one study were *not* reported to favor a package specifically designed for the black market over one designed for a general market (when beer containers were considered).[33]

Automobile ownership by make of car has been a frequent topic in literature on the black consumer. Studies have stated that blacks tend to own higher-priced cars than whites at all income levels.[34] This tends to support the argument that blacks favor prestige products carrying a high degree of social visibility. But there are more recent opinions that upper middle-class are veering away from traditional prestige cars like Cadillacs toward other luxury cars, believing that the Cadillac has become a symbol of the "nouveau riche" black.[35]

Shopping Behavior   While white housewives tend to shop for food on the criteria of quality and pricing, black housewives appear more concerned with store friendliness and convenience.[36] Blacks rate supermarkets in general as much less appealing than whites do, citing high prices, crowded and unsanitary facilities, and rude employees.[37] This is largely due to the condition of supermarkets in low-income black neighborhoods, and helps explain the phenomenon that blacks who own cars will drive farther to shop than whites.[38] Blacks are also more inclined to shop at discount houses than whites of the same income level, who prefer department stores. But this finding tends to disappear where upper-income blacks are concerned.[39]

Persuasive Communications   In studies of recall and attitude change, black consumers are generally depicted as more receptive to advertising appeals than whites.[40] Blacks tune into the general media for products addressed to both black and white markets and to "black" media for black-oriented products.[41] The effectiveness of integrated advertising using both white and black models is still subject to controversy. Blacks respond more readily to all-black or integrated ads than to all-white ads in some studies.[42] But other researchers note that integrated messages may not work as well as might be expected. Maggard offers the example of two toothpaste brands—one, the market leader with blacks, used only Caucasians in its television commercials while the other, a less-favored brand, experimented with integrated advertising. Black consumers failed to respond to the integrated commercials by increasing that brand's share of market, indicating in this case that brand loyalty was stronger than an integrated message.[43] And one study indicates that some young blacks may resent the use of black and white models in the same ad.[44]

Black consumers do appear to favor persuasive communications backed by reports of equal employment opportunities by the advertisers, the use of black sales representatives in black areas, and a willingness on the part of advertisers to identify with the problems of the black community.[45]

During the 1960s, a number of black advertising agencies were established specifically to reach the black consumer with effective ad communications. But today, few of these agencies survive. One reason appears to be that clients felt they could get the same kind of advertising from their general agencies. But another frequently mentioned problem is the fact that few principles in the black agencies had received broad-based administrative training in the general agencies where they had worked previously.[46]

Reaching Black Markets

Despite the vast research into patterns of black consumers, black market segmentation remains something of a mystery to marketing practitioners. Part of the problem is the tendency to view all blacks as a single market. Another difficulty is the result of historical discrimination and exploitation by the white community, injustices not easily forgotten by many blacks. Thus what plagues many whites in positions of marketing decision making is an unspoken fear of being offensive to black consumers. Controversy over advertising appeals (should interracial couples be shown in ads?), frustrations expressed by low-income blacks over second-rate shopping conditions in black neighborhoods, and other dilemmas are both real and potential.

There is a serious need for segmentation of black markets according to such variables as income, age, social class, and other determinants of purchasing behavior. This would permit effective positioning of existing products and services, new product development to meet the needs of the black consumer, and intelligent media selection.

Positioning Products in Black Markets Income segmentation may be the first step toward understanding black markets. One major consideration is the fact that 20 percent of blacks in the United States account for 45 percent of black income. But middle- and upper-class blacks do not necessarily aspire to the values of the white middle class. Wall notes that:[47]

A decade ago, the typical successful black adopted the white man's middle-class style. The black from Tuskegee was more Ivy League than the Brahmin from Yale. Blacks are no longer emulating whites. They are expressing their black consciousness. More important, they are not monolithic. They are using different products to differentiate among themselves.

Positioning products for black markets means finding out which black consumers maintain life styles amenable to those products, how target segments feel about those products already, which of their benefits will be most appealing to the segment, and how the merchandise may be best distributed. In new-brand development, additional questions come to mind: What are the real needs of that segment of the black community the product is supposed to serve? Is the pricing consistent with what that segment can afford? How does the sector in question respond to other products in that class? The differences between the ways in which blacks and whites use products affect marketing decisions dramatically. Say that a breakfast cereal is being positioned for consumption by a black segment. It is important to recognize that black mothers are reported to place more emphasis on nutrition than white mothers and stress a hearty breakfast because they don't always trust the lunches their children receive in school. Despite the fact that many black mothers work and would seem to prefer foods that are easy to prepare, they will not sacrifice nutrition for convenience. In a slightly different context, if a new soft drink is considered for black segments in Northern markets, it helps to remember that black tastes tend to reflect Southern origins; for example, in the South cola, grape, and orange drinks are preferred, while root beer is virtually unknown.[48] Again, effective positioning relies heavily on research.

Media Selection   In selecting the most potent advertising medium, the marketer seeking to reach black consumers must be alert to the particular ways in which black Americans react to television, radio, newspapers, and magazines—ways apt to differ sharply from whites' reactions.

Television   Blacks emerge as heavy television viewers, as measured by the number of television sets in black communities.[49] Preferred shows are adventure, medical, and legal dramas. Shows that stress essentially white problems—situation comedies and the like—are less popular.[50] News programs and sportscasts are viewed much more heavily in black homes than in white. The effectiveness of television in black markets is subject

to some question for, although blacks watch television frequently, there is evidence that commercials do not draw positive responses. This may be due to a lack of black-oriented messages, disapproval of integrated models, feelings that the commercials that do feature blacks do so unrealistically, or a combination of these factors.

Radio   Research indicates that radio may be the best overall medium for reaching black segments. While only 51 percent of the white families surveyed in one media study listened to radio, 71 percent of the black families questioned listened frequently. Black-oriented stations were especially popular, with 57 percent of black listeners preferring this programming to general radio.[51] Black programming also appears to carry a high level of credibility within the black community, possibly because other sources of communication may be considered white-slanted.

Newspapers   On an average weekday, 61 percent of black households are reported to read a newspaper, contrasted with 80 percent of white households. Young blacks read more than older blacks; and readership is significantly higher outside the low-income South. Although fewer blacks than whites read newspapers, more black readers than white "look forward" to reading advertisements.[52] The emerging pattern is that black readership of daily papers is largely related to age and income.

Magazines   With a circulation of approximately 1.5 million, *Ebony* is the most popular magazine in the black community. But general interest periodicals such as *The Reader's Digest* and special interest magazines like *Sports Illustrated* are also heavily read.[53] Due partially to the high cost of magazine space, most advertisers have been slow to experiment with black-oriented magazine advertising.

Much of the demographic and life-style research necessary to evaluate media for black market segments has yet to be conducted, but the amount of advertising aimed at blacks is growing in both print and broadcast media.

Regional Subcultures

Those who have ventured to parts of the country other than their own have seen that people display different patterns of behavior according to where they live.

Many Californians and New Yorkers like to view themselves as innovators, and much of what other Americans receive by way of fashion, entertainment, news, and advertising reflects that attitude. California has been described as a weathervane for the nation at large—what happens "on the Coast" politically, socially, and in popular culture, some say, will eventually sweep over the rest of the United States. This has seemed to hold true over the past several years for conservative politics, campus unrest, condominium apartments, surfboards, and Walt Disney entertainment centers. New York remains the communications center for television, publishing, and the advertising industry, thus determining to some degree the products that people everywhere will see and want to consume. In general, when cultural change occurs, it is likely to be noticed first in New York and California. Thus, these are regions unto themselves, each with its unique subcultural patterns.

Between the two coasts, each region has its own ethos and personality. The West and the Southwest retain an aura of the American frontier, rugged and individualistic. The Middle West is still considered America's heartland, and has come to be characterized by phrases such as "Middle America." Here people are reputed to be more conservative in religion, politics, social integration, and even new-product innovation relative to other parts of the country. New Englanders regard themselves as shrewd consumers; are protective of their region's natural beauty; and resent (to varying degrees) intrusions by tourists, skiers, "summer people," and real estate developers. The South, traditionally afflicted by high rates of poverty and other difficulties, has sought and achieved a change of image in recent years, becoming more urbanized and reflective of mass communications. Reed has compared the enduring regional subculture of the South with that of the North, concluding that Southern attitudes are more supportive of the private use of violence than Northern, that attachment to a local community is more common in the South, that religious practices there are more strongly denominational, and that family and church are more influential in the South than schools and the mass media.[54]

While some behavioral characteristics of people in different regions may seem stereotypical, real differences apparently exist in consumption patterns. In beverage preferences alone, Tucker notes that people on the West Coast drink more gin and vodka, while the East consumes more scotch and the South downs more bourbon. In New England, birch beer and cream soda are popular soft drinks, yet these beverages are virtually unheard of in the South. And even coffee drinkers vary according to region—Maxwell House is one manufacturer who brews a stronger, darker blend for the West than for the East.[55]

Some of the differences attributed to regional subcultures tend to disappear as people achieve greater mobility and exposure to mass communication. Other profound differences, such as the ways in which people earn their living and regard institutions like religion and the family, persist more stubbornly.

The Subculture of the Aging

While marketers scramble to anticipate new developments in the youth market, they have largely overlooked a segment with even greater spending power. This is the over–65 age group, now about 10 percent of the population and increasing faster than the under–65 group. Yet this subculture has suffered significant alienation from the rest of society. One-fourth of them live below the poverty level; two-thirds of those who live alone or with nonrelatives are poor.[56] And the youth orientation of our culture has made many feel useless, unwanted, and a burden to others. Among the special problems that confront the aging are inadequate pensions and social security, deteriorating health, emotional difficulties, lack of employment, rehabilitation of the disabled, and unique considerations affecting older members of disadvantaged groups—blacks, American Indians, and others.

The Elderly: An Emerging Market

But not all those over 65 are suffering from deprivation. Changing patterns of aging in the United States have altered the life styles of many retirees, thereby creating new markets for a variety of products and services. These changes have been brought about by greater affluence, improved living conditions, and emerging new attitudes toward old age.

Greater Affluence At age 65, today's retiree may receive income from several sources: a pension, Social Security, interest and/or dividends, and possibly wages (one-quarter of all the men over 65 are now working full or part time). If a spouse is working or has retired, there is additional income. Finally, benefits such as national health insurance and tax advantages help to cover the reduced expenses of the retired couple. There is also the possibility that they own their own home and car. While not all elderly people by any means are enjoying these benefits, a significant proportion do. And rising pension and Social Security payments will help to achieve realistic incomes for the aged.[57]

Improved Living Conditions Several decades ago, the elderly were apt to live with their children, or at least nearby. Now they are more likely to live away from their families. For many of the aging, this has meant clinging to their own homes, which may be badly in need of repair; entering nursing homes; or moving into trailers or other forms of low-cost housing. But a growing number of persons past retirement age have settled into planned communities designed for leisure living in comfortable climates. The state of

Florida has become a notable retirement haven, with half the permanent residents of Miami Beach over 65. Other cities in Florida are following that trend.[58] Most of the newer "Senior Citizen" communities offer good housing, security, and recreation.

Changing Attitudes Toward Aging   There is a cultural tendency in the United States to regard the aging as sedentary, melancholy, and resigned to uselessness. But a newer breed of retirees (exemplified by a "militant" group known as the Gray Panthers) are rejecting such a dismal view of growing old. Today's elderly are better educated, have higher incomes, and have learned to be shrewder consumers than their counterparts of previous generations. Many want to continue working in some fashion. Most wish to enjoy some of the hedonistic pursuits they may have missed out on when they were younger, especially travel.

The Aging as Forgotten Consumers

As well as buying most of the necessities younger people do, the elderly form a distinct market for special housing, health products, travel and leisure services, tailored insurance protection, investments, and diet foods. Marketers who have recognized the unmet needs of older people reap considerable successes. One company, specializing in services for the elderly, offers health, life, and auto insurance geared toward people over 55; worldwide travel operations with tours designed for a more leisurely pace; and a temporary employment service.[59]

In magazine and newspaper ads and television commercials for most products, the aging are conspicuous by their absence. A few exceptions include advertising for dental adhesives or laxatives, but most mass communications ignore the over–65 market in favor of youthful appeals.

Problems in Communication With the Elderly
One major reason that old people are seldom addressed directly in advertising is that they resent being depicted as old. A baby-food manufacturer, recognizing that elderly individuals were eating the product because of dental problems, introduced a new line of *senior* foods. This nearly proved disastrous because older people preferred to claim that they were buying the baby food for their grandchildren.[60] Due to the negative attitudes about aging still common in American culture, people dislike to admit to themselves or others that they are no longer young. Thus the over–65 market does not like being segmented as such. The most successful communications are those that show a mixture of age groups using the product.

Over-65 Consumption Patterns   Few research projects have been conducted in this area, but certain buying patterns have been observed among the elderly. Older people have been shown to be careful consumers, with established preferences for certain brands and a greater tendency toward comparison shopping. There is an inclination to buy nationally-known, "name" brands; to prefer large chain stores to specialty shops (presumably for greater values); and, particularly, to shy away from shops they feel cater exclusively to older customers.[61] In using buying information, older people seem to rely on personal judgment while younger people depend more on informed sources of knowledge about products.[62] This pattern is reportedly true with new products as well.[63] Older families have been found to deliberate less before making purchases, probably as a result of accumulated buying experience.[64]

Future Marketing Prospects

As more individuals retire before age 65, the market comprised of people with high discretionary incomes will continue to expand. The next few years will no doubt mark the transition to a prevailing retirement age of 55, creating a sizable group not yet old but ready to enjoy the fruits of leisure. This will particularly affect the travel, clothing, and entertainment industries, as well as many others. As advertising executive Richard Seclow points out:[65]

Too many marketers still consider retirees as part of a Geritol Market, consisting mainly of people in front porch rockers who are financially dependent on their families and society. Realistically, the median income of the retirement market continues to rise as younger people who are receiving more extensive benefits make up an increasing proportion of the total group.

And the time to anticipate new life styles through appropriate research is at hand.

The Singles Subculture

One fast-growing segment of American society is the "singles" subculture—well established in urban areas and increasingly found in suburban and small towns as well. The factors behind this swelling population include a new tendency to postpone marriage, higher divorce rates, and a trend away from quick remarriage after divorce. These patterns are closely related to emerging cultural values that place less emphasis on youthful marriage and child-rearing and encourage the emancipation of women, personal gratification, and the pursuit of pleasure for its own sake, particularly with regard to sexual mores. As consumers, single people defy generalization. They remain subject to the same segmentation by age, sex, income, social class, and regional location that must be applied to any subculture.

The "Affluent" Singles Market

Some singles are more visible than others, and have attracted considerable attention from the mass media since the 1960s. These are the urban men and women, usually in their twenties or thirties, who enjoy high-income life styles and for various reasons choose to remain unmarried for an indeterminate period of time. Some prefer to concentrate on career rather than family responsibilities. Others may be carefully scouting for a more permanent involvement with one partner. Still others simply enjoy short-term multiple relationships. As a well-publicized subculture, these singles are responsible for a growing industry offering an array of specialized products and services. Some examples are singles nightclubs, travel accommodations, dating services, and even country clubs where married couples are not accepted for membership. One successful singles club offers its members such luxury diversions as weekend excursions to Majorca, parties aboard rented commercial jets, and premium seats at popular shows and sporting events.[66]

Housing for Singles

Housing patterns in large cities have reflected this growth in the affluent singles population. Los Angeles pioneered the first singles-only apartment complex, and new high-rise apartment construction in New York City has turned away from the two-bedroom "family" emphasis to concentration on studio apartments designed for single occupancy. Professional roommate-finding services also abound in urban areas. Now there are indications that single people have become prospects for suburban homes. One reason is that banks are adopting more favorable loan practices toward singles, especially women. Another is the tendency to regard single status as a more permanent condition than it once was, and unmarried people's desire to profit from the investment and tax advantages of home ownership.

In addition to supporting the singles services industry, which has enhanced the attractiveness of unmarried life through innovative services, singles are heavier-than-average consumers of other products and services. Some examples include clothing, products that promise sex appeal, convenience foods, sports equipment, and restaurants.

The Subculture of Poverty

On the bleaker side, there is a distinct subculture in the United States characterized by deprivation—the households where total annual income is less than $5,000. In the United States, about one out of every five families can be included in this category.[67] The subculture of poverty tends to overlap considerably with Black America, the aging, and ethnic subcultures such as Chicano and Puerto Rican. It also includes American Indians, migrant farm workers, and other groups generally described as disadvantaged. Almost all of the poor live in rural areas or in the large cities, and have established a pattern of migration from dying farms to urban ghettos. Regionally, the South maintains the highest proportion of poor people in the nation.[68]

Lewis characterizes this subculture by: a lack of participation in the institutions of the larger society; a family structure marked by the absence of childhood as a prolonged, protected state; a strong predisposition to authoritarianism; a lack of privacy; and—above all—an individual feeling of inferiority and helplessness.[69] Among the factors keeping this subculture alive are limited educational opportunities coupled with low motivation to learn, discrimination, and a determination on the part of most Americans to keep the poor at a physical distance.[70]

Consumption Patterns of the Poor

Not surprisingly, this deprived subculture has evolved patterns of consumption markedly different from those of more comfortably situated Americans.

Attitudes toward Products and Services As consumers, people living below the poverty level spend larger shares of their incomes on the necessities—food, shelter, and medical care—than people with higher incomes. They spend less on transportation and clothing relative to their incomes, and about the same proportionately on recreation, personal care, and household equipment.[71] A surprisingly large percentage of their incomes is spent on "durables," particularly large appliances. Caplovitz found in a study of poor families in New York that 93 percent owned television sets, 63 percent owned phonographs, and 41 percent owned automatic washers.[72] Other appliances that accounted for large outlays were radios and smaller kitchen equipment. But these figures seem understandable when we consider the desire of poor people to emulate the middle-income life styles seen in the media, the persuasive selling by neighborhood merchants and the "easy" credit they offer, and the disproportionate number of young families among the poor who are making their first appliance purchases.

While the poor almost always buy these appliances new, they tend to buy used cars rather than new models. In furnishing their homes, they are inclined to purchase "sets" of furniture rather than individual pieces, both as a taste preference and as a reflection of what their area merchants choose to offer them.[73] When shopping for food, low-income families appear to place more emphasis on fairly low-cost, fresh staple items than on prepackaged, more expensive convenience products.[74] In Caplovitz's study, 81 percent of the poor families reported using credit and installment buying.[75] And the ratio of debt to annual income is approximately *twice* as high among poor families as in higher-income households.

Shopping Behavior Impoverished urban families are reported to pay more in real cost for their goods and services than people who live outside ghetto areas.[76] This is not necessarily due to discrimination, but to the economics of inner-city marketing. They have fewer outlets to buy from, higher credit costs from unscrupulous merchants, and take home merchandise of generally inferior quality to what they would find elsewhere.[77] Thus, the fact that prices themselves may actually be lower in ghetto areas does not mean that poor people are getting any bargains. Compounding the problem of fewer supermarkets and other shopping facilities to choose from is the fact that poor consumers are seldom shrewd customers. There is a tendency to rely on merchants or relatives for purchase information, to fail to deliberate and compare prices before making purchases, to use stores that are close by,[78] and to disregard free or reduced-rate programs provided for them.[79]

Future Prospects

It is doubtful that the problems of the subculture of poverty will be alleviated without fundamental changes in our attitudes toward the poor. Traditionally, our society's posture has been one of rewarding people in direct proportion to their productivity. But a growing awareness that many of the poor are old, sick, or otherwise handicapped has led to greater acceptance of principles such as a guaranteed annual income for those who cannot work and tax incentives for those who can.

In the meantime, marketers might anticipate the needs of the poor and meet them more effectively by understanding the dynamics of poverty, seeking solutions to such problems as inner-city distribution of goods and services, and supporting ghetto enterprises that enable the poor to serve themselves and their communities.

To emphasize a recurrent theme in subcultural consumer research, subculture information alone is seldom all that is needed to segment markets. Members of any given subculture vary markedly in their behavior, and never act in lockstep conformity. Relevant variables of age, sex, income, and social class must be applied to obtain meaningful portraits of people.

By the same token, subcultures overlap with one another. We might say that a black retiree living below the poverty level in a Southern state belongs to no less than four different subcultures.

Finally, subcultural patterns are constantly changing. Regional subcultures seem to be decomposing over time, while fairly recent developments such as the singles phenomenon create new subcultures. The counterculture so evident during the 1960s appears to have scattered almost into oblivion, but undoubtedly some new youth subculture will emerge in its place.

When a subcultural segment is under scrutiny for its receptivity to some product or service, the same principles apply as in marketing to a large culture. These are (1) an analysis of the product needs exhibited by the subculture in question; (2) a determination of how well an existing product may meet those needs, how it could be adapted to do so, or how a new product might be developed to accomplish the objective; (3) deciding how best to communicate information about the product in line with subcultural values and norms; and (4) establishing an optimal means of distribution for the product consistent with subcultural realities.

Summary

To distinguish small cultural segments from the dominant culture, anthropologists refer to *subcultures*. A subculture may be described as any cultural patterning that preserves important features of the dominant culture but provides values and life styles of its own. Subcultures are studied by means of the cross-cultural research methods discussed in chapter 4. Six subcultures found in the United States today are *religious and ethnic, Black America, regional, the aging, singles,* and *the subculture of poverty*. Each offers a basis for segmentation by marketers when other variables such as age, sex, social class, income, and other factors are taken into consideration. Positioning a product or service for a subcultural segment involves analyzing what its members' real needs are, how a product may best meet those needs, what the most effective communication about the product may be, and how the product should be distributed.

NOTES

1. David O. Arnold, "A Process Model of Subcultures," in *Sociology of Subcultures*, ed. D. O. Arnold (Glendessary Press, 1970).

2. Nathan Glazer, *Beyond the Melting Pot* (Cambridge: Harvard University Press, 1964).

3. Milton M. Gordon, *Assimilation in American Life* (New York: Oxford University Press, 1964).

4. Milton M. Gordon, "The Subsociety and the Subculture" in Arnold, *Sociology of Subcultures*.

5. Robert L. Brown, "Social Distance Perception as a Function of Mexican-American and Other Ethnic Identity," *Sociology and Social Research*, Vol. 57, No. 3 (April 1973), pp. 273–87.

6. John H. Burma, ed., *Mexican Americans in the United States: A Reader* (Cambridge, Mass.: Schenkman Publishing Co., 1970), pp. xvi–xvii.

7. Perry Alan Zirkel, "A Sociological Survey of Puerto Rican Parents in Connecticut," *American Journal of Orthopsychiatry*, Vol. 43, No. 2 (January 1970), pp. 190–208.

8. "Fever and Froth," *Time*, 26 July 1976.

9. Milton Alexander, "The Significance of Ethnic Groups in Marketing New Type Packaged Foods in Greater New York," *Proceedings of the American Marketing Association*, ed. Lynn H. Stockman, 1959.

10. Douglas J. Dalrymple, Thomas S. Robertson, and Michael J. Yoshino, "Consumption Behavior across Ethnic Categories," *California Management Review* (Fall 1971), pp. 65–73.

11. Raymond A. Bauer and Scott M. Cunningham, "The Negro Market," *Journal of Advertising Research*, Vol. 10 (April 1970).

12. Kelvin A. Wall, "Positioning Your Product in the Black Market," *Advertising Age*, 18 June 1973.

13. Thomas E. Barry and Michael G. Harvey, "Marketing to Heterogeneous Black Consumers," *California Management Review* (Winter 1974).

14. John P. Maggard, "Negro Market—Fact or Fiction," *California Management Review*, Vol. 14, No. 1 (Fall 1971), p. 71.

15. Helen Axel, *A Guide to Consumer Markets*, (New York: The Conference Board, 1975), p. 142.

16. Raymond O. Oladipudo, *How Distinct Is the Negro Market?* (New York: Ogilvy and Mather, Inc., 1970).

17. Reynolds Farley and Albert I. Hermalin, "Family Stability: A Comparison of Trends between Blacks and Whites" *American Sociological Review*, Vol. 36, No. 1 (February 1971), pp. 1–17.

18. "Blacks' Progress: A Story of Opportunities Grasped," *US News and World Report*, 1 June 1970.

19. Thomas F. Pettigrew, "Racial Segregation and Negro Education," in *Toward A National Urban Policy*, ed. Daniel P. Moyaihan (New York: Basic Books, 1970).

20. Marcus Alexis, "Some Negro-White Differences in Consumption," *American Journal of Economics and Sociology*, Vol. 21 (January 1962).

21. Thomas S. Robertson, Douglas J. Dalrymple, and Michael J. Yoshino, "Cultural Compatibility in New Product Adoption," in *Marketing Involvement in Society and the Economy*, ed. Philip R. McDonald (Chicago: American Marketing Association, Fall 1969).

22. Raymond H. Bauer, Scott M. Cunningham, and Lawrence H. Wortzel, "The Marketing Dilemma of Negroes", *Journal of Marketing*, Vol. 29 (July 1965), p. 72.

23. Robertson et al., "Cultural Compatibility," p. 72.

24. Donald E. Sexton, Jr., "Black Buyer Behavior," *Journal of Marketing*, Volume 36, October 1972, p. 38.

25. Oladipudo, *The Negro Market*, pp. 30–34.

26. Wall, "Positioning Your Product", p. 75.

27. S. Roxanne Hiltz, "Black and White in the Consumer Financial System," *American Journal of Sociology*, Vol. 76, No. 6 (May 1971), pp. 987–99, and Alexis, "Negro-White Differences."

28. Frank G. Davis, *Differential Factors in the Negro Market*, (Chicago: National Association of Market Developers, 1959).

29. W. L. Evans, "Ghetto Marketing—What Now?" *Marketing and the New Science of Planning*, ed. Robert L. King (Chicago: American Marketing Association, Fall 1968), p. 528.

30. Sexton, "Black Buyer Behavior," p. 39.

31. Lawrence P. Feldman and Alvin D. Star, "Racial Factors in Shopping Behavior," in *A New Measure of Responsibility for Marketing*, ed. Keith Cox and Ben M. Enis (Chicago: American

Marketing Association, June 1968).

32. Robert L. King and Earl R. DeManche, "Comparative Acceptance of Selected Private-Branded Food Products by Low-Income Negro and White Families," in McDonald, *Marketing Involvement*, p. 22.

33. Herbert E. Krugman, "White and Negro Responses to Package Designs," *Journal of Marketing Research*, Vol. 3 (May 1966).

34. Fred C. Akers, "Negro and White Automobile Buying Behavior: New Evidence," *Journal of Marketing Research*, Vol. 5 (August 1968), pp. 283–90.

35. Wall, "Positioning Your Product," p. 74.

36. Burgoyne Index, Inc., *Twelfth Annual Study of Supermarket Shoppers*, (Cincinnati, 1965).

37. Robert F. Dietrich, "Know Your Black Shopper," *Progressive Grocer* (June 1975), p. 44.

38. Charles S. Goodman, "Do the Poor Pay More?" *Journal of Marketing*, Vol. 32 (January 1968), pp. 18–24.

39. Feldman and Star, "Racial Factors," p. 222.

40. B. Stuart Tolley and John J. Goett, "Reactions to Blacks in Newspapers," *Journal of Advertising Research*, Vol. 11 (April 1971), pp. 11–17.

41. John V. Petrof, "Reaching the Negro Market: A Segregated vs. a General Newspaper," *Journal of Advertising Research*, Vol. 8 (April 1968), pp. 40–43.

42. Arnold M. Barban, "The Dilemma of Integrated Advertising," *Journal of Business*, Vol. 42 (October 1969), pp. 477–96.

43. Maggard, "Negro Market," p. 77.

44. John W. Gould, Normal B. Sigband, and Cyril E. Zoerner, Jr., "Black Consumer Reactions to Integrated Advertising: An Explanatory Study," *Journal of Marketing*, Vol. 34 (July 1970), pp. 20–26.

45. Maggard, "Negro Market," p. 76.

46. "Black Agencies: Their Quiet Demise," *Advertising News of New York*, 18 June 1976.

47. Wall, "Positioning Your Product," p. 74.

48. Wall, "Positioning Your Product," p. 76.

49. Maggard, "Negro Market," pp. 77–80.

50. James W. Carey, "Variations in Negro-White Television Preferences," *Journal of Broadcasting*, Vol. 10, No. 3 (Summer 1966), pp. 199–212.

51. Maggard, "Negro Market," pp. 77–78.

52. Lee Templeton, "Approaching the Black Market," Templeton Stores, June 1970.

53. Maggard, "Negro Markets," p. 78.

54. John Shelton Reed, *The Enduring South: Subcultural Persistence in Mass Society* (Lexington, Mass.: D. C. Heath and Co., 1972).

55. William T. Tucker, *The Social Context of Economic Behavior* (New York: Holt, Rinehart and Winston, 1964).

56. "The Power of the Aging in the Marketplace," *Business Week*, 20 November 1971.

57. "The Over–65 Set: A Bonanza for Business?" *Nation's Business*, Vol. 59, No. 11 (November 1971), pp. 34–6.

58. Business Week, "Power of Aging," p. 57.

59. Nation's Business, "Bonanza," op cit. p. 35.

60. Business Week, "Power of Aging," p. 55.

61. Business Week, "Power of Aging," p. 56.

62. Sidney Feldman and Merlin C. Spencer in *Marketing and Economic Development*, ed. Peter D. Bennet (Chicago: *Proceedings of the Fall Conference of the American Marketing Association*, 1965).

63. Leon G. Schiffman, "Sources of Information for the Elderly," *Journal of Advertising Research* (October 1971).

64. George Katona and Eva Mueller in *Consumer Behavior*, ed. Lincoln H. Clark (New York: New York University Press, 1955).

65. Richard Seclow, "Coming Boom in Early Retirement Offers Big Market for Travel, Apparel, Housing," *Advertising Age*, 5 May 1972.

66. *New York Times*, July 10, 1976, p. 32.

67. U.S. Bureau of the Census, *Statistical Abstract of the United States*, 1971 (Washington, D.C.: Government Printing Office, 1971), p. 316.

68. U.S. Census Bureau, *Statistical Abstract*, p. 71.

69. Oscar Lewis, *La Vida*, (New York: Random House, 1966).

70. Henry O. Pruden, F. Kelly Shuptrine, and Douglas S. Longman, "A Measure of Alienation from the Marketplace," *Journal of the Academy of Marketing Science*, Vol. 2, No. 4 (Winter 1974).

71. Louise G. Richards, "Consumer Practices of the Poor," in *Low Income Life Styles*, ed. Lola M. Irelan; U.S. Department of Health, Education and Welfare Administration: Division of Research (Washington, D.C.: Government Printing Office, 1969).

72. David Caplovitz, *The Poor Pay More* (New York: Free Press, 1963).

73. Caplovitz, *The Poor Pay More*.

74. Richards, "Consumer Practices," p. 74.

75. Caplovitz, *The Poor Pay More*, p. 75.

76. U.S. Bureau of Labor Statistics, *A Study of Prices in Food Stores Located in Low- and Higher-Income Areas of Six Large Cities*, (Washington, D.C.: U.S. Government Printing Office, 1966).

77. Leonard L. Berry and Paul J. Solomon, "Generalizing about Low-Income Food Shoppers: A Word of Caution," *Journal of Retailing*, Vol. 47, No. 2 (Summer 1971).

78. Arieh Goldman, "Do Lower Income Shoppers Have a More Restricted Shopping Scope?" *Journal of Marketing*, Vol. 40, No. 1 (1976).

79. Richards, "Consumer Practices," p. 74.

MARKETING APPLICATIONS

Conclusion 1   *With changing immigration patterns, ethnic subcultures in the United States arise, exhibit characteristic modes of consumption, and eventually become assimilated to some degree into the mainstream culture.*

Application   Marketers should recognize new subcultural developments early, to meet the needs of ethnic consumers which reflect different cultural biases and behavior. This means conducting consumer research in subcultural markets while they are still becoming established. This approach has proven successful for marketers such as *Goya* in gaining the total Puerto Rican market in New York City by offering ethnic food products and directing communications solely through Spanish-language print media, radio and television stations.

Conclusion 2   *The elderly represent a burgeoning subculture neglected by most marketers, reflecting a cultural bias against the aged in the United States.*

Application   There is a great opportunity for marketers to meet the changing needs of the elderly by careful research into their needs, interests, and buying patterns. Such research must involve testing different communications approaches—for example, advertisements and product packaging—to aim products specifically to this subculture and extend existing product appeals to include elderly consumers.

Conclusion 3   *In the United States, consumers who form the subculture of poverty are penalized by higher prices, fewer product choices, and greater exploitation by marketers than middle-class consumers who buy the same products.*

Application   One of the highest priorities in macromarketing over the next decade will be to develop greater responsiveness to poor consumers. At the micromarketing level, individual marketers must open new channels of communication with the poor through "omsbudsmen"-type services, develop distribution strategies which will lower prices in poor neighborhoods, and impose sanctions against retailers who take advantage of the poor through fraudulent credit practices and other unethical marketing policies.

ASSIGNMENTS

Research Assignment

Background   As a Market Research Analyst for Crimmins, a research organization specializing in profiling magazine readers, you are assigned to a project for *One+One,* a new "singles" magazine directed toward unmarried men and women between 21 and 35. To attract advertisers for the new publication, *One+One's* publishers want to compile some demographic and product-use information about the singles market—how old they are, what they do for a living, how much money they make, where they are concentrated geographically, how well educated they are, and what products and services they are most inclined to use.

Methodology   Because few "scientific" studies of the singles market exist, it will be necessary to check the latest sociological and marketing journals for information. The best sources for data in this case, however, remain the mass media. From readings (and perhaps a trip to some local singles haunts) draw a profile based on the demographic and product-use data you have uncovered.

Extrapolation   From your profile, make some suggestions to the publishers of *One+One* about the kinds of advertisers they will be most likely to attract with your data. What variables have you found in the singles subculture with respect to age, income, and occupation? Which "singles" would be most likely to pay $1 for a magazine that discusses, from a relatively sophisticated point of view, such topics as travel, meeting people, housing, politics, money management, books and films for the unmarried?

Creative Assignment

As an advertising copywriter with the McAnany, Lippman and Bien Agency, you are assigned a special project for a highly prized account—Natural Food Products, Inc. The Natural line features a breakfast cereal known as Nature's Wheat, which has been advertised successfully to a market of young consumers, 18 to 35, and has achieved a significant share of the breakfast cereal market.

Now the management of Natural Foods wants to test its winning cereal brand's appeal to the burgeoning market of consumers over 65. Your assignment is to develop a campaign for the natural cereal specifically directed to older consumers.

The challenges that marketers have encountered in communicating with the elderly have been noted in the preceding chapter, and are discussed in detail in two other sources:

• "The Power of the Aging in the Marketplace," *Business Week,* 20 November 1971.

• Leon G. Schiffman, "Sources of Information for the Elderly," *Journal of Advertising Research,* October 1971.

But like all good copywriters, you are not content to rely on written research alone. You are also in the habit of confronting real people in the target group you wish to reach. Thus, you should ideally speak to two or three older consumers about their feelings toward natural cereal (as well as their personal reactions toward any ads you do) in developing your campaign.

Your ads may focus on any of several appeals—health, vitality, association with younger consumers, or a desire to get back to a natural rather than an artificial life style.

With these considerations in mind, prepare three space ads that will meet the objective of selling Nature's Wheat to older consumers.

Managerial Assignment

The Fisher Pant Company of Hartford, Connecticut, is a youth-oriented manufacturer whose most profitable line is Apache Jeans—high-fashion trousers, shirts, and accessories. The Apache line is presently sold at retail through clothing and department stores as well as Fisher's own franchise outlets, known as Apache Trading Stores.

Fisher wants to expand in large urban markets, concentrating specifically on black segments noted for fashion innovation. Fisher also has an eye toward social responsibility as it approaches the study of black markets, and is eager to do some good in the black community with its new marketing direction beyond increasing its own share of market.

As one of several Product Managers for the Apache line, you are asked for your own recommendations about expanding into this market. Specifically, your views are sought on the following questions:

1. What kind of consumer research should be conducted in the black community?

2. Should Apache franchises in these markets be black-owned?

3. What other types of stores should be considered for these markets?

Your recommendations should be based on information in chapter 5 as well as on a review of some literature in this chapter's notes and bibliography.

SELECTED READINGS

Barry, Thomas E. and Michael G. Harvey. "Marketing to Heterogeneous Black Consumers." *California Management Review,* Winter 1974, pp. 50–57.

Block, Joyanne E. "The Aged Consumer and the Market Place: A Critical Review." *Marquette Business Review,* Summer 1974, pp. 73–81.

Magrabi, Francis M., et al. "An Index of the Economic Welfare of Rural Families." *Consumer Research,* Vol. 2, No. 3 (December 1975), pp. 178–87.

Mason, Joseph B. and Brooks E. Smith. "An Exploratory Note on the Shopping Behavior of the Low Income Senior Citizen." *The Journal of Consumer Affairs,* Winter 1974, pp. 204–10.

Walker, C. K. "The Single Pay More." *The Journal of Consumer Affairs,* Winter 1974, pp. 211–16.

OBJECTIVES

SIX

Social Organization and Reference Groups

Social organization *means, basically, our patterns of interaction with other people. So the influences that a person's* reference groups—*family, friends, coworkers, and others*—*bring to bear on consumer behavior are one important focus of this chapter.*

Everyone knows from personal experience how various forms of pressure from others affect what is acceptable to buy at some given time. This holds especially true for visible items like clothing, which, if not deemed acceptable by a certain peer group, may cause personal embarrassment.

Not all social group influences on consumer behavior are so obvious—some influences are subtle, even quite insidious. For example, this chapter examines such topics as:

• *Why early socialization affects lifetime consumer preferences.*

• *How a person's "self-concept" affects buying behavior.*

• *Why consumers are often unaware of conformity pressure (even when they're succumbing to it).*

• *The emerging woman-as-consumer versus the stereotyped woman-as-consumer.*

• *Social trends that will affect consumption by the year 2000 and how business should interpret them.*

This discussion introduces two specific (and particularly influential) kinds of reference groups, examined more closely in chapters 7 & 8: Social Class and the Family.

Society and the Consumer

We have already come to recognize *culture* as patterns of behavior practiced and passed down by the members of a given *society.* More specifically, these patterns are shaped by values and ideas that set the boundaries for social interaction. Because the American culture stresses values such as social mobility and material gain, we may reasonably expect that much of our social interaction will revolve around enhancing our own status needs and monetary well-being. As we interact with others while striving to maintain a desired level of achievement rewards, we tend to cultivate friendships that will further our needs for money and prestige. These are accepted patterns against the backdrop of traditional American values. Because a consumption ethic is very much a part of American culture, a considerable portion of our daily activities is devoted to producing goods and services for others, purchasing for ourselves, and deciding on the basis of numerous influences from people with whom we associate what we will wear, eat, or drive; how we will entertain ourselves; and how much of our time and money we will spend on various merchandise and diversions.

Researchers have identified several kinds of social organization and patterns of group interaction that influence the individual consumer's behavior.[1] These include socialization, reference groups, and social change.

Socialization

Members of a society learn their culture through *socialization,* defined as *"the process by which a person strives to acquire characteristic ways of behaving, the values, norms, and attitudes of the social unit of which he is a part."*[2] Beginning practically at birth, socialization trains individuals to play their assigned social roles correctly. A number of different institutions play parts in this process, including *the family, schools,* and *religious institutions.* Often their teachings complement each other, but sometimes different institutions can instill independent or conflicting values. Yet such conflict is necessary in a highly diversified society to provide *options* for different life styles and, consequently, different consumption patterns.

The Family

This institution remains the most important to an individual's acquisition of culture. Within the family, there are three major goals of socialization: instilling *self-control, values,* and *role behavior.*[3]

Living in society demands a high degree of *self-control.* Demands for self-control come when the child is asked to put off an immediate pleasure for a future one, or to change some behavior to make it more socially acceptable.

To help the child develop self-discipline, *values* are usually taught at the same time.

For example, a small boy who resents being asked to share his toys with his sister is helped to acquire the self-control necessary for such an action when his parents teach him the value of "cooperation." They explain that his sister will then share her toys with him; they also make it clear that this cooperation is *helpful* to him and *approved* of by others.

The third important aspect of socialization by the family is the *learning of role behavior* through family interaction. Shortly after the child begins to develop a self-image by comparison and contrast with others in the family, he or she also learns that certain behavior is appropriate to this image, while different behavior may be called for in other family members.

Some roles a child learns are soon outgrown and forgotten. But other role behavior learned in the first years lasts considerably longer, and a prime example of this is sex differentiation. Differences that may be learned early in life (that is, men usually go to work, women usually stay home) will color an individual's concepts of male and female roles all through life, and it may be very difficult to change these views. This can cause difficulties in times of widespread or rapid social change, as is taking place right now with women's emancipation in business and social interaction.

The crux of socializing children is *motivating* them to learn culturally patterned behavior. In our society, material rewards are often used in socialization. Upper-income parents may show their approval by buying new toys for their children, rewarding a daughter's excellent grades by giving her a car for her sixteenth birthday, or other practices that build a social connection between personal approval and material objects. This lesson is well-learned by many middle-class children, who are likely to grow up demon-strating their own approval of others' behavior through consumption rather than emotional means.

Self-Concept   In the course of the interaction between child and parents, the child is learning to *define himself or herself as a person.* A personality or sense of self; an awareness and feeling about personal and social identity, is being developed in these early years. Later, others' attitudes and behavior toward the individual will contribute to this emerging sense of self.

Cooley has referred to this reflection in the eyes of others as the "looking-glass self." He suggests that it has three main components: (1) our perception of how our behavior appears to others; (2) our perceptions of their judgments of this behavior; and (3) our feelings about these judgments.[4] Through a large number of encounters with others, the *self* is formed as a social product. The need for social interaction to define the self continues throughout life. We learn new roles and gradually alter our self-image by using the feedback we receive from others.

Mead contends that there is a difference between the social demands and expectations made by those with whom you have a close personal relationship (and whose judgments are important to you), and the impersonal demands made by society. The first type he calls demands of *significant* others, such as those made by parents. The other type embraces the demands of *generalized* others. A child learns to respond first to the demands of significant others; response to generalized others comes at a later stage of development.[5]

Self-Concept Seen in Consumption Patterns
Individuals tend to express their self-concepts through their life styles, hence through the products and services they use. A woman

who views herself as attractive and desirable to men will exhibit different patterns of buying clothes and cosmetics than a woman who sees herself as rather frumpy and uninteresting. A businessman who sustains a self-concept of personal competence and confidence will use his consumption patterns to reinforce that concept. Similarly, some individuals may wish to project an "idealized" self-concept through consumption patterns. Through their choice of homes, automobiles, clothing, and other purchases, they hope to influence others' perceptions of them as contemporary, successful, interesting, or otherwise admirable. "Self-concept" has been studied in consumer research as a determinant of automobile choice,[6] packaged goods purchases,[7] retail store selection,[8] and preference for beer or wine.[9]

The Educational Institution

The first agency outside the family responsible for socializing individuals is the school. Here children learn the behavioral techniques and intellectual heritage of their culture so that each new generation will be able to benefit from their forebears' hard-won experience and discoveries. In a society as complex and technologically advanced as ours, the transmission of this aspect of culture is a most important and lengthy undertaking; thus education remains an integral part of our lives for up to fifteen or twenty years.

Education and Values   The influence of educational institutions in changing people's values has been noted by Louis Harris:[10]

In the regular surveys which the Harris organization has conducted, the impact of educa-

tion in forming people's attitudes has proven to be decisive. On the key issues of the day, those with the least education tend to hold a harder line on U.S. foreign policy, favoring a "fortress America" view, and are keenly suspicious of "too much involvement" abroad. The college educated, by contrast, are more in favor of limiting the use of American military power abroad, and are much more inclined to commit the nation's resources to international organizations and agreement with the communist world. On racial matters, educated whites are far more amenable on the subject of integration than the less well educated. Concerning young people and their tastes and styles, the college educated are far more open-minded than the less well educated.

There is some evidence to indicate, on the average, a much wider difference between the attitudes of those with only a grade school education and those who completed high school, than between high school and college graduates. Thus, a high school education may be somewhat more important than a college education in its effects on attitudes.

Religious Institutions

The existence and observance of *social norms* is the foundation of social organization and socialization. Religion usually supports these norms and values—indeed, often makes them sacred.

In the United States, there are about 250 different religions; yet the largest of these share certain features in common. One, according to Milton Yinger, is a general acceptance of the "American way of life," including tenets of work, material reward as desirable, and other characteristics of the

Education as Consumption: Is the Consumer Always Right?

All of us are, or have been, consumers of education. Families pay for their children's "free" education in the public school system through taxes, from kindergarten through college. Private universities must charge high tuition to supplement funds from alumni grants and other sources. Educational institutions, however, do not usually view students as "consumers" in the marketing sense, or themselves as sellers who must embrace a philosophy of "the customer is always right."

Some thorny questions have arisen in recent years from this dichotomy of values:

In Public Schools
- Should schools have the right to enforce dress codes?
- Should schoolchildren be bussed to achieve racial balance?
- Should parent pressure groups be able to block sex education from the classroom?
- Should teachers be forbidden to abuse students verbally?
- Should a controversial teacher (for instance, a self-proclaimed Marxist) be fired in response to parent demands?

In Universities
- How much freedom should students have to choose programs of study?
- Should any courses be required and, if so, which ones?
- Should professors' career advancement be subject to students' evaluations of their performance?
- Should colleges impose any restrictions on resident students' behavior?
- Should grading be replaced with another kind of progress evaluation?

familiar Protestant ethic.[12] Another is the sense that a religious doctrine should be appealing to people, as expressed by Berger:[13]

. . . putting it in a somewhat oversimplified way, the "product" of the religious institution must be "salable." It is one thing to threaten a captive audience of medieval peasants with hell-fire and damnation. It is quite another thing to market a doctrine of this sort in a population of suburban commuters and housewives. In other words, the "needs" of the consumer must now be taken into consideration.

The kind of religious training, or lack of it, that a person receives during socialization will affect consumer behavior in three ways. First, religious practice may dictate the use of some products and services, or frown upon consuming others. Chapter 4 noted that orthodox Jews buy kosher products and that

Mormons are not supposed to drink liquor or smoke cigarettes. Second, some religions are more traditional than others in forming attitudes about what is good and what is immoral.[14] For example, the person who comes from a strict, conservative religious background may view using credit cards, buying expensive clothing, or driving a flashy car as symbols of a materialistic approach to life inconsistent with a strong spiritual upbringing. Third, there is some evidence that in the United States religious affiliation is related to both family income and educational attainment.

Religion and Income Gallup reports that 69 percent of Jews fall into a relatively high income category, closely followed by 59 percent of Episcopalians. Among the lower ranking denominations are Methodists (42 percent) and Baptists (26 percent).[15] One reason may be regional differences. Most Episcopalians and Jews live in the northeastern United States, where income levels are generally high. The Baptists are more numerous in the South and Midwest, where income levels are lower.

Religion and Education Studies indicate that there is a difference in the average educational level reached by members of different religious groups. A young person appears to have the best chance of going to college if his parents are Jewish or Episcopalian, or if they subscribe to no religion. In a study of school dropouts, it was found that Jewish students were least likely to drop out of school, followed by Protestants and then Catholics, which may be another explanation of the greater financial success of Jews and Protestants.[16]

Thus the institutions of family, school, and religion serve to socialize an individual in American culture. An emerging institution which may become as important as the more traditional ones is the *mass media,* particularly television. The influence of television on consumer behavior is treated thoroughly in chapter 14.

In addition to their socialization by institutions, people learn social (and consumer) behavior from a variety of formal and informal groups.

Reference Groups: Primary and Secondary

"I don't care what other people think, I buy (wear, read, listen to) what *I* want" is a popular refrain that actually applies to very few people in our society. The groups a person associates with exert considerable influence on how their members will behave. And this influence becomes apparent when we analyze our reasons for buying the clothes we happen to have on at the moment, the books and magazines we read, and the music we listen to, to

cite just a few examples.

To the individual, the most important group is the one that helps to define his or her own beliefs, values, attitudes, and opinions. This is known as the *reference group,* which may be defined as *the group whose perspective an individual assumes in forming attitudes and overt behavior.*

According to Bourne, reference groups influence consumer behavior in two ways.

For one, they set *levels of aspiration* for the individual—offering cues as to what life style (and related purchasing patterns) one should strive to achieve. Second, they define the actual items considered acceptable for displaying this level of aspiration, the kind of housing, clothing, automobile, and so on that will be deemed appropriate for a person wishing to remain a member in good standing of the group.[17]

Two kinds of reference groups exist—primary and secondary. The term *primary group* denotes any group, even in adult life, that contains relationships somewhat like those within the family, such as *peer* groups and closely knit *work* groups.[10]

Characteristics of Primary Groups

The primary relationship has five basic characteristics: (1) It includes a *variety of roles and interests* for each individual in the relationship. In a primary relationship, a man and woman may be husband and wife. They may also be coworkers in the backyard garden—and partners in the decision making process of buying a new microwave oven. (2) It involves *the whole personality*. Within a work primary group, the members know each other as workers; but through meetings outside the office and conversation during office hours, they get to know each other as fathers, husbands, wives. They each know something of the way the others handle their finances, behave as consumers, enjoy their leisure time, and relate to their children. (3) It involves *free and extensive communication*. A basic assumption about those who have entered into a primary relationship is that they should communicate a great deal and with relative freedom. (4) It is a *personal and emotion-laden relationship*. Each mem-

ber accepts the uniqueness of the other and is concerned for that person's welfare. But in a primary group, there may well be members who dislike some of the others. The members who do not like each other maintain their primary relationship because they are getting some personal satisfaction from the group other than affection—respect, emotional support, status, or economic benefit. (5) It is *not an easily transferable relationship*, because it demands a special response to the unique attributes of another individual. When you are in a department store buying a television set and you don't like the way a salesperson behaves, you can simply take your business to another salesperson, that is, transfer the relationship to another person who plays the role of seller in that store. However, in the close primary group relationships, the feelings involved cannot quickly or easily be transferred to another individual.

Functions of Primary Groups

One of the chief values of a primary relationship is that it gives each individual a chance to *develop a larger part of his or her total personality* than other relationships do. Each member is able to form a deeper self-image, which transcends the demands of whatever role or roles that member is currently playing. Although the self-image formed by any one primary relationship (particularly in the family) may change under the influence of later evaluations or new attachments, elements of that self-image may persist far beyond the life of the relationship.

Primary relationships also serve as *teachers* and *interpreters* of societal values and norms. The primary relationship and the primary group are the main channels through which the individual learns the major beliefs and expectations of society, and the patterns of behavior necessary for successful adaptation to that society. Since the primary relationship implies an acceptance of the whole individual, it is a source of security during conflicts with other individuals or groups and even with society in general.

Secondary Groups

In contrast to the personal, primary group we interact with many, less emotional, sec-ondary groups. The secondary relationship is instrumental in determining behavior, but by its very nature requires less personal involvement than the primary group.

Large organizations, religious organizations, and trade unions qualify as secondary groups, since they are most often *formal* in structure and function. Unlike the fluid primary group, a secondary group expects its members to carry out specialized, standardized tasks. No matter what position an individual holds within an organization, his or her official job or function is usually spelled out in an easily discernible fashion.[19]

Reference Group Norms and Conformity

A "norm" has been defined as a rule of behavior for meeting societal expectations; all members of a group must adhere to the *normative system* established for that group. To enforce normative systems, groups tend to exert conformity pressures, direct or indirect, on their members. A teenage peer group may find one's choice of clothing unacceptable and subject the member to a good deal of kidding before he or she accepts group norms of dress. Or a serious-minded church group may bring considerable pressure to bear on a member who is earning a reputation as a heavy drinker.

While conformity pressure is common to everyone's personal experiences, its existence has also been identified empirically in two classical studies from social psychology. In one, Sherif asked small groups to identify the direction of "movement" of a light that appeared to move in a dark room (an "autokinetic" illusion); his findings showed that, due to conformity pressure, group members tended to share the same perceptual distortions.[20] In the second study, Asch asked small groups of subjects to compare the lengths of various lines and influenced their judgments by having experimental confederates call out wrong answers. Even when group answers were obviously erroneous, individual subjects would defer to the group judgments by calling out wrong answers themselves.[21]

Degree of Conformity

The extent to which individuals will conform to group norms depends largely on the nature and characteristics of the group situation.

Cohesiveness and Attractiveness   The more stable and cohesive the group, Festinger points out, the more tendency it will have to exert conformity pressure on its members. Similarly, the more attractive an individual believes group membership to be, the more likely he or she will be to conform to that group's norms.[22]

Group Consensus Asch notes that in his own research into inducing group members to give incorrect responses, the extent of conformity by individuals increased according to the number of group members agreeing on the wrong answer.[23]

Stimulus Ambiguity In Crutchfield's experiments measuring conformity pressure, individuals were more likely to conform as the stimuli became more ambiguous and called for greater "interpretation."[24]

Profit of Interaction Homans explains group interactions in terms of an "Equation of Human Exchange."[25] According to this equation, individuals relate to each other for certain *rewards* such as companionship, sympathy, and other positive reinforcements, but run the risks of incurring *costs* like associating with someone who will not maximize rewards. The value of an interaction (*profit*) is determined by subtracting the cost of an exchange from the reward. And the extent to which an individual will succumb to conformity pressure is directly related to the profit he or she perceives in the process of conforming.

Conformity Pressure in Consumer Behavior

The phenomenon of group conformity pressure upon individuals was introduced to consumer behavior research by Lewin.[26]

Attempting to change consumers' attitudes toward using "less desirable" kinds of meat during the World War II rationing years, he found that group discussions were more influential in effecting attitude change than simple lectures. He attributed this to the fact that groups were exerting conformity influence on individuals in the more successful format.

In another early study, Whyte investigated purchase patterns for air conditioners (then an innovative product) in a suburban setting.[27] He concluded that adoption of the *product* itself was indeed influenced by group interaction, but that brand and retail store preference were not.

More recent research suggests a relationship between the *kind* of product and the degree to which individuals using it will be subject to conformity pressure. This relationship has been established for automobiles, cigarettes, and various packaged goods like beer and after-shave lotion.[28] As noted earlier by Bourne, the extent of group influence is directly related to the *conspicuousness* of the product—that is, when it is immediately noticeable and identifiable by others, its purchase is more likely to be influenced by group conformity pressure.[29]

Social Control and Deviance

Groups enforce the normative system of a culture by establishing rewards and punishments for behavior deemed acceptable or unacceptable. Deviance may be defined as the process of breaking down rules and norms of a society. A deviant can be a barefooted businessman, a marijuana smoker, or a shoplifter.

Consumer behavior enters the realm of

deviance most commonly when goods or services desired by a segment of the population are prohibited by a society's normative system. In the United States, gambling, prostitution, abortion, and marijuana have fallen into this category. (Abortion is the only one of these to be legalized.) When the demand for such items is not met through the conventional marketing channels, they usually become available through organized crime or deviant subcultures.[30]

Implications of Reference Group Influence

Evidence of group influence may be summarized as:

1. Bourne found that the amount of reference group influence is related to the *kind of product* under consideration. He concludes that to become a focal point for a friendship group, a product must be easily seen and identified by others. Products which elicit strong reference group influences include cars, cigarettes, beer, and drugs. Products which are less subject to influence include soap, radios and refrigerators.[31]

2. Stafford discovered that housewives developed preferences for brands of bread preferred by their peers, (although all brands were actually identical in content but wrapped differently).[32]

3. Venkatesan uncovered similar findings in business students' selection of business suits. Although the suits offered were identical, subjects yielded to conformity pressure in deciding that one was "better" than the others.[33]

4. Cook, in a study of attitudes toward the Volkswagen, revealed that groups whose members exhibited similar social charac-

teristics were more susceptible to attitude change than groups whose members were less homogenous.[34]

5. But Burnkrant and Cousineau, in an investigation of how group norms affect purchasing decisions for coffee, caution that people may frequently buy products that others in their group buy, not to establish a role relationship or seek reward from the group, but rather to acquire what they perceive as a good product.[35]

If reference group influence is felt to be important in marketing a specific product, the first objective should be to identify characteristics of that group. It will then be possible to design effective communications. Bourne offers this advice for advertising strategy:[36]

Where reference-group influence is operative, the advertiser should stress the kinds of people who buy the product, reinforcing and broadening where possible the existing stereotypes of users. The strategy of the advertiser should involve learning what the stereotypes are and what specific reference groups enter into the picture, so that appeals can be "tailored" to each main group reached by the different media employed.

For instance, many advertisers use both a national ad campaign and local ones for large urban markets such as New York and Chicago. Winston cigarettes ran such a campaign, using models in each ad whose appearance would appeal to different segments of the 25–30 age group. In the national campaign, the models tended to be more clean-cut, characteristic of young adults as usually portrayed in national advertising. But in urban markets, readers could identify with a more sophisticated, stylish (and ethnic) type of model who reflected young adult reference groups in cities.

Social Change

In chapter 4, *technology* was identified as the major force in sociocultural change. The effects of technological development on a society are summarized in the process known as "modernization." There are several ways in which modernization may affect social organization, all creating profound changes in life styles and consumption:[37]

1. *Geographic and social mobility* increase because of new occupational roles. New jobs are often in the city, requiring rural families to leave their traditional surroundings and relocate in new ones—the process of urbanization. This move to cities and new occupations results in an increase in skills and a rise in income, leading to upward mobility and higher social status.

2. *The existing system of stratification* is changed. Wealth and occupation become more important determinants of status, and birth and kinship relatively less important. "Ascribed" status is replaced by "achieved" status, based more on merit, and a closed system of social stratification becomes more open.

3. The *nuclear family* (mother, father, and children), better adapted to industrial society than the extended family (nuclear family plus other blood relatives), becomes the normal mode of living. The very old and very young become unproductive because they are unsuited for highly skilled jobs. Women are able to find employment outside the home in large numbers. Their greater independence alters the nature of the husband-wife relationship, which in turn alters the structure and the experiences of family life. The family becomes less of a center for all activities and more of a "home base" to which one returns after pursuing activities outside the house. Its structure becomes more democratic and less authoritarian.

4. *Religious beliefs* give way to secular rationality and science, a process called "secularization." As religion becomes less important, the church is increasingly separated as an institution from other aspects of life.

5. Finally, *mass communications, mass education,* and, ultimately, *mass culture* grow prominent. Political appeals and popular art forms tend to become standardized, commercialized, and widely distributed throughout the population. This does not necessarily mean that cultural forms degenerate, but rather that they are communicated in new ways and to a wider audience.

Such developments can be readily seen in the United States after its industrialization. They are also characteristic of emerging, technologically advancing nations that are opening up great opportunities in international marketing.

Urbanization: Its Life Styles

With modernization, American society has become increasingly *urbanized* in population and outlook. The attitudes of the city tend to dominate those of the small town and rural areas in forming American culture. It is not just that a certain percentage of the population lives in cities; it is also that the viewpoint and interests of the city are diffused to the entire society by mass media. Each week, millions of Americans all over the country read *Time* and *Newsweek*, watch the news and other programming produced by the three national networks, and possibly spend Saturday night enjoying a movie made in New York or Hollywood. All of these are the products of people who live in major urban centers, and they tend to impart the values of the city rather than those of the small town.

Gans has identified five different life styles that can be found in the typical American city:[38]

1. *The "cosmopolites":* This group tends to be well educated and to work in the professions or those industries allied with literature and art such as advertising, publishing, designing, and so on. On the average, their incomes are quite high. They choose to live in the city so as to be near its "cultural" facilities; they do not have strong ties to a local neighborhood.

2. *The unmarried or childless:* They also live in the city by choice, primarily because of its advantages as a place to meet people and to live an active but not home-centered social life. They move frequently, and usually leave the city altogether when they marry and have children. For these people the city is a temporary stopover in their journey to some suburb, and they typically have little sense of commitment to it.

3. *The "ethnic villagers":* These are the immigrants from other countries who remain largely unintegrated, continuing in many respects the way of life of the rural villages from which they came. In most cases they stay strictly within their own neighborhoods and have little interest in, or information about, the rest of the city.

4. *The deprived:* These are the poor, the nonwhite, the economically marginal, the divorced mothers of large families. They live in the city because they can find cheap housing in the slums and rooming houses, because welfare payments in the city are usually larger than in rural areas, and because they hope that the city will provide a chance to find employment and improve their economic situation.

5. *The "trapped":* They are usually old people who cannot afford to move and who are living out their lives on their pensions. They often have lived in the city all their lives. Like the ethnic villagers, they identify strongly with their own neighborhood and seldom leave it.

Suburbanization

Today, over a third of all Americans live in communities that are classified as suburban. What is more important, suburbs are the *fastest growing* communities in America; if the present trend continues, more than half of all Americans will soon be suburban dwellers.[39]

The suburb, a relatively small community adjacent to and dependent upon a central city, is a creation of the twentieth century, the product of rapid urban growth, advances in transportation (especially the automobile and mass transport), and rising personal incomes. The central cities have more or less remained stable in population since 1950, and many have even declined, while the *actual* growth of metropolitan areas is taking place in suburbia.

The central city and its suburbs are interdependent. The city looks to the suburbs for a significant part of its labor force and its retail shoppers; the suburbs, in turn, rely upon the central city for employment opportunities and for many cultural activities as well as for colleges and universities. There is a growing movement of central city jobs and facilities to the outskirts, however, along with the people. Industries are moving out, attracted by open space and lower taxes. Local shopping centers are giving serious competition to central city commercial districts; local newspapers and radio and television stations make suburbs less dependent on urban communications media. This dispersion may be noted particularly in the newest American cities such as Houston and Phoenix. These centers exhibit only minor downtown areas; they are actually composed of a connected series of separate residential areas interspersed with offices and shopping developments.

Suburbs tend to be stratified along lines of class and income differences. Some such as Evanston, Illinois; Arlington, Virginia; or Palo Alto, California, have a high percentage of residents with college degrees and large incomes; they are upper middle-class suburbs. There are also decidedly *upper* class suburbs, where incomes average considerably more than in upper middle-class communities. Greenwich, Connecticut, and Beverly Hills, California, are luxurious examples of this type. Others are middle or upper-lower income in composition.

Thus, modernization of American society is proceeding in the direction of urbanism in cultural values but toward suburbanization in actual population settlement.

Changing Social Roles

Modernization has also brought about significant changes in social roles, the most profound is the emergence of women in business and in formerly all-male occupations. However, there is much evidence that women are still subject to discrimination in business and industry.

Women in the Work Force Women, comprising 51 percent of the population, cannot really be described as an oppressed "minority group." In fact, one-third of the nation's work force is composed of women—approximately 30 million. But the strength of their numbers is misleading when one considers how they are rewarded for their contribution to the nation's economic output.

In a recent study only 7 percent of the working women in the United States earned a salary of more than $10,000, a poor showing in comparison with the 41 percent of working men who make more than this amount. Nor did the average salary of the female high school graduate measure up to that of male workers with the same educational background, and the difference was no niggling sum—$5,200 for women compared with $9,100 for men. One could argue that this is because only 17 percent of the women who work are managerial personnel, but actually income figures for women in all occupations are lower than those for men in the same occupations. Another assumption is that women work only for extra money to buy personal luxuries while their husbands support their families, but this is not the case. About 6 million families today are headed by women, more than half of these women are in the labor force, and more than three-fifths of them provide the total family income. [40]

The Emerging Female Consumer There are more women in the work force every year, a trend that promises to continue as day care centers are established, families have fewer children, and half of all new marriages end in divorce. The female consumer of the next decade will undoubtedly be a phenomenon far removed from the stereotyped housewife devoted to soap operas. She will more likely be a woman with a career and family, dual responsibilities that will require new time-saving products and services. She will increasingly be less receptive to the stereotyped "houswife" advertising appeals so prominent in home products promotion today.[41] And she will be likely to play a weightier role in the family decision process[42] (see chapter 8).

How Social Trends Will Affect Consumption

The social changes that accompany modernization are reflected in new demographic patterns. And these patterns will affect consumption of products and services through the 1970s and 1980s. Four areas of particular interest to marketers include *family structure, distribution of age groups, education,* and *geographic mobility.*

Family Structure

American families are growing smaller, the result of social and economic changes such as the availability of effective birth control, the escalating cost of raising children, and concerns about overpopulation and the deteriorating environment.

The institution of marriage appears to be statistically declining, and there is a distinct trend toward delaying marriage. Traditionally, a middle-class family pattern has been early marriage, three or four children, a house in the suburbs, two cars, and a wife removed from the work force until children are grown. Now, however, middle-class couples are tending to marry later, have only two children, and allow mothers to return to their careers while children are quite young. As consumers, these families have larger incomes and greater options than before; they may save more, spend more on recreation and travel, or increase their selection of goods such as clothing and durables.[43]

Distribution of Age Groups

Recent declines in American birth rates arising from changing family structures will tend to raise the average age of the population. This trend will continue as the number of children and young adults shrinks and the children of the post-World War II baby boom approach retirement (Table 6.1). Marketers might reasonably expect certain consumption patterns to reflect this trend:[44]

More Retirees The population segment of people 65 and older will increase to the year 2000, both in absolute members and in percentage of the total population. As this group exerts greater political influence, its members will undoubtedly receive larger Social Security and pension payments from both the government and their employers. This will mean that older people will have more money for more goods and services, a condition that should benefit the retirement home, travel, entertainment, and leisure industries. In addition, because the elderly will own a significant share of the nation's wealth, lifestyle changes will probably reflect a trend away from rapid social change and toward maintaining the status-quo.

**Table 6-1 Projected Age Distributions for Selected Age Brackets
(in millions and as percent of total population)**

	1970	1980	2000
65 and up	20,156	24,427	32,100
	9.3%	11.2%	13.5%
25–64	90,321	104,357	132,857
	44.1%	48.0%	54.6%
5–24	77,142	74,366	61,461
	37.7%	34.1%	25.6%
15–24	36,461	41,579	30,404
	17.8%	19.1%	12.7%
Under 5	17,184	14,816	14,869
	8.4%	6.7%	6.3%

Source: Data for 1970 from U.S. Bureau of the Census, Statistical Abstract of the United States: 1072 *(Washington. U.S. Gov't. Printing Office, 1972), p. 8; for 1980 and 2000, Projection III.*

Figure 6-1 A trend toward educational equality.

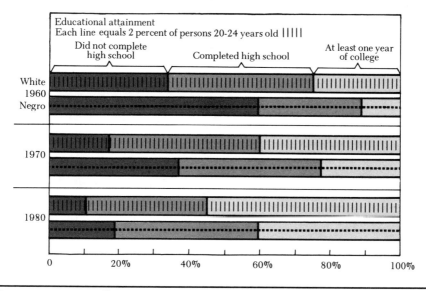

Source: Lawrence A. Mayer, "New Questions About the U.S. Population," Fortune, *February, 1971. Reprinted by permission.*

Fewer Children Marketers offering baby products, like Johnson and Johnson, are already redirecting their efforts to reach new growth segments. Baby powder, for example, is now advertised for adults.

More Workers The 25-to-64 age group, which makes up the bulk of our work force, will increase dramatically in the next thirty years. Demand for goods and services is expected to be sufficiently high to minimize unemployment, and a national four-day work week seems a likely development. The industries that will probably benefit most will be those offering leisure facilities and expensive recreational products. Also, an aging work force may create unprecedented growth in warm-weather resort areas.

Education

Due to the declining birth rate, enrollments in elementary and secondary schools will drop off as well. This will yield some financial relief for the American public school system, but may also mean that our increasing oversupply of teachers could virtually glut the market.

Table 6-2   How Your State's Population Will Change
(projected population change from 1973–1990)

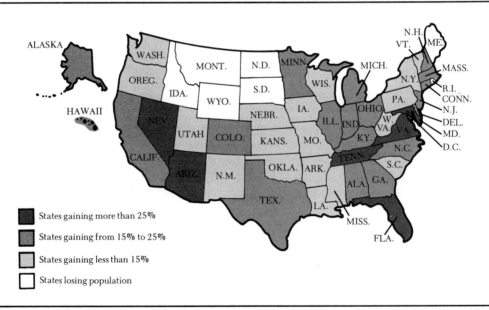

States gaining more than 25%

States gaining from 15% to 25%

States gaining less than 15%

States losing population

Source: Reprinted from U.S. News & World Report, July 15, 1974, p. 57. Copyright 1974 U.S. News & World Report, Inc.

At the college level, however, it is likely that a greater number of people will be able to take advantage of higher education, since colleges and universities will have expanded to handle large enrollments.[45] This would suggest that nonwhites will be able to attain greater educational equality, as indicated in Figure 6-1 (p. 161).

Geographic Mobility

It seems inevitable that geographic shifts of the next few decades will continue to favor the suburbs and small cities rather than the huge megalopolis. The largest areas of growth promise to be the West and the South.[46] Growth projections for all the states from 1970 to 1990 are shown in Table 6-2.

Implications for Consumer Markets

Table 6-3 summarizes the likely growth of consumer markets created by these social trends. *Durable* goods will be especially benefited by the movement toward greater affluence, smaller families, suburbanization, and leisure products. *Nondurable* goods have generally declined in their total share of the American family's budget. Although rising income will affect all consumer spending, demand for nondurables continues to respond lazily to higher earnings. Dollar expenditures for *services* have doubled over the past decade, although inflation may account for some of this juggernaut growth. The services most likely to capture the greatest share of consumer dollars over the next few decades include medical and personal care, foreign travel, and leisure services.[47]

These projections are, of course, subject to considerable refinement as new economic and social trends develop. Yet, at any time emerging social changes offer marketers some useful insights into new directions for consumer research and new product or service development.

Table 6-3   Growth in the Consumer Market
(personal consumption expenditures)

	1970 BILLIONS OF DOLLARS	PERCENT INCREASE 1970–1980
Disposable income	$687.8	53.8%
Total expenditures	615.8	53.1
Durables	88.6	82.5
Nondurables	264.7	39.7
Services	262.5	56.8
Durables	88.6	82.5
Cars	31.5	75.7
Tires, accessories	5.6	108.0
Furniture	8.0	39.7

Table 6-3   (Continued)

	1970 BILLIONS OF DOLLARS	PERCENT INCREASE 1970–1980
Appliances	8.5	84.2
Television, radios, records etc.	8.3	152.4
Other household durables	12.4	69.2
Boats, sports goods	4.9	106.1
Other durables	9.4	69.2
Nondurables	264.7	39.7
Food at home	100.5	30.5
Restaurant food	28.4	24.3
Alcoholic beverages	17.7	39.7
Tobacco	11.2	21.9
Women's apparel	28.8	55.3
Men's apparel	15.5	48.0
Footwear	8.1	29.3
Housefurnishings	6.4	74.1
Household supplies	5.5	50.9
Drugs	6.7	89.5
Toilet goods	6.1	89.5
Gas and oil	22.9	56.8
Other nondurables	6.9	4.4
Services	262.5	56.8
Shelter	91.2	64.4
Household operations	36.1	58.3
Gas and electricity	15.1	72.4
Telephone, telegraph	9.8	106.1
Transportation	17.9	28.0
Automotive services	12.4	34.4
Intercity travel	3.0	74.1
Medical services	38.7	64.4
Physicians	12.4	52.3
Dentists	4.4	42.4
Personal care	4.0	39.7
Foreign travel	5.4	98.6
Higher education	5.2	93.1
Other services	64.0	43.4

Sources: U.S. Department of Commerce; Fabian Linden, "The Consumer Market in 1980: An Overview," The Conference Board Record, June 1972.

Summary

Members of a society learn their culture through *socialization*, which is accomplished by institutions such as the family and educational and religious institutions. Individual behavior is further influenced by *reference groups*, with whom we interact in both primary and secondary relationships. Reference groups affect consumer behavior by stressing conformity to group attitudes, although some products are more susceptible to this influence than others. In the United States, the process of modernization has brought about changes in our society, notably in the *urbanization* of American values and the suburbanization of our population. It has also redefined the role of women as workers and consumers, a shift that will change the ways in which marketers approach the female consumer. The social trends most likely to affect consumption during the next few decades are changes in family structure, age distribution, education, and geographic mobility.

NOTES

1. Yoram Wind, "Preferences of Relevant Others and Individual Choice Models," *Journal of Consumer Research*, Vol. 3, No. 1 (June 1976), p. 50; and Gordon R. Foxall, "Social Factors in Consumer Choice: Replication and Extension," *Journal of Consumer Research*, Vol. 2, No. 1 (June 1975).

2. S. Stryker, "The Interactional and Situational Approaches," in *Handbook of Marriage and the Family*, ed. H. T. Christensen (Chicago: Rand McNally, 1964).

3. Leonard Broome and Philip Selznick, *Sociology*, (New York: Harper and Row, 1973).

4. Charles Cooley, *Human Nature and the Social Order* (New York: Schocken Books, 1964).

5. George H. Mead, in *Mind, Self, and Society*, ed. Charles W. Morris (Chicago: University of Chicago Press, 1934).

6. Edward L. Grubb and Gregg Hupp, "Perception of Self, Generalized Stereotypes, and Brand Selection," *Journal of Marketing Research*, Vol. 5 (February 1968).

7. Ira J. Dolich, "Congruence Relationships Between Self-Images and Product Brands," *Journal of Marketing Research*, Vol. 6 (February 1969).

8. Joseph Mason and Morris L. Mayer, "The Problem of Self-Concept in Store Image Studies," *Journal of Marketing*, Vol. 34 (April 1970).

9. E. Laird Landon, Jr., "Self-Concept, Ideal Self-Concept, and Consumer Purchase Intentions," *Journal of Consumer Research*, Vol. 1, No. 2 (September 1974), p. 44.

10. Louis Harris, "Many Feel Uneducated," *New York Post*, 30 April 1970.

11. Lewis B. Whitman, ed., *Yearbook of American Churches* (New York: Council Press, 1976).

12. Milton Yinger, "Religious Pluralism in America," in *Sociology Looks at Religion*, ed. J. M. Yinger (New York: The Macmillan Co., 1963).

13. Peter Berger, "Religious Institutions," in *Sociology: An Introduction*, ed. Neil J. Smelser, (New York: John Wiley & Sons, 1967), p. 375.

14. Charles J. Coleman, William C. Toomey, and Richard L. Woodland, "Cognition, Belief, and Behavior: A Study of Commitment to a Religious Institution," *Religious Education*, Vol. 70, No. 6 (November-December 1975)

15. *Gallup Opinion Index*, No. 44, (Princeton, N.J.: Gallup International, February 1969), pp. 22, 32.

16. Gerhard Lenski, *The Religious Factor* (New York: Doubleday, Anchor, 1963) pp. 84–85.

17. Francis S. Bourne, "Group Influence in Marketing and Public Relations," in *Some Appli-*

cations of Behavioral Research, ed. Rensis Likert and Samuel P. Hayes (Paris: UNESCO, 1957).

18. George Homans, *The Human Group*, (New York: Harcourt, Brace, and World), 1950.

19. Harold W. Berkman, *The Human Relations of Management*, (Encino, Calif.: Dickenson Publishing Co., 1974).

20. Muzafer Sherif, "Group Influences Upon the Formation of Norms and Attitudes," in *Readings in Social Psychology*, ed. Elanor Maccoby (New York: Holt, Rinehart and Winston, 1958), pp. 219–32.

21. Solomon E. Asch, "Effects of Group Pressure Upon the Modification and Distortion of Judgments," in Maccoby, *Social Psychology*, pp. 174–83.

22. Leon Festinger, "Informal Social Communication," *Psychological Review*, Vol. 57 (1950).

23. Asch, "Group Pressure."

24. Richard Crutchfield, "Conformity and Character," *American Psychologist*, Vol. 10 (1955), pp. 191–98.

25. George C. Homans, "Social Behavior as Exchange," *American Journal of Sociology*, Vol. 63 (1958), pp. 597–606.

26. Kurt Lewin, "Group Decision and Social Change," in Maccoby, *Social Psychology*, pp. 197–211.

27. William Whyte, "The Web of Words of Mouth," *Fortune*, November 1954, pp. 140–43.

28. Robert E. Witt, "Informal Social Group Influence on Consumer Brand Choice," *Journal of Marketing Research*, Vol. 7, November 1970.

29. Bourne, "Group Influence."

30. John I. Ketsuso and Malcolm Spector, "Social Problems and Deviance: Some Parallel Issues," *Social Problems*, Vol. 22, No. 5 (June 1975).

31. Bourne, "Group Influence."

32. James E. Stafford, "Effects of Group Influence on Consumer Brand Preferences," *Journal of Marketing Research*, Vol. 3 (February 1966), pp. 68–75.

33. M. Venkatesan, "Experimental Study of Consumer Behavior Conformity and Independence," *Journal of Marketing Research*, Vol. 3 (November 1966), pp. 384–87.

34. Victor J. Cook, "Group Decision, Social Comparison and Persuasion in Changing Attitudes," *Journal of Advertising Research*, Vol. 7 (March 1967), pp. 31–37.

35. Robert E. Burnkrant and Alain Cousineau, "Informational and Normative Social Influence in Buyer Behavior," *Journal of Consumer Research*, Vol. 2, No. 3 (December 1975), p. 206–15.

36. Bourne, "Group Influence."

37. Niel J. Smelser, *Essays in Sociological Explanation* (Englewood Cliffs, N.J.: Prentice-Hall, 1968).

38. Herbert J. Gans, "Urbanism and Suburbanism as Ways of Life: A Re-evaluation of Definitions," in *Human Behavior and Social Processes*, ed. Arnold M. Rose (Boston: Houghton Mifflin, 1962), ch. 2.

39. Reynolds Farley, "Suburban Persistence," *American Sociological Review*, Vol. 29, No. 1 (February 1964), pp. 38–47.

40. Harold W. Berkman, *Human Relations*, p. 253.

41. Louis C. Wagner and James B. Banos, "A Woman's Place: A Follow-Up Analysis of the Roles Portrayed by Women in Magazine Advertisements," *Journal of Marketing Research*, Vol. 10, May 1973; and Lawrence A. Wortzel and John M. Frisbie, "Women's Role Preferences in Advertisements: An Empirical Study," *Journal of Marketing*, No. 38 (October 1974).

42. Robert T. Green and Isabella C. M. Cunningham, "Feminine Role Perception and Family Purchasing Decisions," *Journal of Marketing Research*, Vol. 12, No. 3 (August 1975).

43. Lawrence A. Mayer, "New Questions about the U.S. Population, *Fortune*, February 1971.

44. James D. Foust and Al D. Southwood, "Profiles of the Future," *Business Horizons*, February 1973.

45. Foust, "Profiles."

46. "Where Americans Will Live in 1990," *U.S. News and World Report*, 10 April 1972.

47. Fabian Linden, "The Consumer Market in 1980: An Overview," *The Conference Board Record*, June 1972.

MARKETING APPLICATIONS

Conclusion 1 *Reference groups, which fulfill a number of social functions for individuals, exert varying degrees of influence over consumer attitudes and behavior.*

Application Research has pointed out that reference groups have the most influence on product choices that are highly visible or that reinforce an individual's sense of "belonging" to a group through conformity pressure. These findings have been applied effectively in communications which stress group membership and acceptance revolving around some product choice; for example, the group of fun-loving volleyball players on the beach who greets one of their members with open arms for appearing with the "right" brand of beer.

Conclusion 2 *The role of women in society is changing dramatically as they continue to achieve greater opportunities for career mobility. Thus the traditional marketers' portrayal of female consumers as obsessed with housework and family care is becoming obsolete.*

Application Marketers must reevaluate the existing stereotypes of female consumers to accommodate the shifting emphasis from housewife to career-homemaker roles. This approach is already evident in commercials for household products which stress benefits such as convenience and time-saving and depict women as consumers who must cope with their new dual roles.

Conclusion 3 *The demographic composition of our society, reflecting patterns of social change, is moving toward smaller families and a rising average age of the population.*

Application Marketing efforts over the past several years have been geared toward youth-oriented society, with children as the focal point of family life. But as the products of the post-World War II baby boom reach middle age, the great majority of people in the country will demand a new attention to the preferences of adults. Thus, marketers might expect the rate of innovations to fall somewhat in favor of products and services aimed at a more settled, conservative population. Also, child-centeredness will probably become less of a sociological phenomenon as adult consumers lose their fascination with youth and devote more time as consumers to their own creative and recreational interests. Probable growth areas include adult education, travel, cultural entertainment, and hobby products.

ASSIGNMENTS

Research Assignment

Background   Since the decline of student enrollments in the 1970s (as well as earlier pressures for greater student participation in setting school policies), colleges and universities have become more concerned with attracting and keeping students. Hence, students have tended to emerge in a new role—as consumers.

As an independent marketing consultant, you are hired by your school to analyze its performance as a marketing institution from the viewpoint of increasing enrollment by effectively reaching and recruiting good students and satisfying their educational needs.

Methodology   You are primarily interested in the following questions:

1. What exactly is your school doing to attract students in the first place? Does it advertise? Work with student placement agencies?

2. Has your school exhausted all of its possibilities for attracting students? What other vehicles might be used? Are courses for adults offered? Could more courses be made available that would appeal to people already pursuing careers?

3. Once students are enrolled, how do they evaluate the school's performance in meeting their needs?

Your research should include an analysis of current marketing activities as well as interviews with at least five students in other curricula.

Extrapolation   How might your school be evaluated along the three criteria stated above? What recommendations could you make for improving the school's performance from the view of students-as-consumers? If feasible, try to put your prescriptions into actual practice.

Creative Assignment

Since the growth of women's consciousness over the past decade or so, much criticism has been directed at advertisers for stereotyping American women as household drudges whose most important considerations in life are dust-free coffee tables and shiny floors, or as helpless individuals dependent on men for social support.

As a Creative Consultant to the National Organization for Women (NOW), you have been hired to help bring this problem to the attention of advertisers in a constructive way. To meet this objective you must find three ads which stereotype women in a sexist way and three others which effectively appeal to women without resorting to such stereotypes. Write a brief rationale for each of your choices. What factors account for the differences?

Managerial Assignment

Consumer behavior may be viewed as *deviant* when consumers seek services that are prohibited by law. Gambling is perhaps one of the most prevalent forms of this type of behavior. There is a general trend toward legalizing certain forms of gambling, have them regulated by government and used as a source of revenue by a municipality or state.

As a member of the City Planning Board of a midwestern city (population about 200,000) you find the prospect of legalizing gambling in the municipality increasingly attractive. You are aware that many forms of gambling are going on every day on a covert basis. Bets are constantly placed on horse races through bookmakers, for example. And the experiences of certain states in legalizing off-track betting have caused the Planning Board to talk seriously of adopting some kind of off-track betting in your city (encouraged by the realization that the city is in troublesome financial straits).

Assuming that the state government would approve such a move, you have been asked to make a recommendation pro or con legalized racetrack betting. As one source of information, you may consult literature on off-track betting in New York State. But you also feel that some form of consumer research should be conducted to find out how widespread acceptance of such a proposal would be.

Make a recommendation for a research project that would help you make that decision including considerations of how the research should be conducted, what questions should be asked, who should participate as respondents, and what other factors should be weighed in making a final determination.

SELECTED READINGS

Douglas, Susan P. "Cross-National Comparisons and Consumer Stereotypes: A Case Study of Working and Non-Working Wives in the U.S. and France." *Journal of Consumer Research*, Vol. 3, No. 1 (June 1976), pp. 12-20.

Hale, W. Daniel and Bonnie R. Strickland. "Induction of Mood States and Their Effect on Cognitive and Social Behaviors." *Journal of Consulting and Clinical Psychology*, Vol. 44, No. 1 (February 1976), pp. 155.

Ross, Ivan. "Self Concept and Brand Preference." *Journal of Business*, Vol. 44, No. 1 (January 1971), pp. 38–50.

Seclow, Richard. "Coming Boom in Early Retirement Offers Big Market for Travel, Apparel, Housing." *Advertising Age*, Vol. 43, No. 69 (15 May 1972).

VanDusen, R.A. and E.B. Sheldon. "The Changing Status of American Women: A Life Cycle Perspective." *American Psychologist*, (February 1976), pp. 106–116.

Ward Scott. "Consumer Socialization." *Journal of Consumer Research*, Vol. 1, No. 2 (September 1974), pp. 1–14.

OBJECTIVES

1. Describe the *six variables* that enter into social class.   *173*

2. Define *social class* and describe the four *determinants* of social class membership.   *173–174*

3. Discuss the three research *methodologies* for investigating social class.   *175*

4. Discuss Hodges's *five social classes* found in the United States.   *176*

5. Discuss four theories of why the social classes may be breaking down.   *178*

6. Compare the *social class differences* in media use, brand preferences, shopping behavior, leisure pursuits.   *184*

SEVEN

Social Class

Most Americans have only the vaguest awareness of social classes in the United States, except that all very rich people seem to belong to one class, all "middle class" people to another, and some "poor" people to a third. But marketers have learned in recent years that social class membership is much more complicated and may determine what a person buys even more than income.

Social class is a form of reference group that pervades an individual's choice of housing, automobile, clothing, education, leisure, and a number of other consumer goods and activities.

To offer a view of social class that will be useful in decision making, this chapter introduces topics such as:

• How to identify and measure social classes in the United States.

• Two views of the American social class structure.

• Four ways in which social classes may be slowly breaking down.

• Why life-style characteristics of the social classes affect consumer behavior.

• How social classes differ in purchasing, store selection, media patterns, and credit card use.

Investigating Social Class

It wasn't until the Great Depression that behavioral scientists began investigating social classes in the United States. The pioneer studies of the 1930s and 1940s—"Elmtown," "Jonesville," and "Yankee City"—contributed both a systematic means of investigating American social stratification and a vast amount of data on the subject. By the 1960s, sociologists could distinguish a class hierarchy of six distinct levels in most communities, beginning with an established, privileged elite entrenched in the loftiest position. Another group could be observed, probably living close by, who had accumulated enough money to join the elite but were tacitly excluded because of other considerations. A corps of professional and managerial people comprised an upper middle class, and a larger group of white collar workers a somewhat lower middle class. Skilled blue collar workers formed another stratum. And finally, those who remained very poor in a nation of affluence occupied the bottom rung.

Today, changing economic and social relationships are complicating this system. Through unionization and specialized, valuable skills, many blue collar workers have achieved income levels far above their white collar counterparts. Some have even moved their families into traditionally white collar suburbs. Groups such as blacks, Italians, and Jews are rapidly advanced into high status occupations once reserved for WASPS (white, Anglo-Saxon Protestants). And young people representing all social strata have moved toward an alternative culture that appears to reject class consciousness. In spite of these developments, most social scientists agree that class distinctions in the United States remain basically intact.

Much evidence confirms relationships between class membership and consumer behavior. This chapter explores these relationships, examining how stratification operates, what social class means in America, recent developments in lifestyle theory relevant to class-linked behavior, and the impact of social class on consumer purchasing decisions.

Social Stratification

The concept of stratification was popularized by Karl Marx, with decidedly negative undertones. He found in it an unnatural system through which some members of a society exploit the others:[1]

The history of all hitherto existing society is the history of class struggles. Freeman and slave, patrician and plebeian, lord and serf, guild-master and journeyman, in a word, oppressor and oppressed, stood in constant opposition to one another, carried on an uninterrupted, now hidden, now open fight, a fight that each time ended either in a revolutionary reconstitution of society at large, or in the common ruin of the contending classes.

Every society we know of distributes responsibilities and rewards unequally among different people. Kingsley Davis explains this phenomenon as a logical means of motivation.[2]

Any society must distribute its individuals in the positions of its social structure and induce them to perform the duties of these positions. It must therefore solve the problem of motivation at two levels: to instill in the proper individuals the desire to occupy certain positions and, once in these positions, the desire to perform all duties attached to them. (The duties of these positions are not all equally difficult or equally pleasant.) Inevitably, then, a society must have some kind of rewards that it can use as inducements and some way of distributing these rewards differently according to positions . . . In a sense the rewards are "built into" the position. They consist in the "rights" associated with the position, plus what may be called its accompaniments or prerequisites . . . If the rights and prerequisites of different positions in a society must be unequal, then the society must be stratified because that is precisely what stratification means.

Max Weber developed a scheme for stratifying any complex society that has been further refined by Kuhl on the basis of six variables:[3] (1) *Prestige* granted to an individual implies an attitude of deference on the part of others; some individuals command more prestige than others do. (2) *Occupation* represents a social role receiving a certain amount of prestige. (3) *Possessions* provide an especially useful basis for stratification in countries such as the United States. (4) *Interaction* consists in differential contact with others, and people are stratified according to their patterns of personal contact. (5) *Class consciousness* refers to the level at which people are aware of themselves as belonging to a distinctive social grouping. (6) *Value orientations* reflect convictions shared by people, defining the ends of life and means of achieving them.

Each one of these variables can be applied to the task of stratifying a population, and all of them influence one another. But *prestige* tends to predominate because it underlies all the rest.

Defining Social Class

The concept of social class remains especially difficult to pinpoint. Kuhl notes that stratification into social classes involves families rather than individuals: "A family shares many characteristics among its members that greatly affect their relationships with outsiders: the same house, the same income, the same values. If a large group of families are approximately equal to one another and closely differentiated from other families, we call them a social class."[4]

This description hints at the tendency to confuse social class considerations with demographics. Income fails to offer a true indication of class membership today, since a construction foreman, a corporate lawyer, and a relatively successful chicken farmer could all earn $42,000 a year. Yet they probably spend their money quite differently and are perceived as belonging to different social strata. Income neither determines nor explains social stratification.[5] Occupation may provide a more accurate measure, but this is another demographic characteristic rather than an indicator of class membership. The sharpest distinctions among social classes occur on the basis of life style, as Levy demonstrates.[6] People conceptualized as members of the same classes tend to share common values and behave much alike. And these last criteria best serve the interests of students concerned with consumer behavior.

Thus, social classes could be defined as *large groups in a population sharing approximately the same life styles, who are stratified hierarchically according to their social prestige.*

The qualified terms "*large* groups" and "*approximately* the same life styles" deserve special emphasis. People who have rejected the traditional American family structure to live in communes certainly share the same style of life. But numerically they represent too small a fraction of our total population to be recognized as a distinct social class. Also, the life styles of various people within a class are never totally homogeneous. The upper middle class includes doctors, advertising account executives, Kiwanis Club officials, college professors, airline pilots, and interior designers. Their attitudes and overt behavior could be quite divergent, without even considering the variables of region, educational diversity, and income discrepancies. Yet the similarities that grant them membership in this particular class tend to overshadow their differences.

Determining Class Membership

In the United States, four principal factors determine who belongs to what class: occupation, artifacts, associations, and influence.

Occupation This may be the most accurate single indicator of a person's class membership. For one, occupation dictates to a large degree the variables of income, personal associations, status, and influence. Secondly, the fact that many see occupation as almost synonymous with class membership influences the data obtained in studies of social stratification. Most of us are predisposed to identify professionals with the upper middle class, automobile mechanics with the blue collar working class, and people on welfare with the lowest level in our class hierarchy.

Artifacts These represent the most useful symbols of class identification for consumer behavior study. The type of home a person buys or rents usually depends upon the social class he or she belongs to. (One intriguing example is the organized crime figure who, despite vast wealth and influence, continues to live quietly in a two-family house among working-class neighbors.) Home furnishings are commonly linked with class membership,

as are clothing and appliances. In choosing possessions, people both define and reflect their life styles.

Associations These tend to occur in class-related patterns. Interactions with friends and relatives vary according to class membership. So do the kinds of people with whom a person associates in the course of work. Most people continue to date and marry people from approximately the same social class.[7] Furthermore, an individual's sense of belonging to a particular class is reinforced one way or the other by the people with whom that person interacts. The "social climber" knows this all too well.

Influence With its implications of power and authority, influence is wielded more by some classes than others. W. Lloyd Warner notes that, in complex societies, people who perform coordinating functions usually exert the most influence:[8]

Those who occupy coordinating positions acquire power and prestige. They do so because their actions partly control the behavior of the individuals who look to them for direction. Within this simple control there is simple power. Those who exercise such power either acquire prestige directly from it or have gained prestige from other sources sufficiently to be raised to a coordinating position.

The coordinators, of course, are managerial and professional in the highest social strata and because they control mass communications—television, the motion picture industry, and publishing—they influence the attitudes and consumption behavior of other groups.

These are by no means the only criteria for assigning people to various social classes. In research practice, class membership is usually defined by whatever procedure is used to measure it.

Measuring Social Class

Investigators use three principal methods to place individuals at the most appropriate class level. These are *reputational, subjective,* and *objective.*

The *reputational* technique means inviting people to rank the social positions of their neighbors.[9] This interview procedure normally draws willing responses, and most respondents are aware of a class system in their community. Since they are asked to rank only people with whom they are familiar, however, this protocol best lends itself to small communities.

The *subjective* approach asks individuals to rank *themselves* with respect to social class. Centers pointed out a major difficulty with this technique—people like to overrate their own positions.[10] This approach seems most useful (in conjunction with some other method) for comparisons of how people see their class level against others' ratings of them.

Objective methods include single- and multiple-item indexes. The single-item variety rates individuals along a single dimension; the most popular dimension is occupation. Multiple-item ratings are highly preferable to this type. Warner's *Index of Status Characteristics* (ISC) represents a sophisticated multiple-item approach. Here individuals are ranked according to occupation, source of income, type of house, and dwelling area. (The original ISC included size of income and education, but both were deleted with no apparent impact on predictive success.)[11] Hollingshead developed a similar *Index of Social Position* (ISP), utilizing occupation, area of residence, and education.[12] Carman employs an *Index of Cultural Classes* in marketing research; power, status, and culture are his variables.[13] Of the three available methods, multiple-item indexes receive the most attention from researchers.

Armed with these techniques, investigators have attempted to locate and define social classes in the United States.

Research Models of Social Class

Warner's trail-blazing "Yankee City" study was published in 1949, an exhaustive and significant portrait of social class structure in a small New England community. Today, the six-level class hierarchy he reported remains the definitive classification system to most sociologists. A skeleton version of that system appears here. Another major study under Warner's guidance confirmed most of his Yankee City findings for the Chicago area in the mid-1950s.[14] But the most recent exploration of social class in a metropolitan complex was published by Hodges in 1963.[15] Because its urban and suburban orientation comes closer to America today, this research will be covered in somewhat greater detail.

Warner: The Local Community

After classifying 99 percent of Yankee City's families, Warner identified the following social classes:[16]

Upper-upper   This group consisted of an old-family elite, characterized by wealth inherited over one generation or more.

Lower-upper   These individuals were actually wealthier than the upper-uppers, but could not claim equal lineage. Their money had been made more recently; they lacked the carefully polished manners exhibited by the higher group; and their sense of security could be described as less pronounced.

Upper-middle   This group was composed of reasonably successful businessmen and professionals, less affluent than the lower-uppers and less concerned with lineage or their lack of it.

Lower-middle   The small businessmen, minor professionals, and less successful white collar workers at this level were described as superpatriotic, lodge members, and tending toward religious fundamentalism.

Upper-lower   Solid laboring people occupied this level, hard-working and primarily concerned with respectability.

Lower-lower   In Yankee City, these were rather slovenly, disreputable individuals engaged in ventures such as digging clams and living on public assistance.

Warner indicated that the divisions between these classes were clean-cut, except for the break between the lower-middle and upper-lower groups, where distinctions became somewhat blurred. However, this study was actually conducted in 1933, while the country was weathering out the Great Depression. Unemployment soared to more than 70 percent for the lower-lowers, and annual incomes ranged from $882 for the lower-lowers to $6,400 for the upper-uppers.[17] The depression factor could have created sharper distinctions between haves and have-nots than might have been observed under a more stable economic climate.

Hodges: The Metropolitan Complex

A three-county area around San Francisco, populated by about 2 million people, was the setting for Hodges' study during the late 1950s and early 1960s. Unlike Warner, he reported fairly overlapping, imprecise distinctions among the classes. His divisions were essentially the same as Warner's except that only five levels were delineated.[18]

Upper   Hodges merged Warner's two upper classes into one—characterized by "eccentricity, ancestor worship, and insouciance."[19] He found that this group leaned toward inconspicuous consumption—tweeds, battered station wagons, and quiet parties, as opposed to chauffered limousines and furs. A minority jet set (perhaps Warner's missing "lower uppers") lived a flashier, ultra-fashionable life, but the upper class as a whole was not described in these terms. Members of this group received their college education at Stanford, Harvard, Vassar, and other traditionally elite schools. As adults, they spent much of their time in a round of parties, charity balls, skiing, and flying to resort homes at Lake Tahoe. Because the group remains quite small in proportion to other classes, its members are usually glossed over in marketing schemes for most products. However, they do form a desirable market for investment services and expensive specialty products.

Upper-Middle   These were the professionals and semiprofessionals, independent businessmen, and corporate executives. Membership in this class implied preoccupation with one's education and career. Usually graduates of state universities, they hoped their offspring would go to Harvard, Yale, or Bennington, but recognized that admissions were limited to the very bright. Thus, a distinct upper middle-class pattern of obsession with children's education became apparent. Hodges found "organizational proneness" a feature of this group. Men joined professional societies, Rotary, and Chambers of Commerce. Women were active in garden and bridge clubs, neighborhood improvement meetings. Both men and women tended to take religion more socially than literally. People of the upper middle class exert much more influence on the market place than their limited numbers would suggest. These are the "upscale" families to whom many marketers gear product development and promotion.

Lower-Middle Hodges summed up this group with the words "frugality, puritanism, and the Bible." These were the salesmen, clerical workers, foremen, lathing contractors, and the owner of the corner drugstore, a group that has been described as setting "the level of the common man." Members of this class tended to own tract homes in the suburbs or comparable accommodations, and were considerably more traditional in orientation than people belonging to the upper middle class. A high school diploma was considered standard educational achievement. Lower-middle families distinguished themselves by excessive concern over morals, religion, and acceptance of the Protestant Ethic. Yet Hodges noted a pattern which has been described as the emergence of a "new middle class."[20] Younger members who were apt to work for large corporations appeared to behave more self-indulgently, spending beyond their means on clothing, furnishings, and cars. Today, several years after Hodges' research, this "hedonistic" subgroup seems to have grown and now predominates. Today's average Americans spend and use credit with a zeal that would horrify their 1963 counterparts.

Upper-lower These skilled and semiskilled blue collar workers were the "hardhats" of the 1960s, outspoken in their intolerance for blacks, Mexican-Americans, and intellectuals. A focal point of the upper-lower existence was the promise of "raising one's social position."[21] In fact, the blue collar people whom Hodges contacted were doing just that. With a newly discovered affluence, (average wages rose 50 percent between 1950 and 1960) upper-lowers began arriving in lower middle-class suburbs by the time of this study. In other research, Coleman identified certain members of this group as "overprivileged," earning more than most blue collar workers but spending the extra money in traditional upper-lower patterns.[22] These individuals would remain in blue collar neighborhoods but drive larger cars and enjoy more home appliances than their neighbors. With considerably more money to spend today than in the early 1960s, the upper-lower group represents the most populous market in America and an increasingly attractive one to marketers.

Lower-lower Occupying the bottom of the hierarchy were "lower blue collarites," unemployed persons, and families on welfare, inhabiting dilapidated tenements or suburban slums. Hodges described this group as victims of "cultural deficiency": geared to an essentially middle class form of reference by the mass media, but thwarted or stifled in their attempts to achieve middle-class goals. Consequently, this class was marked by "despair, anger, and apathy."[23] In the past marketers seldom paid much attention to this group, although this pattern may be changing. The poor use food products and packaged goods as well as television, automobiles, and home appliances. And in buying these products from retail establishments close to home, they often pay more than others along the class hierarchy.

Warner and Hodges agree fundamentally on how social classes distribute themselves in the United States. Lower-middle and upper-lower groups form the distinct majority we have come to think of as Middle America, as can be seen in Table 7-1. Percentages for each group are expressed in terms of the total population:[24]

The differences reported could simply reflect different representation of the classes in the two communities. They may also be affected by the depression factor overshadowing Warner's figures. The lower-lower category could, in harsh economic times, embrace unemployed persons who would normally populate higher levels, particularly upper-lower and lower-middle.

Are Classes Breaking Down?

The question "Are classes breaking down?" can only be answered by yes and no. Several indicators point to confusion surrounding class identity and a steady chipping away of barriers separating the classes. Empirical research into this question seems conspicuously absent; what evidence does exist supports the view that social classes in the United States remain essentially permanent. The changes that many authors see occurring could be summed up as follows:

Democratization of the Elite

Some observers believe a widespread social leveling is taking place, a democratization of the elite. This premise states that upper classes are gradually eroding due to greater societal participation by groups traditionally suppressed.[27]

The centralization of people in cities, of workers in unions, of manufacturing and finance in gigantic combines, of regulatory functions in government, have created parallel shifts in America's social classes. One accompaniment of the technological revolution underlying these changes has been the gradual "democratization of the elite"—a sharing of privilege noticeable in the graduated income tax, the more even application of laws, the spread of welfare programs, and lately, the vociferous demands of college students, workers, and oppressed minorities for

Table 7-1 Distribution of Social Classes in the United States: Two Studies

	WARNER (1933) (PERCENT)	HODGES (1968) (PERCENT)
Upper-upper	1.4	.2
Lower-upper	1.6	—
Upper-middle	10.2	10–15
Lower-middle	28.1	35
Upper-lower	32.6	35–40
Lower-lower	25.2	15–20

R.O.C.I.: *Segmenting by Social Class and Income*

At each social class level, there are fortunate families whose income falls above the median income for that class. Coleman calls these consumers "overprivileged." But there are also "underprivileged" families whose household incomes are below the average. The relationships of a family's total income to the median for that occupational class has been termed Relative Occupational Class Income (R.O.C.I.). Many researchers think that R.O.C.I. is a useful variable for segmentation, both for durable goods such as automobiles[25] and non-durables like food products.

In one experiment, it proved possible to predict which consumers would pay high or low prices for coffee based on their R.O.C.I.[26]

Table 7-2   A. Percentage Makeup of Coffee Markets by Relative Occupational Income Status (actual purchases)

| | COFFEE CLASS | | | |
INCOME STATUS	LOW PRICE N:138	AVERAGE PRICE N:451	HIGH PRICE N:437	EXPECTED
Underprivileged	43%	41%	33%	38%
Average	11	16	15	15
Overprivileged	46	43	52	47
Total	100	100	100	100

Table 7-2   B. Percentage Variance of Actual from Expected Purchases of Each Coffee Class by Each Income Status Group*

| | COFFEE CLASS | | |
INCOME STATUS	LOW PRICE	AVERAGE PRICE	HIGH PRICE
Underprivileged	+13	+8	−13
Average	−26	+7	0
Overprivileged	−2	−9	+11

*Variance computed as follows: $\dfrac{\text{actual \% — expected \%}}{\text{Expected \%}}$ (100)

Source: R. Eugene Klippel and John F. Monoky, "A Potential Segmentation Variable for Marketers: Relative Occupational Class Income," Journal of the Academy of Marketing Science, Vol. 2, No. 2, Spring 1974, p. 354. Reprinted by permission of the Academy of Marketing Science, Copyright © 1974.

This suggests that the different R.O.C.I. groups tend to behave alike across occupational levels . . . blue collar workers in the relative class groups buy like their counterparts in the white collar ranks.

The Rich New Working Class

Today, American workers can earn $15,000 . . . $20,000 . . . $25,000, and more in traditional blue collar occupations like truck driving, plumbing, and factory work. Such earnings far surpass what many white collar employees can expect in banks, insurance companies, and other office environments. It is also substantially more than upper-strata professional people earn in European countries (even compensating for monetary differences).

This affluence permits blue collar families with good credit to enjoy $60,000 suburban homes, four-wheel drive "Scouts" with expensive custom tires and citizen band radios, MFG fibreglass boats with Evinrude outboard motors, and luxuriously fitted Winnebago campers with Sony color TVs operating on battery packs inside.

Tom Wolfe has remarked that blue collar workers don't even wear blue collars anymore, but "$35 superstar Qiana shirts with elephant collars."[32]

greater participation in decisions affecting their life chances.

What happened to some elements of the upper class during the period of change might be called a "trickle-up" effect. Or, since the late 1960s, chic has come from the streets and not from Paris. Tom Wolfe first articulated the pattern in *Radical Chic*, describing fund-raising parties thrown for the revolutionary Black Panthers by members of New York City's upper Park Avenue elite.[28] There are signs everywhere that children of the privileged classes may be breaking away from rigid class-consciousness. The runaway popularity of denim clothing, cutting across all class lines, offers visible evidence. Upper-strata "prep" schools acknowledge that they are in financial trouble.[29] The elite universities and colleges—Harvard, Yale, Vassar—were among the first to experience student demands for "democratization" a decade ago.

Massification of the Middle Class

Another position maintains that the life styles of all social classes are becoming more and more like that of the middle class. Those who see this pattern of massification usually attribute it to factors such as industrial democratization and mass merchandising:[30]

With the rise of mass marketing (especially franchising), an American can have tacos in Duluth, chow mein in Dallas, and Coney Island hot dogs in San Diego. The franchised tacos are the same in Albuquerque and Duluth; thus food becomes uniformly bland. . . . The theme in American mass merchandising is uniformity, quantity, and mediocrity. In air-conditioned suburban shopping malls from coast to coast are found "hippie boutiques" selling mass-produced psychedelic posters, plastic love beads, and peace-symbol dresses, necklaces, and roach clips. The mass market is not a recent development in the United States; neither is criticism of it.

Some observers find massification a consequence of blurred distinctions between white collar and blue collar workers,[31] due to closer income levels and a new tendency for blue collar families to move into white collar suburbs.

The Blueing of America

This theory, authored by the Bergers, maintains that the "green" revolution of the 1960s (as described in Charles Reich's best-seller the *Greening of America*) concerned only children of the upper middle class. Whenever a member of this group "drops out" to pursue countercultural activities, room at the top is created for some upwardly mobile member of a lower class:[33]

Precisely those classes that remain most untouched by what is considered to be the revolutionary tide in contemporary America face *new prospects of upward social mobility.* Thus, the "revolution" (hardly the word) is not at all where it seems to be, which should not surprise anyone. The very word *avant-garde* suggests that one ought to look behind it for what is to follow—and there is no point asking the *avant-gardistes*, whose eyes are steadfastly looking forward. Not even the Jacobins paid attention to the grubby tradesmen waiting to climb up over their shoulders.

Thus, if Yale and Harvard were to become totally "greened," Wall Street would draw its recruits from Fordham and Wichita State.

Empirical Views

Studies launched to investigate breakdown of class structure have been few, but what findings there have been support continued differentiation among classes. Glen studied Gallup and National Opinion Research Center polls for evidence of class-linked responses and concluded that class differences still exist.[34] Recent research into children's perceptions revealed that children ranked occupational prestige (the favorite one-item index of social class) in the same order as their parents. They also did not believe that people share equal opportunity to achieve valued rewards in America.[35]

The New Affluence

Despite these findings, observations of shifting economic patterns suggest that changes have occurred across class lines during the last couple of decades. For instance, the following trends emerged between 1960 and 1970:[36]

1. *A generally higher standard of living.* Despite erosion of purchasing power, the "typical" American family could buy a third more in the way of goods and services in 1970 than it could in 1960. Half the families in the United States earned more than $10,000 in 1970. One of every four families made between $10,000 and $15,000 a year, compared with only 11 percent in 1960; and three families out of every 100 earned more than $25,000.

2. *Emphasis on more desirable occupations.* Less work being done in 1970 was in the unskilled, low wage, normally unpleasant

jobs. Of the 13 million jobs that had opened up since 1960, nearly 4 million were in professional and technical occupations, 4 million in clerical positions, 1.8 million in service work, and half a million in sales.

3. *More widespread educational opportunities.* The proportion of high school students who enrolled in college rose to 30 percent in 1970, up from 22 percent in 1960. Percentage of high school graduates across the country went from 61 to 75 percent for the same period.

These developments lead us to believe that our entire class structure may have shifted somewhat since the major studies of stratification were conducted.

Life Style Differences in Social Class

As mentioned earlier, Levy contends that variations in social class are really differences in life style. These differences may be subtle to those who stress the similarity between, say, a prosperous working-class family's kitchen and an upper middle-class family's kitchen. But even though the same brands of appliances might be found, the purchasing patterns that brought them there originate in different values, thought processes, and decisions. From a number of studies, Levy has devised a conceptual framework for these lifestyle differences based on values, interpersonal attitudes, self-perceptions, and daily life routines.[37]

Values

Lower status people tend to value education less than middle-class people. They are also more apt to seek immediate gratification, to depend on luck for opportunities, and to avoid risking their security. Lower-class women, who feel trapped at the less desirable end of the social scale, are not likely to take pride in the work they do. Middle-class people place more emphasis on doing things right, on morality, and on respectability. They tend to believe that they can govern their destinies and achieve success by applying these values to their lives and work. Because they have achieved more, there is a greater feeling of accomplishment and pride in their activities among the middle class. The higher one progresses up the social strata, increasingly broad values, a sense of participation in the community, and self-expressive activities such as painting and sculpting can be observed.

Interpersonal Attitudes

Upper middle-class husbands and wives are inclined to function as teams. Women in this group demand much from themselves as child therapists, organization workers, and intellectually stimulating wives. Upper middle-class people try to develop bright, active, precocious children, and look for products that will enhance their success as parents. Lower middle-class parents are more likely to emphasize control and conformity in raising their children, and place great value on teaching them standards of cleanliness, politeness, and order. Members of the lower middle class are most prone to say they want babies who are well-behaved, well-scheduled, and manageable. Working-class mothers express a strong need to enjoy their babies, while working class fathers prefer to remain fairly distant from young children.

In other relationships, lower-class women usually say that they dress to please themselves; lower middle-class women are more concerned with what other women think of their clothing; and upper middle-class women tend to dress for themselves, their husbands, other women, and other men. Lower-class families maintain the least adventurous social boundaries, preferring to socialize with relatives. They are more prone to spend vacations staying home, visiting relatives, or letting the husband take off by himself than upper middle-class people, who spend vacations as family groups.

Self-Perceptions

Lower status women understand their bodies least of women in any class and maintain a sense of taboo about them. Higher status women reveal more pride in their bodies and think of themselves as fastidious. Upper middle-class women are less concerned with products such as deodorants, feeling less anxiety about offending others. They express the most personal pride and self-esteem in grooming, while lower middle-class women respond to social motives and general self-consciousness. Working-class women think of immediate needs in personal care, such as getting ready for "tonight's date" or a special occasion. Upper middle class men see themselves as clean, fastidious, and well-groomed, and relate these traits to career

success. Masculine know-how is defined as sophistication about business, restaurants, travel, and so on. Lower middle-class men find masculine identity in being good fathers, building a solid home life. They are characterized as serious, rather depressed, fearful of being displaced by lower-class individuals, and concerned that their children get a good education to achieve upward mobility. Men in this group are most traditional in matters of clothing and grooming and appear most resistant to innovative fashions. Working-class men see themselves as sturdy guys who make decent livings for their families. They value manual adroitness, physical skills, and appreciate their leisure time. These men are inclined to feel that life uses them up faster than it does males from other social strata.

Daily Life

Lower-class women wake up earlier in the morning and feel they can get by with less sleep. A chronic dilemma of the working-class household is wanting to stay up for the late movie but needing to retire earlier than those who keep office hours. Middle-class housewives tend to manage their housework, to plan ahead and feel a sense of mastery over chores. Working-class women, by contrast, are more likely to complain that woman's work is never done. At higher status levels, more time is spend outside the home and more hours are devoted to expressive activities such as reading, art, and music. Time management patterns also vary by social class. Lower-class people eat earlier, spend less time at the dinner table and more in front of the television than do upper middle-class people.

Social Class and Buying Behavior

Because social classes embrace groups of people who share similar life styles, market segmentation by class may be highly useful in strategy planning. Kuhl notes that:[38]

Prestige tends to be bestowed through consumption behavior rather than income, for only that which can be seen can be judged. Consumption patterns and interaction networks are intimately linked; people spend their leisure time with others who share their tastes and recreational activities, and they learn new tastes from those with whom they associate.

But controversy surrounds the question of whether social class is a more useful basis for segmentation than income.[39] Wasson found the class concept more relevant than income to patterns of spending for food, shelter, and education.[40] But Myers, Stanton, and Haug failed to observe a significant relationship between social class and purchases of low-ticket packaged goods.[41] And, in yet a third analysis, Plummer concluded that income is as valuable an indicator as social class in studying credit card use patterns.[42]

However, social class as a determinant of consumer behavior has been documented in the following areas:

Media

Levy remarks that media are approached and used in contrasting as well as similar ways by different class groups.[43]
Newspapers and Magazines   Lower-class people are less likely to subscribe to newspapers than middle-class people. When they do subscribe, they tend to prefer the morning paper, while middle-class individuals read the afternoon paper.[44] Hodges discovered that lower middle-class readers identify with *Readers Digest* and the *Ladies Home Journal*, while those of the upper middle class lean toward *Time, Sports Illustrated, New Yorker,* and *Saturday Review.*[45]
Television   Studies in fifteen major cities reveal that members of the upper middle class consistently prefer the NBC channels while lower middle-class viewers favor CBS.[46] Tastes in programming run to quiz shows, variety shows, Westerns, and late movies for lower-class audiences, while middle-class respondents enjoy dramatic fare, movies, and late night talk shows.[47] As might also be expected, lower-class families spend more time in front of the television than their upper middle-class counterparts.[48]

Advertising Acceptance

The symbolic nature of advertising becomes important to creative strategy when addressing members of different social classes. Levy's studies indicate that lower status people are more receptive to advertising that depicts activity, on-going work and life, impressions of energy, and solutions to practical problems in daily life and social relationships. They also prefer advertising of a strong visual character.[49]

Upper lower-class women respond to promotion offering coupons or other special inducements. Such appeals make them feel shrewd and economical. Lower middle-class women may feel the same attraction, but are more inclined to question their need for the products offered. They wish to feel sensible about offers and promotions. Upper middle-class women more often tend to reject coupons, sensing lower-class implications and recognizing no great appeal in the usually insignificant premiums and savings.

Upper middle-class people generally are more critical of advertising, suspicious of emotional appeals, and skeptical of claims. They tend to be insulted by the straightforward and literal selling approaches aimed at lower class groups. What does seem to appeal to upper middle-class tastes are advertisements that are individual in tone, witty, sophisticated, stylish, and that offer objects and symbols related to their status and self-expressive pursuits.[50]

Shopping Behavior

In retail store selection, social class determines to some degree where people prefer to shop. Martineau discovered that lower status women were quite aware they would be punished for shopping in a high status store.[51]

"The clerks treat you like a crumb," one woman expressed it. After trying to be waited on, another woman bitterly complained that she was loftily told, "We thought you were a clerk."

Thus, the same products and brands may be purchased in different places by members of different social classes. Lower-class women are the most impulsive about shopping, and the least organized. They like to shop as an excuse to get out of the house, and prefer retail stores where they can find easy credit and a friendly reception.[52] Lower middle-class women, according to Levy, "work" more at their shopping. They display more anxiety about it and find the decision-making process fraught with uncertainties. They are particularly oriented toward finding the best buys for their money and are more likely than other groups to shop comparatively. Upper middle-class women manage their shopping excursions more purposefully than women of lower status. They are more knowledgeable about what they want, know where to look for it, and cover a wider range of territory in their shopping than other women.[53] The upper middle class goes shopping more often than other groups and are more inclined to favor stores with "pleasant" environments.

Department stores maintain images, and consumers will choose the store that seems most appropriate to their social status for the bulk of their purchases. Although any store attracts customers from all social strata, shopping patterns differ among the classes.[54] An upper middle-class shopper may fight the crowds at a discount house for low-visibility products such as home appliances, but she probably wouldn't be caught buying her jewelry there. Lower status people may find themselves in Neiman-Marcus or Bergdorf Goodman, but probably just to buy gifts. Food chains are also characterized by Levy as varying in status appeal.[55]

Purchasing Hard Goods

People may express class membership when they buy automobiles, furniture, and appliances. Peters reports that "overprivileged" members of a social class (those with greater income than other members of that class) flaunt more medium-sized and luxury cars. "Average income" families in all social classes, he claims, own more foreign, intermediate, or economy cars than would be expected.[56]

Laumann and House discovered that traditional home furnishings were preferred by the established WASPS of the upper-upper class, while non-Anglo Saxons with an eye toward upward mobility leaned toward expensive contemporary furnishings.[57]

Lower-class housewives, Sommers learned, express themselves through the appliances they owned, rather than products such as clothing.[58]

Enjoying Leisure

Not surprisingly, leisure activities were found to vary with class membership. Bowling, television, and boxing were identified by Bishop and Ikeda as lower-class pursuits, while tennis, ice skating, and bridge drew upper-class participants.[59] These authors suggest that time may be a factor in leisure preferences—most activities enjoyed by upper-strata people were less time-consuming than lower-strata choices. They also indicate that lower status individuals were less inclined to "work" at leisure. Television, bingo, and the like do not require great spurts of energy, while tennis and ice skating are more active and participatory. This may reflect a desire to escape routine, which for lower-class people probably means physical labor and for upper-class individuals some form of brain work.[60]

Using Credit Cards

This subject area provides an interesting contrast between so-called "lifestyle" research and traditional social class studies.

Using psychographic techniques, Plummer investigated the relationships between lifestyle patterns and heavy bank charge card usage.[61] Findings were reported for both men and women who charged purchases on Mastercharge and BankAmericard accounts. The male users indicated active, upper-income, urban orientations in line with their income and educational status. They tended to belong to several organizations, considered reading a source of information and entertainment, and expressed willingness to take risks in buying decisions. Female users also reported lively, upper-income life styles and concern with appearance, plus the added dimension of a fantasy orientation about travel, luxury items, and self-aspirations. The women's interests outside the home, risk-taking, and perceptions of themselves as managers of their purchases were consistent with male responses. Both men and women reflected attitudes, interests, and opinions that could be characterized as contemporary rather than traditional.

Plummer's findings contribute some new insights to those gained from earlier studies by Mathews and Slocum. These researchers concluded that members of lower social classes tended to use their cards for installment buying while upper-class individuals used them for convenience. They also indicated that upper-class purchasers were inclined to use their cards for luxury items, whereas lower income users bought durables or essentials with their charge cards.[62]

Plummer's study reinforces the profile of heavy users as high-income, "upscale" people, but points out that credit cards are used by many segments of the population. Plummer also suggests that habitual charge card users are best characterized as having a contemporary state of mind and rejecting conservative, traditional concepts—a viewpoint that may also cut across the class hierarchy. In addition, he notes that a definition of luxury purchases must be seen in the context of particular life styles and roles, not broadly categorized for all groups.[63]

Thus, there are products and services that may lend themselves to market segmentation by social class. As the study of consumer behavior grows more sophisticated, research will determine whether the stratification concept "pays for itself" as a useful tool for marketers.

Summary

Stratification of American society creates social classes—large groups of people sharing approximately the same life styles who are ranked according to social prestige. Class membership is determined on the basis of occupation, artifacts, association, and influence. Classes themselves are measured empirically through reputational, subjective, and objective techniques. The most popular models of American class structure provide for five or six distinct social strata. In recent years, however, divisions have become somewhat blurred by the spread of affluence and rapid social change. Social class appears to determine buying behavior for some products and services, and may be useful as a basis for market segmentation.

NOTES

1. Karl Marx and Frederick Engels, *Manifesto of the Communist Party* (New York: International Publishers, 1932).

2. Kingsley Davis, *Human Society* (New York: The Macmillan Co., 1949), pp. 366–68.

3. Joseph A. Kuhl, *The American Class Structure* (New York: Holt, Rinehart and Winston, 1967).

4. Kuhl, *Class Structure*.

5. Egon E. Bergel, *Social Stratification* (New York: McGraw-Hill Book Co., 1962).

6. Sidney J. Levy, "Social Class and Consumer Behavior," in *Buyer Behavior*, ed. John A. Howard and Lynn E. Ostlund (New York: Alfred A. Knopf, 1973).

7. Levy, "Social Class."

8. Warner, as cited in Kuhl, *Class Structure*.

9. Arun K. Jain, "A Method for Investigating and Representing Implicit Social Class Theory," *Journal of Consumer Research*, Vol. 2, No. 1 (June 1975), p. 53.

10. Richard Centers, *The Psychology of Social Classes* (Princeton, New Jersey: Princeton University Press, 1949).

11. W. Lloyd Warner, Marchia Meeker, and Kenneth Eels, *Social Class in America* (Chicago: Science Research Associates, 1949).

12. A. B. Hollingshead, *Elmtown's Youth* (New York: John Wiley and Sons, 1949).

13. James M. Carman, "The Application of Social Class in Market Segmentation," (Berkeley, Calif.: Institute of Business and Economic Research, 1965).

14. Pierre Martineau, "Social Classes and Spending Behavior," *Journal of Marketing*, Volume 23 (October 1968).

15. Harold M. Hodges, "Peninsula People: Social Stratification in a Metropolitan Complex," in *Permanence and Change in Social Class*, ed. W. Clayton Lang (Cambridge, Mass.: Schenkman Publishing Co., 1968). See also Harold M. Hodges, *Underdogs and Middle Americans* 2nd Edition (Morningside, New Jersey: General Learning Press, 1976).

16. Hodges, "Peninsula People," p. 5.

17. Kuhl, *Class Structure*, p. 116.

18. Hodges, "Peninsula People," p. 5.

19. Hodges, "Peninsula People," p. 7.

20. G. W. Domhoff, *Who Rules America?* (New York: Spectrum Books, 1967), p. 5.

21. Hodges, "Peninsula People," p. 15.

22. Coleman and Newgarten, *Social Status in the City*, (San Francisco: Jossey-Bass, 1971).

23. Hodges, "Peninsula People," p. 20.

24. From Warner, *Social Class* and Hodges, "Peninsula People."

25. William H. Peters, "Relative Occupational Class Income: A Significant Variable in the Marketing of Automobiles," *Journal of Marketing*, No. 34 (April 1970), p. 74.

26. R. Eugene Klippel and John F. Monoky, "A Potential Segmentation Variable for Marketers: Relative Occupational Class Income," *Journal of the Academy of Marketing Science*, Vol. 2, No. 2 (Spring 1974), p. 351.

27. W. Clayton Lane, *Permanence and Change in Social Class* (Cambridge, Mass.: Schenkman Publishing Co., 1968).

28. Tom Wolfe, *Radical Chic and Mau-Mauing the Flak Catchers* (New York: Farrar, Straus and Giroux, 1970).

29. Harold W. Berkman and Christopher C. Gilson, "Schools of the Super-Affluent," Unpublished pilot study, C. W. Post Center of L.I.U., Greenvale, N.Y., 1976.

30. S. D. Feldman and G. W. Thielbar, *Life Styles: Diversity in American Society* (Boston, Mass.: Little, Brown and Co., 1972).

31. R. A. Nisbet, "The Decline and Fall of Social Class," *Traditional Revolt*, ed. R. A. Nisbet (New York: Random House, 1968).

32. Tom Wolfe, "The Me Decade," *New York*, 23 August 1976.

33. Peter L. Berger and Brigette Berger, "The Blueing of America," *The New Republic*, 3 April 1971.

34. Norval D. Glenn, "Massification vs. Differentiation: Some Trend Data from National Surveys," *Social Forces*, (December 1967).

35. R. G. Simmons and M. Rosenberg, "Functions of Children's Perceptions of the Stratification System," *American Sociological Review*, Vol. 36, No. 2 (April 1971), pp. 235–49.

36. "The Spread of Affluence," *U.S. News and World Report*, June 1970, pp. 16–18.

37. Levy, "Social Class."

38. Kuhl, *Class Structure*, p. 56.

39. William W. Curtis, "Social Class or Income?" *Journal of Marketing*, Vol. 36 (January 1972), p. 67.

40. Chester R. Wasson, "Is it Time to Quit Thinking of Income Classes?" *Journal of Marketing*, Vol. 33 (April 1967) pp. 54–56.

41. J. H. Myers, R. R. Stanton, and A. F. Haug. "Correlates of Buying Behavior: Social Class vs. Income," *Journal of Marketing*, Vol. 35 (October 1971), pp. 8–15.

42. Joseph T. Plummer, "Life Style Patterns and Commercial Bank Credit Card Usage," *Journal of Marketing*, Vol. 35 April 1971 pp. 35–41.

43. Levy, "Social Class," p. 56.

44. Levy, "Social Class," p. 56.

45. Hodges, "Peninsula People," p. 15.

46. Levy, "Social Class," p. 59.

47. Hodges, "Peninsula People," p. 16.

48. Levy, "Social Class," p. 62.

49. Levy, "Social Class," p. 58.

50. Levy, "Social Class," p. 59.

51. Martineau, "Spending Behavior," p. 152.

52. Levy, "Social Class," p. 61.

53. Levy, "Social Class," p. 62.

54. V. Kanti Prasad, "Socioeconomic Product Risk and Patronage Preferences of Retail Shoppers," *Journal of Marketing*, Vol. 39, No. 3 (July 1975).

55. Levy, "Social Class," p. 62.

56. Peters, "Relative Occupational Class Income," p. 75.

57. E. O. Laumann and J. S. House, "Living Room Styles: The Patterning of Material Artifacts in a Modern Urban Community," *Sociology and Social Research*, Vol. 54, No. 3 (April 1970) pp. 321–42.

58. Montrose S. Sommers, "The Use of Product Symbolism to Differentiate Social Strata," *University of Houston Business Review*, Vol. 11 (Fall 1964) pp. 1–102.

59. D. W. Bishop and M. Ikeda, "Status and Role Factors in the Leisure Behavior of Different Occupations," *Sociology and Social Research*, Vol. 54 (January 1970), pp. 190–208.

60. Bishop and Ikeda, "Status and Role," p. 200.

61. Plummer, "Life Style Patterns," p. 41.

62. J. W. Slocum, Jr., and H. L. Mathews, "Social Class and Income as Indicators of Consumer Credit Behavior," *Journal of Marketing*, Vol. 34 (April 1970) pp. 69–74.

63. Plummer, "Life Style Patterns," p. 41.

MARKETING APPLICATIONS

Conclusion 1 *Retail shopping behavior differs along social class lines. Lower strata people are inclined to favor different stores for different products than upper strata consumers.*
Application A store's image should be developed to reflect the people it wishes to attract. Because a store has nurtured a "lower-class" image does not detract from, and, in fact, may enhance, its profitability. One successful marketer of low-cost appliances in the New York area used to appear in his own commercials wearing a hardhat, shouting that the "way below retail" prices in his stores were available "only to union members and their families." Catering to consumers in the lower strata was the formula behind today's successful discount chain stores. And the advertising, store layout, personnel, and pricing of these chains should be studied carefully as guidelines for retailers who wish to reach lower-strata retail shoppers.

Conclusion 2 *Consumer patterns of exposure to media and susceptibility to advertising messages are related to class membership.*
Application In designing communication for any given product or service, it is important to find out what social class profile is associated with the target market. For reasons that reflect generally greater intelligence, education, and sensitivity to stimulus differences, upper-strata people respond to more subtle appeals than people at the other end of the spectrum. It is possible to "upscale" a product by changing the advertising messages, although the process may take some time if the product is too closely associated with lower-strata consumption. One car manufacturer attempted for years to upgrade its image by introducing more expensive models and running more sophisticated ads. But the approach was unsuccessful because the name had become firmly established as a low-end product which middle-class consumers were reluctant to be seen driving during the status-conscious 1950s.

Conclusion 3 *The products which are purchased to lend prestige differ by social class.*
Application Consumers in lower-class households tend to view expensive kitchen appliances as a source of status. This is related to the home and kitchen-centered nature of socializing. Upper-strata people are less concerned with owning the newest and highest-priced refrigerator with special features like a built-in ice-water dispenser. To a marketer of kitchen appliances, this is an important consideration in how top of the-line models are designed and promoted.

ASSIGNMENTS

Research Assignment

Background   Student Marketdata, Inc., a research organization specializing in campus polls, has been commissioned to investigate college students' perceptions of occupational prestige. The client, Worldwide Publishing, produces textbooks for business and professional students and requires this information for new textbook development. Worldwide's marketing department has formed an untested hypothesis that perceptions of occupational prestige have changed considerably over the past few years. Therefore, the client is specifically interested in comparing the responses of business school seniors with those of business school freshmen.

Research Input   In 1963, Hodge, Seigel and Rossi obtained prestige ratings for 90 different occupations. Student Marketdata has decided to use 25 of these occupations in their study:

OCCUPATION	ORIGINAL RANK*	NEW RANK**
Physician	2	1
College professor	8	2
Lawyer	11	3
Dentist	14	4.5
Architect	14	4.5
Psychologist	17.5	7
Minister	17.5	7
Member of the board of directors of a large corporation	17.5	7
Banker	24.5	9
Sociologist	26	10
Captain in the regular army	27.5	11
Accountant for a large business	29.5	12.5
Public school teacher	29.5	12.5
Building contractor	31.5	14
Artist who paints pictures exhibited in galleries	34.5	16
Musician in a symphony orchestra	34.5	16
Author of novels	34.5	16
Policeman	47	18
Reporter on a daily paper	48	19
Insurance agent	51.5	20
Machine operator in a factory	62.5	21
Singer in a nightclub	74	22

Filling station attendant	75	23
Taxi driver	80.5	24
Bartender	83	25

*Among the original 90 occupations
**25 occupations condensed for this study

Source: Robert W. Hodge, Paul M. Seigel, and Peter H. Rossi, "Occupational Prestige in the United States: 1925–1963", in Reinhard Bendix and Seymour Martin Lipset (eds.) Class, Status and Power, 2nd edition (New York: Free Press, 1966), pp. 324–325.

Methodology Each researcher duplicates the list above and selects two subjects: one business school freshman and one senior. Subjects are tested individually, both instructed to order the occupations on the list from 1 to 25 as to *prestige* or *status*. Subjects are to indicate the order of prestige by placing a corresponding number from 1 to 25 next to each occupation. Of course, the higher the number, the lower the status of the occupation.

Researchers then pool their data and perform the following statistical analysis comparison of freshman versus seniors:

For the pooled data, comparisons will be made thus:

(a) freshmen versus seniors

(b) present year (freshmen and seniors combined) versus 1963 rankings

Freshmen vs. Seniors

1. For the freshmen, sum the rankings for each occupation to determine its score. Do the same for the seniors. You can now give a pooled ranking for all the occupations for freshmen and seniors.

Example:	FRESHMAN 1 RANKINGS	FRESHMAN 2 RANKINGS	SENIOR 1 RANKINGS	SENIOR 2 RANKINGS
OCCUPATION 1	1	2	1	3
OCCUPATION 2	4	3	2	2
OCCUPATION 3	2	4	4	1
OCCUPATION 4	3	2	3	4

For this example of 4 students (2 freshmen and 2 seniors) with 4 occupations, we get the following pooled rankings:

	FRESHMEN SCORE	RANK	SCORE	RANK
OCCUPATION 1	3	1	4	1.5 *
OCCUPATION 2	7	4	4	1.5 *
OCCUPATION 3	6	3	5	3
OCCUPATION 4	5	2	7	4

---

*When scores are tied, take the average of the Ranked Positions. Ex.: Ranks 1 and 2 are tied, so average = 1.5 each.

2. Using the *pooled rankings* calculate the *difference between the ranks* for each occupation (ignore sign) and square each difference.

Example:	POOLED FRESHMEN RANKS	POOLED SENIOR RANKS	DIFFERENCE (D)	DIFFERENCE SQD (D²)
OCCUPATION 1	1	1.5	.5	.25
OCCUPATION 2	4	1.5	2.5	6.25
OCCUPATION 3	3	3	0	0
OCCUPATION 4	2	4	2.0	4.0
			$\Sigma D^2 =$	10.50

3. Add up the squared differences (ΣD^2).
   Example: $\Sigma D^2 = 10.50$, sum of squared differences.
4. If $\Sigma D^2 \geq 1638$, (For this problem, 5200 is maximum value of ΣD^2) the 2 *groups do not agree* on rankings. In fact if $\Sigma D^2 \geq 3563$, the groups tend to rank in opposite order. If $\Sigma D^2 < 1638$, the *groups do agree* on rankings.

Extrapolation   Occupational prestige is the most popular index of social class for research purposes. Discuss the significance of your Marketdata findings for social class. Compare your findings with occupational prestige ratings obtained by Hodge, Seigel, and Rossi for 1963 from a social class perspective. Are social class distinctions breaking down, or are they basically intact?

Creative Assignment

The Marlborough Beach Club is a new California resort that wants to attract affluent consumers to fill its rooms and suites for $150 to $1,200 a day. In addition to luxurious accommodations, the Club offers all resort activities such as golf, tennis, an indoor squash court, a private beach, a yacht basin, an excellent restaurant, and a nightclub.

As Assistant Director of the Club, you are responsible for developing promotional ideas which will reach the kind of clientele who will fit the Club's profile in income and social class associations.

Your ideas might include some unusual services such as helicopter and limousine service from nearby airports, a London hairstylist on the premises, or guest chefs from four-star French restaurants. Come up with a list of ten ideas, and be prepared to support them with what you know of your market.

Managerial Assignment

Milloff's, a Midwestern department store chain, has achieved much success through directing its stores' "image" and merchandise toward consumers at the lower end of the socioeconomic scale. The chain now has a new president who has just succeeded his father. Young Milloff has been trained in retailing at the University of Chicago, is familiar with consumer research, and is aggressively making plans to establish new store locations in other Midwestern cities.

As a Management Trainee in the Milloff corporate organization, you are asked to help put together data that will aid management in selecting new locations. Your specific assignment is to organize the research available on social class and buying behavior (since Milloff was intrigued with social class studies while he was studying for his MBA) in a comprehensive presentation form.

Your analysis should focus on the product buying behavior, media habits, and store selection criteria of consumers in the lower-middle social class and below, since it is this market Milloff's is most successful in reaching. Material may be found on pages 184–187 of the preceding chapter, as well as in Sidney J. Levy, "Social Class and Consumer Behavior," in *On Knowing the Consumer,* ed. Joseph W. Newman, (Chicago: John Wiley and Sons, 1966).

SELECTED READINGS

Foxall, Gordon R. "Social Factors in Consumer Choice: Replication and Extension." *Journal of Consumer Research*, Vol. 2, No. 1 (June 1975), pp. 60–64.

Goldman, Arieh. "Do Lower-Income Consumers Have a More Restricted Shopping Scope?" *Journal of Marketing*, Vol. 40, No. 1 (January 1976), pp. 46–54.

Jain, Arun K. "A Method for Investigating and Representing Implicit Social Class Theory." *Journal of Consumer Research*, Vol. 2, No. 1 (June 1975), pp. 53–59.

Klippel, R. Eugene and John F. Monoky. "A Potential Segmentation Variable for Marketers: Relative Occupational Class Income." *Journal of the Academy of Marketing Science*, Vol. 2, No. 2 (Spring 1974), pp. 351–56.

Prasad, V. Kanti. "Socioeconomic Product Risk and Patronage Preferences of Retail Shoppers." *Journal of Marketing*, Vol. 39, No. 3 (July 1975), pp. 42–47.

OBJECTIVES

1. Discuss *husband and wife influences* on buying decisions. *198*

2. Discuss the *cultural and social* factors in family decision making. *202*

3. Relate the nine stages in the *family life cycle* to consumer needs. *204*

4. Describe the influences on *children's consumption patterns*. *208*

5. Explain how children *learn* to be consumers, develop *brand* loyalties, and establish *media* patterns. *209–210*

6. Discuss children's influence on the family's purchases of *food* and *durables*, and explain the *gatekeeper* role. *212*

7. Discuss the *five questions* that will help determine the family member who dominates any given consumer decision process. *213*

EIGHT

The Family

Focusing on the family as a reference group lets marketers discover two important variables in how consumer choices are made:

• Which family member makes the final purchasing decision.

• Who else gets involved in the process and what they say contribute to the eventual decision.

Neither determination is simple. Many variables enter into each purchasing process where more than one family member becomes involved (which is nearly always the case for considered-purchase products and services).[1]

This chapter offers some guidelines for evaluating the influence of various family members and deciding when information about family decision processes may be most effectively used. Sample topics include:

• Roles members play in making family purchasing decisions.

• The nine stages of a family's life cycle and characteristic buying behavior at each stage.

• How changing family structures will affect consumption.

• How children behave as consumers—media use, brand choice and loyalty.

• Five important questions to help determine which family member will ultimately purchase a given product.

These considerations aid marketers in deciding on the right family member to approach through product development, persuasive communications, media selection, and retail assortments.

A Sociological Look at the Family

Several different groups may affect an individual's behavior, but the family remains the most pervasive and tenacious influence of all. From our first conscious experiences with our environment, the family is present—determining what we see and hear. When we become exposed to other influences as children, the family stays close by to filter our perceptions. And even as mature adults, we apply many of the behavior patterns learned as children to the tasks of interacting with others and, ultimately, to establishing families of our own.

All of us remember some of the earliest purchasing decisions we made with other family members: which brand of cereal, television set, or make of automobile to buy. What we cannot always recognize in our consumption behavior are the subtler influences of family upon our decision making. We regard some products favorably (or unfavorably) because our parents swore by (or at) them. A number of advertising appeals have focused on this theme, associating brands with a message that says, in effect, "Your

mother trusted our detergent, and so should you."

As an individual's primary frame of reference, the family determines the kind of socialization he or she receives. This includes such critical elements as the cultural norms and values the family accepts or rejects, the subcultural influences (if any) it transmits to the individual, and the social class with which the individual identifies. The family also serves as the principal arbiter of individual personality development, governing such variables as early learning environment, birth order differences, and role acceptance.

These factors are instrumental in shaping people's life styles and the products or services reflecting their behavior patterns. In this chapter, the family is analyzed as a *consumption unit*. We will consider how family decision making is influenced by role specialization, cultural and social factors, and the personalities of its members; the family life cycle concept; how children behave as consumers and influence purchasing decisions; ways in which marketers may best utilize information about family consumption.

Family Definitions

All families function as groups, whether they are large aggregates of related people living together or the simple husband-and-wife teams common in our culture.

Cooley describes the family as one type of *primary group* ". . . characterized by face to

face association and cooperation . . . fundamental in forming the social nature and ideas of the individual."[2] In such a group, relationships ideally are marked by mutual commitment, intimacy, and affection. Each family also represents a unit of *social organization* that defines the roles of its members and sets limits upon their behavior.

The family based upon blood relation into which we are born is known as the *consanguine* family (or "family of orientation"). The family formed by marriage is termed the *conjugal* family (or "family of procreation").[3] The *nuclear* family is made up of a conjugal pair and their children. In the United States, the isolated nuclear family long ago replaced the *extended* family, consisting of the nuclear family and their relatives, as the most common mode of living. This occurred simultaneously with the urbanization of America.

The nuclear family retains a large measure of freedom and independence, but demands greater responsibility for the care of children. These heavier responsibilities, coupled with the absence of supportive relatives, leave the isolated family particularly vulnerable to divorce and other disintegrating stresses. This problem has been discussed by sociologists in analyzing limited human resources. Because there are only two adult members in the nuclear family, each is reliant upon the other for cooperation in solving family problems. When serious tensions exist between them, their decision making ability as the responsible family members is severely impaired. And in times of accelerated social change, they may often be unable to draw on personal experience in handling family problems caused by changing norms and behavior.[4]

For our purposes, the isolated nuclear family will be the frame of reference throughout this chapter.

Influences on Family Decision Making

As a consumption unit, the family functions in ways similar to other groups faced with problems to solve and decisions to make. Each member plays some role, not necessarily active, and the relative importance of each may vary according to the kind of product or service under consideration, its cost, and other variables.

In some purchasing behavior, husband and wife perform together with virtually equal weight. Where children are part of the family, their influence may or may not be felt. (The role of children in family purchasing decisions is considered at length later in this chapter.) Because the family is also functioning as a sociological unit, the roles of its members are partially shaped by cultural and social determinants—including the mass culture, subcultural influences, social class, and other reference groups. In addition, each family undergoes a *life cycle* that imposes certain buying expectations at various stages. Finally, the personalities of family members themselves may exert a notable influence on purchasing decisions.

Cultural Influence

In Section 2 the impact of the dominant culture and various subcultures in the United States were analyzed for purposes of market segmentation. Both anthropological concepts offer insights into the consumption patterns of families.

Mass Culture The fundamental values of

our culture stress social and occupational mobility, education, organized religion, and conventional marriage with the goal of having children. But these values are being modified, with emphasis increasing on leisure, personal religious experiences, and experimentation with different conjugal styles. These *emerging* values have changed the structure of families dramatically.

One major development is a spiraling divorce rate that leaves many children with single parents, most often mothers. Because women are finding greater career opportunities, working mothers are spending less time with their children. Youngsters are entrusted to nursery schools or day care centers at an earlier age. There is also a marked trend toward fewer children; smaller families can devote more of their resources, emotional and financial, to each child. And growing numbers of couples are deciding to postpone having children indefinitely, which vastly increases their discretionary income.

All of these patterns are expected to continue for some time, meaning that less emphasis will be placed on traditional child-rearing practices in the future. Thus, children may be expected to learn fewer of their values from parents and more from educational institutions and their peer groups. While children are becoming more susceptible to educational influences, the nature of education itself is changing. Traditional modes of instruction— such as making children memorize data to pass tests— are disappearing as more value is placed on learning to question intelligently and to solve problems.

Specialization of Roles Our cultural values have also emphasized specific, discrete roles for men and women. Kenkel observes that men in our culture learn "goal directed" beha-

vior, while women learn "emotional" and "expressive" roles. This would suggest that husbands wield more influence in relating products to family needs and women concern themselves more with aesthetic features.[5] Actually, purchasing influence is largely situational and varies according to the product or service considered. *Husbands* traditionally have dominated most of the purchasing discussions about automobiles,[6] tires, radios, record players, and photographic equipment.[7] *Wives* have dominated the decision making process about washing machines, sewing machines, vacuum cleaners, rugs and carpets, pet foods, frozen juice, and toothpaste.[8] In these instances, the person who uses the product most heavily is likely to control the choice process.[9] In shopping for services, the same relationship holds true. Husbands usually choose the family automobile insurance agent, while wives are more likely to select supermarkets. *Collective*, or joint, decision making between husband and wife is more frequent when the step is a major one—buying a home,[10] large appliances, life insurance, and making *final* purchase decisions about automobiles are examples.[11]

However, these traditional patterns may be changing. As more women enter on their own careers and contribute significantly to the family income, role differences may be moderated. Husbands are gradually learning some of the homemaking skills formerly the sole province of women and wives are revealing greater concern about how *their* money is spent. Research suggests that women who see themselves as more liberated tend to make *more* purchase decisions than women who view their role as the more traditional housewife. Conversely, the husbands of the more assertive women make fewer purchasing decisions than the husbands of the more homebound ones.

Husband-Wife Involvement in Family Decision Making

Most of the studies probing family decision making have focused on just husband and wife. The most recent research has attempted to identify family money management patterns and the degree of each partner's involvement in buying decisions.

Who Handles the Money?   How a family saves, spends, and invests its resources indicates a great deal about its consumer behavior. Ferber has, in fact, divided all family economic decisions into financial and consumer choices as the basis of his own decision making model.[12] This model reveals how a family's objectives and attitudes influence its financial decisions, and how handling of its assets will come to affect future objectives (Figure 8-1).

Figure 8 1   Interrelation of saving and spending decisions.

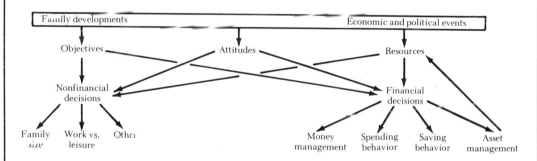

Source: R. Ferber, "Family Decision Making and Economic Behavior" in Family Economic Behavior: Problems and Prospects, *ed. E.B. Sheldon, (Philadelphia: J.B. Lippincott Company, 1973), p. 31. Reprinted by permission of the publisher.*

Delving further into the American family's financial affairs, Ferber and Lee devised the useful segmentation concept "Family Financial Officer" (FFO for short). They used this concept to study young married couples and discovered two interesting patterns:[13]
1. Most couples act jointly as FFO immediately after marriage, then shift to a single FFO— usually the wife.
2. Where the husband becomes FFO, the couple can be expected to save *more* of its income and invest more of its assets in real estate and negotiable securities (Table 8-1).

Because role specialization appears to be more complex than was originally believed and roles change throughout the choice process, marketers who wish to address decision makers should consider:
1. Who will *initiate* the choice process?

Table 8-1 Percent of Couples Owning Selected Assets by Identity of FFO

	IDENTITY OF FFO		
ASSET	HUSBAND	WIFE	BOTH
	OWNERSHIP OF ASSET		
Savings accounts	83%	78%	69%
Government bonds	17	24	22
Insurance	87	84	89
Marketable securities	28	14	26
Real estate	64	53	55
	DISTRIBUTION OF PORTFOLIO		
Savings accounts	9%	7%	9%
Government bonds	*	1	*
Insurance	10	17	17
Marketable securities	3	17	5
Real estate	79	58	69
Total	100%	100%	100%

*Less than 0.5 percent.

Source: Robert Ferber and Lucy Chao Lee, "Husband-Wife Influence in Family Purchasing Behavior," Journal of Consumer Research, Vol. 1 (June 1974). Reprinted by permission of the American Marketing Association.

2. Who will dominate the *search* process?

3. Who will make *price* decisions?

4. Who will make the *final* purchasing choice?

5. Who will actually make the *purchase*?

Who Really Makes the Decisions?   There are three important guidelines to understanding who dominates decision processes and makes the final choices, according to Davis:[14]

1. Husband-wife involvement varies widely by product category.

2. Husband-wife involvement within any product category varies with the specific decision at hand.

3. Husband-wife involvement is likely to be quite different for different families.

Davis and Rigaux investigated the decision roles of husbands and wives in Belgian families. On that basis they classified purchasing choices as Husband-Dominant, Wife-Dominant, Autonomic (usually involving just one party), and Syncratic (usually made by both parties).[15]

Their model, Figure 8-2, indicates who is likely to govern choices of a wide range of products.

Figure 8-2 Extent of role specialization in family decision making.

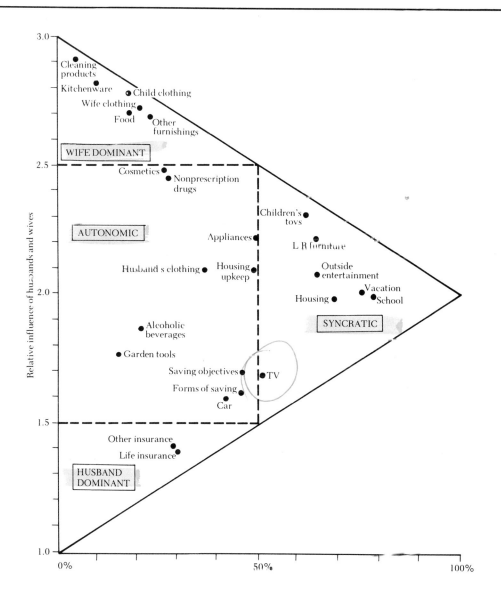

Subcultures   As outlined in chapter 5, diversity in American culture creates widely different purchasing patterns across subcultural groups. These differences tend to affect family purchasing decisions.

Ethnic subcultural investigations suggest that black families lean toward mother and grandmother dominance; thus women here may wield more purchasing clout than in white families. Japanese-American families are reported to be dominated by husbands, who make virtually all the important decisions.[16] The Mexican-American subculture also seems to be male-dominant for consumption purposes.[17] But there is some evidence that subcultural influences in family role specialization diminish with assimilation into the larger culture.

Religious subcultural values may also help shape family buying behavior. For example, members of the Mormon church do not smoke, gamble, or drink tea, coffee, or alcoholic beverages. In addition, they are expected to maintain a year's supply of food, clothing, and other essentials in case of some catastrophe and to offer an annual tithe to their church equal to 10 percent of family income.[18] Other religious faiths impose similar sanctions on the use of certain products, which may increase a family's discretionary income for other purposes.

Regional subcultural patterns also affect the ways in which a family will spend its money. Climate dictates housing and clothing consumption to some degree and regional convention helps to influence fashion consciousness and product use. A California family may consider their swimming pool an absolute recreational and social necessity, while a Midwestern family would balk at such extravagance. In some large cities middle-class parents view the public school system with alarm and consider private education for their children an expensive fact of life. *Urban* areas

in general are more appealing to childless families, whereas *suburbs* are almost overrun with children. In *rural* areas, wives are reported to exert less overall influence on buying decisions than their husbands.[19] This probably results from a more traditional observance of role specialization and the limited opportunities for women in those areas to pursue their own careers.

Social Influence

Beyond cultural determinants, societal influences come into play when families make consumer decisions. The two major sociological variables are (1) social class membership and (2) other reference groups.

Social Class   Because social class is related to the amount of money a family has and its perceived status in the community, the impact of this variable may override other group influences. The life style a family maintains is almost always tied to class membership, especially for socially mobile families striving to better their position through occupational attainment and consumption patterns. But virtually all families look to their peers in the same social stratum for purchasing information.

In role playing and decision making, lower-strata wives tend to make a greater number of purchasing decisions for their families than do middle-class wives. In middle-class families, husbands and wives are more inclined to reach buying decisions jointly, while in upper-strata families the husband seems to dominate.[20] Komarovsky contrasts the attitudes toward money management and consumption she uncovered in lower-class neighborhoods with those of the middle class:[21]

At one pole stands a working-class family. . . The wife paid the rent, insurance and food bills and bought all the food and household sundries for the home. She also set aside regular amounts for clothing, loan payments, and Christmas Clubs. Husbands for the most part did not know how much housekeeping money was spent. This was evident from the number of married men interviewed who had to turn to their wives for information about rent, insurance, and sums spent on coal. Women talk of financial arrangements between themselves and their children as though the husband was not a party to them at all . . . In contrast to this stands what has become known as the "companionship" marriage. In such families, the division of labor between the spouses is more flexible; there is less division and more direct cooperation instead. There is more consultation on . . . decisions and more communication of personal feelings . .

Social class also influences the leisure activities a family will pursue and determines which family members will participate. At the lower end of the scale, husbands and wives are reported to enjoy their leisure independently, because wives are busy with household duties and their husbands would rather spend recreation time with other men.[22] Middle-class husbands and wives spend more time together in recreational activities, and there seems to be a slight decline in husband-wife participation in the upper classes.[23]

As discussed in chapter 7, class membership affects family purchasing of clothing, automobiles, and home furnishings. These are all visible items of social prestige and their selection reflects the social position a family perceives itself as holding. In service consumption, financial investments such as stocks, bonds, and real estate are generally middle- and upper-class phenomena. Services such as Beneficial Finance and Greyhound bus travel are most often associated with low-strata families. When selecting media, marketers should take into account lower-strata families' heavier television viewing and the significantly higher magazine readership among middle- and upper-class families.

Other Reference Groups Families also consume products and services according to their own parents' way of making purchasing decisions, their friends' consumption behavior, and husbands' and wives' associations with peers in work organizations.

To some degree, all families reflect the buying behavior that husband and wife learned from their *respective parents*. This becomes particularly evident in role specialization. Where a husband's father assumed an authoritative role, we may expect that husband to follow that model with his conjugal family. If his wife learned her role-playing behavior in a similar father-dominant family, it is even more likely that family decisions will bear a strong male influence. With more and more women seeking careers, however, traditional roles become somewhat blurred, requiring adjustment on the part of males who feel a strong need to control. Many children are now being raised by parents who both work, and their models predispose them to greater equality in decision making. This equality is expected to predominate among all social strata as these young people mature and establish conjugal relationships.

Families receive important consumption cues from their close *friends and acquaintances*. The "keeping up with the Joneses" cliché born during the 1950s has not lost its relevance—families still like to maintain a life style comparable with that of their peers. Pity the parents who cannot afford the same summer camp their children's friends will be enjoying. More families are regarding travel as a form of leisure to be shared with friends, and will readily plan to go camping with other families or fly on a group tour to some exotic beach. In making major purchases such as appliances, a car, or a house, families look to their friends for buying information and advice. They are also attuned to the clothing fashions and other new products adopted by their peer group. Wives who shop with friends exchange product information on even the most incidental packaged goods purchases, and husbands considering some male-oriented purchase such as an outboard motor swap technical information with their friends. Marketers providing family services like life insurance and mutual funds recognize the value of a referral from a prospective customer's close friend or neighbor and use these contacts extensively when making calls.

Work associations are also reference groups possibly influencing family purchases. Some large corporations tacitly encourage homogeneous life styles for white collar employees, especially in dress, housing, and entertainment. In most tightly structured organizations that have given birth to "company towns," executives associate with each other socially and consume the products and services that augment their company way of life. In less formal and demanding organizations, workers may still receive cues as to which styles of consumption are deemed appropriate for a given occupation or job level; clothing is the most common example. Some executives and salesmen have grown so accustomed to expense-account living that they overspend their own incomes precariously to maintain the high-rolling business life style.

The Family Life Cycle

The members of a conventional nuclear family go through a number of stages in the course of their lives known as the *life cycle*. This concept has been developed by a number of researchers and a summary of their findings appears here. (See John B. Lansing and Leslie Kish, "Family Life Cycle as an Independent Variable," *American Sociological Review*, October 1957, pp. 512–19; and William D. Wells and George Gubar, "The Life Cycle Concept in Marketing Research," *Journal of Marketing Research*, Volume 3, November 1966, pp. 355–63).

Stage 1: Single Phase   While not all young unmarried individuals are swinging singles, their consumption patterns lean toward personal care items, clothing, an apartment, a car, and whatever leisure and entertainment facilities are available to them. (A more detailed description of singles' life styles appears in chapter 5.)

Stage 2: The Newlywed Game   Once two singles have found each other and wed, both may continue their careers and enjoy a relatively large aggregate income. Without children, they are free to spend their money on furniture, appliances, clothing, and housing, and to invest a portion of their income to build a reserve for the future. They may also travel and devote much of their nonoccupational time to leisure pursuits. (Many young couples are now recognizing the advantages of the newlywed stage and prolonging it; some even decide to do without children altogether.) Families at this stage are frequent targets for marketers of real estate, insurance, and other "newlywed services" as well as luxury and entertainment goods and services.

Stage 3: Expanding I   This stage commences when the couple have their first child and ends when the youngest child becomes six years of age. The first child dramatically alters consumption patterns as the family moves to a larger apartment or buys a house and begins assembling the paraphernalia young children require. Physicians' bills are only one consideration; others are furnishings for the child's room and an assortment of baby items such as carriages, toys, baby food, babysitting services, and medications. At this point, the family is usually no longer so financially secure as it was in the newlywed stage. Each new baby demands most of the same expenditures, and the growing children continue to need clothing, food, and toys.

Stage 4: Expanding II   The family's youngest child is now six or over and child-oriented purchases continue. But the family's financial status may have improved somewhat. As the husband's career progresses, his salary is rising and the family may once again receive extra income if the wife returns to work. Now the parents may begin saving for their children's education and make longterm financial plans.

Stage 5: Contracting   At this stage of family life, children are well into adolescence, and consumption patterns reveal the heavy expenses of supporting teenagers. Clothing costs, as well as educational expenditures and allowances, are high. The husband's salary has increased and his wife has probably returned to her own career, so aggregate family income continues to rise. Now there may be enough money for luxuries such as home redecoration or a second car; however, financial planning becomes particularly acute as children approach college age.

Stage 6: Post-parental, Childless   The children have left home, no longer dependent on their parents, and family income may again be spent solely on husband and wife. This stage marks the period of greatest financial security, since both parents' incomes have peaked. Purchases now include travel and leisure pursuits, as they did during the newlywed stage. Money may also be allocated for home decorating, an automobile, and new appliances.

Because retirement is not too far away, the couple may now think seriously of protective investments with which to support themselves.

Stage 7: Childless, Older Married   Once the husband retires, any financial cornucopia enjoyed during the post-parental, childless stage becomes negligible. Yet if the wife continues to work, family income is still satisfactory. At this juncture, the couple may decide to relocate in a smaller home or apartment. Expenditures reflect a pattern of aging as more is spent on health care.

Stage 8: The Working Lone Survivor   Usually the lone survivor is the wife, who continues to work until retirement and earns a reasonably good income to support just herself. Health purchases increase, but discretionary income is now spent almost solely on leisure and entertainment.

Stage 9: The Retired Lone Survivor   Out of the work force, the lone survivor must now concentrate on making ends meet with a smaller fixed income. This may come from a pension, Social Security, and interest on investments. An increasing number of retired people are also finding part-time work to supplement their income. Eventually, the lone survivor must confront the reality of aging, and move to a retirement community or nursing home. Medical expenses now demand a large portion of income, and the unique problems of the aging in the United States, loneliness and a feeling of uselessness, no doubt emerge.

It is probably evident that the family life cycle described here applies for the most part to relatively affluent middle-class families. Many lower-strata families never realize such comfortable growth in income over the years or share the same option to retire to a warm climate. Also, the life cycle stages may be upset by such common occurrences as divorce and remarriage or the premature death of one spouse. But as a general schema for marketing decisions, the life cycle concept serves as a valid basis of segmentation when weighed with such variables as social class, subcultural influences, and demographic data.

Personality Traits of Family Members

An important variable in how a family behaves as a unit is its members' individual behavior. The concept of personality will be developed more fully in chapter 11, but two family-related characteristics affecting decision making are discussed briefly here: birth order differences and conformity orientation.

Birth Order Differences Research in social psychology indicates that individuals may develop certain traits as the result of their birth order in the consanguine family. These characteristics, listed below, remain with a person to maturity and influence even a parent's "role playing" with his or her conjugal family:[24]

1. Firstborns exhibit less confidence in tasks than those born later.

2. Firstborns show stronger susceptibility to influence by others than do those born later.

3. Younger siblings express a greater need to have their anxiety reduced by others (especially parents) than do first children.

To translate these conclusions to the family decision-making front, we might expect a firstborn family member to hold less confidence in his or her ability to make correct buying decisions. The same individual may also be more susceptible to influence by others whose confidence is manifest. A family member born later might exude greater confi-

dence, but would simultaneously feel the need to have decisions approved by whoever is perceived as the "parent." In this way, anxiety over the decision-making task would be reduced.

Conformity Orientation In small group tasks such as family buying decisions, conforming behavior seems to be related to certain personality traits. For example:[25]

1. Persons with low self-esteem tend to conform more readily than others.

2. For persons who conform compulsively, conformity behavior reduces anxiety.

3. Individuals who could be described as "authoritarian personalities" (characterized by conventionalism, submission, destructiveness, and strong parent needs) tend to exhibit more conformity behavior than others.

Barron distinguishes conformity oriented individuals (Yielders) from nonconformists (Independents) on the basis of these traits:[26]

Independents see themselves primarily as original, emotional, and artistic. Yielders characterize themselves as obliging, optimistic, efficient, determined, patient, and kind. Yielders tend to be practical-minded, somewhat physicalistic in their thinking, and group oriented; Independents placed higher values on creativity, close interpersonal relations, and the individual as opposed to the group.

Thus, one or more members of the family may exhibit strong predispositions to be influenced by others regardless of their private feelings. They may feel that by asserting themselves they will suffer a loss of esteem or increase their anxiety. The more pragmatic family members may be more subject to influence than those who maintain strong individual and original biases.

Children and Family Consumption

To this point, our discussion has focused mainly upon husband and wife in the family decision making processes. But, as the family life cycle concept illustrates, the presence of children alters consumption patterns dramatically as spending shifts from adult-centered to child-oriented purchases. Kenkel notes that the appearance of children tends to reduce the amount of joint decision making because new roles are created, the set of interaction patterns becomes more complex, and the egalitarian nature of family role structure may be subdued when husband and wife accept the more directive "parent" roles.[27]

Children affect family consumption in a number of ways. For one, they are *expensive dependents* whose long-term needs must be anticipated and provided for until they are able to support themselves. The total cumulative cost for an *upper middle-class* family of raising a child today from conception to graduation has been estimated at $188,949 for a male and $200,713 for a female.[28] Secondly, older children are *key family members* whose preferences are usually taken into account when major purchases are contemplated. And finally, children are *independent consumers* themselves, buying specific kinds of products on their own. The range of these purchases becomes larger and more diverse as children grow older. (See Table 8-2.)

Styles of child-rearing have changed markedly over the last few decades. Among the trends identified by social psychologist Urie Bronfenbrenner are:[29]

1. A tendency toward greater permissiveness and less authoritarian control that extends across all social classes.

2. Increased emphasis on indirect means of control such as rational discussion rather than direct means such as scolding or physical punishment.

3. A readiness to express affection more freely with children and encourage them to be expressive in return.

4. Declining differences among the social classes in child-rearing practices, which have

Table 8-2   The High Cost of Childhood

STAGE IN LIFE CYCLE	MALE	FEMALE
Conception to age 1	$ 5,462	$ 5,402
Babyhood: ages 1 through 5	25,540	25,540
Childhood: ages 6 through 11	55,807	56,938
Adolescence: ages 12 through 17	54,389	56,282
College: ages 18 through 21	47,751	56,551
TOTAL	$188,949	$200,713

Source: Adapted from "The High Cost of Children" by Terry Clifford, Esquire *(March 1974), pp. 119–121). Reprinted by permission of* Esquire *magazine.* © *1974 by Esquire, Inc.*

veered toward the middle-class techniques described here.

5. Changing roles of parents, reflected in less authoritarian and more affectionate fathers, and more disciplinarian mothers—a move away from the "wait until your father gets home" school of discipline.

These trends are generally indicative of the child oriented home which has become prevalent in our culture. And the importance we place upon the happiness of our children exerts a hefty influence upon a family's purchasing patterns.

This section investigates the roles of children as members of the family consumption unit and as independent consumers—the influences that shape their buying behavior, how they behave in the market place, and how they affect family decision making.

Influences on Children's Behavior

As children, we form the primary attitudes and values that shape our consumer behavior as adults. Influencing the formation of these basics are such variables as parent and peer group inputs, social class and subcultural considerations, and sex differences.

Parents versus Peer Groups   Popular wisdom has it that children rely less on parents and more on their peer group for behavioral models as they reach their teen years. Peer group functions are described as two-fold: (1) to enable the individual to develop a clear self-identity in relationships with others and (2) to fulfill the individual's physical, social, and psychological needs.[30] Research into parent as opposed to peer influences suggests that even as peer pressure increases with age,

parental influence may still be an overriding factor.

In a study of children from the fourth to tenth grades, an increasing tendency to associate with the peer group and, to a lesser degree, accept its values as norms could be noted each year. However, a decline in orientation to the family was *not* an inevitable outcome. Only in cases marked by poor adjustment among family members did this orientation diminish. Also, peer and family orientations were hardly mutually exclusive, but as children spend more *time* with their peers, they spend less time in relationships with family members.[31] Other research indicates that high school students are not less concerned with their parents' approval than elementary school students are.[32] As a matter of fact, in purchases of clothing, sports equipment, small appliances, and some food products, 16- to 19-year-olds were influenced to a greater degree by parents than friends.[33]

Whether children lean toward parents or peers in decision making depends on the problem context. Adolescents see peers as competent judges in some areas of conduct, and parents in others. In matters such as taste in clothes and feelings about school, a sample of adolescent girls was more inclined to reflect peer pressure. When the same girls were questioned about an adult role-playing situation (for example, reporting someone who had destroyed property), they adopted parent-favored alternatives.[34] Another study points out that children comply with parents over peers when choices are considered difficult and important.[35] Although parents are more influential in serious matters, in most purchases that children make as independent consumers, such as clothing, candy, and entertainment, peers seem to exert more influence over their behavior.[36]

Differences between parents and peers are

also affected by the youngster's sex. Peer groups seem to be more important to boys and wield more influence over their behavior, while girls exhibit a tendency to see peer groups as a source of friends and intimate relationships.[37]

Social Class and Subcultural Differences Within the overall attitudes listed on p. 208, the treatment children receive from their parents and the attitudes they form vary according to their social class. In lower-strata families, children are given more freedom relative to their age in buying clothes, making doctors' appointments, and deciding whom they will date as adolescents. Children from middle-class families revealed that, while their parents give them more credit for good judgment, they are subject to greater supervision in their activities—including what they buy.[38]

Subcultural influences have been discovered along ethnic and regional dimensions. Black children, as reported in many studies, suffer from a deprecatory self-image, a lack of black awareness, discrimination, a relatively high degree of family instability, and undereducation.[39] But with the growth of a black middle class (described in chapter 5), deprivation is becoming less a part of the black experience. On the other hand, children of more recently established subcultures such as Mexican-American groups may suffer discrimination in social contact with children of the dominant subculture.[40]

A number of *regional subcultural* studies have been conducted with rural youth to determine whether they behave differently from urban and suburban youth. As portrayed in the findings, adolescents living in rural areas are less likely than urban youth to approve of teenage drinking and smoking. Young people living on *farms* are said to be even more traditional and intolerant of permissiveness than other rural adolescents. These differences are due primarily to family background, in that rural families usually live on low incomes and in sparsely populated areas with limited access to products and services. Rural families are also likely to belong to religious subcultures of an emotional and Evangelical bent. They are often forbidden to smoke, drink, or sample other small vices enjoyed throughout the land, and may easily develop a rigid, nonmobile orientation.[41]

Sex Differences The role specialization of males and females still so much a part of our culture begins early in childhood. When parents select toys for young children, they still tend to buy dolls for little girls and junior sports equipment for little boys. This consumption behavior is deeply ingrained and, though changing, will be with us for some time.

All these variables set a general context for the range of childrens' behavior. But marketers are specifically interested in how children behave as consumers themselves and how they contribute to family purchasing decisions.

How Children Behave as Independent Consumers

Some findings have surfaced over the past few years concerning how children learn money managing and purchasing skills, how they regard brands, and how they respond to various media.

Learning to be Consumers Young children begin developing consumer skills early and improve them gradually as they mature.

McNeal's study of five-, seven- and nine-year-olds concludes that:[42]

1. The youngest age group recognized that money could be used to buy things but expressed little interest in it. Less than half of the five-year-old subjects shopped alone—when they did, they were restricted to nearby stores.

2. By age seven, children received a regular allowance, which they used both for immediate purchases and for savings. A majority of them had been questioned by their parents as to their food preferences. At this age, interest in toys for prestige and personal satisfaction emerged.

3. The nine-year-olds could be described as true practicing consumers, spending money from an allowance and income from performing household chores. They shopped alone for both personal and family items, and looked for the products they wanted themselves rather than requesting them from parents.

Surprisingly enough, giving children an allowance does not appear to help them develop knowledge about money or give them money-managing skills.[43] The differences are among *parents*—those who give their children an allowance differ in other practices and attitudes about money from parents who supply their children's money needs in other ways. Parents who manage their own money wisely seem to serve as good models, since their children tend to acquire their parents' expertise.[44]

While children learn the basic essentials of consumption from their families, they seem to learn prestige and other *symbolic* functions of products from the media and their peer groups.[45]

Brand Awareness and Loyalty   First-grade children, in one study, were found to be not particularly susceptible to brand loyalty.

Among older children brand loyalty seems to apply to some products but not others; it increases slightly in children of higher socioeconomic groups.[46] The greatest preferences for brand names appear to focus on food products and soaps,[47] and brand loyalty seems to develop earliest for simple, inexpensive products such as soft drinks.[48] Teenagers have been reported as relatively cautious, insecure consumers who look for assurances of quality.[49] In this respect, they may favor nationally advertised brand names.[50]

Media Patterns and Preferences   *Television*
The home screen usually offers children their first exposure to media and remains the most popular form of entertainment. Before age three, children watch television but see only movement, making no distinction between programming and commercials. By their third year, they are watching from five to forty-two hours per week.[51] Extensive studies have revealed the following average weekly viewing times for children of nursery school age:[52] boys—34.56 hours; girls—32.44 hours.

Children of low income families spend considerably more time than more affluent youngsters in front of the television, and the set is often left on when children are not actually viewing.[53]

Wells offers these conclusions from research into television advertising for children:[54]

1. Children's programming preferences change dramatically between the ages of five and twelve. But while older children are no longer interested in cartoon programs, they will still look at cartoon commercials.

2. Children are willing to suspend disbelief to a point, but are alienated by obvious misrepresentations of what they know to be reality.

3. Motion pictures are more effective than still pictures in attracting and holding children's attention.

Money Managing Kit for Children

Shortly after Christmas, a New York City savings bank directed a special promotion to children and their parents. The give-away was a "Free Money-Managing Kit for Kids," including a budget guide, a record-keeper, a guide to free children's activities in New York, and a savings account application.

A popular child star announced the promotion in a television commercial, addressing parents with the appeal, "Listen . . . did your children get some money for the holidays? Here's how you can help them hold onto it . . ."

The promotion was well-received by parents interested in developing their children's ability to handle their own money, and the bank was rewarded with number one rank among all savings banks for that period for new deposits.

1. SFX: BANK INTERIOR AMBIENCE

2. MASON:

Listen. Did your children get some extra money for the holidays? Here's how you can help them hold onto it.

3. The Manhattan Savings Bank has this Money Managing Kit. Just for kids.

4. It's got a Budget Guide that shows you how to manage your money...how to save...how to earn extra cash...and how to be a shrewd consumer

Courtesy Manhattan Savings Bank.

4. Children respond well to advertising that announces new products or shows someone demonstrating the product.

5. Children are inclined to draw generic reactions to food commercials—they desire the food category rather than the specific product advertised. With toys, they are more inclined to desire the actual item advertised.

Radio   As children become teenagers, radio becomes an important medium. Younger adolescents are relatively light listeners while older children could be described as true radio enthusiasts. Youth marketers generally consider radio the most efficient medium by which to reach adolescents of both sexes, indicating that both straight spot announcements by favorite disc jockeys and taped commercials with music are the most effective kinds of messages.[55]

Print   Newspapers and magazines have proven useful with older children and teenagers. Youngsters begin to read newspapers at about seven years of age, with comics the principal attraction. Interest in comics tends to peak at about the fourth grade and decline afterwards. Around seventh and eighth grades, daily newspaper reading becomes common and increases through adolescence.[56] Older teenagers' reading patterns are similar to adult preferences, including mass magazines such as the *Reader's Digest* and specialty publications aligned with individual interests. Magazine readership tends to be heaviest among children whose families reflect high socio-economic and educational levels.[57]

How Children Influence Family Consumption

Wells notes that children influence family purchasing behavior in two ways—as *direct*

agents and as *passive dictators*. In the passive role, they need not be present when decisions are made because, for example, a mother will select certain brands since she knows which ones her children like.[58] Two categories in which children have been shown to exert special influence are food and durables.

Food Products   The number and ages of its children dictate the specific kinds of foods a family will buy. Prepared baby foods are purchased most heavily when children are from six to eighteen months old. Other products reflect children's maturing preferences. Cereal, for example, is most appealing to young children when it is bland. From six to twelve years they prefer wheat flakes and shredded wheat as well as presweetened varieties. Among teenagers wheat cereal and corn flakes enjoy the greatest popularity. One study of mothers' choices of cereal for their children reported that a mother's child-centeredness was *negatively* related to her children's preferences. This was explained by the mother's concern for nutritional needs, which they did not feel were adequately met by the children's favorite, the presweetened cereals.[59] In this instance, the mothers adopted a *gatekeeper* role. As "purchasing agents" for their children, they found it necessary to restrict certain kinds of consumption. (Other examples of the gatekeeper role include parents who keep their children from seeing certain movies or who refuse to buy "war toys.")

Children tend to accompany their parents to the supermarket and influence purchases there by making both suggestions and brand choices. But their influence usually varies with the product—for example, children affect twice as many cereal as detergent purchases.[60] The kinds of foods youngsters are most likely to ask for are fruits and vegetables, cereals, meats, and snacks. And their reasons for requesting them tend to revolve around taste, nutrition (in response to ads promising the bulging muscles favored by boys, or the clear complexions and trim figures girls are more concerned with), and to enjoy as a snack. In the classic gatekeeper role, mothers are inclined to refuse snack purchases more than any other kind.[61]

Durable Goods Children are, logically enough, instrumental in the purchase of toys and sports equipment, and help to create needs for appliances like washing machines and garbage compactors. Life cycle research indicates that the appearance of children positively influences consumption of durables like television sets but has a negative effect on new automobile purchases. In later stages of the life cycle, the family still consumes durable goods and considers the input from older children when buying a car.[62] Wickstrom found that children are also influential in purchases of record players, cameras, radios, and other home entertainment appliances. In about 20 percent of his cases, children actually initiated the decision process for these goods, although only five percent made the ultimate brand choice. Again, some purchases were reported to be more child-influenced than others; as one example, children were three times as important in decisions involving record players as they were in decisions about radios.[63]

Using Family Concepts in Marketing

Every product or service is aimed at some member of a family or combination of members. When role structure and decision making within the family are considered, influences are usually described as (1) husband only, (2) wife only, (3) children only, (4) husband more than wife, (5) wife more than husband, or (6) husband and wife together. To determine *which* family member(s) will be most likely to need, desire, and consume a product, a marketer should pose five relevant questions:

1. *Who will initiate the decision process?* If the product is along the lines of an automobile, a power tool, or a fishing outfit, the husband will probably initiate discussion. If the product is a sewing machine or a new carpet, the wife will no doubt begin the discussion. And if there is a television set or stereo system at stake, the children will quite possibly bring the matter up. It is reasonably safe to assume that those who will be deriving the most use or pleasure from a product will initiate the decision process, except in the case of gifts to other family members. This relationship holds true for inexpensive packaged goods as well as considered-purchase products.

2. *Who will dominate the evaluative process?* In this stage of decision making, the family gathers information to make comparisons among brands; there may also be some discussion if the product is a considered purchase. Role structure may again dictate husband or wife dominance for certain products, but if the purchase is important, this stage may reveal collective decision making. There is also a tendency for the partner who was passive in the initiation stage to become suddenly active at

this point. Children may play active or passive roles influencing evaluation.

3. *Who will make price decisions?* Either husband or wife may prevail here, depending on the nature of the product and the role structure of the household. If the product falls within the budgetary realm customarily the husband's, he will usually dominate, as will the wife with products traditionally assigned to her domain. Social class differences are important at this stage, as well as subcultural norms of dominance and submission. Children are usually subdued in this phase of weighing important purchases, unless the product or service directly concerns them.

4. *Who will make the final purchasing decision?* Sometimes a major purchasing decision is dominated by one party until this stage, but its importance will bring other family members into the process for final arbitration. This is especially true with automobiles, where husbands tend to initiate and dominate through the early decision stages, but wives surface in the final selection of make and model. When a new car is the outcome, older children are usually heard from at this point as well.

5. *Who will actually do the purchasing?* The ultimate consumer, or any combination of family members, may be the final decision maker(s). Here the gatekeeper effect may also arise, as one family member acts as purchasing agent for other family members. If the item in question is an automobile insurance policy, the husband will probably contact the agent to sign the contract even though the wife may have been active in the decision process. If the product is available at a supermarket, the wife will no doubt act as purchasing agent.

All of these questions are based on the cultural, sociological, and psychological considerations discussed throughout the chapter. They are the determinants that must be weighed to use family concepts properly in marketing.

Summary

The usual family in the United States is an *isolated nuclear* entity consisting of husband, wife, and their offspring. The family exists as a sociological unit for acculturating children, and also as a *consumption unit* engaged in the purchase of products and services. Decision making within the family is influenced by an interrelated network of cultural and social variables such as subculture, social class, life cycle, and the personality characteristics of its members. Family *role specialization* determines who is likely to dominate decision making about the product in question. This may be the husband, wife, children, or any combination of family members. Children are important to the family unit as dependents, key members, and independent consumers. Their buying behavior is learned in the context of parent versus peer influences, subculture, social class, and sex differences. To use family concepts effectively, marketers must consider who will initiate the decision process, who will dominate the evaluative process, who will make the price decisions, who will make the final purchasing decision, and who will actually do the purchasing.

NOTES

1. Harry L. Davis, "Decision Making within the Household," *Journal of Consumer Research,* Vol. 2, No. 4 (March 1976), p. 241.

2. Charles Horton Cooley, *Social Organization* (New York: Charles Scribner's Sons, 1909), p. 23.

3. Leonard Broome and Philip Selznick, *Sociology* (New York: Harper and Row, 1973).

4. Eugene Litwak and J. Figueira, "Technological Innovation and Theoretical Functions of Primary Groups and Bureaucratic Structures," *American Journal of Sociology,* Vol. 73 (January 1968), pp. 468–81.

5. William Kenkel, "Family Interaction in Decision Making and Spending," in *Household Decision Making,* ed. Nelson N. Foote (New York: University Press, 1961), pp. 140–164.

6. Harry L. Davis, "Decision Making," p. 254.

7. Elizabeth H. Wolgast, "Do Husbands or Wives Make the Purchasing Decisions?", *Journal of Marketing,* Vol. 22 (October 1958), pp. 151–158.

8. Fabian Linden, ed., *Expenditure Patterns of the American Family* (Prepared by the National Industrial Conference Board and sponsored by *Life Magazine,* 1965).

9. D. J. Hempel, "Family Buying Decisions: A Cross-Cultural Perspective," *Journal of Marketing Research,* Vol. 11 (August 1974).

10. R. F. Kelley and M. B. Egan, "Husband and Wife Interaction in a Consumer Decision Process" (Paper presented at the American Marketing Association Fall Conference, Cincinnati, Ohio, 1969).

11. Robert T. Green and Isabella C. M. Cunningham, "Feminine Role Perception and Family Purchasing Decisions," *Journal of Marketing Research,* Vol. 12, No. 3 (August 1975).

12. Robert Ferber, "Family Decision Making and Economic Behavior," in *Family Economic Behavior: Problems and Prospects,* ed. E. B. Sheldon (Philadelphia: J. B. Lippincott Company, 1973).

13. Robert Ferber and Lucy Chao Lee, "Husband-Wife Influence in Family Purchasing Behavior," *Journal of Consumer Research,* Vol. 1 (June 1974).

14. Davis, "Decision Making," pp. 246–247.

15. Harry L. Davis and Benny P. Rigaux, "Perception of Marital Roles in Decision Processes," *Journal of Consumer Research,* Vol. 1 (June 1974).

16. Douglas S. Dalrymple, Thomas S. Robertson, and Michael Y. Yoshino, *Consumption Behavior across Ethnic Categories,* (Graduate School of Business, Indiana University, 1969).

17. John H. Burma, ed., *Mexican-Americans in the United States: A Reader* (New York: Schenkman Publishing Co., Inc., 1970, pp. xvi–xvii).

18. Michael Creedman, "The Bountiful Life in Bountiful Utah," *Money,* April 1974.

19. Wolgast, "Husbands or Wives," p. 154.

20. Mira Komarovsky, "Class Differences in Family Decision-Making," in *Household Decision Making* ed. Nelson N. Foote (New York: University Press, 1961), pp. 255–265.

21. Komarovsky, "Class Differences."

22. Lee Rainwater, Richard P. Coleman, and Gerald Handel, *Workingman's Wife. Her Personality, World and Life Style* (New York: Oceana Publications, 1959).

23. Bert N. Adams and James E. Butler, "Occupational Status and Husband and Wife Social Participation," *Social Forces,* Vol. 45 (June 1967), p. 506.

24. Adapted from Kenneth Ring, C. E. Lipinsky, and Dorothy Braginsky, "The Relationship of Birth Order to Self-Evaluation, Anxiety Reduction, and Susceptibility to Emotional Contagion," *Psychological Monographs,* 1965, 79, No. 10.

25. From Crutchfield, R., "Conformity and Character," *American Psychologist,* 1955, Vol. 10, pp. 191–198; Hoffman, M. L., "Some Psychodynamic Factors in Compulsive Conformity," *Journal of Abnormal and Social Psychology,* Vol. 48, pp. 383–389; and Janis, I. "Personality Correlates of Susceptibility to Persuasion," *Journal of Personality,* 1954, Vol. 22, pp. 504–518.

26. F. K. Barron, "Some Personality Correlates of Independence of Judgement," *Journal of Consulting Psychology,* 1953, Vol. 121, pp. 287–289.

27. Kenkel, "Family Interaction," pp. 140–164.

28. Terry Clifford, "The High Cost of Children," *Esquire,* March 1974, pp. 119–121.

29. Urie Bronfenbrenner, "The Changing American Child—A Speculative Analysis," *Journal of Social Issues,* Vol. 17 (1961), pp. 16–18.

30. Muzafer Sherif and Carolyn W. Sherif, *Reference Groups: Exploration into Conformity and Deviation of Adolescents,* (New York: Harper and Row, 1964).

31. Charles E. Bowerman and John W. Kinch, "Changes in Family and Peer Orientation of Children between Fourth and Tenth Grades," *Social Forces,* Vol. 37 (March 1959).

32. David C. Epperson, "Reassessment of Indices of Parental Influence in the American Society," *American Sociological Review,* Vol. 29 (February 1964).

33. Paul Gilkison, "What Influences the Buying Decisions of Teenagers?" *Journal of Retailing,* Vol. 41 (Fall 1965).

34. David Gottlieb, "College Climates and Student Subcultures," in W. B. Brookover, *The College Student,* (New York Center for Applied Research in Education, 1965).

35. Russell L. Langworthy, "Community Status and Influence in a High School," *American Sociological Review,* Vol. 24 (August 1959).

36. Elizabeth Dorvan and Joseph Adelson, *The Adolescent Experience* (New York: John Wiley and Sons, Inc., 1966).

37. Dorvan and Adelson, *Adolescent Experience.*

38. George Psathas, "Ethnicity, Social Class, and Adolescent Independence from Parental Control," *American Sociological Review,* Vol. 22 (August 1957).

39. Hans Sebald, *Adolescence: A Sociological Analysis,* (New York: Appleton Century·Crofts, 1968).

40. Robert F. Peck and Corro Galliani, "Intelligence, Ethnicity and Social Roles in Adolescent Society," *Sociometry,* Vol. 25, No. 1 (March 1962), pp. 64–72.

41. James H. Copp, "Family Backgrounds of Rural Youth," in *Rural Youth in Crisis: Facts, Myths, and Social Change* ed. L. G. Burchinal (Department of Health, Education, and Welfare, U.S. Government Printing Office, 1965).

42. James U. McNeal, *Children as Consumers* (Bureau of Business Research, University of Texas, 1964).

43. Helen R. Marshall and Lucille Magruder, "Relations Between Parents, Money, Education Practices and Children's Knowledge and Use of Money," *Child Development,* Vol. 31 (June 1960).

44. Gladys K. Phelan and Jay D. Schraneveldo, "Spending and Saving Patterns of Adolescent Siblings," *Journal of Home Economics,* Vol. 61 (February 1969).

45. Del I. Hawkins and Kenneth A. Coney, "Peer Group Influences on Children's Product Preferences," *Journal of the Academy of Marketing Science,* Vol. 2, No. 2 (Spring 1974).

46. Lester P. Guest, "Brand Loyalty Revisited: A Twenty Year Report," *Journal of Applied Psychology,* Vol. 48 (April 1964).

47. Penelope Orth, "Teenagers: What Kind of Consumers?", *Printer's Ink,* Vol. 284 (September 20, 1963).

48. *Advertising Age,* March 22, 1974, p. 62.

49. *Advertising Age,* January 16, 1975, p. 31.

50. *Advertising Age,* March 22, 1974, p. 62.

51. J. P. Murray, "Viewing Behavior of Young Boys," in *Television and Social Behavior, Vol. 4* (Department of Health, Education, and Welfare, U.S. Government Printing Office, 1971).

52. A. Stein and L. Friedrich, "Television Content and Young Children's Behavior," in *Television and Social Behavior, Vol. 4* (Department of Health, Education, and Welfare, U.S. Government Printing Office, 1971).

53. Murray, "Viewing Behavior."

54. William D. Wells, "Communicating with Children," *Journal of Advertising Research,* Vol. 5 (June 1965).

55. "The U.S. Market," *Sponsor,* Vol. 22 (January 1968).

56. Wilbur Schramm, Jack Lyle, and Edwin B. Parker, "Patterns in Children's Reading of Newspapers," *Journalism Quarterly,* Vol. 37 (Winter 1960).

57. Ellis I. Folke, "Teenagers and Print Media," *Media/Scope,* Vol. 11 (December 1967), pp. 117–118.

58. William D. Wells, "Children as Consumers," in *On Knowing the Consumer* ed. J. W. Newman (New York: John Wiley and Sons, Inc., 1966).

59. Lewis A. Berey and Richard W. Pollay, "The Influencing Role of the Child in Family Decision Making," *Journal of Marketing Research,* Vol. 5 (February 1968).

60. Wells, "Children as Consumers."

61. Dorothy Dickins and Alvirda Johnston, "Children's Influence on Family Food Purchase Decisions," Bulletin 671 (State College, Mississippi: Mississippi State University, 1973).

62. John B. Lansing and Leslie Kish, "Family Life Cycle as an Independent Variable," *American Sociological Review,* Vol. 22 (October 1957).

63. B. Wirkstriim, *Kosumentens Markesval* (Gothenburg, Sweden: Gothenburg School of Economics and Business Administration Publications, 1965).

MARKETING APPLICATIONS

Conclusion 1 *Role specialization within the family is changing as women devote more of their time to careers and men assume a more active interest in child rearing and home care.*

Application As roles become less specific, patterns of decision-making influence are altered. Products traditionally advertised to women must now appeal to men as well—in both household and child-care categories. Conversely, purchases of products such as automobiles and cameras, which have tended to be husband-selected, are increasingly influenced by wives who wield purchasing power of their own. Decisions about a wider range of products are made collectively, and marketing communications must reflect the new role structures.

Conclusion 2 *The family life cycle is a means of differentiating families according to the products and services they are likeliest to buy at any given stage.*

Application A marketer of any specific product—refrigerators, packaged travel, or diapers—can best define a target market by knowing the kind of activities, interests, and problems found in the prime consumer's family environment. Knowing the particular stage in the family life cycle of the consumer can be used with demographic facts such as age and income in designing communications and enhancing retail performance. One particularly active consumer stage in the life cycle is the newlywed period when, as Wattenberg notes, couples in the process of setting up a household are responsible for 58 percent of all sterling silverware sales, 25 percent of the bedroom furniture sold, and 41 percent of all the stereo and high fidelity equipment purchased.

Conclusion 3 *Children learn consumer preferences at an early age from parental, peer group, and media sources.*

Application Marketers should utilize every opportunity to develop favorable attitudes among children and teen-age consumers. Some successful examples include a retail store's extending limited credit card privileges to teenagers and sponsorship of "worthwhile" children's entertainment in the media in addition to the usual cartoons on Saturday morning TV. Of course, as well as appealing to children themselves, such positive initiatives are duly noted by parents who are also likely to form positive attitudes toward concerned marketers.

ASSIGNMENTS

Research Assignment

Background The Dynamic Electric Company has just perfected a major product breakthrough, a 72-inch television system consisting of a large home-movie type screen and a projection module. Unlike similar sets on the market, Dynamic's model has been priced at $995 rather than several thousand dollars. Thus the Dynamic S72 is competitive with some of the more expensive "small screen sets" from other manufacturers.

Assignment   As a Research Designer for Family Research, Inc., you are responsible for designing the research instrument that will be used to identify the family influences likely to affect purchasing of the Dynamic S72.

Your assignment is to write a brief questionnaire that could be administered separately to husbands and wives while both are at home in the evening. You want to find out:

1. Whether husband or wife would be the more influential in the buying decision. Who would be the more likely to initiate discussion about purchasing the product? Who would make the final decision to buy it? Who would decide where to buy it (if it were available from several retail outlets)?

2. To what extent children (if any) would be involved in the purchasing process.

Write a questionnaire of 15 items or fewer that will obtain that information. Decide whether an interviewer should (1) give the questionnaires to husband and wife at the same time to answer in written form or (2) take husband and wife aside separately to ask the questions verbally and record the spoken answers.

Creative Assignment

You are the recently appointed Marketing Manager of the Freedom Savings Bank, a savings and loan institution. Your bank receives its deposits from two principal sources: *passbook* savings accounts (which pay a lower rate of interest but let people take their money out when they need it), and *savings certificates* (which pay depositors higher interest rates but require a minimum deposit of $250 and stipulate that deposits must be left in the bank for at least one year).

The bank is anxious to increase the number of people who purchase savings certificates, since their money will be committed to the bank for one year or more and may be used to make profitable loans to other customers. Your research indicates that certificate purchasers tend to be married women in their forties and fifties, which suggests that they are acting as "gatekeepers" for their families' savings.

With this knowledge in mind, make some creative recommendations to your advertising agency for reaching more women in this age group and appealing to them in their "gatekeeper" role.

Managerial Assignment

Creative Toys, Inc., is both a manufacturing and retail company developing toys for children ages one through twelve. The staff of Creative Toys includes several consultants trained in child psychology who are employed to design playthings that help children develop their intellectual and conceptual skills. Thus each toy product sold at Creative Toys outlets throughout the country is the result of scientific research and careful consideration of an individual child's developmental needs.

As Store Manager of the new Creative Toys retail outlet in your city, you will be responsible for training your sales staff to present your product line to parents as being different from other playthings sold in toy and department stores.

Prepare a strategy that outlines techniques your salespeople should use in (1) justifying the relatively high cost of Creative Toys (25 percent to 50 percent higher than toys from other manufacturers), and (2) convincing parents that Creative Toys will be as much fun for their children as others designed only for play.

Once you have devised your sales strategy, set up a role-playing situation between a salesperson and a "customer" that covers those points.

SELECTED READINGS

Cox, Eli P. "Family Purchase Decision Making and the Process of Adjustment." *Journal of Marketing Research*, Vol. 12, No. 2 (May 1975), pp. 189–95.

Davis, Harry L. "Decision Making Within the Household." *Journal of Consumer Research*, Vol. 2, No. 4 (March 1976), pp. 241–60.

———— and Benny P. Rigaux. "Perception of Marital Roles in Decision Processes." *Journal of Consumer Research*, Vol. 1, No. 1 (June 1974), pp. 51–62.

Ferber, Robert and Lucy C. Lee. "Husband-Wife Influence in Family Purchasing Behavior." *Journal of Consumer Research*, Vol. 1, No. 1 (June 1974), pp. 43–50.

Munsinger, Gary M., Jean E. Weber and Richard W. Hansen. "Joint Home Purchasing Decisions by Husbands and Wives." *Journal of Consumer Research*, Vol. 1, No. 4 (March 1975), pp. 60–66.

III
INDIVIDUAL INFLUENCES

Learning
Perception
Motivation and Personality
Attitudes
Attitude Change

OBJECTIVES

NINE

Learning

This chapter introduces the consumer as an individual rather than as a member of a group—subject to an almost endless array of personal idiosyncrasies and predispositions. Of course, such purely personal influences guarantee that any statements made about how consumers will act must, at best, be generalizations. But these psychology-based generalizations provide most of our knowledge about why people behave as they do and form the cornerstone of consumer research today.

Because psychology is the study of individual human behavior, it is not surprising that our knowledge of individual consumer behavior comes from this discipline. And one basic assumption of psychological theory today is that human behavior is learned. Thus, our discussion of the individual influences on purchase behavior also starts with this premise.

Two conflicting theories of learning—behaviorist and cognitive—merit a careful discussion here because of their prominence in consumer behavior study. Other learning topics include

• How psychologists can sometimes "condition" people to behave in prescribed ways (and why marketers generally can't).

• How certain learning principles have been used successfully in advertising.

• How commercials may encourage consumers to crave the wrong product.

• How consumers learn "loyalties" to certain brands or stores, but may switch for a few purchases before returning to the brand to which they're attached.

• How probability models can be used to predict brand loyalty with a fair degree of accuracy.

The overview of learning presented here also serves as a background for viewing perception, motivation, personality, attitudes, and attitude change—the related individual attributes developed in this section.

Learning and Experience

Psychologists agree that our responses to what we find in our environment are acquired through experience. Consider the urban market research executive who has developed a habit of drinking two martinis before lunch. To arrive at this behavior, he first must have acquired a taste for alcohol, possibly learned from his parents or his adolescent peer group. At some point he made the transition from drinking liquor as a generalized behavior to the more specific preference for gin and vermouth. Because martinis are rarely enjoyed for taste alone, he has probably come to like this drink for its soporific effect, and no doubt has learned through trial and error that two martinis will provide maximum pleasure without distorting his behavior. In brief, this executive has learned how to achieve a desired goal (a form of tension reduction) and still avoid an undesirable outcome (returning to the office in a condition that would raise eyebrows) through a specific kind of consumption behavior. Furthermore,

he may have developed a loyalty to a particular brand of gin, ordering, for example, a "*Beefeater* martini" rather than just a martini. He may even frequent a given restaurant solely because (he swears) the bartender has perfected the exact proportion of gin to vermouth that our executive prefers—"Nobody makes a martini like Charlie." Thus, the factors of brand loyalty and a "retail" preference are included in his total learning process. Many of the same factors affect other consumption patterns, including the boy who loves Fruit Loops and the housewife who always uses Viva paper towels.

This chapter focuses on the role of learning in individual consumer behavior, beginning with a discussion of two basic learning theories, progressing to the possibilities for behavioral modification in marketing and the development of brand loyalty, and concluding with an evaluation of probability models in predicting consumer behavior.

Behaviorist versus Cognitive Learning Theory

As noted earlier, the direction of mainstream psychology has shifted in recent years from a "behaviorist" to a "cognitive" orientation.[1] This new emphasis is felt most noticeably in the realm of learning, since this terrain was theoretical home base for the behaviorists during their days of greatest influence.

The Behaviorist Approach

The basic tenet of behavioral psychology is that all human behavior can be reduced to a simple relationship of some stimulus (S) from the environment evoking a desired response (R). This "S-R" phenomenon was described succinctly by John Watson, the father of behaviorism:[2]

In each adjustment there is always both a response or act and a stimulus or situation which calls out the response . . .The stimulus is always provided by the environment, external to the body, or by the movements of man's own muscles and the secretions of his glands . . . The responses always follow relatively immediately upon the presentation or incidence of the stimulus.

If such a relationship appears rather a simplistic explanation of behavior, this was by design. The guiding premise of behaviorism was to consider as worthy of serious investigation only those aspects of behavior that could be readily observed. This reductionism was, in fact, a "scientific" reaction on the part of many experimental psychologists to what they perceived (and often rightfully so) as the theoretical excesses of Freudian psychology, offering such blatantly unmeasurable concepts as the superego and sublimation. Thus, the ideal for behaviorists was rigorous empirical control. And research results tended to be confined to the responses of laboratory animals, eminently more controllable subjects than even college students.

B. F. Skinner, the most prominent theorist and spokesman for the behaviorist community, conceptualized learning as a *change in the probability of a response*.[3] This definition can be illustrated by the kind of learning known as *trial and error*. Here some stimulus (Sd) has characteristically produced a given response (R_1) that is gratifying. But for some reason, conditions have changed and the original response is no longer so gratifying. Now the individual is cast into variable trial and error behavior and tries responses R_2, R_3, and so on until finding one that "works."

This new response, possibly R_4, now becomes the established one:[4]

$$
\begin{array}{llll}
 & & R_1 & \\
Sd\text{-}R_1 & \quad Sd & R_2 & \qquad Sd\text{-}R_4 \\
 & & R_3 & \\
 & & R_4 &
\end{array}
$$

Example of Behaviorist Theory As an example of the trial and error process, envision a ten-year-old boy who has developed the typical habit of reading comic books because they evoke a great sense of reading pleasure. But one day, the thrill of finding a new issue of his favorite comic on the magazine rack isn't quite as intense as before. This young reader is ready to sample a more sophisticated kind of entertainment. Searching through the rack, he is attracted to the *National Lampoon* and buys it. Unfortunately, the arch humor of this publication leaves him more baffled than amused. So he tries again and brings home a *1000 Laughs* joke magazine. The problem with this is, there are plenty of jokes but no pictures to hold his interest, so he gives up on this magazine as well. But on the very next trial, he discovers *Mad* magazine—the perfect choice for his entertainment needs. He has finally selected the most gratifying choice, and this is the one that becomes established until his needs again change.

Limitations of Behaviorist Theory The problem with behaviorist explanations of learning is that they assume a mechanistic view of the consumer, much like the old-style economic theorists: Present a certain stimulus and elicit a fairly predictable response. Behaviorists tend to overlook internal, *covert* behavior—thinking, perceiving, and the like—because it cannot be as readily observed in an experimental setting as external, *overt* action. (Even the above example of the boy and his search for new reading matter involved factors the behaviorists would ignore: attitudes, perceptions, "humor," and other internal variables.) For this reason, cognitive theory has deposed behaviorism as the current psychological "establishment" view. But behaviorist theories about how learning occurs through *conditioning* offer several applications to consumer behavior; these will be discussed shortly.

The Cognitive Approach

The basic difference between behaviorist and cognitive theory is the way in which the human organism is depicted. While the behaviorists see humans as not too different from laboratory rats, protoplasm that will respond when prodded with a stimulus, cognitivists think of them as *adaptive problem solvers*.[5] The human being is a highly complex "sensory processing and data-gathering organism . . . pulled to acts of choice by his goals and aspirations."[6]

Cognitive theorists acknowledge that some learning is simply an association between S and R factors, but maintain that most learning, particularly in consumer behavior, is not that simple. It is instead an expression of adaptive problem solving: making use of the processes of reasoning, forming concepts, and acquiring knowledge about the environment.[7] Markin summarizes the cognitive orientation to learning as a holistic (total) and humanistic portrayal of human endeavor:[8]

The behaviorist is inclined to ask, "What has the subject learned to do?" The cognitivist, on the other hand, would be inclined to ask, "How has the subject learned to perceive the situation?" The cognitivist is interested in examining a learning situation in terms of such factors as motivation, the perceived goals, the aspiration level, the overall nature of the situation, and the beliefs, values, and personality of the subject—in short, the entire range of a subject's psychological field.

Cognitive theory will be expanded more fully in following chapters, as it serves to integrate all psychological influences throughout the process of consumer information seeking and decision making.

Learning and its Components Defined

Learning may be defined for consumer study as the *acquisition of new responses to behavioral cues in the environment, occurring as the result of reinforcement*. This definition includes the generally recognized components of learning: drives, cues, and reinforcement.

Drives   A *drive* is an arousal mechanism that causes an individual to act. *Primary* drives include such physiological motivators as hunger, sex, and the avoidance of pain. *Secondary* drives are acquired through previous learning and reflect social and cultural influences upon the individual. Examples are the desire for prestige, anxiety, and the need for affection.

Cues   A *cue* is any stimulus found in the individual's environment that may potentially trigger a drive. An advertisement is a cue, with the intention of inducing a drive to purchase the product or service in the person who sees it.

Reinforcements   A reinforcement serves

as a reward for some response and reduces an individual's drive. The reduction of a primary drive by a reinforcement is known as a *primary* reinforcer; for instance, a hungry animal (or person) may be rewarded for some activity by being fed. A *secondary* reinforcer reduces a secondary drive; the most obvious example of this type in our society is money.

These concepts are integrated in the model of learning developed by Hull, which may be reduced to the equation:[9]

$$E = D \cdot K \cdot H \cdot V$$

Hull represents *behavior* by E, which he refers to as "action potential." This potential is activated by the cumulative effect of a *drive* (D), multiplied by the incentive of a *goal* (K),

times reinforcement (H), times the intensity of the *cue* (V).

In other words, Hull sees the learning situation as a case of an individual organism that wants to satisfy its needs or reach certain goals responding to specific cues in the environment. The cues and responses that are associated when reinforcement occurs are strengthened. And the individual learns to make a similar response again when forced with a similar cue. In addition to the cue-response association actually reinforced, the pairs of cues and responses leading *up to* that reinforcement are also strengthened to a progressively lesser degree, according to the length of time that they preceded the reinforcement.[10]

Behavior Modification in Psychology and Marketing

Conditioning (simple S-R learning) principles are still interesting to those who wish to modify or change behavior, such as psychiatrists, teachers, and marketers. Two kinds of conditioning, classical and operant, have been the subject of much theorizing and research in the behavioral sciences, and both may account for some specific behaviors and behavioral patterns associated with consumption.

Classical Conditioning

This type of learning was first demonstrated by the Russian physiologist Pavlov and his famous salivating dogs. In his original experiments, Pavlov noted that when meat is placed in a dog's mouth, saliva begins to flow

as a natural and automatic behavior. He termed this an "unconditioned reflex." An "incidental stimulus" such as a ringing bell would, by itself, create no reason for a dog to salivate. But if the bell is rung immediately before each feeding, before long the ringing alone will be sufficient to make the dog salivate. This new response to the bell was termed a "conditioned response" and the bell a "conditioned stimulus." A relationship had been established between the bell and the food, so that a response originally made to the food would now be made to the bell.[11]

Initially, we might conclude that buying behaviors (such as going out of one's way to shop at a particular store or choosing a specific model of automobile) cannot be classically conditioned because they are voluntary and have no unconditioned stimuli that would automatically produce them. But a closer analysis suggests that classical conditioning may be responsible for some consumer decision making.

Consider the food advertisement portraying a lavish buffet so realistic in "appetite appeal" it makes one's mouth water (just like a Pavlovian dog). This associative relationship is also the hope of many advertisers, who wish to create a highly favorable awareness of a product by picturing it in a pleasure-producing context. One example was the humorous television campaign for a felt-tip pen named the "Bic Banana." By evoking a pleasurable sensation through the humor of Mel Brooks in the Bic commercials, the advertiser hoped it would logically follow that a consumer spotting the pen in a retail store would recall the "fun" sensation and buy the pen on that impulse.

Operant Conditioning

This form of learning was demonstrated by B. F. Skinner. The basic procedure was to place a hungry animal in a "Skinner Box" equipped with a food dispenser activated by a lever. Eventually, the animal would press the lever purely by accident, and a pellet of food would drop into the box. After several "accidents" of this sort, the animal would learn that pressing the lever was somehow connected with the appearance of food, and would depress the lever more and more frequently.

Operant conditioning, then, refers to "a process in which the *frequency of occurrence* of a bit of behavior is modified by the *consequences of the behavior.*"[12] Much behavior, and especially much consumer behavior, is operant in nature—like driving a car, choosing a brand off a supermarket shelf, eating a meal, and making a telephone call.

The Use of Reinforcement By definition, operant conditioning is largely a matter of reinforcement, or consequences of behavior. This distinguishes operant learning from classical conditioning, where no reinforcement occurs. But reinforcement in this context does not mean only reward; in operant terminology, a desirable outcome or reward is a *positive* reinforcer, while a punishment or undesirable outcome is called a *negative* reinforcer. There are several ways in which reinforcers determine operant learning:[13]

1. *If a positive reinforcer follows each occurrence of a particular response, that response will occur with growing frequency.* A young woman may pick up an issue of *Cosmopolitan* for the first time and find features in it that appeal to her. The next month, she buys the magazine again and finds other articles that hold her interest. As the months go by and the magazine continues to intrigue her, "that *Cosmopolitan* girl" will maintain her behavior.

2. *If a negative reinforcer regularly follows a response, that response will occur less frequently.* A motorist who uses a neighborhood gas station for convenience will probably look elsewhere if "punished" by surly, discourteous service.

3. *When a negative reinforcer that has usually followed a response is regularly withdrawn, the frequency of that response should increase.* The same motorist will probably return to the neighborhood station more frequently if new management steps in with a friendlier service policy.

4. *When a response acquired through operant conditioning is allowed to continue but is no longer reinforced, it will become less and less frequent and finally cease.* This is known as "extinction" of a response. If a consumer patronizes a distant supermarket because the prices are significantly lower than in other

markets, but the store suddenly raises all its prices to the same levels as (or even slightly higher than) other food outlets, it is likely that the consumer will ultimately stop buying there.

Reinforcement does not have to be *continuous* (every correct response rewarded) in operant learning to be effective. The kind of reinforcement that is most resistant to extinction once the reinforcement ceases is called *intermittent*, which means reinforcing only some correct responses. One way to accomplish this is to reinforce the first response after a set time period, and another is to deliver the reinforcer after a certain number of responses have occurred. An often-used example of intermittent reinforcement is the Las Vegas slot machine—the gambler continues to play because a few coins do fall out as a reward from time to time. The most *efficient* use of reinforcement in operant learning is to begin with continuous reinforcement so that the response will occur frequently, then switch to intermittent reinforcement to keep the response from being extinguished. [14]

Shaping Behavior This is a special kind of operant conditioning used by "trainers" to produce a desired response in their subjects. It consists of *reinforcing closer and closer approximations to the response ultimately desired*. [15] Theoretically, it is possible for students to make their instructor stand in any section of the classroom they want during the class, without the teacher's awareness of the maneuver. According to university folklore, a professor of psychology was once so "trained" by his class, who appeared bright and attentive while he stood in certain locations, bored and sluggish while he stood in others. Thus the professor unconsciously "learned" to stand in specific spots and, the

story goes, was finally conducting his lectures backed into one far corner of the classroom.

"Superstitious" Behavior In studies with animals in which intermittent reinforcement is administered at set time intervals, the subject may associate the reinforcement with whatever behavior is occurring at the time. In other words, a pigeon who happens to have cocked its head just as a food pellet appears will associate head-cocking with food and make this a permanent part of its behavioral repertoire. By the same token, a high school girl may be wearing a new hair style on the day that some boy she has been attracted to happens to notice her for the first time. It is conceivable that she would attribute this reinforcement to the way she was wearing her hair, even though the encounter was probably by chance. In an even more "superstitious" vein, a junior executive may wear a bow tie to the office for the first time in his career, and unexpectedly receive a promotion along with a sizable salary increase. Although he recognizes objectively that the bow tie had nothing to do with his good fortune, he may nonetheless spend some of his raise stocking up on bow ties.

Reinforcement in Advertising Research Advertisers are necessarily concerned about the reinforcement value of their messages on the television screen and in print media. The more positively reinforcing a message is, the more likely a person will be to watch or read it; this represents an important criterion for creative and media decisions by advertising agencies. To measure the reinforcement power of various advertising messages in laboratory situations, researchers have developed a machine known as CONPAAD, "Conjugately Programmed Analysis of Advertising." [16] By pressing a foot pedal as the operant response, subjects can control whether or not a segment of a television commercial stays on or fades away. Because the subject keeps a message in view for as long as it is rewarding, the advertisements with the most highly rewarding stimuli receive the highest rate of operant responding.

Some experimental findings from the use of CONPAAD are:

• A test of two commercials for coffee concluded that a greater degree of information about the product was more reinforcing than a lesser degree.[17]

• When tests of detergent commercials by operant methods were compared with sales studies, the commercial identified as more reinforcing by CONPAAD also obtained the most coupon responses. Thus the operant approach may hold a significant predictive value.[18]

Generalization and Discrimination

Two learning concepts relevant to consumer behavior are *generalization* and *discrimination* of stimuli. Through these processes, consumers make decisions about new circumstances based upon their previous learning.

Generalization   When a new stimulus is similar to one previously learned, one tends to respond to it in the same way as to the old one. And the more the new stimulus resembles the earlier one, the stronger the response will be.[19] This tendency to make the same responses to similar stimuli is called *generalization*. Consumers make generalizations in a number of ways.

Howard points out that generalization occurs when a buyer shifts his or her purchase response from one brand to a new one because it is similar.[20] (For this reason a brand that does not have the largest share of market may be packaged similarly to the market leader.) Variation in the extent of a transfer to new brands is called the gradient of generalization, as shown in Figure 9-1.

Here D_1 indicates one level of drive, and D_2 a higher level. As drive increases, the gradient of generalization also increases; in other words, the more a housewife feels the need to buy a household product, the greater her tendency will be to choose a brand similar to the one she ordinarily uses if the former is more readily available. This relationship suggests two implications:[21]

• An advertiser building up a desire (or drive) for his product must be careful not to create just a desire for the *generic* product—a craving for ice cream in general, say, rather than specifically for Carvel ice cream.

Figure 9-1   Gradient of generalization.

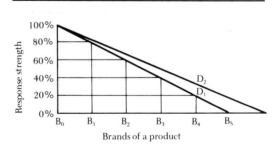

Source: John A. Howard, Marketing Theory, *p. 109. © Copyright 1965 by Allyn and Bacon, Inc., Boston.*

• Under the generalization principle, a company's product should be readily available. If it is not, the buyer is apt to settle for a similar brand to avoid both the delay and inconvenience of looking elsewhere for the preferred brand.

So, in most cases, from the marketing standpoint generalization is an unwanted variable in consumption. Marketers want their specific brand to be the drive reinforcer rather than the generic product.

Discrimination In psychology, *discrimination training* involves teaching a subject who is generalizing from two different stimuli to respond differently to them. This is ordinarily accomplished by presenting the two stimuli and conditioning the response to one of them while extinguishing the other.[22] Consumer discrimination is a major goal of marketers—convincing people that one brand of aspirin is more effective than another, that one kind of corn flakes tastes better than its competitors, or that Xerox stock is a better buy for investors than IBM. In this sense, discrimination is a process through which consumers restrict their range of responses and attach themselves to a particular brand.

When product differences are easily recognizable, such as those between a Chevrolet Vega and a Volkswagen, it is relatively easy for consumers to discriminate. But when products are generically equal and undifferentiated, as is the case with most competing brands in a product category, the problem is to develop the marketing strategy that will make consumers perceive one brand as different from others. *Positioning* (see chapter 1) refers to the strategy of establishing a "position" for a product in the consumer's frame of reference, differentiating it from others in the same category. Thus Excedrin became "the extra-strength pain reliever" to distinguish it from simple aspirin. In the household-cleaner category, a product was positioned as the "industrial-strength cleaner," with the appropriate name "Janitor in a Drum" (and packaging to match—an industrial-looking green plastic drum). Perhaps the most effective positioning to date occurred in the highly competitive car rental field, when all companies were offering essentially the same cars at the same rates. Because Hertz was the market leader and Avis a distant second, Avis advertising adopted the slogan "We're only Number Two, so we try harder," and built a highly successful campaign with what would seem to be an unenviable position.

When products within a category are undifferentiated and a positioning strategy is neither possible nor effective, it may become necessary to offer lower prices, special premiums, or other incentives to facilitate discrimination on the part of the consumer.

One rather intriguing discrimination experiment commissioned by a drug company was teaching pigeons to inspect pill capsules. In this case, the birds had to respond to pills of the correct shape or color by letting them pass and rejecting the wrong capsules. At the primary stage of training, the pigeons were reinforced with food when they responded to red capsules on the conveyer belt by pecking a reject button and were not reinforced for discarding white ones. After one week, the pigeons were responding correctly 99 percent of the time. Unfortunately, the project was dropped by the sponsoring company for fear of how its competitors and consumers might respond to the use of pigeons as quality control inspectors.[23]

How Commercials Use Learning Concepts

Aspects of learning theory have been identified by marketing psychologist Steuart Henderson Britt in two recent television and radio campaigns:[24]

Covert Involvement   Through this process, consumers can experience some of the benefits of a product just by thinking or fantasizing about them. This was the concept behind the "Nestea Plunge" campaign, which featured hot, sweating individuals on a blistering day who take a sip of iced tea and miraculously fall backwards, fully dressed, into a swimming pool. Viewers could take a bit of a "plunge" themselves just by watching this spectacle and, it was hoped, associate the momentary sensation of refreshment with Nestea.

Mental Completion   People want to complete their experiences, to give them "closure." Thus, something that has not been completed is more unsettling, and also better remembered, than something finished and done with. In a radio campaign, Salem cigarettes used a jingle that went "You can take Salem out of the country but . . . (long pause) . . . you can't take the country out of Salem." During the pause after the first part of the jingle, people would finish the message themselves by soundlessly phrasing the second half. Such viewer involvement in a commercial is rare and highly desirable from the marketer's standpoint.

Retention and Advertising Messages

Needless to say, not all learned material is remembered; memory is selective and varies according to a number of factors. Psychologists refer to *retention* as "the amount of material previously learned that is remembered." The opposite is *forgetting*, "a loss in retention of material previously learned." The most important implications of retention are in the area of advertising effectiveness.

Experimental Findings on Retention   Extensive laboratory work in retention was pioneered by Herman Ebbinghaus and has been carried on by many other researchers. Some generally accepted findings state that:[25]

1. Repetition of learned material increases retention.

2. Retention is greater with meaningful material than with nonmeaningful material. (In studies of learners' ability to memorize lists of words as against lists of nonsense syllables such as GRE or ETP, retention of familiar words is greater.)

3. Retention is greater the more thoroughly material is learned originally.

4. Forgetting occurs as a "logarithmic function" of time elapsed since material is learned. If two associations are of equal strength, the older one (in elapsed time) will lose strength more slowly with the passage of time.

5. Forgetting occurs through "interference." A learned message may be forgotten when new learning occurs afterwards.

6. Most forgetting occurs immediately after learning.

Advertising Implications Of the lessons marketers might draw from learning research, one of the most indisputable is the effectiveness of repetition in advertising.

Repetition As early as 1885, an observer of consumer behavior offered this counsel to advertisers:[26]

The first time a man looks at an advertisement, he does not see it.
The second time he does not notice it.
The third time he is conscious of its existence.
The fourth time he faintly remembers having seen it before.
The fifth time he reads it.
The sixth time he turns up his nose at it.
The seventh time he reads it through and says, "Oh brother!"
The eighth time he says, "Here's that confounded thing again!"
The ninth time he wonders if it amounts to anything.
The tenth time he thinks he will ask his neighbor if he has tried it.
The eleventh time he wonders how the advertiser makes it pay.
The twelfth time he thinks perhaps it may be worth something.
The thirteenth time he thinks it must be a good thing.
The fourteenth time he remembers that he has wanted such a thing for a long time.
The fifteenth time he is tantalized because he cannot afford to buy it.
The sixteenth time he thinks he will buy it some day.
The seventeenth time he makes a memorandum of it.
The eighteenth time he swears at his poverty.

The nineteenth time he counts his money carefully.
The twentieth time he sees it, he buys the article, or instructs his wife to do so.

It is axiomatic that the greater the frequency of the commercial message, the better people will remember that message. This holds true even for commercials people say they dislike. A Charmin bathroom tissue campaign featuring a grocer who cautions customers not to "squeeze the Charmin" was reportedly unpopular with many viewers, but the brand's share of market increased dramatically through sheer repetition of the theme. Most "slice of life" commercials for home products, those showing housewives discussing and using the product, are less than memorable as single events, but gain awareness after being noticed again and again.

Identical Ad Versus Campaign Approach When the same advertisement is repeated continuously, it may reach a point of diminishing retention. Thus, advertising "campaigns" comprised of several different extensions of a central theme are judged to be more effective.[27] Repetition of the same ad too often may, in fact, produce a negative effect. One reason may be that consumers "tune out" to a single message observed too frequently, and another may be antagonism to the tiresome repetition of the same ad.

Stewart found that the point at which repetition loses effectiveness varies according to the ad or product in question.[28] This points to another axiom: The more effective an ad in attracting notice, the less repetition is necessary to drive its message home.

Continuous versus Concentrated Messages Advertising that runs over a length of time appears to be more effective than advertising concentrated into a short time period. This generalization may vary for the product advertised, however. *New products* demand the attention-getting impact of a "saturation" campaign, as do special promotions such as free gifts at a new savings bank or a limited-time special airline fare to Hawaii. For older, familiar brands seeking long-term awareness, continuous messages remain the most effective.[29]

The Problems of Commercial Clutter "Interference" has been identified as a cause of forgetting. This raises the question of "clutter" in television commercial programming; the consumer is simply bombarded with a huge number of messages. And the problem grows more pressing as sixty-second segments (traditionally allotted for one commercial) are broken down into thirty- and ten-second messages. The most effective way an advertiser can deal with this problem is by making outstanding commercials, especially if the media budget is modest. Advertisers who can afford to spend large sums on media are generally not as concerned with a striking "creative" execution as are small-budget advertisers, who must make every exposure count.

Comparing Two Ads Ebbinghaus, as noted earlier, was first to identify the relationship between forgetting and elapsed time (see Figure 9-2, and other researchers have elaborated on his findings.

Ebbinghaus also suggested that, given the same amount of repetition, a lengthy, complex message will be forgotten more readily than a shorter, less complicated one. That is, a more involved product story or

Figure 9-2 Relearning and forgetting (Ebbinghaus).

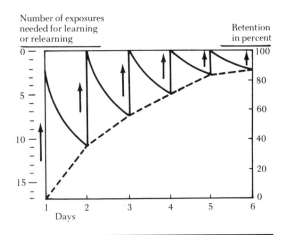

Source: William T. Moran, "Methods of Psychology in Marketing," Paper presented to the European Society for Opinion and Marketing Research, June 2, 1973.

concept must be repeated more frequently to ensure the same degree of retention. This may also help to explain a recent finding from direct response advertising for book clubs on television: A message offering three specific books for one dollar as an incentive to join is more successful than a message asking the viewer to choose three from several books shown, when both commercials were aired the same number of times. The "choice" message was more complicated and probably required additional repetition to gain the same retention as the "no choice" message.[30]

Habit Formation and Brand Loyalty

Marketers are particularly concerned with learning as it applies to habits of product, brand, and store selection. A major goal of their efforts revolves around getting consumers to develop loyalties to their products, to prefer a given brand consistently over others.

How Habits Are Formed ╲╲〇

Psychologists contend that one of the most powerful variables in determining the strength of a habit is the amount of reinforcement the individual receives.[31] A traditional statement of this principle is Thorndike's Law of Effect (as quoted by Kingsley and Garry), which says basically that:[32]

. . . when a connection is accompanied by a satisfying state of affairs, its strength is increased [and] the probability of its recurrence is greater. Inversely, when the connection is accompanied by an annoying state of affairs, its strength is reduced or weakened. . . . [a]n organism tends to repeat that which has previously been satisfying and avoid that which has been dissatisfying.

In consumer decision making, this would suggest that the person who buys an Oldsmobile every two years does so because the purchase of that brand continues to gratify his or her needs. The same conclusion could be drawn for the habitual Marlboro smoker and the housewife who buys only Ivory Soap. In practice, however, the question of brand loyalty is subject to many variables.

Brand Loyalty

A number of studies have investigated the nature of learning brand loyalty—how it is developed, variation of loyalty among product categories, and specific applications in areas such as consumer appliance and industrial buying. Some of their findings are summarized here.

What Brand Loyalty Means Tucker has illustrated the meaning of brand loyalty by showing that a consistent pattern of brand choice behavior can occur even between virtually identical brands. He conceives brand loyalty as simply *biased choice* behavior with respect to branded merchandise:[33]

If there are two cola drinks offered to a person a number of times, his degree of brand loyalty can be stated in terms of the relative frequency with which he chooses one brand rather than the other. If he selects Pepsi Cola rather than Coca-Cola (and both are equally available) enough of the time to persuade the statistically sophisticated observer that the difference in frequency is not due to chance, he may be said to be brand loyal.

In early research, Tucker offered the following tentative conclusions about brand loyalty:[34]

1. Brand loyalty will develop in some consumers even when no discernible difference exists between brands other than the trademarks themselves.

2. Although brand loyalty appears to be based on trivial and superficial differences (for example, packaging and labeling), the bias may be firmly established and is not easily modified.

3. Consumers vary greatly in degree of susceptibility to brand loyalty.

4. Brand loyalty and preferences for specific product *characteristics* are two different considerations, but together make up what is normally termed brand loyalty.

5. Although *exploratory* consumer behavior is hard to identify, some consumer purchasing

selections are clearly exploratory in nature and may indicate that a repeat purchase is unlikely.

Variation in Brand Loyalty among Products   A number of researchers have concluded that there are significant differences in measured brand loyalty among product categories. This has been attributed to differences in the products themselves and to differences in consumer attitudes toward products.[35]

Farley has identified several factors that may account for this variation:[36]

1. *Price.* In a market where prices fluctuate greatly, price activity may be a significant variable. With greater flexibility in pricing, some switching to lower priced brands should occur.

2. *Product Importance.* People presumably put greater effort into "shopping" for products important to them than for relatively unimportant products. Theoretically, the greater the importance, the more likely that brand-switching will occur.

3. *Different Product Uses.* Consumers may be loyal to a number of brands for different users or uses. Families might be expected to enjoy variety in, say, food products and prefer different food brands for their different flavors.

4. *Brand Distribution in the Market Place.* Consumers tend to spread purchases of household products among several stores over a period of time. Combined with a tendency toward repeat purchase of a brand bought last, this suggests that consumers will be less likely to switch brands if many are widely available.

Farley concluded from a study of numerous food product categories that consumers tend to be *less* loyal to products where many brands available, frequency of purchase and expenditures are high, prices are active, and where consumers might simultaneously use a number of brands of the same product. They exhibit a tendency toward *greater* loyalty where brands are widely distributed and where market share was concentrated heavily in a leading brand.[37]

Correlates of Brand Loyalty   Carman studied the interaction of numerous variables in brand loyalty through a model known as the Morgan-Sonquist Automatic Interaction Detector (AID), illustrated in Figure 9-3.

His conclusions are summarized here:[38]

1. *Store loyalty* is the single most important predictor of brand loyalty. Because frequenting a single store restricts the number of brand alternatives available, the store-loyal customer will consequently appear more brand-loyal.

2. Consumers who are described as not "shopping-prone" will shop in a *small number of stores* and remain loyal to a *small number of brands* rather than making choices among values offered by those stores. Non-shoppers have been shown to belong in general to lower income groups than shopping-prone consumers.

3. *Personal characteristics* of consumers may explain differences in store loyalties. Loyal shoppers tend to be busy women with jobs and children who are newer in the neighborhood and know fewer store employees.

4. The degree to which housewives *socialize* with neighbors tends to influence loyalty. Brand- and store-loyal consumers report moderate to heavy socialization with their neighbors and say that neighbors are a source of food-purchasing information.

5. The characteristics of consumers associated with brand loyalty *differ among products.* In purchases of coffee, consumers inter-

Figure 9-3   The AID model.

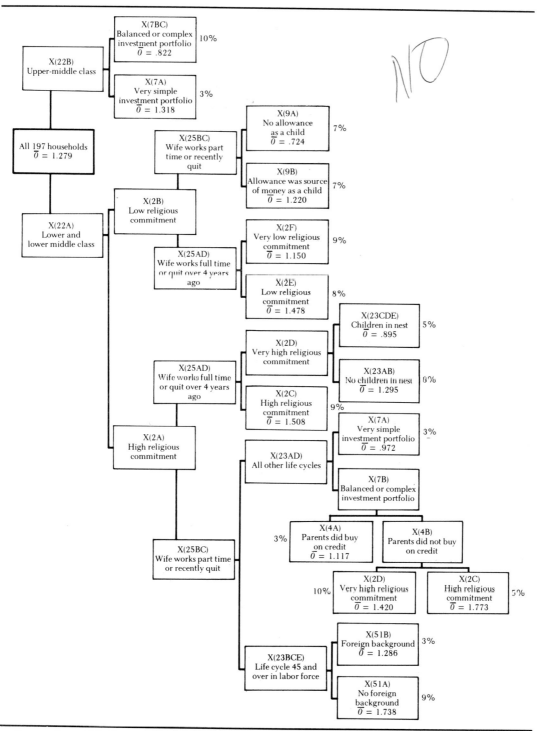

Source: James M. Carman, "Correlates of Brand Loyalty: Some Positive Results," Journal of Marketing Research, *Vol. 7 (February, 1970), p. 69. Reprinted by permission of the American Marketing Association.*

ested in status were most loyal. Orange juice and canned fruit purchases, however, did not reveal similar reference group influences. This finding tends to support conclusions of other researchers that brand loyalty varies according to product category.

The Role of Image in Store Loyalty   In line with the finding that brand loyalty is closely related to store loyalty, Lessig has investigated consumer loyalty across chain stores as a function of store image. He notes that consumer loyalty may be more a question of *avoiding* certain stores than of being attracted to particular retail outlets and concludes that:[39]

• If patronage of one store is the result of "other store avoidance," the retailer is vulnerable to store switching by customers. Since they are not drawn to the store out of any particular liking for its characteristics, they will readily switch to another whose image is consistent with their desires.

• Store loyalty is not only a function of how the image of the store patronized is perceived but also of how consumers perceive the images of other stores. Thus retailers must find out how their own and competing stores are perceived to develop an image consistent with the consumers they wish to attract.

Brand Loyalty and Durable Goods   On the basis of available evidence, research has indicated that brand loyalty is lower for hard goods than for packaged goods. In one study, Newman and Werbel investigated the variables in brand loyalty associated with major household appliances, using the scoring system shown in Figure 9-4.

These researchers concluded that:[40]

1. *Brand loyalty varies directly with perceived satisfaction reported for the old brand.*

This indicates that the satisfied owner is reluctant to spend the time searching for alternatives, a finding well within the implications of brand loyalty theory for packaged goods.

2. *Brand loyalty is less marked in households where more or less than a median price was paid for a major appliance.* We might assume that those who paid less had greater tendencies to shop for appliances, while those who paid higher prices were "trading up."

3. *Brand loyalty appears to be greater in older than in younger households.* Because younger families are growing and exhibit changing needs, they are probably more in-

Figure 9-4   Brand loyalty model for household purchases.

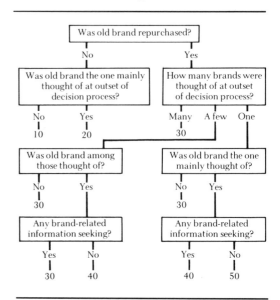

Source: *Joseph W. Newman and Richard A. Werbel, "Multivariate Analysis of Brand Loyalty for Major Household Appliances,"* Journal of Marketing Research *(November 1973), p. 405. Reprinted by permission of the American Marketing Association.*

clined to purchase different brands. Additionally, their generally lower incomes may dictate more studious shopping for greater values.

Industrial "Source" Loyalty While much research has been devoted to consumer brand and store loyalty, few investigations have entered the realm of industrial purchasing. One study of "source" loyalty exhibited by industrial buyers was conducted by Wind, who provides the first model for source loyalty analysis (Figure 9-5).

Wind contends that the probability of strong source loyalty is high when:[41]

1. *Pricing is constant or reduced from the previous buy.* Thus the buyer has no reason to look elsewhere for cost savings.

2. *The dollar value of the order is small.* When no significant cost savings can be expected from other sources, the buyer is reluctant to pay for investigating alternatives.

3. *The past cost-savings are high.* When there is little pressure upon the buyer to cut costs, less motivation to look for savings from other sources exists.

4. *The specific brand is recommended by the actual user.* Usually the purchaser receives either no specific brand information or a number of possible brands from the person(s) who will use the item. But when a specific brand is recommended, the buyer tends to accept the user's judgment. This holds implications for the direction industrial marketing might follow in finding and persuading the ultimate user.

Figure 9-5   A simplified model of industrial source loyalty.

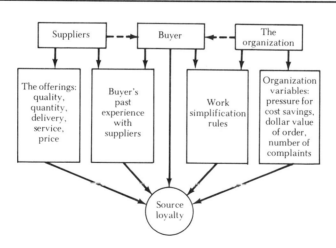

Source: Yoram Wind, "Industrial Source Loyalty," Journal of Marketing Research, *Vol. 7 (November 1970), p. 451. Reprinted by permission of the American Marketing Association.*

Probability Models

One sophisticated development in consumer learning research is the use of *stochastic* or *probability* models to predict purchasing behavior. A probability measure rests on the learning proposition that a buyer's previous (and particularly most recent) purchasing behavior will determine future behavior. Numerous stochastic models have been designed to quantify this relationship. Stochastic models have, to date, been applied to studies of brand loyalty, brand acceptance, brand switching, and new product forecasting.

Brand Loyalty In an early application of a stochastic model to consumer behavior, Kuehn arrived at the following conclusions about predicting purchases of frozen orange juice:[42]

1. Frequent purchasers of frozen orange juice are the consumers who will most probably develop brand loyalties.

2. The greater the time interval between purchases, the smaller the probability that the same brand will be purchased.

3. Purchasers of frozen orange juice do not form brand loyalties strong enough to negate the probability of brand switching.

Brand Acceptance When probability is applied to consumers who are trying a new or existing brand for the first time, it provides a measure of potential *brand acceptance*. Such measures are useful to marketers who must introduce a new brand with some indication of its future, or monitor the strength of an existing brand with an eye toward probable future sales.[43]

Aaker applied stochastic methodology to a study of brand acceptance by new users and found that:[44]

• High volume users of a product are more difficult to win over to a new brand (once they have tried it) than average users.

Figure 9-6 Projected new subscriptions and cumulative subscriptions of cable television, based on 1963–1972 data.

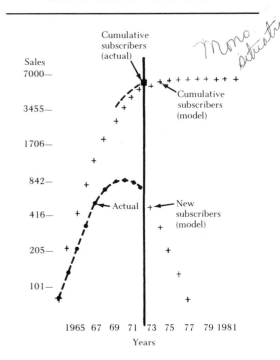

Source: Wellesly Dodds and Arnold M. Durham, "An Application of the Bass Model in Long-Term New Product Forecasting," Journal of Marketing Research, *Vol. 10 (August 1973), p. 310. Reprinted by permission of the American Marketing Association.*

• Buyers who tend toward brand loyalty are more likely to accept a new brand once they have tried it.

Brand Switching   Bass concluded that brand choice may be predicted through stochastic preference, and that brand switching in one study confirmed the probabilistic nature of choice.

Through analyzing the soft drink choices of students and secretaries over a three-week period, he made the following observations:[45]

• There is substantial brand switching in the soft drink market; thus the brand loyalty factor is well below average.

• The three brands achieving the largest market share are fairly close in preference, but substantially different from the brands gaining smaller shares. The variance in shares among the three majors is an indication of substantial switching.

New Product Forecasting   Dodds has adapted a Bass model of first-purchaser activity to the forecasting of new subscriptions for cable color television units. Observing data from subscriptions for cable installations from the years 1963 to 1972, he notes that the market is rapidly reaching saturation and contends that an earlier forecast based on initial new-user data would have provided a reasonably good forecast of peak sales *four years* before the event (Figure 9-6).[46]

The use of stochastic models is now gaining momentum and promises great utility in other related areas—multibrand buying, segmentation by stochastic preference, the influence of decision variables on stochastic preference, and similar applications.[47]

Summary

Learning is a major influence on consumer behavior, important to marketers who wish to find out how buying preferences and habits are formed, how choices might be predicted, and how advertising messages may be "learned" more efficiently.

There are two theories of learning, behaviorist (S-R learning) and cognitive (human beings as adaptive problem-solvers). Learning may be defined as *the acquisition of new responses to behavioral cues in the environment, as the result of reinforcement.*

Generalization describes a tendency to respond to similar stimuli in the same way, while *discrimination* means choosing prefer-

ences. Both are useful concepts to marketers. Research into *retention*, or remembering material, and *forgetting* holds lessons for advertisers about repetition and the quality of advertising messages.

Habit formation occurs when responses are reinforced; this is the basis for *brand loyalty*, biased choice behavior with respect to branded merchandise. *Probability models* have increasingly been applied to studies of brand loyalty as well as other predictive measures of behavior, and promise to be a useful methodology evolved from learning theory.

NOTES

1. William J. McGuire, "Some Internal Psychological Factors Influencing Consumer Behavior," *Journal of Consumer Research*, Vol. 2, No. 4 (March 1976), p. 302.

2. J. B. Watson, as cited in John A. Barlow, *Stimulus and Response* (New York: Harper and Row, 1968).

3. B. F. Skinner, "Are Theories of Learning Necessary?", *Psychological Review*, Vol. 57, No. 4 (July 1950).

4. O. Hobart Mowrer, *Learning Theory and Behavior* (New York: John Wiley and Sons, 1960), p. 16.

5. Robert Ferber, ed. *A Synthesis of Selected Aspects of Consumer Behavior* (Washington, D.C.: National Science Foundation, 1976).

6. Rom J. Markin, Jr., *Consumer Behavior: A Cognitive Orientation* (New York: The Macmillan Co., 1974), p. 113.

7. L. W. Gregg, ed., *Knowledge and Cognition* (New York: John Wiley and Sons Inc., 1974).

8. Markin, *Consumer Behavior*, p. 239.

9. Ernest R. Hilgard and Gordon H. Bower, *Theories of Learning* (New York: Appleton-Century-Crofts, 1966).

10. Howard L. Kingsley and Ralph Garry, *The Nature and Conditions of Learning* (Englewood Cliffs, N.J.: Prentice-Hall, 1957).

11. G. S. Reynolds, *A Primer of Operant Conditioning* (New York: Scott, Foresman and Co., 1968), p. 1.

12. David S. Austin and James M. Johnson, *Explaining Behavior* (Encino, Calif.: Dickenson Publishing Co., 1974).

13. Howard H. Kendler, *Basic Psychology* (New York: Appleton-Century-Crofts, 1968).

14. Austin and Johnson, *Explaining Behavior*, p. 60.

15. B. F. Skinner, *The Behavior of Organisms: An Experimental Analysis* (New York: Appleton-Century-Crofts, 1966).

16. Lewis C. Winters and Wallace H. Wallace, "On Operant Conditioning Techniques," *Journal of Advertising Research*, Vol. 10, No. 5 (October 1970).

17. Lewis C. Winters and Wallace H. Wallace, "Operant Behavioral Measures of the Effect of Advertising Content and Placement" (Speech at American Psychological Association Convention, Chicago, 1965).

18. D. Z. Newman and W. H. Wallace, "Validation of an Operant Conditioning Technique Through Induced Sales Data" (Speech at Eastern Psychological Association, Boston, 1967).

19. G. S. Reynolds, *Operant Conditioning*, p. 439.

20. John A. Howard, *Marketing Theory* (Boston: Allyn and Bacon, 1965, p. 109).

21. Howard, *Marketing Theory*, p. 109.

22. Austin and Johnson, *Explaining Behavior*, p. 69.

23. T. Verhave, "The Pigeon as a Quality Control Inspector," *American Psychologist*, No. 21 (1966), pp. 109–115.

24. Steuart Henderson Britt, "Applying Learning Principles to Marketing," *MSU Business Topics*, No. 23 (Spring 1975), pp. 9–16.

25. Adapted from: Herman Ebbinghaus, *Memory* (Teachers College, Columbia University, 1913); D. O. Hebb, *The Organization of Behavior* (New York: John Wiley and Sons, 1949); Carl I. Hovland, Irving L. Janis, and Harold H. Lelley, *Communication and Persuasion* (Yale University Press, 1953).

26. Thomas Smith, *Hints to Intending Advertisers*, London, 1885, as cited in Herbert E. Krugman, "An Application of Learning Theory to TV Copy Testing," *Public Opinion Quarterly*, Vol. 26 (1962), pp. 626–634.

27. Leo Bogart, *Strategy in Advertising* (Harcourt, Brace, and World, 1967).

28. John B. Stewart, *Repetitive Advertising in Newspapers* (Boston: Harvard University, 1964).

29. James H. Myers and William Reynolds, *Consumer Behavior and Marketing Management* (Boston: Houghton Mifflin, 1967).

30. Doubleday Advertising Company, 1977.

31. Kendler, *Basic Psychology*, p. 284.

32. Kingsley and Garry, *Learning*, p. 95.

33. W. T. Tucker, "The Development of Brand Loyalty," *Journal of Marketing Research*, Vol.3 (August 1964), pp. 32–35.

34. Tucker, "Brand Loyalty," p. 35.

35. George H. Brown, "Brand Loyalty—Fact

or Fiction," *Advertising Age*, No. 23, June 9, 1952; and Ross M. Cunningham, "Brand Loyalty—What, Where, How Much?", *Harvard Business Review*, No. 34 (January–February 1956).

36. John V. Farley, "Why Does Brand Loyalty Vary Over Products?", *Journal of Marketing Research*, Vol. 1 (November 1964), pp. 9–14.

37. Farley, "Brand Loyalty," p. 14.

38. James M. Carman, "Correlates of Brand Loyalty: Some Positive Results," *Journal of Marketing Research*, Vol. 7 (February 1970), pp. 67–76.

39. V. Parker Lessig, "Consumer Store Images and Store Loyalties," *Journal of Marketing*, Vol. 37, No. 4 (October 1973), pp. 72–74.

40. Joseph W. Newman and Richard A. Werbel, "Multivariate Analysis of Brand Loyalty for Major Household Appliances," *Journal of Marketing Research* (November 1973), pp. 404–408.

41. Yoram Wind, "Industrial Source Loyalty," *Journal of Marketing Research*, Vol. 7 (November 1970), pp. 450–457.

42. Alfred A. Kuehn, "Consumer Brand Choice as a Learning Process," *Journal of Advertising Research*, Vol. 2 (December 1962), pp. 10–17.

43. David A. Aaker, "A Measure of Brand Acceptance," *Journal of Marketing Research*, Vol. 9 (May 1972), pp. 160–167.

44. Aaker, "Brand Acceptance," p. 167.

45. Frank M. Bass, "The Theory of Stochastic Preference and Brand Switching," *Journal of Marketing Research*, Vol. 11 (February 1974), pp. 1–20.

46. Wellesley Dodds, "An Application of the Bass Model in Long-Term New Product Forecasting," *Journal of Marketing Research*, Vol. 10 (August 1973).

47. Roger J. Best, "The Predictive Aspects of a Joint-Space Theory of Stochastic Choice," *Journal of Marketing Research*, Vol 13, No 2 (May 1976).

MARKETING APPLICATIONS

Conclusion 1   *Behavior which is reinforced is likely to be learned, just as behavior which is not reinforced is likely to be extinguished.*
Application   This basic tenet of learning is applied to many marketing functions. It is apparent in the retail environment where incentives are offered to try new brands. It is operative in the repetition of the same advertising message. It is also the basis of marketers' attempts to ensure satisfaction with purchases and thus influence further purchasing activity.

Conclusion 2   *Brand loyalty is the marketing term for consumer habit formation—a consistent preference for one brand or store over all others in the market domain.*
Application   Marketers may encourage brand loyalty for a specific item by (1) segmenting the market to distinguish the consumers who are most likely to develop loyalties (i.e., higher income consumers who do not feel it necessary to "shop" for lowest prices), and (2) reinforcing a consistent purchasing pattern by maintaining quality standards, maintaining competitive exposure with other brands in advertising, packaging, and distribution, and keeping prices fairly well in line with competitive brands.

Conclusion 3   *"Source" loyalty refers to consistent purchasing behavior at the industrial level, which appears to be influenced by factors that may be marketer-controlled.*
Application   A strategy for industrial marketers to enhance repeat sales would include constant (or reduced) pricing, costs which are competitive with other sources, and strong recommendations from other users of the industrial product. A representative selling computerized accounting services to hotel comptrollers, for example, would be wise to offer several "references" from other hotel financial executives who have benefited from the service.

ASSIGNMENTS

Research Assignment

Background   As a psychologist who is a nonsmoker (or a smoker who wants to quit), you have decided to offer your community a service called Smokebreakers to help people give up the habit through "unlearning" principles. You visualize your service as a group session a few nights a week that will offer your clients social support as well as behavioral techniques.

To decide upon the most effective ways to help people stop smoking, you are interested in the factors they feel contributed most heavily to their developing the habit to begin with. Thus, your research prior to forming Smokbreakers will focus on consumers' own perceptions of how they "learned" to use a popular product.

Methodology   You wish to determine through interviews with at least 5 smokers how important they perceive each of several factors to have been in the formation of their habits. So you work with a questionnaire that includes these items:

Rank the reasons for your starting to smoke cigarettes from the most (1) to the least (5) important.
I was influenced by advertising.
My friends got me to smoke.
My parents and their friends smoked.
I wanted to be more "adult."
I wanted to be like people I saw on TV or in the movies.
After you began smoking, how important was each of these factors in your continuing to smoke? (rank from 1 to 5.)
I felt addicted to tobacco.
I liked the taste.
Smoking relaxed me when I felt nervous.
I liked to have something to do with my hands.
I liked the sensation of the smoke in my lungs.
When do you always (or almost always) reach for a cigarette now?
After eating.
When I'm with other people who are smoking.
When I feel nervous about being with other people.
When I'm under pressure.
When I'm drinking coffee.
When I'm drinking liquor.
When my hands are unoccupied.

Extrapolation   What are the most common reasons for learning to use cigarettes and the most common reinforcements for continuing their use? Are there other products whose use is learned in similar ways?

Creative Assignment

You have been appointed Director of a group called Consumers for Better TV, which addresses itself to the challenge of obtaining better programming from the networks and less "objectionable" commercials from advertisers.

One of your main projects is to discuss with advertisers and their agencies different possibilities for creating TV commercials that will not "turn off" viewers through their constant repetition. You are familiar with the reasons for frequent repetition of commercial messages and the need for commercials that will "intrude" on the consumer's consciousness to break through commercial clutter on the air. But you are also well-grounded in the argument that, if commercials were better-conceived in the first place to tell the product story, they would not have to be so "objectionable" and would not have to be repeated so often.

As an example to use in bolstering your argument, pick a commercial that seems to lack a good persuasive message for buying the product and relies totally on repetition to be effective. Reconceive that commercial so that it will be more effective and less objectionable to the viewer. Use the same product advantage stressed in the objectionable commercial.

Managerial Assignment

As a Brand Manager for the United Beverage Company, you are responsible for marketing a carbonated soft drink known as Yodel. This drink has been distributed in the Southern states for some years with notable success—now *United* wishes to market it nationally to compete with Coca-Cola, Pepsi-Cola, Dr. Pepper, and Seven-Up.

Yodel has a tart, distinctly lemon taste that has proven popular with the 18–25 market, and advertising appeals have maintained a Country and Western music flavor to give the drink a personality.

To position the brand for the national market, you are concerned with patterns of brand loyalty for carbonated soft-drink products—a category in which consumers have been quite fickle, frequently switching brands.

For your positioning recommendations to management, prepare a report on brand loyalty patterns for the soft drink category, including all brands for which data is available. Use as your sources page 231 of the preceding chapter, as well as relevant articles from the chapter bibliography, marketing journals, and trade magazines from the beverage industry.

From your research, develop a report on brand loyalty among consumers of soft drinks and make a positioning recommendation on this basis. Should you maintain the folksy Country and Western theme effective in the South or reposition the brand for the national market?

SELECTED READINGS

Dawson, Michael E. and John J. Furedy. "The Role of Awareness in Human Differential Autonomic Classical Conditioning: The Necessary-gate Hypothesis." *Psychophysiology*, Vol. 13, No. 1 (January 1976), pp. 50–53.

Moore, Roy L. and Lowndes F. Stephens. "Some Communication and Demographic Determinants of Adolescent Consumer Learning." *Journal of Consumer Research*, Vol. 2, No. 1 (September 1975), pp. 80–92.

O'Hara, Martin et al. "Creative Memory: Five Suggestions for Categorization of Adult Learning." *Adult Education*, Vol. 26, No. 1 (Fall 1975), pp. 32–52.

Lawrence, Raymond J. "Consumer Brand Choice—A Random Walk?" *Journal of Marketing Research*, Vol. 12, No. 3 (August 1975), pp. 314–24.

Ward, Scott. "Consumer Socialization." *Journal of Consumer Research*, Vol. 1, No. 2 (September 1974), pp. 1–14.

OBJECTIVES

TEN

Perception

The last chapter pointed out that learning takes place when a cue in the environment, such as an ad, triggers a drive that elicits a response. As consumers scan their market domain at any given time, thousands of stimuli are available. Yet only a few of these stimuli bring forth responses, no matter how greedy consumers may be for product information.

Perception is the process through which certain cues are first noted, permitting learning to occur. And perception is, in turn, affected by what a person has already learned about particular cues. Thus, perception and learning are interrelated concepts.

Applied to problems of consumer behavior, perception means considerably more than seeing and hearing. This chapter treats such current topics as:

• How selective perception works to block out important information we do not "want" to receive.

• Whether there is really "subliminal seduction" in advertising.

• Why the reasons behind consumers' brand image of a packaged goods product may have nothing to do with what's inside the package.

• How consumers perceive the relationship between price and quality.

• Why the perception of "risk" can complicate the purchase of even a 39-cent item (and how consumers form strategies to reduce risk).

A thorough understanding of perception becomes extremely useful in decisions affecting packaging, pricing, and enhancing retail display performance. On a more immediate level, perception is a critical variable in the consumer decision-making process discussed in the next section—influential in both product choice and retail purchasing.

Types of Consumer Perception

What makes a consumer prefer one brand of hand soap over another? Hand soaps are most often parity products—99 percent physically alike—so the differences among them must be that consumers perceive one branded product as somehow different from others. Some differences such as packaging, color, and scent, are readily apparent. Others are not so obvious. A consumer's perception of a brand's *image*—what kind of people use the brand and why?—will affect the purchasing process. Part of that image comes from ways in which the product is advertised. Which consumers respond to the ads for a particular brand? Do they remember the soap brand as a quality product used by people with whom they identify? Another important consideration is how consumers view the *price* of a product. Are they buying the brand because it is inexpensive, or do they select one because they are willing to pay more for quality factors or a certain kind of packaging? Finally, how much *risk* do consumers identify with that brand? Although it seems strange to think of buying hand soap as a risky proposition, risk perception does play a significant role in much consumer purchasing behavior.

The way in which a product is perceived is intricately tied to the share of the market it gains. Advertisers work very hard to create distinct images for the products they want to sell. Influencing the consumer's perception of the product, of its effects and its value, is part of image creation.

Just as some kinds of perception direct positive purchase choice, risk perceptions will lead to avoidance of products. Although we all enjoy taking a chance once in a while (if the consequences are not likely to be dire), we usually try to minimize the discomfort induced by bad decisions. If a shampoo does not result in gorgeous hair, we simply throw that 89-cent product away and resolve not to buy it again. If, however, a new automobile proves unreliable, we become much more concerned and aggravated. In buying behavior the consumer tries to avoid risk by acquiring as much information as possible.

The information we receive comes through the process of perception. Perception thus forms the basis for a great deal of decision-making. Understanding the process of perception, both sensory and social, is therefore fundamental to understanding consumer behavior.

This chapter explores some of the major theories, modes, and characteristics of perception, and factors determining how we perceive. Finally, various findings from perception research in consumer behavior are scrutinized.

Definition of Perception

Measuring stimuli and responses associated with the five senses was the traditional study of perception. But the old use of the term to designate simply the use of eyes, ears, nose, mouth, and hands, or other areas sensitive to touch, is no longer sufficient. For our purposes, we may define perception as the *way in which an individual gathers, processes, and interprets information from the environment.* The senses, of course, play a large part in human *apprehending* and *comprehending* of experience, but many phenomena indicate that *interpreting* goes on as well. Beyond interpretation, the process by which an individual organizes sensations of, for instance, brownness, smoothness, fizziness, coolness, and wetness into the meaningful unit, "bottle of beer in my hand," seems to demand a higher level of perception. *Analytic introspection* is one name for putting together, or synthesizing, a group of stimuli into a form or structure or whole.[1]

Gestalt and Cognitive Theories of Perception

Two major theories that have shaped current thinking about perception are the older Gestalt and more recent cognitive approaches.

The Gestalt Tradition

Gestalt theorists contend that a whole object cannot be predicted simply by adding up our perceptions of the parts. The parts may, in fact, become unobservable when combined with other parts. The term "gestalt" means "whole form, or configuration," and the Gestalt theory holds that we perceive *form* above all else. When the key of a certain advertising jingle is changed, for example, the melody does not cease to be recognizable. "I'd Like to Buy the World a Coke" is recognized as the same song whether it is professionally sung by children on a mountaintop in the familiar commercial, or hummed by someone sitting next to us on the bus. Or in Gestalt terms, the form we perceive remains constant even though specific points may be changed. The Gestalt approach is considered especially useful in understanding how individuals *process* perceptual data into meaningful wholes.

A contemporary branch of philosophy that deals with perception, *phenomenology,* carries this view one step farther. Phenomenologists assert that deep meditating can bring us to "eidetic reduction," that is, a perception of the qualities of form used to represent an object that are so basic that they make the object represented perceivable as itself. This principle seems evident even in the evolution of corporate logos. Note how the Bell Telephone bell symbol has become simpler over the years until it is now a mere simplified outline, yet it is clearly recognizable as a bell. International road sign symbols operate under the same principle.

Since the *lower* order variables—individual points of color, single tones, and the like—can change without affecting our perception of form, the determinants of perception must be *higher* order variables. Gestaltists have isolated experimentally some of the higher order variables that affect visual perception. Foremost among these are the concepts of *figure* and *ground.* Any contour divides stimulation of the eye into two regions, and the shape of both cannot be perceived simultaneously. At a given moment only one shape will be seen. That is the "figure." It will appear to be interposed between viewer and some indeterminate backdrop, the "ground" (Figure 10-1).

Certain laws of organization emerge from Gestalt experiments. When visual stimuli are ambiguous, that is, capable of being interpreted in two or more ways, these laws determine perception of shape.[2]

1. *Area.* The smaller a closed region, the more it tends to be seen as figure.

2. *Proximity.* Dots or objects that are close together tend to be grouped together.

3. *Closedness.* Areas with closed contours tend to be seen as figures more than do those with open contours.

4. *Symmetry.* The more symmetrical a closed region, the more it tends to be seen as a figure.

5. *Good continuation.* That arrangement of figure and ground tends to be seen that will show the fewest changes or interruptions in straight or smoothly curving lines or contours.

Hochberg notes that most of the above "laws" can be contained under the Law of Simplicity:[3]

We are what is simplest to see. Whether by early perceptual learning or by inborn arrangement, our nervous systems seem to choose those ways of seeing the world that keep perceived surfaces and objects as simple and constant as possible.

The Cognitive View of Perception

Cognitive psychology accepts the Gestalt model of a total, holistic approach to behavior, and recognizes perception as an important part of cognitive activity.

First of all, these theorists use the term *cognitive structures* to identify the attitudes, beliefs, and ideas that individuals use to

Figure 10-1 Figure (white) and ground (black).

distinguish, and make sense out of, different stimuli in the environment.[4] It is through these cognitive structures that the process of *cognition*—acquiring and using knowledge—actually occurs. The consumer, it will be remembered, is an adaptive information processor and decision maker. ("Information" now refers not just to how to buy articles, but to all stimuli.) Somehow, this adaptive organism must constantly change its cognitive structures to accommodate new information, and this is the role of perception.

Markin represents the relationship between cognitive structures and perception by the following model (Figure 10-2).

Stimuli from the environment (Cell 1) are fed to the central nervous system (Cell 2), where cognitive structures (values, attitudes,

Figure 10-2 Cognitive model of perception.

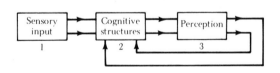

Source: Rom J. Markin, Jr., Consumer Behavior: A Cognitive Orientation, *(New York: Macmillan Publishing Co., Inc. © 1974), p. 199. Reprinted by permission.*

beliefs, and images) are stored. Through these structures, the individual may interpret and react to the stimuli in some meaningful way, resulting in perception (Cell 3). The perception of those stimuli is then fed back (and stored) as a new addition to the cognitive structures, which will help filter future experiences.[5]

For instance, a person casually walking by a popular "bargain basement" style discount store notices a commotion as an apparent shoplifter bursts out of the door and makes a wild dash down the sidewalk. But in hot pursuit is a uniformed security guard who races behind, gains steadily on his target, and suddenly tackles the shoplifter, pulls him to his feet, and drags him by the collar back into the store. Now the observer of this episode filters this sensory stimulus through cognitive structures of attitudes and beliefs. The fact is, this person has always seen that store as a pretty sleazy shopping environment, with rude salespeople, untidy displays, and a fairly low-end clientele. The perception that emerges is that the *shoplifter* was somehow victimized ("Look how that guard treated him, and he probably just forgot to pay for something"). This perception in turn becomes a part of the person's cognitive structures, so that in interpreting future stimuli about that store, he will weigh all his previous attitudes *plus* the most recent perception that the store personnel actually brutalize innocent customers.

Modes of Perception

The basic modes of perception are visual, aural, olfactory, and tactile; we see, hear, smell, taste, and touch the world around us. Also, we perceive in a *kinesthetic* mode, using muscles and joints, and in a *vestibular* mode through our internal organs. These are the senses that react to energy-emitting external stimuli: mechanical, chemical, or electromagnetic energy. The pressure of a stubbed toe or a swallow of bad coffee, for example, generally produces a somewhat painful perception when it impinges on the senses.

Visual

From a physiological standpoint, vision consists in the retinal reaction to external stimuli. Biochemically triggered messages race to the brain along the optic nerve each time the cells "fire."

Visual perception is a crucial input for consumer decision making, and product advertising and packaging are all designed to provide visual cues. In packaging, for example, laundry detergents are dressed in bright, even garish, boxes with design elements such as lightning bolts and prominent, hard-hitting names like DUZ, BOLD, or BIZ. Their jarring appearance is designed to compete with the other detergents in the same supermarket display. Expensive cosmetics, however, are usually found in sophisticated, often award-winning packages to enhance the glamorous image.

Aural

Like vision, hearing can be measured scientifically. "The human ear is sensitive to sounds with frequencies between about 20 and 20,000 cycles per second . . . the upper limit for a normal adult being about 12,000-15,000 cps."[6] Yet such statistics do not reveal why some sounds are mere noise and others create sensations of pleasure, why one person's favorite music is another's severe irritant.

Swedish researcher Lage Wedin conducted an investigation of perceptual-emotional qualities in music, finding that there was indeed some agreed upon correlation between technical properties—tempo, pitch, and the like—and the emotions they induce—solemnity, triviality, gaiety, dignity, and so on.[7] Some music has rather narrow appeal (such as acid rock when it was first introduced) but other forms are perceived as enjoyable by large and diverse groups of people. Among the highest paid individuals in the advertising world are the jingle composers who can create tunes so catchy that people will make them a part of their humming or whistling repertoire. The jingle has developed into a major awareness technique for advertisers who want a certain tune associated, through repetition, with a certain product or service.

Olfactory

Since smell and taste are closely entwined, they can be discussed jointly as the "olfactory" mode of perception. The tongue is the physiological organ of taste, containing nerve endings sensitive to bitterness, sweetness, saltiness, liquidity or solidity, heat and cold. That smell is crucial to taste is obvious to anyone whose nose has been stuffed up with a bad cold. The old trick of pinching a child's

nostrils shut while spooning down some foul-tasting medicine is still an effective measure for alleviating the nasty flavor.

Perceptions of smell and taste may not be as well developed in human beings as in other animals, but their role in everyday existence is greatly influenced by cultural and social factors. The many advertisements for products that deodorize bodies and change mouth odors from pizza to mint show how aroma-conscious we are. As Doty points out, odors are ". . . more than experiences tallying with the chemical composition of substances . . . Odors involve emotional and other conditioned responses which may be too varied and diverse to catalog."[9]

Some intriguing conclusions about olfactory perception include:[10]

1. While agreement is unanimous on what smells are dreadful, it is not so strong on what smells are desirable.

2. Children dislike oily smells but the smell of onions and chives are enjoyed most by young adults.

3. One cannot predict odor preference on the basis of personal temperament, but introverts are more receptive to strange odors than extroverts. Males are more stable in odor preferences than females.

Tactile

Perceptions of the "feel" of things are important to people. Fingertips are particularly sensitive perceptors, because nerve endings are clustered very closely there. Other parts of the body, the lower back, for example, have nerve endings widely spaced. A pin prick readily perceived on finger or forearm

The Great Coke and Pepsi Taste-Test War

During the summer of 1976, a pitched advertising battle raged between the two soft drink giants, Coke and Pepsi.[8]

It all started when Pepsi began running commercials in Dallas, where its share of market was low, claiming that in blind taste tests, more Coke drinkers actually preferred Pepsi than their own brand.

"Foul!" cried the Coke people. The reasons for those results, they argued, had nothing to do with taste but with the fact that Pepsi was always labeled *M* in the blind test and Coke *Q*. And there is a distinct consumer bias for the letter *M* over the letter *Q*. Pepsi then replaced those letters, labeling Pepsi *L* and Coke *S*. "Foul again!" Coke spokesmen retorted. "The very same bias applies to those letters as well."

What began as a single-market initiative was growing to national proportions, as Pepsi introduced the campaign in other large urban markets like Los Angeles and New York, where ads began claiming that consumers preferred Pepsi over Coke 2-to-1. The campaign, called "The Pepsi Challenge," invited Coke drinkers to try Pepsi for themselves and compare. It was believed to be the first competitive advertising for a major company in which superiority claims were based strictly on taste.

Coke quickly retaliated with a defensive campaign, bringing to the consumer's attention the question of people's biases for some letters over others in taste-test labeling. This rejoinder campaign escalated along with "The Pepsi Challenge," until Coke was finally running commercials spoofing the whole business of taste tests as irrelevant—the theme was "One Sip Isn't Enough." One commercial, for example, showed a woman taking the taste test, explaining that she preferred *Q* because her spirits told her to. Many observers thought that Coke's strategy was to muddy the waters so that consumers would distrust all taste-testing, in which case Coke as the market leader would continue to prevail.

There will be more on taste-testing later in this chapter.

is far less noticeable on the back or thigh.

Psychological studies of perception by touch are scarce, but some conclusions may be drawn about tactile stimuli. Perceptions of the textures of clothing, car upholstery, hand lotion, and carpets impinge on our sense of touch constantly. Even those far-spaced nerve endings in the lower back take notice of a tack on the seat. But, as with odors and tastes, our responses are to a large extent *conditioned* ones. Manufacturers of fabric softeners and synthetic fibers cater to our learned responses because interpretation of tactile stimuli vary according to individual and also social learning. In the United States a soft bedsheet is considered desirable. In other countries a coarse cotton sheet is considered more pleasing than a silky percale. And a perception such as "the skin you love to touch" varies from one culture to another.

Factors Determining Perception

Two distinct sets of factors—stimuli and responses—determine an individual's perception process. *Stimulus factors* are the physical, chemical, electromagnetic, and all other observable characteristics of the person, object, or situation perceived. *Response factors* are determinants of perception within the perceiver.

Stimulus Factors

Stimulus factors important to the discussion of consumer behavior include: *color, contrast, size, frequency, intensity, motion, position, and isolation.*

Color and Contrast Although a color advertisement in print or on television generally captures greater attention than one in black and white,[11] it loses impact when seen in a context of many color ads. The principle of contrast would suggest that, in a full-color context, a black and white ad is more likely to be noticed. Color perception involves subjective judgments. While "day-glo" or fluorescent colors may gain attention, they may also be highly irritating to some consumers. Some products seem to have very limited ranges of acceptable color. Would you wash your hands with jet black soap? Our perception of body cleanliness traditionally demands white or pastel colors although new soap products in brown and green are gaining acceptance today. Shampoos, on the other hand, have always come in deep and varied colors.

Size Large sizes tend to attract greater attention than small, but the ratio of size increase to attention gained is not a simple one. The larger an object is, the greater any enlargement must be to be perceived. The amount of size increase needed for its perception is proportionately related to the initial size of the stimulus.

Intensity Intensity, the loudness of sounds or brightness of colors, gains attention. As with size, however, doubling the intensity of a stimulus boosts the attention given it only by a percentage of the increase. Doubling the intensity of the sound does not guarantee that it will get double the degree of attention.

Movement Movement, or its illusion, secures attention, and such forms of movement as neon lighting have traditionally been used to attract consumers. Billboards with rotating vertical bars that spell out a different message on each surface may even constitute traffic hazards because of their ability to catch the eye.

Position Position is one of the most interesting determinants of perception. The upper half of a page gets more attention than the lower half, the left-hand side more than the right. (However, Orientals, Arabs, and those used to reading Hebrew will give perceptual emphasis to other portions of a page.) Some research suggests that people "read" the design of a car from rear to front, a tendency that may cause interference when a person sees a picture of a car facing to the left in an ad. In addition, a sculpted line or chrome strip that starts from a low point at the rear of a car and ends at a high point at the front is seen as an *ascending* diagonal and seems to connote speed. Conversely, a line high in the rear and low in the front appears to droop.[12]

Isolation Aloneness, too, projects strong attraction. Centering a small object in a virtually blank page draws the eye to it immediately. One television advertisement for an antacid began with a tiny rotating white sphere in a dark space—a dramatic use of the isolation principle.

Individual Response Factors

Stimulus characteristics are only one aspect of the perception process. Perception factors unique to the individual also play a vital role, even though the internal response factors of perception cannot be gauged with the scientific precision of the external stimuli cited above. Physiological capacity to respond can be measured, but interest, attention, needs, memory, experiences, values, and cognitive set are less quantifiable.

Interest Interest varies from individual to individual, and there have been research generalizations about differences among groups. The perceptual interest of more women than men can be stimulated by depictions of children and babies, and of more men than women by power tools, cars, and athletes, regardless of size, color, or other stimulus factors. Interest also accounts for brand perception to some degree. A Honda owner is more likely to notice Honda ads than Yamaha ads, and fewer consumers pay attention to ads for less popular, less widely owned items than to ads for popular brand names.

Sometimes consumers get "hooked" on ads that stimulate interest by repetition with minor variation. For a while school children took great interest in the next version of the campaign for Alka Seltzer, "Try it, you'll like it," and "I can't believe I ate the whole thing," although they probably did not suffer from stomach upset.

Attention Attention to stimuli changes frequently, at the rate of about one shift every five seconds. Given a large perceptual field, a person pays attention over a longer period by shifting his or her focus to different areas. Attention, in fact, can be defined as focusing narrowly on an incoming stimulus.

Researchers have contended that attention can be objectively measured by ascertaining fine differences in galvanic skin response (GSR) and in pupil dilation. GSR is the measurement of a change in the skin's electrical resistance to a current and of a difference in electrical potential between two different areas of body surface. It provides an indication of arousal and attentiveness. Measurement of the infinitesimal dilations and contractions of the pupil of the eye also indicates focusing attention to stimuli (chapter 3).

Needs Psychological experimentation has indicated that internal need states do, within certain limits, affect perception. Three early experimenters made their subjects undergo a period of hunger while showing them blurry and unrecognizable food pictures. As the fast continued, the subjects' tendencies to see the obscure visual stimuli as food increased. After twelve hours of food deprivation, however, the stimuli produced fewer "food" responses.

A young woman in American society is likely to *overestimate* perceptually the effects of various cosmetic products because of cultural pressure to be good-looking. Similarly, Marlboro ads cater to many men's needs for orthodox signs of virility.

Memory Because we select carefully the information we are going to retain from our daily bombardment of stimuli, we remember very few of the hundreds or thousands of ads we perceive. Many advertising authorities feel, therefore, that the best ad is the one with a single, simple proposition, for instance, "The one beer to have when you're having more than one."

Experience generates perceptual readiness for expected sequences of events. We see the pained woman swallow the pill and "expect" the consequent look of relief. Experience also tends to dictate future perceptions. No matter how strong an airline's claims of passenger service may be, if that airline once bumped you from a scheduled flight, you will probably perceive those claims as untrustworthy.

Values The influence of values on perception has become evident through a number of studies. Postman, Bruner, and McGinnies developed the concept of *perceptual defense*—a means of blocking out perceptions that are repugnant to an individual for various psychological or sociopsychological reasons.

The effect of social status on perception has also been demonstrated. Children from a settlement house in a slum consistently overestimated the sizes of coins of greater value in one study, while children from middle-class homes showed less of this value distortion than the poor children.

Bruner draws this conclusion about the effects of social and cultural values on perception:[13]

. . . once a society has patterned a man's interests and trained him to expect what is likely in that society, it has gained a great measure of control not only on his thought processes, but also on the very material on which thought works—the experienced data of perception.

Cognitive Set Cognitive set is a primary determinant of perception. It is the "map" one makes of one's world, through which some persons, skills, experiences, needs, values, and goals are elevated and others flattened. But this map takes into account the individual's physical and mental capabilities and sociocultural background and environment. One young woman's New York may be composed of a brokerage firm's office on Wall Street, the theater, French restaurants, tennis courts, Bloomingdale's, and exclusive Sutton Place. Another's may comprise Spanish Harlem, secretarial school, the *Iglesia Pentecostal,* and a tiny *groceria.* A person's cognitive set underlies all perception.

Cognitive set accounts for the *selectivity* of perception in that the same objective event is perceived very differently by different observers. Children play a game in which some message is whispered from one to another, with the last person saying it out loud. The distortion from original to final version is often hilarious. The distortions that affect eyewitness reports of accidents or crimes when they appear in court may not be so amusing.

One popular example cited by Hastorf and Cantril points out the differences in perception of a Princeton-Dartmouth football game. The whole game was exceedingly rough. Referees were kept hopping. Princeton's star player received a broken nose and a Dartmouth player suffered a broken leg. The "same" sensory impingements coming from the same football field, transmitted through the visual mechanism to the different viewers, gave rise to different interpretations by different people. Those rooting for Princeton saw Dartmouth as the aggressor while Dartmouth fans blamed the mayhem on Princeton. The authors conclude that "a person selects perceptual stimuli that have some significance for him from his own egocentric position in the total matrix."[14]

Features of Perception Affecting Consumer Behavior

There are four characteristic features of perception that influence how an individual will process and interpret information. These are called perceptual *cues, selectivity, organization,* and *thresholds.*

Perceptual Cues

Cues are stimulus associations, or symbols, that influence perception of a given stimulus. People use perceptual cues to make judgments about what they find in the environment. Stereotyping, for example, is the result of relying on only a few cues about a person to form our attitudes. Standing in a used car lot by a car that interests us, we might suddenly be approached by a fast-talking, cigar-chomping salesman who fits the old stereotype of the less-than-honest used car salesman (although such a hustler would probably be difficult to locate today). From our few cues about this individual's character, we might back away from what was probably a very acceptable purchase.

Consumers use cues like store names, brand names, packaging, and price to help them make buying decisions. These are known as *relevant* cues when they are actual indicators of the store or product's identity or value. We can usually make judgments about a store that are fairly accurate from its personnel (helpful or detached) and decor (expensive or utilitarian) or the advertising it runs (image oriented or bargain basement). But some researchers note that consumers may rely on *irrelevant* cues during complex perceptual problems, especially where information is ambiguous.[15] Buying an expensive piece of jewelry in a foreign country, for example, one may not find the quiet, plush store environment for precious jewels that we are used to in the United States, but a noisy outdoor bazaar. Thus, we might rely on what we perceive as a salesperson's apparent goodwill, or lack of it, in making our decision.

Perceptual Selectivity

Consumers are faced with a staggering variety of stimuli every day. It has been estimated that a person is exposed to more than 300 advertising messages daily, although he or she may be consciously aware of very few of them. Bauer and Greyser have found that a consumer actually perceives only seventy-six advertising messages each day and responds to perhaps a dozen.[16] Similarly, we are confronted with thousands of items when we enter a fairly large drugstore to buy a can of shaving cream, but the chances are that we will walk out with only the shaving cream if we did not perceive something else that triggered a desire-to-purchase reaction.

The process of coping with the dazzling number of stimuli around us by perceiving only some of them is known as perceptual *selectivity.* This process operates through the factors of needs, interests, value and cognitive set, which have been discussed earlier in this chapter. Brand and store preferences invoke selective perception, as do brand and store loyalty. If we "know" that we can rely on the flavor quality of Heinz catsup or the cleanliness of a roadside MacDonald's, then we have made the processes of buying ketchup or stopping off the freeway for a hamburger much easier by narrowing the choices.

Perceptual Organization

Perceptual stimuli occur in a field, only taking on meaning as we organize them. Thus, once some stimulus has gained our attention, we struggle to organize it, to resolve its ambiguity, through our personal frame of reference. We want to know where a sound is coming from and what it means; we want dots, lines, and other shapes to have meaning.

In advertisements, *unification* of the copy headline and visual (or soundtrack and visual if it is a commercial) aid the consumer in organizing the message. An example is the classic Volkswagen ad with a picture of the car and the single-word headline "Lemon." The consumer organized this message immediately and wanted to know "Why is it a lemon?" The persuasive selling copy told readers that a paint bubble had been discovered on this car's glove compartment before it left the factory. And, in line with perfectionist VW standards, the "lemon" had to be made right before it was offered for sale.

Repetition also contributes to perceptual organization, as noted in a fashion publication:[17]

An innovation first makes its appearance and because it is new, it is startling; then a modification of the idea, or a duplication of it is seen—then another, and another. Finally, the observer asks herself: "Can it be that we are actually going to wear these things?" Even as the words are being spoken the idea grows less startling and she is gently coerced into ordering something similar for the first days of autumn.

When as consumers we confront a product in a retail store, our perceptual organization process enables us to consider advertising for that product, brand associations, and such fine discriminations as the size of the package compared with that of a competing brand's package next to it.

Perceptual Thresholds

A threshold is a point of minimum stimulus needed to produce perception. Table 10-1 describes, in lay terms, lower thresholds for the five senses. In the case of hearing, there is also an upper threshold, a limit above which sound is not perceived. In addition to a lower threshold and a *terminal* threshold—the point beyond which increases in stimulus intensity or frequency produce no greater sensation—there is a "difference threshold."[18] The smallest increase in a given stimulus that can be perceived as an increase is

Table 10-1 Some Approximate Detection Threshold Values in Commonplace Terms

SENSE MODALITY	DETECTION THRESHOLD
Light	A candle flame seen at 30 miles on a dark clear night (ca. 10 quanta).
Sound	The tick of a watch under quiet conditions at twenty feet (ca. 0.0002 dynes/cm²).
Taste	One teaspoon of sugar in 2 gallons of water.
Smell	One drop of perfume diffused into the entire volume of a 3-room apartment.
Touch	The wing of a bee falling on your cheek from a distance of 1 cm.

Source: R. H. Day, Human Perception, *John Wiley & Sons, Inc., Sydney, Australia, 1969. Reprinted by permission.*

called the JND, the Just Noticeable Difference.

Weber's Law quantifies the JND as a constant percentage of any given stimulus intensity. If you can just barely perceive a sweeter taste in a soft drink when the original sweetness is increased by 10 percent, then that 10 percent increment will be needed to make you notice a difference no matter what the absolute sweetness.

As another example, Weber's Law may be applied to price perception. An increase of $250 in the price of a $6,000 Buick is perceived as less significant than a $250 price increase on a $1,000 motorcycle.

Subliminal Perception

Prominent in the literature of perceptual thresholds is the curious problem of subliminal perception; that is, can stimuli that are presented at levels below the "limen," or lower threshold of the individual, be somehow perceived and can they affect behavior? One experiment in the mid–1950s appeared to reveal that "subliminal" perception existed and could motivate consumers. While showing movies, a theater projected "Eat Popcorn" and "Drink Coca-Cola" on the screen for 1/3000 of a second. Sales figures jumped 57 percent for popcorn and 18 percent for Coca-Cola during the six-week term of the experiment. However, this study has never been replicated successfully; in addition, variables other than the subliminal messages were in play during the experiment.[19] Among other factors, the movie being shown during the experiment period was *Picnic*, which included many scenes of people eating and drinking in hot summer weather.[20]

If it were possible to persuade people "against their will," by subliminal advertising, profound ethical questions would be raised. But there is general agreement that it is not possible. For one, thresholds vary among individuals. Secondly, no galvanic skin response can be detected during subliminal-perception "states." If a message is below the threshold of visual perception, then, in fact, it is *not* perceived at all. And even if a message were perceived, it would necessarily be easily distorted.[21] "Drink Coke" might make a viewer "go smoke" or "think jokes" or wonder what a "brink stroke" is.

Sexy Ice Cubes?

The subliminal perception controversy was rekindled recently with the publication of a book that accused advertising people of planting hidden sexual messages in print ads—particularly in the ice cubes portrayed in liquor advertising.

Subliminal Seduction (subtitled "Here Are the Secret Ways Ad Men Arouse Your Desires to Sell Their Products") was the result of painstaking research by Wilson Bryan Keys, who offered numerous examples of sexual symbols, four-letter words, and pornographic pictures buried in the otherwise bland content of various ads.[22] He concluded that such "hidden persuaders" were carefully contrived by major advertisers and their agencies to seduce consumers at a subliminal level.

But to people who have worked in ad agencies, there would seem to be a simpler explanation. Much photography for advertising art is sent to professional retouching studios, where artists set to work correcting photographic imperfections and adding visual effects not captured by the camera. Ice cubes in ads, for example, are completely the work of retouching artists, since real ice cubes would melt under the hot lights of the photographer's studio. Retouchers, like most artistic people in commercial fields, want to add something of their own creativity to their work. Some even find it humorous to introduce carefully disguised sexual elements to an ad that must be puritanically straightlaced for the mass market.

Thus such concealed symbols and words in ads (and, indeed, there are numerous examples) are most likely the work of individual creativity, boredom, or mischievousness rather than the cunning and insidious strategy of marketing decision makers that Professor Key suggests.

Perception Research in Consumer Behavior

The multidimensional role of perception in consumer behavior can be examined most directly in three areas: *perception of brand image, price perception,* and *perception of risk.* A consumer is stimulated to select a given product or service from among the plethora of alternatives not so much by the product's intrinsic qualities as by perception of its qualities as they are linked with its brand name.

One of the first problems marketing experts confront in capturing or increasing their brand's share of market is that of gaining brand *recognition.* Once recognized, a brand must be accepted into the consumer's system of buying needs and alternatives. *Brand acceptance* depends in part upon *price perception.* The question of a product's worth is closely linked to the consumer's perception of the product's value. For instance, no price will be too high for the drug that can save your life. For the sake of social acceptability,

Can these ice cubes seduce you?

esteem, and status, some consumers will perceive that a higher price defines a more desirable product. Would a Cadillac Eldorado seem luxurious if it cost as little as a Chevrolet Vega? Furthermore, in every buying experience, a consumer must face *risks*. Buying an old familiar brand is far easier than switching. One cigarette company even went so far as to assert that consumers who developed loyalty to their brand "would rather fight than switch."

Brand Image

One research project that revealed most strongly the effects of brand image on percep-

tion was conducted for a brewing company. Beer drinkers were accepted as subjects on the basis of their ability to discern differences in certain qualities of beer.[23] Specifically, these characteristics included aftertaste, body, foam, aroma, carbonation, bitterness, sweetness, strength, and lightness. Results indicated that these drinkers could *not*, overall, distinguish taste differences in the beers on a brand basis when they drank from unlabeled bottles. Indeed, none of them rated their preferred brands above the others. Only in the variable "perceived carbonation" did the subjects report any significant differences among all the beers tasted. When the same subjects drank from *labeled* bottles, however, the overall ratings of the beers improved and drinkers of one brand of beer gave their brand a whopping 18 percent increase in rating. The study concluded that "product distinctions or differences, in the minds of the participants, arose primarily through their receptiveness to the various firms' marketing efforts rather than through perceived physical product differences."[24]

Similar experiments with cigarettes and cola beverages[25] have obtained comparable results. Consumers do not usually detect significant differences from one brand of a given product to another. The presence of brand labels does affect olfactory perception in that users express preference for "their" brands over others on the basis of "taste." Thus, both *external* factors—such as color or design of labels, packaging, advertising—and *internal* factors—such as mental set, past experience, self-esteem, risk reduction—are interrelated in brand perception.

Recent research has examined the effect of *added information* on consumers' brand perceptions of cars. Differences in brand perceptions did, in fact, change when consumers were exposed to descriptions and performance record profiles of a specific make of automobile's weight, horsepower, service record, and other characteristics.[26]

Other research has assessed the effect of ecological concern on perception of brands of laundry detergents.[27] Some buyers do perceive detergents within a framework of ecological concern, and marketing people may find that segment a steadily growing phenomenon.

Generalizations about the effect of ecological concern include: (1) The greater the concern, the greater the perceived similarity of the nonpolluting brands of detergent; and (2) a large number of consumers perceive these products on the basis of nonecological dimensions (cleaning ability and the like).

One aspect of brand perception is *quality* perception. In research investigating consumers' perception of the quality of tape recorders, a "complex, multidimensional product," overstatement of quality tended to produce more favorable evaluations. Exaggerated claims, or "puffery," produced high *expectations* of performance. Understatement, conversely, produced low expectations. Consumers with high expectations rated tape recorder performance higher than subjects with low expectations even when the recorders did not perform well.[28] Surprisingly, the expected development that high expectations might lead to keen disappointment over standard performance and hence to very *low* product evaluation did not occur.

Price Perception

There is much research evidence that price is a factor in brand sales performance.[29] Generally, higher actual prices suggest greater *risk* to the consumer because the hazard of financial loss looms larger if the product does not satisfy. Consumer perception of price may be *distorted*, like perception in any other area. Also, consumers interpret and respond *differentially* to price information.

A Price-Quality Relationship? In one study probing the effect of price perception on choice behavior, consumers chose products on the basis of price alone.[30] Seven product types (tape recorders, portable stereo sets, molded luggage, tennis rackets, toothpaste, coffee, and suntan lotions) were presented. Three price levels—low, medium, and high—existed for each product type. In choosing tennis rackets and portable stereos, more than 50 percent of the people tested selected the "high"-priced item, while some 60 percent selected the "low"-priced toothpaste, coffee, and suntan lotion. Selections of tape recorders and molded luggage were distributed fairly evenly in all price categories.

Price was perceived to be an indication of *quality* in high-ticket items such as stereo sets and tennis rackets; both perceived risk and social considerations were operating here. Selection of those products entailed greater financial risk than, say, buying a tube of toothpaste. Also, one's toothpaste is not on public display, but one's tennis racket carries social information.

Subjects who selected the *lower* priced items perceived very little price-quality relationship and felt that consequences of unsatisfactory choice would be mild. They expressed belief that brand choice would have little social meaning and also indicated that their purchasing experience was relatively limited.[31]

Are Price Perceptions Always Valid?   Since food purchases constitute some of the most frequent product choices, studies of price perception in the supermarket arena prove especially pertinent. One study concludes that shoppers who "place great emphasis" on price have more *valid* price perceptions than those "not at all price conscious." However, no generalizations could be made about the larger group of consumers between these two extremes.[32] Patrons of the lowest priced stores revealed the most value-price perceptions. Brown cites "a critical attitude of one's own shopping ability, a similar attitude toward others' ability, and the use of price considerations in choosing a supermarket" as indicating consistent perceptual validity. In demographic terms, "the married, full-time housewife" reveals very low price perception validity. Consumers working full

time exhibited more valid price perceptions, as did those who were older and enjoyed higher incomes. Studies such as this indicate that useful market segmentation on the basis of price perception are probably not possible with the information presently available. But one small yet distinct market segment does appear to exist:[33]

The *price conscious* shoppers constitute a distinct market segment. They have not fooled themselves or idealized their own actions. They perceived price levels validly and were not easily misled.

Most shoppers base their supermarket choices on perceptions of convenience, service, quality of meat, and other matters both rational and emotional. Customers do not consistently patronize low priced stores. A nationwide survey on shopping behavior in selected cities reveals that in many urban areas, shoppers are more likely to patronize higher priced stores than lower priced ones. Only in one city did a large majority of shoppers frequent the lowest priced store.

Monroe, surveying the literature of price perception, reports that a significant number of studies do substantiate a perception of *price-quality* relationship.[34] There is also price snobbery. One cosmetic product, for example, showed a poor market performance at a low price but, when reintroduced at a higher price, did well. In the fall of 1974, a perfume manufacturer decided to market the most expensive lipstick ever (priced at more than $6.00 for a single tube), and successfully promoted it as "an affordable luxury." The inverse price-demand relationship (the less it costs, the more people will buy it) is a cornerstone of classical economics, but there also appears to be much evidence of the high price-desirability relationship for some products.

Risk Perception

The perceived quality-price relationship is related to the compelling desire to minimize risk. While brand image usually works strongly in a positive-choice direction, price perception can work in either a positive or negative direction when a product is considered.[35] Consumers react differentially to prices of varying product types. The choice of suntan lotion or cleansing cream, for example, is not usually predicated on a "high price equals high quality" decision. Why do some products sell better when priced higher no matter what their other attributes?

The answer lies in the phenomenon of *risk* perception. Just as the human organism works hard to maintain physiological balance and comfort, it also seeks to avoid psychological insecurity. Consumers abhor uncertainty, yet every decision to purchase will produce consequences the consumer cannot anticipate. Some purchasing decisions result in unpleasant consequences. If a consumer decided to buy an expensive record album set containing two records with thirty-two songs, she might be disappointed to find that she enjoyed listening to only three or four of the songs. So when she purchased the album without listening to it all the way through, she took the risk of paying $10 or $12 for nine minutes of actual enjoyment. She may decide to reduce record purchase risk in the future by listening to friends' records before purchasing her own.

With the shrink-wrap seal around the records, this consumer probably did not experience what is called *performance risk* in buying the album. She could be reasonably sure that the records were not scratched or otherwise damaged and that they had been manufactured properly. She may, however, have given a thought or two to the *psychosocial risk* involved in the purchase—especially if her friends had remarked that the album was a creative failure. Some products are relatively low in functional risk—a new telephone, a pair of jeans or sneakers. Cold remedies and other products that may or may not work are fairly high in functional risk. Clothing purchases are high in psycho-social risk, as they profoundly affect your self-image and the opinions others hold of you. Purchase of a car usually involves perception of both functional and psycho-social risk. Thus perceived risk is a multidimensional phenomenon.

Risk Reduction

To reduce risk, consumers engage in *information seeking*. Uncertainty about possible consequences of a purchase choice can be reduced by talking, asking "the man who owns one," reading use tests in consumer journals, reading or listening to advertisements, examining the article in a store display, or sampling the product (if possible).[36] The midget jars of instant decaffeinated coffee and the sample bars of soap left hanging on your doorknob give you a chance to try a new product with very little risk. If a consumer is already brand-loyal to one instant decaffeinated coffee, a free sample may be the only way to get that consumer to take the risk of trying a new one. Most people would not rush out and snap up the giant economy size jar of a product they knew nothing about. Brand loyalty, discussed in chapter 9, is a risk reduction strategy, for consumers cling to a reliable brand to reduce or eliminate uncertainty and possibly unhappy consequences.

Two different modes of risk reduction may be synthesized in two hypothetical consumer statements. One who perceives *price-quality* relationships as valid says, "I think it pays to get the more expensive of two things. If it costs more, it must be made better. You can be sure it's good. Things that have been on the market a long time must be dependable." Another might say, "I ignore brand names and advertising claims. I just try to get the most for my money. The most expensive item is not always the best. When I need something big, I see what *Consumer Reports* has to say about it, and I compare prices at different stores. I shop around for the best buy."

Risk perception is a highly individual matter, varying greatly from one consumer to the next and depending upon the product under consideration. This variance is due to many factors; *prior product experience, ego involvement* in buying, and general *self-esteem* are among the most important. One researcher found that the features most closely correlated with *high* risk perception

were brand loyalty, disinclination to purchase private or house brands, low willingness to buy new products, and immunity to fellow consumers' product judgments.[37] On the other hand, there are consumers who seem to enjoy taking a chance on new products and make purchase decisions with little or no attempt at risk reduction.

One major goal of most consumers is to feel satisfied that the goods and services they have purchased are fulfilling their needs. Much of a consumer's perceptual energy is directed toward that goal. Out of his or her economic, social, physical, and psychological background arise the determinants of perception—the abilities, needs, and desires to respond to certain stimuli in certain ways. The American market place offers a wide range of choices of any given product, and innumerable stimuli bombard a consumer. This situation, far from confusing and frustrating, may go far to satisfy a person's need to feel competent. Or in Jellison and Harvey's words, "in situations in which they have high perceived choice, they get maximal information about their competence."[38]

Summary

Perception is the way in which individuals gather, process, and interpret what they encounter in the environment. It has traditionally been the study of psychologists—particularly Gestalt, and now cognitive, theorists—and has come to be recognized as an important determinant of individual consumer behavior. The basic modes of perception are visual, aural, olfactory, and tactile. Two distinct sets of factors determine

an individual's perception process. *Stimulus* factors (attributes of the stimuli perceived) include color, contrast, size, frequency, intensity, motion, position, and isolation. *Response* factors (attributes of the perceiver) are physiological capabilities of the sense organs, interest, attention, needs, memory, experiences, values, and cognitive set. Four characteristic features of perception influence how information will be processed and interpreted. Perceptual *cues* are stimulus associations or symbols that aid consumers in making judgments. Perceptual selectivity leads to such an effect as responding to only a dozen of the 300 or so commercial messages we are exposed to every day. Perceptual *organization* creates meaning out of isolated situations perceived. And perceptual thresholds are points at which perception no longer occurs, or changes in degree go unnoticed. Research in consumer behavior has focused on perception of *brand images, price* perception, and perception of *risk* in purchasing decisions.

NOTES

1. See E. C. Carterette and M. P. Friedman, eds., *Handbook of Perception*, (New York: Academic Books, 1974); and Robert Ferber, ed., *A Synthesis of Selected Aspects of Consumer Behavior*, (Washington, D.C.: National Science Foundation, 1976).

2. Julian E. Hochberg, *Perception* (Englewood Cliffs, N.J.: Prentice-Hall, 1964).

3. Hochberg, *Perception*, p. 99.

4. B. F. Anderson, *Cognitive Psychology: The Study of Knowing, Learning, and Thinking* (New York: Academic Press, 1975).

5. Rom J. Markin, Jr., *Consumer Behavior: A Cognitive Orientation*, (New York: The Macmillan Co., 1974), p. 199.

6. R. H. Day, *Human Perception* (Sydney: John Wiley and Sons, Australasia Pty., Ltd., 1969).

7. Lage Wedin, "A Multidimensional Study of Perceptual-Emotional Qualities in Music," *Scandinavian Journal of Psychology*, Vol. 13, No. 4 (1972), p. 241ff.

8. See "Coke Touts 2 to 1 N.Y. Margin as Pepsi Changes Dallas Letters," *Advertising Age*, June 28, 1976; "Pepsi: We're Preferred," *Advertising Age*, July 19, 1976; and "One Sip Not A Taste Test, Coke Tells New Yorkers," *Advertising Age*, August 16, 1976.

9. Richard I. Doty, "The Role of Olfaction in Man: Sense or Nonsense?" in S. Howard Bartley, *Perception in Everyday Life* (New York: Harper & Row, 1972), p. 143.

10. Doty, *Role of Olfaction*, p. 159–161.

11. "Are Color Television Commercials Worth the Extra Cost?" (New York: Association of Color Advertisers, Inc., 1966).

12. James H. Myers and William H. Reynolds, *Consumer Behavior in Marketing and Marketing Management* (Boston: Houghton Mifflin Company, 1967), p. 12 ff.

13. L. Postman, J. S. Bruner and E. McGinnies, "Personal Values as Selective Factors in Perception," *Journal of Abnormal and Social Psychology*, Vol. 43, No. 2 (April 1948), pp. 142–154.

14. Albert H. Hastorf and Hadley Cantril, "They Saw A Game: A Case Study," *Journal of Abnormal and Social Psychology*, Vol. 49, No. 1 (January 1954), pp. 129–34.

15. S. S. Zalkind and T. W. Costello, "Perception: Some Recent Research and Implications for Administrators," *Administrative Science Quarterly*, Vol. 7 (September 1962).

16. Raymond A. Bauer and Stephen A. Greyser, *Advertising in America: The Consumer View* (Cambridge, Mass.: Graduate School of Business Administration, Harvard University, 1968).

17. Diana Vreeland, "Inventive Clothes 1909–1939", (New York: The Metropolitan Museum of Art, 1974), p. 1.

18. Myers and Reynolds, *Consumer Behavior in Marketing*, p. 11.

19. Myers and Reynolds, *Consumer Behavior in Marketing*, p. 14.

20. Richard P. Barthol and Michael J. Goldstein, "Psychology and the Invisible Sell," *California Management Review*, Vol. 1, No. 2 (Winter 1959).

21. Barthol and Goldstein, "The Invisible Sell," p. 92.

22. Wilson Bryan Key, *Subliminal Seduction* (New York: Signet, 1975).

23. Ralph I. Allison and Kenneth P. Uhl, "Influence of Beer Brand Identification on Taste Perception," *Journal of Marketing Research,* Vol. 1 (August 1964).

24. Allison and Uhl, "Beer Brand Identification," p. 85.

25. Myers and Reynolds, *Consumer Behavior in Marketing,* pp. 16–19.

26. Vithala R. Rao, "Changes in Explicit Information and Brand Perceptions," *Journal of Marketing Research,* Vol. 9 (May 1972), pp. 209 ff.

27. Thomas C. Kinnear and James R. Taylor, "The Effect of Ecological Concern on Brand Perceptions," *Journal of Marketing Research,* Vol. 10 (May 1973), pp. 191–197.

28. Richard W. Olshavsky and John A. Miller, "Consumer Expectations, Product Performance, and Perceived Product Quality," *Journal of Marketing Research,* Vol. 9 (February 1972), pp. 19–21.

29. Kent B. Monroe, "The Influence of Price Differences and Brand Familiarity on Brand Preferences," *Journal of Consumer Research,* Vol. 3, No. 1 (1976), p. 42.

30. Zarrel V. Lambert, "Price and Choice Behavior," *Journal of Marketing Research,* Vol. 9 (February 1972), pp. 35–40.

31. Lambert, "Price and Choice," p. 40.

32. F. E. Brown, "Price Image Versus Price Reality," *Journal of Marketing Research,* Vol. 6 (May 1969), pp. 185–191.

33. F. E. Brown, "Who Perceives Supermarket Prices Most Validly?", *Journal of Marketing Research,* Vol. 8 (February 1971), p. 111.

34. Kent B. Monroe, "Buyers' Subjective Perceptions of Price," *Journal of Marketing Research,* Vol. 10 (February 1973), pp. 70–80.

35. J. Paul Peter and Michael J. Ryan, "An Investigation of Perceived Risk at the Brand Level," *Journal of Marketing Research,* Vol. 13, No. 2 (May 1976).

36. Thomas L. Brown and James W. Gentry, "Analysis of Risk and Risk-Reduction Strategies—A Multiple Product Case," *Journal of the Academy of Marketing Science,* Vol. 3, No. 2 (Spring 1975), p. 148.

37. James R. Bettman, "Perceived Risk and Its Components: A Model and Empirical Test," *Journal of Marketing Research,* Vol. 10 (May 1973), pp. 184–190.

38. Jerald M. Jellison and John H. Harvey, "Determinants of Perceived Choice and the Relationship between Perceived Choice and Perceived Competence," *Journal of Personality and Social Psychology,* Vol. 28, No. 3 (1973), p. 382.

MARKETING APPLICATIONS

Conclusion 1 *While items in some product categories can readily be distinguished from one another, perceptible differences in other categories are practically nonexistent. The latter are referred to as "parity" products.*

Application In categories where differences are not easily perceived, marketers must rely on distinctive positioning through packaging, pricing, more widespread distribution, or other factors which will give the product a competitive advantage. All vodka brands, for instance, contain the same ingredients and there is no real taste difference. Thus, a vodka brand might be priced lower than the rest and be promoted on the basis that "as a shrewd consumer, you know that all vodkas are alike—buy Siberian Vodka because it is cheaper and spend the money you save on good caviar."

Conclusion 2 *Stimulus factors such as color, contrast, size, intensity motion and isolation affect consumer perception of market items.*

Application Point-of-purchase materials must be designed to attract attention away from competitive items in a retail environment and to focus attention directly on the product in question. Thus, the most effective point-of-purchase materials are those which use colors in an arresting way not found in the surrounding environment, command a large space, actually move or create the illusion of motion, or are separated from other displays either physically or through some means of bracketing (for example, using color borders around a product display).

ASSIGNMENTS

Research Assignment

Background You are a Marketing Professor and Research Consultant who has been retained by the Regional Brewers' Group, a trade association of local beer manufacturers and bottlers. The brewers are interested in finding out whether consumers can actually distinguish their local beers from those of national competitors by taste alone, since many consumers of local beers swear by their superior brew and others are unfailingly loyal to national brands such as Schlitz and Budweiser.

Research Input Investigations into perceived differences in taste within categories of similar branded products have usually yielded the same findings—consumers cannot normally distinguish their preferred brands from others if they have no cues other than taste.

For a classic study of beer-taste perception, refer to Ralph I. Allison and Kenneth P. Uhl, "Influence of Beer Brand Identification on Taste Perception," *Journal of Marketing Research,* Vol. 1, August 1964, pp. 36–39.

Methodology Your research project will be designed to answer two questions:
· Can beer drinkers distinguish among various brands in a blind test?
· Can beer drinkers identify their "preferred" brands in a blind test?

Your procedure will be as follows:
· Select at least 5 subjects who are beer drinkers and who have tried both regional and national brands.
· Buy a sufficient quantity of four brands of beer—two national brands and two regional brands—to give each subject two separate glasses of each.
· Instruct each subject to taste four unmarked, unidentified glasses, each containing one of the brands, and have them rank each from Most Preferred (1) to Least Preferred (4).
· Then instruct each subject to name his or her brand out of the four unidentified glassfuls tasted.

Extrapolation How do your findings compare with the Allison-Uhl study? What conclusions can you draw about taste preferences for beer and other product categories involving similar branded products?

Creative Assignment

As a designer for the All Creation Art Studio, you have been commissioned to design a package for the new laundry detergent Pro-Clean. The product is so named because it is a commercial-type cleaning formula that gives consumers the same quality wash in their automatic washers as that obtained at an expensive professional hand laundry.

Your research should include a trip to the local supermarket to study your competitors' packages in the laundry detergent section. Your Pro-Clean package should be so designed that consumers will be able to notice it among the sea of other detergents occupying nearby shelf space.

Additionally, you need to consider that your product is an innovation, which the package design can help to position. For examples of how this has been done effectively with other products, note the packaging for Janitor-in-a-Drum and Liquid Plumber.

From your research, design a package of any reasonable size and shape you wish, using a rough sketch to show the brand name off to best advantage so that it will stand out among all the rest. You may also include descriptive copy on the package, along the lines of "The first professional cleaner you can use in your washer."

Managerial Assignment

As a new Sales Representative for the Premier line of industrial piping, you call on industrial buyers in the manufacturing industries who are likely to be familiar with your product. While your product line is generally well regarded by those who have used it, Premier is also considerably more expensive than your competitors' pipe. And the price difference is less a reflection of better quality than a function of the large advertising budget your company wisely maintains to keep Premier's name in front of your prospective buyers.

You are vaguely familiar with the concept of a price-quality relationship that consumers perceive and use as a strategy for reducing risk in purchasing consumer products. But you wish to find out as much about the phenomenon as possible to have in mind as you make your sales calls. Thus you refer to these studies of consumer price-quality perceptions: Zarrel V. Lambert, "Price and Choice Behavior," *Journal of Marketing Research*, Vol. 9, February 1972; Kent B. Monroe, "Buyers' Subjective Perceptions of Price," *Journal of Marketing Research*, Vol. 10, February 1973.

What conclusions can you draw from these studies that might prove useful to you in your sales calls? Or, would you expect the industrial buyer to be unaffected by that perception?

SELECTED READINGS

Davis, Harry L. and Benny P. Rigaux. "Perception of Marital Roles in Decision Processes." *Journal of Consumer Research*, Vol. 1, No. 1 (June 1974), pp. 51–62.

Lawrence, Janet H. "The Effect of Perceived Age on Initial Impressions and Normative Role Expectations." *International Journal of Aging and Human Development*, Vol. 5, No. 4 (Fall 1975), pp. 369–391.

Ostlund, Lyman E. "Perceived Innovation Attributes as Predictors of Innovativeness." *Journal of Consumer Research*, Vol. 1, No. 2 (Sept. 1974), pp. 23–29.

Robertson, Thomas S. and John R. Rossiter. "Children and Commercial Persuasion: An Attribution Theory Analysis." *Journal of Consumer Research*, Vol. 1, No. 1 (June 1974), pp. 13–20.

Sawyer, Alan G. "Demand Artifacts in Laboratory Experiments in Consumer Research." *Journal of Consumer Research*, Vol. 1, No. 4 (March 1975), pp. 20–30.

OBJECTIVES

1. Define *motive* and *motivation* in consumer behavior.   277

2. Discuss the marketing implications of consumers' *physiological* and *social-personality* needs.   278

3. Summarize *psychoanalytic, Gestalt,* and *cognitive* explanations of motivation.   279

4. Discuss and criticize *projective techniques* used in Motivation Research.   285

5. Define *personality* for consumer behavior study.   286

6. Summarize the *major theories of personality.*   287

7. Describe *personality measures.*   290

8. Discuss and criticize the methodologies used in four types of personality research: (1) *product-use studies,* (2) *interpersonal concepts,* (3) *multivariate analysis,* and (4) *psychographic segmentation.*   292

ELEVEN

Motivation and Personality

Learning and perception have been portrayed in the last two chapters as interrelated elements in the consumer's cognitive structure. Somehow a button is pressed and the process of selecting cues, evaluating the situation, and making an appropriate response is activated. The question then arises: What started it all? And the generally accepted explanation is a phenomenon we refer to as motivation.

Motivation is, in turn, the dynamic aspect of a second variable that has come to be called personality.[1] A given individual's personality is popularly believed to be the traits that make that person unique. In consumer behavior research, personality is the total set of responses that make that consumer unique across a variety of market stimuli.[2]

Both of these terms were first used by psychiatrists to help discover the reasons for their patients' deviant behavior. But a growing fascination with psychiatric thought (and jargon) during the 1950s caused some mar-keters to wonder whether these concepts could also uncover consumers' "unconscious" motives for buying things, or whether personality theories purporting to explain behavior in general could offer new insights into consumer behavior in particular.

Although the theories and tests generated by this interest have not offered the magical key to consumer behavior marketers once hoped they might, motivation and personality remain two areas of constant investigation.

This chapter explores such topics as:

• Why a best-selling book warned the public against "motivation research" (MR) during the 1950s.

• Whether MR can uncover people's "hidden" motives for consumption.

• What Freud told us about personality and consumer behavior.

• Which measures of personality are most promising for consumer research and how the findings are used.

275

*• What personality characteristics are asso-
ciated with cigarette smoking, using mouthwash, and after shave lotion.*

*Some of the theoretical topics discussed in
this chapter may appear a bit quaint to advocates of the more scientific, cognitive psy-*

*chology practiced today. But the basic prin-
ciples of motivation are essential to a complete
view of the psychological determinants influencing consumer behavior. And certain
personality measures may yet prove their
usefulness in segmenting consumer markets.*

Theory and Research

The front page of the *Wall Street Journal*
recently carried an intriguing finding from
a Rand Youth Poll:[3]

38% of teen-agers say they buy ridiculous
products to satisfy their egos and salve frustrations; two-thirds believe their contem-
poraries are always making foolish purchases.

Ego-support and frustration-reduction are
only two examples of what psychologists
call *motives*. And just as psychologists have
long attempted to identify the motives responsible for an infinite variety of human
behavior, so have students of consumer behavior in the market place. Theories of *motivation* are derived to explain why individuals are compelled to behave as they do,
especially when their behavior seems "irrational." Behind our discussion of motivation
exists the even broader questions of *personality*—how can an individual's personality
be measured in the first place and how are
personality characteristics related to motivation and ultimate behavior?

In 1957, *The Hidden Persuaders* by Vance
Packard purported to "cast a penetrating
light into the murky world of the motivational
researchers," and answer such questions as
"Why men think of a mistress when they see

a convertible in a showroom window" and
"Why women in supermarkets are attracted
to items wrapped in red." The rationale behind the use of motivation research, or MR
for short, has been identified in Packard's
book, by Louis Cheskin:[4]

Motivation research is the type of research
that seeks to learn what motivates people in
making choices. . . . Actually in the buying
situation the consumer generally acts emotionally and compulsively, unconsciously
reacting to the images and design which in
the subconscious are associated with the
product.

Cheskin, who worked with MR as long ago
as 1935, and Ernest Dichter, for many years
president of the Institute for Motivational
Research, Inc., were pioneers in techniques
known as "depth-probing methods for merchandising."

The "depths" that were probed were the
so-called subconscious levels of the mind.
The belief that there existed "hidden motives" for sexual, oral, or other kinds of needs
to be satisfied by purchased objects, led to
some curious identification of consumer goods
with exotic personality constructs. Powerful
cars came to be viewed as phallic symbols
and enhancers of virility. "The most success-

ful breakfast cereals were building crunch into their appeal to appease hostility by giving outlet to aggressive and other feelings." In one chapter of his book called "Back to the Breast, and Beyond," Packard concluded that smoking represented to the MR people "only one thing: the infant's pleasure in sucking."[5]

Before wondering too hard how such facts about buying motives can be uncovered, one should note that this type of research has not held up well under the scrutiny of time and empirical testing. Motivation research has, in most cases, been found lacking in both useful explanations for marketing decisions and predictive ability.

Motivation, like personality, is a difficult variable to define and use. Yet, both enter into any total conceptualization of the individual influences affecting behavior.

This chapter first considers the theories of motivation and reviews some methods of motivational research. Then personality is examined from several theoretical positions and evaluated as a variable in consumer research that has seen much application but should be used quite selectively in segmentation attempts.

An Overview of Motivation

Motivation is related to the concept of motion—something that has *motive* force can move you. "Motives," at the simplest level, are prime movers of human beings.

Some motives are physiological. Biological needs for food, liquids, warmth, shelter, oxygen obviously produce strong motivation. The drive to satisfy these needs is as strong as the will to survive. Other motives are social rather than biological. The urge for security, the desire for comfort, the yearning to love and be loved, and the need for status and achievement are among these.

As a foundation on which to rest the concepts that will follow, motives may be considered the impelling and compelling force behind all behavior.

Regarding the behavior of consumers, *motivation is the drive to satisfy perceived needs by purchases and to enhance self-image by specific object and brand selection*. It is the cognitive state that can be said to channel a consumer's time, money, and energy into pursuit of some definite market goal.

The Role of Needs

Since all responses to given market stimuli are not identical from one human being to the next, there must be a variable that intervenes between stimuli and responses. Psychologists identify motivation as this intervening variable.

Every organism experiences tension when certain *needs* are unmet. The energy generated by this tension is most rationally directed toward meeting those needs. Psychologists use such a basic motivating force as *hunger* with great effectiveness in their experiments with learning in laboratory animals. When their desire for food is sufficiently great enough, these animals can be trained to accomplish surprising tasks. Some white rats, for example, were trained to dig over three and one-half pounds of sand a day for a food reward.[6] Because they maintained a state of tension—hunger—they could be described as highly motivated to get food through meeting any strange demands of the experimenters.

People's needs may also emanate from the social environment. Sociologists discuss the need people feel to be accepted by their family and peer groups.

Need States

Physiological needs must be met if the human organism is to survive; hence, motivation to reduce physiological tension states is considered *primary*. Biological need systems include such basics as the need for air, food, and water; for sleep and elimination of wastes; for relatively constant internal body temperature and freedom from pain. The nature of biological needs is quite specific: about 70 grams of protein per day for the average adult male, eight hours of sleep, and similar basic physical requirements. The cultural influences to which these needs are subject become obvious when one examines, say, the diet preferences of a hungry Eskimo versus those of a hungry American businessman.

The *social environment* is a second major source of human needs. Socially determined motivations spring from parental pressures, society's expectations, and religious and political laws.

As noted in chapter 2, Abraham Maslow postulated a hierarchical structure of human motivation on the basis of tension-creating needs. His need categories are:[7]

1. *The Physiological Needs:* The body strives constantly for homeostasis—to maintain in the bloodstream the optimum amounts of salt, sugar, protein, fat, calcium, oxygen, acid-base balance, and heat. Moreover, sleep, activity, sex, and other physiological drives exist.

2. *The Safety Needs:* Protection from danger, security against threats, and reliable order and routine in daily affairs are necessary to infants and adults alike. The drive for security is nearly as strong as the need to satisfy physiological needs.

3. *The Love Needs:* The desires to give and receive affection and love, to be lovingly accepted as one who belongs in a family and with a group of friends—these drives are also important motivators.

4. *The Esteem Needs:* People are driven, too, by the need both for self-respect and the esteem of others. They need to be competent, confident, important, appreciated, to have status and worth.

5. *The Need for Self-Actualization:* Because people perceive potential for achievement in themselves, they are motivated by the need to actualize their potential, to achieve in reality what they *think* (believe) they can do.

6. *The Desire to Know and Understand:* The search for meaning and for analyses which will systematize knowledge and enable the construction of a value system is another motivating drive.

7. *The Need For Beauty:* At some level, the aesthetic needs also are strong. Even primitive peoples barely above subsistence living embellish their crude pots and baskets, and their bodies.

Maslow believed that these motivating forces

operated more or less sequentially. That is, as needs at one level were satisfied, those at the next were felt more intensely. Although any given level of needs may never be 100 percent satisfied, as the amount of satisfaction at one level increases, more of the *next* higher level of needs come into play as motivating drives. But the lower level needs *must* be met if the higher ones are to emerge and become salient.

For most consuming Americans, the needs at levels one and two are not problematical. The drives of levels three and four, however, may be strong. Foods are advertised not as means of preventing one's family from starving, but as vehicles for winning the family's love and esteem. Even soft drinks may be associated with these rather than thirst-quenching needs, as seen in the slogan "Ginger ale tastes like Love—find someone and share it."

Levy has characterized products designed to meet needs at the levels higher than simple biological and security needs as "symbols for sale."[8] Merchandise is frequently meant to satisfy psychological longings as well as functional purposes. The cosmetic industry is certainly a potent example. A man does not buy a hair spray; he buys charm and sex appeal, and maybe a status symbol for his bathroom sink. Brand image, as we have seen, contribute more to sales than product qualities or pricing.

A second set of needs was defined by Edwards, who extended several of Maslow's higher levels as specific *personality* needs:[9]

1. Achievement: To do one's best, to accomplish something of great significance.

2. Deference: To find out what others think, to accept the leadership of others.

3. Exhibition: To say witty and clever things, to talk about personal achievements.

4. Autonomy: To be able to come and go as desired, to say what one thinks about things.

5. Affiliation: To be loyal to friends, to make as many friends as possible.

6. Intraception: To analyze one's motives and feelings, to analyze the behavior of others.

7. Dominance: To be a leader in the groups to which one belongs, to tell others how to do their jobs.

8. Abasement: To feel guilty when one does something wrong, to feel inferior to others in most respects.

9. Change: To do new and different things, to participate in new fads and fashions.

10. Aggression. To attack contrary points of view, to get revenge for insults.

11. Heterosexuality: To become sexually excited, to be in love with someone of the opposite sex.

The ways in which an individual responds to these needs are considered indications of "personality," which will be discussed later in this chapter.

Motivation Theory

The theories that have shaped current thinking about motivation in consumer behavior[10] come from three theoretical origins in psychology—*psychoanalytic*, *Gestalt*, and *cognitive*.

Psychoanalytic Theory The psychoanalytic approach to psychotherapy, which Sigmund Freud conceived in the late nineteenth century, underlies a traditional approach to motivation. In his work with disturbed patients, Freud discerned three fundamental forces at work in the human psyche: the id, the ego, and the superego. The *id* is a force that drives a person to pleasure-seeking, aggression, and destruction, and is present at birth. The id says, in effect, "I want what I want when I want it and I'll kick and scream until I get it!" The *superego*, in opposition to the id, is the force impelling a person toward conformity with all of the moral principles learned from society. The superego is thus thought of as a sort of "conscience." Arbitrating between the two polar forces of the id and the superego is the ego, "the reality principle." Through reason, the ego strives to balance the impulses of the id and the inhibitions of the superego. Thus, individuals will vary in motivation and behavior according to the force that is ascendant, according to this conceptual scheme.

Subconscious Motivation   One of the most important legacies of Freudian theory concerning motivation is the concept of the subconscious or unconscious forces in human beings. The role of the subconscious became the focal point for motivational research at about the same time that psychoanalytic treatment became the popular mode of psychotherapy (as well as a source of much cocktail party conversation) during the 1940s and 1950s. Subconscious motivation was also said to be responsible for the so-called Freudian slips people make in speech. A wealthy man addressing a graduating class at a private school said, "Now I want you to take just three million—I mean three *minutes*—to think about . . ." Sometimes calling other people by the "wrong" names is not entirely accidental. We may really be expressing strong emotions we cannot entirely conceal.

Defense Mechanisms   According to Freudian thought, one can resolve conflicts and protect one's self-image by using *defense mechanisms*. *Repression* is the technique of relegating threatening or unacceptable feelings "back" into the unconscious. To the extent that repression is successful as a way of dealing with anxiety, a person may never realize that he or she is actually experiencing a given fear. *Displacement* allows a person to substitute an acceptable object for a morally or socially unacceptable one in the search for pleasure or tension resolution. In buying behavior, strong feelings may be attached to some new purchase as a substitute for affection. *Projection* is the attribution of one's own disliked characteristics to others. Not wishing to admit feeling deep or even unconscious racism, a person may cast aspersions on "bigots." The huge success of the Archie Bunker television character of "All in the Family" may be partially due to the mechanism of projection. A fourth defense mechanism is *identification.* The rationale behind using popular heroes and heroines as "authorities" in advertising is the human tendency to imitate and copy those we admire—to identify with them by being like them. This may be expressed through seeking to use products or brands we think they use. When Joe Namath shaved off his famous mustache with a razor, sports fans who wanted to emulate his various strengths might have identified that razor with them and bought it. The use of such mechanisms as identification, projection, displacement, and repression always occurs below the conscious level, in Freud's view. We are never aware that we are protecting ourselves from what may lurk in our subconscious.

Neo-Freudian Theories   Various disciples of Freud disagreed with his theory that motivation involved strictly id, ego, and superego determinants. Alfred Adler, Erich Fromm, and Karen Horney were among those who saw other forces of motivation molding an individual's behavior. Adler thought that the basic human drive was the urge to achieve superiority. He believed that the very nature of childhood makes any child feel inferior (the "inferiority complex") and imperfect, and that the rest of life is shaped by the struggle to become perfect and superior. Erich Fromm believes that the prime motivation of human beings is to escape from "freedom" and loneliness. The urge toward love and security, toward full and warm relationships with fellow human beings, he conceives as the strongest force. Karen Horney felt that all human behavior was guided by the profound desire to alleviate the anxieties and insecurities of childhood. She believed that coping with and reducing anxieties determines behavior to a greater degree than any other desires; the behavior patterns formed out of the need to reduce anxiety are the personality patterns a person carries through life. In some cases, buyer behavior may be determined by needs to reduce *anxiety*, (such as fear of "offending" with dandruff flakes on one's shoulders.)

Gestalt Theory A very different approach to motivation is that of the "field" or Gestalt theorists, among them psychologist Kurt Lewin. Gestaltists see behavior as a function of the total of forces that exist simultaneously in the psychological "field" of an individual. The situation at the time of some action is made up of all the facts that exist for a person, his or her *life space*. The person's world, as the individual perceives it, is the impinging reality, or life space—made up of that person's past, goals, experiences both positive and negative, and the encompassing environment. Understanding behavior, then, necessarily involves understanding all of the forces in the life space of a person, the compelling desires, the restraining fears, the inhibiting blocks or barriers.

The individual exists in a state of tension when needs are unfulfilled and goals unreached. When a goal is achieved, tension is released and equilibrium reigns. Various areas of the field possess differing "valences" of either positive or negative attraction. An object in the life space may have positive or negative valence, depending on the individual's state of tension. To relieve tension, an individual exerts *energy*, which combines with *valence* to create a force impressing itself on the individual. That force, if strong enough, leads to behavior in some direction. The combination of direction and strength of a force, is a *vector*, and usually more than one vector is directed upon an individual to generate behavior.

One example of field theory is the set of purchase alternatives faced by an individual who must choose between an expensive and an inexpensive product. A positive valence for price may have to be balanced against a negative valence for style or convenience. When a purchase decision has been reached, the positive valences of one product have outweighed the negative valences of the others and the vector has impelled the shopper to the choice. Motivation, then, emerges as the basis of operation of all these forces.

Cognitive Theory Today, motivation is usually viewed as an integral part of the individual consumer's cognitive structure. In line with the approach of the cognitive theorists described throughout this text, motivation is thought to affect the nature and intensity of information processing. This includes the consumer's need for information about a product or service, his or her expectancy that the processing of "messages" will help acquire information relevant to that need, and the evaluation of messages as a credible and useful source of knowledge.[11]

Kagan defines *motive* in this context as "a

[handwritten margin note: not a stimulus motivation response.]

cognitive representation of a future goal state that is desired . . . an event in the future that the person believes will permit him to feel better."[12] This can apply as easily to the consumption of information as to the goal of, say, satisfying thirst with a Seven-Up.

Because the cognitivists see consumer behavior as problem solving in nature, it is necessarily goal-oriented. Markin effectively summarizes the cognitive approach through a series of propositions based on the consumer's needs for self-enhancement and identity:[13]

1. The consumer is an integrated and organized whole. . . . We understand the mechanism of motivation not in terms of the mechanism per se but in terms of the holocentric nature of behavior.

2. Consumers have an enormous capacity for acquiring motives and these numerous motives often manifest themselves in simultaneous clusters rather than single-file entries. Thus, the purchase of most goods probably does not involve a single motive, but because of the complex symbolic significance of goods, they are purchased to satisfy multiple motivators.

3. Consumer behavior is human behavior. Thus, motivation studies based upon animal data are not applicable. . . . To understand consumer motivation, we had best study human organisms.

In brief, cognitivists stress the aspects of motivation that are oriented toward a consumer's self-actualization and gratification of needs for communication with what the environment has to offer.[14] Such goals as self-enhancement and ego-integration may seem a bit lofty as motivators for most purchasing decisions of the type we make at the supermarket, but this would be too literal a reading of the cognitive theory. Those goal-directed behaviors (for instance, buying a frozen pizza) must be viewed in the larger context of problem solving to reduce our basic maintenance needs.

Motivation Research Methods

Research into consumer motivation, identified before as MR for short, became the most highly popularized form of market research during the 1950s. Based almost entirely on psychoanalytic theories of motivation, MR practitioners have adapted techniques of psychiatric interviewing to probe consumers' "unconscious" motivations in seeking products and services.

Thus, MR investigators have reported exotic findings such as "soup is a profoundly emotion-charged food. Moods of nostalgic reverie characterize the way respondents recall the soups of their childhood. Highly emotional associations center around . . . mother's love."*

Some of the techniques of motivation research discussed in chapter 3—direct questioning, depth interviewing, and projective techniques[15]—will be reviewed briefly here, along with various criticisms of these methods in consumer research.

*An encyclopedic collection of MR conclusions may be found in Ernest Dichter, *Handbook of Consumer Motivations* (New York: McGraw-Hill, 1964).

Frustration as a Motive for Buying

When consumers are frustrated from obtaining some goal, a motivation exists to resolve that frustration. This appeal is frequently used in communications that set up some problem situation, and offer a particular product or service as a solution to that problem.

One such strategy was used in the area of business problem solving. Many companies today are plagued with poor "receivables" performance. Customers are simply paying their bills later and later, which interferes dramatically with the cash flow of the companies to whom they owe money. This ad was directed at businessmen who are faced with that problem. The appeal was an immediate identification with a situation virtually all had faced—calling someone who owed them money and being told some variation of the old refrain, "Your check is in the mail," which is almost never true.

To obtain an "emotional" reaction to the ad, a rather sleazy-appearing individual was depicted who was obviously lying to the reader over the telephone. This is, in fact, the way most businessmen trying to collect the money rightfully due them like to envision people who exhaust a catalog of excuses rather than actually sending payment. Thus, the sense of righteous anger induced by the ad was a highly successful motivator in getting readers to send the coupon for more information about the service (a system for computerizing and speeding up receivables collection).

"Sure I mailed you that check."

Courtesy The Service Bureau Company.

Question and Interview Techniques

Direct questions are formal and structured and represent an attempt to learn about direct and overt motives. Most consumers can give reasonable answers to direct reason-for-purchase questions—citing price, availability, quality, past experience, and so on. The fact that people do wish to appear intelligent and rational, however, may prevent them from admitting some of their actual motives for buying. Responses may be misleading, and may say more about the person's self-image or aspirations than why he or she bought the brand or product.

The *depth interview* is a means of examining a few subjects in great detail. Sometimes the interviewer can use a *free associative* technique. Freud believed that if a person could be made to blurt out the first impression that came to mind following a given stimulus word or picture, the defenses of the conscious mind could be overcome and the unconscious would express itself. Hence, subliminal areas of personality and motivation would be revealed.

Another device used is the *open-end questionnaire,* which leaves room for a latitude of response. The interviewer asks formal questions, but may follow them with unstructured reactions such as repeating the respondent's answers, waiting expectantly, or giving brief assenting comments to probe more deeply. Sometimes groups are asked to respond to a single stimulus such as an ad, a television program, or a film. Each member of the group can then relate the situation portrayed in the stimulus to his or her own attitudes or predispositions.

Projective Techniques

The *projective techniques* of motivation research are based upon clinical psychology methods. It was felt that projection enabled a respondent to reveal motives that were subconscious, and not readily verbalized because of some threat to the person's ego.

The *word-association test* remains one of the simplest projection techniques. If a new product is about to be launched, several possible brand names may be under consideration. Subject consumers would then be enlisted to obtain their "free-flow" reactions to these names. If a new floor wax is about to be announced with the brand name "Glitter," the subjects would be asked to begin rattling off their associations with this name. If the responses were along the lines of "all show and no substance" or "looks cheap," marketers would probably have some misgivings about the negative connotations of that product name.

Somewhat more informative is the *sentence completion test.* The incomplete sentences may begin, "People who use Squeaky shampoo . . . ," "Snack foods . . . ," or "Lots of people shop in Super Stores because . . . ," and subject consumers complete the sentences as they see the product or service in question. Data from this type of test may be more plentiful and easier to interpret than data from simple-word association, but may still not be amenable to rigorous quantification and statistical application.

The *semantic differential test* is a more recent attempt to measure the meaning or significance of words for brand names, situations, persons, or other stimuli. If reactions to slogans or packaging or characters impersonated in ads can be actually measured along a quantitative dimension, then consumer choices may be more easily predicted. In this test, the respondent is given a concept and a set of adjectives that are pairs of opposites—happy/sad, beautiful/ugly, large/small. Between each pair of opposites is some number of spaces (usually seven) measuring degrees of "tilt" toward one side or the other. Subjects indicate their feelings about the brand, store, or other concept under scrutiny by marking a position along the seven-point scale. Thus, the meanings attached differentially to various stimuli can be examined and treated with factor analysis methods.

The *cartoon test* portrays people conversing. The balloon over one figure is filled with some comment affecting the others, whose balloons are blank. Respondents fill in the blank balloons. If the balloon statement or situation is frustrating to one of the figures, this may be called the "picture frustration" test.

Finally, *psychodrama* provides the respondent a chance to project by role-playing. Here the subjects are placed in hypothetical real-life situations, such as a discussion between husband and wife about breakfast food. Circumstances surrounding the role the participant is to play must be described comprehensively and must give a good "feel" of the situation. Then the subject can "Guess and Imagine," or "Play and Personify," projecting his or her own personality and motivations.[16]

In 1950, one study utilizing an unusual projective technique was conducted by Mason Haire.[17] Shown two shopping lists that differed only by the inclusion of Nescafe Instant Coffee in one and Maxwell House Regular Coffee in the other, women were asked to imagine and describe the types of women who would have such shopping lists. The finding that respondents overwhelmingly described the instant coffee user as lazy, slovenly, and a poor housekeeper points up how greatly attitudes and motives toward convenience products have changed in the last quarter-century.

Criticisms of Motivational Research Techniques

One objection to all of the projective techniques as methods of market research is that they were originated for use with disturbed personalities in the offices of clinical psychologists. Thus, they may not be entirely applicable to most consumers. Secondly, getting people to project themselves adequately into the roles experimenters may wish them to take may prove difficult. The information respondents are willing to give out may be irrelevant to their motivations as consumers. Third, interviewers may themselves distort the test situations, and it is very difficult to perform projective tests with statistically significant samples. Finally, there may be some distorting selection factor at work in that some people are willing to participate in these tests while others are not. Sometimes experimenters find themselves using only college students as their subjects, and generalizing from the responses of such a distinct group to the buying public in general is risky, to say the least.

Although motivation research has directed attention to factors other than simple demographics—such as age, income level, and occupation—that might influence purchase decisions, MR seems on the whole to have limited utility in most research problems.

Consequently, interest in motivation research has waned considerably over the last decade or so. MR techniques in general, and particularly focused interviews, are generally used today only for generating hypotheses that will then be subjected to more precise measurement.

The Concept of Personality

Behavior is not usually determined by a single variable such as learning, perception, or motivation. Instead, it tends to emerge from the patterned interaction of different variables.

Personality is a common organizational concept used to place behavior in that larger psychological perspective. Like motivation, the meaning of personality depends very much on whose theoretical orientation one adopts. Several are presented here. And there is some question about whether the large amount of research into personality found in the literature on consumer behavior has really contributed that much for marketers to use in actual decision making. A sampling of personality research may be overviewed here, along with some of the more likely areas for future development.

One of the most widely used definitions of personality is Gordon Allport's concept:[18]

Personality *is* something and *does* something. It is not synonymous with behavior or activity; least of all is it merely the impression that this activity makes on others. It is what lies *behind* specific acts and *within* the individual. The systems that constitute personality are in every sense *determining* tendencies, and when aroused by suitable stimuli provoke those adjustive and expressed acts by which the personality comes to be known.

But most interesting to students of consumer behavior is the possibility of predicting behavior on the basis of knowledge about an individual's personality:[19]

. . . personality is that which permits prediction of what a person will do in a given situation. . . . It is concerned with all the behavior of the individual, both overt and under the skin.

As a concept applied to consumer research, personality may be viewed as an individual *set of more or less consistent response tendencies to items in the market place.*

Personality Theory

Theories of personality abound in the literature of psychology and social psychology, ranging from fairly exotic constructs to personality traits that may be objectively measured. The major theoretical orientations may be classified as (1) orthodox Freudian, (2) sociopsychoanalytic, (3) Gestalt, (4) stimulus-response, (5) cognitive, and (6) trait theory.

The Orthodox Freudian View of Personality

Some major elements of Freud's personality theory have already been discussed in relation to motivation. Personality, he believed, is determined by the interaction of the id, ego, and superego. In particular, the energy (libido) generated by the demands of the id must be channeled toward socially acceptable and morally responsible goals by the ego and superego. The ego utilizes the mechanisms of rationalization, projection, repression, and identification to handle destructive impulses and relegate them to lower levels of consciousness.

In addition, Freud maintained that the individual, as a very young child, undergoes four definable, sequential stages in development; and the amount of frustration and anxiety the child experiences at any one of these stages may dictate the personality characteristics of the adult.

During approximately the first year of infancy, an individual experiences the *oral* stage, when such activities as sucking, eating, and swallowing are most vital. Excessive anxiety at the oral stage will "fixate" the personality to a pattern of talkative, passive, greedy, and selfish behavior. Years two and three of infancy comprise the *anal* period. Strains and difficulties in the process of being toilet-trained will predispose the child to develop as stubborn, authoritarian, scrupulously neat, and stingy. As the child reaches years four and five, he enters the *phallic* stage during which his chief focus is sexual. Males supposedly fantasize about sex with their mothers (the so-called "Oedipus complex") and females entertain fantasies of sex with their fathers. Freud theorized that fixation at this stage would lead to abnormal

sexual attitudes toward the opposite sex or deviant attitudes toward authority. Finally the *genital* stage arrives in which the child shifts from self-centeredness to awareness of others, interest in the outside world, and "normal" socialization. According to the dictates of society, the person is attracted to the opposite sex, takes up a career and starts a family of his or her own.

While orthodox Freudian personality theory has attracted many critics on the psychological front, his influence continues to appear in our literature, our entertainment media, and everyday conversation. In the United States, the popularization of Freud's views focused primarily on their sexual aspects. Thus we might conclude that the gradual introduction of sexual themes in marketing (and particularly advertising) occurred in part through the cultural diffusion of Freudian sexual consciousness into our traditionally puritan atittudes towards sexuality.

Horney's Sociopsychoanalytic View

Many disciples of Freud expanded upon his original theories to include other personality dimensions. Karen Horney was one who viewed the child's development in social interaction as a prime determinant of personality.

Horney classified individuals into three general orientations: compliant, detached, and aggressive.[20] *Compliant* individuals need most of all to be accepted, loved, needed, and appreciated. They will subordinate themselves to others to avoid conflict and gain companionship. The compliant person is a conformist.

The *detached* individual wants to remain free from obligations and dependence on others. People of this type consider themselves intelligent and rational, and believe that they possess talents that should be recognized and applauded whether or not they actually display them. Self-sufficiency is a high-ranking value to this individual, who may actively distrust others.

The *aggressive* individual competes eagerly to gain prestige, success, excellence, and admiration. Such a person values strength and power, and, while seeing others as competitors, manipulates them to reinforce his or her own self-image. This kind of individual discounts emotions as motivators, and believes that everyone operates on the basis of self-interest alone.

Like Freud, Horney believed that whatever strategy for dealing with parents, peers, and authorities was most successful for the child would lead to the adoption of similar adult values, attitudes, and responses—those that would be most consistently reinforced with feelings of security and self-confidence. Eventually an individual would become better skilled in some strategies than in others, and one of the three personality types would emerge. An application of Horney's theory to consumer research is discussed shortly.

Gestalt Theory

In personality theory, Gestaltists refer once again to the totality of a given situation, and suggest that the whole is more than the sum of its parts.[21] Consideration of separate personal characteristics, they contend, cannot possibly give an accurate rendition of personality. One's internal characteristics interact with one's entire "life space" to form personality.

An individual's psychological field, with its objects of positive and negative *valence*, interacts with motivations and attitudes to create *tension* when *barriers* (psychological or physical) prevent moving along vectors toward objects of positive valence, or away from those of negative valence. Kurt Lewin postulated this scheme of personality structure and development as *individually patterned totalities*, as described by Clawson:[22]

They are individual because attention is centered above all on the interplay of many desires within a specific person and on the way in which these desires affect his behavior. They are patterned because the person's behavior possibilities are seen as a unified system of choices related to one another in a definite fashion. They are viewed as totalities because account should be taken of *all* the factors actually or potentially affecting the person at a given moment, both from within and from without, whether these factors happen to be called economic, political, social, religious, or psychological.

Lewin's theory has also been presented as a model of consumer behavior (Figure 11-1). The model includes, briefly, (1) a *life-space* consisting of the individual's environment, (2) a *motor-perceptual* region through which the individual selectively perceives the environment, and (3) an inner-personal region composed of internal desires, each of which may be satisfied by pursuing a number of different behavioral directions.

Stimulus-Response Theory

As discussed in Chapter 9, stimulus-response theory states that personality is the sum of response habits conditioned (or learned) over time. As responses to given cues

Figure 11-1 Lewin's consumer behavior model.

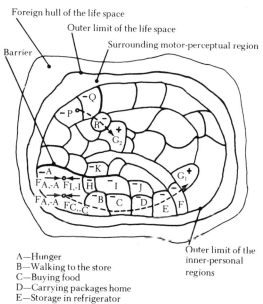

Foreign hull of the life space
Outer limit of the life space
Surrounding motor-perceptual region
Barrier

Outer limit of the inner-personal regions

A—Hunger
B—Walking to the store
C—Buying food
D—Carrying packages home
E—Storage in refrigerator
F—Cooking
G₁—Eating
G₂—Seeing motion picture
H—Buying vegetable seeds and chicks
I—Raising vegetables and poultry
J—Pulling vegetables, killing and plucking chickens
K—Patronizing unlicensed or black market store
P—Tired and bored
Q—Walking to the theater
R—Buying ticket to movie

Source: Joseph Clawson, "Lewin's Psychology and Motives in Marketing," in Theory in Marketing, *ed. R. Cox and W. Alderson (Homewood, Ill.: Richard D. Irwin, 1950). Reprinted by permission.*

or stimuli are reinforced or rewarded, they become part of a person's behavioral repertoire. As they are punished, they are extinguished. They may also be eliminated simply from lack of reinforcement over a period of time. Thus, classical behaviorist learning theory defines personality as the aggregate of all acquired habitual responses.

Any stimulus, if it reaches sufficient intensity, may become a *drive*. Drives energize, but do not direct, behavior. While biological drives are relatively simple, as we have seen, the drives that culminate in a purchase response to a certain product stimulus may be very complex. Yet, it remains quite difficult to measure the intensity of market stimuli in individual consumers by personality.

Cognitive Theory

As in all other realms of psychological influence, cognitive theorists see the stimulus-response approach to personality as hopelessly limited and unable to explain the complexities of consumer behavior. The current trend is to view personality as a systems or structural concept, which comprises two sets of aspects—directive and dynamic.

Directive Aspects of Personality McGuire describes this set as embracing the "information processing" function, which may be further broken down into a series of steps.[23] Briefly, the first step, *exposure*, refers to habits that will determine the information to which a consumer will be exposed. In the second step, *perception*, the consumer uses attention and other factors of informational selectivity. In the third, *comprehension*, the consumer focuses on the process of finding meaning in the communication. Fourth, the consumer registers some level of *agreement* with the message. Fifth, *retention* may or may not occur. Sixth, there may be *retrieval* of the information for use in the seventh step of *decision making*. Then *action* occurs as some activity is directed to purchasing. Mostly, these aspects have been discussed in the preceding chapter.

Dynamic Aspects of Personality This refers to the role of *motivation* in getting consumers moving toward goal-oriented behavior. Motives are visualized as the forces that initiate the processing of information to solve some problem for the consumer. Cognitive theorists are generally more concerned with the directive aspects of personality, since those are the ones directly concerned with information processing.

In addition, some cognitivists identify *dispositions* that may be isolated and evaluated in an individual consumer's behavior.[24] These dispositions include some characteristics other theorists identify as "traits" or personality "types," such as *dogmatism* (inability to hold an open mind), *anxiety* (excessive fear), susceptibility to *persuasion,* and *achievement*-orientation.

Trait Theory

This orientation may be traced back to concepts expounded by the ancient Greeks. In the Middle Ages, scientists, influenced by Greek philosophers, believed that human personality was determined by the predominance of one of four "humors"—a phlegmatic person was lethargic, a choleric person irritable and cross, a melancholic person depressed and pessimistic, and a sanguine person optimistic and happy. In modern trait theory, Allport asserts that traits are the attributes that make a person functional and identify him as a given person.[25] Caution and deliberateness are traits that may produce a high level of risk perception and an attitude of unwillingness to try new products. As traits, caution and deliberation will be evident in social and interpersonal behavior as well as in consumer behavior. If a large group of consumers possesses traits in common, it may be possible to define them as a market segment. Traits may also be sources of motivation.

Usefulness of Trait Theory Most consumer behavior research in the realm of personality has consisted of some applications of trait theory. Because the "traits" comprising personality can be given names or labels and empirically measured, this approach is more useful than the generally esoteric psychoanalytic schemes or the rather limiting stimulus-response orientation. There is no general agreement as to one set of traits that characterize all individuals. Instead, traits are operationally defined by the various instrument used to measure them; and there is some evidence that these measures work as well even when shortened or otherwise modified.[26]

Measurement of Personality Traits One popular yardstick used to distinguish different groups in terms of personality traits is the *Thurstone Temperament Schedule*. This scale delineates individuals along seven dimensions, described by Westfall:[27]

1. Active. A high score in this area suggests you like to be "on the go." You probably speak, walk, write, drive, work, and eat fast even if you do not have to.

2. Vigorous. A high score here indicates you enjoy active sports, work requiring use of the hands or tools, and outdoor occupations. You usually enjoy physical activity requiring a lot of energy.

3. Impulsive. If you score high in this area you are usually happy-go-lucky. You probably like to take chances, and can make decisions quickly.

4. Dominant. A high score shows capacity for taking the initiative and assuming respon-

sibility. You probably enjoy organizing social activities, promoting new projects, and persuading others.

5. Stable. If you have a high stability score you probably remain calm in a crisis, can disregard distractions while studying or working, and are not irritated if interrupted when concentrating.

6. Sociable. If you are sociable, you usually enjoy the company of others, make friends easily, and are sympathetic, cooperative, and agreeable in your relations with others.

7. Reflective. A high score in this area indicates you like meditative thinking and enjoy dealing with theoretical rather than practical problems. You usually prefer to work alone with material requiring accuracy and fine detail.

Personality *inventories* may invoke any number of trait factors. One of the most widely used today is the *California Psychological Inventory* (CPI), consisting of 280 items for subjects to designate True or False and yielding scores on eighteen scales (see Table 11-1).

Table 11-1   Scales of the California Psychological Inventory

INVENTORY

I. *Measures of Poise, Ascendancy, and Self Assurance*
   1. Dominance (Do)
   2. Capacity for status (Cs)
   3. Sociability (Sy)
   4. Social presence (Sp)
   5. Self-acceptance (Sa)
   6. Sense of well-being (Wb)

II. *Measures of Socialization, Maturity, and Responsibility*
   7. Responsibility (Re)
   8. Socialization (So)
   9. Self-control (Sc)
  10. Tolerance (To)
  11. Good impression (Gi)
  12. Communality (Cm)

III. *Measures of Achievement Potential and Intellectual Efficiency*
  13. Achievement via conformance (Ac)
  14. Achievement via independence (Ai)
  15. Intellectual efficiency (Ie)

IV. *Measures of Intellectual and Interest Modes*
  16. Psychological-mindedness (Py)
  17. Flexibility (Fx)
  18. Femininity (Fe)

Source: H. Gough, CPI Manual *(Palo Alto, Calif.: Consulting Psychologists Press, 1957.)*

The *Gordon Personal Profile* and *Gordon Personal Inventory* are both twenty-item lists designed to measure four personality factors each. The profile measures Ascendance, Responsibility, Emotional Stability, and Sociability. The Inventory measures Cautiousness, Original Thinking, Personal Relations, and Vigor.

In the following section, specific applications of trait factor theory are presented in the context of their contribution to the consumer behavior literature.

Personality in Consumer Behavior Research

Generally, studies relating personality theories and measures to buying behavior focus on how product or brand choices correlate with personality variables.

Automobile Choice

Variations in automobile buying, according to hypotheses by Pierre Martineau, were related to three basic personality "types": *conservatives, moderates* (or *sociables*), and *attention-getters.* Martineau concluded that personality structure had direct relevance to predicting buyer behavior, because "purchase choices are an expression of an individual's personality."[28]

In the same year, 1959, Franklin B. Evans investigated the personality structure of Ford and Chevrolet owners. Evans administered the Edwards Personal Preference Schedule to 869 Ford owners and 770 Chevrolet owners in Park Forest, Illinois, and concluded that:[29]

. . . in almost two-thirds of the cases, the individual projects his greatest need into the brand he happens to have. In this sense then, automobiles are extensions of the owner's personality; they are used to satisfy certain important personality needs.

Although only the need called "achievement" on the Edwards scale revealed significant difference in range between the two car brands, Cohen suggests that it was meaningful for personality research because at least one personality need was "a powerful predictor."[30]

Later studies by Westfall and by Evans found no personality differences significant enough for prediction between Ford and Chevrolet owners. Westfall, using the Thurstone Temperament Schedule (see above), did find that "the characteristics of *active* and *impulsive* were predictive of convertible ownership and those of *stable* and *sociable* of standard and compact automobile ownership."[31] Westfall broadens the scope of his conclusion:[32]

The fact that personality differences were found between the owners of two car types indicates that, at least in some cases, measurable personality differences do exist between owners of different products serving the same basic function.

Food and Beverage Purchases

The classic "shopping list" study of Mason Haire, discussed earlier in this chapter, is often referred to in discussions of personality. Haire concluded that a product's physical attributes alone do not account for purchase decisions—consumers take into account far more than that in making their choices. "Underlying" motives were apparently responsible, in the 1950 study cited earlier, for subjects' descriptions of women who bought instant coffee as lazy and not very good housewives.

Webster and Von Pechmann conducted research eighteen years later based on the hypothesis that "convenience foods in general and instant coffee in particular have become much more acceptable to the American housewife."[33] Replicating Haire's study, they uncovered no significant differences between characteristics ascribed by subjects to the regular coffee versus the instant coffee buyer. (However, a fairly large number of the subjects felt that the instant coffee shopper was a busy, active person in contrast to the woman preferring regular coffee, who was seen as dull, rural, unadventuresome, and not very elegant.)

Thus, two different research teams using an unstructured research technique largely separated in time came up with different results in the American market. (However, a recent Canadian replication of Haire's study concluded that the original findings still hold true with a sample of French-Canadians in a middle-class suburb of Montreal.)[34]

Coffee, tea, and beer were the food products under scrutiny in a study conducted by Frank, Massy, and Lodahl. They concluded that personality and socioeconomic data taken together "account for between one and four percent of the variance of purchasing behavior" of the three products, and that trying new predictors along those lines seems worthwhile. Yet, their general conclusion is negative for personality variables in consumer research:[35]

. . . it is felt this study is definitive in showing that temporal averages of purchasing behavior are measures not predictable in any simple and direct way from personality and socioeconomic status variables.

Cigarette Use

A study of male cigarette smokers by Koponen found that smokers expressed greater needs than the average male for sex, aggression, achievement, and dominance. The smokers fell below the average for order, compliance, association, and self-depreciation. And for heavy smokers, these relationships were even more noticeable. Use of the Edwards Personal Preference Schedule raised methodological questions in this study. Should Edwards' "abasement" scale be used as equivalent to "self-depreciation"? Should the affiliation scale be translated into "association"?

Recent research by Fry did reveal significant relationships between smokers' personality traits and brand preferences. Moreover, Fry took into account the vital role of moderator variables. He found that the personality variables "made sense" in their match with brand characteristics, while respondents' sex, self-confidence, and social class importantly moderated one or more of those relationships. He believes, therefore, that[36]

Personality variables as measured by standard tests appear to have considerable potential for improving understanding of the psychological basis of brand choice.

Analysis could be refined, Fry believes, by obtaining better descriptions of the perceived differences among various brands, by grouping respondents giving common descriptions and by isolating the effects personality variables may exert on the nature of brand discrimination.

Interpersonal Concepts and Product Use

An interpersonal approach to personality research is based on the fact that most purchases are used in the presence of other people, or with consideration of the opinions of others. The things people buy carry dimensions of personal and social meaning above and beyond their functionality. Thus, the way people perceive their own personalities—conformist, dominant, sociable, aggressive, affiliative, or striving—will in some ways influence what they buy to fit in with that perception. Their purchases will no doubt express in personal relationships what the buyer feels is his or her own personality. Interpersonal response traits can be thought of as enduring dispositions to respond to others in characteristic or typical ways.

As indicated earlier, from the theoretical approach of Karen Horney, three clusters of traits may be derived categorizing individuals as compliant, aggressive, or detached. It is possible to measure these traits on a Likert-type instrument of thirty-five items, called a CAD Scale.

Cohen's study, based on the concept of "interpersonal man," hypothesized that *compliant* types should show more favorable response to products designed to enhance social relationships, *aggressive* types are most likely to choose products with high status and success images, and *detached* individuals would probably respond to appeals to their independence.[37] Instruments, including the CAD, were used to measure both product and brand usage for fifteen items and media preferences (Table 11-2).

Cohen found differential preferences generally consistent with the theoretical expectations. Gasoline, largely irrelevant to interpersonal goals and values, revealed no differences among the subjects, but manual razors appealed to 75 percent of the students rated as aggressive while only 62 percent of those categorized as compliant and detached subjects made that choice. Aggressive individuals scored highest on use of cologne or after shave lotions. Users of mouthwash included a significantly greater number of compliant than detached students. Cohen concludes that interpersonal needs should receive major emphasis in studying personality correlates of buyer behavior.

Multivariate Personality Analysis

Sparks and Tucker applied a distinctly gestaltist approach to the problem of finding significant personality-product use relationships. They noted that most personality measurement techniques are based upon a concept of personality comprised of discrete, independent traits. These researchers investigated complex trait interactions through *canonical analysis*—a methodology for correlating sets of predictor variables.* They measured a sundry list of products including mouthwash, headache remedies, hair spray, men's cologne, shampoo, *Playboy*, antacids, complexion aids, alcoholic beverages, vitamins, coffee, cigarettes, chewing gum, and after shave lotion. A correlation analysis of the data produced weak relationships between personality traits and particular prod-

*A basic description of canonical analysis may be found in Paul E. Green and Donald S. Tull, *Research for Marketing Decisions*, 3rd ed. (Englewood Cliffs, N.J.: Prentice-Hall, 1975).

uct use. But they found that canonical analysis provided more of a positive case for the relationships under scrutiny, for example:[38]

. . . not a simple connection between sociability and early fashion adoption, but a more complex one in which sociability combined with emotional stability and irresponsibility is oriented toward one sort of action while sociability combined with emotional instability and cautiousness is oriented toward its opposite.

Sparks and Tucker suggest that even a simple model based on trait *interaction* could prove higher in predictive validity than a trait-by-trait approach.

Table 11-2   Compliant, Aggressive, and Detached Personality Traits and Product Use

PRODUCT	WITHIN-TRAIT COMPARISON[a]	BRAND OR CATEGORY	N	PERCENT OF HIGH GROUPING IN EACH BRAND OR PRODUCT CATEGORY		
				C(n = 66)	A(n = 67)	D(n = 75)
Cigarettes	NS	Smoker	47	40	40	32
		Nonsmoker	83	60	60	68
Men's dress shirts	NS	Arrow	26	20	15	22
		Van Heusen	21	16	25	20
		Brand not known	15	8	5	12
		Other	67	56	55	46
Mouthwash	Compliant	Used	91	74	64	56
		Not used	54	26	36	44
Men's deodorant	Aggressive	Old Spice	33	34	41	24
		Right Guard	53	45	38	52
		Other	33	21	21	24
Men's cologne and after-shave lotion	Aggressive	At least several times a week	119	88	91	82
		Several times a month or less	25	12	9	18
Toilet or bath soap	Compliant	Dial	50	47	36	31
		No preference	39	19	23	38
		Other	46	34	41	31
Men's hair dressing	NS	Not used	46	41	43	39
		Other	65	59	57	61

Table 11-2 (Continued)

PRODUCT	WITHIN-TRAIT COMPARISON[a]	BRAND OR CATEGORY	N	PERCENT OF HIGH GROUPING IN EACH BRAND OR PRODUCT CATEGORY		
				C(n = 66)	A(n = 67)	D(n = 75)
Toothpaste	NS	Crest	77	61	60	60
		Colgate	28	16	24	20
		Other	29	23	16	20
Razors	Aggressive	Electric	48	38	25	38
		Manual	92	62	75	62
Beer	NS	Coors	54	41	49	35
		Not consumed	29	19	19	24
		Other	60	40	32	41
Tea	Detached	At least several times a week	41	26	22	33
		Several times a month or less	116	74	78	67
Wine	Compliant	At least several times a month	38	35	33	23
		Several times a year or less	119	65	67	77
Metrecal and similar diet products	NS	At least a few times a year	18	15	12	11
		Never	139	85	88	89
Gasoline	NS	Standard	32	17	23	19
		Shell	32	28	18	23
		Other	83	55	59	58
Headache remedies	NS	Bayer aspirin	44	32	38	30
		Other aspirin	33	13	23	21
		Bufferin	23	18	11	15
		Other remedy	47	37	28	34

[a]High and low groupings on each trait were compared using the chi-square test. Differences significant at the .05 level are reported by trait designation.

Source: Joel B. Cohen, "An Interpersonal Orientation to the Study of Consumer Behavior," Journal of Marketing Research *(August 1967), p. 276. Reprinted with permission of the American Marketing Association.*

How relevant is personality theory to consumer behavior research? The question is still debatable. Far more research is needed, with new techniques and more sophisticated use of the ones now available.

Intuitively, it seems obvious that there are "types" of personalities, and that knowing a person's "personality type," permits some predictions of his or her reactions in certain situations. It also seems apparent from our own experience that we express our personality in the objects we buy and use, and that purchase decisions take into account what these objects will tell others about us. Yet, precise measures of personality and correlations between personality and product or brand choice have been difficult to obtain. Most research reveals some variance of buyer behavior, explained by personality variables, but not enough to be statistically significant. For example, ownership of Fords as against Chevrolets could be predicted on the basis of personality factors in only two-thirds of the members of the sample. And predictability reached just 75 percent for the use of manual razors by highly aggressive types in another group. Thus, personality-purchase relationships must be more complex than most studies have been designed to measure.

Problems in Personality Research

Difficulties in two major areas face personality researchers. One is the problem shared by all investigators in determining the nature and structure of personality. Even the basic area of trait definition leads to semantic differences yet to be made uniform. And if there are dominant attributes over a market segment or population or sample, these attributes may very well not be consistent or enduring. People do modify, revise, and change their behavior over time. The total environment must always be considered in describing personality because under different conditions—stress, elation—the same person will behave in different ways. Identical personality attributes may lead to different buying behavior. One highly compliant woman, for example, may focus her approval needs on clothing, while another feels that her family's approval of her cooking is more important.

The second set of difficulties lies in the tests, scales, and measures of personality customarily used. In many instances they are derived from instruments used in clinical psychology to measure deviant behavior patterns. Finally, the tests may be lacking in reliability or validity; they may not measure what they purport to measure and may not provide consistent results through repeated use.

Personality and Life Style

Personality traits that characterize an individual may be seen as determinants of life style. A person who scores high on traits such as vigorousness and sociability, for example, probably exhibits a life-style pattern quite divergent from one who maintains a lower profile on these factors. The differences are likely to be reflected in an individual's career choice, attitudes, and buying behavior.

Psychographic segmentation is a relatively new approach to distinguishing between heavy and light users of different products, services, and media on the basis of life styles. The research technique involves an activity, interest, and opinion (AIO) inventory to classify consumers along these variables.

This information is taken in conjunction with facts about product use and demographic data to draw "life-style portraits" of different market segments.

AIO inventories are similar to personality inventories like the California Psychological Inventory in the types of items used, including statements with which subjects either agree or disagree, such as:[40]

"I think I have more self-confidence than most people."

"I like bright, splashy colors."

"I would like to be an actress."

"I stay home most evenings."

Thus, information obtained by AIO inventory is largely personality data. In this application, personality concepts seem to have a bright future, as life-style research promises to become increasingly important in market segmentation. (This approach is discussed thoroughly in chapter 19.)

Motivation and personality research in general are greatly in need of methodological refinement. First, some standardization of terms is in order to bring uniformity to personality research. Second, the problem of reliability and validity must be overcome by modifying existing measurement instruments or, more likely, by developing new ones that hold greater promise for quantification.

Summary

Motivation is the compelling force behind behavior, which arises out of both physiological and psychological needs. Human needs can be seen as hierarchical, in that satisfaction of needs at one level will permit operation of needs and motives at a higher level. Consumers turn to brands or products as the items increase the satisfaction of basic or higher needs. Major theories of motivation are those of Freud, neo-Freudians, the Gestaltists, cognitive theorists. *Motivation research* was a technique for probing unconscious, "hidden" motivations for buying which was highly popularized in the 1950s, but has since waned due to significant problems in concept and measurement.

Personality refers to a set of relatively consistent internal and external consumer responses to market stimuli. Theories of personality include the orthodox Freudian, socio-psychoanalytic, Gestalt, stimulus-response, cognitive, and trait approaches.

Most personality research in marketing has been based on the use of trait theory to find links between traits and specific purchase choices. Success has not been extravagant in these attempts, but sufficient progress has been made to suggest that personality research could be refined to become highly useful in predicting buyer behavior, especially in the area of life-style research.

NOTES

1. William J. McGuire, "Some Internal Psychological Factors Influencing Consumer Choice," *Journal of Consumer Research*, Vol. 2, No. 4 (March 1976), p. 302.

2. Robert Ferber, ed., *A Synthesis of Selected Aspects of Consumer Behavior*, (Washington, D.C.: National Science Foundation, 1976).

3. "Irrational Buying Needs Claimed by Youth," *Wall Street Journal*, October 17, 1974, p. 1.

4. Vance Packard, *The Hidden Persuaders* (New York: Pocket Books, Inc., 1958).

5. Packard, *Hidden Persuaders*, p. 5.

6. Dalbir Bindra, "An Overview, A General Problem, and Human Motivation" in *Motivation: A Systematic Reinterpretation*, ed. Joseph McVicker Hunt (New York: The Ronald Press Co., 1959, p. 296).

7. Abraham H. Maslow, *Motivation and Personality*, 2nd ed. (New York: Harper and Row, 1970).

8. Sidney J. Levy, "Symbols for Sale," *Harvard Business Review*, Vol. 37 (July–August 1959), pp. 117–124.

9. A. L. Edwards, "The Relationship between the Judged Desirability of a Trait and the Probability that the Trait Will Be Endorsed," *Journal of Applied Psychology*, Vol. 37 (1953), pp. 90–93. See also *Edwards Personal Preference Schedule*, The Psychological Corporation, New York, N.Y.

10. Philip Kotler, *Marketing Management* (Englewood Cliffs, N.J.: Prentice-Hall, 1967), p. 88.

11. Robert E. Burnkrant, "A Motivational Model of Information Processing Intensity," *Journal of Consumer Research*, Vol. 3, No. 1 (June 1976), p. 21.

12. J. Kagan, "Motives and Development," *Journal of Personality and Social Psychology*, No. 22 (1972), p. 54, as cited in Burnkrant, "Motivational Model," p. 22.

13. Rom J. Markin, Jr., *Consumer Behavior: A Cognitive Orientation*, (New York: The Macmillan Co., 1974), p. 189.

14. William J. McGuire, "Psychological Motives and Communication Gratification," in *The Uses of Mass Communications: Current Perspectives on Gratifications Research*, ed. J. G. Blumler and E. Katz, (Beverly Hills, Calif.: Sage Publications, 1974).

15. Discussion adapted from David J. Luck, Hugh G. Wales, and Donald A. Taylor, *Marketing Research* (Englewood Cliffs, N.J.: Prentice-Hall, 1961).

16. Luck et al., *Marketing Research*, p. 402.

17. Mason Haire, "Projective Techniques in Marketing Research," *Journal of Marketing*, Vol. 14 (April 1950), pp. 649–656. (noted in Luck, Wales, and Taylor, p. 403).

18. Earl E. Baughman, *Personality: The Psychological Study of the Individual* (Englewood Cliffs, N.J.: Prentice-Hall, 1972), p. 8.

19. Baughman, *Personality*, p. 9.

20. Joel B. Cohen, "Toward an Interpersonal Theory of Consumer Behavior," in *Perspectives in Consumer Behavior*, ed. Kassarjian and Robertson (Glenview, Illinois: Scott, Foresman, 1968).

21. Uri Bronfenbrenner, "Toward an Integrated Theory of Personality," in *Perception, An Approach to Personality*, ed. Robert R. Blake and Glenn V. Ramsey (New York: The Ronald Press, 1951), p. 216.

22. Joseph Clawson, "Lewin's Psychology and Motives in Marketing," in *Theory in Marketing*, ed. R. Cox and W. Alderson (Homewood, Illinois: Richard D. Irwin, 1950).

23. McGuire, "Psychological Motives," pp. 303–315.

24. Markin, *Consumer Behavior*, pp. 345–348.

25. G. W. Allport, *Personality, A Psychological Interpretation* (New York: Holt and Co., 1937).

26. Kathryn E. A. Villani and Yoram Wind, "On The Usage of 'Modified' Personality Trait Measures in Consumer Research," *Journal of Consumer Research*, Vol. 2, No. 3 (December 1975), p. 223.

27. Ralph Westfall, "Psychological Factors in Predicting Product Choice," *Journal of Marketing*, Vol. 26 (April 1962), p. 36.

28. Pierre D. Martineau, "The Pattern of Social Classes," in *Proceedings of the American Marketing Association*, ed. Robert L. Clewett, American Marketing Association (1957), pp. 233–247.

29. Franklin B. Evans, "Psychological and Objective Factors in the Prediction of Brand Choice," *Journal of Business*, Vol. 32 (October 1959), pp. 340–369.

30. Joel B. Cohen, "Theory of Consumer Behavior," p. 74.

31. R. Westfall, "Psychological Factors in Predicting Product Choice," *Journal of Marketing*, Vol. 26, No. 2 (1962), pp. 34–40.

32. Westfall, "Predicting Product Choice."

33. Frederick E. Webster, Jr., and Frederick von Pechmann, "A Replication of the 'Shopping List' Study," *Journal of Marketing*, Vol. 34 (April 1970), pp. 61–77.

34. George S. Lane and Gayne L. Watson, "A Canadian Replication of Mason Haire's 'Shopping List' Study," *Journal of The Academy of Marketing Science*, Vol. 3, No. 1 (Spring 1975), p. 48.

35. William E. Massy, Ronald E. Frank, and Thomas Lodahl, *Purchasing Behavior and Personal Attributes* (Philadelphia: University of Pennsylvania Press, 1968), p. 123.

36. Joseph N. Fry, "Personality Variables and Cigarette Brand Choice," *Journal of Marketing Research*, Vol. 8 (August 1971), pp. 298–304.

37. Joel B. Cohen, "Theory of Consumer Behavior," p. 78.

38. David L. Sparks and W. T. Tucker, "A Multivariate Analysis of Personality and Product Use," *Journal of Marketing Research*, Vol. 8 (February 1971), pp. 67–70.

40. Joseph T. Plummer, "Life Style Patterns and Commercial Bank Credit Card Usage," *Journal of Marketing*, Vol. 35, No. 2 (1971), p. 40.

MARKETING APPLICATIONS

Conclusion 1 *According to Maslow's hierarchy, people strive for self-actualization once physiological, safety, love, and esteem motives are gratified.*

Application In American culture, a seemingly endless variety of "self-actualizing" opportunities have been marketed to people seeking different forms of self-expansion. In the mid-1970s, a number of popular books directed themselves to helping timid people become more assertive—such as *When I Say No, I Feel Guilty* and *Winning Through Intimidation.* Consumers interested in consciousness raising could choose from therapies and activities like est, ARICA, primal therapy, T-groups, transcendental meditation, and other highly organized marketers of self-enhancement.

Conclusion 2 *Appeals to achievement needs may be less common in product positioning and advertising than in the more "status-striving" 1950s, but are nonetheless effective when directed toward the proper segments.*

Application In the wake of social change during the late 1960s, which deemphasized an upwardly-mobile "making-it" approach to life, many marketers turned from this appeal in communicating with consumers. Yet people on their way up still formed a highly visible (and high-earning) segment for some marketers. Johnny Walker Black Label Scotch whisky was positioned for this segment through elegant ads with headlines such as "Now that you've made it to the top, you must be thirstier than ever," and "The road to success is paved with rocks . . . let us smooth them for you" (accompanied by a photograph of an empty glass full of ice). This appeal proved effective for the high-ticket Scotch, even in an economic climate that favored cost-conscious purchasing of lower-priced brands.

Conclusion 3 *Success in using personality measures as a predictor of consumer behavior has not been extravagant to this point. Yet personality traits* interact *with other variables which influence buying behavior.*

Application Personality measures may be used in conjunction with other predictive tools to draw profiles of target consumers. For example, chapter 19, on life style and psychographics research, shows how demographic data, product use information, and personality statements combine to paint vivid portraits of consumers who are heavy users of specific products, services, and media. The personality aspects of these profiles help marketers communicate more effectively by identifying prime prospects as traditional or contemporary, sociable or withdrawn, family and home-centered or oriented to activities outside the house.

ASSIGNMENTS

Research Assignment

Background   The American Potato Growers Association wants to determine what personality differences might be associated with the consumers who buy real potatoes as against those who purchase the instant variety. As their research consultant, you recall the classic study conducted by Mason Haire in 1950 which compared "shopping lists" of people who bought real versus instant coffee (page 285 of this chapter). You also recall that a more recent study did not substantiate Haire's findings, concluding that instant coffee purchasers were not perceived as lazier than those who bought ground coffee. Instant coffee had become the norm.

In the shopping lists shown to subjects in those two studies, one item held constant was "5 lbs. potatoes." Thus, you decide to adopt Haire's shopping list to your purposes, holding all items constant on the "shopping lists" but the kind of potatoes purchased.

Research Input   For a description of both studies in question, see Frederick E. Webster, Jr., and Frederick Von Pechmann, "A Replication of the 'Shopping List' Study," *Journal of Marketing*, Vol. 34, April 1970, pp. 61–77.

Methodology   Select at least 6 representative, willing housewives and give them the following instructions:

Read the shopping list below. Try to project yourself into the situation as far as possible until you can more or less characterize the woman who brought home these groceries. Then write a brief description of her personality and character. Wherever possible indicate what factors influenced your judgment.

Then show one of the following lists to half of your sample and the other list to the other half. (Your subjects should not be aware of the existence of two lists.)

Shopping list 1	*Shopping list 2*
Pound-and-a-half of hamburger	Pound-and-a-half of hamburger
2 loaves of Wonder bread	2 loaves of Wonder bread
Bunch of carrots	Bunch of carrots
1 pkg. French's Instant mashed potatoes	5 lbs. potatotes
Nescafe instant coffee	Nescafe instant coffee
2 cans Del Monte peaches	2 cans Del Monte peaches

Compare responses to the two lists and draw a profile of the "consumer" who bought instant potatoes contrasted with the one who bought real potatoes, according to your subjects' perceptions of their personality traits.

Extrapolation   Compare your findings with those of the Haire and Webster-Von Pechmann studies. Have instant potatoes become an acceptable substitute for real potatoes?

On the basis of your findings, make a marketing recommendation to the Potato Growers Association. How can these findings help them in reaching consumers?

Creative Assignment

As a partner in a creative marketing agency, you are approached by a major cosmetics and packaged goods company with a special assignment: how to reintroduce a man's hair spray that captured a fairly large market share when it came out but has fizzled in recent years.

You have decided that the problem is in the brand's name, "The Dry One." Although the name was successful in positioning the product when man's hair spray was an innovation, men are used to "dry" hair products now and the name lacks excitement.

Without changing the product itself, rename it to be more competitive in today's market place. Bear in mind that cosmetic products are purchased for motivations other than keeping one's hair in place.

Managerial Assignment

At National Motors, one of the nation's major automobile manufacturers, a heated controversy is raging through the marketing department: Should additional money be spent for market research probing such factors as personality variables in consumer automobile choice?

In one corner, cost-cutting hardliners are finding much to criticize about research projects that have already been conducted. Their argument is, "What good do these expensive findings do a salesman who has the prospect in front of him and wants to move a car?"

But another faction is defending consumer research into personality (correlated with car buying) from a different perspective. Their argument is, "If we don't know enough about consumers to give them the kinds of cars they want, prospects will never get to the salesman."

As a member of the *National* marketing group, you are expected to take a stand on this issue, on the basis of information on pages 286–292 of this chapter, as well as on the basis of a search of the recent marketing literature on personality research in general and car-buying correlates of personality in particular.

Put your thoughts on paper and be prepared to back up your argument with specifics when you confront another manager who holds the opposite view.

SELECTED READINGS

Burnkrant, Robert E. "A Motivational Model of Information Processing Intensity." *Journal of Consumer Research*, Vol. 3, No. 1 (June 1976), pp. 21–30.

Johnson, Charles D. and Anne V. Gormly. "Personality, Attraction, and Social Ambiguity." *Journal of Social Psychology*, Vol. 97, No. 2 (December 1975), pp. 227–232.

Lombardo, John P., Michele Syeigleder, and Richard Feinberg. "Internality-Externality: The Perception of Negatively Valued Personality Characteristics and Interpersonal Attraction." *Representative Research in Social Psychology*, Vol. 6, No. 2 (1975), pp. 89–95.

McGuire, William J. "Some Internal Psychological Factors Influencing Consumer Choice." *Journal of Consumer Research*, Vol. 2, No. 4 (March 1975), pp. 302–319.

Villani, Kathryn E. A. and Yoram Wind. "On the Usage of 'Modified' Personality Trait Measures in Consumer Research." *Journal of Consumer Research*, Vol. 2, No. 3 (December 1975), pp. 223–28.

OBJECTIVES

TWELVE

Attitudes

Because consumer attitudes are considered to be the most accurate predictor of actual buying behavior, no other single influence is quite so important to the study of consumer behavior today.[1]

Attitudes refer to inclinations we hold toward various products or services and the places where we buy them. If we are favorably inclined toward some product stimulus and respond by buying it, our positive attitude becomes reinforced when the experience is rewarding. But most situations where attitudes come into play are considerably more complicated. If our favorable attitude toward the item were not reinforced—if, for example, the "instant suntan" product we were eager to use turned our skin yellow—we would be forced to change our attitude toward the product.

In the consumer's cognitive structure, attitudes are interrelated with the other psychological variables discussed thus far.

First, they are learned like other behaviors. Second, they are affected by selective perception and, in turn, influence new perceptions of the market environment. Third, attitudes are subject to different motivations, and help determine how efficiently consumers solve problems and achieve their goals. Finally, attitudes shape the set of consistent responses we refer to as personality.

Consumer attitudes are also a source of great (and often grave) concern to every kind of marketer. The business person wants to know what "our customers" are thinking about the firm, the product, the advertising, the salespeople. Politicians turn nervously to opinion polls to tell them how the voters seem to feel about issues. Your professors make an effort to instill positive attitudes in students toward their courses.

In this chapter and the next, on attitude formation and change, consumer attitudes are subjected to close analysis for use in marketing. *The current chapter probes the nature, organization, and measurement of attitudes including topics such as:*

• *Why attitudes are supposed to be the best predictors of buying behavior.*

• *How attitudes are organized (and may be broken down).*

• *The relationship between product attributes and attitudes toward that product.*

• *Techniques for measuring and comparing attitudes.*

• *How the attitudes of domestic small-car owners compare with those of foreign small-car owners.*

This discussion will provide a basis for understanding the principles and strategies of changing consumer attitudes in chapter 13.

Influence of Attitudes

Every decision a consumer makes involves, at some level, the phenomenon psychologists refer to as "attitude." We are all favorably disposed towards some products, services, media, and retail establishments and unfavorably disposed toward others. The nature of these dispositions will affect the choices we make in the market place.

Consider the business student who is thinking about buying a pocket calculator to navigate the maze of mathematical computations all business students confront. Through the perceptual process, he or she evaluates the information that calculators are designed to solve challenging math problems, that there are scores of these mini-brains on the market with a variety of different features, and that a number of retail outlets offer them at competitive prices.

At this point, the individual's attitudes determine what the final buying outcome will be. Does the student view the calculator as an essential tool for the person who is learning business math procedures, or somehow feel that an electronic helpmate is "cheating" because it eliminates learning to do the computations oneself? And what are the attitudes of the students' instructors and peers toward using calculators at this point in the learning process? Once these questions have been resolved, there is the problem of which brand to buy. What is the student's attitude toward the commercial for the Bowmar Brain, positioned as an aid for "the dummy in all of us?" Is there a positive disposition toward the company that wants to help him or her be less of a dummy, or a more favorable inclination to Texas Instrument's machines because their ads talk to the competent professional? Finally, how does the student feel about the stores that are offering the brand he or she wants to buy? Attitude will determine whether the purchase will be made at the discount house offering the lowest price or at a more expensive specialty shop the student believes will provide more personalized sales help and better service. On the basis of these attitudinal determinants, our student will choose the brand and store that should add up to the greatest personal satisfaction with the calculator.

While this example concerns a considered-purchase product, packaged goods, foods and other low-priced purchases bring attitudes into play as well.[2] Marketers pay close attention to the role of attitude research in predicting consumer behavior since generally accepted findings reveal that:

1. As consumers' attitudes toward a product become more favorable, product usage tends to increase. And as attitudes grow less favorable, usage tends to decline until people actually stop buying the product.[3]

2. Consumer attitudes offer a useful variable in explaining the different market shares captured by different brands.[4]

3. Attitudes may be changed through persuasive communications (advertising), but many variables determine the effectiveness of advertising in accomplishing such changes.[5]

4. As the number of new products in the market place increases, marketers must constantly reinforce attitudes which are already favorable.[6]

This chapter explores the meaning of attitude derived from psychological theory, the organization of attitudes, the functions they serve, how attitudes are measured, and the current state of attitude theory in consumer research.

Understanding Attitude

Attitude has evolved from a relatively simple concept in psychology to one of the most complicated. A sampling of how attitude has been viewed through the years illustrates this development.

Psychological Origins

An early description is attributed to Bem:[7]

Attitudes are likes and dislikes. They are our affinities for and our aversions to situations, objects, persons, groups, or any other identifiable aspects of our environment, including abstract ideas and social policies.

A more recent explanation from social psychology reflects many years of empirical refinement:[8]

Operationally, an attitude may be defined as the individual's set of categories for evaluating a stimulus domain, which he has established as he learns about that domain in interaction with other persons and which relate him to various subsets within the domain with varying degrees of positive or negative effect.

Every individual approaches a "stimulus domain" (say, a supermarket or cocktail party) with a *learned* set of values, opinions, or beliefs. There is an act of perception. The person then "relates" or reacts to the situation, people, product, with "varying degrees of positive or negative effect." That is, he or she has feelings of acceptance or rejection, favor or disfavor, pleasure or irritation. And, after cognition and feeling, the individual probably completes the structure by some sort of behavior—by buying the supermarket's house brand or staying at the party until 2 a.m.

But attitudes are not fleeting likes and dislikes.

An attitude is a *relatively enduring* organization of beliefs around an object or situation predisposing one to respond in some preferential manner.[9]

At times, a momentary predisposition may appear to be attitudinal. After a long, hot day on the beach, a confirmed wine-only drinker may reach gratefully for a gin and tonic. A woman who has always disliked the color green may choose a green scarf or purse if it is the prevailing high fashion color. But these behaviors may or may not bring about an enduring attitude.

Defining Attitude for Consumer Behavior

For the purpose of consumer research, attitude may be defined as *a consumer's evaluative inclinations toward or against any element in his or her market domain.* This may include products, services, ideas, people, stores, media, brands, or any other item that enters into the purchasing process.

Additionally, Howard and Ostlund distinguish between two types of attitudes possibly affecting purchasing decisions.[10] First there are *personal* attitudes—the preference evaluations of the buyer considered just from an individual perspective. Secondly, the individual buyer may take into account the attitudes of those important to him or her; these are known as *situational* attitudes. Situational attitudes are important because consumer behavior seldom occurs in isolation (as in the case of the student buying a calculator who had to consider the attitudes of instructor and peers).

Opinions, Beliefs, and Values

"Values," "beliefs," and "opinions" are distinct from attitudes, although closely related. *Opinions* are commonly held to be the verbal expression of attitudes. One may, of course, express an attitude nonverbally in very clear ways, like sniffing loudly at the smell of a particular perfume or talking to a companion during a boring movie.

Beliefs are those portions of a person's cognitive structure that are founded more on faith than on reason. One may believe that musk oil makes a woman more attractive and, hence, have a favorable attitude toward women who use it. Beliefs are sometimes prescriptive, as, "I believe that manufacturers should take full responsibility for injuries caused by their products," and sometimes ethical, as in "I believe that capitalism is the only right and good economic system." Some beliefs are descriptive: "I believe in you." Beliefs can be considered among the important elements underlying attitudes. A belief long-standing in our culture—that the harder a woman drudges around her house the better a person she is—once led to a widespread attitude that instant foods and low-effort cleansers were not really desirable.

Values differ from both beliefs and attitudes and may be arranged into hierarchical structures, as discussed in chapter 4. Like beliefs, they can be components of attitudes. They contribute to the preferential nature of attitudes, often determining dispositions toward or against objects, persons, or philosophies. Values may also relate to so-called "end states" of existence—for example, valuing a world at peace or a society free from prejudice. Attitudes closely connected with values may be said to have *centrality*. Given a high value ranking on the attribute "beautiful body," a person may exhibit favorable attitudes toward exercise equipment; high-protein, low-fat foods; cosmetics, and the like. Central attitudes may be so fully developed as to be a major portion of personality.

Bem draws beliefs and values together in the term "evaluative beliefs."[11] Evaluative beliefs can determine attitudes in part, but they are not synonymous with attitudes. One may believe that disobeying the law is bad for society and that inhaling smoke is bad for the lungs, and still hold the attitude that smoking marijuana makes for a pleasant evening.

Attitude Organization

The key to understanding how attitudes actually work is in their organization. An attitude has a composition, or structure. And the processes of measuring, gauging, and changing attitudes depend heavily on how an attitude may be broken down into simpler parts.

There are two current views of attitude structure, both of which are popularly accepted and used in current research. The traditional view holds that attitudes have three separate components. A more recent formulation that has generated great enthusiasms and a flurry of application studies is the "multiattribute" model.

Three-Component Attitude Model

One way to view the organization of any given attitude is to think of it as the conclusion of a simple syllogism.

Major premise: Whole grain foods are very nutritious.
Minor premise: Being well-nourished makes me feel great.
Conclusion: I really like whole grain foods best.

The first premise is a matter of *cognition*. A person can study health books or journals of nutrition research, or learn the facts of human metabolism from class lectures. The second premise is *affective:* a matter of feeling or emotion. The conclusion contains a strongly implied *behavior* pattern. Liking whole grain foods should logically motivate purchase of, say, granola-type cereals and whole wheat breads.

Thus, the traditional approach to attitude structure conceived by Kretch, Crutchfield, and Ballachey identifies three components—cognitive, affective, and action-tendency.[12]

The Cognitive Component This segment of a given attitude consists in the way an individual evaluates some object or class of objects. Attitudes toward a food product such as spaghetti include cognitive beliefs about spaghetti itself, about Italy and Italians, about other people who eat spaghetti, about the difficulty people have eating the slippery strings, and other elements of the attitude-object. These cognitive beliefs include certain *evaluative* aspects—whether the object is seen favorably or unfavorably—and prescriptions about what should be done about the object if it is viewed unfavorably. For instance, an individual consumer may hold a highly negative attitude toward X-rated movies, believing that they are degrading, that they undermine the moral fabric of American culture. A part of this cognitive component would be this person's view of how X-rated movies should be dealt with: outlawed, controlled, or burned publicly in their film cans.

The Affective Component This aspect of attitude refers to its emotional aspects, like feelings of pleasure or displeasure, love or hate.

One problem in consumer attitude measurement studies, identified by Will and Hasty, is that subjects are sometimes asked to respond to a single stimulus, and this forces them to use "rational" thought processes they do not use exclusively when forming an attitude in real life situations.[13] An emotional response is evident in the case of Ivory soap. "Ninety-nine and 44/100 percent pure" does not provoke the rational response, "Pure what?" Rationally, a buyer might fear that the soap contains pure lye, a common ingredient of soaps, or pure lard, given the color of some soaps. But the common attitude is that Ivory soap is one of the least irritating, suitable even for the skin of a newborn infant.

The Action-Tendency Component This aspect refers to a disposition to behave in a certain way toward the attitude object—a readiness to respond. If a consumer's attitude toward a television commercial for some product is positive, he or she may chuckle, comment on what a great commercial it is, or actually make a mental note to purchase the brand. If the reaction is negative, the viewer may groan, make coarse remarks about the sponsor, and vow never to purchase the brand. Because the action-tendency component seems most closely related to consumer purchasing behavior, the majority of studies probing attitude structure have focused on this aspect. But Day cautions that too many research efforts leap to the third component without a full understanding of the cognitive and affective aspects.[14] Attitudinal effects on behavior are complex, and require sufficient knowledge of cognitive and emotional processes before sensible predictions may be made.

Valence and Multiplexity Kretch et al contend that each attitude component carries a certain *valence:* the degree of positive or negative disposition toward or against the attitude object. The stronger the valence, the more enduring and tenacious that attitude will be.[15]

Each component also maintains a degree of *multiplexity,* a measure of the complexity of elements within a single attitude. Some attitudes are relatively simple matters of approve-disapprove, love-hate, or act positively-act negatively. Buying a can of shaving cream requires simple attitudinal activity. But searching for the right doctor to perform cosmetic surgery on one's face would bring into play a range of cognitive, affective, and action-tendency variables.

Organizational Consistency

The three-component model suggests that there is a high degree of consistency both within the structure of a given attitude and among the various *clusters* in an individual's attitude *system.*

Intra-attitude Consistency It is logical to expect that the cognitive, affective, and action-tendency components of an individual attitude will be consistent with one another. In other words, a consumer who visits the same haircutter month after month (action-tendency) probably believes that the stylist gives good haircuts (cognitive) and that there is a personal rapport extending at least to a mutual feeling about how the consumer's hair should look after the trim (affective). Rosenberg notes that consonance between the affective and cognitive aspects must exist for an attitude to be maintained because an individual cannot tolerate an inconsistency between these components. When the two are not in accord, a threshold is reached and the attitude dissipates. To reaffirm the old attitude, the cause of the inconsistency must be isolated and rejected as insignificant by the individual.[16] In the example cited above, if the hairdresser should become surly and uncommunicative while styling the consumer's hair, the consumer must either decide that a personal rapport with one's haircutter really isn't needed to get a good haircut or else change attitudes toward the stylist and find a new one.

Interattitude Consistency Similarly, the clusters of attitudes within an individual's system should also be consistent. Suedfeld divides consistency theories into three categories: *balance* theory, *congruity* theory, and *cognitive dissonance* theory.[17]

Balance theory states that imbalance leads to change only if the individual is aware of it and is motivated to reduce it, while recognizing that different persons may have different thresholds of tolerance for imbalance. To achieve balance when forced to face an imbalanced situation, we adjust either or both of our conflicting attitudes. If an individual savors the "underground" gourmet cuisine of an out-of-the-way restaurant, but finds

the decor somewhat tacky and secretly suspects that the chef doesn't always wash up before serving, the diner can either decide that the food isn't such a treat after all or that sparkling cleanliness doesn't really count.

Congruity theory is based on the asumption that attitudes tend toward simplicity—that they tend to lie at the extremes of the good-bad dimension. This theory adds that, when two differently rated objects become related they achieve more nearly identical ratings on a continuum. A previously unliked store may begin to appeal to a consumer who discovers that it is the only one in town to carry a hard-to-find but dearly loved brand.

Cognitive dissonance theory asserts that people perpetually strive for harmony among all their beliefs, values, attitudes, feelings, and actions. Whenever they perceive that one area is out of line with the others, or dissonant, they will modify all systems until harmony is achieved. Thus, a man who desires to see himself as rugged and tough but who genuinely likes the taste of Virginia Slims better than that of Marlboros will have some adjusting to do. Or a middle-aged person who wants to be thought of as a young swinger but who can't stand to listen to any music composed since 1970 must change either musical appetite or self-image. The theory of cognitive dissonance will be discussed in greater detail as a basis for attitude change strategies.

Fishbein's Multiattribute Model

A second way to view the structure of consumer attitude toward a product is to assume that there are not three but only two components:

• *Beliefs* about the specific attributes of a

product, such as price, design, packaging, durability, and other characteristics of the object itself.

• *Evaluative* aspects of those beliefs—how the consumer evaluates the *importance* of each attribute in satisfying his or her product needs.

This is the basis for multiattribute models of attitude. The most widely used today is the Fishbein Model, expressed as:[18]

$$A_b = \sum_{i-1}^{N} W_i B_{ib}$$

where:

A_b = the attitude toward a particular brand b

W_i = the weight or importance of attribute i

B_{ib} = the evaluative aspect or belief toward attribute i for brand b

N = the number of attributes important in the selection of a given brand in the given product category

In more familiar terms, consumers grant different weights to different attributes of a given product. Buying paper towels, one shopper may want Bounty's advertised "extra" absorbency, another may look for Viva's colorful prints, a third may believe price alone to be the most important feature and buy the cheapest house brand available. But seldom is a single attribute the only important one. Generally, consumers weigh a number of attributes, and the *evaluative attitude* toward any product is the sum total of attitudes toward each attribute perceived as important.[19]

Because product attributes are readily identifiable and consumers may indicate the relative salience each attribute possesses for them, the Fishbein model lends itself particularly to studies probing the effects of attitude on brand preference. Some examples for different kinds of products appear later in this chapter.

The Fishbein Behavioral Intention Model

But as Fishbein himself notes, his Multi-attribute Model was conceived to explain attitudes toward objects (products) rather than relationships between attitudes and behavior:[20]

I think this distinction between attitude toward an object and attitude toward a behavior is a very important one. . . . Even though I may think that some product has all kinds of good characteristics, qualities and attributes, I may not believe buying or using that product will lead to valued outcomes. That is, even though I may have a positive attitude toward "Brand X," I might not have a positive attitude toward "buying Brand X," and according to behavioral decision theory, it is this latter attitude that should be related to buying behavior. For example, a woman might believe that "high pile carpeting" is "warm," "comfortable," "luxurious," and "prestigious," and since she positively evaluates those attributes, she is likely to have a positive attitude toward "high pile carpeting." However, what do you think the consequences of "buying high pile carpeting" are for that woman if she has two dogs, a cat, and three children under nine?

To meet this need, he adapted a cognitive theory of Dulany's to create the Fishbein Behavioral Intentions Model, stated in a very simplified form as:[21]

$$\text{Aact} = \sum_{i}^{n} {}_1 B_i a_i$$

where:

Aact = the attitude toward performance of a specific act

B_i = beliefs about the consequences of a specific act

a_i = the evaluative aspect of B_i

n = the number of relevant consequences.

This means, again in a simplified way, that a consumer's intention to perform a particular purchasing act is a function of that person's beliefs and evaluations of the consequences (the probability that they will be gratifying), in the context of the buying situation, and further considering his or her desire (or lack of it) to do what appears should be done.

At the time of this writing, the Behavioral Intentions Model is being tested, and modified, by researchers on purchases such as Ultra-Brite toothpaste,[22] the Mustang II,[23] and commercially prepared term papers.[24]

Functions of Attitudes

But the organizational structure of attitudes does not tell everything about how they serve the individuals who hold them. In a general way, attitudes superimpose an order and structure on an individual's environment because, like perception, attitudes are highly selective. Our attitudes toward the dizzying array of products and services available to us prevent us from being inundated by them. We are attracted to some items because we are positively disposed toward them and we reject the rest because we are unfavorably disposed or just indifferent.

Four Psychological Functions of Attitudes

In a now-classic article, Daniel Katz specifies four basic functions attitudes perform for individuals.[25] The first, "adjustment" function, is related to the action-tendency component of attitudes mentioned earlier. Two other functions, "ego-defense" and "value-expression," are connected to the affective component in that they allow for the operation and expression of emotions in self-realization situations. The fourth, or "knowledge," function expands the cognitive component of attitude formation and definition.

Adjustment Katz describes the *adjustment* function as the development of attitudes that will lead most efficiently (in any situation) toward perceived rewards, and avoid most conveniently any punishments involved. If a conservative family moves into a neighborhood where their closest neighbors are strongly liberal, and they yearn for lots of neighborly contact, they will probably adjust their political attitudes somewhat to agree rather than argue with the neighbors. A consumer who has learned from past experience that electric hair rollers cause split ends in hair will probably not readily accept electric hairbrushes or single-wand electric curlers.

Ego Defense The *ego-defensive* function helps the individual to realize the goals and image he or she desires. A consumer may ward off threats to self-image by developing positive attitudes toward self-enhancing products such as fashions, grooming aids, an impressive car, and other visible indications that the consumer is a competent, attractive person. In some cases, ego-defense leads to projections of one's own weaknesses onto others, and development of an unfavorable attitude toward *them*, rather than toward one's own shortcomings.

Value Expression   A third function of attitudes is to give *positive expression* to the external world of an individual's own values. Attitudes of ecological concern may be expressed in buying a bicycle, using cold water for laundry, bundling the Sunday paper off to the recycling center, and drinking beer in returnable bottles.

Knowledge   The fourth function of attitudes is designated as *knowledge*. This may have both positive and negative effects on personal adjustment. It can lead to racial or national stereotyping because it is a shortcut to "knowing" just what the next member of some ethnic subculture one meets is going to be like. It can also serve as an information filter, making it easier to sort out what one will read and agree with and what one will reject from the plethora of news items about some controversial issue. Attitudes serving this

function thus provide frames of reference for understanding the world. The efficiency of the knowledge function of attitudes is readily observable in consumer behavior. Attitudes lead a purchaser to "know" that she will prefer denims to dresses. She does not have to reexamine her values, habits, and life style each time she wants to buy an article of clothing.

Attitude Salience

When one attitude fulfills certain functions for an individual to a greater degree than another, it is said to be more *salient* (important or relevant) to the person. And attitudes that are most salient are the most enduring and resistant to change. Generally, attitudes about consumer products and services are not especially salient to individuals until the felt need for a purchase arises.

How Attitudes Are Measured

In psychological and consumer research, attitudes have been gauged by such techniques as scale ratings of verbal statements about objects, people, and self (measured by degree of esteem or accomplishment). They have also been measured by rankings of the *value* of objects, ratings of mood, willingness to endorse a product, and likelihood of some subsequent behavior. Behavioral measures rather than pencil and paper sessions have also been used to elicit verbal reports of attitudes.

The techniques that will be reviewed here

are scaling methods, attribute ratings, and longitudinal analysis. (See chapter 3 for additional discussion.)

Scaling Techniques

Thurstone and Likert have devised two of the most widely used scaling techniques.

The Thurstone Scale   In Thurstone's method of *equal-appearing intervals,* a group of state-

What They "Like" Depends on How You Ask the Question

One of the thorniest problems in attitude measurement concerns phrasing statements or questions so that they do not affect the subject's responses.

Say the measurement problem at hand is gauging attitudes toward orange soda. The logical question to ask is, of course:

"Do you like orange soda?"

But the problem is that most people will respond positively to a question phrased in that fashion. "Sure," comes the answer, although this consumer's vague memory of tasting orange soda may be of an occasion ten years before. Yet, on the survey report, he would have been recorded as an orange soda enthusiast.

The most open-ended way to pose the question is:

"What kinds of soda do you like?"

The trouble now concerns the consumer's probable inability to remember all the sodas he or she happens to like. Even though this person may enjoy orange soda and buy it often, the likeliest response will be "Coke" or "Pepsi," since these heavily advertised brands are usually first to come to mind.

Thus, the best solution is to offer alternative choices of this nature:

"Which kinds of soda do you like?"

1. Cola

2. Root Beer

3. Orange

4. Grape

5. Cream

since this mode of questioning lets the consumer focus on specific items for further analysis.

This technique employs a multiattribute approach such as the Fishbein model discussed earlier. The procedure involves gauging the *importance* of each attribute of a product and the consumer's *evaluation* of the product on that attribute alone. Then the sum of those evaluations is represented as the consumer's overall attitude toward the product. Tables 12-1 and 12-2 represent a measure of attribute importance for economy cars, and consumer ratings of four different models on those attributes. The model receiving the lowest average score across all the attributes is the one which is said to elicit the *most* favorable overall attitudes. The reason the lowest score is the most desirable is that consumers were asked to rate on a scale of 1 to 6, with a score of 1 denoting a highly favorable rating on that attribute and 6 a highly unfavorable rating. Thus, Model B, with an average score of 2.04, obtains the most positive overall attitude rating.

Table 12-1 Measuring Attribute Importance in Consumer Attitudes Toward Economy Cars

(handwritten margin note: "ppl sure of what they liked then didn't like")

	RANKING OF ATTRIBUTE IMPORTANCE (SHOWN IN % OF RESPONDENTS)				
ATTRIBUTE	1ST *(most important)*	2ND	3RD	4TH	5TH
Styling	9.2	12.7	18.2	22.6	37.3
Gas Mileage	31.3	31.4	19.6	8.1	3.6
Price	32.1	30.6	10.3	12.1	10.9
Performance	17.1	11.3	38.5	23.1	10.0
Comfort	10.3	14.0	13.4	34.1	38.2
	100%	100%	100%	100%	100%

Table 12-2 Attribute Ratings of Different Economy Car Models (Average Scores)

MODELS	STYLING	GAS MILEAGE	PRICE	PERFORMANCE	COMFORT
Car A	2.43	2.86	2.51	2.75	1.82
Car B	1.71	2.17	2.38	1.93	2.03
Car C	2.56	2.77	2.34	2.14	2.51
Car D	2.86	2.74	2.31	2.66	2.68
Car E	2.33	1.97	2.65	2.34	2.77

ments about some given topic (detergents' effects on ecology, cuts in defense spending, tastiness of luncheon meats, harmful effects of smoking, or whatever) is arranged on an attitude continuum from least favorable (category 1) to most favorable (category 11). Judges arrange the statements so that each positive or negative statement is an equal distance from the ones on either side of it. Attempts are made to make the statements as unambiguous as possible. Subjects are scored on the median of the scale values of the statements with which they agree.

The Likert Scale The Likert scale enables consumers to choose from five degrees of agreement with a large number of positive and negative statements expressing attitudes about some topic. These are: Strongly agree, Agree, Undecided, Disagree, Strongly disagree. For the positive statements the responses are weighted with values 5, 4, 3, 2, 1, respectively. Responses to negative statements are valued 1, 2, 3, 4, 5, so that "Strongly agreeing" with a positive statement and "Strongly disagreeing" with a negative statement provide the highest numerical scores.

A person's score, then, is the sum of his or her scores on all items of the scale. Likert scales are somewhat easier to design than Thurstone scales (as they do not require unbiased judges to construct the attitude statements), yet they are considered comparable in reliability. Although other attitude scaling procedures exist, some highly mathematical, most attitude scales have been constructed by the Thurstone and Likert methods.

Methodological Questions One of the difficulties encountered with scaling techniques in attitude research is that oppositely polarized attitude statements may evoke not only huge differences in response *intensity* but also reversals in attitude *direction*.[26] In other words, what one says about oneself tends to reflect whether statements are phrased positively or negatively. Use of polarized statements in attitude research is useful in many cases, but marketers should be aware that polarized statements are generally "loaded."

Longitudinal Studies

A third method for measuring attitude is particularly intriguing because it lets researchers measure attitude shifts over a period of time. This approach permits gauging of attitude change and patterns of brand loyalty (or disloyalty).

The basic method consists of successive interviews with the same subjects at various times and plotting their responses toward a product or brand along a consistent scale of "favorable," "neutral," and "unfavorable." Both positive and negative changes are recorded, and it is possible to determine the exact proportions of a sample which retained the same attitudes, developed more favorable attitudes, or adopted a more negative disposition to the product in question.[27]

Attitude Theory in Consumer Research

As an indication of the kind of attitude research marketers may profit from in the next few years, some representative studies and findings are included here. These focus particularly on two areas: attitude as a predictor of *brand preference* and attitude as a *segmentation variable*.

Attitudes and Brand Preference

This has been one of the most fruitful avenues of research for attitude theorists in predictive ability and identifying salient product attributes.

Testing Attitude Models The multiattribute model developed by Fishbein has received the greatest current research interest and application to date. Bass and Talarzyk found that, comparing Fishbein's attitude model with three other predictive tools, brand preference was most often predicted correctly by the attitude measure (see Table 12-3).[28]

In a representative study of soft drinks using Fishbein's model, Bass, Pessemier, and Lehman found that choice behavior is

Table 12-3   Probability of Correctly Predicting Most Preferred Brands For Various Models

MODEL	PRODUCT					
	FROZEN ORANGE JUICE	MOUTH-WASH	TOOTH-PASTE	TOILET TISSUE	LIP-STICK	BRASSIERES
Attitudes	.67[a]	.69[a]	.75[a]	.63[a]	.70[a]	.72[a]
Multiple discriminant analysis (using beliefs)	.58	.58	.63	.56	.63	.58
Multiple discriminant analysis (using demographics)	.52	.49	.57	.42	.53	.56
Market share	.53	.44	.46	.36	.46	.39
Random	.20	.20	.20	.20	.20	.20

[a]Significant at the .01 level when compared with all of the other models.

Source: Frank M. Bass and Wayne Talarazyk, "An Attitude Model for the Study of Brand Preference," Journal of Marketing Research, Vol. 9 (February 1972), p. 95. Reprinted by permission of the American Marketing Association.

not constant even when attitudes are unchanged, suggesting that attitude-based predictions of change must be probabilities. However, when subjects did not actually choose the brand they most preferred, they were more likely to choose a similar brand than a dissimilar one.[29]

Multiattribute models, and particularly Fishbein's, are constantly being tested, adapted, and refined by researchers. (Two examples for the curious reader are Ahtola's Vector Model of Preferences[30] and the concept of Cognitive Algebra in Multiattribute Models put forth by Bettman et al.[31]

Market Segmentation by Attitude

It may be possible to segment markets on the basis of consumer attitudes, as shown in studies weighing attitudes with other psychological variables and in determinant attitude analysis.

Attitude and Motivational Segmentation

Combining these two variables Cunningham and Crissy discovered that the small car market is really two markets—one for foreign cars and one for American compacts.[32]

Maverick owners and foreign car buyers were found to differ significantly on four out of five motivation and attitude variables:

1. Maverick owners were significantly more status-conscious than the owners of foreign compact cars.

2. Owners of foreign compact cars were less conservative than Maverick owners.

3. Maverick owners tended to have a more positive attitude toward big business than did foreign compact car owners, although the differences were not significant.

4. Owners of foreign compact cars were less dogmatic than Maverick owners.

5. Foreign compact-car owners were more positive in their attitudes toward foreign products than were Maverick owners.

These findings hold interest for both American and automotive car marketers, particularly in positioning and designing communications for their target markets.

Determinant Attitude Segmentation While a consumer holds many attitudes toward a service or product, Myers and Alpert contend that only a few are *determinant attitudes* or "Attitudes toward features which are most closely related to preference or to actual purchase decisions . . ."[33]

Determinant attitude *segmentation* rests on assumptions that (1) consumers' *beliefs* about the attributes of a product are the most highly predictive aspect of the Fishbein-type multiattribute models, (2) demographic variables may reveal groups of consumers who maintain different relationships between their beliefs and behaviors, and (3) various demographic categories may hold different *determinant* attributes regarding the purchase of a market item.

In a Canadian study, Sweitzer used determinant attitude segmentation to portray target consumer groups for four different commercial banks.[34] Consumer groups were categorized on the basis of their life cycle. Then the different segments were studied to find out which displayed the determinant attributes were looked for at the different banks (Table 12-4). On this basis, the banks were able to position their services and benefits for the segments they wished to reach.

Behavioral prediction and segmentation are two of the uses marketers have found for attitude models. The third area that has generated much exploration is the whole question of attitude change, which will be the subject of the next chapter.

Summary

All consumer decisions entail the psychological concept of *attitude*, defined for consumer research purposes as a consumer's evaluative inclination toward or against any element in his or her market domain. There are two theories of attitude organization. One states that there are three components of attitude: *cognitive*, *affective*, and *action-tendency*. Each component, in turn, carries both *valence* and *multiplexity*. The individual strives for consistency (as a rule) both in the components of a single attitude and in the interaction of attitudes within the person's system. The second theory holds that attitudes are comprised of *beliefs* about the specific attributes of a product and the evaluative aspects of those beliefs—how consumers evaluate the importance of each attribute in satisfying product needs. This view is advanced in the currently popular *Fishbein Multiattribute Model*. Attitudes are functional in that they are of four types, which meet needs for *adjustment*, *ego-defense*, *value-expression*, and *judgment*. When one attitude meets a given need to a greater degree than others, it is said to be more *salient*. Attitudes are measured by *scaling techniques*, *attribute ratings*, and *longitudinal studies*. Current attitude research in consumer behavior focuses upon such topics as prediction of *brand preference* and determinant attribute *segmentation*.

Table 12-4   Determinant Attitude Segmentation

		DETERMINANT ATTRIBUTE MARKET SEGMENTS			
	DEMOGRAPHIC CATEGORIES	CANADIAN BANK	BANQUE CANADIENNE	BANK OF CANADA	BANQUE DU CANADA
I.	Getting Started:				
	College	Cheque Charges	Cheque Charges	Emphatic Manager	Loan Policy
	High School	Good reputation Helpful personnel Empathic manager Loan policy Accessible manager Financial advice	Cheque Charges	—	Good Reputation
II.	Early nest: College	Good reputation	Accessible manager Empathic manager Financial advice Loan policy Innovative financial services	—	Accessible manager Financial advice Helpful personnel Empathic manager
	High school	—	Loan policy Innovative financial services Speed of service Helpful personnel Financial advice Good reputation	—	—
III.	Full nest: College	—	Helpful personnel Speed of service	Speed of service Good reputation Helpful personnel Loan policy Cheque charges	Innovative Financial services Cheque charges
	High School	—	Empathic manager Good reputation	—	—
IV.	Empty nest: College	Empathic manager Speed of service Innovative financial services	—	Cheque charges Loan policy Accessible manager Financial advice Speed of service Innovative financial services Empathic manager Good reputation	—
	High School	Accessible manager Speed of service Innovative financial services Cheque charges	—	—	Cheque charges Good reputation

Source: Robert W. Sweitzer, "Determinant Attribute Segmentation," Journal of the Academy of Marketing Science, *Vol. 3, No. 1 (Winter 1975), p. 95. Reprinted by permission of the Academy of Marketing Science.*

NOTES

1. Martin A. Fishbein, *Belief, Attitude, Intention, and Behavior: An Introduction to Theory and Research*, (Reading, Mass.: Addison-Wesley, 1975).

2. See E. H. Bonfield and Marvin J. Karson, "Attitude, Social Influence, Personal Influence, and Intention Interactions as Related to Brand Purchase Behavior," *Journal of Marketing Research*, Vol. 11 (November 1974), p. 379; and Michael J. Ryan and E. H. Bonfield, "The Fishbein Extended Model and Consumer Behavior," *Journal of Consumer Research*, Vol. 2, No. 2 (September 1975), p. 118.

3. Alvin Achenbaum, "Knowledge is a Thing Called Measurement" in *Attitude Research at Sea*, ed. Lee Adler and Irving Crespi (Chicago, American Marketing Association, 1966), p. 123.

4. Henry Assael and George S. Day, "Attitudes and Awareness as Predictors of Market Share," *Journal of Advertising Research*, Vol. 8, December 1968, p. 10.

5. Frederick W. Winter, "A Laboratory Experiment of Individual Attitude Response to Advertising Exposure," *Journal of Marketing Research*, Vol. 10, May 1973, p. 140.

6. Steward W. Bither, Ira J. Dolich, and Elaine B. Nell, "The Application of Attitude Immunization Techniques in Marketing," *Journal of Marketing Research*, Vol. 8, February 1971, pp. 56–61.

7. Daryl J. Bem, *Beliefs, Attitudes and Human Affairs* (Belmont, Calif.: Brooks/Cole Publishing Co., 1970, p. 14.

8. Muzafer Sherif and Carolyn Sherif, "Attitude as the Individual's Own Categories: The Social Judgment-Involvement Approach to Attitude and Attitude Change," in *Attitude, Ego-Involvement, and Change* ed. Sherif and Sherif (New York: John Wiley and Sons, 1967), p. 115.

9. Milton Rokeach, *Beliefs, Attitudes, and Values: A Theory of Organization and Change* (San Francisco: Jossey-Bass Inc., 1970), p. 112.

10. John A. Howard and Lyman E. Ostlund, eds., *Buyer Behavior* (New York: Alfred A. Knopf, Inc. 1973), p. 255.

11. Bem, *Beliefs, Attitudes*, p. 15.

12. David Kretch, Richard S. Crutchfield, and Egerton L. Ballachey, *Individual in Society* (New York: McGraw-Hill, 1962).

13. R. Ted Will and Ronald W. Hasty, "Attitude Measurement Under Conditions of Multiple Stimuli," *Journal of Marketing*, Vol. 35, No. 1 (January 1971), p. 66.

14. George S. Day, "Evaluating Models of Attitude Structure," *Journal of Marketing Research*, Vol. 9 (August 1972), p. 279.

15. Kretch, Crutchfield and Ballachey, *Individual in Society*, 12.

16. Milton J. Rosenberg, "Inconsistency Arousal and Reduction in Attitude Change," in *Current Studies in Social Psychology* ed. I. D. Steiner and M. Fishbein (New York: Holt, Rinehart and Winston, 1965).

17. Peter Suedfeld, ed., *Attitude Change: The Competing Views* (Chicago: Aldine Atherton, 1971), p. 1.

18. Martin Fishbein, "A Consideration of Beliefs and Their Role in Attitude Measurement," in *Readings in Attitude Theory and Measurement*, ed. M. Fishbein (New York: John Wiley and Sons, 1967).

19. Neil E. Beckwith and Donald R. Lehmann, "The Importance of Differential Weights in Multiple Attribute Models of Consumer Attitude," *Journal of Marketing Research*, Vol. 10 (May 1973), p. 141.

20. Martin A. Fishbein, "Some Comments on the Use of 'Models' in Advertising Research," in *Proceedings: Seminar on Translating Advanced Advertising Theories into Research Reality* (Amsterdam, The Netherlands: European Society of Market Research, 1971), p. 245, as cited in Michael J. Ryan and E. H. Bonfield, "The Fishbein Extended Model and Consumer Behavior," *Journal of Consumer Research*, Vol. 2, No. 2 (September 1975), p. 120.

21. Martin A. Fishbein, "Attitude and the Prediction of Behavior," in *Readings in Attitude Theory and Measurement*, ed. M. Fishbein (New York: John Wiley and Sons, 1967, pp. 477–492.

22. Michael J. Ryan, "An Empirical Test of a Predictive Model and Causal Chain Derived from Fishbein's Behavioral Intention Model and Applied to a Purchase Intention Situation" (Unpublished doctoral dissertation, University of Kentucky, 1974).

23. Ryan, "Test of Predictive Model."

24. David E. Weddle and James R. Bettman, "Marketing Underground: An Investigation of Fishbein's Behavioral Intention Model," in *Advances in Consumer Research*, Vol. I, ed. Scott Ward and Peter Wright (Association for Consumer Research, 1973).

25. Daniel Katz, "The Functional Approach to the Study of Attitudes," *Public Opinion Quarterly*, Vol. 24, 1960, pp. 163–204.

26. In Philip Zimbardo and Ebbe B. Ebbesen, *Influencing Attitudes and Changing Behavior: A Basic Introduction to Relevant Methodology, Theory and Applications* (Reading, Mass.: Addison-Wesley Publishing Co., 1969).

27. Peter D. Bennet, ed., *Marketing and Economic Development* (Chicago: American Marketing Association, 1966).

28. Frank M. Bass and W. Wayne Talarzyk, "An Attitude Model for the Study of Brand Preference," *Journal of Marketing Research*, Vol. 9 (February 1972), p. 93.

29. Frank M. Bass, Edgar A. Pessemier, and Donald R. Lehmann, "An Experimental Study of Relationships between Attitudes, Brand Preference, and Choice," *Behavioral Science*, Vol. 17, No. 6, November 1972, pp. 532–541.

30. Olli T. Ahtola, "The Vector Model of Preferences: An Alternative to the Fishbein Model," *Journal of Marketing Research*, Vol. 12 (February 1975), p. 52.

31. James R. Bettman, Noel Capon, and Richard J. Lutz, "Cognitive Algebra in Multi-Attribute Attitude Models," *Journal of Marketing Research*, Vol. 12 (May 1975), p. 151.

32. William H. Cunningham and William J. E. Crissy, "Market Segmentation by Motivation and Attitude," *Journal of Marketing Research*, Vol. 9 (February 1972), pp. 100–102.

33. James H. Myers and Mark I. Alpert, "Determinant Buying Attitudes: Meaning and Measurement," *Journal of Marketing*, Vol. 32 (October 1968), pp. 13–20.

34. Robert W. Sweitzer, "Determinant Attribute Segmentation," *Journal of the Academy of Marketing Science*, Vol. 3, No. 1 (Winter 1975).

MARKETING APPLICATIONS

Conclusion 1 *Attitudes registered by consumers as prospective voters are considered important indicators of voting behavior in the "marketing" of political candidates.*

Application The term marketing applied to politics remains controversial—most people do not like to consider candidates for the presidency, governorships, and congressional seats as commercial products. Yet marketing techniques such as voter segmentation and carefully-prepared "image" advertising have been well-documented in political contests. Perhaps one of the earliest and most successful applications of marketing methodology was made by the public relations firm hired on behalf of Ronald Reagan for the 1965 California gubernatorial contest. In this case, voter attitudes were probed to uncover the "gut," emotional issues most troubling Californians at the time—such as racial unrest in Watts and student unrest at Berkeley. This information was skillfully employed in developing the candidate's positions and speeches and was considered a critical factor in his victory.

Conclusion 2 *Attitude salience is an important factor in gauging consumer attitudes toward specific products and brands.*

Application When making decisions about marketing a certain product—say, a dishwasher detergent—it is important to find out how important various product attributes are. Thus, it may be useful to set up a "focus group" of representative consumers who are heavy users of dishwasher detergent. By placing twelve or so in a discussion group under the direction of a skilled moderator, these consumers may express what they feel about (1) dishwasher detergents in general and (2) your brand in particular. Through this dialogue, it will be possible to determine what product features are considered salient (or most important) and how well your product measures up in those areas. For instance, is it important for any detergent to eliminate water spots on glasses? And how do people think your product performs at leaving their glasses crystal clear? The salient areas uncovered are those that should be stressed in product development and communications.

Conclusion 3 *The importance of different product attributes may be measured by attribute ratings, with the sum total indicating a consumer's overall attitude toward the product.*

Application With an attribute rating of his product in hand, the marketer of a professional-type hotcomb obtains several kinds of useful information. He knows whether or not consumers reveal a favorable overall rating of the appliance. And he knows how his product compares to several others on the basis of attributes such as "power," "dries fast," "easy to handle," "price," "styling," and "durability." If the product is rated lower than its competition on power—even though it is actually just as powerful as the brands rated higher—

325

there is something wrong with the product design in that consumers do not perceive it as being so powerful. Thus, the product, which was carefully designed to be less noisy, might be redesigned to make it as loud as its competitors, and unveiled as the new "super" unit.

ASSIGNMENTS

Research Assignment

Background   The Midwestern Brands Company offers a dog food line known as Dogourmet, which consists of the usual flavors—beef, liver, chicken, cheese. Dogourmet's share of market has been slipping somewhat due to unknown factors, and management wants to do something unique with the line to make it more attractive to dog owners.

You are hired as a research consultant to test a proposition some of Midwestern's management feel is quite valid (if not scientifically proven)—that pet owners tend to hold the attitude that their pets will like exactly the same foods that the owners like. Under this assumption, it would be desirable to add new flavors to the Dogourmet line such as Filet Mignon, Fried Chicken, Cheeseburger, and other human favorites.

Methodology   Select a sample of at least 5 dog owners and ask them to rate the following flavors in the order they would be most likely to buy them for their pets, based on their attitudes toward what their dogs would find tasty:

a. Beef
b. Cheeseburger
c. Filet mignon
d. Liver
e. Liver and bacon
f. Chicken
g. Fried chicken
h. Cheese
i. Roast beef

Items b,c,e,g, and i are all flavors that reflect human attitudes toward what tastes good. The other items are existing dog food flavors.

Extrapolation   On the basis of your findings, what recommendations would you make to Midwestern about their proposed Dogourmet line? What do your findings suggest about dog owners' attitudes toward their pets?

Creative Assignment

As a young partner in a California poster company whose market is the 15-to-25 age group, you are interested in the attitudes that are most salient to young people at the moment so that you can create a new product line. Because your research budget is virtually zero, you do your own market research through contact with consumers in your prime target group.

Interview an "unscientific" sample of five people in the age group 15–25, and ask them to select the three poster themes they would most likely be attracted to and buy:

1. A favorite political figure
2. A disliked political figure making a hypocritical statement
3. A contemporary film star
4. A 1930s film star
5. A nude couple
6. A poster graphic that spells "LOVE"
7. An ecology symbol

Determine the three most popular and the three most unpopular themes by utilizing either the Likert or Thurstone scale.

On the basis of your findings, make a creative recommendation for seven new poster themes.

Managerial Assignment

One underground marketing scheme that has achieved some notoriety in academic services is the rash of "research" services selling term papers to college students to meet course requirements.

As the Dean of Students at a large urban university, you are naturally concerned about the practice. Your first impulse is to follow the route of some educators by approaching local legislators to outlaw these services. But you are fundamentally concerned with the kind of student attitudes that create a market for this service. Attempt to identify the attitudes toward education that would be amenable to using such a service (whether on a continuing or situational basis). Evaluate the probable extent of the problem and make a recommendation to the university administration.

SELECTED READINGS

Ahtola, Olli T. "The Vector Model of Preference: An Alternative to the Fishbein Model." *Journal of Marketing Research*, Vol. 12, No. 1 February 1975, pp. 52–59.

Bruno, Albert V. and Albert R. Wildt. "Toward Understanding Attitude Structure: A Study of the Complimentarity of Multi-Attribute Attitude Models." *Journal of Consumer Research*, Vol. 2, No. 2 (September 1975), pp. 137–145.

Hulbert, James. "Information Processing Capacity and Attitude Measurement." *Journal of Marketing Research*, Vol. 12, No. 1 (February 1975), pp. 104–106.

Ryan, Michael J. and E. H. Bonfield. "The Fishbein Extended Model and Consumer Behavior." *Journal of Consumer Research*, Vol. 2, No. 2 (September 1975), pp. 118–136.

Wyckham, Robert C. "Spending Attitudes of Consumers: Pilot Studies in French and English Canada." *Journal of the Academy of Marketing Science*, Vol. 3, No. 1 (Winter 1975), pp. 109–118.

OBJECTIVES

THIRTEEN

Attitude Change

As the preceding chapter explained, marketers maintain a keen interest in consumer attitudes, because they are the best-known predictors of brand preference and actual purchasing behavior.

It is relatively easy to reinforce favorable consumer attitudes toward some market items by keeping product quality high enough to satisfy most customers and using communications to reassert the features or attributes people already like about the product. Ivory Soap, for instance, has long held its position as a pure, no-frills brand for people who want a quality soap without perfumes, deodorants, and other adornments. Advertising for Ivory is shrewdly directed to young women interested in achieving today's sought-after look of "natural" beauty.

But how can marketers build positive attitudes toward a product that isn't already blessed with Ivory's established following? Here the problem becomes one of persuading consumers to budge from a posture of stubborn indifference, or possibly of confronting negative attitudes previously formed through disappointing product use or unfavorable

associations. Because attitudes serve worthwhile functions for people in their problem solving activities, they are not shed easily. So attitude change, while a very desirable marketing goal in many instances, is not easily accomplished.

This chapter presents the major theoretical approach to attitude change, with the strategies considered to be most effective in modifying consumer attitudes through persuasive communications. Topics include:

• How successful drug education programs and courses in sexuality have been in effecting attitude change.

• Why marketers try to create "dissonance" to change consumers' attitudes.

• What personal qualities are important in a communicator who wants to change attitudes.

• What kinds of information are most effective in modifying attitudes.

Because communication is the key to attitude change, this discussion offers an introduction to the chapters that follow on the use of mass media and interpersonal communications.

A Realistic Goal?

There is still some controversy over whether or not attitude change is a realistic goal for marketers. Consider some of the successes (and failures) in recent attempts to modify consumers' attitudes toward products, services, and social behavior.

1. The Pepsi-Cola Company reports that, when Coca Cola drinkers were persuaded to sample both products in taste tests, many Coke drinkers actually preferred Pepsi, expressed a favorable new attitude toward the product, and claimed that they would buy Pepsi in the future. This served as the basis for an advertising campaign in several major markets to persuade Coke drinkers to try Pepsi—which the Pepsi-Cola Company deemed quite successful.[1]

2. After discovering that it had acquired a rather stodgy image over the years, a New York savings bank redirected its advertising to offer special accounts for career women and young singles. A sampling of "new" consumer attitudes produced highly favorable ratings on attributes such as "a fun place to save" and "unstuffy banking."

3. Despite the vast amount of interest and resources devoted to drug education programs in recent years, one study concluded that representative programs in New York, Boston, Chicago, and Detroit had no significant effect in changing attitudes toward drug use.[2]

4. Investigating the currently popular courses in sexuality for men and women, researchers concluded that one such program did induce attitude change in both sexes—toward a more "experimental" approach to sensual expression.[3]

Much evidence indicates that attitude-change strategies may be effective in persuading consumers to try new products or reevaluate their attitudes toward existing ones. Yet, the dynamics of attitude change are complex, and even the most ambitious attempts may yield meager results. This discussion focuses on the basics of attitude change, the theories that attempt to explain how it works and the role of communication in strategic planning, thus setting a context for analyzing mass media and interpersonal communications in the next section.

Recalling the definition of "attitude" in chapter 12, attitude change may be seen as *the modification of a consumer's evaluative inclinations toward or against any item in his or her market domain.*

The question of how this modification actually operates has generated many explanations. (One psychologist points out that a recent survey counted thirty-four distinguishable models of attitude change.)[4] However, most fall under three classifications—*cognitive dissonance* theory, *functional* theory, and *multiattribute* theory—all based on concepts introduced in the previous chapter. Each theory will be presented here with implications for marketing strategy.

Cognitive Dissonance Theory

The *fundamental* premise of attitude change is that *dissonance reduction*—the felt need for cognitive consistency—is primarily responsible for modification of consumer attitudes. An assumption of cognitive consistency, that one's cognitions must be in balance with one another, underlies all theory in cognitive psychology, the most widely accepted orientation to consumer behavior.

Whenever a consumer is exposed to information that creates inconsistency or *dissonance* with attitudes or knowledge already held, his or her personal attitudes are adjusted by the revision of old ones, the adoption of new ones, or, in extreme cases, by modifications of the entire personal value system.

Internal Dissonance   According to the traditional three-component theory of attitude (cognitive, affective, and action-tendency) most intra-attitude dissonance is caused by conflict between the cognitive and affective components.[5] One traditional marketing approach for bringing about attitude change has been to attempt to influence people's cognition—to change their beliefs about some attitude-object. Persuasive communications such as ads, commercials, and the arguments of salespeople are often designed to explain why a product or service should be perceived as good and useful when the consumer has not previously regarded it as such. A related approach is the attempt to change the affective component, the feelings about a product, by presenting them in a highly favorable emotional context. In line with dissonance theory, once a single component of an attitude has been altered, attitude change may follow as the consumer strives for internal "balance." Thus, creation of dissonance is seen as one marketing goal to effect attitude change.

Interattitude Dissonance   As individuals attempt to balance the components of a single attitude, they also strive for congruity among attitudes and attitude clusters. The theory of cognitive dissonance devised by Festinger

states that a modification of overt behavior making it inconsistent with held attitudes will force those attitudes into congruity with the new behavior.[6] The classical example of Festinger's theory is the man who buys one automobile (overt behavior) and experiences the dissonance of having passed over others which also impressed him favorably. To resolve this dissonance, the buyer will seek out information which reinforces his brand choice—looking only at ads for the model he purchased rather than ads for the competitive models he passed by.

How Cognitive Dissonance Occurs

Festinger suggests a wide variety of consumer situations that can produce dissonance. Just a few of these include:[7]

1. *A consumer's final buying decision between two (or more) alternatives.* Using the example above, the man who ultimately buys a Jaguar XJS for $22,000 may have also considered (and test-driven) a Mercedes 450SL for $21,000 and a Porsche Super Carrera for $25,000—and been impressed with all three. Now he will resolve the dissonance between his positive attitude toward the cars he did *not* choose and his actual decision by seeking information providing additional "good reasons" for having chosen the Jaguar, and screening out information about the Porsche and Mercedes.

2. *A consumer's exposure to new information that is inconsistent with attitudes already held.* If a consumer who regularly uses Right Guard deodorant because of a belief that it is the best one on the market sees a competitive commercial that "proves" that Ultra Ban is more effective, this exposure may create dissonance between the person's current attitude and the new "evidence."

3. *A challenge to a consumer's attitude by contrary attitudes held by significant others.* Uncomfortable dissonance may result when a young woman highly disposed toward buying Radio Shack stereo equipment finds that her friends disdain that brand in favor of Marantz receivers and Advent speakers.

Other buying situations that may produce dissonance abound in everyday consumption, as illustrated in Table 13-1.

How Cognitive Dissonance May Be Reduced

According to Festinger, there are three essential ways in which a person can alleviate the uncomfortable tension resulting from dissonance:[8]

1. *Change one (or more) of the factors responsible for the dissonance.* The consumer who experiences dissonance between attitudes and behavior may change either one. If there is a discrepancy between, say, a belief that one should be able to wear jeans to work and a current job with IBM requiring three-piece suits and ties, a person may decide that going to the office in Levi's isn't professional, or wear them anyway and accept the (probably unpleasant) consequences.

2. *Seek new information consistent with existing attitudes or behavior.* This is how the Jaguar buyer helped to resolve his dissonance—by actively seeking favorable information, such as glowing road test reports, on his choice.

3. *Decide that the dissonance-producing situation isn't really that important.* This could occur in a situation such as the Right Guard user encountered upon seeing the Ultra Ban "evidence" of greater effectiveness.

"What difference does it make which one I use? They're all the same anyway."

While theoretically a person may be as likely to change behavior as attitude to resolve dissonance, it should be noted that where correlations between attitudes and behavior have been established in research, it is usually because an individual has changed attitudes to conform to overt behavior rather than vice versa.[9]

Strategic Implications

Two approaches to applying dissonance theory have been well documented in marketing: communication and role playing (which may also include the use of communication).

Using Communication to Create Dissonance One useful means of attitude change is offering new information to alter existing attitudes, hence creating dissonance and disposing the consumer to bring the dissonant elements into balance. This is accomplished through marketer-dominated information sources such as advertising, promotional materials at the retail level, sales contacts, and other opportunities to give consumers as much favorable information as possible about a product (often pointing up the benefits lacking in competitive products).

Maintaining Source Credibility A key factor of the informational approach to changing attitudes is *credibility* of source: communicator credibility has consistently been found to be a significant variable in attitude change.[10] Research indicates that when people perceive an intent to persuade in ads, they find the source less persuasive and less credible than when they perceive only informativeness.[11] What makes for consistent source reliability? Part of the answer can be seen in the increased use of "real people" offering testimonials on television commercials. "Neighbors" seem more credible rec-

Table 13-1 Dissonance in Selected Buying Situations

FACTORS AFFECTING DISSONANCE	BUYING SITUATION	CONDITIONS WITH HIGH DISSONANCE EXPECTATION	CONDITIONS WITH LOW DISSONANCE EXPECTATION
1. Attractiveness of rejected alternative	A high school graduate decides which of several pictures to order.	Three of the proofs have both attractive and desirable features.	One of the proofs clearly is superior to the rest.
2. Negative factors in chosen alternative	A man chooses between two suits of clothing.	The chosen suit has the color the man wanted but not the style.	The chosen suit has both the color and the style the man wanted.
3. Number of alternatives	A teacher shops for a tape recorder.	There are eight recorders from which to choose.	There are only two recorders from which to choose.
4. Cognitive overlap	A housewife shops for a vacuum sweeper.	A salesman offers two similarly priced tank types.	A salesman offers a tank type and an upright cleaner.
5. Importance of cognitions involved	A child buys a present for her sister.	The sister has definite preference for certain kinds of music.	The sister has no strong tastes for certain records.
6. Positive inducement	Parents decide to buy a photoenlarger for their son.	The son already has hobby equipment and does not need the enlarger.	The son never has had a true hobby and needs something to keep him occupied.
7. Discrepant or negative action	A man purchases an expensive watch.	The man had never before paid more than $35 for a watch.	Fairly expensive watches had been important gift items in the man's family.
8. Information available	A housewife buys a detergent.	The housewife has no experience with the brand purchased—it is a new variety.	The housewife has read and heard a good deal about the product and has confidence in the manufacturer.
9. Anticipated dissonance	A small boy buys a model airplane.	The boy anticipates trouble at home because of the cost of the model.	The boy expects no trouble at home because of the purchase.
10. Familiarity and knowledge	A family buys a floor polisher.	The item was purchased without much thought.	The item was purchased after a careful selection process.

Source: Robert S. Halloway, "An Experiment in Cognitive Dissonance," Journal of Marketing, *Vol. 31 (January 1967), p. 40. Reprinted by permission of the American Marketing Association.*

ommending household products than distant celebrities (who probably don't do their own cleaning or ironing anyway).

In line with this finding, word-of-mouth communication is usually considered superior to mass media communication in creating attitude change:[12]

. . . word of mouth has a much greater impact on those who are exposed, because (1) there is an opportunity for feedback and clarification, (2) word of mouth is regarded as providing more reliable, trustworthy advice, and (3) personal contacts are generally able to offer social support and encouragement.

However, although ultimate success in creating and reinforcing positive attitudes rests largely with the ability of the brand to generate favorable word-of-mouth communications,[13] roughly three times as many consumers still hear about a new product through media communications as hear about it from other people.

The characteristics of the communicator are important to source credibility and attitude change in several ways:

Source Likeability This consideration involves a number of factors such as pleasantness, perceived honesty, and, yes, physical attractiveness. The attractive communicator has emerged in research as more likely to effect attitude change.[14]

Source Similarity Generally speaking, communicators are most effective when they are perceived by the listeners as similar to them in appearance and other personal characteristics.

The Unexpected Source Sometimes it may be useful to choose a communicator who seems *least* likely to be advocating the argument at hand. In one study of the effect of similarity between the communicator and the recipient consumer, Lowry found that

greater similarity did not necessarily lead to greater credibility and increased attitude change.[15] He notes, surprisingly, that the communicators least like their audience were the most favorably evaluated by the recipients. This was due to the "disconfirmation of negative expectations": the subjects had expected to hear from a supposed "Communist" a message that was contrary to their own attitudes. When the "Communist" expressed views that differed from their own only moderately, they reacted more favorably to what he had to say. Similarly, unexpected communicators were rated more "sincere" and "honest" in a study where "hippies" spoke against marijuana and seminarians advocated it.[16] The best theoretical spokesman for General Motors, say, would be Ralph Nader—just because people know he would never accept the job!

Using communications, both in mass media and interpersonal situations, to greatest advantage is a more complicated business than this brief introduction would suggest. Chapters 14 and 15 cover this topic in detail.

Role Playing Through role playing psychologists have experimented with dissonance and subsequent attitude change. The hypothesis is that one's perception of others is changed when one assumes their roles. When a member of a tactical police force, for example, takes on the character of a ghetto resident, he may evolve a different attitude toward people in the ghetto. And research indicates that enacting a role at odds with one's present beliefs has proven to be an effective tactic for the modification of attitudes and behavior.[18]

Many advertisements draw the consumer into vicarious role playing. Television commercials depicting a scene with the viewer implicitly present at the kitchen table over

The "Censored" Message and Attitude Change

As everyone knows, censorship usually increases people's desire to see whatever is being kept from them. Now there is research evidence that they are also inclined to develop a positive attitude toward a message that is censored in some fashion.[17]

This principle has long been used in persuasive communications seeking to arouse consumers' interest and possibly make them more favorably disposed to the product. For instance:

- An ad headlined "Why Won't *The New York Times* Run This Ad?" for a recent book that purported to implicate high government figures in political payoffs and other chicanery. (*The Times* and other newspapers had, in fact, declined to run the ad.)

- A commercial for Royal Crown Cola in which the announcer was "bleeped" out each time he mentioned the two market leaders. (Royal Crown Cola is half the price of "bleep" and "bleep".)

- Any number of retail ads that promise sale prices so low on big-name, nationally advertised merchandise that "the manufacturers won't let us use their names in this ad" (often because you wouldn't recognize them if they did!).

The fact that people respond with such interest to censored messages is probably due to curiosity and a reluctance to let anyone else decide what they may see or hear—qualities which appear to work for ads as well as books and films.

a cup of coffee, or at a party in someone's living room, enlist the consumer in the role of "neighbor" or "friend." Some ads ask questions specifically designed to cast the viewer or listener into the role of confidant. "Aren't you glad you use Dial? Don't you wish everyone did?"

Functional Theory Katz, who introduced the concept of four distinct attitude functions, has also indicated how attitudes that serve each function may be modified.[19] Attitudes fulfilling an *adjustment* need may best be changed when a product no longer meets those needs or when the consumer's level of aspiration has changed. *Ego defense* attitudes are most resistant to change by marketers,

although communications that pose threats to a consumer's ego defenses may be removed. Attitudes that aid in *value expression* may be changed when the consumer is somehow dissatisfied with his or her self-concept. And *knowledge*-serving attitudes may change when the consumer is presented with new information inconsistent with prior knowledge, thus creating dissonance.

Ego Defense Factors Sherif and Sherif contend that ego involvement is one crucial variable to take into account in attempting to bring about attitude change:[20]

Low (ego) involvement, unstructured stimulus situations, and highly valued sources increase the range of assimilation, within which communication is increasingly effective in producing attitude change. High ego involvement, structured communications, and less valued sources restrict the range of assimilation, beyond which decreasing frequency and extent of attitude change occur as the communication becomes more discrepant . . .

Katz, Sarnoff, and McClintock have investigated ego-defense variables and attitude change in feelings toward others. In an experiment that dealt with stereotyped attitudes towards blacks, these researchers found that subjects scoring high in ego defensive-ness were less amenable to change both on the measure of beliefs about blacks and on the Bogardus scale (a measure of the "social distance" a subject perceives between himself or herself and others).[21] Although attempts to change attitudes through self-insight were not effective with high ego-defensive types, attitudes were changed with that group as easily as with the low ego-defensive groups by giving them more information about attitude-objects.[22] This suggests that some ego-defense functioning attitudes might be modified with much the same approach as that used in changing knowledge-related attitudes.

Multiattribute Theory

The concept of multiattribute models of attitude structure was introduced in chapter 12 as the most sophisticated means to date of predicting brand preference and purchase intentions. But this approach is also useful for tracking information processing in attitude change.[23]

Fishbein's Extended Behavioral Intentions Model, it will be remembered, postulates that a consumer's intention to perform a specific purchasing activity is a function of that person's beliefs and evaluation of the consequences of the activity, in the context of the buying situation. This was stated as:

$$\text{Aact} = \Sigma_{i=1}^{n} B_i a_i$$

where:

   $Aact$ = the attitude toward performance of a specific act
   B_i = beliefs about the consequences of a specific act
   a_i = the evaluative aspect of B_i
   n = the number of relevant consequences

Lutz devised three possible strategies from Fishbein's model to change brand attitudes by modifying cognitive structure.[24]

Strategic Implications   Viewing the concept of attitude as based on the structure of the Behavioral Intentions Model, Lutz suggests these modifications:[25]

1. Change an existing B_i element. In a consumer behavior context, this strategy most closely parallels typical mass media advertising: An attempt is made to change the consumer's perception of the brand on one or more attributes (for example, "Cadillac gets good mileage").

2. Change an existing a_i element. This strategy represents an attempt to convince the consumer to reassess the value (that is, the goodness or badness) of a particular attribute (as an example, with regard to mouthwash, Listerine claims that "bad taste" is a good quality).

3. Add a new $B_i a_i$ combination. This is an-

other common advertising tactic: introducing a new attribute into cognitive structure in an attempt to increase the overall attractiveness of the brand (for instance, "Magnavox color TV automatically adjusts itself to changes in room lighting").

Testing the a_i and B_i strategies, he found (1) a greater potential for the B_i and (2) that *negative* information has a greater impact on attitude change than positive information. This, Lutz concludes, is a reflection of the fact that negative information is still a novelty for most consumers, since it is usually in the form of "corrective" advertising demanded by regulatory agencies to make up for fraudulent claims and the like.[26]

Salience   It has been noted that the salience of both consumer attitudes and product attributes varies across products and is highly situational. For example, salience of attitudes toward Campbell soups is quite low until a consumer is in the mood for soup or is actually shopping for some. And the packaging attributes of cosmetics are usually more salient than packaging factors in purchasing a garden hose. Winter's research into brand attitude change concludes that a brand's possession of certain salient attributes can be more crucial to the consumer than possession of other attributes. Beliefs about the relative amounts of attributes each brand possesses will also affect attitude. Through advertising, Winter notes, consumers less familiar with a given brand and its attributes can be more

influenced than those already somewhat familiar with it. However, while first and second advertisement exposures create a significant level of attitude change, successive exposures lead to decreasing effectiveness and "the more unfavorable the attitude prior to exposure, the greater the favorable attitude change produced by the advertising."[27]

In using salience to effect attitude change toward a given brand, Boyd, Ray, and Strong offer five prescriptions:[28]

1. Affect those forces that influence strongly the choice criteria used for evaluating brands belonging to the product class;

2. Add characteristic(s) to those considered salient for the product class;

3. Increase or decrease the rating for a salient product class characteristic;

4. Change perception of the *company's* brand with regard to some particular salient product characteristic; or

5. Change perception of *competitive* brands with regard to some particular salient product characteristic.

It cannot be stressed too strongly that our knowledge of attitude change, while sophisticated enough to offer a few presumptions, should not be accepted as laws carved in stone.

To make any impact at all, an attitude-change strategy should be (1) tied to a product's carefully considered positioning, (2) brilliant in concept and execution, (3) backed by a huge budget.

Summary

Marketers are necessarily interested in the possibilities for *attitude change:* the modification of a consumer's evaluative inclinations toward or against any object in his or her market domain. There are three theoretical orientations to explaining the dynamics of attitude change. First, *cognitive dissonance* theory, based on the assumption that consumers strive to maintain consistency among attitudes and between attitudes and behavior. Strategically, this theory is usually applied to *persuasive communications* that attempt to create dissonance by offering new information. *Role playing* is a method by which dissonance may be generated. Second, *functional theory* explains attitude change by the functions attitudes serve: adjustment, ego defense and value expression. *Ego involvement* is critical to attitude change in this context. Third, *multiattribute theory* suggests new uses of the Behavioral Intentions Model to change attitudes by modifying cognition structure. Using the multiattribute approach, it is necessary to identify the attributes that are most salient to the consumer.

NOTES

---

1. "Pepsi Co. Ad Insists: No Question—Coke Drinkers Prefer Pepsi," *Advertising Age*, July 19, 1976, p. 2.

2. Edward H. Brown and Andrew L. Klein, "The Effects of Drug Education Programs on Attitude Change," *Journal of Drug Education*, Vol. 5, No. 1 (1975), pp. 51–56.

3. Marvin Zuckerman, Richard Tushrup, and Stephen Finner, "Sexual Attitudes and Experience: Attitude and Personality Correlates and Changes Produced by a Course in Sexuality," *Journal of Consulting and Clinical Psychology*, Vol. 44, No. 1 (February 1976), pp. 7–19.

4. Daryl J. Bem, "Self-Perception Theory," in *Advances in Experimental Social Psychology*, ed. L. Berkowitz (New York: Academic Press, 1972), p. 45.

5. Milton J. Rosenberg, "Inconsistency Arousal and Reduction in Attitude Change," in *Current Studies in Social Psychology*, ed. I. D. Steiner and M. Fishbein (New York: Holt, Rinehart and Winston, 1965).

6. Leon Festinger, *A Theory of Cognitive Dissonance* (New York: Harper and Row, 1957).

7. Leon Festinger and Dana Bramel, "The Reactions of Humans to Cognitive Dissonance," in *Experimental Foundations of Clinical Psychology*, ed. Arthur J. Bachrach (New York: Basic Books, 1962), pp. 261–262.

8. Festinger, "Cognitive Dissonance," p. 264.

9. Martin Fishbein, "Attitude and the Prediction of Behavior," in *Attitude Theory and Measurement*, ed. M. Fishbein (New York: John Wiley and Sons, 1967).

10. Dennis T. Lowry, "Demographic Similarity, Attitudinal Similarity, and Attitude Change," *Public Opinion Quarterly*, Vol. 37, No. 2 (Summer 1973), p. 192.

11. Thomas S. Robertson and John R. Rossiter, "Children and Commercial Persuasion: An Attribution Theory Analysis," *Journal of Consumer Research*, Vol. 1 (June 1974), p. 19.

12. George S. Day, "Attitude Change, Media, and Word of Mouth," *Journal of Advertising Research*, Vol. 11, No. 6 (December 1971), p. 31.

13. Day, "Attitude Change," p. 39.

14. Alice H. Eagly and Shelly Chaiken, "An Attribution Analysis of the Effect of Communicator Characteristics on Opinion Change: The Case of Communicator Attractiveness," *Journal of Personality and Social Psychology*, Vol. 32, No. 1 (1975), pp. 136–144.

15. Lowry, "Demographic Similarity," p. 192.

16. Robert W. McPeck and John D. Edwards, "Expectancy Disconfirmation and Attitude Change," *Journal of Social Psychology*, Vol. 96, No. 2 (August 1975), pp. 193–208.

17. Stephen Worchel, Susan Arnold, and Michael Baker, "The Effects of Censorship on Attitude Change: The Influence of Censor and Communication Characteristics," *Journal of Applied Social Psychology*, Vol. 5, No. 3 (July–September 1975).

18. Robert E. Matfey, "Attitude Change In-

duced by Role Playing as a Function of Improvisation and Role-Taking Skill," in *Journal of Personality and Social Psychology*, Vol. 24 (No. 3 (1972), p. 343.

19. Daniel Katz, "The Functional Approach to the Study of Attitudes," *Public Opinion Quarterly*, Vol. 24 (1960), pp. 163–204.

20. Muzafer Sherif and Carolyn Sherif, "Attitude as the Individual's Own Categories: The Social Judgment-Involvement Approach to Attitude and Attitude Change," in *Attitude, Ego-Involvement, and Change*, ed. Sherif and Sherif (New York: John Wiley and Sons, 1967), p. 135.

21. Daniel Katz, Irving Sarnoff, and Charles McClintock, "Ego-Defense and Attitude Change," in *Study of Attitude Change*, ed. Richard V. Wagner and John J. Sherwood (Belmont, Calif.: Brooks/Cole, 1969), p. 51.

22. Katz, et al. "Ego-Defense," p. 55.

23. James R. Bettman, Noel Capon, and Richard J. Lutz, "Information Processing in Attitude Function and Change," *Communication Research*, Vol. 2, No. 3 (July 1975), pp. 267–278.

24. Richard J. Lutz, "Changing Brand Attitudes through Modification of Cognitive Structure," *Journal of Consumer Research*, Vol. 1, No. 4 (March 1975), pp. 49–59.

25. Lutz, "Changing Brand Attitudes," p. 48.

26. Lutz, "Changing Brand Attitudes," p. 58.

27. Frederick W. Winter, "A Laboratory Experiment of Individual Attitude Response to Advertising Exposure," *Journal of Marketing Research*, Vol. 10 (May 1973), p. 140.

28. Harold W. Boyd, Jr., Michael L. Ray, and Edward C. Strong, "An Attitudinal Framework for Advertising Strategy," *Journal of Marketing*, Vol. 36 (April 1972), p. 28.

MARKETING APPLICATIONS

Conclusion 1   *Cognitive dissonance is a generally accepted explanation for attitude change that may be useful in forming marketing strategy. One example of dissonance occurs when a consumer is exposed to information that is inconsistent with his or her existing attitudes. To reduce uncomfortable dissonance, one may adjust attitudes to conform to the new information.*

Application   One of the most common marketing problems that may be attacked with an attitude-change strategy surfaces when consumers identify a certain product with an "image" they don't feel is relevant to them. Geritol, for example, is an iron supplement traditionally seen as a tonic for older people who tire easily. Some marketers have even referred to older consumers as the "Geritol market." The Geritol people wanted to change this image and appeal to a younger, more affluent group of consumers. So television commercials began featuring models in their early thirties—as young couples who say they use Geritol just to be bright and vivacious for each other. Theoretically, a younger consumer who sees this commercial will process the new information ("People like me use Geritol") and experience dissonance with the existing attitude ("Geritol is only for grandparents with tired blood"). The outcome could well be that the consumer will form a positive new attitude toward the product to reduce the dissonance.

Conclusion 2   *Multiattribute theory states that a consumer's intention to purchase is directly related to (1) beliefs about specific product attributes and (2) evaluation of the consequences of the purchasing activity. This suggests various strategies for changing attitudes toward products and brands.*

Application   By using the measure of attribute ratings presented in chapter 12, page 318 it is possible to determine which product attributes are viewed favorably and which arouse antipathy. This may suggest product changes, or a different advertising or selling strategy. For example, if a refrigerator brand makes a poor showing on "freezing performance", because it melts customers' ice cream, a physical modification is in order. If its performance scores are adequate but the styling is regarded as less than breathtaking, a different advertising approach might cast the styling in a more favorable light (a rather old-fashioned looking model, for instance, might be pictured in a nostalgic 1950s setting, one that seems to have positive associations for many people today).

ASSIGNMENTS

Research Assignment

Background   Decision makers in the fashion merchandising industry have usually relied on intuitive thinking, or "shrewd instinct," rather than consumer research to determine what customers will be buying at any given time. As a research consultant to the *American Garment Manufacturers Trade Association,* you are asked to develop a research model to show people in this volatile business that research can be (1) timely enough to keep marketers ahead of rapidly changing fads and shifting trends and (2) inexpensive enough to use as often as it might be necessary.

Most of the great fashion innovations are ahead of their time. In other words, if everybody liked a new fashion right away, it would already be outdated. Thus, there must be attitude change involved in fashion acceptance as people who are at first reluctant to try a style finally come to accept it.

Methodology   Design a research instrument—a questionnaire, for instance—that you could use to measure consumers' changing attitudes toward new fashions, and discover how attitude change contributes to purchasing fashion merchandise.

Also, recommend a survey procedure outlining how you plan to reach the consumers you are most interested in hearing from.

Creative Assignment

Aruba is a Caribbean island that has, until recently, been as popular a vacation spot with U.S. tourists as Jamaica or the Virgin Islands. But political unrest in the Caribbean, and a few specific incidents in Aruba, have induced negative attitudes toward the island in a number of potential visitors.

Some tourists, having heard isolated stories of political violence in some of the Caribbean islands, worry about their personal safety. Others, because of the news media reports, have simply adopted the attitude that Arubans will not be as friendly to U.S. tourists as in the past.

As Creative Supervisor on the Aruba account at the Weaver and Fitzgerald advertising agency, you are responsible for developing a new campaign that will change these attitudes and convince potential vacationers that they will still enjoy a safe trip and a friendly welcome from the island's natives.

Develop a campaign strategy to meet this objective.

Managerial Assignment

As Campaign Manager for one mayoralty candidate in a city of 75,000, you are faced with the problem of how best to position your candidate—Alison Wilheim—to the major share of the registered voters.

Ms. Wilheim is 24, a student, and ultra liberal in her life style, thus representing about 20 percent of the electorate. The remaining 80 percent tend to be older, blue-collar, conservative. And most of the voting males are not favorably disposed toward the idea of a young student, let alone a woman, as mayor.

To aggravate the situation, the local media have made much of precampaign comments by your candidate such as "most of the voters in this town are politically to the right of Genghis Khan."

Thus you must change some decidedly negative attitudes toward your candidate before election day. You are considering two possible areas of concentration:

1. As a graduate business student, Ms. Wilheim is well trained in management and cost accounting. Her opponent is a local lawyer who is well liked, although not notably successful in his own practice. The media have noted this difference between the two candidates, and lean slightly toward Ms. Wilheim. Furthermore, Ms. Wilheim is a classical libertarian who believes in minimal government. She would, in fact, lay off all city workers concerned with essential services (except firemen) and hire private contractors to provide police protection, collect garbage, and so on. Because the city is presently mismanaged financially and municipal services are virtually at a standstill, most voters' attitudes are even more hostile toward the present city government than toward Ms. Wilheim. (The incumbent mayor is not seeking reelection.) Thus some voters might be receptive to this position, since your opponent has taken no substantive stand on how to improve city services.

2. Ms. Wilheim seems to have some appeal for women—your polls conclude that even those women who are opposed to her are slightly more receptive to her candidacy than male voters. Of the fifty percent of voters who say they are going to vote for your opponent and the 30 percent undecided, about half are women.

From these considerations, decide upon a good "marketing" position for your candidate, develop a campaign slogan, and make recommendations for changing enough voters' attitudes to achieve an upset victory in this election.

SELECTED READINGS

Bennett, Peter D. and Gilbert D. Harrell. "The Role of Confidence in Understanding and Predicting Buyers' Attitudes and Purchase Intentions." *Journal of Consumer Research*, Vol. 2, No. 2 (September 1975), pp. 110–117.

Bettman, James R. "A Threshold Model of Attribute Satisfaction Decisions." *Journal of Consumer Research*, Vol. 1, No. 2 (September 1974), pp. 30–35.

———, Noel Capon, and Richard J. Lutz. "Cognitive Algebra in Multi-Attribute Attitude Models." *Journal of Marketing Research*, Vol. 12, No. 2 (May 1975), pp. 151–164.

Lutz, Richard J. "Changing Brand Attitudes through Modification of Cognitive Structure." *Journal of Consumer Research*, Vol. 1, No. 4 (March 1975), pp. 49–59.

McGann, Anthony F. and Michael F. Foran. "Attitude Models Revisited: An Individual Level Analysis." *Journal of Consumer Research*, Vol. 1, No. 3 (December 1974), pp. 16–21.

IV
CONSUMER INFORMATION PROCESSING AND DECISION MAKING

Media Communications
Interpersonal Communications
Consumer Choice Behavior
Purchasing and Postpurchase Behavior

OBJECTIVES

1. Discuss the two ways in which *mass media* influence consumer behavior.   *350*

2. Compare demographic and psychographic *profiles* of heavy newspaper readers, magazine readers, radio listeners, and television viewers.   *351*

3. State the *three objectives of advertising* directed to consumers.   *360*

4. Describe three *pretesting* and two *posttesting* techniques for measuring advertising effectiveness.   *362*

5. Describe the *three variables in the presentation* of an ad that influence consumer acceptance.   *365*

6. Summarize research findings on consumer responses to (1) *humor*, (2) *fear*, (3) *sex*, and (4) *two-sided* appeals in advertising.   *367*

7. Discuss *three internal consumer response* variables that may determine acceptance of a persuasive communication.   *369*

8. Discuss the relationship between consumers' *intent to buy* and actual purchasing behavior.   *373*

FOURTEEN

Media Communications

To this point, the sociocultural and individual variables that enter into a consumer's decision making process have been the focus of discussion. Now information processing and decison making themselves will be analyzed, beginning with the media influences that offer people information about the products and services they will want to consume.

It will be helpful throughout this section of the text to visualize the decision process as shown in Figure 14-1.*

The mass media provide a continuous showcase of consumer goods, services, and ideas. Media information may enter directly into choice behavior, but it may also be filtered through interpersonal communication from opinion leaders to the mass of consumers. In choice behavior, a market item is selected to

*Bear in mind that this visualization does not purport to be a definitive model of how consumer purchases occur in the real world. Various steps may be bypassed or there may be greater interaction, as we shall see in the following chapters. It is rather a representation of the basic stages and elements that can enter into the decision process, in the theoretical sequence that will be followed here.

the exclusion of others, a decision influenced heavily by cultural, social, and psychological variables. This leads to actual purchasing. And evaluation of postpurchase satisfaction will in turn affect future choices.

This chapter concentrates on how both consumers and marketers use media, with special attention to the influence of "persuasive" communications. Topics covered include:

• How much TV people really watch and how they feel about the programs they see.

• How some consumers determine the ads and commercials the rest of us will be exposed to.

• Why the most "obnoxious" ads are often the ones considered most effective.

• How consumers respond to humor, sex, and "truth" in advertising.

• What a single ad can accomplish in actual sales.

There is practical information here for anyone who plans to deal with marketing communications, as well as research findings of interest to critics of media and advertising today.

Figure 14-1   Visualization of the decision process.

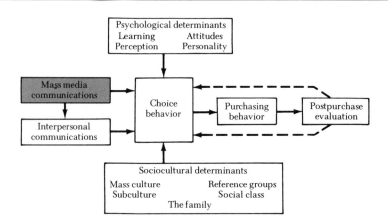

The Dual Roles of Mass Media

In the United States, life styles and buying behavior are continuously shaped by the mass communications media. The term "mass media" in this context refers to the newspapers and magazines we read, the radio programming we listen to, and—most important today—television.

Mass media in America have two major thrusts. On one hand, they serve as a major *socializing* institution in our culture. Individuals pick up a variety of behavioral cues from *newspapers* and *magazines*, for example, as to what people are thinking, what they are wearing, how to spend their time, and other facets of acceptable life styles. *Radio*, both reflecting and determining our musical preferences, has in the past few decades helped to create a distinct youth subculture first through rock and roll, then folk rock, then hard rock themes. These forms have now been assimilated into the culture at large,

and new themes such as ethnic music and nostalgia for the 1940s and 1950s are contributing to the life styles of another generation.

The pervasive influence of *television* as an entertainment and information medium has affected the childhood, adolescent, and adult experiences of most readers of this book. Increasingly more than the other media, it is a powerful force for homogeneity in American society. By watching "the tube," people throughout the country become aware of social change and behavioral innovations once confined to metropolitan centers. New opinions, appearances, and values are diffused throughout the society immediately. Conversely, television has been cited as a medium geared to "the lowest common denominator" in intellectual and aesthetic preferences, through the underlying assumption that some kinds of programming are too sophisticated or controversial for the bulk of the television audience. This criticism is valid in the sense that most television programs today tend to reflect values of mainstream American culture, with new or subcultural themes generally presented on the news, in late evening rather than prime-time shows, in special presentations, and in feature films. Still, television both introduces and reinforces values and behavioral patterns to a large segment of our population.

On the other hand, mass media serve as the vehicles for *persuasive communications*—to reach people as consumers and predispose them to buy the products and services of the marketing system. This is the function of *advertising* as a communications system, and a medium's attractiveness to marketers is based upon the market segments which that medium can deliver to advertisers who wish to get their message across. Not surprisingly, media vary in their effectiveness to attract groups of consumers interested in different kinds of products. *Family Circle* readers exhibit consumption patterns quite removed from readers of *Town and Country*. *Meet the Press* fans are not usually heavy viewers of television game shows like *The Price is Right*. Some recent findings from life-style and psychographic research as to which consumers respond to which media are explored in this chapter.

Similarly, consumers respond differently to various kinds of print ads and broadcast commercials. Different kinds of advertising for the same product utilizing various creative approaches and media strategies have obtained a wide range of effectiveness results. Advertisers are necessarily concerned with such problems, and spend huge research budgets to determine which commercials and print ads are (or are likely to be) most successful. The frequency of presentation and size of an advertisement can affect consumer responses. So can its content. Also, consumer variables such as "resistance" come into play where persuasive communications are involved.[2] And, while most mass media advertising is designed to build favorable attitudes toward a brand image or a predisposition to buy when the purchasing occasion arises, some ads are supposed to affect consumer purchases directly within a short time period. Thus, the effectiveness of certain persuasive communications may be directly measured by coupon return or retail purchases, rather than by research indications of attitude change or other psychological constructs.

This chapter investigates mass media influences through consumer exposure patterns, measurement of advertising effectiveness, message presentation and content, consumer response variables, and effects upon actual purchasing behavior.

Consumer Exposure to Mass Media

Patterns of media exposure have traditionally been drawn from *demographic* studies, that is, creating profiles of heavy users of different media by age, sex, income, and other purely objective criteria. But more recently, *psychographic* studies have served to identify people who use the various media through a combination of demographic information; personality characteristics; life-style variables such as interest, activities, and opinions; and product use.

Both demographic and psychographic find-

How Consumers Process Media Communications from Marketers

Principles of consumer information processing have been discussed with respect to attitude change (chapter 13) and personality (chapter 11).

Marketers' communications directed through media to large numbers of consumers all share some common aspects, whether appearing in print or beamed over the airwaves. They all require a *communicator* (the marketer), a *message* (usually an ad), a *channel* (the medium—whether print, radio, television, billboard, or matchbook), and a lot of *receivers*, as shown in Figure 14-2.

Figure 14-2 Mass communication.

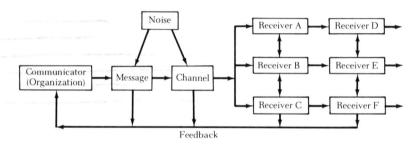

Source: Promotional Strategy, *by Engel, Wales, and Warshaw, Rev. Ed. (Homewood, Ill.: Richard D. Irwin, 1971 C.) p. 24.*

From the consumer's standpoint, each persuasive communication is accepted or rejected according to the usual steps of information processing.

As Figure 14-3 indicates, first there must be an *exposure* situation—the presentation of the ad. How does the marketer ensure that the right consumers will be exposed to the ad? By selecting the best possible medium on the basis of demographic and psychographic profiles of its readership or audience.

Second, the consumer must *attend* to the communication if it is to have an impact. It must break through the barrier of the consumer's selective perception. Advertisements attempt to gain attention through startling headlines, loud noises, or unusual situations (like an attractive model curled up with a snarling tiger).

Third, the perceived message must be *comprehended* as meaningful. In other words, the beautiful woman with the tiger must somehow relate the product to consumers' needs.

Fourth, there must be some agreement or *yielding* on the part of consumers if the message is to make a difference in their lives. This depends on such factors as message credibility and timeliness.

Fifth, the consumer must retain the information agreed to long enough to do something about it. This is one reason why television commercials sign off with the name of the sponsor clearly presented on the screen while the announcer repeats it yet another time.

Finally, for a message to achieve complete acceptance, the consumer has to act in some way, usually by buying the product. Even if consumers have acquiesced in all other aspects of the process, there may be many intervening variables between intending to buy and actually purchasing—new information, insufficient retail distribution, or a reduced need for the product.

Figure 14-3   Indexes of advertising effectiveness related to the behavioral steps in being persuaded.

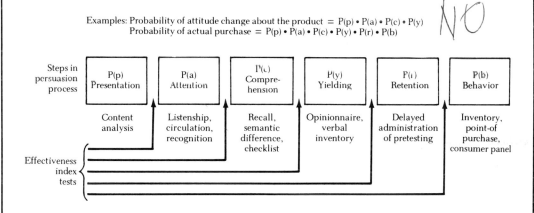

Examples: Probability of attitude change about the product $= P(p) \cdot P(a) \cdot P(c) \cdot P(y)$
Probability of actual purchase $= P(p) \cdot P(a) \cdot P(c) \cdot P(y) \cdot P(r) \cdot P(b)$

Steps in persuasion process	P(p) Presentation	P(a) Attention	P(c) Comprehension	P(y) Yielding	P(r) Retention	P(b) Behavior
	Content analysis	Listenship, circulation, recognition	Recall, semantic difference, checklist	Opinionnaire, verbal inventory	Delayed administration of pretesting	Inventory, point-of purchase, consumer panel

Effectiveness index tests

Source: William J. McGuire, "An Information-Processing Model of Advertising Effectiveness, a paper presented at the Symposium of Behavioral and Management Science in Marketing, Center for Continuing Education, The University of Chicago, July, 1969.

ings are applied here to the question of how consumers are likely to differentiate themselves on the basis of reading and viewing patterns

Print Media

The term "print media" refers to newspaper and mass-appeal magazines, including those magazines designed for special market segments such as *TV Guide, Playboy,* and *Better Homes and Gardens.* Limited interest publications—coin collectors' magazines, scholarly journals, and other narrowly focused periodicals—are not considered mass media.

Newspapers   Virtually everyone reads newspapers to some degree, according to various studies, which number 84 percent to 90 percent of the adult population in the United

States as regular readers or those who "have read a newspaper in the past week."[3] Leo Bogart suggests an explanation for this almost universal appeal:[4]

No medium comes closer to expressing . . . sense of community than the daily newspaper. Only in the newspaper is there a daily display of the concerns that are shared, the problems that are faced, and the little dramas that are played among those who live within the same boundaries of interest. The display of merchandise in the daily newspaper ads represents a catalogue of the information to which consumers in this area look for necessary guidance as they plan their shopping business each day. The area of a newspaper's primary circulation is generally synonymous not only with civic identity but [also] with the market as sales executives can best describe and plan for it.

Demographically, people who registered high in newspaper readership and low in other forms of media involvement in one study were profiled as predominantly male, least likely to be married, and enjoying the greatest household income and education level.[5]

Psychographic explorations of newspaper readership have found that different groups of consumers with markedly different life-style patterns do not reveal great variances in newspaper reading.[6] A substantial majority of all the groups studied see at least four issues of the daily paper from Monday to Friday, and even people in groups that are highest in magazine readership tend to read the newspaper frequently. However, the consumers who reported highest newspaper readership of all groups leaned toward these characteristics:[7]

• The heaviest male readers could be described as well educated, of middle or upper-socioeconomic status, usually middle-aged or older, interested in culture and social reform, and generally concerned about people's needs.

• The heaviest female readers were portrayed as of *lower* education, average socioeconomic status, somewhat younger than the average; they are usually outgoing women who enjoy life, love to shop, and buy impulsively.

Magazines   The fifteen most frequently read magazines[8] for both men and women are shown in Table 14-1.

Magazine readership draws a richer variety of data than newspaper readership because the choice of magazines is quite large and people can better define themselves by which ones they prefer to read. In general, people who report high exposure to magazines are highest in total media exposure, exhibit the greatest tendency to be married, and are generally older than other media groups.[9]

Psychographic profiling offers several interesting contrasts among consumers who read specific magazines. Not surprisingly, magazines that are quite different in style and content appeal to groups sharply divergent in life styles. *Reader's Digest* readers, for example, are more conservative, more religious, less permissive, and less optimistic than *Playboy* readers.[10]

However, it is surprising that people who read *Time* magazine regularly are quite different in demographic characteristics and life-style variables from regular *Newsweek* readers, an essentially similar news magazine. Those who read *Time* regularly tend to be younger, better educated, and at a higher level occupationally and economically than those loyal to *Newsweek*. *Time* readers are also less interested in security, less conservative, less concerned about health, and are more inclined to travel abroad. *Newsweek* readers, by comparison, are more price con-

Table 14-1   The 15 Most Frequently Read Magazines (1974)

BY MALES	BY FEMALES
Reader's Digest	Reader's Digest
TV Guide	Better Homes & Gardens
National Geographic	Family Circle
Newsweek	TV Guide
Time	Woman's Day
Better Homes & Gardens	Good Housekeeping
U.S. News & World Report	McCall's
Popular Science	Ladies' Home Journal
Popular Mechanics	Redbook
Field & Stream	American Home
Sports Illustrated	National Geographic
Mechanix Illustrated	Newsweek
Outdoor Life	Time
Playboy	Cosmopolitan
Esquire	True Story

Source: W. R. Simmons and Associates, New York, N.Y.

scious, more likely to complain about merchandise, and more amenable to products like beer, guns, and camping equipment. Also, *Newsweek* readers are more distrustful of advertising than their *Time* counterparts.[11]

Broadcast Media

The electronic media of radio and television are called broadcast media. While very little research has focused on radio listeners, a great number of studies are designed to probe the television audience for information about this huge mass of consumers.

Radio   Except for individual stations seeking to attract advertisers with facts about their special audiences, few investigators are presently concerned with radio. One reason is that advertisers themselves have not been particularly curious, since either their radio budgets are relatively small or they are not using radio at all. Many advertisers shy away from the medium because they can't show their products, while others see it primarily as a means of building brand awareness through musical jingles.

However, this situation is likely to change as the more expensive media become less efficient through "commercial clutter." Already Gallup notes that radio commercials received an 8 percent registration (in a test for measuring recall) against a 10 percent level for television. And when car radios were considered, that level rose to 12 percent.[12] Orson Welles offers another advantage of consumer involvement with radio. "TV . . . leaves precious little room for the audience's imagination to get into the act (but) radio is a coloring book. It supplies the words, the sounds. The audience will become the artist—visualizing the total picture and coloring it in to bring it to life."[13]

Adults who report much radio listening (and little attention to other media) in research studies emerge as primarily female, relatively young, and fairly low in household income. Less than half are married. In personality variables, this group is depicted as significantly less conservative and possessing fewer achievement and deference needs than other groups.[14]

Television   Because television is the only medium that has been seriously studied for its socializing influence as well as its commercial applications, there is considerably more information available on patterns of consumer exposure.

Amount of Viewing   Hardly anyone in the United States lacks the opportunity to watch television, since between 96 and 99 percent of all homes boast at least one set.[15] And these home sets are turned on for an average of six hours and eighteen minutes every day.[16] Averages for *individual* viewing time, however, are considerably less. Most adults watch daily for at least two hours, but on any given day up to 20 percent of the United States population will not watch television at all. Women tend to watch more than men, presumably because more women work at home and have the opportunity to see daytime shows.[17] Children's viewing patterns are more complex, but by the time children begin school also tend to reflect sex differences in program preferences. Most youngsters watch at least two hours every day, but many spend considerably more time. As mentioned previously, a study with nursery school children documented an average

weekly viewing time of 34.5 hours for boys and 32.4 for girls.[18] The amount of viewing actually increases from that figure through the elementary years, then decreases during high school to approximate the usual adult viewing time.

Why People Watch Television   When respondents in a national survey were asked why they watched television, over 60 percent gave more than two reasons; "entertainment" and "relaxation" were the most frequent. Another 18 percent offered "killing time" as the chief reason, yet a minority placed a more constructive perspective on viewing such as "to keep up with what is going on."[19] Table 14-2 illustrates the principal reasons cited by participants in the study.

Level of Attention   Evidence points to television watching as a rather disjointed activity. For one, people do other things while they

Table 14-2   Main Reasons for Watching Television

	100%
For entertainment	32%
For relaxation	26
To kill time	18
To keep up with current events	8
For learning or self-improvement	4
For social reasons	4
To see specific show	2
Other	2
No answer, no reason	4

Source: Leonard A. LoSciuto, "A National Inventory of Television Viewing Behavior," in Television and Social Behavior, *Vol. 4 (Washington, D.C.: U.S. Government Printing Office, 1971).*

are viewing and, for another, only a percentage of viewing follows a given show from beginning to end. Most people spend the major portion of their television time with other people, and both adults and children engage in conversation while they watch. About 34 percent of viewing occurs while people are doing other things. Work and housework are the most frequently mentioned, followed by eating, talking, reading, and child care. Other activities mentioned fairly often are sewing, personal care, hobbies, and schoolwork. Furthermore, only 10 percent of all programs watched are viewed from beginning to end by the vast majority of the people who watch them. So the audience for the average television show cannot be described as very attentive. Interestingly enough, only about half the viewers watch a program to the end when it is the last one viewed, "probably reflecting the role of television as a sleep-inducing agent."[20]

Attitudes toward Programming People's favorite programs are most often comedy and variety shows, with crime, adventure, dramatic shows, and soap operas close behind. Less than 20 percent of those who responded to this survey listed a news program, documentary, or other educational program as one of their favorites, reinforcing the view that people use television for entertainment above all. However, game shows and news programs account for a good share of *actual* viewing, and the *attention* value of a program is not necessarily related to its audience size or expressed popularity.

In spite of the frequent criticisms directed at network programming, most viewers express positive attitudes toward what they see. Few programs are dismissed as a waste of time; one-fifth of the viewers surveyed even expressed the desire to see a program they had seen the day before a second time.

What people dislike about television most vehemently are—yes—commercials. Three-quarters of those questioned in the national survey feel there are too many, compared with less than one-half who complain about too much violence and one-third who are worried about too much sex. Table 14-3 quantifies the complaints about television registered most frequently.

This finding correlates with a growing intensity of negative feelings toward commercials—especially among the young, the better educated, and blacks—reported by the National Association of Broadcasters.[21] Such a trend in consumer opinion could create dramatic changes in the familiar methods of advertising products and services.

Profiles of Heavy Television Viewers Some viewers watch television considerably more than others, and psychographic profiling identifies the "heavy viewer" groups for eight evening shows as follows:[22]

• Males tend toward a low educational level and low or middle socioeconomic status, are the oldest of the groups profiled, follow conventional rules of social behavior, feel secure, and are conservative as shoppers—favoring popular brands and well-known manufacturers.

• Female heavy viewers are characterized as conventional, quite rigid and intolerant toward social change. They tend to belong to the lowest education groups of those profiled, the lowest socioeconomic status, and are in the oldest group sampled. As shoppers, they find reassurance in traditional brand names and take pride in hunting down bargains.

Psychographic and life-style distinctions have also been drawn to compare heavy viewers of certain *types* of programs. Tigert has contrasted people who rate fantasy-comedy

Table 14-3   Percentage of Respondents Giving Various Complaints about Television

	ANYTHING YOU WOULD LIKE TO SEE CHANGED?*	AGREE AS A COMPLAINT
Too many commercials	25%	73%
Too much violence	11	43
Too much sex	5	33
Too many news programs	2	13
Fewer particular types of programs (Westerns, sports, etc.)	19	Not asked
More educational or cultural programs	5	Not asked
More particular kinds of programs	6	Not asked
Poor scheduling of programs	5	Not asked
Greater variety of programs	5	Not asked
Better children's programming	4	Not asked
Better or less biased news coverage	4	Not asked
Other complaints (e.g., too many blacks, irrelevant content)	11	Not asked

*Multiple answers are included, so figures add to more than 100%.

Source: Leonard A. LoSciuto, "A National Inventory of Television Viewing Behavior," in Television and Social Behavior, *Vol. 4 (Washington, D.C.: U.S. Government Printing Office, 1971).*

shows as their favorite programs with people who rate late-night talk shows among their favorites.[23]

Fantasy-Comedy enthusiasts are less affluent and well educated, with life-style characteristics that tend toward:

1. A strong traditional-conservative orientation expressed in concern about religion, youth, drugs, and permissiveness.

2. A more pronounced view of life as a defeat, both personally and financially.

3. A decided commitment to television to the exclusion of print media or outside activities.

4. A price-conscious, bargain-seeking approach to consumer decisions, but a willingness to pay extra for nationally advertised brands.

Talk show heavy viewers revealed a dramatically different life-style profile, including:

1. A strong interest in new products.

2. A need for excitement in their lives.

3. A strong interest in fashion and personal appearance.

4. An inclination to seek out, and share, information about innovative products.

Thus, marketers can obtain a range of useful knowledge about media exposure patterns from "life-style" research—an approach discussed in some detail in chapter 19.

The New Television: What Consumers Will Be Watching

While the familiar, commercially sponsored television programming of CBS, ABC, and NBC promises to be with us for some time, there are stirrings of revolution everywhere in the television industry. And changes in the kind of programming consumers will be exposed to should dramatically alter the nature of persuasive communications in this medium.

Cable TV   This increasingly popular service, paid for by subscriptions, offers consumers two advantages: (1) improved reception in most areas and (2) alternative programming not found on free (commercial) stations.

More than 8 million homes are now plugged into cable TV systems. The impact of cable is greatest in large urban areas such as New York, which has several channels for cable transmission. New Yorkers are regularly treated to an intriguing mix of shows referred to in the industry as "narrowcasts" appealing specifically to small audience segments not reached by commercial television. These include the *Chinese TV Program* (totally incomprehensible to anyone who does not speak Chinese), *Movie Watch* (which gives viewers the opportunity to call in and rebuff film critics), and *Midnight Blue* (considered to be television's first "soft core" pornography show).[24] It is even possible for viewers to produce their own shows in New York under that city's "free access" regulation; two cable channels and production studios are provided, free of charge, subject to availability. Time is available to advertisers on cable stations, which now feature a smattering of local commercials but no national advertising of consequence. Market researchers have probed cable subscribers to see if they reveal different life-style and psychographic patterns than nonviewers. So far, no such differences are apparent.[25]

Home Box Office   The concept of paying a fee for special, premium programs—sports events, first-run movies, and the like—has been around for some time without much fanfare (except for angry notices the managements of movie houses put up asking for signatures on petitions to ban Pay TV). But it is only since the growth of cable TV that the idea has reached national proportions.

Today, Home Box Office (HBO) from Time, Inc., supplies over 80 percent of the approximately 900,000 homes enjoying pay television. HBO offers a full schedule of feature films (usually several months after theatrical distribution, but still far ahead of their commercial television debuts), sports, concerts, plays, and performances by celebrities—all beamed via satellite to any home that has a cable and optional HBO hookup.

HBO, of course, does not offer time to advertisers.

International Programming   In 1976, New York's independent station, WOR/Channel 9, broadcast an entire week of programs from Britain's *Thames TV*. These shows ranged from "quality" productions to crime shows loosely patterned, it seemed, after the American thrillers so popular in Britain. The commercials run during that week focused on British stores and products (Harrod's department store in London, the new Jaguar car, etc.) and, especially, British tourism. It was clear at week's end that WOR had located a new television audience—better educated, more affluent, and influential.[26]

The next instance of international television also occurred in New York, but this time on a cable station—*Telefrance-USA*. A potpourri of French films, news, interviews, and dramas from French television was offered, sponsored by prestigious French firms such as Cartier (jewelry) and Yves St. Laurent (fashions). Such programs may be evidence of a trend toward multinational television, which would direct advertising toward more sophisticated viewers than may be reached through conventional programming.

The Persuasive Message: An Overview

A persuasive message in mass media is, of course, a print advertisement or a broadcast commercial. Most advertising urges the consumer to think about, remember, or actually purchase some product, brand, or service; this type of message is prepared for marketers by their advertising agencies.

Other persuasive messages are of the institutional, public service, or "cause" variety. *Institutional* messages are sponsored by regular advertisers to position any given company in a certain way, to tell consumers what good the company is doing, or simply to keep the company name in front of the public. For example, as the American Bicentennial drew near, Shell Oil sponsored a series of interesting messages recounting historical happenings of the 1770s. Other companies have used ads and commercials to call attention to a social problem such as drunken driving or racial inequality, closing simply with a presentation of the company name and logo. *Public service* messages are usually designed to raise money for nonprofit organizations like the American Cancer Society or the United Negro College Fund. These ads, also

prepared by advertising professionals, can be startling and effective. *Cause* advertising is a relatively new phenomenon, tackling social issues that are usually too controversial for advertisers or conventional public service organizations to sponsor. One New York advertising agency deals exclusively in cause marketing for such groups as Other Woman, Ltd., (to abolish alimony laws), Friends of the Earth (environmental group), and maverick political candidates.[27] An example of a cause advertisement is shown in Figure 14-4.

Because they form the bulk of persuasive communications in mass media, advertisements specifically designed to market consumer goods and services will be the primary focus of this discussion. Persuasive messages in this broad category are conceived and executed to meet any one of three objectives:

1. *To create and reinforce awareness of a product or brand name.* Most consumer advertising rests on the assumption that, when people become aware of a brand and that awareness is reinforced through repetition, the desired message will influence the consumer when a purchasing decision is

consumer product brand recognition

Figure 14-4 A cause advertisement.

Send us $1 to help us get your ex-wife a job. Or a husband.

It had to happen.

A citizen's group to rehabilitate ex-wives.

The kind of unmarried, childless, able-bodied ex-wife who believes her ex-husband is obligated to support her for the rest of her life.

Enter The Other Woman, Ltd.

To mend these ladies, a unique group of women formed the Other Woman, Ltd. (O.W.L.)

They're unique because:

1. They're self-sufficient.

2. They work hard at acquiring a meaningful relationship with a man.

3. They don't believe in alimony — the maintenance money an ex-wife gets. However, they strongly endorse child support payments for mothers.

O.W.L. women are concerned that the destructive behavior of ex-wives has begun to affect their own lives. In these ways:

1. So many men are paying alimony, available solvent males are in short supply.

2. If a woman marries a man paying alimony, she's an accomplice to "legalized bigamy"—a situation where a man has to support two women even if he's only married to one.

3. A new wife must accept a reduced standard of living when the ex-wife refuses to work or re-marry.

4. A second marriage will be under constant pressure from the ex-wife as she initiates more court hassles for more alimony handouts.

In short, O.W.L. wants divorced men to be financially free to re-marry.

The high cost of leaving: a life-long ball and chain.

If a man commits murder he could be free in twenty years.

If two people call it quits on a luckless marriage, the man nevertheless must support the woman forever.

Think about that for a minute.

Even the U.S. Constitution prohibits involuntary servitude.

Some women want to be equal, but not too equal.

Some ex-wives expound the necessity for equal rights with men.

But these same women will look to the Alimony Court Judges to acknowledge their own inequality. Their helplessness. Their second-class citizenship.

The Judges, in turn, help perpetuate the myth of male superiority. They confirm that these women really *aren't* able to be financially independent.

Pennsylvania and Texas, however, decided women *could* control their own destinies and threw out alimony laws.

80% of the women in those states support themselves.

Meanwhile, New York City still retains its own remnant of the Middle Ages on West 37th Street: a debtor's prison called Alimony Jail.

To re-educate women against the idea of alimony we need money and names.

To help you get your ex-wife back to working and loving, we need money. For brochures, lectures and demonstrations. And for more ads like this one.

If alimony is taking too big a bite, just send us your name. We can use your moral support.

If we get enough names, we might be able to persuade enough people that 30 million divorced American men and women deserve to be emancipated.

And that divorce should mean just what the name implies — the complete dissolution of a marriage with no strings attached.

Help America reach full employment. Send in the coupon.

The Other Woman, Ltd. Penny Thompson, President
153 E. 18 St., New York, N.Y. 10003
I agree with your aim to get ex-wives self-supporting and remarried.
☐ Here's my contribution of $_____
$10.00 to $99.99 will make you a member of O.W.L. $100 or more will make you a charter member. All contributions are tax deductible.
☐ Send me_____reprints of this ad at $1.00 each.
☐ I need your help in getting my ex-wife a job or a husband.
☐ I want to participate in your work. Let me know if there's anything I can do. Special skill or background_____.
☐ I've made_____copies of this ad and distributed them.
Name_____
Street_____
Home, business telephone_____
City, State, Zip_____

Advertisement prepared by the New School for Social Research Workshop: "Social Change Through Issue Advertising".

Courtesy John Ziegler, Inc.

made. This is the basis for the "slice-of-life" commercials usually associated with detergents and other packaged goods. While there is little persuasion impact in most ads where two women are discussing a laundry product, constant repetition is expected to drive the brand name "Dash" or "Cheer" into the consumer's consciousness.

2. *To position a new product or reposition an existing one.* A popular marketing thesis states that people establish "positions" for products in their cognition because those products promise to serve some need. One brand of soft drink, Dr. Pepper, was introduced to new markets by dramatically positioning it as something people were *afraid* to try. Thus consumers attributed rather exotic, alluring characteristics to that fruit-flavored soda. Another beverage, Seven Up, dragged far behind cola drinks until it was repositioned as the *Uncola*, serving consumers' needs to try something different for a change. Repositioning is a strategy for changing consumers' attitudes toward an existing product, a process discussed in chapter 13.

3. *To obtain direct orders or immediate purchases.* The entire discipline of direct response advertising is concerned with persuading consumers to grab the nearest sharp object and clip a coupon, or to telephone an order for some product or premium. Thus, effectiveness is determined by actual responses received. Other advertising attempts to bring consumers directly into a retail outlet by announcing a special sale or some other inducement. Messages geared toward these purposes will be discussed later in this chapter.

Testing the Persuasive Message

Sales figures are one measure of advertising's persuasiveness, but they do not usually indicate consumer acceptance or rejection of ads until a good deal of money has been spent on print space or broadcast time. Also, factors other than advertising may affect a product or brand's performance—changes in the economy, product quality, and distribution are only a few critical variables. Thus, advertisers conduct consumer research with campaign concepts before the ads are actually run and/or when they are first introduced in a "test" area. These measurement techniques, which provide us with much of our information about consumer responses to media persuasion, are applied to both print and broadcast media.[28]

Pretesting Techniques

One form of testing is administered before an ad or campaign actually appears. This is known as pretesting and is designed to indicate strong and weak points of the ad strategy and execution before media space or time have been purchased. Three representative pretests are the consumer jury, the eye-camera test, and the GSR procedure—all measures of attention or arousal.

The Consumer Jury In the consumer jury technique, a group of consumers, selected as representative of an advertiser's target market, are shown several proposed ads in individual or group interviews. Each juror then ranks the ad according to personal preference, expressing likes and dislikes in the process. In a variation of this protocol, consumers are asked to make paired comparisons (stating preferences for one ad over another) or to rank ads along a scale (several ads in order of preference). The difficulties with these techniques revolve around the objectivity of the juror, who sees the ads in a highly artificial situation and may be affected by his or her role as arbiter rather than consumer.

The Eye-Camera Test   In the eye-camera test, consumers are asked to read advertisements while a hidden camera tracks their eye movements over the ads. The point of immediate contact with the ad, eye movement over the elements of the ad, and time spent in the viewing process are all recorded for analysis. The problem with this technique is that consumers' verbal reactions pointing to attitude change or predisposition to buy the product are not recorded.

GSR Testing   A physiological measure of consumer response, GSR testing uses the index of galvanic skin response on essentially the same principle as the lie detector test. A change in GSR rating while the subject is viewing an ad is equated with emotional involvement or *arousal*. However, it is difficult to say what feature of the ad actually produced the response.

Posttesting Techniques

In posttest procedures, consumers living in areas where they might reasonably be exposed to it are contacted after the adver-

tising has been run. The tests, which may follow immediately after the ad has been published or shown, are designed to measure *penetration*, that is, recognition or recall.

Recognition Tests   In recognition tests consumers who have read publications where an ad has appeared are asked whether they remember the editorial context or the ad itself. The consumer is shown the magazine and asked, "Did you read this page?", and then "Did you see this ad?" The interviewer discovers through questioning which ads produce recognition. One limitation of this approach is that consumers are likely to confuse ads in an ongoing campaign or, when ads in the same publication are quite similar, pick the wrong ones.

Recall Tests   Through this procedure, consumers reveal the impact of various ads by indicating which ones are most easily remembered. There are two variations on this theme, aided and unaided recall. In *aided* recall, the interviewer mentions a generic product to see whether the consumer can remember an ad for a specific brand. "Have you seen an ad for an automobile recently?" is a typical question and, "Yes, I saw one for the new Buick" is a favorable answer if the interviewer happens to be testing for Buick. *Unaided* recall means asking a vague question such as "Have you seen any ads lately that interested you?", but unaided recall can produce disheartening results unless a campaign is spectacularly memorable. Thus it is used less frequently than aided recall.

Testing in Print and Broadcast Media

The oldest and most popular *print* media test is the *Starch Advertisement Rating Re-*

port. It is a posttest recognition procedure in which consumers are first asked to remember an advertisement and then questioned specifically about points in the body copy. This test is applied to both newspaper and magazine ads. Other organizations that direct their testing to magazine advertising are *W. R. Simmons*, *Alfred Politz*, and *Gallup and Robinson*. The Gallup and Robinson method is basically an aided-recall test with five steps:[29]

1. Making the respondent recall and describe at least one feature in the unopened magazine at hand

2. Handing the consumer a group of brand names and asking for a description of the ads he or she has seen for the brands.

3. Asking for a recollection of the ad's sales message.

4. Opening the magazine and asking whether "This is the ad you were thinking of."

5. Obtaining demographic data.

In testing television commercials, the Schwerin Research Corporation offers the most widely used pretest technique. Through inducements such as free prizes, several hundred consumers are brought to a theater where they watch new commercials in the context of a television program and express their like or dislike for the commercial. A chart of their opinions is then gauged against a standard for past commercial tests, and that particular ad is given a rating that will render it usable or not usable. Among the criticisms of this approach is the question of representative sampling. Do people who select themselves for such an event on the basis of a "free prize" or "free show" really reflect the consumer market to whom a commercial is directed? A second question is whether the

audience situation may be too artificial a replication of the home viewing situation.[30]

On-air testing of television commercials is a posttest operation in which a group of test cities are selected for showing the new commercial and both a test and a control group of viewers are chosen through sampling techniques. These respondents are interviewed by telephone as follows:[31]

1. All respondents are screened for eligibility on demographic and product-class usage characteristics. In addition, they are asked a series of questions concerning their television viewing frequency and attitude toward the program on which the commercial is to be aired.

2. The control group is asked a series of questions regarding their specific attitudes and brand preferences prior to watching the program of interest.

3. The test group is asked to watch the program. Subsequent to this, the test group is asked the same kinds of questions presented to the control group about specific brand attitudes and preferences. In addition, this group is asked a series of questions regarding the commercial itself, for example, copy points recalled, as well as general likes and dislikes about the commercial.

The effectiveness of a commercial is then established by measuring brand awareness and attitude measures of the test group versus the control group.

These various testing procedures, in conjunction with other consumer research, suggest certain conclusions about consumer responses to persuasive messages in media. Generally, differences in response may be attributed to *message presentation, message content,* and *individual consumer variables.*

Message Presentation

There are three variables in the actual presentation of a message that will influence its effectiveness: frequency, size or duration, and repetition.

Frequency

Frequency refers to the number of times that a viewer sees the ads in a campaign, a measure expressed by media buyers as Gross Rating Points, or GRPs. Traditional wisdom holds that there is an ideal frequency for every campaign, irrespective of what other competitive advertisers are doing in the same time period, that will produce the desired brand-awareness or intent to purchase. However, Geiger has challenged this contention with a concept of "share of messages seen," computed by a specific brand's GRPs compared with all competitive CRPs. This approach is the first to consider the relative frequency of commercials for heavy, medium, and light viewers. Very heavy viewers may see ten times as much advertising as light viewers in a seven-day period. And the more *specific brand* commercials a person sees, the more *competitive* commercials he or she sees. Thus, more brand commercials are needed to maintain competitive "balance" for some viewers. Through juggling frequency to produce higher "pressure rates," measured by share of messages seen, Geiger achieved the following results with seven brands in seven days:[32]

1. Heavy television viewers, the people who see the most advertising, show sharper "would buy" patterns than other viewers.

2. Among any group of viewers, brands operating at average or better pressure levels achieved better "would buy" patterns than brands operating at below-average rates.

3. When a brand's share of pressure is higher than average among certain viewers, its "would buy" scores tend to be higher among these viewers.

Thus, consumers apparently respond to a brand's frequency relative to other commercials they see, rather than to an "ideal" frequency for any product or brand campaign.

Message Size or Duration

There have been no absolute correlations established between the size of a print ad or length of a television commercial and their impact upon consumers. In fact, the findings have been contradictory.

Starch found that a half-page direct-response ad produced 70 percent as many coupon returns as a full-page ad.[33] However, more recent direct-response ads for considered-purchase products indicated that larger size (full-page) ads drew disproportionately greater responses.[34]

Studies of television commercials of varying lengths suggest that differences in recall and recognition are not significant for thirty-second and sixty-second messages. Table 14-4 illustrates the findings of one such study.

For this reason, consumers are exposed to a greater number of commercials now than they were five years ago, as advertisers buy thirty-second units more frequently than sixty-second time slots. Ironically, this may

Table 14-4   Audience Responses to Test Commercials of Varying Lengths

CRITERIA	30-SECOND COMMERCIAL IN CLUTTER POSITION	60-SECOND COMMERCIAL IN CLUTTER POSITION	60-SECOND COMMERCIAL IN ISLAND POSITION
Adjective check list score	23.08	31.12	28.61
Brand identification	78.48	79.59	85.25
Mean number of sales points recalled	1.08	1.24	1.30
Product desire score	3.43	3.47	3.53
Prepost attitude change score	9.90	12.83	13.23
(Sample size)	79	49	61

Source: Julian L. Simon, The Management of Advertising *(Englewood Cliffs, N.J.: Prentice-Hall, 1971), p. 73. Reprinted by permission.*

have contributed to the finding cited earlier in this chapter that consumers are increasingly annoyed at commercial messages on television.

Repetition

The question of repetition was introduced in chapter 9 in the discussion of learning and forgetting behavior. A vast amount of research has been generated to determine the effects of repetition—how many presentations are necessary for "learning" a brand image and at what point repetition may produce diminishing interest. The general conclusions suggested by several studies are summarized here:

1. Stewart found that repetition produces a pattern of high brand awareness that becomes stable, then drops off once repetition ceases. The figure of fifteen consecutive reiterations was established for optimal results in this study.[35]

2. Zielske simulated a saturation campaign by mailing thirteen ads to a small sample— one every week—and concluded that recall was increased by one-third over mailings at monthly intervals.[36]

3. Schwerin reports that diminishing interest with repetition is related to *initial impact* of the advertisement, which must be high to sustain attention during repeated exposure; *content factors* such as humor, which tends to wear out quickly; *competitive advertising* which, if new and innovative, may subdue the repeated campaign; and the *pattern of exposure,* which must be altered to avoid too-predictable repetition.[37]

Some advertisers such as Procter and Gamble are almost religiously devoted to the strategy of repetition; although consumers may groan at an individual commercial for Charmin or Comet, enough people buy Charmin and Comet to indicate that the strategy must be working. However, the campaigns for these heavily advertised brands always consist of several individual commercials, each somewhat different but conveying the same campaign theme.

Message Content

The content of an advertising message refers to a number of variables: its selling or positioning strategy; its creative execution seen in its headline and/or visual; and its body copy (if any), which elaborates on the proposition or concept advanced in the ad. Most people like some ads better than others. Some messages are humorous, disarmingly straightforward, warm, friendly, erotic, informative, or otherwise arresting. Others are silly, contrived, insulting, or just unmemorable. While it would be difficult to tackle the relative effectiveness of ads that represent all of these characteristics, certain advertising appeals have come under empirical scrutiny in consumer behavior research. These include humor, fear, sex, and two-sided messages.

Humorous Appeals

A continuing controversy rages in advertising circles over the effectiveness of humor in print ads and commercials. Some campaigns have proven highly successful through creative uses of humor—Volkswagen and Alka Seltzer are two often-cited examples. Yet other attempts to amuse consumers into brand acceptance have fallen flat or produced chuckles at the expense of the product advertised.[38]

In a thorough review of the rather limited research into the use of humor in advertising messages, Sternthal and Craig draw these conclusions:[39]

1. *Humorous messages attract attention.* Most advertisers accept this premise, but note that too much repetition dramatically reduces the attention-getting factor. If a humorous commercial relies on an unexpected punch line, for example, the humor will have been given away by the second exposure—an "I heard that one before" phenomenon.

2. *Humorous messages may hamper comprehension.* If a humorous execution complicates a selling story unduly, or rests on "borrowed" interest remote from the product, comprehension may be reduced.

3. *Humor may distract the audience, yielding a reduction in counterargumentation and an increase in persuasion.* This is in line with the hypothesis that people are inclined to argue under their breath with persuasive communication. Therefore, interference with this subvocal counterargument will result in more agreement with the position taken in the communication.[40]

4. *Humorous appeals appear to be persuasive, but the persuasive effect is at best no greater than that of serious appeals.*

5. *Humor tends to enhance source credibility.* Brunet suggests that a previously unidentified source was perceived to have greater attributes of character when he delivered a humorous rather than serious communication in one study.[41]

6. *Audience characteristics may confound the effects of humor,* if, for example, an audience's low intelligence level inhibits comprehension.[42]

7. *A humorous context may increase liking for the source and create a positive mood.* This may enhance the persuasive effect of the message.

8. *To the extent that a humorous context*

functions as a positive reinforcer, a persuasive communication placed in such a context may be more effective.

Fear Appeals

Since an early study indicating that fear appeals were negatively related to message effectiveness, the use of "scare tactics" in advertising has been treated rather gingerly. But a number of more recent studies have suggested that fear appeals might be conducive to persuasion in certain kinds of messages and with certain consumers segmented on the basis of personality variables.

Ray and Wilkie cite the possible connection between antismoking advertisements using fear stimuli (such as a testimonial from a well-known actor who announced that he was dying of lung cancer caused by cigarette smoking) and a concurrent national drop in smoking. They conclude that *high* fear appeals, once regarded as counterproductive, may be persuasive with audiences consisting of people who are "low in anxiety and high in self-esteem, who exhibit coping behavior, who normally find the topic or category of low relevance, and who normally see themselves as having low vulnerability to the threat in the fear message."[43]

From the findings available, fear appeals seem most useful when the audience is similar in composition to the profile developed by Ray and Wilkie, and when the source credibility of the advertiser is unquestioned on the specific topic.[44]

Sex Appeals

Much to the chagrin of the women's movement, female models are increasingly used in advertising to express underlying (or more blatant) sexual themes. The highly controversial "Fly Me" campaign for National Airlines posed that headline above various attractive stewardesses, which many viewed as a sexual euphemism. (However, the advertising agency that created the campaign remained adamant that it conveyed a friendly invitation to fly a personalized airline and nothing more.) Nudity has become fairly commonplace in cosmetic and fashion advertising; a more recent development is the use of male models as "sex objects" in some advertising directed at women. But in spite of the popularity of sex appeals in ads, little consumer research has been advanced to measure their effectiveness in persuasion.

There has been some empirical evidence that sexual *illustrations* may evoke immediate interest from readers of both sexes,[45] but later research points out that, while that may be true, readers do not relate the illustration to the brand name.[46]

Steadman studied the relationship of sexual illustrations to brand name recall and found that:[47]

• Nonsexual illustrations were more effective in producing recall of brand names than were sexual illustrations, a response that became more pronounced with the passage of time.

• Individuals already favorable to the use of sex appeals in advertising recalled a greater number of correct brand names than those who were unfavorable to sex themes in ads.

Morrison and Sherman, noting that other researchers used their own definitions of sexual appeal in conducting their studies, allowed consumers themselves to judge the inherent sexual connotations of various ads on the different factors of degree of nudity, realism, romantic content, sexual overtones in printed words, and sexual arousal stimulated by the ad. These researchers observed that:[48]

• Suggestiveness of copy is rather uniformly noticed by women but not by men.

• Men are less inclined to report awareness of nudity, although different groups of men can be segmented on the basis of their responses to sexual themes in advertising.

These findings tend to discredit our traditional view of responses by men as against women toward sexual themes. Suggestive copy, it seems, might be used more effectively in advertising to women, while nudity seems to be barely noticed by a significant number of male consumers.

Two-Sided Arguments

Most advertising messages could be described as strictly *one-sided*—statements of a product or brand's superior qualities and the benefits that will come to the consumer who purchases it. *Two-sided* communications, on the other hand, express arguments both pro and con, a persuasion strategy that may predispose consumers toward the product in question. Faison first analyzed the use of a two-sided argument in an advertising context for products as diverse as floor wax and automobiles, concluding that two-sided appeals facilitated persuasion to a greater degree than one-sided appeals.[49] Since then, consumers have responded favorably to a number of persuasive messages offering a two-sided approach.

One cogent example has been identified by Twedt: an advertising strategy adopted by Renault after the automobile's sales had plunged drastically due to mechanical problems and unsatisfactory dealer service.[50]

To explain the rather startling headline, "The Renault for people who swore they would never buy another one," the body copy admits:[51]

We cannot blame anyone who swore they would never buy another Renault. When we first sent our cars into this country we ran into a sad situation   Our cars were not fully prepared to meet the demands of America, where sustained high speeds are normal, where a heavy foot on the clutch is normal, and where people are not used to fixing their own cars. More than a fair share of things went wrong with our cars. Less than a fair share of our dealers were equipped to deal with what went wrong . . .

This approach enabled the advertiser to continue selling Renaults in the United States. Evidently, consumers may view an honest admission of product shortcomings as enhancing source credibility.

Consumer Response Variables

We know from personal experience that some persuasive messages move us more deeply than others, and it is not always a function of the message itself. Three explanations for this phenomenon that have been scrutinized in consumer research are *perceptual screening*, the *distraction hypothesis*, and the *self-confidence persuasibility* relationship.

Perceptual Screening

It is axiomatic that people screen out huge blocks of advertising messages. The most recent estimates in *Advertising Age* suggest that, out of a daily exposure to approximately 150 messages, the consumer can only count between eleven and twenty of which he or she is aware. Similarly, an advertising agency once exposed viewers in their homes to a show in which three commercials appeared, without notifying them that they were actually being tested for exposure to commercials. When the subjects were contacted the next day and asked if they had noticed any commercials, over one-third could not recall any—even under those highly memorable circumstances. Thus peoples' perceptual screens seem to work very well indeed where commercial messages are concerned! Furthermore, perceptual screening goes to work early in a campaign—after an initial peak during the first couple of exposures, attention declines considerably.[52]

Haley points out that consumers are using their screening processes more and more to avoid commercials and ads.[53]

A number of reasons have been suggested for the increased use of perceptual screening during recent years. These include commercial clutter, boredom with television, erosion of product protection policies, increased commercial time, copy restrictions, more advertising messages per capita, more advertisers pushing more products.[54] All of these reasons might be summarized as the steadily increasing problem of too many persuasive messages.

The Distraction Hypothesis

The distraction hypothesis, first advanced by Festinger and Maccoby, means essentially that people are inclined to argue subvocally with a persuasive communication, and this counterargumentation diminishes the effect of any communication not consistent with the perceiver's view of things.[55]

Maccoby rests the hypothesis on an as-

sumption that a communication is received and understood, and that:[56]

. . . persuasive communications are 100 percent effective at the moment they are perceived and understood and that the belief in them would be permanent if it were not changed by some subsequent influence.

This "subsequent influence" was postulated as the recipient's counterarguments. If the communication is consistent with the recipient's own perception of the world, little counterarguing takes place and the communication is accepted. But if the communication fails to reflect the perceiver's world view, he or she begins to counterargue subvocally and either becomes less accepting of the communication or rejects it completely.

Allyn and Festinger concluded that communicators could reduce counterargumentation by building some form of distraction into the message, such as background noise or music.[57] The receiver will be so distracted by this extra element, the theory holds, that he or she will forget to counterargue and will thus be more susceptible to the persuasive communication.

This hypothesis has generated some controversy. Venkatesan and Haaland, applying both visual and behavioral forms of distraction, found that subjects who were not distracted were most susceptible to the message, while those who were, experienced the least attitude change.[58] Similarly, Gardner discovered that as subjects' attention was diverted, they were able to recall significantly less about a communication to which they had been exposed. Gardner notes that one problem arises in determining what distraction really means. If an element like music or artwork in a communication is designed to support it, the line between distraction and communication support becomes a very fine one,[59]

The Self-Confidence\Persuasibility Relationship

A relationship has been reported between consumers' self-confidence and their susceptibility to persuasion that may be described as curvilinear. Consumers who were characterized as most and least self-confident emerged as more resistant to persuasion than those who were only moderately self-confident. Cox and Bauer found this relationship to hold true for middle-aged women

purchasing stockings,[60] and Bell arrived at the same conclusion for both male and female purchasers of automobiles.[61]

Bither and Wright have investigated this relationship in conjunction with the distraction hypothesis discussed previously, concluding that the relationship between a receiver's self-confidence and his or her attitudinal acceptance of a television commercial depends on the level of potential distraction contained in the ad. More specifically, they found that people with medium self-confidence and, to a lesser degree, those with high self-confidence tended to change their attitudes under conditions of distraction. And this facilitating effect was strongest when the distraction was of moderate intensity.[62]

Effects of Media Persuasion on Purchasing Behavior

In the wake of consumers' mounting perceptual screening defenses and much contradictory evidence as to advertising effectiveness, one might wonder whether an ad can persuade people to buy at all.

The most positive means for tracing actual sales results of a single ad remains in the province of direct response advertising, where a response mechanism (such as a coupon) is built right into a communication and consumers may order the product directly. Because this form of advertising offers immediate accountability, it is becoming quite popular with advertisers. A direct response ad is shown in Figure 14-5.

In national advertising for packaged goods brands, attempts to determine the direct purchasing results of individual ads have also been successful.

"What One Little Ad Can Do"

One study conducted by Bogart, Tolley, and Orenstein compared measures of advertising readership (the traditional research approach) with actual sales data to determine the relationship between immediate purchasing behavior and measures of recall or attitude responses to communications.[63] In contrast to the conventional wisdom that consumers carry around an assortment of brand images that are triggered at the time of purchase, these researchers hypothesized that a consumer's "set" toward a brand may be built more upon previous use than on advertising exposures. Thus, an ad's mission may be to produce an immediate effect on the people

Figure 14-5 A direct response ad.

Bargain Book Club saves you more than anyone [almost].

Start with any 6 books for 99¢ when you join.

Just list your selections on the coupon and mail it today.

FIRST CLASS
Permit No. 3
Garden City
New York

BUSINESS REPLY MAIL
No Postage Stamp Required if Mailed in the United States

Postage Will Be Paid By

Doubleday Bargain Book Club
Garden City, New York
11530

Courtesy Doubleday & Co.

who are already predisposed to buy (whether they know it or not).

This study's findings indicate that:[64]

1. A relationship exists between recall scores of single ads and actual purchasing behavior (Table 14-5).

2. Individual ads may produce negative results as well as no results when people are unconvinced or their attention is distracted by too much "creative technique."

3. An ad may arouse widespread attention and readership without persuading people to buy, but, conversely, an ad may rank low on appeal and still exert a strong sales effect.

"Intent to Buy" and Purchasing Effects

In another study investigating the relationship between traditional advertising research and actual sales, Stapel explored the measure "intent to buy" as an indicator of actual buying behavior. For a variety of packaged goods brands and considered-purchase products, this researcher found that:[65]

• Roughly one out of every two respondents who claimed a "buying intent" put his or her name on an order coupon for home delivery.

• People recalling an ad exhibited approximately twice the intention to buy and produced twice the order coupons as consumers who did not recall the specific ad (Table 14-6).

Thus there appears to be justification for the popular research measurements of advertising effectiveness as indications of consumer purchasing behavior. The problems in making persuasive communications actually persuasive, however, increase almost daily as consumers are exposed to even greater numbers of ads. And consumers are giving marketers signals, through their growing use of perceptual screening and negative responses to commercial clutter, that some of the traditional advertising techniques—especially repetition and intrusiveness—may be due for reevaluation.[66]

Table 14-5 Purchase of the Advertised Brand Among Those Who Recall It to Varying Degrees

AMONG THOSE WHO:	(BASE NUMBER OF INSTANCES)	NUMBER/1000 SUBSCRIBERS WHO BOUGHT ADVERTISED BRAND
Made a "connection" with ad message	(129)	8
Proved recall of ad	(682)	9
Recognized ad (when shown)	(2,565)	4
Read something on page other than ad	(8,649)	3
Opened page, read nothing	(7,896)	2
Did not open page with ad	(6,003)	2
(X^2 for "proved recall" against "did not open page" = 10.50; $P < .002$)		

Source: Leo Bogart, B. Stuart Tolley and Frank Orenstein, "What One Little Ad Can Do," Journal of Advertising Research, Vol. 10, No. 4 (August 1970), p. 8. © Copyright 1970, by the Advertising Research Foundation.

Table 14-6 Buying Behavior Among Different Ad Perception Groups

PRODUCT	PERCEPTION GROUP	SHARE (%) OF PERCEPTION GROUP	
		GIVING VERBAL CERTAIN-TO-BUY	COMPLETING ORDER COUPON
Supra Coffee, A	With Ad Recall	40%	20%
	No Ad Recall	24	10
	No Ad Recognition	21	6
Supra Coffee, B	With Ad Recall	32	21
	No Ad Recall	26	14
	No Ad Recognition	19	11
Duel Cleaner	With Ad Recall	37	9
	No Ad Recall	12	1
	No Ad Recognition	12	2
Philips Tape Recorder*	With Ad Recall	24	17
	No Ad Recall	10	9
	No Ad Recognition	10	7
Castella-Matic Detergent	With Ad Recall	21	8
	No Ad Recall	10	7
	No Ad Recognition	9	8
Supra Coffee, C	With Ad Recall	25	10
	No Ad Recall	10	2
	No Ad Recognition	5	1
Average Product	With Ad Recall	30%	14%
	No Ad Recall	15	7
	No Ad Recognition	13	6

*The "order coupon" was for a brochure to be sent by the company to the customer rather than immediate delivery of the tape recorder itself.

Source: Jan Stapel, "Sales Effects of Pring Ads," Journal of Advertising Research Vol. 11, No. 3 (Junr 1971). © Copyright 1971, by the Advertising Research Foundation.

Summary

The communications media exert influence over consumer behavior as both vehicles of socialization and mechanisms for marketer communications. Different market segments are exposed differentially to individual media, and the factors that distinguish target segments may be identified through demographic and psychographic techniques. *Persuasive communications* are usually designed to market consumer goods and services, although they may also be used to position a company favorably in the consumer's frame of reference or persuade people to respond to some public service appeal. These communications are tested through measures such as *recall* and *recognition*. There are variables in the presentation of messages that may determine their effectiveness—*frequency*, *size* or *duration*, *repetition*, and *message* content. There are also variables that are functions of the perceiver such as *perceptual screening*, *distraction*, and *self-confidence*. Research indicates that, in addition to building awareness, ads may also accomplish short-term direct sales results in some relationship to the traditional measures of their effectiveness.

NOTES

1. Bent Stidsen, "Market Segmentation, Advertising, and the Concept of Communications Systems," *Journal of the Academy of Marketing Science*, Vol. 3, No. 1 (Winter 1975), p. 69.

2. Peter Wright, "Factors Affecting Cognitive Resistance to Advertising," *Journal of Consumer Research*, Vol. 2, No. 1 (June 1975), p. 1.

3. American Newspaper Publishers Association, 1974.

4. Leo Bogart, "Reaching People Where They Buy," *Sales Management*, September 1, 1971, p. 54.

5. Robert Peterson, "Psychographics and Media Exposure," *Journal of Advertising Research*, Vol. 12, No. 3 (June 1972).

6. Rapp & Collins, Division of Doyle Dane Bernbach, 1977.

7. *Psychographics: A Study of Personality, Life Style and Consumption Patterns* (New York: Newspaper Advertising Bureau, Inc., September 1973).

8. W. R. Simmons and Associates, New York, N.Y.

9. Peterson, "Psychographics," p. 19.

10. Douglas S. Tigert, "Psychographic Profile of Magazine Audiences: An Investigation of a Medium's Climate" (Working paper presented at the First Annual Conference of the Association for Consumer Research, Ohio State University, Columbus, Ohio, August 1969).

11. Tigert, "Psychographic Profile."

12. *Broadcasting*, May 21, 1973.

13. "Why Radio Keeps Gaining Power," *Broadcasting*, June 14, 1971.

14. Peterson, "Psychographics," p. 19.

15. U.S. Census Bureau, 1973.

16. *Broadcasting Yearbook*, 1971.

17. Leonard A. LoSciuto, "A National Inventory of Television Viewing Behavior," in *Television and Social Behavior, Volume 4: Television in Day-To-Day Life: Patterns of Use* ed. Eli A. Rubenstein, George A. Comstock, and John P. Murray (Washington, D.C.: U.S. Government Printing Office, 1971).

18. A. Stein and J. Friedlich, "Television Content and Young Children's Behavior," *Television and Social Behavior, Vol. 2*, (Washington, D.C.: U.S. Government Printing Office, 1971).

19. LoSciuto, "Television Viewing Behavior."

20. LoSciuto, "Television Viewing Behavior."

21. "Public Wants More T.V. Without Ads, NAB Study Shows," *Broadcasting*, February 28, 1973.

22. Newspaper Advertising Bureau, Inc., "Psychographics: Personality, Life Style, Consumption."

23. Douglas J. Tigert, "Are Television Audiences Really Different?" (Paper presented at the 54th International Marketing Congress, American Marketing Association, San Francisco, California, April 1971).

24. Carol. E. Brown, "Tired of TV? Try Cable," *Village Voice*, September 20, 1976.

25. Christopher C. Binkert, James A. Brunner, and Jack L. Simonetti, "The Use of Life Style Segmentation to Determine if CATV Subscribers Are Really Different," *Journal of the Academy of Marketing Science*, Vol. 3, No. 2 (Spring 1975).

26. John. O'Conner, "Are There Options for

-the Selective Viewer?" *New York Times*, September 19, 1976.

27. John Ziegler, Inc., New York, N.Y., 1977.

28. Portions of this discussion are adapted from Evelyn Konrad and Rod Erikson, *Marketing Research—A Management Overview* (New York: American Management Association, 1966); and David J. Luck, Hugh G. Wales, and Donald A. Taylor, *Marketing Research* (Englewood Cliffs, N.J.: Prentice-Hall, 1961).

29. Luck et. al., *Marketing Research*, p. 419.

30. Konrad and Erikson, *Management Overview*, p. 144.

31. Yoram Wind and Joseph Denny, "Multivariate Analysis of Variance in Research on the Effectiveness of T.V. Commercials," *Journal of Marketing Research*, Vol. 11 (May 1974).

32. John A. Geiger, "Seven Brands in Seven Days," *Journal of Advertising Research*, Vol. 11, No. 5 (October 1971).

33. Julian L. Simon, "The General Pattern of Response to Different Amounts of Advertising," in *The Management of Advertising* (Englewood Cliffs, N.J.: Prentice-Hall, 1971).

34. Rapp & Collins Division of Doyle, Dane, Bernbach, 1977.

35. John B. Stewart, *Repetitive Advertising in Newspapers* (Cambridge, Mass.: Harvard University, 1964).

36. H. A. Zielske, "The Remembering and Forgetting of Advertising," *Journal of Marketing*, Vol. 23, No. 3 (January 1959), pp. 239–243.

37. *Schwerin Research Corporation Bulletin*, October 1966.

38. J. Weingarten, "Is 'Far-Out' Advertising Entertaining The Public More But Selling It Less?", *Dun's Review*, Vol. 90 (July 1967).

39. Brian Sternthal and C. Samuel Craig, "Humor in Advertising," *Journal of Marketing*, Vol. 37 (October 1973), p. 17.

40. David M. Gardner, "The Distraction Hypothesis in Marketing," *Journal of Marketing Research*, Vol. 10 (December 6, 1970).

41. C. Brunet, "A Further Experimental Study of Satire as Persuasion, in "Sternthal and Craig, op. cit. 39.

42. Sternthal and Craig, "Humor in Advertising."

43. Michael L. Ray and William L. Wilkie, "Fear: The Potential of an Appeal Neglected by Marketing," *Journal of Marketing*, Vol. 34 (January 1970).

44. M. Hewgill and G. Miller, "Source Credibility and Response to Fear-Arousing Communications," *Speech Monographs*, Vol. 32 (1965).

45. Stephen Baker, *Visual Persuasion* (New York: McGraw-Hill, 1961).

46. Anne Anastasi, *Fields of Applied Psychology* (New York: McGraw-Hill, 1964).

47. Major Steadman, "How Sexy Illustrations Affect Brand Recall," *Journal of Advertising*, Vol. 9, No. 1, pp. 15–19.

48. Bruce J. Morrison and Richard C. Sherman, "Who Responds to Sex in Advertising?", *Journal of Advertising Research*, Vol. 12, No. 2 (1972), pp. 15–19.

49. E. W. Faison, "Effectiveness of One-Sided and Two-Sided Mass Communications in Advertising," *Public Opinion Quarterly*, Vol. 25 (1961).

50. Dik W. Twedt, "How Does Brand Awareness-Attitude Affect Marketing Strategy?", *Journal of Marketing*, Vol. 31 (October 1967).

51. Twedt, "Brand Awareness-Attitude," p. 64.

52. Russell I. Haley, "Beyond Benefit Segmentation," *Journal of Advertising Research*, Vol. 11, No. 4 (August 1971), pp. 3–7.

53. Haley, "Segmentation."

54. Edward H. Myer, "Is The Golden Goose Beginning to Lay Leaden Eggs?", Television Advertising Management Seminar sponsored by the Association of National Advertisers, April 1970.

55. Leon Festinger and Nathan Maccoby, "On Resistance to Persuasive Communication," *Journal of Abnormal and Social Psychology*, Vol. 68, No. 4.

56. Nathan Maccoby as cited in David M. Gardner, "The Distraction Hypothesis in Marketing," *Journal of Marketing Research*, Vol. 8 (May 1971), p. 26.

57. J. Allyn and L. Festinger, "The Effectiveness of Unanticipated Persuasive Communications," *Journal of Abnormal and Social Psychology*, Vol. 62 (1961).

58. M. Venkatesan and Gordon A. Haaland, "An Experimental Study of the Effect of Distraction on the Influence of Persuasive Marketing Communications (Paper presented at the Consumer Behavior Conference, Columbia University Graduate School of Business, 1967.

59. Gardner, "Distraction Hypothesis."

60. Donald F. Cox and Raymond A. Bauer, "Self-Confidence and Persuasibility in Women,"

Public Opinion Quarterly, Vol. 28 (Fall 1964).

61. Gerald D. Bell, "Self-Confidence and Persuasion in Car Buying," *Journal of Marketing Research,* Vol. 4 (February 1967).

62. Stewart W. Bither and Peter L. Wright, "The Self-Confidence-Advertising Response Relationship: A Function of Situational Distraction," *Journal of Marketing Research,* Vol. 10 (May 1963).

63. Leo Bogart, B. Stuart Tolley, and Frank Orenstein, "What One Little Ad Can Do," *Journal of Advertising Research,* Vol. 10, No. 4 (August 1970).

64. Bogart et. al., "One Little Ad."

65. Jan Stapel, "Sales Effects of Print Ads," *Journal of Advertising Research,* Vol. 11, No. 3 (June 1971).

66. See, for example, Gordon H. G. McDougall and Joseph N. Fry, "Source and Message Content Credibility in Retail Advertisements," *Journal of the Academy of Marketing Science,* Vol. 3, No. 1 (Winter 1975), p. 60; and James R. Bettman, "Issues in Designing Consumer Information Systems," *Journal of Consumer Research,* Vol. 2, No. 3 (December 1975), p. 169.

MARKETING APPLICATIONS

Conclusion 1 *Consumers who are most likely to prefer a given medium may be identified through demographic and psychographic information.*

Application To send persuasive messages to consumers, marketers must first be certain that they are talking to the right people. Many an effective ad or commercial has been wasted because it found itself in the wrong environment to reach the consumers it was designed for. For instance, a new product which will rely heavily on a large number of consumers who are willing to try innovative items will probably be introduced most effectively on television (to obtain the largest numbers) and on talk shows (to reach innovators). Also there are often subtle differences among similar media, such as those found between the news magazines *Time* and *Newsweek* (see page 354 of the preceding chapter.) Marketers should use all demographic and psychographic facts available when making media decisions.

Conclusion 2 *Two-sided arguments may be effectively used in some advertisements, since they can offer greater source credibility than the usual one-sided persuasive message.*

Application This type of advertising can change unfavorable attitudes toward a product or service. First, the ad admits that something about the product has been found less than satisfactory, with which consumers who have tried and rejected the product will be inclined to agree. Now the stage is set for the positive side of the argument—how the product has improved or the consumer problem solved.

Conclusion 3 *Advertising should, wherever possible, offer some form of accountability, so marketers can see clearly whether it is working or not before waiting for market share to rise or decline.*

Application The simplest way to test the effectiveness of an ad is to include some mechanism which the consumer can respond to. This is most often a coupon for more information, a cents-off coupon to bring to the retailer, or a telephone number to call in broadcast advertising. Once a base response level for an ad is established, other ads may be tested against it to determine which ones are drawing the greatest response from consumers.

ASSIGNMENTS

Research Assignment

Background   Sadly enough for people who like to sport natural suntans, the sun's damaging effect on skin has been increasingly cited by medical authorities. The Totalcare Beauty Company has noted this fact and wants to introduce an artificial cosmetic tanning cream that will give consumers a natural-looking tan without exposure to the sun, and will actually moisturize skin without drying it out.

As the Research Director for the Rosemary Samuels Advertising Agency, you are assigned the task of finding out how consumers in your target group will respond to this product idea so you can offer guidelines to your creative department for preparing an advertising campaign.

Research Input   Because this product represents a form of consumer problem solving, you wish to uncover consumers' feelings about the problem of skin damage under the sun. You also want to determine how they feel about artificial tanning agents and to suggest a name for the product. Thus, you decide upon a focus group of consumers in your target segment—women 18 to 30. A focus group involves getting several people representing your market together in a session where they may freely discuss both the problem and the product designed to solve it. This is a popular form of advertising research at major agencies both prior to and after a campaign is developed.

Methodology   Assemble a group of at least five women 18 to 30 and direct their conversation along these guidelines (with a tape recorder going so you may analyze the dialogue afterwards):

1. Medical evidence points out conclusively that the sun does damage your skin, and in ways that show up after just a few years of heavy exposure. Are you worried about that? Do you limit your exposure to the sun because of it?

2. My client is developing a new product that will give you a *cosmetic* tan that looks as natural as one you could get in the sun. How would you feel about using it sometimes? How often would you use it?

3. Have you had experience with artificial tanning creams that look artificial? This product uses a new process to give you an absolutely natural-looking tan. Would you believe that if you saw it in an ad? What would convince you that it's true?

4. How do you feel about these names for our product? (Note: leave time for discussion after each one).

Instant Tan	Miami Tan
Unsun Tan	Malibu Tan

Perfect Tan	The Better Tan
Moisture Tan	Safe Tan

Extrapolation   Record the range of responses to each item and draw conclusions about the problem, how well the product is perceived as solving it, and the most favorably-received name for the product.

Creative Assignment

You are the Creative Director on the Totalcare account at the same agency. From the data supplied by your Research Director after the focus group session, develop a rough campaign of three space ads and a television commercial that will:

1. Introduce the product to the target consumers.

2. Address itself to the most important consumer problem identified during the focus group.

3. Focus on either the advantage of skin care or the benefit of an instant tan—whichever the focus group expressed as the product's most desirable feature.

4. Overcome negative feelings (such as resistance to artificial tanning creams) uncovered during the research.

Your campaign should stress one central theme, which will depend upon the feelings expressed by the people most likely to buy the product. Too many secondary themes, while useful as copy points, will tend to weaken your message.

Managerial Assignment

The proper use of humor in advertising remains a thorny problem in marketing. Some agencies, such as Doyle, Dane, Bernbach and Wells, Rich, Green, have been wildly successful with brilliant, humorous executions that have entertained consumers while they were selling products. Other agencies consciously avoid humorous appeals as "frivolous" and "ineffective."

As an account executive trying to convince a rather humorless hot dog manufacturer to use humor in his upcoming campaign, you must marshall a persuasive rationale for the impact of humorous advertising in breaking the consumer's boredom threshold and gaining awareness of this product. Prepare this rationale from information on pages 367–368 of this chapter, as well as searching relevant literature such as *Advertising Age* and the *Journal of Advertising Research.*

Cite reasons based on improved advertising performance rather than a need to entertain consumers alone.

SELECTED READINGS

Berning, Carol A., et al. "Patterns of Information Acquisition in New Product Purchases." *Journal of Consumer Research*, Vol. 1, No. 2 (September 1974), pp. 18–22.

Darden, William R. and William D. Perreault, Jr. "A Multivariate Analysis of Media Exposure and Vacation Behavior with Life Style Covariates." *Journal of Consumer Research*, Vol. 2, No. 2 (September 1975), pp. 93–103.

Goldberg, Marvin E. and Gerald J. Gorn. "Children's Reactions to Television Advertising: An Experimental Approach." *Journal of Consumer Research*, Vol. 1, No. 2 (September 1974), pp. 69–75.

McDougall, Gordon and Joseph N. Fry. "Source and Message Content Credibility in Retail Advertisements." *Journal of the Academy of Marketing Science*, Vol. 3, No. 1 (Winter 1975), pp. 60–68.

Stidsen, Bent. "Market Segmentation, Advertising, and the Concept of Communication Systems." *Journal of the Academy of Marketing Science*, Vol. 3, No. 1 (Winter 1975), pp. 69–84.

OBJECTIVES

1. Discuss how *interpersonal communications* are processed.   385

2. Describe the *two-step flow hypothesis.*   387

3. Discuss four means for identifying *opinion leaders.*   388

4. Compare *product-specific and generalized* opinion leadership.   390

5. Summarize the research findings about *industrial and institutional* opinion leadership.   393

6. Discuss *four strategies for using opinion leadership* in marketing.   395

FIFTEEN

Interpersonal Communications

Each time we see a new film, read a best-seller, or try a different brand of headache remedy solely on someone else's recommendation, a direct form of personal influence has prompted us to spend time and money on something we had not intended to do. And these are among the most obvious examples; other purchasing events may be affected quite subtly by what people say about the market items they've bought and used.

Interpersonal communications shape consumer choice behavior in two ways. They may serve as a primary source of influence when consumers seek or receive unsolicited advice about market items from others. They may also act as a filter through which information

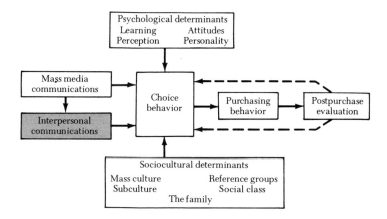

from media sources is absorbed by opinion leaders who pass their evaluations on to larger groups of consumers.

This chapter examines interpersonal influence through such topics as:

• The self-serving reasons why people enter into communication with one another.

• Why word of mouth is the most convincing source of information about products and services.

• How to identify opinion leaders who influence other consumers.

• Strategies for reaching opinion leaders (or creating new ones) through persuasive communications.

Because marketers realize the strength of personal influence in purchasing behavior, research into how communications affect attitudes, opinions, and choices is a major contribution to our knowledge of consumer decision making. [1]

The Importance of Face-to-Face Interactions

While most communications research concentrates on marketer-dominated sources of information, face-to-face interactions play an equally important role in consumer decisions. Word-of-mouth communications, in fact, were described in chapter 14 as generally more credible to consumers than advertising messages, and a number of advertisers consciously use this axiom in their own messages. Consider the number of television commercials that present slice-of-life conversations about products between actresses portraying housewives as compared with the number of "standup" commercials in which an announcer holds up the product and addresses the consumer directly. The popularity of the slice-of-life technique with marketers rests on the assumption that people are influenced by what their neighbors, relatives, or friends say about certain products or brands.

Thus we witness, in a typical hour of television viewing, a housewife, mortified because her guests snicker over odors in her house, being assured by her one true friend

that a brand of air freshener will solve her problem; a young woman chided by her roommate to stop spending money on clothes to attract men because a particular toothpaste is really what she needs; a clumsy salesman who spills his coffee in a diner lectured by a waitress on a paper towel's effectiveness; and, for a brand of chocolate, a delightful spoof of the whole approach—a woman who gushes sympathy over the viewer who hasn't tried Cadbury's, "Oh, my dear," (choking back a sob), "you've missed so much!"

While such portrayals of word-of-mouth communications may strike the viewer as less than authentic, the effects of interpersonal influences on consumption are apparent from everyday experience. Everyone has been predisposed toward buying certain products or patronizing specific retail outlets through others' appraisals. Sometimes advice may be actively sought, as when someone considering a make of cars asks present owners for their opinions. And impromptu testimonials for brands occur between friends and relatives over choice of wine, shampoo, television shows, floor wax, and any other item that happens to be important for a consumer at any given time. Consumers generally see others' evaluations as significant in trying to decide whether to buy what they perceive as a good product.[2]

This chapter discusses interpersonal influences in a *communications* context, beginning with an overview of interpersonal communications, both verbal and nonverbal. The concept of *opinion leadership,* a generally accepted framework for viewing influence, is then analyzed from the standpoints of consumer, product, and perceived-risk variables. Finally, some questions for future research and prescriptions for using interpersonal concepts in marketing come under scrutiny.

The Interpersonal Communication Process

Interpersonal communications in the marketing sense may be defined as *the flow and exchange of information among consumers in face-to-face interaction.* Personal *influence* is the degree to which an interpersonal communication affects one or more consumers' attitudes or behavior toward a product, service, store, or purchasing decision.

Verbal Communications

Engel, Wales, and Warshaw have summarized the verbal aspects of the interpersonal communication process in a working model shown in Figure 15-1.[3]

In this basic overview of the process, Communicator A arranges words in a sequence to be presented to Receiver B, an activity known as *encoding. Receiver B* then *decodes* the message, which may be filtered through perceptual screening and is subject to *noise,* which may distort the message. Communicator A ultimately receives *feedback* from Receiver B and decides whether the communication has been received as intended.

The nature of such a communication is affected by a number of variables including the *demographic* characteristics of both com-

Figure 15-1   Basic interpersonal communication model.

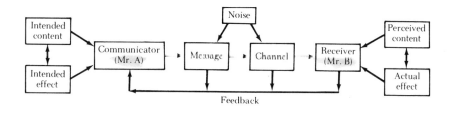

Source: *J. F. Engel, H. G. Wales, and M. R. Warshaw,* Promotional Strategy *(Homewood, Ill.: Richard D. Irwin, 1971), p. 19.*

municator and receiver, their *perceptual* attributes, *attitudes* held by both parties toward each other and toward the communication, and the *motivation* which each party brings to the communication milieu.

Nonverbal Aspects of Communication

Hulbert and Capon have furthered this research through a model that takes into account both verbal elements and nonverbal "signs." These signs are characterized as physical events generated by one individual in the process and available for reception by the other.[4] Nonverbal signs include the use of facial expressions (such as the raised eyebrow) to augment a message and the phenomenon popularly known as "body language"—a communication through posture and mannerisms that may be sent inadvertently by the communicator (Figure 15-2).

In this model, some stimuli do not require deliberation before responding; these are known as *habit-determined* responses as distinguished from *deliberated* responses. The flow of physical signs (body language) may be referred to as the syntax of the communication, or *syntactic* domain. Perception and encoding (interpreting the message) occur in a semantic realm. And the functions involving the way the receiver uses the information are known as the *pragmatic* category.

Functions of Interpersonal Communication

According to a sociological "theory of exchange" developed by Homans, people enter

Figure 15-2   The individual in communication.

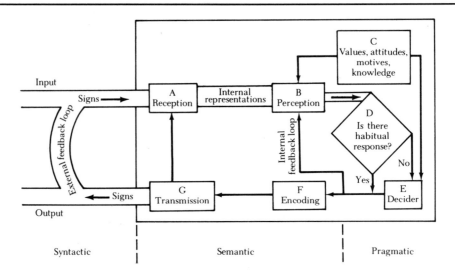

Source: James Hulbert and Noel Capon, "Interpersonal Communication in Marketing: An Overview," Journal of Marketing Research, *Vol. 9 (February 1972), p. 32. Reprinted by permission of the American Marketing Association.*

into face-to-face interactions for some perceived reward or reinforcement that will be derived from the contact.[5] An individual's decision to interact with someone else and follow that person's advice or directives will be based upon his or her perceptions of:[6]

• The *frequency* of reward. The more often within a period of time an individual is reinforced by interaction with another, the more frequently that individual will initiate a contact.

• The *magnitude* of reward. The greater the degree of reward an individual receives from complying with the advice or directives of another, the more likely the individual will be to comply.

Homans' theory has been applied to subjects such as romantic attraction and conformity, and might logically be extended to consumer interactions that concern information about products and services. If a consumer perceives some reward in an encounter with someone else (as in the case of the person considering a certain make of car who comes across a present owner of that make), he or she will initiate a communication. This suggests that some consumers will be sought after by other consumers for information and opinions, which elevates the former to the role of opinion leadership in interpersonal communications.

Opinion Leadership in Personal Influence

In the previous chapter, mass media communications were analyzed for their effectiveness in reaching consumers. But are all available consumers "reached" at once in the presentation of a message? Evidence indicates that the flow of mass communications from source to receivers is actually a multistage process.

The Two-Step Flow of Communications

The two-step flow hypothesis, originally presented by Katz and Lazarfield, notes that communications do not flow in a vertical line from mass media to the consumer.[7] Instead, there is a vertical stream from the media to certain consumers designated as opinion leaders, those who are the first to absorb and use the information the media provides. These opinion leaders then transmit the same information horizontally, as described by Nicosia:[8]

Messages channeled through mass media,

books, conventions, shows, and other sources tend to reach mass audiences in two stages: first, they are noted by opinion leaders; and second, are transmitted by the opinion leaders to members of their social milieu through direct contact in its many forms, from casual conversation to deliberate advice seeking. (See Figure 15-3.)

When this concept was first advanced, it was at variance with the generally accepted view of new-product or service adoption— the "trickle-down" effect. While the trickle-down theorists maintained that fashion adoption flowed from upper to lower socioeconomic strata, the two-step hypothesis was supported by much evidence that opinion leadership is largely a horizontal phenomenon within peer groups.[9]

Any consideration of opinion leadership should include recent findings that, although the two-step hypothesis presupposes one-way communication between leaders and followers (or "influentials" and "influencees"), this

Figure 15-3   The two-step flow hypothesis.

is not the only kind of communication that may occur. Studies of fashion acceptance have since concluded that people participating in interpersonal communications tend both to transmit and receive information.[10] A closer examination of opinion leader characteristics will reveal that leadership is a highly situational attribute, and that participation in two-way interpersonal communications is quite broad.

For instance, Cox cites findings that 50 percent of conversations about products are initiated by *non*leaders who are requesting information from opinion leaders, rather than the other way around, as the two-step hypothesis contends.[11] This would suggest that interpersonal exchanges are more closely related to consumer *needs* for information than to unsolicited information passed from leaders to nonleaders.[12]

Distinguishing the Opinion Leaders

Accepting the common assumption that there are opinion leaders, or *influentials*, who act as sources of communication and other consumers who behave as *receivers*, it follows that influentials make up a special market segment of people with particular perceptions, values, attitudes, and other characteristics that distinguish them from most consumers. Because of the effect influentials have on the behavior of other individuals, many researchers believe that directing persuasive communications to this segment is more fruitful than trying to deliver communications to everyone.[13] For this reason, *identifying* opinion leaders has been adopted as a market segmentation strategy.

The most widely used method of identifying opinion leaders has been *self-designation*, or letting leaders identify themselves through self-report inventories posing questions such as "Have you recently tried to convince anyone of your political ideas?" Another, related procedure consists of self-designation questions paired with interviews of the people who have supposedly been influenced. A third procedure entails asking everyone in a certain population some sociometric questions such as "Can you name three or four of your best friends?"[14] To date, the most reliable procedure has been self-designation, although it has certain limitations. For one, individuals are being asked to give self-perceptions—which are notoriously difficult to verify and control. Also, interpersonal communication leading to influence may occur when the people involved are not aware of it or do not recognize it as such. Instruments for self-designation are currently being refined to compensate for some of these difficulties.

Studies investigating opinion leadership for consumer products and services have attempted to identify opinion leaders through patterns of *media exposure, demographics, personality traits,* and *perceived risk.*

Media Exposure As might be expected, opinion leaders reveal greater exposure to media,[16] and this is particularly true of media that reflect their special area(s) of leadership.[17] (The tendency for opinion leaders' spheres of influence to cluster around individual products or groups of products is discussed below under Product-Specific Leadership.) Opinion leaders go to more movies and watch more television.[18] They also read more magazines; this is especially the case for fashion influentials, who appear to study fashion publications more religiously than noninfluentials.[19] Whether they become opinion leaders because of their greater exposure to media or because, as influentials, they feel a greater compulsion to know what is going on remains subject to question.

Demographic Characteristics Opinion leadership has not been closely associated with particular demographic traits. Most studies conclude that the traits of influentials tend to be related to specific products or services, and that social class variables are likely to be equivalent for both influentials and receivers.[20] Education was found to be positively correlated with opinion leadership in politics and home entertainment choice, but negatively correlated with leadership in home upkeep and medical care.[21] Katz and Lazarfield discovered that opinion leaders for *movies* were usually young and single, while those affecting *food* buying were predominantly married and with large families.[22] In selecting medical services, opinion leaders tend to be older than information receivers.[23] Thus, opinion leaders are most easily segmented demographically for specific product profiles; they do not appear to form a particular demographic segment by themselves.

Personality Characteristics One generally accepted finding about influentials' personalities is that they are usually more gregarious than noninfluentials. This is not surprising, since they are active in disseminating information about products and services. Other attempts to link personality traits with personal influence conclude that opinion leaders are more nonconforming, cosmopolitan, self-confident, and socially active than information receivers.[24] Again, most findings suggest that the relevant personality characteristics of these people are related to specific products rather than generalized across all product categories. In a Canadian study probing life-style determinants of influentials, factors such as innovativeness, independence, occupational attainment, community involvement, and fashion consciousness emerged as the attributes and activities of opinion leaders.[25]

Perceived Risk Cunningham investigated opinion leadership in terms of perceived risk, with the expectation that people who perceive greater risk in purchases will be more likely to engage in product-oriented discussions with others.[26] It was hypothesized that influentials would be *less* likely to perceive high risk, since they are supposed to be authorities. But this relationship was not found, instead, those perceiving greater risk were also more inclined to designate themselves as opinion leaders for fabric softeners, laundry products in general, and all supermarket products. As in the case of interpersonal communication, this would suggest that information seeking may be less a leader-receiver pattern than one of two-way communications stimulated by consumer needs for product knowledge.

Product-Specific Leadership and Overlap

It becomes apparent that opinion leadership may be viewed in two ways: (1) as *specific* for certain products or services (a leader in one product arena may not be sought after for information in another) and (2) as a more

generalized phenomenon (leadership overlaps across products and product categories).

Product-Specific Leadership For certain products, researchers have found influentials to dominate in only limited areas:

1. Robertson and Myers concluded that among food, clothing, and small appliances, there is very little overlap of opinion leadership.[27]

2. Silk discovered that opinion leaders in the realm of dental products were not influential in other areas.[28]

3. Katz and Lazarfield point out that opinion leadership is a function of *interest* in a particular area.[29] Thus, leadership is likely to be specific in one area, such as fashion, in which interest would not be associated with another area, such as kitchen appliances.

4. Katz's early study of opinion leadership focused on personal *expertise* as a dominant trait of influentials.[30] Just as personal interest may limit an influential's scope, so expertise may also be confined to a relatively narrow range. The expert on fishing equipment may not be the best person to ask about an upcoming ballet.

While product-specific leadership is indicated in traditional research in this field, there is now mounting evidence that influence may overlap among areas more than was originally suspected.

• King and Summers uncovered a high degree of influence overlap with six product groups: foods, fashions, detergents and cleansers, large appliances, small appliances, and personal care products. The greatest overlap occurred in closely related areas such as large and small appliances and women's fashion and personal care items.[31]

• Montgomery and Silk also found that overlap across product categories was related to products that held similar interest for the same opinion leaders.[32]

The prevailing view today is that, while one individual's opinion leadership is not highly generalized over many products and services, influence may overlap across clusters of products that meet similar needs or fulfill certain life-style requirements. The woman who is extremely fashion conscious, who reads women's magazines, and even *Women's Wear Daily*, to keep herself informed of every new development in the fashion arena, will undoubtedly extend her interest to cosmetics and personal care items. Similarly, a person recognized as an authority on film-making and related equipment may be a good source of information about still-photography cameras as well.

Opinion Leadership and New Product Adoption

Because influentials affect other consumers' purchasing patterns for *existing* products and services, the question of whether opinion leaders are more likely to try *new* products arises. There are several similarities in the profiles of "new product adopters," the term applied to opinion leaders and consumers who tend to try new products before others. (Adoption behavior is discussed in much greater detail in chapter 16.) But whether influentials are a desirable target segment for new-product information remains controversial.

Similarities between "Influentials" and "Adopters" It has already been noted that influentials reveal characteristics of *gregariousness, independence, self-confidence,* and

social activity. Boone found these traits to characterize new-product adopters as well.[33] However, the attribute of *cosmopolitanism* revealed by opinion leaders in one study was identified as *negatively* correlated to new-product adoption in a study by Robertson and Kennedy.[34] It should be noted that this research concerned small appliances, which are probably not as interesting to people reflecting cosmopolitan values as to more home-oriented consumers. New-product adoption is, in fact, product related to a great extent—just as opinion leadership would appear to be.

In keeping a watchful eye turned to the media, new-product adopters resemble opinion leaders in their greater exposure (although Robertson suggests that such adopters tend to read more than watch television,[35] a finding not established for opinion leaders).

Research Evidence Aligned with other similarities between the two groups, there is some evidence that opinion leaders are more likely to adopt new products than other consumers.

Berning and Jacoby note that, in some studies, innovators are shown to enter into more word-of-mouth communications than noninnovators.[36] Other findings suggest that consumers who are later adopters look for more information from interpersonal sources than do earlier adopters;[37] yet another study reveals no real differences between early and late adopters in seeking interpersonal information.[38] One of the strongest evidences of a relationship between opinion leadership and adoption behavior is Corey's finding that 60 percent of the early adopters of a new automobile were opinion leaders.[39] On this basis, we may conclude that:

1. Opinion leadership and new-product

Erhard Seminar Training (est): The Use of Personal Influence

One of the most intriguing self-actualization movements ever devised is the phenomenal *est*, named after founder Werner Erhard (formerly Jack Rosenberg). The highly publicized organization—revolving around the charismatic ex-encyclopedia salesman whose followers call him "Werner"—offers an excellent example of personal influence used to reach mainly well-educated, intelligent, upper middle-class consumers.

Est training means, for the initiate, two grueling weekends sitting on a hard-backed chair among several hundred other men and women in an auditorium, undergoing what some critics have called brainwashing techniques. Trainees go without food, water, and bathroom breaks for many hours on end so that they may better concentrate on the trainer, who stands on a stage loudly describing his assembled listeners as "tubes" and worse.

The reward for all this punishment is "getting it," achieving the satisfying awareness that we are responsible for our own lives and nothing can really prevent us from achieving what we want. Most trainees say they "get it" at some time during the training. Others do not.

But the majority of graduates maintain that *est* has changed their lives for the better. And many of these men and women—all on a voluntary basis, of course—commit some of their time to encouraging others to take the training. The training will cost those who are persuaded about $300.

Thus, *est* needs no national advertising to fill auditoriums. Its converts are sufficiently grateful to want to share the *est* experience with others in their reference groups, and, without really divulging what goes on in the training, to use their personal influence to convince others.

When a curious potential trainee arrives at one of the free *est* get-acquainted seminars, he or she may listen to several enthusiastic graduates tell of their own experiences, and hear questions and answers about such "nuts and bolts" as who gets all the money. The meeting then adjourns and graduates walk up with a friendly smile to help talk out "whatever reasons you might have for not taking the training . . . right now!" The solicitous graduates are always polite, ingratiating, and articulate, the approach is quite persuasive. And a great number of the simply curious usually sign up for the first available training period.

---

adoption are not synonymous, but influentials share several characteristics with early adopters.

2. Opinion leadership may be an indication of innovativeness for certain products (and has been used as a variable in some new-product adoption studies).

3. Early adopters may perform a role as opinion leaders in persuading later adopters to try a new product or service.

Thus, opinion leaders might be considered a useful segment for new product communications, on the basis of research evidence now available.

Opinion Leadership in Industrial and Institutional Markets

Most research on personal influence and opinion leadership has been conducted in consumer markets. But some recent investigations have taken the study of influentials beyond the household consumer level.

Industrial Opinion Leadership Most studies at the industrial level have suggested that opinion leadership is not much in evidence. Webster concludes from two studies that:

• Personal influence tends to be absent in industrial purchasing decisions because buyers receive considerably more information from their suppliers than consumers receive from persuasive marketing communications. Also, buyers do not communicate among themselves, Webster argues, to the degree that consumers discuss products.[40]

• Industrial executives' informal sources of information, such as buyers in other companies and engineers within the company, are not aggressive forces in purchasing decisions.[41]

Ozanne and Churchill, in a study of purchases of automatic machine tools, concur that company associates, friends, and other interpersonal sources wield relatively little influence on buyers in such decision making.[42] But Mantilla, in an investigation of communication within industrial organizations, found both interpersonal purchasing discussions and patterns of opinion leadership.[43]

The contradictory findings in this area signal a need for more research as industrial purchasing becomes increasingly important to marketers.

Institutional Opinion Leadership Schiffman and Gaccione conducted one innovative study of influentials in the nursing home industry in which opinion leadership was defined as "being contacted 'frequently' for advice by persons in other nursing homes."[44] These researchers found that:

1. Opinion leaders in nursing homes reported greater contact with peers in other homes than did nonleaders (indicating that institutional influentials, like household consumer influentials, engage in more widespread interpersonal activity).

2. Opinion leaders whose advice was actively sought by others also solicited advice from peers (again conforming to research evidence on consumer influentials).

3. Institutional opinion leaders tend to be exposed to more media (publications in this case) than nonleaders, but the difference was not significant. Similarly, exposure to sales representatives failed to distinguish leaders from nonleaders.

4. Opinion leadership and innovativeness (new-product adoption) appear to be strongly interrelated in the institutional setting.

Schiffman and Gaccione note that *identifying* opinion leaders may be easier in industrial/institutional markets than in household/consumer markets, because the products and services in the former are more expensive and the population of customers is considerably smaller. Their findings are presented in Table 15-1.

Table 15-1   Institutional Opinion Leadership
vs. Nonleadership Characteristics

A. SUBSCRIPTION TO PROFESSIONAL PUBLICATIONS AMONG NURSING HOME OPINION LEADERS VS. NONLEADERS

	LOW (0 TO 4 PUBLICATIONS)	MEDIUM (5 TO 6 PUBLICATIONS)	HIGH (7 OR MORE PUBLICATIONS)	TOTAL
Nonleaders	56%	48%	38%	47%
Leaders	44	52	62	53
TOTAL	100%	100%	100%	100%
Base	(36)	(46)	(39)	(121)

$x^2 = 2.21$; $p < .40$; 2 d.f.

B. APPROXIMATE NUMBER OF SALESMEN SEEN IN A MONTH BY NURSING HOME OPINION LEADERS VS. NONLEADERS

	LOW (0 TO 5 SALESMEN)	MEDIUM (6 TO 10 SALESMEN)	HIGH (11 OR MORE SALESMEN)	TOTAL
Nonleaders	53%	60%	42%	52%
Leaders	47	40	58	48
TOTAL	100%	100%	100%	100%
Base	(38)	(40)	(38)	(116)

$X^2 = 2.52$; $p < .30$; 2 d.f.

C. APPROXIMATE SOCIAL/PROFESSIONAL INVOLVEMENT OF NURSING HOME OPINION LEADERS VS. NONLEADERS

	NONE	1 TO 3 MEETINGS	4 OR MORE MEETINGS	TOTAL
Nonleaders	73%	54%	31%	50%
Leaders	27	46	69	50
TOTAL	100%	100%	100%	100%
Base	(26)	(46)	(42)	(114)

$x^2 = 11.98$; $p < .01$; 2 d.f.

Source: Leon G. Schiffman and Vincent Gaccione, "Opinion Leaders in Institutional Markets," Journal of Marketing Research, Vol. 38 (April 1974). Reprinted with permission of the American Marketing Association.

Using Interpersonal Communication and Influence

In analyzing interpersonal communication research, certain generalizations emerge that may be useful to marketers in segmentation and communications strategies.

Interpersonal communication and influence occur over a wide range of products and services. Some examples include food, cosmetics, movies, clothing, auto insurance, and particularly, in medical and dental services.[45] The purchase decisions most often influenced by interpersonal communications are those that are highly visible (such as clothing and cosmetics, which make some statement about the person who wears them) and those involving some degree of risk, because they are expensive or because the consumer is inexperienced in using them. Interpersonal communications are not necessarily verbal; they may be transmitted through physical signs that indicate approval or disapproval. To someone considering a certain purchase, the frown of a person whose opinion matters may transmit enough adverse information to predispose the consumer against that purchase.

Interpersonal influence can occur in a number of ways. These include situations in which (1) a person who is regarded as an expert about some product initiates discussion concerning it, (2) a person actively solicits information from someone he or she views as an authority, and (3) two consumers exchange information in such a way that both are influential and both are influenced.

Agents of personal influence— opinion leaders—may form segments for certain products and services. While the two-step hypothesis contends that opinion leaders are the link between media and their "followers" among the mass consumer markets, there is evidence that the term "leader" may be deceptive. Several researchers point out that leaders may be influenced as well as influential, according to the specific needs of people in an interpersonal situation. Additionally, leadership is seldom generalized across a wide range of products; instead, innovative individuals appear to be influential over specific products and product clusters in which they reveal some special interest or expertise.

Marketing Strategies Using Personal Influence

There are four generally recognized strategies for using principles of personal influence in marketing. These are *identifying opinion leaders, simulating opinion leadership, creating interpersonal communications,* and *creating opinion leaders.*

Identifying Opinion Leaders   In some relatively small markets, such as the institutional and industrial settings mentioned earlier, it may be possible to identify opinion leaders and target communications to them through direct mail or carefully selected print or broadcast media.

Most markets are not this small, however, so it becomes necessary to rely heavily on research in finding the influentials for a specific product or service.

Simulating Opinion Leadership   Robertson uses the term "simulating opinion leadership" to describe advertising that initiates word-of-mouth communication.[46] One example of this is the slice-of-life technique mentioned at the beginning of this chapter. Another is the technique of interviewing real consumers to elicit unrehearsed testimonials about a product. A third is the trend toward using actors and actresses who look like people who would actually buy the product rather than like actors and actresses. All of these devices say, in effect, "Our product is used by people just like you—people you can believe when they tell you how great it works." A variation of this theme is using testimonials by celebrities who might be seen as possessing some special expertise about the product. The actor David Niven once appeared in an unusually credible commercial for the "world's most experienced airline," admitting that "when it comes to flying, David Niven . . . bon vivant and world traveler . . . is the world's greatest chicken."

Creating Interpersonal Communication Although they happen rarely, some marketing and advertising strategies successfully encourage people to talk about a product or service. "Want a nice Hawaiian punch?" has become part of almost every child's vocabulary, and other slogans have managed to work their way into the language through memorability and repetition. McDonald's commercials for the New York market announced prizes for consumers who could recite a tongue-twisting jingle listing all of the ingredients of their "Big Mac" hamburger in less than five seconds.[47] When samples of a new product, such as a detergent, are distributed throughout a market area, this device encourages discussion of the product because neighbors may test it together. "Sampling" may be conducted in a different vein for considered-purchase, high-ticket items.

Executives drawn from a credit card mailing list were once invited by personal letter to test drive an expensive car. Rather than having to go to a showroom, these potential opinion leaders could make an appointment to have the car delivered to their homes or offices.

Creating Opinion Leaders Sometimes opinion leaders can be created by marketers to disseminate information about a product. A successful example of this approach is the "Tupperware Party," which uses one homemaker as a sales representative to give a party for her neighbors focusing on Tupperware home products. Mancuso reports one instance of a record company that invited social leaders (although not necessarily product opinion leaders) at high schools and colleges to join a "panel" of judges who would evaluate new record releases. These judges were encouraged to discuss the records with their friends, and the experiment resulted in several hit records for the company.[48]

Personal Influence in Sales Strategies

One type of interpersonal communication that allows marketers an unusual degree of control is the personal sales situation. Yet this area has not received the same research interest as mass communications or interpersonal contacts among consumers.

Evans has demonstrated that a salesperson may play the role of opinion leader when the demographic and life-style characteristics of both salesperson and prospect are similar. In his study of insurance sales, the "attractiveness" of the salesperson to the customer on the basis of these similarities tended to result in a favorable sales outcome.[49]

In a communications context, Pennington found that a salesperson's verbal behavior was related to his or her sales performance.[50] Hulbert and Capon later extended research into sales communication to establish a classification scheme for visual, auditory, tactile, and olfactory elements of a salesperson-customer interview. Their scheme is summarized in Table 15-2.

As Evans found similarity between salesperson and customer to increase sales performance, so Kelman contends that attractiveness and credibility of the salesperson will evoke two interrelated influences—identification and internalization. The greater the salesperson's perceived credibility, the stronger the tendency for a prospect to internalize the influential message.[51]

Woodside and Davenport tested these findings in a study of personal influences in the sale of cleaning units for eight-track tape players. First, they note the interaction of "psycho-social game playing" and "problem solving game playing" in a sales communication:[52]

Psycho-social game playing is the customer's reliance and use of the . . . attractiveness of the communicator in making purchase decisions. Problem-solving game playing can be defined as the customer's reliance and use of the . . . credibility of the communicator in making purchase decisions, with experience and expertise being dimensions of competence. . . .

They confirmed their hypothesis that:[53]

(1) The greater the perceived expertise attached to the salesman, the greater the likelihood of purchase by the customer. (2) The greater the perceived similarity attached to the salesman, the greater the likelihood of purchase by the customer. (3) For an Exten-

Table 15-2 Classification Scheme for Elements of the Salesperson-Customer Interpersonal Communication NO

RECEIVER ROLE	SENDER ROLE			
	A STATIC, UNCONTROLLABLE	B STATIC, CONTROLLABLE	C DYNAMIC (LOW FREQUENCY)	D DYNAMIC (HIGH FREQUENCY)
1. Visual	a. Physical features (race, sex, age, etc.)	a. Clothing (style, neatness) b. Physical features (hair style, facial hair)	a. Posture b. Axial orientation c. Distance	a. Body movement b. Facial expression c. Eyeline d. Gesture e. Head orientation
2. Auditory	a. Voice set	a. Accent	a. Temporal speech patterning b. Accent c. Voice qualities	a. Vocalizations b. Verbal
3. Tactile and Olfactory		a. Personal odor	a. Touching behavior b. Thermal	

Source: James Hulbert and Noel Capon, "Interpersonal Communication in Marketings, An Overview," Journal of Marketing Research, Vol. 9 (February 1972), p. 27. Reprinted with permission of the American Marketing Association.

sive Problem Solving stage in consumer decision making, perceived expertise of the salesman produces a greater likelihood of purchase by the customer than perceived similarity of the salesman.

These studies into the salesperson-customer interpersonal communication process suggest that personal selling might be better controlled by marketers through (1) matching salespeople to target customers in demographics and life style and (2) training salespeople to direct their appeals to the "game-playing" technique appropriate to the specific sales context.

Building on this basic description of interpersonal communication, the following chapter will analyze both media influences and interpersonal influences in consumer choice behavior leading to purchase decisions.

Summary

Interpersonal communication may be seen as the flow and exchange of information among consumers in face-to-face interaction. Personal *influence* is the degree to which an interpersonal communication affects attitudes or purchasing behavior. A basic model of the interpersonal communication process includes the elements known as encoding, decoding, and feedback. But not all communications are verbal; nonverbal "signs" are critical to the communication process as well. Interpersonal communication serves the function of reward or reinforcement, and people enter into contact with others to achieve this objective. As consumers, people look to *opinion leaders* for information about products and services. According to the two-step flow hypothesis, opinion leaders are the link between the media and most consumers. They tend to distinguish themselves along demographic and psychographic lines, and may be segmented for specific products and services. Opinion leadership, however, is often a two-way communication; leaders receive, as well as transmit, information. While opinion leadership is not highly generalized, leaders tend to dominate clusters of related products in which they hold interest or expertise. Opinion leadership may operate at the industrial and institutional level as well as in household decision making, although the extent of personal influence in the former is controversial. Marketers use personal influence principles in identifying opinion leaders, simulating leadership, creating interpersonal communications, and creating opinion leaders. One particular area where personal influence might be used more effectively is in the salesperson-customer relationship.

NOTES

1. See Jacob Jacoby, "Consumer Psychology as a Social Psychological Sphere of Action," *American Psychologist,* 30, October 1975; and Robert Ferber, ed., *A Synthesis of Selected Aspects of Consumer Behavior* (Washington, D.C.: National Science Foundation, 1976).

2. Robert E. Burnkrant and Alain Cousineau, "Informational and Normative Social Influence on Buyer Behavior," *Journal of Consumer Research,* Vol. 2, No. 3 (December 1975).

3. J. F. Engel, H. G. Wales, and M. R. Warshaw, *Promotional Strategy* (Homewood, Illinois: Richard D. Irwin, Inc., 1971).

4. James Hulbert and Noel Capon, "Interpersonal Communication in Marketing: An Overview," *Journal of Marketing Research,* Vol. 9 (February 1972), pp. 27–34.

5. George Homans, *Social Behavior: Its Elementary Forms* (New York: Harcourt Brace, 1961).

6. Paul V. Crosble, "Social Exchange and Power Compliance: A Test of Homans' Propositions," *Sociometry,* Vol. 35, No. 1 (1972).

7. Elihu Katz and Paul F. Lazarfield, *Personal Influence: The Part Played by People in the Flow of Mass Communications* (New York: The Free Press, 1955).

8. Francesco M. Nicosia, "Opinion Leadership and the Flow of Communication: Some Problems and Prospects," in *Reflections on Progress in Marketing,* ed. George L. Smith, *Proceedings of the Fall Conference,* American Marketing Association, 1964, p. 341.

9. Charles W. King, "Fashion Adoption: A Rebuttal to the 'Trickle Down' Theory" in *Toward Scientific Marketing,* ed. Stephen A. Greyser (Chicago: American Marketing Association, 1964).

10. Charles W. King and John O. Summers, "Dynamics of Interpersonal Communication: The Interaction Dyad," in *Risk Taking and Information Handling in Consumer Behavior,* ed. Donald F. Cox (Boston: Harvard Graduate School of Business Administration, 1967).

11. Donald F. Cox as cited in Scott M. Cunningham, "Perceived Risk as a Factor in Informal Consumer Communications," in *Risk Taking and Information Handling in Consumer Behavior,* ed.

Donald F. Cox (Cambridge: Harvard University Press, 1967).

12. Cunningham, "Perceived Risk."

13. Flemming Hansen, *Consumer Choice Behavior, A Cognitive Theory* (New York: The Free Press, 1972), p. 375.

14. Nicosia, "Flow of Communication."

15. Thomas S. Robertson and James H. Myers, "Personality Correlates of Opinion Leadership and Innovative Buying Behavior," *Journal of Marketing Research,* Vol. 6, (May 1969), pp. 164–68; and William R. Darden and Fred D. Reynolds, "Backward Profiling of Male Innovators," *Journal of Marketing Research,* Vol. 11 (February 1974).

16. Charles W. King and John O. Summers, "Overlap of Opinion Leadership across Consumer Product Categories," *Journal of Marketing Research,* Vol. 7 (February 1970).

17. Robertson and Myers, "Personality Correlates."

18. John O. Summers, "Media Exposure Patterns of Consumer Innovators," *Journal of Marketing Research,* Vol. 36 (January 1972).

19. Fred D. Reynolds and William R. Darden, "Mutually Adaptive Effects of Interpersonal Communication," *Journal of Marketing Research,* Vol. 7 (November 1971).

20. Thomas S. Robertson, *Consumer Behavior* (Glenview, Illinois: Scott Foresman, 1970).

21. John G. Myers and Thomas S. Robertson, "Dimensions of Opinion Leadership" (Paper presented at the Workshop on Experimental Research, Ohio State University, 1969).

22. Elihu Katz and Paul F. Lazarfield, *Personal Influence.*

23. Sidney Feldman and Merlin C. Spencer, "The Effect of Personal Influence," in *The Selection of Consumer Services,* ed. Peter Bennett *Proceedings of the American Marketing Association,* Chicago, 1965.

24. Reynolds and Darden, "Interpersonal Communication," and Myers and Robertson, "Opinion Leadership."

25. Douglas J. Tigert and Stephen J. Arnold, *Profiling Self-Designated Opinion Leaders and Self-Designated Innovators Through Life Style*

Research (Toronto: University of Toronto, 1971).

26. Cunningham, "Perceived Risk."

27. Robertson and Myers, "Personality Correlates."

28. Alvin J. Silk, "Overlap Among Self-Designated Opinion Leaders: A Study of Selected Dental Products and Services," *Journal of Marketing Research*, Vol. 3 (August 1966).

29. Katz and Lazarfield, *Personal Influence*.

30. Elihu Katz, "The Two-Step Flow of Communications: An Up-To-Date Report on a Hypothesis," *Public Opinion Quarterly*, Vol. 21 (Spring 1957).

31. King and Summers, "Overlap of Opinion Leadership."

32. David B. Montgomery and Alvin J. Silk, "Patterns of Overlap in Opinion Leadership and Interest for Selected Categories of Purchasing Activity," in *Marketing Involvement in Society and the Economy*, ed. P. R. McDonald (Chicago: American Marketing Association, 1969).

33. Louis E. Boone, "The Search for the Consumer Innovator," *Journal of Business*, Vol. 43 (April 1970).

34. Thomas S. Robertson and James N. Kennedy, "Prediction of Consumer Innovators: Application of Multiple Discriminant Analysis," *Journal of Marketing Research*, Vol. 5 (February 1968).

35. Thomas S. Robertson, *Innovation and the Consumer* (New York: Holt, Rinehart and Winston, 1971).

36. Carol A. Kohn Berning and Jacob Jacoby, "Patterns of Information Acquisition in New Product Purchases," *Journal of Consumer Research*, Vol. 1 (September 1974).

37. Everett M. Rogers and F. Floyd Shoemaker, *Communication of Innovations* (New York: The Free Press, 1971).

38. Zarrel V. Lambert, "Perceptual Patterns, Information Handling, and Innovativeness," *Journal of Marketing Research*, Vol. 9 (November 1973).

39. Lawrence G. Corey, "People Who Claim to be Opinion Leaders: Identifying Their Characteristics," *Journal of Marketing*, Vol. 35 (October 1971).

40. Frederick E. Webster, Jr., "Word of Mouth Communication and Opinion Leadership in Industrial Markets," in *Proceedings of the American Marketing Association*, ed. Robert L. King (Chicago: American Marketing Association, 1968).

41. Frederick E. Webster, Jr., "Informal Communication in Industrial Markets," *Journal of Marketing Research*, Vol. 7 (May 1970).

42. Urban B. Ozanne and Gilbert A. Churchill, Jr., "Adoption Research: Information Sources and the Industrial Purchasing Decision," in *Marketing and the New Science of Planning*, ed. Robert L. King (Chicago: American Marketing Association, 1968).

43. John A. Mantilla, "Word of Mouth Communication in the Industrial Adoption Process," *Journal of Marketing Research*, Vol. 8 (May 1971).

44. Leon G. Schiffman and Vincent Gaccione, "Opinion Leaders in Institutional Markets," *Journal of Marketing*, Vol. 38 (April 1974).

45. James S. West and A. B. Blankenship, "The Physician and the Marketing Concept," *Journal of the Academy of Marketing Science*, Vol. 3, No. 2 (Spring 1975).

46. Robertson, *Consumer Behavior*.

47. Marketing information obtained from Rosenfeld, Sirowitz, and Lawson Advertising Agency, New York, N.Y. (1976).

48. Joseph R. Mancuso, "Why Not Create Opinion Leaders for New Product Introductions?", *Journal of Marketing*, Vol. 33 (July 1969).

49. Franklin B. Evans, "Selling as a Dyadic Relationship," *American Behavioral Scientist*, Vol. 6 (May 1963).

50. Allan L. Pennington, "Customer-Sales Bargaining Behavior in Retail Transactions," *Journal of Marketing Research*, Vol. 5 (August 1968).

51. Herbert C. Kelman, "Processes of Opinion Change," *Public Opinion Quarterly*, Vol. 25 (Spring 1961).

52. Arch G. Woodside and J. William Davenport, Jr., "The Effect of Salesman Similarity and Expertise on Consumer Purchasing Behavior," *Journal of Marketing Research*, Vol. 11 (May 1974).

53. Woodside and Davenport, "Salesman Similarity and Expertise."

MARKETING APPLICATIONS

Conclusion 1 *Interpersonal influence appears to be wielded most heavily by* opinion leaders *who receive and act on marketer communications first, then communicate their experiences to other consumers.*

Application   Opinion leadership offers marketers a credible source for word-of-mouth communication about some product. Thus, opinion leaders should be created whenever possible. For example, the marketer of an information newsletter directed to municipal officials would do well to isolate the influentials, probably the officials in the largest cities. These people could then be approached directly with an incentive (such as getting the newsletter free for a trial period) if they would be willing to discuss how the newsletter helped them and describe their experiences to their counterparts in other municipalities. This is known as a testimonial approach, and it becomes especially useful in industrial or professional markets where different customers have similar problems to solve.

Conclusion 2   *In retail selling, the greater a salesperson's perceived attractiveness to the consumer, the more likely a buyer will be to internalize the selling message.*

Application   The people who consumers usually find most attractive are people like themselves—similar in appearance, age, personal characteristics, and so on. At the retail level, many marketers do not seem to make a conscious effort to take advantage of this truth (although the situation is complicated by the fact that there is a greater demand for retail salespeople than there are people who want those positions). A basic approach to hiring retail salespeople should involve deciding who the target consumers are for the product to be sold and using the customer characteristics as evaluative criteria for hiring.

ASSIGNMENTS

Research Assignment

Background   You are West Coast Research Director of Paragon Pictures, a distributor of feature films. Like Paramount and United Artists, your corporation packages film properties and markets them to theaters across the country. Much of the research you design and conduct consists of testing advertising campaigns for specific films to determine what types of ads will be most effective in reaching the largest audiences. But you are also concerned with launching a new research project that will give Paragon more sophisticated information about *why* people go to see movies. You realize that the phenomenon of interpersonal communication represents a strong influence in determining what films people will leave home to see. You recognize that critical reviews of films may be an important form of *opinion* leadership to moviegoers. But you also suspect that *word-of-mouth* communication may be the deciding factor in the success (or failure) of many Paragon releases. Now you want to test your hypothesis on a sample of moviegoers while they are visiting local theaters.

Methodology   Design a questionnaire that will obtain the following information about *why* people are going to see a film:

1. How important they feel *advertising* was in prompting them to go.
2. How much weight they gave to *critical reviews*.
3. Whether they received information about the film from others who had seen it, and how influential those *interpersonal communications* were in their decision to attend the film.
4. Whether, after having seen the film themselves, they will talk about it with others.

Once the questionnaire is constructed, review it with someone at your school versed in statistics to determine the proper procedure for evaluating your findings. Then administer the questionnaire to at least ten filmgoers who are entering a local theater.

Extrapolation   Evaluate the importance of word-of-mouth communications with other influences in the decision to see a feature film. How could this information be used more effectively in marketing?

Creative Assignment

You are the sole owner of the Bagel Maven, a new delicatessen-style restaurant which serves twelve different varieties of bagels, and sandwiches consisting of different meats and spreads on toasted bagels.

Because you have virtually no advertising budget, you must rely almost entirely on word-of-mouth to attract customers to your restaurant. But you do possess some knowledge of how to reach consumers without advertising. Your first project is to get local media recognition of the Bagel Maven through a creative scheme, thus gaining recognition with opinion leaders and the people they influence.

Develop an idea newsworthy enough to get free media coverage. Possible directions include:

1. Staging a Bagel Benefit for a local charity or youth group.

2. Offering to cater, at a reduced rate, some prominent political or social event where members of the press will be present. (Or, persuade them to hold the event right at the Bagel Maven.)

3. Holding a Senior Citizens' Bagel Night with free bagels and entertainment.

Your activities will be most newsworthy if, in addition to being different, they are beneficial to the community in a dramatic way.

Managerial Assignment

As Sales Manager for the Educational Systems Corporation, you are responsible for a sales force that visits elementary, junior high, and high school teachers to sell audiovisual materials such as films, cassettes, and filmstrips.

Because there are so many teachers in the country and you have so few representatives, you are concerned with finding techniques of selecting the best sales representatives and training them to make every sales contact count in getting orders. Analyzing your representatives' contact reports, you discover that the 20 percent of your force who are most successful seem to consist of people who are young and have had some training or experience as teachers themselves.

Use that finding to make specific plans for improving your sales productivity. Why do your most effective salespeople fit that profile? What does that tell you about the kind of people you should be hiring in the future? Can you think of ways to enhance the performance of the rest of your sales force short of firing them? Prepare a one- to two-page report with prescriptions for changes before the next school year's buying period.

SELECTED READINGS

Burnkrant, Robert E. and Alain Cousineau. "Informational and Normative Social Influence in Buyer Behavior." *Journal of Consumer Research,* Vol. 2, No. 3 (December 1975), pp. 206–215.

Prasad, V. Kanti. "Communications-Effectiveness of Comparative Advertising: A Laboratory Analysis." *Journal of Marketing Research*, Vol. 13, No. 2 (May 1976), pp. 128–137.

Sternthal, Brian and Samuel C. Craig. "Fear Appeals: Revisited and Revised." *Journal of Consumer Research*, Vol. 1, No. 3 (December 1974), pp. 22–34.

Stewart, Daniel K. "Advertising and Consumer Behavior." *Journal of Advertising Research* (Summer 1974), pp. 16–20.

Wright, Peter. "Factors Affecting Cognitive Resistance to Advertising." *Journal of Consumer Research*, Vol. 2, No. 1 (June 1975), pp. 1–9.

OBJECTIVES

SIXTEEN

Consumer Choice Behavior

When a consumer reaches the critical point of choosing one brand or store over others in the market domain, all of the influences discussed so far may come into play.

Choice behavior is set into motion by the awareness of some problem that may be solved through buying activity. This is known as need arousal (illustrated by the problem of an old car pushed to the end of its life span finally breaking down beyond any hope of repair). Need arousal triggers exposure and search behavior, as the consumer seeks information about solutions to this felt need through media and interpersonal sources. And the choice process is further influenced by the entire spectrum of sociocultural and psychological determinants.

This chapter tracks consumer choice behav-

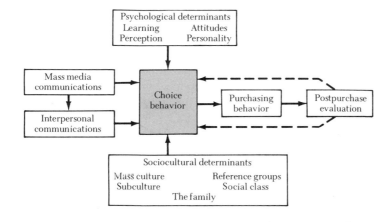

ior from need arousal through exposure and search, the familiar problem of risk, *and the final evaluation of a limited set of alternatives. Specific topics include:*

• *Why interpersonal sources may be as untrustworthy as commercials for giving accurate product information.*

• *How the trend toward informative advertising (nudged along by the consumer protection movement) may be doing consumers a disservice.*

• *How income and social class determine the sources people will listen to.*

• *Why some consumers invariably buy the most expensive brands (even when they can't comfortably afford them).*

• *How a store derives its "image."*

Once a choice has been made, the consumer enters the last two stages of the decision process, which will be discussed in chapter 17— purchasing and post-purchase evaluation.

How Buying Needs Arise

How do consumers finally decide to choose one brand or store over all others, once the various environmental and internal factors point to a final outcome? This question represents the "bottom line" of most consumer behavior theory and research, but marketers still find few reliable answers. What consumer research can now provide is a generalized description of the individual choice process, which must be applied to specific buying decisions and filled in with all available information about the market segment involved, the product, brand, or store itself, and the environmental and situational context in which the choice will be made.[1] This chapter examines consumer choice behavior from the perceived need for buying something, through the dynamics of brand and store choice, and leading to a discussion of actual purchasing processes in chapter 17.

There are three basic explanations of how buying needs arise in a consumer's frame of reference:

1. *The Motivation-Arousal Approach.* According to one popular model of consumer behavior, the need for a purchase is dictated by *motives* "derived from biogenic or psychogenic needs, wants, or desires of the buyer that are related to . . . consuming a product class or category."[2] Motives reflect both personality characteristics of the buyer and social environmental variables. The presence of motives creates a state of *arousal;* and a high state of arousal prompts *overt search* for information that will help the consumer gratify his or her particular motives. Search activities include looking for information from the mass media, from other marketer-dominated sources such as retail outlets, and from interpersonal contacts.

2. *The Problem-Recognition Approach.* A second widely accepted model of the consumer decision process contends that consumers recognize *problems* that must be solved through some buying activity.[3] Typical problems are running out of coffee or facing the dilemma of repairing a broken black-and-white television weighed against buying a much-preferred color set. In each case, there is a discrepancy between an *actual* state (the

problem) and a *desired* state (having the coffee or an operating television) that must be resolved through some form of consumption.

3. *The Conflict-Reduction Approach.* This explanation, taken directly from psychological learning theory, maintains that people respond to situations in relatively consistent ways, but the termination of a response places individuals in *conflict* situations with several different alternatives. And resulting behavior in these situations may be termed *choice* behavior.[4] Again, suddenly running out of coffee illustrates a response that is terminated, creating the need for a buying decision.

All these explanations, which take into account factors of learning, sociocultural influences, perception, attitude, personality, and situation, are widely used in consumer studies. But in the context of this chapter, choice behavior will be treated as *problem solving through information seeking and preference formation for a given brand or store.* From this perspective, choice behavior will be analyzed by examining exposure to information, search processes, environmental and individual determinants of choice, the role of risk perception, and the formation of brand and store choices.

Exposure and Search Behavior

In the preceding chapters, mass media influences and interpersonal communications were described as sources of consumer information. Here the exposure situations in which people confront these communications will be outlined as elements in the search process.

Exposure Situations

Hansen has identified three ways people may internalize communications about consumer goods and services: experience formation, forced learning, and information acquisition.[5]

Experience Formation This type of exposure occurs when a consumer has some direct contact with a product through actual use or engages in interpersonal communication about the item. The effects of experience

formation depend on the degree of conflict aroused, and such conflict comes about on the basis of the product's performance. If a pipe smoker who is "brand loyal" to one brand of tobacco happens to catch the aromatic whiff of another make from someone else's pipe, this experience may set up a conflict the smoker could resolve by trying out the other brand.

Forced Learning If a communication is to effect "forced" learning, it must create a conflict when the consumer is not looking for information. Advertising represents one type of communication "forced" on people, but they may quite effectively use perceptual screening to block out all but the most engaging ads and commercials. When a person who doesn't even chew gum begins inadvertently humming "Lets pick a pack from the Juicy Fruit Tree," we may say that forced learning has been effective. This mode of exposure may also come out of interpersonal communications, such as those between an uninterested customer and an aggressive retail salesperson.

Information Acquisition Here the consumer is actively seeking out information to resolve an existing conflict. Information acquisition will be directed by several variables, including familiarity and degree of conflict. If a consumer is already familiar with the problem at hand, information seeking will not be so extensive—the less familiarity there is with the problem, the more exploring will ensue. And the greater the conflict a consumer experiences, the more information he or she will try to acquire. It is this type of exposure that occurs during the process known as "search" behavior.

Search Behavior

A consumer may conduct two kinds of search processes, internal and external. *Internal* search entails recalling information already exposed to the individual's cognition. This process may include remembering past communications about some product category from either media or interpersonal sources; using past experience with a product as a guide to new decision making; and eliciting preformed attitudes toward the buying decision, product category, or brand in question. *External* search represents a conscious effort to seek out new information through communication with others; by monitoring ads about some product, going to a retail establishment, or clipping a coupon for a brochure; or by a variety of other behaviors directed toward information acquisition.[6] Both types of search may take place in the course of the same choice situation. A person may have some

internal experience to draw on, but still require additional information before making a choice.

Many choices bring only internal search into play. This is the case when a consumer is already experienced in a certain product category or is sufficiently convinced that buying the same brand again will satisfy the conflict causing search behavior.[7] Most purchases of foods and packaged goods that are familiar, convenient, and repetitive do not involve a great deal of external search.

When external search does occur, it is because the consumer perceives some reinforcement in taking the trouble to do it. External search means physical activity—paying attention to a commercial, going to a store, asking someone for information, leafing through a catalogue, and other time- and effort-consuming tasks. In addition, the longer a consumer spends in search behavior, the longer the choice and its resulting benefits are deferred. So the consumer must weigh the reinforcement value of the search against the reinforcement value of making a purchase immediately.[8] Once the decision to engage in external search is made, the next step is choosing the source of the information needed.

Media Selection The sources a consumer may refer to are: (1) *marketer-dominated* sources such as advertising, retail establishments, or promotional materials; (2) *interpersonal* sources drawn from reference groups such as relatives, friends, neighbors, work associates, or contact with salespeople; and (3) *objective* sources like *Consumer Reports* or other product-rating and consumer information services. There are several considerations that will determine the sources to be selected.

Product Considerations The product in question will affect source selection. In most search decisions, interpersonal sources are judged more reliable than marketer-dominated communications, but this is not true for all products and services. In some choice situations involving new or very technical products, product information supplied by manufacturers may be the most extensive, accurate, and readily available.

Source Considerations   The nature of a given source will often determine the circumstances under which consumers will turn to it. It has been emphasized that opinion leaders, for example, are not recognized as authorities on all products and services; instead, their expertise tends to cover a single product category or cluster or products related to their specific interests. Marketer communications are understandably regarded with some skepticism as biased, advocacy communications. Yet interpersonal sources, while seemingly unbiased, still are shaped by subjective factors—a person who asks a friend which motorcycle to buy will receive information that is heavily selective. Maybe the friend bought the one lemon in an otherwise very acceptable product line. Or perhaps the friend's needs which are met by one kind of motorcycle differ widely from the consumer's own needs for buying one. However, while objective sources of consumer information may offer the best rational evaluations of products, they are only ratings of a product's performance, and seldom take into consideration the needs for status, belonging, or life-style enhancement a certain product will meet for an individual consumer.

Research Findings on Search Behavior and Source Selection   Howard and Sheth have referred to a *psychology of simplification* in a consumer's search processes: The more people succeed in simplifying their environment, the less inclined they will be to engage

in external search.[9] Stated another way, consumers may use a "strategy" of simplification to make the decision process less trying.[10] In line with this view, the more a consumer's choices lean toward repeat purchases in a product category, the less time that individual will spend in active search behavior within that category. Bennett and Mandell investigated these hypotheses in a study of automobile choice behavior, assigning "weights" to the different sources a consumer might consult during or before a car purchase.[11] The different weights are used to classify sources by the amount of time and effort a buyer must devote to using them (Table 16-1).

These researchers found that, as the total number of *reinforced* purchases of a brand increases, the extent of active search concerning that particular brand will decrease. In selecting communications throughout the search process, car buyers who are brand loyal to a given make will attend to that marketer's communications to a greater degree than they will to those of competitors.

In a study of search processes associated with food shopping, Bucklin identified *personality* profiles that isolated women who were more likely to search for informtion in newspapers.[12] "Submissive wives," oriented toward satisfying husbands and children, revealed the greatest inclination to search through food advertising. Less likely to read such ads prior to shopping were "traditionalists," who tended to buy and prepare food in pretty much the same ways as their parents. And "liberated" women, who expressed high interest in politics and low regard for housewifely duties, exhibited the least concern with search behavior in food buying.

Bauer and Wortzel probed *media selection* in the highly specialized realm of doctors' preferred sources of information about new

Table 16-1   Weighting Information Sources

INFORMATION SOURCE	WEIGHT[a]
Consumer Reports	18
Dealer visit	18
Expert opinion[b]	12
Friends' opinion	10
Reading brochures[c]	10
Discussion with spouse	9
Auto show	7
Advertisements	7
News articles	6
Discussion with children	3
Total	100

[a]Weights indicate the relative amount of effort required to use the particular source.

[b]Expert could be mechanic or "purchase pal" with special knowledge of automobiles, either of a technical or economic nature.

[c]Indicates the actual reading of brochure, usually picked up at "Dealer Visit."

Source: Peter D. Bennett and Robert M. Mandell, "Prepurchase Information Seeking Behavior of New Car Purchasers: The Learning Hypothesis," Journal of Marketing Research, Vol. 6 (November 1969). Reprinted by permission of the American Marketing Association.

prescription drugs.[13] Because physicians are constantly overloaded with communications from drug manufacturers, colleagues, and medical journals, they are obliged to use selective screening to receive any meaningful information at all. Doctors, apparently, allow advertising to perform their initial screening; they depend upon communications from drug companies to alert them to drugs deserving further investigation. In this exposure situation, doctors devote as much time as possible to high information sources like detail men (pharmaceutical salesmen) and sources that may be quickly screened, such as journal advertising. Medicines for treating severe conditions or whose action may be uncertain are set aside for future search. This usually occurs through interpersonal contacts with colleagues for more information, because: (1) the amount of information provided by drug companies may not be sufficient, and (2) at a high level of prescribing risk, drug manufacturers' communications may not be entirely trustworthy. But Bauer and Wortzel also discovered that the source that first alerts doctors to a new drug is likely to be the source that ultimately leads to their prescribing it (Table 16-2).

Information Load   It has been noted that consumers incur certain costs in seeking out information such as spending time, attending to media, and devoting effort to processing what they see and hear. Since the trend in marketing today is toward giving consumers more information than has ever been available before, the question of how much information a consumer can actually handle arises. In the search process, there is a hypothesized point at which an individual feels confronted with an overwhelming load of information and begins to restrict search behavior accordingly.[14]

One study by Jacoby, Kohn, and Speller tested this hypothesis on the basis of product information in packaging, and concluded that consumers will spend more time acquiring package information as the number of brands increases, up to about sixteen. But they will generally stop their search behavior when the number of informative points about a brand hits twelve or higher, no matter how the information is organized.[15]

Another investigation of information load suggests that the ability to choose a "best" brand was less functional at low and high levels of "load" than at medium levels.[16]

*The Patient as Consumer: Finding the Right Doctor**

Although they seldom admit to it in so many words, physicians are technically in the business of offering medical services for sale to consumers. They seek and make handsome profits. Their practices are frequently incorporated, and many hire staffs of bookkeepers, receptionists, and other personnel to control the flow of their "customers."

Yet a paradox exists in that, as professional people, doctors are barred by the International Code of Medical Ethics from behaving like business people in ways such as advertising their services.

Most physicians say that their patients' wants and needs are their primary concern. But while marketers recognize that customer service is a function of the *total* product or service offering, physicians seem to feel that adequate medical care is all the patient wants. This lack of concern for total patient satisfaction is reflected in common practices such as:

1. Not keeping appointments on time, usually due to overbooking appointments or inefficient processing. The patient, who feels that his or her time is also valuable, waits an hour or more at the mercy of available reading matter—generally out-of-date medical journals.

2. Maintaining a cavalier attitude on the part of physician and staff. In this second manifestation of an attitude which suggests that only the doctor's time is valuable, the patient is made to feel anxious about asking for information that will provide peace of mind about symptoms.

Prescribing medicine by brand name rather than the much more economical generic drugs, which are just as effective. (Some doctors, of course, own drugstores and profit from this loyalty to the expensive brands.)

4. Not making house calls, failing to take phone calls after office hours, and leaving the office at the stroke of 6 p.m., even if there are patients still waiting.

5. Maintaining a double standard on formality—calling a patient by first name while insisting on titles for doctor and staff.

6. Instituting a cash-or-cure basis for payment—no cash, no cure. Fortunately, most doctors offer more liberal credit terms than this, but it is difficult to know unless one asks beforehand.

Because there is a distinct seller's market—fewer physicians per patients than would encourage a more competitive orientation—consumers are advised to note the foregoing considerations. Most become apparent on the first visit to the office, or even on the first telephone contact.

Assuming that all physicians are equally competent, the patient may best be advised to make telephone inquiries of different doctors to determine office hours and house-call policies, credit terms, and other important factors in the doctor-patient relationship.

*James S. West and A. B. Blankenship, "The Physician and the Marketing Concept," *Journal of the Academy of Marketing Science*, Vol. 3, No. 2 (Spring 1975). Adapted with permission.

Table 16-2   Relationship of Original Information Source to "Convincing" Source in Doctors' Search Behavior for New Prescription Drugs

	SOURCE OF FIRST NOTICE				
CONVINCING SOURCE	JOURNAL	DETAIL MAN	MAIL ADVERTISEMENT	OTHER	ALL SOURCES
Journal	63.6%	14.3%	22.1%	9.2%	28.6%
Detail Man	4.6	51.2	5.5	2.3	21.3
Mail Advertisement	5.0	11.6	44.8	5.4	15.5
Other	26.8	22.9	27.6	83.1	34.6
TOTAL	100.0%	100.0%	100.0%	100.0%	100.0%
Base:	(220)	(293)	(163)	(130)	(806)

Source: Raymond A. Bauer and Lawrence H. Wortzel, "Doctor's Choice: The Physician and his Source of Information About Drugs," Journal of Marketing Research, Vol. 3 (February 1966), p. 42. Reprinted by permission of the American Marketing Association.

And a third study probing information load in supermarket items poses three considerations for marketers:[17]

1. *If there is an optimal "load," does it vary according to the market segment under scrutiny?* We might expect a younger consumer group to be able to use more information than the elderly, and highly educated individuals to include more information in their search than the undereducated and economically disadvantaged.

2. *Assuming that the amount of information should be restricted to an optimal level, what kinds of information should be provided?* This question becomes critical as more complete

disclosure of costs, ingredients, contracts, and other variables are demanded by consumer groups and regulated by government agencies.

3. *Once an optimal load of information is arrived at for specific products, how should the information be organized?* This applies to advertising, packaging, and other communications that must draw attention to themselves while conveying information. Advertisers in heavily regulated industries such as drugs, insurance, and banking are finding it more challenging than ever to design provocative advertising when selling propositions must be supported by explanatory copy.

How Environmental and Individual Influences Affect Choice Behavior: A Review

As the decision making component of consumer behavior, the choice process is influenced by virtually all the determinants outlined in the first half of this book: mass culture, subcultures, social class, the family unit; and individual variables of learning, perception, attitudes, and personality. These influences may be analyzed in two broad categories—sociocultural and individual—and a brief review of them will be helpful at this point.

Sociocultural Determinants

Consumer behavior research has traditionally linked choice behavior to sociological theories of reference group influence and family decision making. More recently, cultural determinants of the choice process are

appearing in cross-cultural research for multinational markets.

Mass Culture In any culture, patterns of exposure to information sources reflect the institutions and values of that cultural setting. In the United States, the mass media represent a socializing institution as well as a source of marketer communications. Thus, consumers screen the media for "opinion leader" cues as to what other people are buying to wear, eat, or amuse themselves. Because American culture both sustains and reflects the goals of the marketing system, many interpersonal communications revolve around consumption. "Did you see that movie?" "Have you tried the restaurant where they slice and cook the steak at your table?" So when a conflict occurs that must be resolved with some buying choice, there is no shortage of information to seek out. In fact, there is usually an overabundance of information when we do not need it. This may not be the case in other cultures where people are not so affluent and have learned to be somewhat guarded about their purchase behavior. In underdeveloped nations, such as India, and in Soviet countries, which cling to a more socialistic philosophy, our means of seeking information about purchases would be frowned upon.

Subcultures Because a subculture pursues a life style all its own while adopting features of the dominant culture, there are aspects of choice behavior unique to virtually any subcultural grouping. In the United States, black consumers have generally been described as more brand-loyal than white consumers, which would suggest that blacks devote less time to external search behavior. (However, recent research points to patterns of "disloyalty" emerging.)[18] On the other hand, black consumers are often regarded as more susceptible to advertising appeals than their white counterparts, which would indicate that blacks are more often exposed to the mass media and may lean toward them as an information source.[19] In other ethnic subcultures, there are patterns of differential choice behavior, particularly in brand and store preference. Japanese-Americans appear to be particularly search-conscious, mentioning considerably more information sources than white consumers and other groups in comparison studies. Of all sources, advertising is the one Japanese-Americans are most likely to consult.[20]

The subculture of the aging has also revealed special search behaviors, although they are in the direction of *reduced* search. The elderly tend to choose products and services on the basis of brand loyalty, established store preferences, and reliance on internal search and personal judgment rather than on interpersonal or media communications.[21] In a study of search behavior displayed by low-income households, Block notes that the poor are most likely to seek information from television and newspapers, and that the helpfulness of product information sources in making choices is related to education. The better-educated poor make more use of different sources in search processes. One conclusion from this study is the variation of behavior that takes place even in homogeneous low-income neighborhoods. The poor do not behave uniformly in search processes because of demographic differences among them—in income and, especially, education.[22]

Reference Groups When consumers succumb to conformity pressures, their search activities necessarily become limited. This is the pattern in most reference group influence, where conformity demands restrict search from mass media sources and channel it through the personal interactions of the dominant group. Bourne found that reference group pressure is most likely to affect products and services that are *conspicuous.* These include items such as cars, cigarettes, and beer.[23] Whyte discovered a similar pattern of interpersonal communication dictating choices of air conditioners in one suburban neighborhood.[24] And in a study of attitudes toward the Volkswagen Bug when it was a novelty, Cook noted that members of cohesive groups exhibiting similar social characteristics were more susceptible to interpersonal attitude change than more independent consumers.[25]

Social Class Several differences in the search behavior of various social classes have been isolated by Levy.[26] Lower-strata people are more inclined to view television as an information source than upper middle-class consumers, who lean toward print media, especially magazines. Upper middle-class people in general are more critical of advertising, skeptical about claims, and are often insulted by the straightforwardness and literal selling approaches aimed at lower-class groups. In search behavior at the retail level, lower-class consumers display more anxiety about the decision-making process and like to confine their shopping excursions to neighborhood stores where they are assured a friendly reception and easy credit. Upper middle-class shoppers are less likely to search in the retail setting, since they are more knowledgeable about what they want before they begin shopping. While a number of studies conclude that upper-strata people tend to search less in general, some controversy surrounds this finding.[27] Bucklin has identified two separate groups in the lower social strata who reveal markedly varying search behavior. Families identified as *transient* demonstrate little search activity, which may result from living in temporary, rented apartments they intend to vacate, a general dissatisfaction with their position in life, and low self-confidence. *Bleak future* households, on the other hand, consist of older people in dire economic straits who feel that things will get even worse. This group was the most likely of all to become involved in search behavior.[28]

The Family Unit Considerable attention has been directed to the family as a decision making unit, because marketers want to know which members play what roles at every stage of the choice process. Traditional research suggests that information acquisition and choice are largely product-specific in household decisions.[29] Husbands dominate

search behavior aimed at cars, tires, and photographic equipment.[30] Wives tend to conduct most of the choice process over products like washing machines, vacuum cleaners, and such day-to-day family packaged goods as toothpaste.[31] This hypothesis rests on the assumption that the family member most likely to use the product will be the most directly involved in the choice. However, husbands and wives do not always agree on who is more influential.[32] *Collective*, or joint, decision making thus occurs when decisions are major, such as buying a new home or life insurance.[33] But with changing sex roles, emancipation of women, and other developments affecting family decisions, there is much evidence that traditional roles in choice behavior are changing.

Individual Determinants

Individuals' effects upon their choice process may be viewed in terms of learning, perception, attitude, and personality.

Learning Consumer choice behavior represents selective responses to cues in the product environment. To form responses appropriate to the situation, the consumer acquires new information about the choice problem at hand, investigating the product category and selectively deciding upon one choice over others.

The role of brand loyalty is a popular theme in consumer choice research. Brand loyalty has been described as an *internal* search process negatively related to the need for external search. If a consumer develops a loyalty to some brand of shaving cream, he may be expected to resolve the conflict of needing a new can of Noxzema by buying another can of Noxzema, rather than undertaking the process of acquiring information about Rise and Foamy. In general, consumers tend to be *less* loyal to products with many available brands, where frequency of purchase and expenditure are high, prices are active, and consumers might use a number of brands of the same product simultaneously. Consumers are inclined to observe *greater* loyalty to products with brands widely distributed, and where market share tends to be concentrated in one leading brand.[34]

Perception   The process of perception enters into choice decisions in three ways. For one, *selective* perception operates during information acquisition, screening out sources that deliver irrelevant information and directing attention to communications that are pertinent to the particular choice problem. Secondly, perception of *product attributes* such as price, quality, packaging, and other factors will help to determine the final product choice. Price information has been shown to be positively related to quality judgments about different products; likewise, recognizable brand names generally lead to judgments of higher quality than unrecognizable brands. The role of product attributes in consumer choice will be analyzed later in this chapter. Third, perception of *risk* comes into play at various levels of the choice process—in seeking out and accepting communications, in weighing alternatives, and in making the final product choice. As noted in chapter 10, risk characterizes many purchasing decisions not commonly thought of as "risky" such as packaged goods, food, and other inexpensive items, as well as considered-purchase, high-ticket, or highly visible purchases. The influence of risk perception will also be covered in greater detail later in this chapter.

Personality   One measure of personality is *self-concept* or, more specifically, the distinction between "actual" self-concept (the way we actually see ourselves) and "idealized" self-concept (the way we would *like* to see ourselves and have others see us). When self-concept measures have been applied to brand choice, the common finding is that idealized self-concept explains consumer preferences to a greater degree than actual self-concept.[36] In other words, people choose products that afford them the personality characteristics they would like to possess. A middle-aged housewife chooses sensuous evening dresses to assure herself and others that she is still attractive. A moderate-income individual pays attention to ads that imply a certain product will help that person attain an upper-income life style more in line with his or her idealized preferences.

In the search for information, personality variables also suggest that people with certain characteristics are more susceptible to information than others. Green notes that consumers who are most receptive to information during search exhibit greater confidence, independence, and open-mindedness than those who tend to reject information.[37]

Attitudes   Research suggests that a reliable measure of consumer attitudes may be the most powerful predictor of brand choice. But there are also indications that choice behavior is not consistent even when attitudes are.[38]

Ginter researched attitude change resulting from advertising exposure as one variable in choice of a new product brand, drawing these conclusions:[39]

• Over a period of several weeks, consumers' choice of a new brand was correlated with both a change in attitude toward the brand and their exposure to advertising.

Advertising folk protested vigorously when the French supermarket chain Carrefour introduced its fifty house-brand *produits libres*—products in white wrappers with nothing other than the generic name of what was inside to distinguish them.

But consumers seemed to like the idea, since Carrefour's unbranded products soon accounted for 30 percent of the store's total sales.

Carrefour's Marketing Director contends that:[35]

. . . a growing segment of the public wants simple things, packaged plainly. Coffee called coffee, rice called rice, oil called oil. And not 4 kilos 470, but simply 5 kilos. Packaging, moreover, should give information, not bonuses or trips to the Caribbean.

But critics in the advertising profession argue that the entire business system will collapse if branded merchandise must face "unfair" competition, and particularly if other retailers follow Carrefour's lead.

Reaction in the United States has been quiet, perhaps in anticipation of what finally evolves from the French debate.

Free products from France.

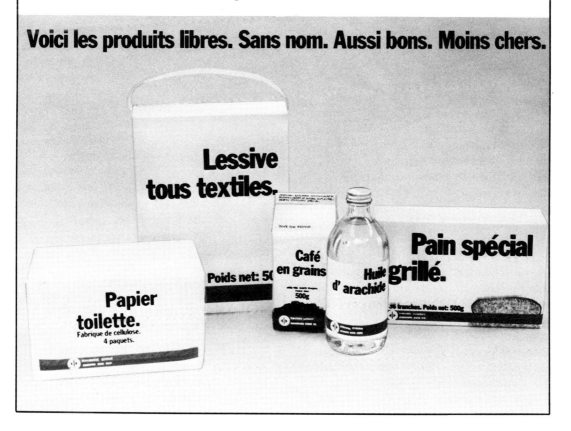

• A significant change in attitude was recorded twice—both before and after the actual choice of the new brand. And choice of the new brand on two occasions increased the probability of choosing it a third time (a development of brand loyalty).

This study was addressed to the question of whether attitude change precedes or follows a new brand choice. The results indicate that change can occur at both times, which offers support for advertising communications designed to effect attitude change. *When such messages are introduced during consumer's search processes in that product category,* there is reason to believe that they may be persuaded to try a new item that would not otherwise enter into their information domain.

The Role of Risk in Choice Behavior

As noted often throughout the text, most buying decisions contain an element of risk, no matter how inexpensive the choice may be. Many people like to leaf through magazines before they actually buy them, because they want to be sure that their 75-cent purchase is going to reward them with something they want to read about. Buying a relatively expensive item like a clock radio multiplies the risks involved. What if it's a lemon? Even if there's a money-back guarantee, the time and effort expended in getting it repaired (let alone the annoyance of being without it for the duration) are possibilities that cross many consumers' minds. And what if some other manufacturer makes a better radio you don't know about yet that might even cost less than the one at hand?

Financial risk is the most obvious chance one takes in making a consumer choice, and it looms larger the longer one expects to live with the choice. The risks in buying a house or condominium guarantee sleepless nights for even the shrewdest consumers. *Performance* risk entails anxiety about whether or not the item under consideration will do what it is supposed to do.

Then there is also the problem of *psycho-* social risk. Even if a consumer reconciles the chancy elements of loss of time or money in a choice decision, will the choice prove embarrassing before family, friends, business associates, or neighbors? The risk that such discomfort will ensue is increased by the conspicuousness of the item under consideration.

A Model of Risk

The study of risk-taking in consumer choice behavior has become sufficiently formalized to warrant a comprehensive model developed by James W. Taylor (Figure 16-1).

Identifying choice as the central problem of consumer behavior, Taylor notes that because risk is anxiety producing and painful, consumers must deal with it in some way in order to make choices:[40]

Any choice situation always involves two aspects of risk: uncertainty about the outcome and uncertainty about the consequences. Uncertainty about the outcome can be reduced by acquiring and "handling" information. Uncertainty about the consequences can be dealt with by reducing the conse-

Figure 16-1 A model of risk-taking in consumer choice behavior.

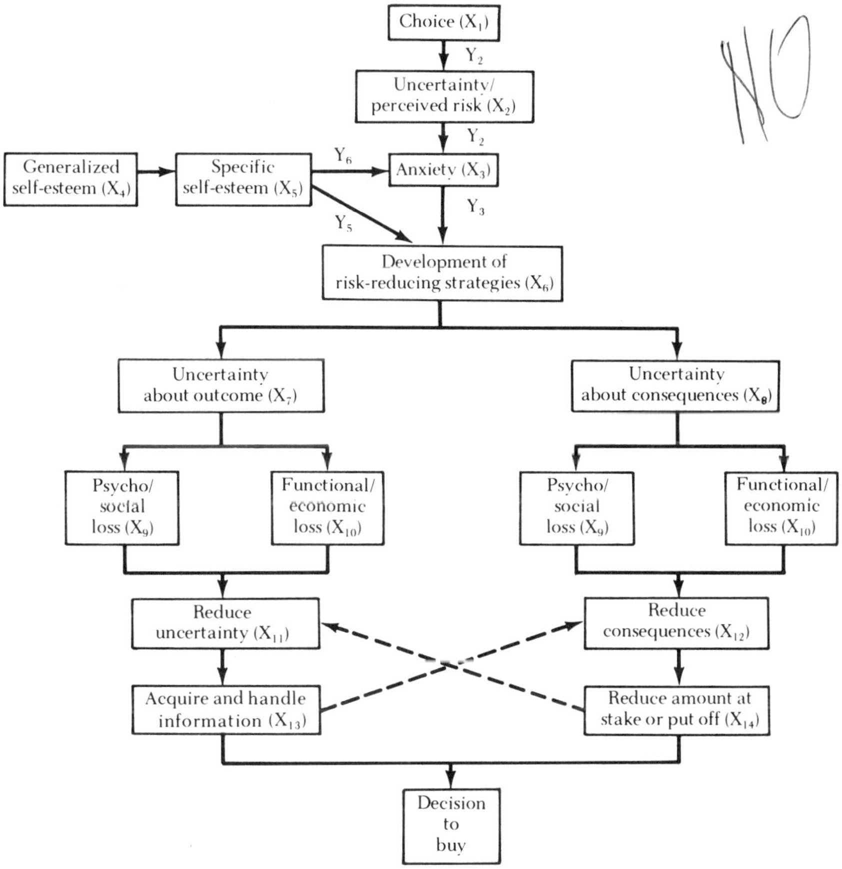

Source: James W. Taylor, "The Role of Risk in Consumer Behavior," Journal of Marketing, *Vol. 38 (April 1974). Reprinted with permission of the American Marketing Association.*

quences through reducing the amount at stake or putting off the choice. In a choice situation, risk can be interpreted in terms of possible loss. The loss can be in psychosocial terms or in functional/economic terms, or in some combination of both forms of loss.

Taylor's model may be used to approximate consumer choice situations by measuring: (1) self-confidence in relation to the given product category; (2) perceived risk in the product category choice; (3) type of loss associated with the product category; (4) perceived risk in brand choice; (5) preferences for various risk-reducing strategies; and (6) the sizes of consumer segments with common characteristics in perceiving risk, self-confidence, and preferred risk-reduction strategies.[41]

Risk-Reducing Strategies

Knoee

Although they may not be fully aware of them, consumers develop "strategies" of risk reduction that enable them to cope with the anxiety of choice decisions.[42] These have been classified by Bauer into six different approaches:[43]

1. *Buying only a certain brand.* This strategy is known as brand loyalty. Bauer suggests that people high in perceived risk should also be high in brand loyalty, since this is one way to control a hazardous choice. Cunningham adds that brand loyalty appears to be related to the type of risk perceived by consumers; the more *serious* the risk, the greater the probability that brand loyalty will be established. However, the relationship between brand loyalty and perceived risk is not as simple as is sometimes thought. Even consumers who score high in risk-perception will try new brands when it seems sensible (usually after a cautionary period). The motivation for this is usually to "find a better brand."[44]

2. *Buying only nationally advertised brands.* Many consumers feel that if a brand is not exposed to the consumer through frequent advertising messages, it is somehow inferior. In some cases, this is true; off-brands may be of poorer quality because they do not undergo the same quality control process that most large manufacturers maintain. But often the little-known or private brand is just as good as, or better than, its mighty competitors who can afford vast advertising expenditures. A supermarket's private brands of foods, for example, come from the same suppliers the nationally advertised brands use. And even a movie camera whose name is unfamiliar may be technically the same as a make whose name

is a household word—because both cameras are also made by the same supplier.

3. *Buying only the cheapest brand.* While the quality of the brand may not measure up to others costing more, the consumer is at least satisfied that it was obtained for the lowest price. For most consumers, this is not their usual strategy. Most Americans believe in a relationship between price and quality and are willing to pay slightly more for brands which they perceive as no better. In some cases, though, buying the cheapest brand is a very effective strategy indeed. Aspirin, the usual example of a generic drug, should be just as effective at 29 cents for 100 as it is in a branded jar at 89 cents for fifty. This is true of other products that are essentially the same no matter what the brand–gasoline and most detergents are examples. But even if the generic product is the same no matter what the price, there may be differences in the retail or service establishment that would predispose consumers to go elsewhere. Local car rental companies, for instance, may rent the same models as Hertz, Avis, and National for less, but probably won't offer as many extras in maintenance, multiple locations, fast airport check-ins, and other conveniences.

4. *Buying only the most expensive brand.* Some consumers who perceive high risk in virtually all choices select only the highest priced brands, under the assumption that if they cost the most, they must necessarily be the best. This amounts to an exaggerated perception of the price-quality relationship, and is not always valid. Many brands are more expensive because of more costly advertising and packaging, or because the marketer consciously wants to present the brand as the "most expensive in the world." Only a small minority of consumers adopt this approach regularly, since most recognize that price

is not the only measure of quality and because, in many choices, they are willing to sacrifice a small measure of quality for a better buy.

5. *Buying only a small amount of the product.* According to this strategy, risk in any choice is minimized by "being stuck with" the least amount of a brand if it is unsatisfactory for some reason. The familiar practice of promoting a new brand in small, "get acquainted" packages is a means of attempting to reduce the risk consumers perceive in trying out some innovative product or new label. Again, this is not a common overall strategy, since most consumers become accustomed to buying standard sized packages, in as great a quantity as they feel they will actually require to meet the need for the choice.

6. *Buying only products with a plain and functional design.* Underlying this approach is the assumption that product "frills" such as design or packaging are expensive and unnecessary. Most consumers are not happy with totally spartan products, though—particularly when they must make choices to meet needs for self-esteem, social acceptance, and other personal life-style requirements.

All consumers use these strategies at one time or another in making choices. But there is a current need for research to indicate when certain strategies are likely to be applied to specific product categories and how they are associated with consumer personality profiles.

[handwritten: (8) warrentees - if product has - then risk is reduced. (7) Dealership - go back to same dealer. professional advice (5)]

Assessment of Product and Store Attributes

In making a product or store choice, consumers must selectively eliminate many alternatives to focus on a few possible choices. The number of possibilities they will consider in search processes is subject to interpretation by different researchers for different product categories, but the consensus is that alternatives are few.

The concept of *evoked set* has been advanced to describe the subset of products or brands a buyer actually considers in a specific brand choice.[46] There is much evidence of a limit on the number of brands in a buyer's evoked set, although this will vary across product categories. Campbell points out that few consumers exhibit an evoked set of more than seven items, and individual buyers are conistent in the size of their evoked sets for different products.[47] Many studies indicate

a small evoked set for purchases of different products. Dommermuth and Cundiff found that 50 to 70 percent of the consumers choosing appliances in one study considered only the brand they finally purchased.[48] Campbell, investigating packaged goods purchases, discovered that consumers in his study limited themselves to between three and five alternatives.[49]

And other research points to a conclusion that the number of product or store *attributes* on which consumers base their choices are just as limited. Katona and Mueller tested one sample to find that more than 60 percent based their brand choices on three attributes or less.[50] Kelly uncovered the same restrictions in store choice; more than 90 percent of the consumers he surveyed con-

"Net Perceived Return" May Be the Best Decision Strategy for Car Choice

A recent study by Peter and Tarpey compared three types of decision-making strategies to explain brand preference for different makes of cars. These were (1) *risk-reduction*—described at some length in this chapter; (2) *perceived return*—maximizing expected gain to the consumer; and (3) *net perceived return*—the expected net "payoff" after gains and losses are weighed.

Net Perceived Return explained more of the variance in brand preference than the other two, with risk-reduction the second most potent explanatory strategy.

Sample questions presented here were used with others to ferret out consumer expectations about the types of risks and gains they perceived for each car choice. (Small and medium-sized models such as the Mazda, Vega, Malibu, and VW Dasher were under scrutiny.) For instance:[45]

IMPROBABLE   PROBABLE

1. I think that it is 1 2 3 4 5 6 7 that the purchase of a (Brand) would lead to a financial loss for me because of such things as its poor warranty, high maintenance costs, and/or high monthly payments.

2. As far as I'm concerned, if this financial loss happened to me, it would be 1 2 3 4 5 6 7
   Important   Unimportant
      Improbable   Probable

3. I think that it is 1 2 3 4 5 6 7 that the purchase of a (Brand) would lead to a social loss for me because my friends and relatives would think less highly of me.

4. As far as I'm concerned, if this social loss happened to me, it would be 1 2 3 4 5 6 7
   Important   Unimportant

IMPROBABLE   PROBABLE

5. I think that it is 1 2 3 4 5 6 7 that the purchase of a (Brand) would lead to a physical gain for me because it would be very safe and would remain safe.

6. As far as I'm concerned, if this physical gain happened to me, it would be 1 2 3 4 5 6 7
   Important   Unimportant
      Improbable   Probable

7. I think that it is 1 2 3 4 5 6 7 that the purchase of a (Brand) would lead to a gain in convenience for me because I would not have to waste much time and effort getting it adjusted and repaired.

8. As far as I'm concerned, if this gain in convenience happened to me, it would be 1 2 3 4 5 6 7
   Unimportant   Important

Consumers apparently hold two kinds of expectations about automobile brands: (1) expected performance, and (2) expectations about how the brand will fit into the buyer's self-image and group image.

sidered three factors or less in making patron-age decisions.[51] What attributes, then, do consumers rely on in making choices?

Product Attributes

The salient characteristics of products to most consumers are pricing, quality, and (to a lesser extent) complexity, durability, visibility, and multipurposeness. The first two attributes are usually considered together as a *relationship.*

The Price-Quality Relationship This rela-tionship, discussed in terms of perception has emerged as an influential factor in choice behavior.[52]

McConnell investigated the influence of consumers' knowledge of price on their appraisal of quality in a widely studied prod-uct—beer.[53] He found that when consumers were asked to rate the quality of three dif-ferent, little-known beer brands (all of which contained exactly the same brew), they per-ceived the highest priced brand as the highest quality beer. And the medium priced brand was seen as marginally better than the lowest priced.

In other research, the price-quality rela-tionship has been shown to influence national brand selections over private brands and perception of recognizable brand names as being of higher quality than unrecognizable brands.[54] Gardner, however, notes in one study that a price-quality relationship may not hold for all products in all situations. He found that perceptions of quality based on price tended to increase with the cost of the item; while toothpaste choices did not reveal the price-quality perception, it became more evident in choice of men's shirts and suits.[55]

Complexity, Visibility, Durability, and Multi-purposeness Settle examined these four attributes by determining the *types of infor-mation* a consumer will pick out in the search process for each attribute. The three criteria he used in "validating" attributes were:[56]

1. *Consistency over time:* Each time the item is present, the individual's reactions must be the same, or nearly so.

2. *Consistency over modality:* The individ-ual's reaction must be consistent even though his or her mode of interaction with the thing varies.

3. *Consensus:* attributes of external origin are experienced the same way by all ob-servers—a form of "social support."

Through this procedure, he found sup-port for hypothesized relationships about how product attributes affect information acquisition:[57]

Complexity When a very complex product is considered (a stereo tuner or wristwatch), a consumer receives more assurance from *consensus* information offered by an expert than from other sources.

Visibility When a highly *visible* product is at stake, (a skirt or sweater), more assurance will be provided from *consensus* information absorbed through personal experience than from other sources.

Durability Given a highly durable product (such as electric hair curlers or earrings), consumers look for assurance in *consistency* information provided by personal experience.

Multipurposeness With a multipurpose product (such as an electric blender), con-sumers receive the greatest assurance from *consistency* information supplied through personal experience over several modes of use.

Store Attributes

In making store choices, consumers assess attributes that include location, physical appearance, size and merchandise assortment, pricing policies, service policies, advertising and promotion, and clientele. Collectively, these attributes may be perceived by consumers as a store's "image."

Location As a general relationship, the greater the distance from a consumer's home to a store, the less likely he or she will be to patronize that store (Figure 16-2). However, there is mounting evidence that more consumers are "out-of-town" shoppers for certain items; these include expensive clothing, items such as men's suits, women's coats and formal dresses, and home accessories.

Figure 16-2 The effect of store distance on demand.

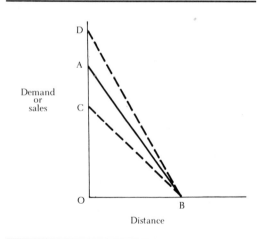

Source: Gunnar Olson, "Central Place Systems, Spatial Interaction and Stochastic Processes," Regional Science Association: Papers, *Vol. 18 (1968), p. 15.*

Profiles of people who shop out-of-town tend to portray them as higher socioeconomically, and younger than those who shop near home.[58]

Physical Appearance How a store looks will determine, to a degree, who chooses to shop there, because appearance tends to reflect pricing and service policies as well as the store's particular ambience, or "image." All other things being equal, an attractive supermarket kept spotlessly clean will draw more consumers than a bleak and shabby one. Appearance becomes especially important in department stores, fashion boutiques, and other establishments where socially visible items are sold. (The effect of internal layout on consumer purchasing will be analyzed in greater detail in chapter 17.)

Size and Merchandise Assortment These attributes are often interrelated—larger stores tend to have more merchandise and, as a rule, a larger assortment will attract a greater number of customers. Stores may be the same size, however, but offer very different assortments of merchandise in quality, pricing, or fashion-consciousness. Department stores, for example, may be classified as "high prestige," "full-line," "chain," or "discount," each adopting somewhat different merchandising policies.

Pricing Policies While pricing will determine, in some instances, the clientele a store attracts, there is no *positive* relationship between price and patronage behavior—except that people in different socioeconomic strata tend to patronize different stores. This finding has been related more closely to other factors, particularly store image.[59] The most popular full-line department store in New York at this moment prices many clothing items above the same merchandise in stores associated with "higher" fashion-consciousness.

Service Policies Included in this category are such variables as the credit plans offered (if any), the type of return and product-service options provided, and the caliber of the salespeople. Availability of credit is important to many consumers, although the ways in which people will use credit plans are related to demographic, social class, and life-style characteristics of individual shoppers.[60] The nature of return and exchange policies and the salespeople employed are also salient attributes that will be discussed more fully in the following chapter.

Advertising and Promotion There are two basic types of advertising stores use to build traffic and store loyalty. One offers specific information about merchandise and pricing; the other is of an institutional variety designed to convey the store's image to the market segment most likely to be attracted by it. It is usually difficult to determine which approach is most effective in stimulating patronage and which is really responsible for building long-term store loyalties. But,

generally, a store's advertising conveys information about its merchandise assortment, pricing, and other factors which is obviously aimed at a particular demographic segment of shoppers. An entrepreneur in New York once built a chain-store empire out of a small appliance shop by directing his advertising appeal only to union members and civil service workers; by showing a union card at the door, consumers obtained discounts, even on fair-traded items.

Clientele People tend to shop where members of their various reference groups shop, including friends, neighbors, and others who reflect the same socioeconomic level and life styles. Because every retail establishment must define some segment of the general shopper population to attract, retailers must weigh all of the attributes their individual stores possess, decide upon their prime segments accordingly, and skew advertising and promotion to those segments.

With this overview of consumer choice behavior for brands and stores as a conceptual framework, the following chapter will analyze actual *purchasing* processes in retail and other environments.

Summary

The central issue in consumer behavior research is how consumers actually choose one brand or store over another, once environmental and individual influences have come into play. Consumer *choice* behavior is described here as the resolution of conflict through information seeking and preference formation for a given brand or store. The first element affecting choice behavior is the *exposure* situation, which may occur through experience formation, forced learning, or information acquisition. The last is referred to as the *search* process. In seeking information about a buying decision that will resolve a conflict, consumers selectively choose the communications they will attend to on the basis of source and situational considerations. When information overwhelms the consumer, this is known as information load, and will bring an end to the choice process if it is not reversed. Choice behavior is also affected by a number of sociocultural and environmental influences, including mass culture and subcultures, reference groups, social class, the family decision unit, learning, perception, and personality. Critical to the problem of choice behavior is the role of *perceived risk,* which consumers may attempt to overcome through risk-reduction strategies. In making choices, consumers limit themselves to a few alternatives known as the *evoked set.* This set includes the attributes of the brands or stores under consideration.

NOTES

1. See Russel W. Belk, "Situational Variables and Consumer Behavior," *Journal of Consumer Research,* Vol. 2, No. 3 (December 1975), p. 157; William J. McGuire, "Some Internal Psychological Factors Influencing Choice Behavior," *Journal of Consumer Research,* Vol. 2, No. 4 (March 1976), p. 302; and Kent. B. Monroe, "The Influence of Price Differences and Brand Familiarity on Brand Preferences," *Journal of Consumer Research,* Vol. 3, No. 1 (June 1976), p. 42.

2. John A. Howard and Lyman E. Ostlund, *Buyer Behavior* (New York: Alfred A. Knopf, Inc., 1973), p. 16.

3. James F. Engel, David T. Kollat, and Roger D. Blackwell, *Consumer Behavior,* 2nd ed. (New York: Holt, Rinehart and Winston), 1973, pp. 352–355.

4. Flemming Hansen, *Consumer Choice Behavior: A Cognitive Approach* (New York: The Free Press, 1972), p. 37.

5. Hansen, *Consumer Choice,* pp. 165–180.

6. G. David Hughes, Seka M. Tunic and Philippe A. Naest, "Analyzing Consumer Information Processing," in *Marketing Involvement in the Society and the Economy,* ed. Philip R. McDonald (Chicago: American Marketing Association, 1969).

7. Robert F. Kelley, "The Search Component of the Consumer Decision Process: A Theoretical Examination," in *Marketing and the New Science of Planning,* ed. Robert L. King (Chicago: American Marketing Association, 1968).

8. John T. Lanzetta and Vera Kanareff, "Information Cost, Amount of Payoff, and Level of Aspiration as Determinants of Information Seeking in Decision Making," *Behavioral Science,* Vol. 7 (1962).

9. John A. Howard and Jagdish N. Sheth, "Theory of Buyer Behavior," in *Changing Marketing Systems: Consumer, Corporate and Government Interfaces,* ed. Reed Moyer, *Proceedings of the Winter Conference of the American Marketing Association,* 1967.

10. Peter Wright, "Consumer Choice Strategies: Simplifying vs. Optimizing," *Journal of Marketing Research,* Vol. 12, No. 1 (February 1975), p. 60.

11. Peter D. Bennett and Robert M. Mandell, "Prepurchase Information Seeking Behavior of New Car Purchases: The Learning Hypothesis," *Journal of Marketing Research,* Vol. 6 (November 1969).

12. Louis P. Bucklin, "Consumer Search, Role Enactment, and Market Efficiency," *Journal of Business,* Vol. 42 (October 1969).

13. Raymond A. Bauer and Lawrence H. Wortzel, "Doctor's Choice: The Physician and His Sources of Information about Drugs," *Journal of Marketing Research,* Vol. 3 (February 1966).

14. Jacob Jacoby, Carol A. Kohn, and Donald E. Speller, "Time Spent Acquiring Information as a Function of Information Load and Organization," *Proceedings of the American Psychological Association's 81st Annual Convention,* 1973.

15. Jacoby et. al., "Acquiring Information."

16. J. Jacoby, D. E. Speller, and C. A. Kohn, "Brand Choice Behavior as a Function of Information Load," *Journal of Marketing Research,* Vol. 11, No. 1 (February 1974), pp. 63–69.

17. J. Jacoby, D. E. Speller, and C. Kohn

Benning, "Brand Choice Behavior as a Function of Information Load: Replication and Extension," *Journal of Consumer Research*, Vol. 1 (June 1974).

18. W. L. Evans, "Ghetto Marketing, What Now?", in *Science of Planning*, ed. Robert L. King.

19. B. Stuart Tolley and John J. Goett, "Reactions to Blacks in Newspapers," *Journal of Advertising Research*, Vol. 11 (April 1971).

20. Douglas J. Dalrymple, Thomas S. Robertson, and Michael J. Yoshino, "Consumption Behavior across Ethnic Categories," *California Management Review* (Fall 1971).

21. Leon G. Schiffman, "Sources of Information for the Elderly," *Journal of Advertising Research* (October 1971).

22. Carl E. Block, "Prepurchase Search Behavior of Low-Income Households," *Journal of Retailing*, Vol. 48 (Spring 1972).

23. Francis S. Bourne in Rensis Likert and Samuel Hayes, Jr., *Some Applications of Behavioral Research* (UNESCO, 1957).

24. William Whyte, "The Web of Word-of-Mouth," *Fortune*, November 1954.

25. Victor J. Cook, "Group Decision, Social Comparison and Persuasion in Changing Attitudes," *Journal of Advertising Research*, Vol. 7 (March 1967).

26. Sidney J. Levy, "Social Class and Consumer Behavior," in *Buyer Behavior*, ed. John A. Howard and Lyman E. Ostlund (New York: Alfred A. Knopf, Inc., 1973).

27. Joseph N. Fry and Frederick H. Siller, "A Comparison of Housewife Decision Making in Two Social Classes," *Journal of Marketing Research*, Vol. 7 (August 1970).

28. Louis P. Bucklin, "Consumer Search, Role Enactment and Market Efficiency," *Journal of Business*, Vol. 42 (October 1969).

29. Harry L. Davis, "Decision Making within the Household," *Journal of Consumer Research*, Vol. 2, No. 4 (March 1976), p. 241.

30. Elizabeth H. Wolgast, *"Do Husbands or Wives Make the Purchasing Decisions?"*, *Journal of Marketing*, Vol. 22 (October 1958).

31. Fabian Linden, ed., *Expenditure Patterns of the American Family*, prepared for the National Industrial Conference Board and sponsored by *Life* Magazine, 1965.

32. Gary M. Munsinger, Jean E. Weber, and Richard W. Hansen, "Joint Home Purchasing Decisions by Husbands and Wives," *Journal of Consumer Research*, Vol. 1, No. 4 (March 1975).

33. R. F. Kelley and M. B. Egan, "Husband and Wife Interaction in a Consumer Decision Process" (Paper Presented at the American Marketing Association Fall Conference, Cincinnati, Ohio, 1969); and Robert Ferber and Lucy Chao Lee, "Husband-Wife Influence in Family Purchasing Behavior," *Journal of Consumer Research*, Vol. 1 (June 1974).

34. John V. Farley, "Why Does Brand Loyalty Vary Over Products?", *Journal of Marketing Research*, Vol. 3 (August 1964).

35. "French Chain's Unbranded Products—Loved by Consumers, Hated by Admen," *Advertising Age*, June 28, 1976, p. 60.

36. Ivan Ross, "Self-Concept and Brand Preference," *Journal of Business*, January 1971.

37. Paul E. Green, "Consumer Use of Information," in *On Knowing the Consumer*, ed. Joseph Newman (New York: John Wiley and Sons, Inc., 1966).

38. Frank M. Bass and Wayne Talarzyk, "An Attitude Model for the Study of Brand Preference," *Journal of Marketing Research*, Vol. 9, February 1972.

39. James L. Ginter, "An Experimental Investigation of Attitude Change and Choice of a New Brand," *Journal of Marketing Research*, Vol. 11 (February 1974).

40. James W. Taylor, "The Role of Risk in Consumer Behavior," *Journal of Marketing*, Vol. 38 (April 1974).

41. Taylor, "Role of Risk," p. 60.

42. Thomas L. Brown and James W. Gentry, "Analysis of Risk and Risk-Reduction Strategies—A Multiple Product Case," *Journal of the Academy of Marketing Science*. Vol. 3, No. 2 (Spring 1975), p. 148.

43. Raymond A. Bauer, "Consumer Behavior as Risk Taking," in *Dynamic Marketing for a Changing World*, ed. Robert S. Hancock (Chicago: American Marketing Association, 1960).

44. Scott M. Cunningham, "Perceived Risk and Brand Loyalty," in *Risk Taking and Information Handling in Consumer Behavior*, ed. Donald F. Cox (Cambridge: Harvard University Press, 1967).

45. J. Paul Peter and Lawrence X. Tarpey, Sr., "A Comparative Analysis of Three Consumer Decision Strategies," *Journal of Consumer Re-*

search, Vol. 2, No. 1 (June 1975), p. 29.

46. Brian Milton Campbell, "The Existence of Evoked Set and Determinants of Its Magnitude in Brand Choice Behavior," (Ph.D. Dissertation, Columbia University, 1967, New York).

47. Campbell, "Evoked Set," p. 242.

48. William P. Dommermuth and Edward W. Cundiff, "Shopping Goods, Shopping Centers, and Selling Strategies," *Journal of Marketing*, Vol. 4, No. 4 (1967).

49. Campbell, "Evoked Set."

50. George Katona and Eva Mueller, *Consumer Expectations* (Ann Arbor, Michigan's Institute for Social Research, 1954).

51. Robert F. Kelly, "Estimating Ultimate Performance Levels of New Retail Outlets," *Journal of Marketing Research*, Vol. 4 (1967).

52. As cited in J. Douglas McConnell, "An Experimental Examination of the Price-Quality Relationship," *Journal of Business*, Vol. 41 (October 1970).

53. McConnell, "Price-Quality Relationship."

54. Richard S. Cimbalo and Adrienne M. Webdale, "Effects of Price Information on Consumer-Rated Quality," *Proceedings of the 81st Annual American Psychological Association Convention*, 1973.

55. David M. Gardner, "An Experimental Investigation of the Price-Quality Relationship," *Journal of Retailing*, Vol. 46, No. 3 (Fall 1970).

56. Robert B. Settle, "Attribution Theory and Acceptance of Information," *Journal of Marketing Research*, Vol. 9 (February 1972), p. 85.

57. Settle, "Attribution Theory," pp. 85–86.

58. John R. Thompson, "Characteristics and Behavior of Out-Shopping Consumers," *Journal of Retailing*, Vol. 47 (Spring 1971).

59. Levy, "Social Class."

60. Joseph T. Plummer, "Life Style Patterns and Commercial Bank Credit-Card Usage," *Journal of Marketing*, Vol. 35 (April 1971).

MARKETING APPLICATIONS

Conclusion 1   *External search, in which the consumer actively seeks out information about a given product, offers marketers a great opportunity to provide data on product features and performance.*

Application   External search is likely to occur in the choice process for considered-purchase products—high ticket items such as appliances, stereos, cars, and so on. One way to take advantage of this opportunity is to include, in each advertisement for a considered-purchase product, an easy means of obtaining a predesigned information package which details the benefits of choosing that particular item. This may be offered in as simple a form as an address to write to.

Conclusion 2   *Consumers perceive certain risks in making product choices: two of these are expressed as financial and performance risks.*

Application   The fear of losing money by choosing a given brand (financial risk) is closely tied to anxiety about the product failing to do what it is supposed to do (performance risk). Both types of fear may be dramatically reduced when a clear and firm guarantee is offered with the product. But such a guarantee must offer the consumer an easy method for exercising his or her right of warranty. Few customers want to take the trouble to write a letter of complaint to a manufacturer. The most persuasive guarantees are those which may be exercised at the retail level. Marketers who offer this type of guarantee should display it prominently in all advertising and promotional communications, since this will be a valid incentive to try the product. The most persuasive guarantees are those which are simple and unequivocal, such as, "If anything goes wrong with your Midas Muffler, we'll fix it free."

Conclusion 3   *Weighing various product attributes in the choice process, consumers tend to see a relationship between price and quality—the more expensive an item, the better it is thought to be.*

Application   The price-quality relationship generally holds true for higher-priced items, but less for inexpensive purchases such as packaged goods. But marketers should be aware that consumers are not usually willing to pay more to obtain the highest-quality merchandise. Thus, an effective marketing appeal is a direct comparison of, say, one brand of luggage which offers many of the same features as the higher-priced "quality" brand but costs significantly less. Side by side comparisons, such as placing one's less expensive suitcase next to the costly one and comparing these feature by feature, are particularly convincing.

ASSIGNMENTS

Research Assignment

Background   You are a partner in the Green Thumb, a florist shop specializing in live exotic plants and trees such as tropical philodendron, palms, and dracaenas for students in your college community. While there is a brisk amount of traffic through the store, sales have not been spectacular. From casual conversation with customers, you believe that many students are afraid to invest in some of your more expensive plants—$15 and up—because they feel that your exotic varieties will not survive for long indoors. To confirm this hypothesis, you wish to conduct some informal research into how people perceive *risk* in buying tropical plants.

Methodology   Administer the following questionnaire to a sample of at least 20 students.

> Exotic plants are popular in many college dormitories and apartments. How would you feel about buying one for yourself?
>
> 1. I would not buy one at any price because _____ .
> 2. I would buy one for ____ under $15, ____ under $25, ____ under $35.
> 3. I would expect the plant to last ____ 1 to 3 months, ____ 6 months to 2 years, ____ indefinitely, with the proper care.
> 4. I would probably have to water or care for the plant ____ every day, ____ every 2 or 3 days, ____ once a week.
> 5. I would feel better about buying the plant if ____ I got free information on how to care for it, ____ I got a guarantee of some kind.

Interpret your findings in the context of what you have learned about risk perception from the preceding chapter.

Extrapolation   If risk perception is indeed a factor, what marketing ideas—in advertising, sales, or informational literature—would you develop to help overcome the problem? What other kinds of products might involve the same kind of risk?

Creative Assignment

As Corporate Communications Director for the Contempo Time Company, you are often called upon to interpret *consumer research* your company receives from outside consultants to management. Your latest assignment is to translate consumer research about general choice behavior into the specific situation of choosing a Contempo watch, which is priced competitively with Bulova and offers a similar range of styles for both men and women. Review the discussion of choice in the preceding chapter and write a description of how the process would theoretically operate in the case of a hypothetical male consumer—beginning with the need to replace a lost wristwatch, through the assessment of brand and store attributes, to the final selection of a $150 digital model from the Contempo line. With your description, include a simple diagram of the process which includes the alternatives and possibilities affecting the final outcome.

Managerial Assignment

The Ethical Pharmaceutical Company markets prescription drugs through *advertising* to prescribing physicians and *direct contact* with doctors on the part of detailers—representatives who visit at regular intervals and leave samples. As a new detailer for Ethical, you are interested in *optimizing* the way doctors get information about the drugs they will prescribe. You are particularly curious about how much information you should be ready to provide in order to solve the doctors' major problem of time management more effectively than your competitors with other drug companies. Refer to the following article: Raymond A. Bauer and Lawrence H. Wortzel, "Doctor's Choice: The Physician and His Source of Information about Drugs," *Journal of Marketing Research*, Vol. 3 (February 1966), p. 42.

From the conclusions drawn in that research, decide how you can improve your company's position in your customers' frame of reference by optimizing the information they receive about *Ethical* products in the minimum amount of time.

SELECTED READINGS

Assael, Henry. "Product Classification and the Theory of Consumer Behavior." *Journal of the Academy of Marketing Science*, Vol. 2, No. 4 (Fall 1974), pp. 539–553.

Brown, Thomas L. and James W. Gentry. "Analysis of Risk and Risk-Reduction Strategies—A Multiple Product Case." *Journal of the Academy of Marketing Science*, Vol. 3, No. 2 (Spring 1975), pp. 148–160.

Granbois, Donald H. and John O. Summers. "Primary and Secondary Validity of Consumer Purchase Probabilities." *Journal of Consumer Research*, Vol. 1, No. 4 (March 1975), pp. 31–38.

Landon, E. Laird, Jr. "Self Concept, Ideal Self Concept and Consumer Purchase Intentions." *Journal of Consumer Research*, Vol. 1, No. 2 (September 1974), pp. 44–51.

Lane, George S. and Gayne L. Watson. "A Canadian Replication of Mason Haire's 'Shopping List' Study." *Journal of the Academy of Marketing Science*, Vol. 3, No. 1 (Winter 1975), pp. 48–59.

OBJECTIVES

SEVENTEEN

Purchasing and Postpurchase Behavior

Making a choice to buy something, as out-lined in the last chapter, does not complete the consumer decision process. It is simply an "intent" to purchase, which may be carried out (or further complicated) through actual purchasing and postpurchase evaluation.

The retail environment offers marketers a natural arena for influencing consumer pur-chases. Thus, recommendations for enhanc-ing retail performance occur frequently in this chapter. In-home buying, an increasingly popular form of shopping, also gives market-ers considerable opportunities to evaluate and respond to consumer needs through strategic planning. Yet, taking full advantage of both kinds of distribution channels calls for a more

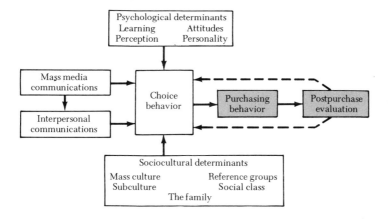

sophisticated knowledge of consumer purchasing variables than many sellers now rely upon. The following discussion combines a theoretical overview of the purchasing process with implications such as:

• *How to use "intent to buy" as a predictive measure.*

• *Why "impulse" buying is usually not that impulsive.*

• *Which store variables make consumers more susceptible to "impulse" purchases.*

• *How "game playing" works in customer-salesperson interaction.*

• *What psychological factors enable some consumers to obtain better deals on their merchandise than others.*

Finally, postpurchase satisfaction should be a dominant goal of marketing activity, since this is the test consumers use to determine their future purchasing activity.[1]

The Purchasing Process

Where the previous chapter analyzed consumer decision processes leading to the choice of a given brand or store, this discussion concentrates on what happens at the actual purchasing level of consumer behavior. Purchasing is sometimes conceptualized as confined to a retail environment, but most researchers view in-store buying as just one event in a continuing process—flowing from an initial *intention* to purchase to actual buying activity to the ultimate consequences of postpurchase evaluation.

Brand choice, selecting one brand over a set of possible alternatives, is one way of forming a purchase intention. A consumer who reduces the conflict of needing a new typewriter by seeking information about different makes and models, weighing the various possibilities, and finally deciding on an Olivetti portable has established an intention to buy that typewriter. Because the item is expensive and

entails a fairly high degree of risk, the formulation of this intention is relatively complex and loaded with variables. But the same process may be invoked at a lower level of complexity for inexpensive, frequently purchased goods like floor wax or shampoo. An intention to buy formed after some degree of problem-solving deliberation is known as a *planned* purchase.

But many purchases are not planned. Every one of us has walked into a supermarket fully intending to buy just a quart of milk or loaf of bread and come home laden with items we didn't "realize" we needed until they happened to catch our eye. Often they include such self-indulgences as canapes, imported chocolates, or other nonessentials that we wouldn't have thought to include on a grocery shopping list. This phenomenon is characterized as "impulse" buying. Clothing and accessories are often purchased on an impulse basis; an unusually designed leather belt may suddenly beckon from a clothing store window, or, while shopping for a sensible pair of slacks, we may notice a sale on high-priced Pierre Cardin shirts too inviting to pass up. *Unplanned* purchases of this nature usually take place in a retail setting, and are influenced by store assortment, layout, special sales, and product packaging variables.

Purchasing itself commonly involves some interaction with retail or outside salespeople, which may affect whether or not a consumer buys at all and what brand will be purchased. In this context, *bargaining* between salesperson and consumer can be an important factor where and when it occurs. But bargaining is typically confined to certain retail environments and products. Since the advent of consumer activism, bargaining has become a topic of much interest to consumers and

researchers; thus it will be analyzed here. And, as mentioned earlier, not all actual purchasing occurs in a retail establishment. Many purchases are made through catalog and mail order systems or over the telephone and bring additional elements of risk into play.

Finally, purchasing behavior implies outcomes and consequences—satisfaction with the purchase and predisposition to buy the same item or brand again; or dissatisfaction and possibly redress, or attitude change. These modes of postpurchase behavior represent an important part of the process[2] and, although some are described in greater detail in other chapters, they will be analyzed here.

Planned Purchases: Intention and Probability

Marketers are necessarily concerned with the nature of buying intentions and are even more interested in ways to predict when and how they will occur. There is also the question of whether a consumer's intention to purchase something will actually culminate in purchase behavior, because many intervening considerations may come into play. There are two generally used constructs for viewing consumers' dispositions to buy: (1) purchase intention and (2) purchase probability. While the latter approach has achieved greater research support in recent years, both have demonstrated predictive usefulness.

The Purchase Intention Approach

"Intention" to buy has traditionally been defined by the research questions used to

measure it. If, for example, researchers want to find out whether consumers think they will buy a car during a projected time period (usually six months to a year), they will pose questions such as "Do you expect to buy a car during the next six months?", or "Do you *plan* to buy a car during the next twelve months?" Then the interviewer places responses in predetermined categories such as "Definitely will buy," "Probably will not buy," and so on. While consumers who report intentions to purchase actually do reveal higher buying rates than those who report that they do not intend to, there are indications that measures of intention may be inefficient in predicting purchase behavior.

Problems with Purchase Intention Prediction

The major problem with this approach is in the nature of the questioning method. For one, answers to questions about car buying intentions, for example, must be affected by the factors that enter into the purchase, such as the current and future economic status of the consumer and the condition of his or her present car. Secondly, many consumers tend to respond that they will "definitely buy" a new car in the next six months when they really mean that they would like to buy a new car if they are able to—a desire rather than a deliberate plan or intention. Very often, circumstances do not afford them the opportunity to act upon that desire.[3]

Psychological Variables and Purchase Intention   Some studies have linked measures of purchase intentions with personality traits, such as Landon's investigation of self-concept and ideal self-concept as determinants of intent to buy. Landon found that:[4]

1. Purchase intentions of some products, such as beer, tend to be correlated with ideal self-image rather than actual self-image (how consumers would like to see themselves rather than true self-concepts).

2. Some consumers characterize themselves by a higher correlation between actual self-image and purchase intention than between an ideal self-image and purchase intention. These subjects were termed actualizers under the theory that healthy individuals strive to fulfill their existing needs.

3. Other consumers reveal higher relationships between ideal self-image and purchase intention, and are conceived of as *perfectionists* because they experience greater needs to improve themselves.

Although the influence of personality upon intent may be a fruitful area of future research, most predictive studies have turned to the construct of purchase probability.

The Purchase Probability Approach

Juster points out that intention might be better thought of as a chance or likelihood that some purchasing event will occur:[5]

Consumers reporting that they "intend to buy A within X months" can be thought of as saying that the probability of their purchasing A within X months is high enough so that some form of "yes" answer is more accurate than a "no" answer.

This approach restructures traditional intent-to-buy questioning procedures by asking consumers to estimate, on an eleven-point scale, their probability of buying some item during a future specified period. Probability estimates of this type have generally provided better forecasting of actual purchase rates than the standard intention survey technique.[6] Table 17-1 illustrates a purchase probability scale adapted to predicting automobile buying over a twelve-month period, viewed against the actual purchasing behavior of consumers who rated their intentions.

Marketing Considerations for Planned Purchases

Applying what is known about planned purchase behavior entails several considerations about the use of "intent-to-purchase" for prediction, factors of deliberation and timing, family roles in planned purchases, and intervening variables that may confound reported intentions.

Predictive Value of Purchase Intentions   It is generally recognized that consumers'

Table 17-1   A Purchase Probability Scale and Purchase Outcomes

LIKELIHOOD OF BUYING A MOTOR CAR, NEW OR SECOND-HAND	ORIGINAL SAMPLE FEBRUARY 1966	REINTERVIEWING EARLY IN 1967, FIGURES OF REINTERVIEWED RESPONDENTS ONLY
	%	
100% (One hundred percent sure)	3,9	79% of these had actually bought
90% (Almost certain)	1,7	
80% (Very big chance)	1,7	
70% (Big chance)	1,7	48% had bought
60% (Not so big a chance)	1,3	
50% (About even)	4,1	36% had bought
40% (Smaller chance)	0,4	
30% (Small chance)	2,8	
20% (Very small chance)	2,2	14% had bought
10% (Almost certainly not)	6,1	
0 (Certainly not)	58	
Nothing indicated	16	Not reinterviewed

Source: Jan Stapel, "Predictive Attitudes," in Attitude Research on the Rocks, ed. Lee Adler and Irving Crespi (Chicago: American Marketing Association, 1968), p. 98.

verbal indications of purchase intentions are useful predictors of actual purchasing behavior.[7] The most efficient means of measuring intentions in current practice is the probability approach, as validated in studies of intent to purchase automobiles, appliances, and food products. The most widespread application of intent-to-buy information today is in advertising research, particularly the *posttesting* techniques discussed at length in chapter 14. In one study comparing "intent-to-buy" measures with actual purchasing behavior, Stapel found that in advertising a variety of products:[8]

• About half the consumers who claimed an intention to buy an advertised item also put their names on coupons for home delivery.

• Consumers who remember an ad in recall testing report twice the intention to buy (and also produce twice as many coupon orders) as those who could not recall the ad.

Thus, planned purchases may be predicted with some degree of accuracy where testing methods are applicable.

Deliberation and Timing Factors   Granbois and Willett report that the amount of deliberation a consumer or family unit engages in when making a purchasing decision will affect the timing of the actual purchase. Deliberation is measured by factors such as the length of a planning period and the degree of contact with information sources, both marketer-dominated and interpersonal. Later purchasers have been shown to spend proportionately more time in deliberation than earlier purchasers. And *non*purchasers appear to spend time consulting nonstore sources, without making the in-store visits judged to be the necessary and final stage of deliberation for consumers who actually do buy.[9]

This would suggest that information sources which marketers can control (specifically advertising) might offer more information to shorten the deliberation process and use more effective means of getting consumers into retail establishments. Incentives such as cents-off coupons, announcements of sales, and other traffic-building techniques have proven useful in bringing consumers directly to dealers. A Chrysler advertising agency once toyed with the idea of a coupon entitling the holder to $150 off the price of a new car, but ultimately decided to give buyers equivalent rebate checks after they had purchased from their dealers—another successful promotion in a flagging new-car market.

Family Roles in Planned Purchases   The different influences of family members is particularly significant at the level of purchase planning. But, although everyone seems to recognize that roles in the decision process are changing, there is some disagreement over what those changes are.

Cunningham and Green compared purchasing roles of family members in 1973 with a similar study in 1955 and found differences in several product categories (Table 17-2).[10] While grocery purchase planning seems to be dominated by wives to a greater degree than in 1955, husbands appear to be exercising more control over life insurance planning. But joint decision making is becoming more evident in automobile, vacation, and housing purchase considerations. Earlier studies have concluded that most purchase planning is conducted by wives, although husbands tend to become involved as the

Table 17-2   Husband-Wife Roles in Purchase Planning Decisions, 1955 vs. 1973

DECISION AREA	1955 (%)	1973 (%)
Food and Groceries		
Husband usually	13	10
Both husband and wife	33	15
Wife usually	54	75
Number of cases	(727)	(248)
Life Insurance		
Husband usually	43	66
Both husband and wife	42	30
Wife usually	15	4
Number of cases	(727)	(247)
Automobile		
Husband usually	70	52
Both husband and wife	25	45
Wife usually	5	3
Number of cases	(727)	(248)
Vacation		
Husband usually	18	7
Both husband and wife	70	84
Wife usually	12	9
Number of cases	(727)	(244)
House or Apartment		
Husband usually	18	12
Both husband and wife	58	77
Wife usually	24	11
Number of cases	(727)	(245)
Money and Bills		
Husband usually	26	27
Both husband and wife	34	24
Wife usually	40	49
Number of cases	(727)	(248)

Source: Isabella C. M. Cunningham and Robert T. Green, "Purchasing Roles in the U.S. Family, 1955 and 1973," Journal of Marketing, Vol. 38 (October 1974), pp. 61–64. Reprinted with permission of the American Marketing Association.

price and complexity of the item in question increase.[11]

The question of who undertakes planning specific purchases has several implications for marketer communications and retail performance. First, much energy and money may be wasted in directing persuasive messages to the wrong family member. Secondly, the way in which a product or service is presented at the retail level requires some consideration of who will be going there to look at it—the "in-store visit" aspect of the deliberation process discussed earlier. Retail environments may be predominantly masculine (the automobile dealerships) or feminine (the infants' department in most department stores) in layout and salespeople. Others are sufficiently asexual to appeal to a husband-wife pair.

Intervening Variables Between a purchasing intention and an actual purchase, a number of circumstances may change to facilitate or inhibit consumers' plans. The most widespread instance of such variables in recent years arose with the energy crisis, inflation, and high unemployment of the mid–1970s. Consumers who had grown accustomed to thinking of our marketing economy as an eternal cornucopia of goods and services were dismayed to find that gasoline was suddenly a precious, high priced commodity. In the housing market, inflation ran rampant and banks withdrew their usual offers of mortgages. A large number of families found their wage earners unemployed, and the pattern of immediate gratification through consumer credit that had developed during the prosperous 1960s reversed itself as people began searching for safe havens for their money in times of grave uncertainty.

These economic and psychological por-

tents, experienced by many Americans, interfered with plans for a number of anticipated purchases. A survey of consumers in 1974 found that, due to these intervening variables:[12]

1. Plans to buy a major electrical appliance were postponed or dropped by 18 percent of the surveyed homes.

2. Two out of five families postponed or cancelled a vacation or pleasure trip by auto.

3. One out of five families started looking for a new car with "better milage." The actual percentage of people choosing a compact car rose from 9 percent to 18 percent.

4. Shopping habits changed radically, with 70 percent of the consumers surveyed making fewer trips to shopping centers because of the gasoline crisis.

It might be well to consider that most published studies of purchase intention and probability were conducted during relatively stable economic times. Studies of intention/purchase relationships undertaken while many families' economic status remains uncertain may draw significantly different findings.

But all intervening variables are not so gloomy—economic circumstances at the individual and household levels may also change for the better, prompting buying behavior that was not anticipated. Similarly, peoples' life styles change in ways not always expected, through marriage, new jobs, and moving in or out of cities and suburbs.

At the micro-level, consumers may switch their intentions to different brands in the same product category or substitute one brand for another. The variables that intervene in these cases are generally found in the retail environment, and may best be understood in the context of "impulse" or unplanned purchases.

Priority Patterns and Consumer Behavior*

If a young married couple were to buy a color television set this month, would it be possible to predict which household durable they are likely to purchase next? It is unlikely, unless the system of *priorities* which consumers maintain relative to household formation is known. A more important question from the point of view of total sales strategy is whether any particular group of homemakers would agree on any general acquisition pattern.

The general implication . . . is that if people think and buy in sets of products, it would seem to be an appropriate strategy to market them together, or at least to follow a marketing program directed toward consumer priorities.

The difficulty of defining such sets . . . is faced by a retailer trying to determine the extent of product set (scrambled merchandising) justifiable in his location. Should his total set of products stocked be a random mixture or a carefully thought out selection based on the purchasing priorities of his customers? If a retailer sells a customer an expensive durable, it may be profitable for him to follow up this sale with direct mail promotion.

In order to provide priority patterns based on consumer intentions, a simple "longitudinal" experiment was conducted in the San Diego area involving two interview periods separated by a five-month interval for the same sample of respondents. The respondents were chosen at the newlywed stage in the life cycle, since it was felt that this was the prime time for the formation of acquisition patterns. The commodity set was a group of twenty-three household durables, "characteristic" in the sense that all made use of electric power in the home. Priority patterns for this set were derived both from the respondents' ownership frequencies and from their stated intentions to buy (Table 17-3).

The priority pattern concept implies that consumers tend to think of their household good purchases in terms of sets to be acquired in a particular order over time. The acquiring of goods in accordance with a priority pattern is not simply an individual process; it is also a group phenomenon. There is growing evidence to support the view that consumer groups can be characterized by high levels of consensus associated with their order of acquisition of durables. In addition, it is true that pronounced differences in the nature of groups may be reflected in the differences of their priority patterns.

What does the priority pattern concept imply for marketing strategy? Certainly, for the purchase of durables, it implies that the idea of an irrational consumer should be discarded. Further, it should be replaced with a picture of a calculating, forward-looking consumer who thinks of whole sets of commodities and who actively plans to acquire them in a particular order. This means that if households think in sets, then perhaps the marketing strategist should match this outlook by adopting a set approach to the marketing of durable goods.

For example, one researcher has suggested that priority patterns may provide guidelines for marketing people in the allocation of promotional activities. The implications are that if

*John McFall, *Journal of Marketing*, Vol. 33 (October 1969), pp. 50–55. Adapted by permission of the author and the American Marketing Association.

the priority pattern relates to commodities *a, b, c, d,* in that order, then the owners of *a* should be exposed to additional promotional pressure in which *b* is emphasized more strongly than *c, c* more strongly than *d,* and so on. Similarly, if a discount were to be offered to a prospective customer on commodity *a,* it would be better to make it conditional (legally, of course) on the purchase of *b* than on the purchase of *c.* That is, market segmentation for durable goods should be conducted not only on the basis of income, social class, and other socioeconomic variables, but also on the basis of the priority patterns of acquisition of the relevant consumer groups.

Table 17.3   San Diego Newlywed Study, Priority Patterns for All Respondents (First Interview); Ownership and Intentions Patterns Compared

PRIORITY PATTERN BASED ON <u>OWNERSHIP</u>	PRIORITY PATTERN BASED ON <u>INTENTIONS</u>
Electric iron	Electric iron
Radio	Radio
Electric toaster	Electric toaster
Food mixer	Vacuum cleaner
Black-and-white T.V.	Refrigerator
Hair dryer	Food mixer
Skillet	Hi-fi
Hi-fi	*Black-and-white TV*
Vacuum cleaner	Hair dryer
Electric blanket	*Automatic washer*
Refrigerator	Skillet
Sewing machine	Garbage disposer
Garbage disposer	Electric blanket
Electric toothbrush	Sewing machine
Electric carver	*Clothes dryer*
Broiler	*Color T.V.*
Oil painting	*Electric carver*
Automatic washer	*Electric toothbrush*
Color T.V.	Broiler
Floor polisher	Oil painting
Room air conditioner	Dishwasher
Clothes dryer	Food freezer
Dishwasher	Room air conditioner
Food freezer	Floor polisher
Pool table	Pool table

give discounts to newly formed households 1st because these are the things they want to buy

Unplanned Purchases: "Impulse" Buying

Because everyone makes "impulse" purchases at one time or another, it would seem that this is a relatively simple phenomenon. A consumer sees some item, finds it appealing, and buys it, although he or she had not planned its purchase before entering the store. Actually, unplanned purchases represent an important but troublesome area of consumer activity. Reseachers and marketers are interested in the dynamics of impulse buying because it accounts for a large proportion of all purchasing behavior. Studies indicate that most purchases in supermarkets are unplanned and that their number increases as the dollar amount of an individual's grocery bill rises, although the proportion tends to taper off over a certain dollar figure (Figure 17-1).[13]

But there is no general accord among researchers as to the nature and role of unplanned purchases. Stern suggests, in one classical study, that there are really four types of "impulse" buying:[14]

1. *Pure Impulse.* This term refers to the act of buying something for the novelty of it, usually when such a purchase is a departure from patterns of brand loyalty or typical buying behavior. Picking up a can of lobster bisque soup instead of the usual Campbell's Tomato or Vegetable is one example.

2. *Reminder Impulse.* When a consumer buys under this impulse, it is because the item is usually purchased anyway but did not happen to be anticipated or noted on a shopping list. While waiting at the drugstore counter to buy a tube of shampoo, a consumer might notice a brand of aspirin on the shelf and remember that the jar at home is practically empty, so the "reminder" of seeing the item triggers this unplanned purchase.

3. *Suggestion Impulse.* A product the consumer encounters for the first time may stimulate a perceived need or use for it. A housewife who spots a jar of concentrated, industrial strength odor repellent in a counter display at Woolworth's may instantly relate the product to her concern about cooking odors around the house and buy the item.

4. *Planned Impulse.* The "planning" aspect of this behavior refers to a consumer's response to some special incentive to buy an

Figure 17-1 Relationship between dollar amount of grocery bills and the percentage of unplanned purchases.

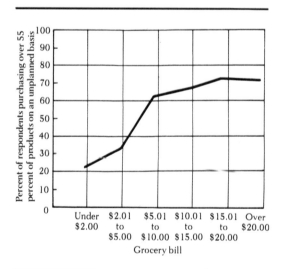

Source: David T. Kollat and Ronald P. Willett, "Consumer Impulse Purchasing Behavior," Journal of Marketing Research, Vol. 4 (February 1967), p. 27. Reprinted by permission of the American Marketing Association.

unanticipated item. The impulse is usually stimulated by a sale announcement, a cents-off coupon, or other compelling offers.

Because different kinds of unplanned purchases may be observed in different contexts, it becomes clear that impulse buying may not be so "impulsive" after all. In many cases, efficient buying decisions cannot be made until the consumer is exposed to the total assortment of alternatives in a store environment. Shaffer argues that:[15]

. . . the observation that many purchase decisions are made in the store does not justify the conclusion that many food purchases are based upon "impulse," that the purchases are irrationally made, and that consumers are subject to substantial manipulation through control of stimuli in the store situation. By referring to in-the-store purchases as "impulse purchases," the implication is made that the purchases are inconsistent with the established preference pattern of the shopper. . . . However, the store may be the most rational place to make many food purchase decisions, since it is there that prices, quality, and availability of substitutes and complements may be best included in consideration.

Although the terms "impulse buying" and "unplanned purchases" are used interchangeably in mainstream consumer research, it must be emphasized that unplanned purchases may involve decision making processes as rational as those associated with planned purchases.

How Unplanned Purchases Occur

A number of explanations for impulse buying activity have been advanced, but most are covered under the broad category of

exposure to stimuli in the store environment. Another recent orientation applies *situational effects* theory to unplanned purchases.

Exposure to Store Stimuli Kollat and Willet have found that impulse purchases (determined by comparison of consumers' purchase intentions and their actual purchases) are caused either by consumers' use of stimuli within the store to remind them of what they should be buying or by the effects of displays, promotions, and other marketer-dominated attempts to create new needs.[16] In the first case, the shopper's need is latent until he or she is in the store and can see the alternatives that will enter into the final purchasing decisions. This is closely related to Stern's formulation of the *reminder* impulse purchase. In the second case, the shopper does not recognize the existence of a need at all; it is created entirely by a new stimulus which is perceived as desirable. Essentially, this describes the *suggestion* impulse.

The same authors investigated possible links between consumer *susceptibility* to unplanned purchases and demographic or personality characteristics, but found few relationships from which marketers might segment different groups of consumers. Factors that did appear to be connected with susceptibility to impulse buying in supermarkets included:[17]

Transaction Size As the number of different products bought increased, the percentage of impulse-purchases also increased.

Shopping Trip A higher percentage of unplanned purchases occurred during major shopping trips than during "fill in" trips.

Frequency of Purchase Unplanned purchases were not as common for frequently purchased products as for those acquired less often.

Shopping List A predetermined list was

related to a higher rate of unplanned purchases, but only when the number of items was large (fifteen or more).

Other studies probing the direct effects of specific products and brands, store layout, and additional in-store factors on unplanned purchases have been largely inconclusive. Some research, however, has focused on the relationship of retail variables such as displays, shelving, and packaging to actual sales. Considering the large proportion of unplanned purchases in shopping trips, it is logical to assume that these factors influence impulse buying.

Displays   Supermarkets reap a large harvest of sales from displays—generally set up at the end of an aisle and featuring reduced prices. Consumers often see display items as special bargains, which enhances impulse purchasing. Displays are also used to create low-price images for stores, since consumers who shop in several supermarkets tend to remember display prices from one to another.[18]

Generally speaking, displays that obtain visibility for an item will increase its sales. This may be accomplished through use of special point-of-purchase setups that organize individual units of a product or brand into one eye-catching stimulus. Bold graphics are typical in point-of-purchase displays, which most marketers attempt to relate to their product image or advertising themes. Another means of obtaining visibility is placing a display where consumers will tend to pass it. At the usual supermarket checkout counter, magazines and small candy items are difficult to overlook because they are placed directly in front of shoppers waiting in line with their carts.

Shelving Techniques   Most retailers will contend that the more space they allocate to a brand in shelving, the higher its sales will be. (Yet this axiom has been refuted in one

study analyzing brands that were rated high in frequency of unplanned purchases.)[19] It is also widely accepted that placing a product at the consumer's eye level will boost sales, although there is some evidence that varying shelf level exerts no influence on a given brand.[20] The general findings on shelving techniques are similar to those concerning displays—the greater visibility a product or brand achieves in the retail environment, the more consumers will be aware of it and pick it up.

• *Packaging*   Major marketers devote a great deal of attention to packaging development, and often test packages still in the design stage to gauge consumer acceptance. Some testing techniques include (1) visibility testing, in which the legibility of design elements is measured by a tachistoscope (a device for measuring visual stimuli) or on a supermarket shelf; (2) behavioral measurements, which mark the speed with which consumers can select the package from a store display; (3) attitude surveys, consisting of open-end questioning of consumers and possibly other projective techniques; and (4) shopping tests, where subjects are consumers who may or may not take the prototype from its display.[21] Exactly how much attention *consumers* devote to packaging is not so evident. But there are some indications that it is an important variable, particularly in personal care products such as cosmetics. Like advertising, packaging is designed to position and convey an image for a product or brand, and some packaging successes have been particularly noteworthy. One often-cited example is L'Eggs Pantyhose, which captured many women's fancy with its plastic "egg" container. In this case, the point-of-purchase display was closely coordinated with the package design and entitled the "L'Eggs Boutique." As an ironic note, one of L'Eggs'

Packaging for Position   NO

Consumers were attracted to package designs that give the product a highly visible difference from others in the same category. One particularly effective design was the innovative bottle for *Macho* cologne—a men's product carrying a frankly masculine image.[22] Another intriguing package rode the crest of the yogurt craze by introducing a soap made from yogurt in the same kind of container usually associated with the food product.[23]

Macho Cologne photo courtesy of Fabergé.

major contenders for share-of-market was introduced as "No-Nonsense" Pantyhose, dressed appropriately in a strictly functional no-nonsense package. And its advertising theme directly challenged L'Eggs by telling consumers, "If you pay more for pantyhose, you're just paying for a package."

Situational Effects   The second theoretical approach to unplanned purchases may be termed "situational analysis," and represents a fairly new research orientation in consumer research. The basic tenet of this theory is that, at the time of purchase, circumstances or situations tend to arise that could not be anticipated in advance. A "situation" in this context has been defined as factors particular to a time and place that cannot be predicted from either the characteristics of the consumer or the attributes of a product, but that wield an observable effect on behavior.[24]

Belk applied situational analysis to consumer purchases of snack products. Unplanned purchase "situations" included such circumstances as:[25]

• You are at the grocery store when you get an urge for a between-meal snack.

• You are at the supermarket and notice the many available snack products; you wonder if you should pick something up in case friends drop by.

• You are at the store to pick up some things for a picnic you are planning with friends and are trying to decide what kind of snack to buy.

These items were tested with other "situations" described as "unplanned *consumption*," "nutrition," and "informal serving situations" stated as:

• You are shopping for a snack that you or your family can eat while watching television in the evenings.

• You are planning a party for a few close friends and are wondering what to have around to snack on.

• Snacks at your house have become a little dull lately and you are wondering what you might pick up that would be better.

• You are going on a long automobile trip and are thinking that you should bring along some snack to eat on the way.

• You suddenly realize that you have invited a couple of friends over for the evening and you have nothing for them to snack on.

• You are thinking about what type of snack to buy to keep around the house this weekend.

• You are thinking about a snack to have with lunch at noon.

Through factor analysis, Belk discovered that consumers could be segmented on the basis of situational effects. The consumers identified as Type I, for example, preferred to serve and eat "substantial" snacks for nutrition, but chose only "light and salty" varieties when making unplanned purchases and avoided the types they usually preferred.

This research represents one of the first successful attempts to segment situational variables in consumption decisions, and points to the possibility of influencing impulse purchasing through persuasive communications aimed at specific consumer groups.

Marketing Considerations for Unplanned Purchases

While some researchers note that estimates of planned purchases may be overrated due to deficiencies in research design,[26] there are areas where information about impulse buying suggests guidelines for marketers. These include increasing the performance of *retail assortment displays* and *creating visibility for products and brands.*

Retail Assortment Displays While studies of the effects of retail assortments and displays upon unplanned purchasing have been largely inconclusive, there are ways in which retailers can "suggest" needs to be fulfilled by impulse buying.

One technique cited in *Progressive Grocer* points up the usefulness of "tie-in" merchandising—relating different items in displays on the basis of how the products will be used. In a supermarket context, this involves finding out consumers' meal patterns, available from sources such as the Market Research Corporation of America's *Menu Census,* and arranging displays to reflect them. Two examples of tie-in merchandising exploiting meal habits include:[27]

Table 17-4 How Often Key Dishes Are Served at Breakfast

		% CHANGE OVER PAST 5 YEARS
Juices	48.7	+12
Fruit	23.3	+ 2
Cold cereals	45.9	+ 7
Hot cereal	11.9	+ 2
Eggs	39.3	−10
Meat, fish, poultry	26.8	−13
Pancakes, waffles	8.6	+12
Yeast breads	62.9	− 7
Muffins, biscuits, rolls, buns	9.1	+11
Fruit spreads	23.0	− 8
Coffee	81.6	− 3
Tea	9.2	+ 8

Source of Table 17-4 and Figure 17-2: Market Research Corporation of America's Menu Census Findings of Breakfast and Lunch Preference Patterns, in Progressive Grocer *(April 1974), p. 115. Reprinted by permission.*

• Noting that breakfast is increasingly eaten on the run (Table 17-4), and that breakfast foods emerging as the most popular are those that can be prepared quickly and easily. This would suggest an assortment display that ties in instant coffee, instant orange juice, and instant breakfast foods to stimulate consumers' recognition of the need for snappy breakfast dishes and their subsequent impulse purchasing to meet this need.

• Observing that lunches eaten at home generate above-average use of certain products—canned soup, for example, which appears two-thirds of the time at midday meals (Figure 17-2). The reason for this pattern is that *age* sets lunches at home apart from other meals; preschool children and adults over 65 make up the largest groups in this meal-time category. Thus, supermarket retailers might tie in lunch items of interest to children and older consumers in appropriate displays.

Enhancing Product and Brand Visibility
Before a consumer can recognize a need to make an impulse purchase, he or she must become aware of the item in the perceptual environment. This axiom gains support from the fact that where shelving, point of purchase displays, and other in-store variables appear to influence impulse purchasing, it is because they gain the product or brand greater visibility through increased shelf space, more conspicuous position, and so on.

From a marketer's standpoint, *packaging* emerges as an important variable in enhancing visibility. Some familiar brands that have gained a large share of market over time come in rather undramatic packages, yet

Figure 17-2 Lunch servings as % of total servings.

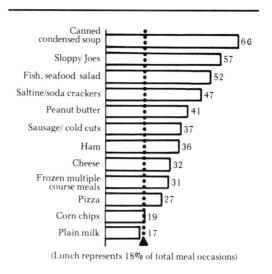

(Lunch represents 18% of total meal occasions)

still prove successful. But new products or brands, and those competing against established market leaders, require thoughtful consideration of how best to present them.

As noted earlier, one growing application of package design is in positioning the brand by suggesting its use or special benefits through the style of the package. A recent entry in the domain of drain openers used a plastic container whose top was in the shape of a drainpipe. The first hair care products using lemon as a highly touted ingredient usually displayed lemons on the package to bring this benefit to the attention of a consumer scanning the hair product shelves in drugstores. And a little-known line of salad dressings that boasted champagne-based recipes was packaged in miniature champagne bottles to dramatize the product difference and set this brand apart from all other commercial salad dressings.

Point-of-purchase displays also represent a critical variable in attaining visibility that is within the province of a marketer's control. It has been mentioned that some marketers effectively correlate point-of-purchase with advertising campaigns, but often this area of communication fails to achieve the same strategic and creative potential as print or broadcast messages. This is due, in part, to a less glamorous image associated with creating point-of-purchase displays in the advertising industry, although some firms who now specialize in point-of-purchase advertising are devoting much time and talent to upgrading the medium.[28]

Overt Purchasing Behavior

Whether purchases are planned or unplanned, certain patterns of behavior have been observed in the actual purchasing process that fall under the heading of consumer-salesperson interactions or "bargaining." The overview of these processes presented here is based on available research, which in some cases is quite meager. Additionally, out-of-store purchasing will be discussed, with considerations for marketers in improving the performance of these vehicles.

Consumer-Salesperson Interaction

As noted in chapter 15 in the context of salespeople as "opinion leaders," findings from this area of communications research are not too extensive, and often conflicting. However, some general conclusions about the nature of customer-salesperson roles might be reached in terms of *similarity, credibility,* and *game-playing.*

Similarity   Consumers are reported to be influenced by salespeople to the degree that they perceive their mutual similarity in demographic and life-style characteristics. Brock, in one classic study, indicated that paint salespeople who expressed product attitudes similar to their customers' were more effective in making sales than those who impressed customers with their expertise about paint.[29] Evans described the same relationship for insurance salespeople and their prospects, stressing the "attractiveness" of a company's representative (seen in similar demographic variables and like opinions) as the best predictor of sales outcomes.[30] Personal experience would suggest that some salespeople are more "attractive" than others in a shopping milieu. A young customer in a clothing store who displays youthful life-style characteristics in dress will be likely to choose a young salesperson who exhibits the same "look" than older, more conservatively dressed salespeople in the same department.

Credibility Kelman has shown that, the greater a salesperson's perceived credibility from the customer's standpoint, the stronger the consumer's tendency to internalize his or her message will be.[31] Because selling is an advocacy form of communication, consumers often expect salespeople to direct their messages toward making a sale rather than giving impartial information. Thus, the personal credibility a salesperson projects in striving to meet the consumer's actual needs will influence how his or her messages are received. The training of salespeople has grown increasingly sophisticated in developing effective communications strategies that will determine consumer needs and gratify them; as one popular text on selling emphasized:[32]

The professional salesman makes this vow: he will not leave the interest stop (expressed by the customer) until he and the buyer are clearly aware of the buyer's needs. He makes this vow to save selling time and effort and have a successful sale. Unless he knows what the buyer wants, he does not know what benefits to offer. Unless the buyer is aware of his needs, he cannot make the need decisions.

Most consumers are aware of the difference between a sales communication designed to manipulate them and one that seeks to meet expressed or latent needs, thus sales effi-ciency is certainly enhanced by the contemporary approach to the sales situation.

Game Playing Woodside and Davenport have applied the concept of "game" analysis to the customer-salesperson interaction and isolated two forms of game playing—"psycho-social" and "problem-solving."[33]

In psycho-social game playing, the attractiveness of the salesperson based upon personal *similarities* is deemed more influential. This type of "game" usually occurs with products that have some social or personal display characteristics. Problem-solving game playing revolves around the salesperson's perceived *competence* or credibility, and tends to arise with purchases requiring some technical expertise or with which the customer is inexperienced.

This conceptualization illustrates the fact that interactions between customer and salesperson are influenced by the *item* under consideration.

Bargaining Behavior

In much purchasing behavior, there is little opportunity for consumers to affect the price of the transaction. Haggling over the price of a tube of toothpaste, for example, is not commonplace in our marketing system. But purchases involving customer-salesperson interaction over high-ticket, considered purchase products and services may include the phenomenon of bargaining, a buyer optimization strategy that has come under some scrutiny in recent research.

Importance of Bargaining Behavior Why do some consumers pay less for identical items than other consumers? Research has pinpointed a number of variables that produce price differences for the same item, including the mode of retail operations, dealer practices, and type of store, as illustrated in Table 17-5.

Of all the reasons for price variations identified by Primeaux, the most significant was differences in consumer knowledge and *bargaining strength*.[34] This finding has implications for both consumers and marketers, and signals a need to understand how the bargaining process works in concept and practice.

Components of the Bargaining Process   Pennington has investigated bargaining in trans-

actions over appliances, and summarizes four observable components in a bargaining situation:[35]

1. Direct offers. Any concession by the salesperson such as reduction of price, more rapid delivery, or extended credit terms; the customer's offer to purchase for concessions such as the above.

2. Presentation of concession limits. Statement of expectations from the transaction by either salesperson or customer, such as statement of prices, desired style, or service policies.

3. Determination of concession limits. At-

Table 17-5   Reasons for Price Differences Among Customers Buying Identical Products*

REASONS FOR PRICE DIFFERENCES	NUMBER OF FIRMS RANKING REASON			
	RANKED FIRST	RANKED SECOND	RANKED THIRD	RANKED LOWER THAN THIRD OR UNRANKED
According to bargaining strength and knowledge of customers	14	4	2	17
Trade-in practices	8	9		20
Discounts to special groups of customers	6			31
Credit rating, trade-in, referral from other stores, customer bargaining strength (all of these factors)	2			35
Because of credit rating of the customer	1			36
To obtain cash needed for floor plan maturity	1			36
Whether referred by another salesman or store		1	1	35
No price differences among consumers	5			32

*Ranked from most important to least important.

Source: Walter J. Primeaux, Jr., "The Effect of Consumer Knowledge and Bargaining Strength on Final Selling Price: A Case Study," Journal of Business, Vol. 43 (October 1970), p. 420. Reprinted by permission.

tempts to determine expectations of the other person in the transaction, such as a salesperson's attempt to determine a customer's delivery schedule.

4. Attempts to change concession limits. Attempts by either customer or salesperson to get the other to change expectations of the transaction.

The variables in Pennington's study that were *positively* correlated with the likelihood of a completed purchase included the frequency of direct offers, the frequency of commitment to concession limits, the frequency of reference to styling, and the relative frequency of reference to a warranty. Although the incidence of bargaining was not especially common, it did appear to exert marked influence on actual outcomes.[36]

Personality Characteristics and Bargaining Strength The influence of personality traits on bargaining activities was scrutinized by Hughes et al., who isolated three trait factors:[37]

1. Efficient personal functioning: intellectual efficiency, tolerance, well-being, capacity for status, achievement via independence, social pressure, psychological-mindedness, flexibility, and risk-taking propensity.

2. Social adaptation: self-control, well-being, good impression, achievement via conformance, sociability, responsibility, and communality.

3. Social striving: sociability, dominance, self-acceptance, and masculinity.

These researchers found that bargaining personality could be viewed according to levels of aspiration and bargaining style. A high *level of aspiration* was related to bargaining strength, and individuals who displayed this trait tended to be more flexible, more socialized, higher in need achievement and less tolerant than others—in other words,

a rather ambitious person determined to look out for his or her own welfare. Bargaining *style* did not lend itself to prediction of success in negotiating as easily as aspiration, except for the conclusion that people with overbearing, impatient styles revealed a "fatalistic" attitude toward the outcome as beyond one's control. The more control over the situation a person might perceive, the more cooperative in the process he or she would tend to be.[38]

Despite the consumer interest in this area, bargaining process research is still at the developmental stage. Future studies may offer additional findings as to the kinds of products most conducive to bargaining, the salesperson and customer traits associated with different purchase outcomes, the possibility of segmenting consumers according to bargaining behavior, and the development of sophisticated negotiating strategies more consumers may adopt to their advantage.

Current findings suggest that bargaining is now confined to knowledgeable, "shrewder" consumers who have pricing information available to them and can psychologically assert themselves with salespeople. As such, they appear to fit the profile of activist consumers, better educated and relatively solvent. It would be extremely useful if bargaining knowledge could be shared by consumers who could most benefit by it—specifically lower income people who pay more for the same products and services that more affluent consumers can purchase for less.

Out-of-Store Purchasing

Purchasing through means other than a store visit includes the modes of catalog, telephone, door-to-door selling, and direct response advertising. There is much evidence that in-home shopping, the classification applied to all of these forms, has increased significantly compared with in-store purchasing. But while in-home shopping offers convenience benefits, it also entails greater risks. A second realm of some interest is the growing use of fast-food franchise outlets by motorists (although some of this purchasing activity may be affected by conditions of gasoline shortages and curtailed use of automobile travel).

In-Home Shopping *Catalog* purchasing has actually grown at a faster rate than retail shopping over the past few years, and is currently estimated at between $10 and $15 billion a year.[39] Reynolds has analyzed catalog-buying behavior as to convenience, type of catalog offerings, and degree of risk, reaching these conclusions about people who tend to shop by catalog:[40]

1. Catalog shoppers tend to be younger, more venturesome, and more self-confident, in line with their willingness to accept the higher degree of risk involved.

2. Catalog buyers enjoy higher incomes than other consumers and prefer more extensive merchandise assortments, which they may not find in local shopping outlets.

3. Life-style profiles may be derived for catalog buyers to aid in developing the catalogs themselves as well as advertising geared toward catalog distribution. Selling copy and graphics approaches could reasonably be directed to better-educated, sophisticated consumers.

Telephone purchasing from retail stores was investigated by Cox and Rich, who found that phone shoppers exhibited greater needs for convenience than other consumers and were more willing to accept the risk of relying on newspaper advertising for purchase information.[41]

Door-to-door selling appeals to a different type of shopper from those who prefer other styles of in-home purchasing. In a study by Peters and Ford, these consumers emerged as lower in income, social class, and education.[42]

Direct response advertising, placing an order directly from an ad, has become a prominent source of in-home purchases. Little research is available in this area, however, because direct response marketers are notoriously secretive about numbers of responses they draw and the characteristics of consumers who respond to their mail order ads. While print advertising is the traditional medium for direct response, television is used increasingly to sell record packages, books, jewelry, new home and personal care products, and instructional courses. This proliferating television advertising usually asks for *telephone* responses from consumers, which adds a new dimension to the use of the phone for in-home purchasing.

Most indications point to no special segment of consumers who are likely to respond to this form of advertising. Instead, the individual ad defines its own segment through the product offered, the appeal, and the medium in which it is placed. One book club that offers substantial discounts on fairly recent best-sellers, for example, is targeted toward housewives who are over twenty-five, have families, have generally attained a high school education with possibly some college, and read magazines such as *Family Circle* and *Better Homes and Gardens*.

The Future of In-Home Shopping The technology to greatly increase in-home shopping and its benefits is at hand, with implications for change in many distribution systems.

Department store shopping is expected to

become more a form for direct response buying through innovations such as ordering by closed circuit television (currently in the experimental stage in some retail chains).[43]

Drugstores may soon automate the dispensing of prescription drugs, and *supermarkets* may offer food items on a direct response order basis.[44]

A *TV bookstore* is being tested at the time of this writing and, if successful, will undoubtedly stimulate purchases of other lei-sure items through television rather than in the traditional retail setting.

Like all technological innovations, these changes in buying patterns are both created and reflected in changing life styles. Consumers have already indicated a keen receptivity to new direct response techniques because these methods conform to work and leisure patterns and fill a desire to simplify certain kinds of purchases through more convenient distribution systems.

Postpurchase Behavior

All purchase behavior, as a continuous process, must entail consequences for the buyer. These occur as the result of *post-decision reevaluation*, and may be categorized as *satisfaction* or *dissatisfaction* with the purchase.

(decision making) processes.[45] These conditions distinguish brand loyalty from other types of repeat purchasing behavior, such as buying the same brand twice but subsequently switching to several purchases of another brand.

Postpurchase Satisfaction

When a purchase expectation is perceived by a consumer as rewarded by the purchase, this is termed *satisfaction*. A condition of satisfaction will tend to prompt repeat purchases because, consistent with the learning theories discussed in chapter 10, such behavior is reinforcing.

Brand loyalty represents one specific form of repeat purchase based on certain criteria—that the "loyal" behavior is a "*biased,* nonrandom *behavioral response* in terms of purchase expressed over *time* by some *decision-making* unit with respect to *one or more alternative brands* out of (an evoked) set of brands and is a function of psychological

Postpurchase Dissatisfaction

When a purchase expectation is *not* seen as rewarded by the purchase, dissatisfaction will result. *Dissatisfaction* is defined as "the degree of disparity between expectations and perceived product performance" by Anderson, who summarizes three behavioral theories about this consequence:[46]

Cognitive Dissonance (Assimilation) When a disparity between performance and expectancy exists, a state of psychological inconsistency or dissonance results. This state is uncomfortable and must be reduced by changing the new product perception to align with the expectancy. Dissonance has been interpreted as a necessary outcome of decision making, with the degree of dissonance experienced a function of several factors:[47]

1. The more important the decision, the greater the dissonance.
2. The greater the number of alternatives considered before the purchase decision, the greater the dissonance.
3. The more attractive the rejected alternatives, the greater the dissonance.
4. The more frequently the product or brand is purchased, the lesser the degree of dissonance.
5. The more irrevocable the purchase, the greater the dissonance.

Theoretically, a consumer may reduce dissonance by seeking out reinforcing information about the item purchased. This has led to the assumption that favorable product information should be dispensed to consumers who have just made a purchase. One study that attempted to help people who had just bought refrigerators reduce their dissonance obtained mixed results; while letters to the new customers appeared to exert a favorable effect, telephone calls did not.[48]

Thus, marketers are left at this stage of research with some uncertainty about dissonance theory and its application to postpurchase situations.

Contrast This theory suggests that the surprise effect of actual product performance that falls short of expectations may cause consumers to *exaggerate* the disparity. Anderson notes that advertising, which usually leans toward overevaluations of product performance, might prompt more realistic evaluation through thoughtfully conceived understatement.[49]

Generalized Negativity According to some researchers, any unfulfilled expectancy creates a negative attitude that tends to extend to other items as well.[50] Under this premise, a consumer dissatisfied with the performance of one product purchased may view other products in the same environment with the same jaundiced eye, although their actual performance may be quite satisfactory. In this case, some products which perform well may suffer guilt by association. Such situations would be extremely difficult for marketers to control.

The realm of postpurchase satisfaction and dissatisfaction remains obviously troublesome. Not enough is known about the dynamics of cognition and behavior after purchase, and what does seem probable is not subject to visible marketing applications. Until better prescriptions are developed, two general guidelines for encouraging postpurchase satisfaction would be to (1) *keep advertising claims in proportion to reality,* in hopes of limiting disappointment and (2) *provide favorable product information* to consumers after they have made purchases likely to result in a high degree of dissonance. This would apply most often to high ticket, considered purchase products and services. A follow-up letter to new car buyers thanking them for purchasing that particular make and furnishing them with additional product information may reduce anxiety created by such an expensive purchase. Conversely, a bank experimented with letters to former customers who had just *closed* accounts, asking whether they were dissatisfied with that bank's services or personnel. A sizable number of the former depositors actually reopened their accounts soon after.[51]

Summary

Purchasing behavior may be conceptualized as a process leading from purchase intentions to postpurchase behavioral consequences. Some purchases are planned beforehand, and research has attempted to predict *planned* purchases through measures of *intent* and *probability*. Estimates of probability, the most common approach, consider factors such as *family roles, purchase timing, personality characteristics,* and *product attributes.* Between intentions and actual purchases, *intervening variables* may come into play— usually changes in financial status or changes in life style. Some purchases are of the *unplanned* or *impulse* variety, which occur in a retail environment and are generally stimulated by in-store factors that marketers and retailers may control to varying degrees. *Retail displays* and *packaging* are two areas where product or brand visibility may be enhanced to stimulate impulse buying. *Overt* purchasing behavior may occur in a retail store where *salesperson-customer interaction* takes place. *Bargaining*, a buyer optimization strategy, has emerged as one kind of interaction explaining why some consumers pay less for identical products than others. *Out-of-store* purchasing represents a growing phenomenon, already reflected in catalog, telephone, and direct response sales figures. *Postpurchase evaluation* encompasses two possible consequences, *satisfaction* and *dissatisfaction*, which are currently at the developmental stage in mainstream consumer research.

NOTES

1. John E. Swan and Linda Jones Combs, "Product Preference and Consumer Satisfaction: A New Concept," *Journal of Marketing*, Vol. 40, No. 2 (April 1976), p. 25.

2. Chem L. Marayana and Rom J. Markin, "Consumer Behavior and Product Performance: An Alternative Conceptualization," *Journal of Marketing*, Vol. 39, No. 4 (October 1975), p. 1.

3. F. Thomas Juster, "Consumer Buying Intentions and Purchase Probability: An Experiment in Survey Design," in *Consumer Buying Intentions and Purchase Probability*, F. Thomas Juster (New York: Columbia University Press, 1966).

4. E. Laird Landon, Jr., "Self Concept, Ideal Self-Concept and Consumer Purchase Intentions," *Journal of Consumer Research*, Vol. 1 (September 1974).

5. Juster, "Buying Intentions," p. 7.

6. Donald H. Granbois and Ronald P. Willett, "An Empirical Test of Probabilistic Intentions and Preference Models for Consumer Durables Purchasing," in *Marketing and the New Science of Planning*, ed. Robert L. King *Proceedings of the 1968 Conference of the American Marketing Association*, Chicago, 1968.

7. Jan Stapel, "Predictive Attitudes," in *Attitude Research on the Rocks*, ed. Lee Adler and Irving Crespi (Chicago: American Marketing Association, 1968).

8. Jan Stapel, "Sales Effects of Print Ads," *Journal of Advertising Research*, Vol. 11, No. 3 (June 1971).

9. Granbois and Willett, "Probabilistic Intentions."

10. Isabella C. M. Cunningham and Robert T. Green, "Purchasing Roles in the U.S. Family, 1955 and 1973," *Journal of Marketing*, Vol. 38 (October 1974).

11. *The Roles of Husbands and Wives in Purchasing Decisions, Life*, 1965.

12. James P. Forkan, "Researchers Find Crises Change Buying Patterns," *Advertising Age*, April 8, 1974.

13. David T. Kollat and Ronald P. Willett, "Customer Impulse Purchasing Behavior," *Journal of Marketing Research*, Vol. 4 (February 1967).

14. Hawkins Stern, "The Significance of Impulse Buying Today," *Journal of Marketing*, Vol. 26 (April 1962).

15. James D. Shaffer, "The Influence of Impulse Buying or In-the-Store Decisions on Consumers' Food Purchases," *Journal of Farm Economics* (May 1960).

16. David T. Kollat and Ronald P. Willett, "Is Impulse Purchasing Really a Useful Concept for Marketing Decisions?", *Journal of Marketing*, Vol. 33 (January 1969).

17. Kollat and Willett, "Impulse Purchasing."

18. Michel Chevalier, "Increase in Sales Due to In-Store Displays," *Journal of Marketing Research*, Vol. 12, No. 4 (November 1975), p. 426.

19. Keith R. Cox, "The Effect of Shelf Space Upon Sales of a Branded Product," *Journal of Marketing Research*, Vol. 7 (February 1970).

20. Ronald E. Frank and William F. Massey, "Shelf Position and Space Effects on Sales," *Journal of Marketing Research*, Vol. 7 (1970).

21. David Schwartz, "Evaluating Packaging," *Journal of Advertising Research*, Vol. 2, No. 5 (1961).

22. *Advertising News of New York*, September 16, 1976.

23. *The Andy Awards Annual*, 1976.

24. Russell W. Belk, "An Exploratory Assessment of Situational Effects in Buyer Behavior," *Journal of Marketing Research*, Vol. 11 (May 1974).

25. Belk, "Situational Effects."

26. Kollat and Willett, "Impulse Purchasing."

27. "Make Your Merchandising Fit Their Lifestyles," *Progressive Grocer* (April 1974).

28. Point of Purchase Advertising Institute, 1977.

29. Timothy C. Brock, "Communicator-Recipient Similarity and Decision Change," *Journal of Personality and Social Psychology*, Vol. 1 (June 1965).

30. Franklin B. Evans, "Selling as a Dyadic Relationship," *American Behavioral Scientist*, Vol. 6 (May 1963).

31. Herbert C. Kelman, "Processes of Opinion Change," *Public Opinion Quarterly*, Vol. 25 (Spring 1961).

32. Earl E. Baer, *Salesmanship*, New York: McGraw-Hill, 1972, p. 51.

33. Arch G. Woodside and J. William Davenport, Jr., "The Effect of Salesman Similarity and Expertise on Consumer Purchasing Behavior," *Journal of Marketing Research*, Vol. II (May 1974).

34. Walter J. Primeaux, Jr., "The Effect of Consumer Knowledge and Bargaining Strength on Final Selling Price: A Case Study," *Journal of Business*, Vol. 43 (October 1970).

35. Alan L. Pennington, "Customer-Salesman Bargaining Behavior in Retail Transactions," *Journal of Marketing Research*, Vol. 5 (August 1968), p. 256.

36. Pennington, "Bargaining Behavior."

37. G. David Hughes, Joseph B. Jushasz, and Bruno Contini, "The Influence of Personality on the Bargaining Process," *Journal of Business*, Vol. 46 (October 1973), p. 599.

38. Hughes et al, "Influence of Personality," pp. 599–600.

39. *Forbes*, March 15, 1972, p. 46.

40. Fred D. Reynolds, "An Analysis of Catalog Buying Behavior," *Journal of Marketing*, Vol. 38 (July 1974), pp. 47–51.

41. Donald F. Cox and Stuart R. Rich, "Perceived Risk and Consumer Decision-Making; the Case of Telephone Shopping," *Journal of Marketing Research*, Vol. 1 (November 1964).

42. William H. Peters and Neil M. Ford, "A Profile of Urban In-Home Shoppers: The Other Half," *Journal of Marketing*, Vol. 36 (January 1972).

43. Calvin Hodock, "Use of Psychographics in Analysis of Channels of Distribution," in *Life Style and Psychographics*, ed. William D. Wells (American Marketing Association, 1974).

44. Hodock, "Use of Psychographics."

45. Jacob Jacoby and David B. Kyner, "Brand Loyalty vs. Repeat Purchasing Behavior," *Journal of Marketing Research*, Vol. 10 (February 1973), p. 2.

46. Ralph E. Anderson, "Consumer Dissatisfaction: The Effect of Disconfirmed Expectancy on Perceived Product Performance," *Journal of Marketing Research*, Vol. 11 (February 1973), pp. 38–44.

47. Sadaomi Oshikawa, "Can Cognitive Disso-

‍

nance Theory Explain Consumer Behavior?", *Journal of Marketing*, Vol. 33 (October 1969).

48. Shelby D. Hunt, "Post-Transaction Communications and Dissonance Reduction," *Journal of Marketing*, Vol. 34 (July 1970).

49. Anderson, "Consumer Dissatisfaction."

50. J. Merrill Carlsmith and Elliot Aronson, "Some Hedonic Consequences of the Confirmation and Disconfirmation of Expectancies," *Journal of Abnormal and Social Psychology*, 66, February 1963, cited in Anderson, "Consumer Dissatisfaction."

51. Christopher C. Gilson and Harold W. Berkman, "Why People Hate Their Banks" (Pilot study in progress, C. W. Post Center, Long Island University, 1977).

MARKETING APPLICATIONS

Conclusion 1 *Purchase probability based on consumer statements of intent-to-purchase offers a useful predictor of planned purchase behavior for automobiles, appliances, and food products.*

Application The measurement of intent-to-purchase should be used to evaluate the effectiveness of marketing communications. Various ads, for example, may be posttested by asking questions such as, "Do you intend to buy the item advertised?" rather than, "Do you remember the headline/photograph/body copy?" Ads which produce the highest measures of intent to buy might be judged best for enhancing purchase probability (other ads may be designed solely to build awareness or to solve specific marketing problems). To produce the best results in this area the ad should offer (1) an incentive to act quickly in making the purchase, (2) clear directions as to where the purchase may be made.

Conclusion 2 *Unplanned purchases of a given item in the retail environment may be enhanced by improving its visibility within the store.*

Application Retailers have traditionally followed this axiom by placing their "impulse" items—candy, souvenirs, and so on—around the cash register where they cannot be overlooked by anyone making a purchase. Special displays may also be created to boost sales of goods which are moving at a very slow pace. A bookstore, for instance, could put up the sign "How to Get Rich (Maybe)," and assemble underneath it books on the stock market, money management, diving for buried treasure, the diary of a counterfeiter, and a real estate sales manual.

Conclusion 3 *In many retail stores, considered purchase items may be purchased by some consumers for less than other consumers pay for the same goods. This is due to the buyer-optimization strategy known as bargaining.*

Application As a consumer, you have probably paid the full ticket price for many items you could have purchased for a reduced amount had you used bargaining techniques. Not all stores will give discounts on this basis—prices in many chain stores are fixed, and individual managers and salesmen are allowed no bargaining flexibility. But you have nothing to lose by initiating a bargaining session the next time you buy a stereo, appliance, a watch, or any other fairly expensive item. Refer to pages of the following chapter, shop for prices at different stores, establish what you want to pay and, when you have selected the item you want, chances are you can buy it for less than you think through bargaining.

ASSIGNMENTS

Research Assignment

Background The phenomenon of bargaining in high-ticket transactions offers one interesting example of how consumer characteristics can affect the outcome of a purchasing event. As an academic researcher, you wish to study the interaction between salesperson and consumer in the bargaining process over a stereo system.

Methodology Your research will be conducted through the medium of role playing in the bargaining game. Select five subjects to play the roles of salespersons and five to act as consumers. The salesperson in each transaction will be given a set of parameters, within which he or she has to operate—including the lowest price at which the stereo system may be sold, the possible delivery dates, and other pertinent information. (Your instructor holds this information so that no subject who plays the consumer role will know these limitations on the transaction.) The consumer's objective in each case is to obtain the lowest possible price and whatever other concessions may be required. Make an anecdotal record of each of the five transactions and note the following:

- Preservation of direct offers and concession limits.
- Characteristics of the consumer in each transaction.

  Compare your records of each transaction and draw conclusions about the effects of consumer behavioral traits in driving the best "bargain."

Extrapolation What do your findings suggest about the bargaining process itself, the "forcefulness" of both salesperson and consumer in the transaction, and additional variables that may have come into play?

Creative Assignment

  The Point-of-Purchase Advertising Institute (POPAI) is a trade association designed to help marketers who use this medium improve their retail effectiveness. You have been hired as a Creative Consultant to demonstrate to their clients how point-of-purchase (P-O-P) can be better conceived by advertisers who run expensive television and space campaigns. The problem is that many of these advertisers fail to tie their P-O-P materials directly into their current campaign strategies, and retailers are often left creating homemade displays that do not perform as well as professionally designed units. You are given considerable latitude in this assignment. Choose any P-O-P display that does *not* reflect a highly visible advertising campaign for a product and design a new one that will gain instant recognition from consumers who have already seen advertising for the product. Consult the preceding chapter for considerations in creating your display.

Managerial Assignment

As the new Store Manager at Kalvan's, a large discount appliance outlet, your first objective is to boost your store's flagging sales performance in five categories—refrigerators, washers and dryers, toasters, and irons. You have the authority to discount each of these items up to 30 percent, as well as to determine which appliances will be featured in local newspaper advertising and in-store promotion.

You have read in a recent trade magazine that consumers tend to establish priority patterns for the durable goods they buy, thinking of appliances in terms of sets to be acquired over a period of time. Now you wish to apply this information in a two-week special promotion directed toward moving those particular items.

Brush up on the concept of priority patterns by reviewing the McFall article on page 440 of the preceding chapter. Then develop an advertising, promotion, and discounting policy that will include:

• Deciding which items to feature most prominently in advertising and promotion.

• Determining which appliances should be discounted most drastically.

• Instructing your sales force to offer special discounts when *two* items are purchased (one as a condition of the other) and advising them on which combinations to push hardest.

SELECTED READINGS

Dash, Joseph F., Leon G. Schiffman, and Conrad Berenson. "Risk and Personality-Related Dimensions of Store Choice." *Journal of Marketing*, Vol. 40, No. 1 (January 1976), pp. 32–39.

Jacobs, Laurence W. "The Continuity Factor in Retail Store Display." *Journal of the Academy of Marketing Science*, Vol. 2, No. 2 (Spring 1974), pp. 340–350.

Newman, Joseph W. and Richard A. Werbel. "Automobile Brand Loyalty." *Journal of the Academy of Marketing Science* Vol. 2, No. 4 (Fall 1974), pp. 593–601.

Samli, A. Coskun. "Use of Segmentation Index to Measure Store Loyalty." *Journal of Retailing* (Spring 1975), pp. 51–60.

Taylor, James W., John J. Houlahan and Alan C. Gabriel. "The Purchase Intention Question in New Product Development: A Field Test." *Journal of Marketing Research*, Vol. 39, No. 1 (January 1975), pp. 90–92.

V
APPLICATIONS AND ISSUES
IN CONSUMER BEHAVIOR

Diffusion of Innovation
Life Style and Psychographics
Consumerism and Social Responsibilities

OBJECTIVES

1. Define *diffusion, adoption,* and *innovation.*
   464

2. Discuss the *four key factors* in the diffusion process. *468*

3. Describe the *eight product characteristics* that determine the success of an innovation. *469*

4. Discuss the *adopter characteristics* associated with consumers who are likely to be the first to try innovations. *472*

5. Analyze the *communications process* in adoption behavior. *477*

6. Summarize researchers' findings relevant to *consumer adoption* behavior. *478*

7. Summarize findings for *retail* adoption. *482*

8. Describe four kinds of *diffusion models* and discuss the problems in using them. *484*

EIGHTEEN

Diffusion of Innovation

The acceptance by an adventurous few of some new mode of behavior, which then begins spreading to increasingly larger groups of people, is known as diffusion.

Social scientists were the first to apply this concept to questions of diffusion from one culture to another (discussed in chapter 4) and the acceptance of innovative social ideas within a society. One striking, if still controversial, example from American society has been the popularization of marijuana smoking. This practice, originally confined to exotic subcultures such as jazz musicians and avant garde creative people, found some favor with counterculture advocates and students during the 1960s. Through media coverage of the phenomenon and interpersonal influences, marijuana smoking has developed into a loosely tolerated middle class activity—to the point where some states have "decriminalized" the behavior with varying degrees of latitude.

Marketers in the business of introducing new products study the diffusion process to determine how it works and, particularly, how the process may be accelerated to reach the greatest number of people with new market items in the shortest possible time. Thus, the following chapter analyzes the theory of diffusion and presents a broad sampling of current research directed to consumer acceptance patterns. Relevant topics include:

• What psychological factors distinguish the people who will readily try new products.

• How probable adopters of different kinds of products may be segmented on the basis of life style.

• Why consumers accepted toothpaste with fluoride but not toothpaste with stripes.

• Why consumers rebelled against the much-touted "midi" look (and changed the "rules" about fashion acceptance).

• How the traditional pattern of diffusion ("trickle-down" from the loftiest segments of society) may be giving way to a new trend ("trickle up" from the less-established segments).

A working knowledge of diffusion principles will prove useful to anyone who wants to know why some bold new ideas enjoy popular success while others are best remembered as Edsels.

The Diffusion Process

Every year in the United States, consumers are exposed to a staggering array of new products and services. Yet, only one fresh commercial concept in sixty is actually successful. Why do some new products, like the digital wristwatch and the bonded razor, find widespread acceptance, while others, such as the Corfam shoe and the midi-length dress, just fizzle out?

From the consumer's standpoint, each new product is an "innovation" that may or may not be deemed useful or enhancing of life style. Thus, innovations may be accepted or rejected. Some products, by virtue of their own attributes, are more likely to be accepted than others. And some consumers, because of individual characteristics, are more inclined than others to accept an innovation. The adoption of a new product and its subsequent spreading throughout a population is studied through a sociocultural concept known as the diffusion of innovations.

This chapter discusses how the diffusion process works, how characteristics of both product and consumer will affect the success of a new product, and how sociocultural influences and communication processes can determine product acceptance or rejection. Because marketers are developing a keen interest in the adoption of retail and industrial innovations, these concepts are also introduced here. In addition, models that have been devised to represent or predict the diffusion process are evaluated for their potential usefulness to marketers.

There are three terms universally accepted for analyzing the diffusion of innovations: *diffusion, adoption* behavior, and the *innovation* itself.

Diffusion

In the language of sociology and anthropology, diffusion is the propagation and spread among a given population of ideas, beliefs, tastes, behavior patterns, and religious practices.[1] From a marketing standpoint, diffusion is the process through which goods and services flow from producer to consumer (industrial as well as individual). This definition includes the important consideration of *rate of acceptance*. And the principal feature of diffusion is that it occurs over a period of *time*.

Adoption

While diffusion refers to the spread of new goods or services, *adoption* is the process by which a *potential* user becomes an *actual* user.[2] The first stage in this process is awareness and perception of the innovation, followed by consideration, trial, use, and continued use. Various models of adoption behavior have been developed,[3] and will be presented, along with discussions of the correlates of adopter behavior for specific goods and services. Because interpersonal information sources are important to adoption, it may be said that diffusion occurs within social systems. The smallest such system might be the individual consumer's friendship group; on a broader level, it would be a given market segment. The individual consumer is not the only significant adoption unit. Industrial or institutional purchasing committees are also buying units. So are families. And although adoption implies a commitment to purchase and then repurchase, the diffusion process must also take into consideration the possibilities of limited adoption and rejection.

Because we know that products exhibit a "life cycle," we can look upon a cumulative diffusion curve as the first half of such a cycle, represented as an S-curve. This curve indicates that a few consumers are early adopters. As time passes and both interpersonal and intersocial communication progresses, more and more adopters should appear. The curve rises, sometimes rather sharply, toward a theoretical 100 percent level, the point at which all potential buyers in a population have become actual users. The data used for diffusion studies underscores the *aggregative* nature of the process. Adoption rates per unit of time and ultimate diffusion levels are described and charted for whole populations (Figure 18-1).

Innovation

While diffusion and adoption are relatively clearcut concepts, innovation is subject to

Figure 18-1   The adoption S-curve.

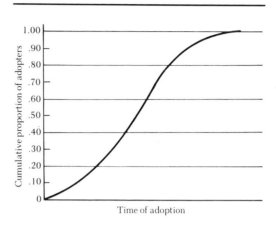

some interpretation. Is new product packaging tantamount to innovation? Does adding a different scent (new lemon-scented Joy) or taking scent away (new unscented Arrid) constitute a new product? How about products requiring new treatment or usage (now *you* add the egg, or mix *and* bake in the same pan)? How innovative are each year's "new" model cars? Or is the consumer's subjective dimension the salient feature—any item or service is new if consumers perceive it as new? Perhaps the time dimension is more crucial: Any form of a product or service that has only recently entered a market is an innovation. The opening of a new branch of some chain store might be an innovation in a given area.

Each description of innovation has applicability to different items. The studies of diffusion of innovations considered in this chapter will show that "newness" has many aspects and depends on the product under examination.

For present purposes, an innovation may be considered along a continuum. The range of the continuum is based on the social impact of the innovation. At one end there exists the *continuous* innovation. Existing patterns of consumption are least disrupted by the alteration of already accepted products. Adding fluoride to toothpaste, menthol to cigarettes, and four headlights to cars are examples. So is introducing shampoos with an acid-alkaline balance and breakfast cereal containing a full supply of daily vitamins.

Innovations that are *dynamically continuous* may disrupt consumer use patterns more than continuous innovations, but still do not radically alter set patterns. "Water piks" and electric toothbrushes fit into whatever dental care habits consumers already had. Even though the pushbutton phone led to publication of a songbook, it still remained fundamentally a telephone. And be it ever so sensational, a waterbed is still a bed.

At the opposite end of the continuum is the *discontinuous innovation,* a new product that necessitates real change in consumption and behavior patterns. Early in this century, the automobile, radio, and telephone were such innovations. In our own time, the computer ranks foremost in its impact.[4]

Discontinuous innovations are infrequent occurrences in the marketplace; most new entries to the market are continuous. It is the exceedingly expensive nature of new product development, among other factors, that makes companies so anxious to win wide acceptance for their products, particularly in an economy where a new product failure can cost as much as $20 million.[5]

Origins and Applications of Diffusion Study

The origins of research in diffusion lie in nineteenth century anthropology and sociology. At first, British and German anthropologists studied the spread of ethnic and religious movements, instances of cultural transfer, and changes in commerce and technology. Economists and sociologists in the early twentieth century were interested in persuading whole populations to accept ideas or products considered "for the good of society," and marketers were beginning to apply this research to the problem of new product acceptance. (See Table 18-1.)

Study of Diffusion in the United States

The study of diffusion became most intense in this country during the 1920s. To learn why some agricultural innovations financed at heavy cost (such as grain and corn hybridization) were adopted by farmers while others were rejected, the U.S. Department of Agriculture channeled sizable research funds into extensive diffusion research. Sociologists have investigated diffusion in voting studies (interaction of mass media communications and informal personal contact), health insurance, and synthetic fibers;[6] one early marketing study focused on the adoption of color television.[7]

The Traditional Research Approach

Two illustrations of diffusion research are Boone's study of the acceptance of cable television in a small Mississippi town and

+ NO
Table 18-1 The Diffusion Research Tradition

TRADITION	MAIN DISCIPLINES REPRESENTED	MAIN METHOD OF DATA GATHERING AND ANALYSIS	MAIN UNIT OF ANALYSIS	MAJOR TYPES OF FINDINGS
Anthropology	Anthropology	Participant observer combined with descriptive analysis	Societies or tribes	How idea diffuses from one society to another; consequences of innovation
Early sociology	Sociology	Data from secondary sources, and a type of statistical analysis	Mainly communities but also individuals	S-shaped adopter distribution; correlates of innovativeness
Rural sociology	Sociology	Personal interviews and statistical analysis	Individual farmers	Correlates of innovativeness, characteristics of ideas related to their rate of adoption; source of information at adoption process stages; S-shaped adopter distribution
Education	Education	Mailed questionnaires and statistical analysis	School systems	Correlates of innovativeness; S-shaped adopter distribution
Industrial	Industrial economists; Industrial engineers	Case studies and statistical analysis	Industrial firms	Correlates of innovativeness
Medical sociology	Sociology; Public Health	Personal interviews and statistical analysis	Individuals	Opinion leadership in diffusion; correlates of innovativeness

Source: Reprinted with permission of Macmillan Publishing Co., Inc., from Diffusion of Innovation *by Everett M. Rogers, Copyright © 1962 by The Free Press, p. 306.*

Gurevitch and Loevy's study of the diffusion of television in Israeli *kibbutzim.*

Boone's aim was to pinpoint behavioral characteristics among all adopters for a period of several years following the actual introduction of some innovation.[8] He identified roughly equal populations of *consumer innovators* (those who bought cable service within three months of the initial offering) and *consumer followers* (those who got on the cable at least six months after first offers went out). He found that the innovators were more likely to be married; change jobs; belong to and hold offices in civic, social, professional, and church groups. Their income levels were also generally higher, enabling them to take more purchasing risks. Innovators who did reveal incomes below the median, however, revealed a higher rank on a number of personality variables—tolerance, sense of well-being, sociability, and dominance, among others. Thus, it appears that high scores on certain personality traits may overcome the inhibitions on innovation adoption attributed to income. In addition, the innovators scored higher than followers in *leadership ability, self-confidence, ascendancy,* and *achievement.*

Gurevitch and Loevy's research attempted to measure the *degree* of innovativeness in a society.[9] Television broadcasting came to

Israel in the spring of 1968, and the kibbutz proved an unusually well-controlled test area for observing its adoption. Since modernity is a prime value to members of the kibbutz, acceptance of such an innovation could be expected. But countervailing values also existed—social collectivism, ideological collectivism, and cultural creativity. All of these values could have been perceived as threatened by the introduction of television sets in individual rooms, exposure to "outside" voices and cultural-spiritual influences, and the inclination to become passive absorbers of culture rather than to create one's own programs for kibbutz weekend entertainment.

This research concluded that cultural incompatibility decelerated the rate of diffusion. It also led to rules demanding placement of television sets in public rooms, prescribing the schedules of viewing, and limiting the amount of individual viewing. Nevertheless, diffusion of television in the Israeli kibbutzim was achieved—the social commitment of members did not appear devastated over time by the introduction of television, suggesting that the social fabric of the kibbutz can stretch to adopt technological and social innovations.

As these studies indicate, diffusion research can be applied in situations requiring varying emphases. A study may focus on (1) the *adopters* at any one of a number of stages of the adoption process, examining their *personality, motivational,* or *demographic* profiles, (2) the *values* of a culture, and (3) the *attributes* of the innovation. Before examining specific findings about these factors, the nature of the diffusion process itself will be discussed.

How the Diffusion Process Works

The key features of the diffusion process are (1) the *innovation;* (2) the *awareness* of the innovation by its potential adopters; (3) the *adopters* themselves, in particular *social* and *cultural* systems; and (4) *time.*

Innovations have already been described as ranging from continuous to discontinuous. They may be developed to meet specific needs or may be marketed to create a felt need for the innovation.

Communication plays a vital role in consumer awareness and perception of innovative goods and services. To a large extent communication is accomplished through media channels, but the rate of diffusion is also affected by consumer awareness from interpersonal and other sources like references from users or trial samples.

Adoption, such as trial use and resulting sustained use, takes place within the boundaries of social and cultural systems. A market segment can constitute a social system. So may a community or an adopter's group of friends. Some adopters are *opinion leaders* in their social systems (discussed in chapter 15).

Time, as applied to diffusion, sorts out the early, middle, and late adopters of an inovation. There is frequently a lag between discovery or development of some innovation and its actual appearance in the marketplace. This time lag can be manipulated to heighten consumer anticipation, as in announcing the coming of a major motion picture or in early "leaking" of features to be included in new model cars.

The four dimensions of diffusion listed

above are referred to as *external.* Also significant in each individual's decision to try, use, and adopt a product or service for continued usage are a number of *internal* dimensions: personality, perception, attitudinal set, and motivation. Rogers portrays as a hierarchical structure[10] (shown in Figure 18-2) the multistage mental and behavioral process that leads a consumer from (1) initial awareness of an innovation through (2) interest, evaluation, and trial to (3) ultimate adoption.

Each feature of the diffusion process—the role of the innovation, the role of the adopter, social and cultural influences, and communications—will be discussed separately. These do, however, function in closely inter-

related ways, as selected *models* of diffusion processes will indicate.

The Role of the Innovation

Assembling data from a vast amount of research, Rogers determined certain characteristics inherent in innovative products that achieve successful diffusion.[11] These include relative advantage, compatibility, communicability, complexity, divisibility (or trialability), availability, fulfillment of felt needs, and immediateness of benefit.

Relative advantage is a critical element in the diffusion of an innovative product. Rela-

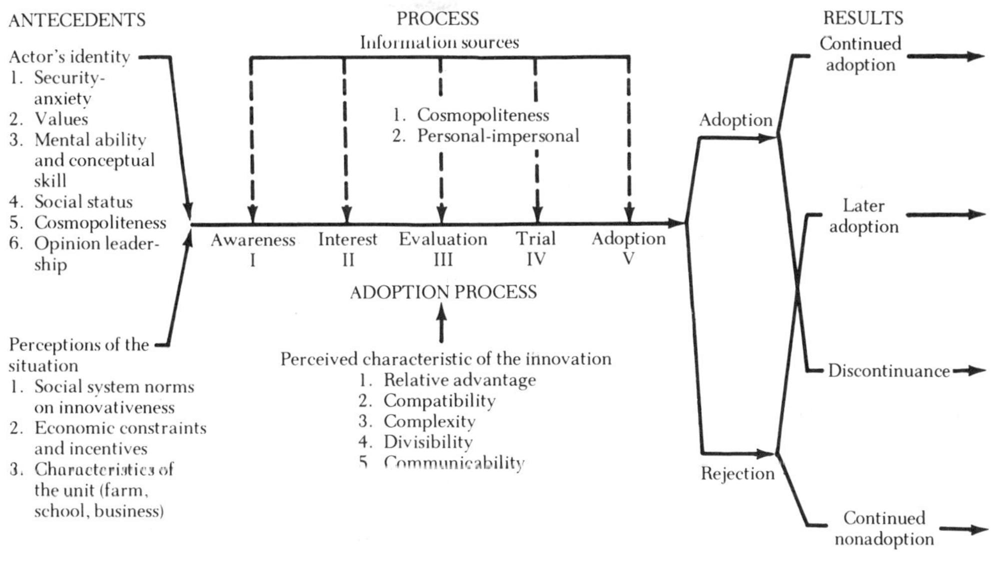

Figure 18-2   Paradigm of the adoption of an innovation by an individual within a social system.

tive to the product it is to supersede, the innovation must offer a perceivable advantage or improvement. When detergent marketers demonstrated that enzymes did make a difference in product functionality, they were rewarded by a successful innovation. But simply changing the scent of a detergent or its form—powder, flake, granule, or liquid—adds no real relative advantage. Striped toothpaste appeared and disappeared in a very short time, while toothpastes with fluoride compounds added have been widely accepted.

At the same time, the innovation must feature *compatibility*. It must not demand of consumers too great a change in their existing behavior and attitude sets, or it will be sluggish in gaining adoption. A new product must not be too disruptive of present values and past experiences. One example of a premature innovation was a red-colored but translucent gel lipstick introduced to consumers in 1963. Startlingly different from any other lipstick at that time, it soon left the market place. The 1970s, however, have seen numerous gel-type cosmetics from every major manufacturer achieve a high degree of compatibility with current consumer experiences.

Complexity refers to the degree of ease or difficulty a consumer may have in understanding and using a new item. If a buyer is required to plow through detailed explanations and instructions before using a new product, he or she is less likely to adopt that product.

Communicability is related to complexity in that the innovation, or the results to be gained from its use, must be easily communicated (visually or verbally) to others. Visibility in social situations enhances diffusion.

Divisibility refers to a product's introduction in small sample packages. The consumer who can try something new with little risk is more likely to do so. Devices for this purpose include in-store sampling, door-to-door distribution of "freebies," and packaging in miniature sizes.

Once a consumer has tried and been satisfied with a new product, repurchase of the item must be easy. Thus *availability* of the item is crucial to diffusion.

Finally, the consumer must perceive that the product tried has indeed met some *felt needs* and has been of *immediate benefit*. The consumer will search for more information about the product and maintain interest to the degree that the product provides those satisfactions.

The Role of the Adopter

Consumers may be segmented on the basis of willingness to adopt new brands, products, or services. Peterson has distinguished *optimal* (most likely) adopter categories by showing Rogers's classification of adopter groups during a time period, based on statistical relationships between the normal or bell curve and the standard deviation measure of dispersion[13] (Figure 18-3).

Although such a distribution of categories of adopters is easily applied in many varying studies and permits generalization and replication, it is arbitrary when applied to marketing situations, and may not apply equally to different types of innovations or to all kinds of innovation environments. Peterson cites fads, such as hula-hoops, and discontinuous innovations as always having skewed, nonnormal or bell-shaped diffusion curves. Discerning situation-specific adopter categories, Peterson feels, may be of more use to marketers, especially as the data on new markets for given items could be accumulated and used for prediction purposes.[14]

How Gillette Keeps Coming up with "New" Ways to Shave

Shaving with a razor would seem to be a fairly simple business, hardly complicated by too many new product innovations.

Yet Gillette manages to maintain its leadership in the shaving market—and boost sales every year—by constantly introducing "better" blades and razors to add to its already impressive collection at every supermarket checkout counter.

Each "innovation" offers some advantage over the previous one. For instance, the Trac II Adjustable razor enables the groggy consumer to inject new blades directly into the razor, avoiding mishaps that may occur by touching the blade. And now a disposable razor eliminates even that necessity, since one only has to throw away the whole inexpensive razor when the blade begins to get dull. It's called, appropriately enough, *Good News.*

As one observer notes, Gillette is no longer just giving away the razor to sell the blade, but is literally throwing it away.[12]

Four Innovations from Gillette.

Courtesy of the Gillette Company, Safety Razor Division, Boston, Mass.

Figure 18-3   Adopter categorization on the basis of relative time of adoption of innovations.

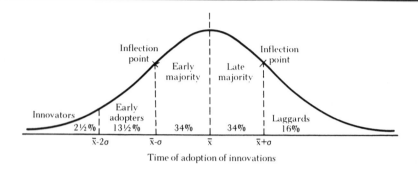

Time of adoption of innovations

Source: Reprinted with permission of Macmillan Publishing Co., Inc., from Diffusion of Innovation *by Everett M. Rogers, Copyright © 1962 by The Free Press. p. 306.*

Identifying Adopters   It is not surprising that consumers, given their widely divergent personalities, incomes, ages, motivations, attitudes, and values, will adopt new market entries at different times. Marketers are concerned with isolating those variables that are most useful in predicting adoption behavior—particularly the role of communicators.[15]

Robertson identified these factors across product categories for adopters versus non-adopters.[16] He found that adopters are younger, better educated, and are found in higher income and occupational strata than non-adopters. They are highly social in formal and informal ways, ascendant, leaders of opinion, and tend to read more than watch television. They are also more venturesome, revealing favorable attitudes toward newness and perceiving less risk in trying things out.

Robertson and Kennedy studied adopter characteristics using a small home appliance as the product innovation.[17] Basing their selection on previous research, they isolated seven factors—venturesomeness, social mobility, privilegedness, social integration, interest range, status concern, and cosmopolitanism—and hypothesized that adopters would rank higher than nonadopters on all seven. These researchers note that two variables accounted for most of the divergence between adopters and nonadopters of the home appliance: venturesomeness and upward social mobility. To a lesser degree, social integration (the extent of doing things with other people), and relative financial well-being (privilegedness), were correlated with readiness to adopt an innovation. Cosmopolitanism, or having an orientation outside the local area, turned out to be *negatively* correlated with adoption. For home appliances, it seems logical that the more provincial a consumer is, the more he or she will be interested in accessories for the home. Conversely, we would expect that adoption of One-Week whirlwind tours through major European capitals would be positively related to cosmopolitanism.

The relationship between adopter characteristics and the innovation under consideration is similarly evident in a study by Pessemier, Burger, and Tigert[18] in which the profile of users of a new brand of laundry detergent proved relatively low-income and blue-collar. Frank, Massy, and Morrison[19] found no distinct profile for adopters of a new brand of coffee, suggesting that some products are so universally used that prime innovator groups would be hard to identify.

Adopter Life-Style Characteristics Profiling suburban male adopters over several product categories, through a multidimensional analysis, yields some insights into the characteristics of such people. Darden and Reynolds hypothesized that there might be more than a single kind of innovator for a group of products, that these various types of innovators would have different media habits and different characteristics even when choosing the same products, and that adoption behavior should be analyzed over several product categories simultaneously.[20] In addition, they felt that characteristics related to adoption behavior in one product class might stimulate adoption in other product categories. They suggest that sets of consumer characteristics different from those of other consumers distinguish innovative behavior groups, and that innovative behavior is multidimensional. However, each product or product type does not represent a separate dimension of innovator behavior.

There were six groups in the Darden and Reynolds study. Suburban males were categorized according to variables like attitude toward change, life-style venturesomeness, and opinion leadership in product category. Innovator Groups III and V are termed "suburban swingers" by Darden and Reynolds, because they score well above average on per-sonal grooming and apparel innovativeness, mobility, and youth, and are below average on home care innovativeness and education. The men in these groups read *Playboy, Penthouse,* and *Men's Wear.* Both groups also rank high on television viewing. As young, self-confident, interested, influential males, it is not surprising that they consume media which are sources of new grooming and fashion ideas.

A member of Innovator Group II—the "house-oriented husband"—buys more new home care products, fewer apparel and grooming items, and ranks lowest of any group on mobility and income. With more education and more children, he is older, less favorable to change and life-style venturesomeness, yet higher in self esteem. *Better Homes and Gardens* appears in this group's media selection.

Clusters IV and VI are designated "suburban conservative," and are similar to the "house-oriented husband" for the most part. They differ from the latter by having above average incomes, below average self-esteem, and, for Group VI, by their readership of *Sports Illustrated, Fortune,* and *Men's Wear.* Their scores were also low on life-style venturesomeness and generalized self-confidence.

The "established suburbanite," or "permanent nester," of Group I reveals heavy innovation in the home care product class, and somewhat less in grooming items. He relaxes in the evening with *Better Homes and Gardens, Consumer Reports,* and sometimes *Gentleman's Quarterly.* Older, less mobile, with more children and higher income, he is basically *average* in adoption behavior. His profile shows few extremes, except for a greater preference for innovative home care products and lower mobility than other groups.

Darden and Reynolds conclude that there

are "natural" groups of adopters who can be determined from measures of adoptive behavior in several product categories. They also suggest that "life style" may be used to segment male suburbanites into the six groups discussed above on the basis of readership, viewing, and listening characteristics.

Dogmatism and Adoption Milton Rokeach has pointed to another characteristic important to the adoption behavior: dogmatism. Dogmatism is the degree of open- or closed-mindedness to information or situations a person exhibits. A relatively undogmatic individual can ignore irrelevant aspects or information, and take the relevant material on its own merits. A highly dogmatic person, however, tends to be closed minded.

Blake, Perloff, and Heslin found that the relationship between a consumer's personality and adoption may depend upon which type of new product is involved—a novel one or a recent one.[21] Dogmatism was significantly related to adoption of recent products, primarily modifications of existing types of products. It was not, however, closely related to acceptance of novel products, those which are more nearly discontinuous innovations (all-terrain vehicles, for example). This would seem to contradict earlier findings that high levels of dogmatism inhibited innovation acceptance.

According to Jacoby, the anxiety to which highly dogmatic people are prone can be reduced by presenting them with "pronouncements of authorities."[22] Highly dogmatic individuals will accept information on the basis of its source. Undogmatic individuals are inclined to make significantly more innovative selections than the opinionated do— although the correlation does not appear too strong. (Jacoby investigated the reactions of women to fifteen products innovative in fashion, function, or brand.) Open-minded women, who revealed more adoption responses toward eleven of the fifteen products, were more likely to prefer *objective* information and facts.

Continuing the study of dogmatism, Coney replicated Jacoby's study with males instead of females.[23] This study tends to support the conclusion that open-minded people are more willing than the closed-minded to try new products.

Perceptual Influences on Adopters Ostlund examined *perceptual* variables in the anticipated diffusion of six new products.[24] Since the products he selected were not actually available for purchase, Ostlund devised a scale to measure "innovative willingness"; this ranged from 0 (absolutely will not buy) to 100 (absolutely will buy). The products included:

1. A plastic bandage with antiseptic in an aerosol can, which, when sprayed on a minor wound, provides a flexible, waterproof, and perspiration-resistant protective covering.

2. A disposable female undergarment

3. A self-layering dessert mix

4. A biodegradable napkin

5. A hot foam aerosol shampoo

6. A fabric treatment solution giving permanent-press characteristics to any washable fabric.

The relationships he hypothesized for the purposes of this study are shown in Table 18-2. Ostlund concludes that perceptual variables overshadow sociodemographic and "predispositioned" factors in predicting innovative behavior.

Social and Cultural Influences

Every culture has its distinguishing values and norms, and these represent strong deter-

Table 18-2 Predictors of Innovative Behavior

VARIABLE	DEFINITION	EXPECTED RELATIONSHIP WITH SURROGATE MEASURE OF INNOVATIVE BEHAVIOR
Predispositional:		
Venturesomeness	Willingness to take risks in buying new products	positive
Cosmopolitanism	Degree of orientation beyond a particular social system	positive
Social integration	Extent of social participation with other members of the community	positive
Privilegedness	Perceived financial well-being relative to peers	positive
Interest polymorphism	Variety and extent of one's personal interests	positive
General self-confidence in problem-solving	Perceived ability to cope with day-to-day problems	positive
General self-confidence in psychosocial matters	Perceived ability to cope with others' opinions of one's decisions	positive
Socioeconomic-Demographic:		
Family income	Total family income	positive
Respondent education	Years of formal education	positive
Occupational status of husband	Social-occupational status, measured by the Duncan scale	positive
Respondent age	Respondent age in years	not specified
Product Perception:		
Relative advantage	Degree to which an innovation is perceived as superior to ideas it supersedes (both economic and noneconomic considerations)	positive
Compatibility	Degree to which an innovation is perceived as consistent with existing values, habits, and past experiences of the potential adopter	positive
Complexity	Degree to which an innovation is perceived as difficult to understand and use	negative

Table 18-2 (Continued)

VARIABLE	DEFINITION	EXPECTED RELATIONSHIP WITH SURROGATE MEASURE OF INNOVATIVE BEHAVIOR
Divisibility	Degree to which an innovation is perceived as available for trial on a limited basis, without a large commitment	positive
Communicability	Degree to which results of an innovation will be apparent and possible to communicate to others	positive
Perceived risk	Degree to which risks are perceived as associated with the product	negative

Source: John A. Howard and Lyman E. Ostlund, Buyer Behavior: Theoretical and Empirical Foundations *(New York: Alfred A. Knopf, 1973), p. 554. Copyright © 1973 Alfred A. Knopf, Inc.*

minants of the rate of diffusion of a new product. A person who departs too far from the norms can be ostracized or even reviled. Heston, describing marketing conditions in India, notes that diffusion of new consumer goods in villages is particularly slow because of social ostracism and shakedowns by local officials who feel it their duty to share in open displays of affluence.[25] In India, language also inhibits diffusion; there are twelve important regional languages, plus Hindi, the official language, and English. Tradition, too, operates to preserve systems which prescribe certain exchanges of goods between different occupational groups; farmers, for example, pay their barbers in annual grain gifts. Still, in spite of social and cultural barriers, two new food items did experience successful diffusion. Hybrid maize was accepted over a three-year period in Mysore, with farming families performing their own experiments in cultivation and preparation

of dishes. While the norm of using rice was so strong that none of the families shared their recipes with each other, they nevertheless devised thirty or forty different methods of preparing maize. The "Peace Corps Chicken" also diffused successfully, causing changes in distribution channels, standardization of quality and supply of frozen chicken and eggs, and a drop in relative price. This is reminiscent of the U.S. Department of Agriculture diffusion studies in the 1920s that were planned to further diffusion of social benefits.

On the other hand, a reluctance to adopt new social structures is apparent in the slow diffusion of birth control in India. Sex mores and taboos have been slow to adjust to contraception and sterilization practices in spite of the widespread problems of severe starvation and resultant disease. Subcultural differences may influence the diffusion of innovations. In the United States, whites are more likely to use new ingredients in cooking than blacks or Japanese-Americans—perhaps because whites have far less compelling ethnic consumption patterns.[26]

Also relevant to diffusion in the United States is social class membership. While upper classes were found to adopt canasta more quickly, lower classes opted for the more passive entertainment offered by television.[27] To optimize diffusion, a strategy must take into account traits of social systems that are potential markets and values of the target culture and class.

The Communication Process

Consumer awareness of innovations arises through two primary channels: (1) interpersonal and word-of-mouth communications and (2) marketer communications. Sheth recounts three areas of research that highlight the interrelation of *both* communication processes.[28] Beginning with a sequence of adoption behavior consisting of Awareness, Interest, Evaluation, Trial, and Adoption, research indicates that initial awareness comes from the mass media but that, at the crucial evaluation stage, the buyer relies on word-of-mouth information and recommendations. A second research finding is based on the "two-step flow of communication" concept (discussed in chapter 15). The first step is the influence of the mass media on a small group of individuals who may be opinion leaders. In turn, they influence many others to adopt. Research in the third area concerns the influence of reference groups in adopting innovations.

The assumption that there is interaction between early and later adopters implies (1) that early adopters must also be influential leaders of opinion, or tastemakers, and (2) that the probability of any person's purchase of an innovation at a given time will be a function of how many other people have already bought. A study of diffusion of a new drug among physicians indicated that "socially integrated" doctors were earlier adopters of the drug than "socially isolated" doctors.[29] Generally, the well-integrated and respected members of any social system seem to adopt earlier than the members who are not. The status risk they incur by being "different" in product use is less. Both opinion leaders and early followers rank high on the personality trait of gregariousness. Robertson found that in small, informal neighborhood groups there was a strong correlation between innovativeness of the members and positive group norms toward trying out new items. And innovativeness is especially high in groups that felt less perceived risk in adopting new products.[30]

In confronting technically complex innovations, consumers may turn to experts or authorities for help in evaluation. Cameras, ski equipment, power tools, and stereo sound equipment are products that send most consumers to authorities with the training or expertise to make judgments and offer advice. Sheth found that 71 percent of the consumers who report being *informed* by a personal source also report being *influenced* by a personal source.

Although Sheth and Howard note that word-of-mouth is generally a more credible source than mass media,[31] the importance of marketer communications should not be underestimated. The role of the mass media in stimulating initial awareness of new products and services has been discussed in chapter 14. Research suggests that, in considering new products, consumers are more susceptible to persuasive messages at the "awareness" stage of the decision process than at later stages such as "interest" and "evaluation."[32]

One would also expect the use and influence of marketer-devised communications to vary over different product innovations.

A fashion innovation is likely to be diffused more rapidly through mass media than a highly technical innovation in the realm of high fidelity equipment.

Adoption Behavior: Consumer, Retail, and Industrial

Most studies of diffusion have focused on products and services aimed at *ultimate* consumers. But in recent years, the adoption of innovations at the *retail* and *industrial* levels has become increasingly important to marketers. Retailers, representing the distribution source of innovations, are a vital component of any diffusion process, and must accept or reject other innovations that may enhance retail performance. Industrial buyers as consumers are daily confronted with innovations that promise to benefit their operations, and the economic impact of industrial adoptions is considerable. If a corporation employing 2,541 secretaries and typists considers adopting a new IBM typewriter to replace its battery of Smith-Corona machines, there is a good piece of business at stake for both typewriter manufacturers and a weighty consumer decision to be made on the part of the corporation.

This section deals with adoption behavior at all three levels of consumption.

Consumer Adoption Behavior

Examples of innovations in the ultimate consumer sphere include acceptance of fashion innovation (and rejection of a specific fashion item—the "midi"), adoption of push-button phones, stainless steel razor blades, and the phenomenon known as "upward" diffusion.

Fashion: The Case of the "Midi"   Few marketers are concerned with the success of as many innovations as those in the fashion industry. Thus the adoption of new fashions and the variables that determine whether or not such innovations will succeed offer a popular source of information about innovation and diffusion.

In 1970, fashion marketers launched an all-out effort to dictate a radical change in the length of skirts and dresses—from the popularly accepted "mini" length to the conservative new "midi." The results were disastrous for the fashion industry, because consumers rejected or simply ignored the innovation in sufficient numbers to send the midi the way of the Edsel for that season. Everyone concerned—designers, manufacturers, and buyers—wanted to know why.

Mason and Bellenger conducted one study of midi adoption on a large college campus, under the assumption that college students are a leading edge in changing attitudes and values.[33] They grouped fifteen independent variables in three categories: demographic variables, mass media exposure variables, and involvement in women's clothing fashions. These were then tested to discover their correlation with midi acceptance and adoption. The profile of the midi buyer showed that most likely she went to four movies a month, three to six fashion shows each year, belonged to a sorority, was not married, and had parents who earned more than $20,000 a year. (The last factor strongly suggests that risk-taking is positively related to income.)

Reynolds and Darden geared another study of the ill-starred midi to finding out if those who expressed purchase intentions could be viewed as innovators and early adopters through whom the style would ultimately diffuse by the process of "social contagion."[34] The social function of early adopters, they note, is to influence those around them by legitimizing the innovative style. Once they have caught the fever of enthusiasm, they spread it to their peer groups. In this study, purchase intentions were considered a surrogate measure of innovativeness. The experimenters then followed up their original research with a survey one year later to learn whether or not the original respondents had actually put a midi into their own wardrobes. They concluded from the first study that the midi would not diffuse in that community. And the subsequent inquiry proved them correct. Contagion seems to have worked in reverse—that is, only two out of twenty-two self-perceived early adopters bought a midi; only two of five self-perceived innovators purchased one.

Several reasons have been suggested for the rapid fall of the midi, a failure that amounted to a consumer rejection of the Paris-directed fashion tradition:

1. After the widespread acceptance of the mini, the dowdy midi seemed an unattractive throwback to less liberated times.

2. Many women had invested a great deal of money in building a mini wardrobe. And minis could not be "let down" to make midis.

For many women accepting the midi was a financial impossibility.

3. The mini fashion cycle was simply thought to have ended too abruptly, rather than allowing consumers "turnaround" time to adjust their attitudes and wardrobes to a totally different look. (In fact, women did come to gradually accept the longer look through the 1970s.)

Fashion Leadership Fashion innovation adoption among college women was also investigated by Painter and Pinegar.[35] A sample of women at a Western university were asked whether or not they owned the following new fashion items: maxicoat, maxidress, midicoat, mididress, safari jacket, and ski pants. The college teenagers most likely to have bought the new fashions read more magazines; belonged to more organizations; were more inner-directed; and reported the incomes, as well as occupational and educational levels of their fathers as higher than average.

Discovering the correlates of fashion opinion leadership in women past the teen years was the focus of a study by John O. Summers. Such influential demographic factors as age, education, and income were not too surprising, nor was the fact that fashion magazine readership was far more strongly related to adoption than listening to radio or viewing television. Personality emerged as a variable in that women who were emotionally stable, assertive, and locally gregarious were more likely to be fashion leaders. Summers concludes that:[36]

The "competitive-exhibitionism" factor may be a particularly strong correlate of opinion leadership in the area of fashion because the concept of fashion involves display or exhibition.

Sociologically, leaders took part in more organizational and social activities, were both more mobile and more cosmopolitan. These life-style aspects suggest high visibility, which, coupled with a strong interest in fashion, stimulates much conversation centered on clothing. That these women receive as well as transmit fashion opinions and information suggests that there is a chain of opinion leaders, or that interpersonal communication involves more *equal* roles for the participants than might be expected.

Economist Sanford V. Berg has developed a model of fashion behavior which points to the interdependency of tastes, economics, technology, and the social framework.[37] One intriguing notation is a mix of motives which includes, on one hand, the desire for exclusiveness and uniqueness ("rarity") and, on the other, a "drive to imitate." Berg counters the sociological argument that adopting changes in the design of things is a simple matter of competition; it was, rather, the intense urge for exclusiveness that made the twenties, for example, a period of juggernaut fashion cycles. Hall reports that "women of all classes adopted the new styles as soon as their pocketbooks made it possible,"[38] in an era where there was so little "lag" distinguishing leaders, it was simply a matter of seeing which member of one group would be first to display a given style.

Wealthier women who received the high-status Paris lines first would change their wardrobes as soon as the look was mass-produced, often only a month or so after it was introduced.

The Pushbutton Phone   The pushbutton telephone is a continuous innovation, and something of a luxury. Robertson and Kennedy investigated consumer adoption of the new telephone by applying multiple discrim-

inant analysis, discussed earlier in this chapter. For purposes of the study, adopters were defined as the first ten percent to buy the phone. These researchers found that the two variables accounting for most of the adoption behavior were venturesomeness and upward social mobility. While social integration and relative financial standing were also important, cosmopolitanism was negatively related. A person who is more home-oriented, then, is more likely to try new products for the home such as the pushbutton phone.[39]

Stainless Steel Razor Blades   A low-risk innovation, the stainless steel razor blade, provided Sheth with an item for comparison.[40] While studies dealing with luxury goods and those investigating dynamically continuous (more radical) product innovations may not fully indicate the effects of word-of-mouth communication on diffusion due to the high-risk nature of the products, stainless steel blades are low-risk, have strong relative advantages, and, as a daily necessity, are purchased frequently. Furthermore, the innovating company of this study did not use mass media marketing communications for some time after introducing the product. Nearly half the individuals of Sheth's sample reported that a personal source influenced their adoption decisions. The same percentage adopted the innovation immediately after becoming aware of it. There was, too, more influence attributable to information from personal sources.

Upward Diffusion   Conventional wisdom has it that innovations, especially those in the fashion sphere, "trickle down" from the top of the status pyramid to the masses at the base. But what do we make of middle-aged men who sport the hair and clothing fashions of young people; whites who adopt

Yogurt: A New Craze Over an Old Culture

One of Soviet Georgia's senior citizens thought Dannon was an excellent yogurt. She ought to know. She's been eating yogurt for 137 years.

Sometimes what is considered an innovation has actually been around for years, virtually unnoticed, until it suddenly appears everywhere through mass consumer acceptance.

Yogurt is just such a product. Originally an undistinguished immigrant dish in the United States, it recently began catching on as a health and snack food.

This is usually credited to (1) an ambitious advertising campaign by the market leader, Dannon, (2) a growing desire for healthful foods on the part of younger consumers, (3) a new sophistication about foreign foods since Americans began flocking all over the world as tourists, (4) a smart move on the part of yogurt marketers to do something about the taste—hence, colorful and flavorful yogurt in strawberry, chocolate, pineapple, and many other flavors.

Today, the yogurt business is flourishing. There are yogurt machines, fast food stands, soft frozen yogurt (called Frostyogurt, and as popular as frozen custard used to be), and chocolate-covered yogurt on a stick.

New Times notes that, in 1975, Americans consumed 415 million pounds of the sour custard—to the tune of $300 million in the pockets of aggressive marketers like Dannon, Hood, and Colombo.[42]

Colombo advertised its product on radio with a character who sounded suspiciously like the popular TV detective of the same name. Dannon used a healthful approach, as in television commercials featuring people from Soviet Georgia who had lived to be over 100 years old—and were found to be heavy consumers of yogurt.[43]

ethnic dances, music, and speech habits; tenth-generation Americans who relish pizza, tacos, and Polish sausage? George A. Field calls the upward diffusion of styles, tastes, amusements, and the like the phenomenon of "status float."[41] From the standpoint of the power structure of a society, it is puzzling to witness this float: adults taking up with the hair styles and garb of reckless youth, men adopting women's tastes in vivid clothing colors and even handbags, business executives purchasing the campers used by blue-collar workers. The changing symbolism of the beard as it moves "upward" is especially curious. Being clean-shaven was at first an imitation of youthfulness, but when younger males took to the hirsute look as a sociopolitical statement, middle-aged men had to adopt beards to look younger! The concept of upward diffusion has been discussed with regard to changes in the American social class structure (chapter 7).

Retail Adoption Behavior

Although the Rogers model of time in the adoption process (Figure 18-3) is general enough to apply to retailing situations as well as to individuals, Reynolds in one study and Swan in another have enhanced the model's applicability by adding considerations of the role of problem-solving in the model's early stages. (See Figure 18-4.)

Adoption of Credit Plans   Reynolds theorized that the adoption process has as a starting point either a problem solving or an innovation orientation.[44] He sampled thirty-one merchants who adopted a new charge account plan operated by a locally owned

Figure 18-4   Problem-oriented adopters' median profiles.

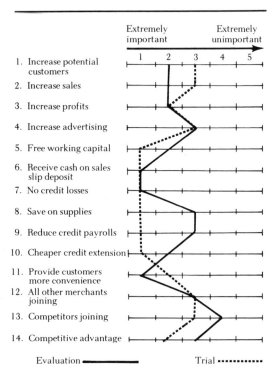

Source: Fred D. Reynolds, "Problem Solving and Trial Use in the Adoption Process," Journal of Marketing Research, *Vol. 8 (February, 1971).* Reprinted by permission of the American Marketing Association.

bank, classifying those who adopted during the first three months as early adopters and the rest as late adopters. The merchants fitted themselves into one of three "situations": (1) "I heard about the plan and decided that it would help my business," (2) "I felt a need to change my credit operation and discovered the bank plan while actively seeking a different way of handling credit," and (3) "I felt a need to change my credit operations and, when I heard about the bank's plan, recognized that it would be good." In other words, the first type consists of adopters who are *innovation* oriented, and the *problem solving* types fell into two categories—active and passive. Profiles of the problem-oriented adopters reveal that the most differentiating factors are those that deal with relative economic advantages of credit operations. The economy factors were generally considered unimportant by the adopters exhibiting the innovation orientation. Moreover, Reynolds found a greater degree of discrimination among factors in the problem-oriented adopters. Differences between early and late adopters did not seem so vital. He suggests that the adoption process model might well be stronger if it were expanded to include a problem recognition stage.

Swan analyzed an innovation in distribution channels for groceries on the basis of a different model, but one which does include in its first step innovation as a response to a problem. This model postulates reorganization of the given retail system to make better use of resources by changing the roles controlling the resources. He concludes that "innovation is more in the nature of a response to a problem rather than a creative insight on the part of entrepreneurs in some unceasing search for profits."[45] Adoption of an innovation is thus a sequential response to a problem.

Adoption of Supermarket Games   Maximizing a small profit margin is one key goal of supermarkets. Allvine analyzed adoption of games by food chains and their competitors in individual markets and diffusion of games within market regions.[46] Markets adopt these innovative "customer games of chance" to gain an edge in sales volume and profits in a highly competitive retailing arena. Early adopters had an attitude of looking to the

future and not caring "what happened yesterday." They were flexible. Later on, nonadopters felt that games were merely gimmicks and that price was a better competitive weapon. Diffusion was quickened when the first adopter had a relatively large share of the market. At the interest stage, word-of-mouth communication among retailers was the most important source of information to three-quarters of the principal market chains who did adopt. It is interesting to note that game use was greatest in the area classified as "Southern markets," while North Atlantic Coast and Western markets were 78 and 88 percent below the median, respectively. This would tend to conflict with regional stereotypes as to "progressiveness" in adopting innovations, at least at the retail level. Allvine concludes that dominance of price strategies among leading chains in an area will deter game adoption, while adoption of that innovation will be more likely in regions with many chain stores. In individual markets, later adopters had more provincial business philosophies, word-of-mouth was the most important communication source (and was operative at both the evaluation and interest stages), and the greater the market share cornered by the early adopters, the faster the diffusion of the game innovation.

Industrial Adoption Behavior

Although industrial adoption involves huge consumer decisions, research in this area has been largely inconclusive. The complexity of accepting new products at this level derives from factors such as group decisions, high potential risk, and difficulty of adequate research design. It has been suggested, however, that the firm most likely to adopt an innovation will be the company that (1) stands to gain the most relative advantage (measured in profit margin increment) from the innovation, (2) can most easily tolerate the investment and loss risk incurred by adoption, (3) has the highest aspiration level (measured in market share, gross sales, and profitability trends), and (4) for which information about the innovation has the highest value.[47]

Ozanne and Churchill, among the earliest researchers to probe industrial adoption, conclude that "the traditional adoption process model can be applied in the industrial setting," but for indivisible innovations, the trial stage might not exist.[48] An automatic machine, for example, may be viewed in operation elsewhere, but a company cannot retool to install it and then just "try it out for a while." It appears in one study that the adopters actually used postpurchase demonstrations for dissonance reduction. Also, personal sources of information (personal selling) were more important at the early stages of adoption, while impersonal sources

(price quotation and tooling proposal) were crucial during the evaluation. Need for information increased as the decision stage neared.

In contrast, Martilla found word-of-mouth communication more important at later stages of adoption.[49] Impersonal sources developed awareness of new products at the early stages. In addition, word-of-mouth *within* firms was an important element in the adoption of new paper by paper-converting firms. Industrial opinion leaders were hard to identify on the basis of demographic data, but in firms which did adopt, opinion leaders were far more frequently and intensively exposed to impersonal information sources.

Czepiel, in view of the controversy over word-of-mouth communication in industrial adoption processes, urges investigation of diffusion in industrial societies as a social and behavioral process. This approach would reflect the rather well-known fact that friendship and other social relationships form the basis for some information spread and innovation diffusion.[50]

Innovation and Diffusion Models

A number of models have been devised to represent the diffusion of innovations in purchasing behavior. Some attempt to illustrate specific features of the diffusion process such as the "innovation boundary," others depict individual changes in consumers during the adoption process.

Innovation Boundary

The *innovation boundary* is a concept that divides innovators from noninnovators. Devised by Dennis P. Slevin, it is a mathematical model with four main variables: S = current success level of a person, T = that individual's target success level, C = costs of innovating, and R = rewards of innovating, or rewards of successful performance of product or practice adopted.[51] Given an individual's estimate of his or her own probable success, one can determine whether that person will or will not adopt. After various trials that give the individual information about the probability of success or failure from using some new "method," a boundary can be plotted that will correctly separate innovators from non-innovators over time. As C (costs of innovating) rises, the boundary shifts back toward nonadoption; conversely as costs lower, adoption increases. The shape and location of the boundary for a given situation can be determined with some degree of precision.

Simulation Models $\mathbb{N}\mathcal{O}$

Simulation models are still in the early stages of development, but may prove useful in tracing consumer behavior during the adoption process. Alba's model assumes that the individual changes from nonknower to knower to knower-adopter.[52] This development will be due to internal or external communications about the innovation. Diffusion will occur as the number of knower-adopters increases over time. Stasch suggests that sample sizes wield important effects in simulation models of diffusion, and concludes that "the average time of adoption of an individual is the measure most capable of identifying the stabilization of a simulation of diffusion innovation." Ranking average times of adoption coupled with periods of most frequent adoption, Stasch has been able to

estimate the most likely path a diffusion will take through a given population. From this simulation technique, he suggests that the web of interpersonal communication forces which influence diffusion is simpler in early stages of adoption.[53]

The BBDO advertising agency developed DEMON (Figure 18-5) to predict new product adoption on the basis of advertising and promotion expenditures.[54] The assumptions of this model are that (1) consumers go through various decision-making stages leading up to actually buying some new item, (2) probability of purchase increases with succeeding stages, and (3) virtually all variables are influenced by advertising.

Problems in Using Models $\mathbb{N}\mathcal{O}$

The fundamental difficulty in designing an accurate model for any process requiring human activity is the almost infinite number of variables that must be taken into account. Bernhardt and Mackenzie find this true of the diffusion models discussed above.[55] Economists, sociologists, psychologists, as well as marketers, struggle to make human behavior more comprehensible by isolating the most important variables and arranging them in models according to their interrelationships. Present models are too limited and restrictive; they do not encompass all the variables a marketing manager has to work with.

These models might also be criticized on the basis of not having been developed along a fully comprehensive and tested theory of adoption and diffusion processes. Differences in social structures and in characteristics of adopters at different times in a product's life

Figure 18-5   The DEMON model.

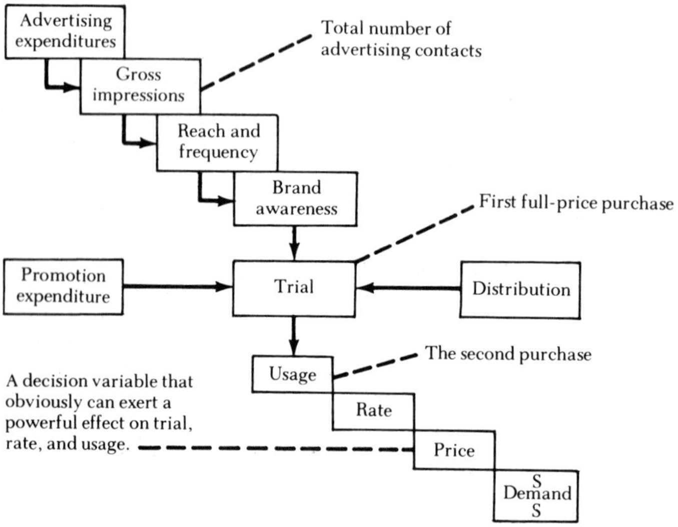

Source: James K. DeVoe, "Plans, Profits and the Marketing Program," in Frederick E. Webster (ed.)
New Directions in Marketing, (Chicago, Ill.: American Marketing Association, 1965).

cycle seem to require further definition. While diffusion studies have tracked a number of successful innovations, marketers might also profit from a look into innovations that have failed. Yet there is a lack of research in this area (although there are several studies of the midi-dress as one glaring example of an unsuccessful innovation, and a number of explanations for the ill-fated Edsel). Bernhardt and Mackenzie call for more checking of whether or not consumers attain "correct perceptions" of innovations. As a further note, the *quantity* of the innovation purchased at given times might also be included.

In spite of such methodological problems, diffusion of innovation is one of the most intriguing of all consumer behavior concepts. The research already accomplished points to new directions for experimenters. Application of mathematics to models of diffusion has proved limited but still of value. Unlike perception and attitudes, for example, the purchase and trial of a new product or service can be determined quite specifically. While motivation, communication, and other influencing factors remain somewhat murky, adoption is concrete and measurable. Considering the vast amounts of energy and money funneled into marketing innovations, the study of how their adoption may be optimized throughout a population should be of considerable interest to marketers.

Summary

The *diffusion of innovations* is the process through which new goods and services flow from producer to consumer, industrial as well as individual. *Adoption* refers to the process by which a potential user of some new item or service—*the innovation*—becomes an actual user. Diffusion study is derived from the fields of anthropology and sociology, and has only recently been applied to marketing problems. In the diffusion process, both *product variables* and *adopter characteristics* interact to determine how readily consumers will embrace an innovation. Key features of the adoption process include the *innovation* itself, the *awareness* of the innovation by potential adopters, the *adopters*

themselves in particular social-cultural systems, the *communication process* through which the adoption is spread, and the passage of *time*. While most studies of diffusion in marketing have focused on the *ultimate* consumer, there is increasing emphasis on this process at the *retail* and *industrial* levels. *Models* of diffusion have been developed to represent the adoption of new products and to gauge the penetration of an innovation in terms of retail purchasing. New models are also being devised to illustrate specific aspects of the diffusion process, and will no doubt prove useful to marketers in making predictions for new-product success.

NOTES

1. Everett M. Rogers, "New Product Adoption and Diffusion," *Journal of Consumer Research*, Vol. 2, No. 4 (March 1976), p. 290.

2. Everett M. Rogers, "Where We Are in Understanding Innovation" (Paper presented at the East-West Communications Institute Conference on Communication and Change: Ten Years After, Honolulu, January 12–17, 1975).

3. For recent advances in mathematical modeling, see David F. Midgeley, "A Simple Mathematical Theory of Innovation Behavior," *Journal of Consumer Research*, Vol. 3, No. 1 (June 1976), p. 31.

4. Thomas S. Robertson, "The Process of Innovation and the Diffusion of Innovation," *Journal of Marketing*, Vol. 31 (January 1967), pp. 14–19.

5. Theodore L. Angelus, "Why Do Most New Products Fail?" *Advertising Age*, March 24, 1969, pp. 85–86.

6. Paul F. Lazarsfeld, Bernard Berelson, and Hazel Gaudet, *The People's Choice*, 2nd ed. rev. (New York: Columbia University Press, 1948).

7. W. P. Gorman, "Market Acceptance of a Consumer Durable Good Innovation: A Socioeconomic Analysis of First and Second Buying Households of Color Television Receivers in Tuscaloosa, Alabama," (Ph.D. dissertation, University of Alabama, 1966).

8. Loui E. Boone, "The Search for the Consumer Innovator," *Journal of Business*, Vol. 43 (April 1970), pp. 135–140.

9. Michael Gurevitch and Zipora Loevy, "The Diffusion of Television as an Innovation: The Case of the Kibbutz," *Human Relations*, Vol. 25, No. 3 (July 1972), pp. 181–197.

10. Everett M. Rogers, *Diffusion of Innovations* (New York: The Free Press, 1962), p. 306.

11. Everett M. Rogers and F. Floyd Shoemaker, *Communication of Innovations* (New

York: The Free Press, 1971), pp. 50–51.

12. Andrew Tobias, "Gillette's New Ploy: Throwing Away the Razor to Sell the Blade," *New York,* July 12, 1976.

13. Robert A. Peterson, "A Note on Optimal Adopter Category Determination," *Journal of Marketing Research,* Vol. 10 (August 1973), pp. 325–329.

14. Peterson, "Optimal Adopter," p. 327.

15. Steven A. Blumgarten, "The Innovative Communicator in the Diffusion Process," *Journal of Marketing Research,* Vol. 12, No. 1 (February 1975), p. 12.

16. Thomas S. Robertson, *Innovation and the Consumer* (New York: Holt, Rinehart and Winston, 1971).

17. Thomas S. Robertson and James N. Kennedy, "Prediction of Consumer Innovators: Application of Multiple Discriminant Analysis," *Journal of Marketing Research,* Vol. 5 (February 1968), pp. 64–69.

18. Edgar A. Pessemier, Phillip Burger, and Douglas Tigert, "Can New Product Buyers Be Identified?", *Journal of Marketing Research,* Vol. 4 (November 1967), pp. 349–354.

19. Ronald E. Frank, William F. Massy, and Donald G. Morrison, "The Determinants of Innovative Behavior with Respect to a Branded, Frequently Purchased Food Product," in *Reflections on Progress in Marketing,* ed. L. George Smith, in *Proceedings of the 1964 Winter Conference of the American Marketing Association,* Chicago, pp. 312–323.

20. William R. Darden and Fred D. Reynolds, "Backward Profiling of Male Innovators," *Journal of Marketing Research,* Vol. 11 (February 1974), pp. 79–85.

21. Brian Blake, Robert Perloff, and Richard Heslin, "Dogmatism and Acceptance of New Products," *Journal of Marketing Research,* Vol. 7 (November 1970), pp. 483–486.

22. Jacob Jacoby, "Multiple-Indicant Approach for Studying New Product Adopters," *Journal of Applied Psychology,* Vol. 55, No. 4 (1971), pp. 384–388; and Carol A. Kohn Berning and Jacob Jacoby, "Patterns of Information Acquisition in New Product Purchases," *Consumer Research,* Vol. 1, No. 2 (September 1974).

23. Kenneth A. Coney, "Dogmatism and Innovation: A Replication," *Journal of Marketing Research,* Vol. 9 (November 1972), pp. 453–455.

24. Lyman E. Ostlund, "Predictors of Innovative Behavior," in *Buyer Behavior,* ed. John A. Howard and Lyman E. Ostlund (New York: Alfred A. Knopf, Inc., 1973); and Lyman E. Ostlund, "Perceived Innovation Attributes as Predictors of Innovativeness," *Consumer Research,* Vol. 1, No. 2 (September 1974).

25. Alan Heston, "Some Socio-Cultural Facets of Marketing and Diffusion of Change in India," in *Proceedings of the American Marketing Association,* No. 28 (1969), pp. 500–503.

26. Thomas S. Robertson, Douglas J. Dalrymple, and Michael J. Yoshino, "Cultural Compatibility in New Product Adoption," in *Proceedings of the American Marketing Association,* 1969.

27. Saxon Graham, "Class and Conservatism in the Adoption of Innovations," *Human Relations,* Vol. 9 (1956).

28. Jagdish N. Sheth, "Word of Mouth in Low-Risk Innovations," *Journal of Advertising Research,* Vol. 11, No. 3 (June 1971), pp. 15–18.

29. James S. Coleman, Elihu Katz, and Herbert Menzel, *Medical Innovation: A Diffusion Study* (New York: Bobbs-Merrill, 1966).

30. Thomas S. Robertson, "The Effect of the Informal Group Upon Member Innovative Behavior," in *Proceedings of The American Marketing Association,* 1968.

31. J. A. Howard and Jagdish N. Sheth, *The Theory of Buyer Behavior* (New York: John Wiley and Sons, 1969).

32. William Lazer and William E. Bell, "The Communication Process and Innovation," *Journal of Advertising Research,* Vol. 6 (September 1966).

33. Joseph Barry Mason and Danny Bellenger, "Analyzing High Fashion Acceptance," *Journal of Retailing,* Vol. 49, No. 9 (Winter 1973–1974), pp. 79–88.

34. Fred D. Reynolds and William R. Darden, "Fashion Theory and Pragmatics: The Case of the Midi," *Journal of Retailing,* Vol. 49, No. 1 (Spring 1973), pp. 31–63.

35. John Jay Painter and Max L. Pinegar, "Post-High Teens and Fashion Innovation," *Journal of Marketing Research,* Vol. 8 (August 1971), pp. 368–369.

36. John O. Summers, "The Identity of Women's Clothing Fashion Opinion Leaders," *Journal of Marketing Research,* Vol. 7 (May 1970), pp. 178–185.

37. Sanford V. Berg, "Interdependent Tastes

and Fashion Behavior," *Quarterly Review of Economics and Business*, Vol. 13 (Summer 1973), pp. 49–58.

38. Linda Hall, "Fashion and Style in the Twenties: The Change," *The Historian*, Vol. 34 (May 1972), pp. 485–497.

39. Thomas S. Robertson and James N. Kennedy, "Consumer Innovators."

40. Jagdish N. Sheth, "Word of Mouth."

41. George A. Field, "The Status Float Phenomenon: The Upward Diffusion of Innovation," *Business Horizons*, Vol. 13 (August 1970), pp. 45–52.

42. Judith Hennessee, "Yogurt: Getting into the Culture," *New Times*, July 23, 1976.

43. *New York*, August 23, 1976.

44. Fred D. Reynolds, "Problem Solving and Trial Use in the Adoption Process," *Journal of Marketing Research*, Vol. 8 (February 1971), pp. 100–102.

45. John E. Swan, "A Functional Analysis of Innovation in Distribution Channels," *Journal of Retailing*, Vol. 50, No. 1 (Spring 1974), pp. 9–90.

46. Fred C. Allvine, "Diffusion of a Competitive Innovation," in *Marketing and the Science of Planning*, ed. Robert L. King, in *Proceedings of the Fall Conference of the American Marketing Association*, Chicago, 1968, p. 431.

47. Frederick E. Webster, Jr., "New Product Adoption in Industrial Markets: A Framework for Analysis," *Journal of Marketing*, Vol. 33 (July 1969).

48. Urban B. Ozanne and Gilbert A. Churchill, "Adoption Research: Information Sources in the Industrial Purchasing Decision," in *Marketing and the New Science of Planning*, ed. Robert L. King, *Proceedings of the Fall Conference of the American Marketing Association*, Chicago, 1968, pp. 352–359.

49. John A. Martilla, "Word-of-Mouth Communication in the Industrial Adoption Process," *Journal of Marketing Research*, Vol. 8, No. 2 (May 1971), pp. 173–178.

50. John A. Czepiel, "Word-of-Mouth Processes in the Diffusion of a Major Technological Innovation," *Journal of Marketing Research*, Vol. 11 (May 1974), pp. 172–180.

51. Dennis P. Slevin, "The Innovation Boundary: A Specific Model and Some Empirical Results," *Administrative Science Quarterly*, Vol. 18, No. 1 (March 1973), pp. 515–531.

52. Manuel S. Alba, "Microanalysis of the Socio-Dynamics of Diffusion of Innovation: A Simulation Study" (abstract), in *Proceedings of the American Marketing Association, Summer Conference*, Denver, Colorado, August 1968.

53. Stanley F. Stasch, "Sample Size and Change in Simulating the Diffusion of Innovation," in *Marketing and the Science of Planning*, ed. Robert L. King, in *Proceedings of the American Marketing Association, Fall Conference*, Chicago, 1968, pp. 360–365.

54. James K. DeVoe, "Plans, Profits, and the Marketing Program," in *New Directions in Marketing*, ed. Frederick E. Webster, Jr. (Chicago: American Marketing Association, 1965).

55. Irwin Bernhardt and Kenneth D. Mackenzie, "Some Problems in Using Diffusion Models for New Products," *Management Science*, Vol. 19, No. 2 (October 1972), pp. 187–200.

MARKETING APPLICATIONS

Conclusion 1 *The factor of divisibility is important in securing the success of an adoption. Consumers like to "sample" new products in some way before they make commitments, thus reducing their risk.*

Application Many new products are introduced through the process of direct marketing: they are advertised in print and TV media with coupons or toll-free numbers for immediate order. A consistent technique in the direct marketing of a new item is some version of the promise "Try it in your own home for thirty days and, if you're not completely satisfied, return it for a full refund." This offers interested consumers an ideal situation for trying out innovations, an opportunity which is not usually available at the retail level. A product which meets the other criteria of a successful innovation should be offered to consumers with a risk-free guarantee. Some successful examples of innovations first sold through direct response ads include an industrial-strength home odor repellent ("Two drops deodorize a skunk"), Crazy Glue ("One drop will hold an automobile to a crane in mid-air"), and a book on financial management entitled *How to Rob Banks Legally*.

Conclusion 2 *In studying industrial adoption behavior, an information-use pattern has been observed. Buyers tend to see personal sources of information about an innovation as critical in the early stages of decision making, with impersonal sources becoming more salient at later stages.*

Application A marketer launching some innovation for an industrial market may apply these findings through a carefully planned introductory campaign. All industrial advertising and direct mail announcements should ask for an appointment for a sales representative. At the same time, a telephone penetration should be conducted to set up meetings for salespeople with key decision makers. Thus, buyers may receive firsthand information about the innovation in face to face contact where they may ask direct questions. These interviews should be followed-up aggressively with mailings of additional product information, which the buyers may use as a ready source at later stages of the decision process.

ASSIGNMENTS

Research Assignment

Background   As a partner in a local cable TV franchise, you have been offered an innovation known as Home Movies. This service offers people in your area the opportunity to receive first-run films, uncensored and without commercial interruption, on a subscription basis. The films are transmitted to their homes over your cable, so the market would include both your current users and whatever additional segment of the homes in your area might be interested in the Home Movies feature. The cost to subscribers would be less than $20 a month. You are excited about the potential of this service to attract new customers, but before you invest in a Home Movies installation, you wish to test the market for its probable acceptance.

Methodology   Prepare a questionnaire as follows:

We would like to find out whether you would be interested in a new concept in home entertainment—one which will bring first-run feature films such as (fill in 3 current films) to your television screen. The films would be uncensored and there would be no commercials. There would be five to six new films a week, which would be repeated at regular intervals so you will be sure to find time to see each film. This service would be on a subscription basis, which you could cancel anytime, and would cost less than $20 a month.

_____Yes, I would be interested right now.
_____No, I would not be interested.
_____Yes, and I will tell my friends about it.
If no, why not?_____
_____Too much money.
_____Not interested in first-run films.
_____Current TV shows are OK.
_____Rather go to the theater.
_____Would rather wait until other people have it.

Administer the questionnaire to a minimum of twenty people at a shopping center and evaluate the results.

Extrapolation   Would this innovation be feasible in your community? If not, why? What information does this offer about adoption and diffusion?

Creative Assignment

Product Innovations, Inc., is a design and development company which prepares new products for industry. Currently, its team of engineers is working to perfect the home holograph unit—an entertainment innovation that will project images in three dimensions instead of two. As a researcher and writer with the company, you are asked to compile a complete profile of the product innovator—including demographic, psychological, and product-use characteristics. This information will be used in designing the entertainment for exhibition in the holographic device. Prepare an analysis of "first adopter" characteristics, using the information in the preceding chapter as well as sources in the bibliography.

Managerial Assignment

You are a Marketing Associate of World Amusements, a company which operates amusement parks across the country. There are rumors that British engineers have designed a small hovercraft that floats at high speed on an air cushion 20 feet above the ground, resembling a flying saucer. While large hovercraft have been in use in Britain for some time, these are the first reports of a small model that could be used as a "Flying Saucer Ride" attraction at World's various parks. You are assigned to decide whether, on the basis of what is known about how product characteristics affect adoption behavior, American families would be "ready" for this innovation. Make a recommendation for or against making an offer for the hovercraft from the information found in this chapter.

SELECTED READINGS

Baumgarten, Steven A. "The Innovative Communicator in the Diffusion Process." *Journal of Marketing Research*, Vol. 12, No. 1 (February 1975), pp. 12–18.

Feldman, Lawrence P. and Gary M. Armstrong, "Identifying Buyers of a Major Automotive Innovation." *Journal of Marketing Research*, Vol. 39, No. 1 (January 1975), pp. 47–53.

Midgley, David F. "A Simple Mathematical Theory of Innovative Behavior." *Journal of Consumer Research*, Vol. 3, No. 1 (June 1976), pp. 31–41.

Reinmuth, James E. "Forecasting the Impact of a New Product Introduction." *Journal of the Academy of Marketing Science*, Vol. 2, No. 2 (Spring 1974), pp. 391–400.

Rogers, Everett M. "New Product Adoption and Diffusion." *Journal of Consumer Research*, Vol. 2, No. 4 (March 1976), pp. 290–301.

OBJECTIVES

1. Describe *four characteristics* of life style and define life style as it relates to *consumer behavior.* *496*

2. Explain how the *life-style concept* is used in analyzing consumer behavior. *498*

3. Summarize the consumer factors that *psychographic research* measures. *499*

4. Compare the two kinds of *life-style research* in methods and advantages. *499*

5. Summarize the psychographic profiles of *beer drinkers, eye makeup users,* and *bank charge card users.* *504, 506–507*

6. Discuss *methodological problems* in psychographic research. *507*

7. Describe *current applications* of life-style research. *511*

NINETEEN

Life Style and Psychographics

The problem of market segmentation—differentiating those consumers who will probably buy a given product from those who probably will not—continues to challenge the most imaginative marketers.

Segmentation has traditionally relied on demographic facts such as age, sex, income, and education to isolate groups of consumers into "target" markets. But how can demographics explain such differences as those found between two consumers who live side by side and share the same demographic profiles, yet reveal extreme divergence in purchasing patterns? One, for example, drives a red sports car on a nightly round of pub-crawling while the other tools a conservative sedan to weekly church meetings.

In recent years, marketers have identified these purchasing differences as reflections of individual life styles. This chapter introduces the concept of life style as a major force in current consumer behavior theory, with an overview of the research techniques that enable researchers to quantify life-style factors and translate them into meaningful profiles of consumers for use in marketing decision making. Some representative topics include:

• Why consumer choices are one of the most important determinants of life style.

• How life-style profiles can offer more meaningful descriptions of heavy users of certain products (shotgun ammunition, for example) than demographic data.

• What questions researchers pose to consumers in probing life-style differences.

• How beer drinkers, eye makeup users, and bank credit card customers emerge in life-style characteristics.

• Why life-style portraits are useful in designing and positioning products, selecting media, developing advertising strategies, and improving retail performance.

Because life style has become such a popular and sought-after source of information, some future applications of this concept are projected for both marketing management and the social sciences.

495

The Life Style Concept in Consumer Behavior

One of the most flamboyant spending sprees of the last decade was accomplished by an eighteen-year-old who, armed with a packet of stolen checks and credit cards and a flair for forging signatures, enjoyed several hundred thousand dollars worth of travel and entertainment in far-flung corners of the globe. When finally arrested by international police, the young bon vivant declared that he was simply "leading the life style I've always wanted to become accustomed to."[1]

While few of us would care to face the consequences of such blissful self-indulgence, we all reveal patterns of consumption that shape the phenomenon sociologists have dubbed "life style." This term, originally coined by Max Weber, encompasses many of the sociological, cultural, and psychological variables under scrutiny in consumer behavior. But even though mass media have popularized the term and most people know roughly what it is supposed to mean, no universal definition is accepted by all researchers.

William Lazer defines life style as referring to a "distinctive or characteristic mode of living, in its aggregate and broadest sense, of a whole society or segment thereof."[2] In other words, a means of characterizing any culture or group to distinguish it from others. This extends logically enough to factors in consumer behavior—attitudes, interests, personality characteristics, demographic considerations, ethnicity, and social class, along with product, service, and media choice. And because a consumer's total life style exerts such influence on his or her likely purchasing decisions, the concept has at-tracted marketers' attention as a formal basis for prediction itself.[3]

The purpose of exploring life style is to obtain more comprehensive and penetrating profiles of how consumers think and act than may be available from more closely defined areas of investigation. First, there is the *concept* of life style, which can organize much isolated data about consumers into a meaningful whole. Secondly, the methodology known as *life style and psychographic research* has been developed to offer a standardized means of obtaining and evaluating life-style information on which marketers can act. Both aspects will be covered in some depth here.

From a sociological viewpoint, Feldman and Thielbar describe life style by the four following characteristics:[4]

1. *Life style is a group phenomenon.* An individual's life style bears the influence of participation in social groups and relationships with significant others. A college student maintains a life style dramatically different from a construction worker's, and an adolescent's life style differs from that of his or her parents. These are easily explained differences. Less obvious at first glance are the divergent patterns exhibited by, say, two clerks who share office space in a corporation. Both earn the same salary, but one maintains his family in a style compatible with his income while the other plunges into debt supporting a wife busily engaged in conspicuous consumption.

2. *Life style pervades many aspects of life.* A person's life style commits that individual, in a sense, to a certain consistency of behavior. Knowing a person's conduct in one aspect

of life may enable us to predict how he or she will behave in other areas. People who prefer oil and vinegar on their salads are more inclined to attend a ballet than people who use commercial French dressing. Individuals who say they are liberal or "left" politically are more likely to see a foreign "art" movie than people who profess to be middle-of-the-road or conservative.[5]

3. *Life style implies a central life interest.* A distinct life style may be identified when some activity or interest pervades other, even unrelated, activities. In the United States, there are many central interests that may fashion an individual's life style; family, work, leisure, drugs, sexual exploits, and religion are some. The upper middle-class life style, for instance, is usually regarded as education and career oriented.

4. *Life styles vary according to sociologically relevant variables.* These include age, sex, ethnicity, social class, region, and a number of other determinants. The rate of social change also has a great deal to do with variation in life styles. America in the 1970s tolerates considerably more diversity than in the 1950s, for example, when life styles were more homogeneous.

A Working Definition

For the purposes of this discussion, life style may be defined as *unified patterns of behavior that both determine and are determined by consumption.*

The term "unified patterns of behavior" refers to behavior in its broadest sense. Attitude formation and other types of subjective activity are not readily observable, but are behaviors nonetheless. Life style is an integrated system of attitudes, values, opinions, and interests as well as overt behavior.

The conclusion that life style "both determines and is determined by consumption" expresses a critical relationship in the study of consumer behavior. Lazer's *life-style hierarchy,* Figure 19-1, helps to illuminate this point.

Cultural and *societal* variables establish the general boundaries of life style specific to our culture. The interaction of *group* and *individual* expectations and values creates a *systematic pattern* of behavior. This is the life-style pattern that determines purchasing decisions. Consumer market reactions are usually favorable when goods and services re-

Figure 19-1 A life-style hierarchy.

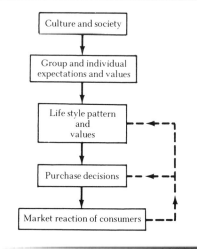

Source: William Lazer, "Life-Style Concepts in Marketing," in Stephen A. Greyser (ed.) Toward Scientific Marketing, (Chicago: American Marketing Association, 1968), p. 132. Reprinted by permission of the American Marketing Association.

inforce life-style patterns and values, usually negative when they do not. And purchases that reinforce those patterns further define individual life styles.

Consider the life styles of two hypothetical consumers. The first, a young, single divorce lawyer living in Los Angeles, views himself as something of a swinger. His attitudes and interests are translated into purchases like an exotic $25,000 Excalibur replica automobile, a custom-fitted wardrobe, and a penthouse apartment in a "singles-only" complex. His monthly credit card statements list an expensive array of nightspots, as well as several plane tickets to Aspen and Las Vegas. All of these purchases tend to reinforce his self-conceptualization—to others as well as to himself. We could predict with some accuracy that he would be an ideal prospect for products such as skis and cameras, rental cars and Hawaiian vacation packages because they would augment his active status-oriented life style. Similarly, we would be most likely to reach him with advertising appeals in media such as *Esquire, Penthouse,* and credit card magazines.

Our second consumer is a tax lawyer and family man living in a small Ohio suburb. His colonial house and Buick station wagon (both selected in consultation with his wife) reflect an orientation toward the home and children. Family vacations tend to be camping trips several times a year and an occasional trip to Europe. Entertainment expenses include food and liquor for cocktails and dinner at home with friends, while clothing accounts for a significantly smaller portion of his budget than his Los Angeles colleague considers sufficient. These purchasing patterns, widely divergent from our first consumer's, both define and reinforce a life style of husband, father, and suburbanite.

We might reasonably predict that this individual would be a prospect for life insurance, a second (economy) car, fishing gear, and possibly a swimming pool. He could probably be reached by advertising in magazines such as *Newsweek, Money,* and the *Reader's Digest.*

Using Life Style

The life-style concept is neither a model nor a theory of consumer behavior. Life style serves here as an *organizational* concept for understanding many of the determinants and processes of behavior. There are two principal reasons for using the concept in this fashion:[6]

• Life style draws a variety of *analyses* together. Data on consumer incomes, age groups, and spending patterns has been gathered and analyzed for some time. Now the objective is to translate these findings into useful information about people. Life style provides a meaningful portrait of how people are individualized and how they identify themselves as members of reference groups, which collectively form patterns of living. This leads us closer to understanding and predicting consumer behavior.

• Life style draws a variety of *disciplines* together. Because it determines and reflects so many aspects of life, the life-style concept is a point of convergence between marketing on the one hand and disciplines such as anthroplogy, psychology, sociology, and economics on the other.

Thus, life style emerges as an organizational systems concept in the study of consumer behavior.

How do you meas. + find out about L.S. (handwritten note)

Life-Style and Psychographic Research

The research methodology generally referred to as life-style and/or psychographic research represents a practical application of behavioral and social sciences to marketing. Basically, psychographics attempts to describe the human characteristics of consumers influencing their responses to market variables—products, packaging, media, and so on—that demographic or socioeconomic measures alone cannot explain.[7]

Dimensions of Psychographics

Because "life style" refers to the ways in which people live and spend time and money, consumers' psychographic profiles are derived by measuring various aspects of individual behavior, such as:[8]

1. Products and services consumed.
2. Activities, interests, and opinions.
3. Value system.
4. Personality traits and conception of "self."
5. Attitudes toward various product classes, which may include the benefits sought in buying items in the category, special problems such items might solve, and the individual's more general attitudes toward brands within the product class.

The advantages of soliciting this kind of information over and above demographics is illustrated by Wells's example of heavy users of a certain product class—people who buy shotgun ammunition[9] (see Tables 19-1 and 19-2). A *demographic* profile of this consumer indicates that he is younger, lower in income and education, and more concentrated in rural areas than nonbuyers. Yet, the *psychographic* portrait of the same consumer yields a richer store of information. He associates hunting with other rugged outdoor activities, suggesting joint marketing ventures between marketers of hunting, fishing, and camping products. He is more prone to take risks. This suggests to public policy makers that it would be ineffective to appeal to his fear of danger in the attempt to limit the use of firearms. And he is more attracted to violence, suggesting media selection criteria (such as "action" television shows) for advertisers who wish to reach him..

Generally, psychographic research may be discussed in two categories—those studies which attempt to isolate consumer "types" and those probing consumers' attitudes, interests, and opinions for specific product or media categories.

Isolating Psychographic Segments Through one approach, researchers draw profiles of groups who reflect similar life-style characteristics. A single product, however, may not necessarily be confined to one "heavy user" group, but may be used by different groups. The advantage of this technique is that products can be developed and advertised to well-defined groups of consumers who exhibit common needs.

The Newspaper Advertising Bureau has conducted such a study, identifying eight male and eight female psychographic segments on the bases of (1) personality, (2) personal aspirations, (3) social roles, (4) product use, and (5) media preferences. These groups are shown in Table 19-3.

The method employed in this type of psy-

Table 19-1   Demographic Profile of the Heavy User of Shotgun Ammunition

	PERCENT WHO SPEND $11+ PER YEAR ON SHOTGUN AMMUNITION: BASE (141)	PERCENT WHO DON'T BUY (395)
Age		
Under 25	9	5
25–34	33	15
35–44	27	22
45–54	18	22
55+	13	36
Occupation		
Professional	6	15
Managerial	23	23
Clerical-Sales	9	17
Craftsman	50	35
Income		
Under $6,000	26	19
$6,000–$10,000	39	36
$10,000–$15,000	24	27
$15,000+	11	18
Population Density		
Rural	34	12
2,500–50,000	11	11
50,000–500,000	16	15
500,000–2 million	21	27
2 million+	13	19
Geographic Division		
New England—Mid-Atlantic	21	33
Central (N, W)	22	30
South Atlantic	23	12
E. South Central	10	3
W. South Central	10	5
Mountain	6	3
Pacific	9	15

Source: Joseph T. Plummer, "Life Style Portrait of the Hunter," as cited in William D. Wells, "Psychographics: A Critical Review," Journal of Marketing Research (May 1975), pp. 198–99. Reprinted by permission of the American Marketing Association.

Table 19-2   Psychographic Profile of the Heavy User of Shotgun Ammunition

(handwritten annotation: (Likert Scale) agree, strongly agree... get a better sense of intensity)

	PERCENT WHO SPEND $11+ PER YEAR ON SHOTGUN AMMUNITION BASE (141)	PERCENT WHO DON'T BUY (395)
I like hunting	88	7
I like fishing	68	26
I like to go camping	57	21
I love the out-of-doors	90	65
A cabin by a quiet lake is a great place to spend the summer	49	34
I like to work outdoors	67	40
I am good at fixing mechanical things	47	27
I often do a lot of repair work on my own car	36	12
I like war stories	50	32
I would do better than average in a fist fight	38	16
I would like to be a professional football player	28	18
I would like to be a policeman	22	8
There is too much violence on television	35	45
There should be a gun in every home	56	10
I like danger	19	8
I would like to own my own airplane	35	13
I like to play poker	50	26
I smoke too much	39	24
I love to eat	49	34
I spend money on myself that I should spend on the family	44	26
If given a chance, most men would cheat on their wives	33	14
I read the newspaper every day	51	72

Source: Joseph T. Plummer, "Life Style Portrait of the Hunter," as cited in William D. Wells, "Psychographics: A Critical Review," Journal of Marketing Research *(May 1975), pp. 198–99. Reprinted by permission of the American Marketing Association.*

chographic segmentation is Q factor analysis—a statistical method for correlating responses people give that tend to group them with other consumers. For the purpose of this study, 4,000 respondents scaled 300 questions about the five items mentioned above.[11] The questions posed were essentially the same as those used in Activities, Interests, and Opinions (AIO) Research (see below).

Activities, Interests, and Opinions   The investigation of activities, interests, and opinions, known as AIO research, seeks to determine the differences between light and heavy users of a given product or medium.

Three types of information are analyzed in this procedure, involving survey forms of 300 questions sent to a sample of approximately 1,000 consumers: (1) each respondent's level of agreement with each AIO

Table 19-3   Two Representative Groups from a Psychographic Segmentation Study

GROUP I.   "THE CONFORMIST" (8% OF THE TOTAL FEMALES)

This woman is more conventional, is quite rigid and intolerant when it comes to change. She likes the familiar and finds reassurance in familiar brand names. She takes pride in hunting down bargains.

She belongs to the lowest educated group, lowest socioeconomic status and the oldest group in this sample.

Most users of: Mouthwash
                 White bread

Fewest users of: Instant coffee; regular or decaffeinated
                   Toothpaste
                   Deodorants
                   Headache remedy
                   Bourbon
                   Domestic wine
                   Domestic and outside U.S. air travel

GROUP VII.   "THE HE-MAN" (19% OF TOTAL MALES)

He is gregarious, likes action, seeks an exciting and dramatic life. Thinks of himself as capable and dominant. Tends to be more of a bachelor than a family man, even after marriage. Products he buys and brands preferred are likely to have "self-expressive value," especially a "Man of Action" dimension.

Well educated, mainly middle socioeconomic status, the youngest of the male groups.

Most users of: Beer
                 Toothpaste
                 Deodorants
                 Shaving cream

Fewest users of: Decaffeinated ground and instant coffee

Source: Psychographics: A Study of Personality, Life Style, and Consumption Patterns *(New York: Newspaper Advertising Bureau, 1973).*

How the Right Demographics Can Help Find the Wrong Consumers[10]

Using the most revealing demographic data, a direct marketer of life insurance can say, "Look, here are two families living side by side. In both households, there's a husband who's 27.2 years old, finished 3.8 years of college, earns $24,783 a year, has 2 kids and .6 of a dog. Those guys are two of my prime prospects and demographics located them for me."

But taking a closer look, we find that he has uncovered only one prime prospect. True, the fellow living in the solid colonial to the right conducts himself as a model of sober family devotion, whose happiest moments occur when he can point his station wagon home from the office early to spend an extra hour with the kids. This consumer couldn't be sold on a life insurance policy *under* $150,000, and would no sooner miss a premium due date than he would kick his .6 of a dog.

But the consumer living next door orders his life around a different set of priorities. This husband and father enjoys nothing more than to hop into his yellow Corvette Sting Ray and race noisily off for a round of pub-crawling. His wife and children dress in near-rags because he spends most of the family income indulging his taste for expensive stereos, golf clubs, and other personal luxuries. That's why his marriage is on the brink of divorce. And why he is such an unlikely candidate for life insurance.

The behavioral differences between these two "prospects" reflect *life-style* patterns that didn't show up in the demographic numbers. Yet they will predetermine the effectiveness of a life insurance ad or salesperson in each household—welcomed by the first family man as relevant to his needs and self-image, dismissed by the second as irrelevant to his.

statement, (2) each respondent's indicated "average use" of some 125 products, and (3) demographic data on each respondent.[12] The following are twenty representative AIO statements:

I enjoy going to concerts.
A woman's place is in the home.
In my job I tell people what to do.
I am a good cook.
My greatest achievements are ahead of me.
I buy many things with a charge or credit card.
We will probably move once in the next five years.
Five years from now the family income will probably be a lot higher than it is now.
Good grooming is a sign of self-respect.

Women wear too much makeup today.
Young people have too many privileges today.
I love the outdoors.
There is too much emphasis on sex today.
There are day people and there are night people; I am a day person.
I would like to have my boss' job.
A party wouldn't be a party without liquor.
When I must choose between the two, I usually dress for fashion, not comfort.
Movies should be censored.
I spend too much time talking on the telephone.
My days seem to follow a definite routine.

The advantage of this approach is that it enables marketers to position given products directly to the group that is likely to find the product most appealing.

Life-Style Portraits

To illustrate the substantial information obtained from delineating the life style of heavy users, three case histories for a range of products and services—beer, eye makeup, and bank credit cards—are presented.

The Heavy Beer Drinker Because so much beer is consumed in the United States, the beer drinker has long been a subject of keen interest to beverage marketers and their advertising agencies. An early breakthrough was achieved when Roper research discovered that only 23 percent of the people who drink beer consume 80 percent of the beverage sold. The Batten, Barton, Durstine, and Osborn Advertising Agency (BBDO), impressed with this finding, began conducting group interviews with beer drinkers who downed several cans (or six packs) a day. This heavy consumer became the advertising target, and BBDO's client, Schaefer Beer, adopted the positioning slogan, "The one beer to have when you're having more than one." The Schaefer campaign proved highly successful in the New York market.

Many other approaches directed at beer drinkers have emerged and disappeared as less than productive. One campaign for Ballantine Beer portrayed a beer company president reclining on a psychoanalyst's couch in a parody of the one-time best seller *Portnoy's Complaint*. His beer, he explained to the therapist, had deteriorated in quality when his relatives were minding the brewery

for him, but was much improved now that he was back at the helm. This appeal held little interest for the largely nonliterary and unanalyzed beer-drinking audience. Another campaign, also aimed at the New York market, focused upon the city's ethnic groups enjoying Rheingold Beer, with a different subculture featured in each commercial. Again, it was reported that beer drinkers did not respond favorably—this time because the groups represented did not appear willing to identify with the others' consumption patterns.[13]

Because the heavy beer drinker's attitudes and behavioral patterns seemed to elude so many marketing experts, this consumer presents an intriguing subject for life-style research. (See Table 19-4.)

Plummer applied this AIO methodology to beer drinkers and found heavy consumers to be middle class economically but engaged in traditional blue collar occupations. The major life-style patterns revealed the serious beer drinker as more pleasure-seeking and hedonistic in his approach to life than the nonbeer drinker. He seemed less concerned about responsibilities such as family and job, and preferred physical, male-oriented activities. He also exhibited a more pronounced tendency to fantasize. Not too surprisingly, he enjoyed drinking and regarded beer as a real man's drink. The Leo Burnett Advertising Agency used these findings to develop a new campaign for Schlitz Beer, stressing virile models engaging in male-type activities and thoroughly enjoying themselves.[14]

The considerations of hedonistic outlook, casual attitudes toward responsibility, and willingness to consume several beers in one sitting seem well-reflected in the slogan,

Table 19-4 Male Beer Drinkers

	PERCENT AGREEMENT		
	NON-USERS	LIGHT USERS	HEAVY USERS
He is self-indulgent, enjoys himself and likes risks			
I like to play poker	18	37	41
I like to take chances	27	32	44
I would rather spend a quiet evening at home than go out to a party	67	53	44
If I had my way, I would own a convertible	7	11	15
I smoke too much	29	40	42
If I had to choose, I would rather have a color TV than a new refrigerator	25	33	38
He rejects responsibility and is a bit impulsive.			
I like to work on community projects	24	18	14
I have helped collect money for the Red Cross or United Fund	41	32	24
I'm not very good at saving money	20	29	38
I find myself checking prices, even for small items	51	42	40
He likes sports and a physical orientation.			
I would like to be a pro football player	10	15	21
I like bowling	32	36	42
I usually read the sports page	47	48	59
I would do better than average in a fist fight	17	26	32
I like war stories	33	37	45
He rejects old-fashioned institutions and moral guidelines			
I go to church regularly	57	37	31
Movies should be censored	67	46	43
I have old-fashioned tastes and habits	69	56	48
There is too much emphasis on sex today	71	59	53
Beer is a real man's drink	9	16	44
Playboy is one of my favorite magazines	11	21	28
I am a girl-watcher	33	47	54
Men should not do the dishes	18	26	38
Men are smarter than women	22	27	31

Source: Joseph T. Plummer, "Life Style and Advertising: Case Studies." Paper presented at the 54th Annual International Marketing Conference, American Marketing Association, 1966.

"You only go around once in life—you've got to grab all the gusto you can."

More recently, Alpert and Gatty probed beer drinkers' life styles through factor analysis.[15] This study revealed definite groupings of behavioral styles in purchasing when heavy users of one brand were compared with heavy users of another. Here, "factors" referred to how the different groups used a variety of products, and categories such as the following were established:

Factor I: The Hard Drinker
    rye whisky
    Canadian whisky
    bourbon
    scotch
    gin
    vodka
    highball mixers
    beer
Factor II: The Car-Conscious Man
    car wax and polish
    motor oil
    antifreeze
    miles driven
    gasoline
Factor IV: The Cosmopolitan Traveler
    plane trips in past year
    car rental in past year
    gas credit cards
    other credit cards
    foreign trips last year
Factor VII: The Dress-Conscious Man
    suits
    shoes
    dress shirts
    sport shirts

The findings disclosed that beer drinking in general was aligned with "Hard Drinking." Heavy beer drinkers were more clearly defined than light beer drinkers, and were unlikely to be either "Liquor or Wine Connoisseurs." Among heavy beer drinkers, brand distinctions became quite apparent. For instance, Brand Y beer drinkers could be described as "Outdoorsmen," thus were more inclined to be "Hard drinkers." Brand W drinkers formed a different profile entirely. These subjects were more likely to be "Cosmopolitan Travelers," "Dress-Conscious Men," "Cocktail Drinkers," and "Car-Conscious Men." Brand W subjects also tended to be "Candy Consumers" and "Cigar and Pipe Smokers," which led the authors of this study to conclude that Brand W people seemed to look for more oral satisfaction.

The User of Eye Makeup Wells and Tigert used an AIO inventory to probe the heavy user of eye cosmetics.[16] Demographic data revealed that such women were inclined to be young, well-educated, and metropolitan. Working wives used more eye makeup than full-time homemakers. Predictably enough, the heavy eye makeup user emerged as a frequent purchaser of other cosmetics. But she also tended to be a heavy smoker and more inclined than the average to use gasoline and make long-distance telephone calls. Her television tastes ran to movies and "talk shows." In magazines, she preferred fashion, news, and general interest periodicals to *True Confessions.*

From responses to AIO statements, she appeared to be more interested in fashion than the nonuser of eye cosmetics, and indicated that being attractive to others, especially to men, formed an important part of her self-image. She was likely to fantasize about a trip around the world, enjoy going to art galleries, the ballet, and to parties where there is much excitement and talk. Her attitudes toward home were style-conscious as opposed to utilitarian. She liked to serve unusual dinners, did not like housework or grocery shopping, and would furnish a home for style rather than comfort.

The heavy eye makeup user could be described as a person who accepts contemporary rather than traditional ideas. She likes to think of herself as a bit of a swinger, enjoys bright splashy colors, and genuinely believes that "blondes have more fun."

Bank Credit Card Users   In a study by Plummer applied to Mastercharge and Bank-Americard usage, male and female users of charge cards were profiled separately.[17] (See Table 19-5).

Male Heavy Users   These affluent males were described as urbane and active, with high income, occupational, and educational achievements. The male heavy user places a high value on personal appearance consistent with his career and life style. He tends to buy at least three new suits a year, to belong to several organizations, and to reveal contemporary rather than traditional attitudes and opinions. This individual is not terribly concerned with security and so is willing to take risks. He does not feel that investing in the stock market is too risky for most families, that it is important to shop around before buying a car, or (obviously enough) that buying anything but a house or car on credit is unwise.

Female Heavy Users   The woman who uses bank charge cards extensively also leads an active life, is concerned with her appearance, and is likely to belong to several organizations. In contrast to the nonuser, she seems to place less value on the traditional skills of the housewife, and takes a "managerial" approach to homemaking. She would appreciate having a maid do the housework, would not enjoy knowing how to sew like an expert,

and does not feel that she is a homebody. Instead, she exhibits a pronounced "fantasy life" of world travel, flying her own airplane, and becoming an actress. Like her male counterpart, the heavy female user expresses a willingness to take risks and a contemporary rather than a traditional orientation.

Methodological Considerations   Like any relatively new research technique applied to the study of human behavior, AIO portraits are subject to methodological questions and problems. Wells and Tigert have identified three areas in which findings have not proven as dramatic as marketers may wish.[18]

Thin Products   The most significant problem confronting life-style researchers is that not all products correlate with a large number of activity, interest, and opinion statements. Cable TV subscribers, for instance, were not found to be significantly different from nonsubscribers.[19]

Overlapping Portraits   This occurs because the products themselves overlap and indicate pretty much the same life styles. One example of similar products that do reveal significantly different profiles are fresh oranges and fresh lemons.

Multiple Product Uses   Some products may be used heavily for two or more different purposes, and different life-style portraits of consumers could be obtained for each purpose. Mouthwash, for example, can serve for cold prevention or as a cosmetic.

But the great bulk of evidence indicates that life style is here to stay as a research technique, and that the problems facing researchers are less formidable than in other methodologies not offering such comprehensive portraits of consumers. Today, life-style studies are in great demand for a variety of products, services, and media.

Vacation Behavior: Life Style Versus Media Exposure Influences

What determines how consumers plan and spend their vacations? Traditionally, media exposure was thought to be a prime consideration, since travel is expensive and would supposedly cause consumers to seek special information from selected media. Yet Darden and Perrault found, in a study comparing media with life style, that life-style criteria may be a more powerful influence on vacation decisions.[18]

This study selected different media groups on the basis of exposure patterns, profiling them as in Figure 19-2.

1. *Median Exposures* (Middle Americans) comprised 50 percent of the sample. They reported high exposure to *Time, Newsweek,* and special interest magazines such as *Field and Stream, National Geographic,* and *Sports Illustrated.*

2. *Home Centereds* (Traditionalists) had the highest exposures for *Woman's Day, Good Housekeeping, Ladies Home Journal, Reader's Digest,* and *TV Guide.*

3. *Low Exposures* (Lowbrows) reported low exposure to magazines, but spent much time watching TV.

4. *High Exposures* (Highbrows) reported the highest exposure for all but the home magazines.

These groups were compared, by means of a Multivariate Analysis of Variance Model (MANOVA), with life-style groups selected on the basis of response to the statements in Table 19-6. The finding that vacation behavior is more influenced by total life style than media exposure suggests that travel marketers should direct more money to life-style and psychographic research and proportionately less to media spending. But it will probably take many more studies to convince even the most avant garde marketers to move away from a long-standing travel marketing strategy of big media, low research budgets.

Table 19-6 Life Style Covariates

SCALE	SAMPLE STATEMENT
Generalized Self-Confidence	I think I have more self-confidence than most people.
Opinion leadership	I sometimes influence the type of places my friends visit for a vacation.
Plan-ahead Traveler	I would never leave on a vacation without reservations at my destination.
Information seeker	My friends give me good advice on where I should spend my vacation.
Camper traveler	My family enjoys camping.
Relaxing traveler	A vacation should not be hectic but quiet and relaxing.
First-class traveler	I would not vacation in an area where first class accommodations were not available.
National traveler	I really like to get to know the people and places when I'm on vacation.
Jettsetter-Vagabond traveler	I always try to visit as many action-packed locations as possible during my vacation.
Historical traveler	Visiting historical locations is an important consideration in planning any vacation.

| Sports-spectator | I normally plan my vacations around watching my favorite sporting event. |
| Functional Gregarious | The most important part of any vacation is meeting new people. |

Source of Table 19-6 and Figure 19-2: Adapted from William R. Darden and William D. Perreault, Jr., "A Multivariate Analysis of Media Exposure and Vacation Behavior with Life Style Covariates," Journal of Consumer Research, *Vol. 2, No. 2 (September 1975), p. 95. Reprinted by permission of the American Marketing Association.*

Figure 19-2 Profiles of media exposure groups.

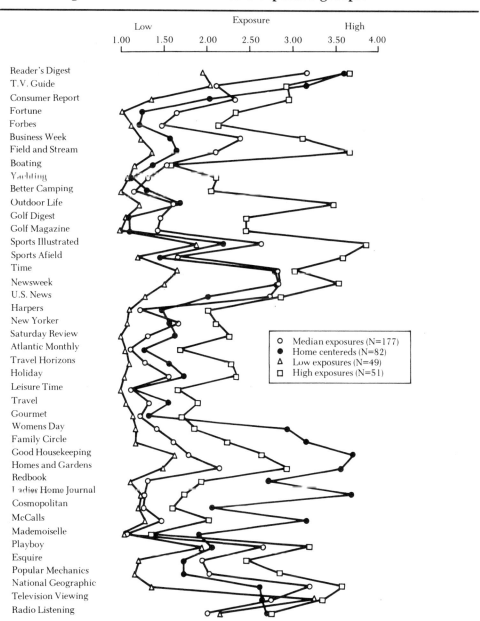

Reader's Digest
T.V. Guide
Consumer Report
Fortune
Forbes
Business Week
Field and Stream
Boating
Yachting
Better Camping
Outdoor Life
Golf Digest
Golf Magazine
Sports Illustrated
Sports Afield
Time
Newsweek
U.S. News
Harpers
New Yorker
Saturday Review
Atlantic Monthly
Travel Horizons
Holiday
Leisure Time
Travel
Gourmet
Womens Day
Family Circle
Good Housekeeping
Homes and Gardens
Redbook
Ladies Home Journal
Cosmopolitan
McCalls
Mademoiselle
Playboy
Esquire
Popular Mechanics
National Geographic
Television Viewing
Radio Listening

Exposure
Low   High
1.00   1.50   2.00   2.50   3.00   3.50   4.00

○ Median exposures (N=177)
● Home centereds (N=82)
△ Low exposures (N=49)
□ High exposures (N=51)

Table 19-5   Cross-Tabulation Results of AIO Agreement with Female Bank Charge Card Usage

STATEMENT	CARD USERS DEFINITE AND GENERAL AGREEMENT	NONCARD USERS DEFINITE AND GENERAL AGREEMENT
I enjoy going to concerts.	41%	32%
The next car our family buys will probably be a station wagon.	32	18
I usually have my dresses altered to the latest hemline levels.	52	39
There should be a gun in every home.	13	27
I buy many things with a credit or charge card.	64	28
If I had my way, I would own a convertible.	17	7
I would like to own and fly my own airplane.	17	10
I would like to be a fashion model.	22	10
I would like to take a trip around the world.	70	57
I enjoy going through an art gallery.	51	42
I like to pay cash for everything I buy.	33	64
I bowl, play tennis, golf or other active sports quite often.	28	14
I would like to be an actress.	16	6
I have more than ten pairs of shoes.	47	37
To buy anything other than a house or car on credit is unwise.	21	36
Our family travels quite a lot.	44	29
I belong to one or more clubs.	55	41
I must really admit I don't like household chores.	40	32
I like to play bridge.	29	16
I like to be considered a leader.	33	22
I'd like to spend a year in London or Paris.	40	28
I would rather spend a quiet evening at home than go out to a party.	31	45
I would like to know how to sew like an expert.	68	77
I would rather live in or near a big city than in or near a small town.	47	28
I sometimes bet money at the races.	16	5
I like to think I am a bit of a swinger.	24	11
I am a homebody.	44	58
I stay home most evenings.	63	73
I often have a cocktail before dinner.	21	9

Table 19-5 (Continued)

STATEMENT	CARD USERS DEFINITE AND GENERAL AGREEMENT	NONCARD USERS DEFINITE AND GENERAL AGREEMENT
I like ballet.	27	18
I like danger.	13	3
I do volunteer work for a hospital or service organization on a fairly regular basis.	27	11
I am an active member of more than one service organization.	26	16
I enjoy most forms of housework.	36	47
I do more things socially than most of my friends.	23	11
Clothes should be dried in the fresh air and sunshine.	26	37
Movies should be censored.	55	65
I would like a maid to do the housework.	41	27
It is good to have charge accounts.	62	41

Source: Joseph T. Plummer, "Life Style Patterns and Commercial Bank Credit Card Usage," Journal of Marketing, Vol. 35, No. 2 (1971), p. 40. Reprinted by permission of the American Marketing Association.

Using Life-Style Research

The life-style profiles cited earlier point out that market items across a wide spectrum lend themselves to psychographic analysis. Beer represents a largely male market whereas eye makeup is, with few exceptions, used only by women. Bank charge cards reflect both male and female usage. While beer and eye makeup are packaged goods and their purchase is both frequent and repetitive, bank credit cards illustrate a "considered purchase" service. Other life-style studies have been applied to automobile choice,[21] furniture preference,[22] sugar,[23] fast food franchises,[24] ecological concern,[25] and many additional areas of interest to marketers, policy makers, and social scientists.

Current Applications

The most striking advantages of using the life-style concept and aligned research today are found in presenting research findings, selecting media, formulating creative strategies, positioning products, and improving retail performance.[26]

Presenting Research Findings   Because research in consumer behavior has traditionally used the methods and jargon of the behavioral sciences, turning data over to business clients can create problems. The marketing director confronted with a complicated model may wonder how such a scheme could ever be made practical. The copywriter/art director teams faced with reams of statistics on their target audience are inclined to wince in agony and generally ignore the data provided. But the life-style concept, as a framework for research recommendations, offers marketing practitioners understandable portraits of people engaged in recognizable patterns of consumption. In addition, the life-style approach draws upon sociological and psychological determinants of purchasing behavior as well as demographic facts. An AIO portrait for heavy users of, say, men's after-shave lotion not only tells us how old they are, where they live, and what socioeconomic groups they belong to, but also points out what other products they are likely to buy, what their interests and opinions are, how they feel about their daily activities, and which media are most likely to reach them. This provides an unusually rich body of data to use in marketing decision making.

Selecting Media   Media salespeople attract advertisers through glowing demographic descriptions of their readers or viewers. These statistics are useful for information such as median incomes, amounts of liquor readers of a given magazine say they drink, and purchasing patterns of audiences. Yet, few insights about people's attitudes and opinions emerge from this data. A demographic analysis of the regular *Playboy* reader may portray him as essentially the same person who savors *Ramparts*, but there are probably sharp differences in the ways that these two consumers view advertising and products. As discussed at some length in chapter 14, life-style analyses provide considerably more information about the personality characteristics, attitudes, opinions, and product use patterns of people who are heavy users of newspapers, magazines, and television. And consumers are further differentiated on the basis of which magazines or kinds of programs they are most likely to read or watch.

Formulating Creative Strategies   In most major advertising campaigns, responsibility for communicating with consumers ultimately rests with an advertising agency's creative department. Here, research is finally sifted through the intuition of people who must come up with a "strategy" or "concept" that will make the ads effective.

Life-style information about the consumers they are trying to reach may be helpful to creative people in three ways.[27] For one, it gives them an idea of what *type* of consumer will be at the other end of the communication. This is useful in choosing the kinds of people who will be shown using the product, and placing them in an appropriate setting. Secondly, life-style data suggests what tone of voice and style of language should be used—whether humorous or serious, contemporary or traditional. Third, information about life style indicates how the product or service fits into people's lives, how they feel about it, and how they may be using that item to communicate something about themselves to other people.

Positioning Products   As noted in chapter 1, establishing a product or service in the consumer's frame of reference calls for some understanding of what that frame of reference actually is. Here life-style research may serve quite handily.

Consider the example of a parity packaged goods product—a toothpaste brand—that lacks distinguishing characteristics other than an extra whitening ingredient. To position this product effectively against Ultra Brite, Macleans, and similar brands would demand some hard research into heavy users of toothpastes that promise sparkling white teeth. If, as might be expected, the target consumers turned out to be teenagers and young singles, advertising and media strategies would probably sell sex appeal in *Seventeen*, *Cosmopolitan*, and in a heavy television and radio schedule. But AIO research might just as readily uncover surprising data on heavy users of "whitening" toothpaste. If they emerged not as adolescents but as young married professionals, the approach adopted by both creative and media departments could be skewed toward this unexpected target group.

A case history of such a development occurred in AIO investigation of people who bought carry-out fried chicken frequently.[28] Colonel Sanders' Kentucky Fried Chicken had been advertised as a folksy, down-home product when no consumer information was available. Yet research revealed that women who purchased the Colonel's chicken regularly were active, somewhat self-indulgent housewives who expressed a much more contemporary state of mind. The product was repositioned accordingly in subsequent advertising.

Improving Retail Performance Just as life style can differentiate consumers who are likely to use certain products, psychographic information can point up differences in shopping behavior. An early study by Demby identified two different types of consumers with regard to purchasing patterns, passive and creative.[29] Creative consumers are more

likely to respond to new modes of distribution than their passive counterparts. They were found in the vanguard of people who first popularized innovative retail environments such as the supermarket and the shopping center. Creative shoppers are also expected to contribute to the types of retail shopping experience projected for the near future and described in chapter 17.

Future Applications

Consumer behavior is still a young discipline, and most of the research now available has been generated only during the past fifteen years or so. Innovations such as the life-style concept and AIO research represent ways to move the study of consumers away from isolated, often unrelated projects toward broader systems and better-integrated research techniques. Consider the potential of life-style research in just two areas of recent interest—studying ethnic subcultures and analyzing small group segments.[30]

Because blacks make up the largest ethnic subculture in the United States, the bulk of consumer research exploring subcultural differences has focused on the black market. Yet, most urban populations also include healthy slices of Jewish, Italian, Chicano, or Puerto Rican life-style patterns that affect shopping and buying decisions. These segments have largely been ignored. AIO research offers the opportunity to study a variety of ethnic life styles in some depth and discover how members of specific subcultures actually feel about the products and services they use, what advertising appeals they tend to find most persuasive, and what new products could be developed to fit subcultural patterns of living. A number of successful specialty products have emerged in response to black consumer demand alone; two obvious examples are black cosmetic lines and African-style clothing. Presumably other ethnic groups have similar needs that could be anticipated through more aggressive market research.

In addition to ethnic groups, there are a number of small market segments ordinarily submerged in traditional mass market research. These include such diverse groups as urban singles, communal organic farmers, individuals engaged in unusual occupations, transient people, families with more than twelve children, couples with no children but high disposable incomes, and parents single by choice. All exhibit life styles that predispose them to be heavier-than-average users of certain products and services. And AIO research is highly suitable for probing both the similarities between these groups and other markets and the differences that would suggest special marketing considerations.

Any concept or research technique attempting to predict behavior bears its limitations, and the life-style approach is no exception. But as an organizational concept drawing on the theories of many disciplines, life style has earned increasing acceptance. It is, at least, a means through which academic and business resources have found some compatibility in tracking the elusive consumer.

Summary

Marketers are increasingly turning to the concept of *life style* as a means for segmenting consumer markets. Life style, originally a sociological term, may be defined as unified patterns of behavior that both determine and are determined by consumption. It is a systems concept that serves to organize the theories and findings of many disciplines. *Life-style and psychographic* research has emerged in recent years as a methodology offering deeper and more comprehensive profiles of consumers than are available through demographics alone. One type of life-style research attempts to isolate *psychographic segments* of consumer groups who reflect similar characteristics. Another—Activity, Interest, and Opinion (AIO) research—is used to distinguish light from heavy users of a given product or service. Life-style portraits are presented here for consumers of beer, eye makeup, and bank charge cards. The current applications of life-style research fall into the areas of presenting research findings, selecting media, developing creative strategies, positioning products, and improving retail performance.

NOTES

1. "Around the World at Eighteen on Credit and A Golden Pen," *New York Post*, October 26, 1973.

2. William Lazer, "Life Style Concepts and Marketing," in *Toward Scientific Marketing*, ed. Stephen A. Greyser (Chicago: American Mar-

keting Association, 1964), p. 130.

3. See Harold W. Berkman and Christopher C. Gilson, "Consumer Life Styles and Market Segmentation," *Journal of the Academy of Marketing Science,* Vol. 2, No. 1 (Winter 1974); and Joseph T. Plummer, "The Concept and Application of Life Style Segmentation," *Journal of Marketing,* Vol. 38 (January 1974).

4. Saul D. Feldman and Gerald W. Thielbar, *Life Styles: Diversity in American Society* (Boston: Little, Brown and Co., 1972), pp. 1–8.

5. Feldman and Thielbar, *Life Styles,* p. 2.

6. Lazar, "Life Style Concepts."

7. Emanuel Demby, "Psychographic and from Whence It Came," in *Life Style and Psychographics,* ed. William D. Wells (Chicago: American Marketing Association, 1974), p. 13.

8. Jerry Wind and Paul Green, "Some Conceptual, Measurement, and Analytical Problems in Life Style Research," in Wells, *Life Style and Psychographics.*

9. William D. Wells, "Psychographics: A Critical Review," *Journal of Marketing Research,* Vol. 12 (May 1975), pp. 196–199.

10. Christopher Gilson, "How the 'Right' Demographics Can Help You Find the Wrong Consumers," *Direct Marketing,* forthcoming issue, 1977.

11. *Psychographics: A Study of Personality, Life Style, and Consumption Patterns* (New York: Newspaper Advertising Bureau, 1973).

12. Joseph T. Plummer, "Life Style and Advertising: Case Studies" (Paper given at 54th Annual International Marketing Conference, American Marketing Association, 1966).

13. Harry W. McMahon, "Beer: One Industry Where Advertising Can Do Serious Harm," *Advertising Age,* October 8, 1973.

14. Plummer, "Life Style and Advertising."

15. Lewis Alpert and Ronald Gatty, "Product Positioning by Behavioral Life Styles," *Journal of Marketing* (April 1971).

16. William D. Wells and Douglas J. Tigert, "Activities, Interests, and Opinions," *Journal of Advertising Research,* Vol. 11, No. 4 (August 1971), pp. 27–35.

17. Joseph T. Plummer, "Life Style Patterns and Commercial Bank Credit Card Usage," *Journal of Marketing,* Vol. 35, No. 2 (1971).

18. William R. Darden and W. D. Perreault, Jr., "A Multivariate Analysis of Media Exposure and Vacation Behavior with Life Style Covariates," *Journal of Consumer Research,* Vol. 2, No. 2 (September 1975).

19. Wells and Tigert, "Activities, Interests, and Opinions," p. 36.

20. Christopher C. Binkert, James A. Brunner, and Jack L. Simonetti, "The Use of Life Style Segmentation to Determine if CATV Subscribers Are Really Different," *Journal of the Academy of Marketing Science,* Vol. 3, No. 2 (Spring 1975), p. 129.

21. Ruth Ziff, "The Role of Psychographics in the Development of Advertising Strategy and Copy," in *Life Style and Psychographics,* ed. William D. Wells (Chicago: American Marketing Association, 1974).

22. Walter S. Good and Otto Suchland, *Consumer Life Styles and Their Relationship to Market Behavior Regarding Household Furniture,* East Lansing, Mich.: Michigan State University Research Bulletin No. 26, 1970.

23. *New Information on Sugar User Psychographics* (Chicago: Leo Burnett, 1972).

24. Douglas J. Tigert, Richard Lathrope, and Michael Bleeg, "The Fast Food Franchise: Psychographic and Demographic Segmentation Analysis," *Journal of Retailing,* Vol. 47 (Spring 1971).

25. Thomas C. Kinnear, James R. Taylor, and Sadrudin A. Ahmed, "Socioeconomic and Personality Characteristics as They Relate to Ecologically-Constructive Behavior," *Proceedings of the Third Annual Conference of the Association for Consumer Research,* 1972.

26. Berkman and Gilson, "Consumer Life Styles."

27. Ruth Ziff, "Role of Psychographics."

28. Plummer, "Life Style and Advertising."

29. Emanuelle Demby, "Going Beyond Demographics to Find the Creative Consumer" (Paper presented at Market Research Section, American Marketing Association, New York Chapter, June 1967).

30. Berkman and Gilson, "Consumer Life Styles."

MARKETING APPLICATIONS

Conclusion 1 *For market segmentation purposes, life style and psychographic data provides a richer lode of information about groups of target consumers than demographics alone.*

Application A marketer of, say, tours to the Far East may point to two different households and note that the family in each is in their thirties, enjoys an annual income over $40,000, has two children, and reveals other demographic traits that would make that family a prime prospect for foreign travel. But a psychographic study probing the same market would distinguish more clearly between the two neighbors on the basis of attitudes, product use, activities, interests and other life style dimensions. While one of the two families may emerge as an ideal candidate for travel because its members are venturesome and curious about other peoples, members of the other tend to shy away from the unfamiliar and prefer to stay at home, representing a poor prospect indeed for a travel marketer.

Conclusion 2 *New possibilities for life-style segmentation include probing subcultures, small market segments for specific products or services, and other groups of interest to marketers and sociologists.*

Application A consumer magazine, for example, which directs itself to the interests of young, single women could pioneer a life-style segmentation study with a representative sample of all single women of ages twenty-one through thirty-five. This would serve the magazine directly in making decisions about editorial content and would offer persuasive information for attracting advertisers. Additionally, it would provide comprehensible profiles of this diverse market for all marketers who hope to meet the needs of single women. And finally, such a study would further our sociological understanding of an impressively large (and growing) segment of the population.

ASSIGNMENTS

Research Assignment

Background The management of McKenna Paper Co., a consumer products corporation, has invited your marketing consulting firm to make a presentation on life-style and psychographic research. McKenna wants to invest considerable sums of money in major projects to help them isolate heavy users of their different products and direct their marketing efforts accordingly. The management is quite sophisticated about research, however, and recognizes that any segmentation technique must entail certain limitations. Thus, the glowing predictions of your presentation must be balanced with some honest admissions of where life style may *not* draw useful profiles.

Methodology   Refer to the preceding chapter, as well as:

William D. Wells, (ed.), *Life Style and Psychographics* (Chicago: American Marketing Association, 1974).

William D. Wells and Douglas J. Tigert, "Interests, Activities, and Opinions," *Journal of Advertising Research*, Vol. 11 (August 1971).

Organize an explanation of life-style and psychographic research that includes what it measures, the kinds of profiles it offers (with examples), the methodological considerations, and applications to current marketing problems.

Extrapolation   What other uses could life-style research be turned to, both in marketing and policy-making or the social sciences?

Creative Assignment

The Barnett, Bixby, and Boyle Advertising Agency has just acquired the Fidelity National Bank account. Fidelity is a full-service, multibranch bank offering its customers credit privileges through its Cashcard service. Cashcard is a standard bank credit card accepted nationally by all major airlines, car rental firms, and hotels. It is also recognized locally by most restaurants, department stores, and shops. In addition, Fidelity's customers may obtain cash advances simply by showing the Cashcard at any branch office.

Cashcard holders have two payment options: (1) They may pay the entire balance on each monthly statement and avoid a finance charge, or (2) they may pay a smaller portion of the balance each month, with a finance charge of 1½% per month added to the unpaid balance. In the second option, cardholders are actually receiving a loan from the bank and are paying interest accordingly.

Although a number of Fidelity's customers hold Cashcards and use them regularly, bank executives are deeply troubled at the generally poor return on their credit privilege investment. The problem is that many cardholders pay the full balance on their statement each month rather than taking the extended payment option. Fidelity is not lending them money in this case and cannot realize any profit on interest.

Fidelity has explained this problem to Barnett, Bixby, and Boyle, and has demanded a new advertising strategy that will *promote the extended-payment advantages of Cashcard to existing and potential cardholders.*

Barnett, Bixby, and Boyle have assured Fidelity that a new campaign, based on life-style data from their research department, will solve the bank's problem. As Creative Supervisor, you are assigned to do a Cashcard campaign for Fidelity National consisting of three newspaper ads (full-page) that will meet the stated objective.

Research Input Refer to Plummer, Joseph T., "Life Style Patterns and Commercial Bank Credit Card Usage," *Journal of Marketing,* Vol. 35, No. 2 (1971).

Managerial Assignment

As a Corporate Public Relations executive for Stanley Brothers, a major recreation products company, you are asked to write a convincing explanation of how this company is using the life-style concept to better meet consumer needs. Your comments will ultimately appear in a Stanley Brothers executive's article in *The Wall Street Journal.*

This explanation, roughly two pages, should draw upon information in this chapter. Additional material may be found in the following sources:

William Lazer, "Life-Style Concepts in Marketing," in *Toward Scientific Marketing,* ed. Stephen A. Greyser, (Chicago: American Marketing Association, 1964).

Joseph T. Plummer, "The Concept and Application of Life-Style Segmentation," *Journal of Marketing,* Vol. 38 (January 1974).

Harold W. Berkman and Christopher C. Gilson, "Consumer Life Styles and Market Segmentation," *Journal of the Academy of Marketing Science,* Vol. 2 (Winter 1974).

SELECTED READINGS

Binkert, Christopher C. et al. "The Use of Life Style Segmentation to Determine if CATV Subscribers are Really Different." *Journal of the Academy of Marketing Science,* Vol. 3, No. 2 (Spring 1975), pp. 129–136.

Lovell, M. R. C. "European Developments in Psychographics" in *Life Style and Psychographics,* ed. W. D. Wells. Chicago: American Marketing Association, 1974, pp. 257–276.

Plummer, Joseph T. "Applications of Life Style Research to the Creation of Advertising Campaigns" in *Life Style and Psychographics,* ed. W. D. Wells. Chicago: American Marketing Association, 1974, pp. 157–169.

Villani, Kathryn E. A. "Personality/Life Style and Television Viewing Behavior." *Journal of Marketing Research,* Vol. 12, No. 4 (November 1976), pp. 432–439.

Wells, William D. "Psychographics: A Critical Review." *Journal of Marketing Research,* Vol. 12, No. 2 (May 1975), pp. 196–213.

OBJECTIVES

1. Profile the people identified with *consumer activism*. 523

2. Discuss the three general areas of *consumerist demands*. 523

3. Summarize the concepts of *expectancy* and *alienation*. 528

4. Discuss three *implications of consumerism* for marketers. 532

5. Explain how *socially conscious* consumers might be segmented as a special market. 533

6. Summarize some implications of the study on *consumer ecological concern*. 535

7. Explain the roles of *demarketing*, buyer *optimization strategies*, and *social marketing* in redefining the marketing concept. 538

TWENTY

Consumerism and Social Responsibility

The current popularity of consumer behavior study may be traced, in some part, to changes in consumers themselves over the past few years. Buyers now express a growing (and often noisy) rejection of the old market place adage, "Let the buyer beware." Response to their demands by government regulatory agencies has provided good reasons for sellers to beware in making product claims, setting the quality standards of their merchandise, and communicating with disgruntled customers.

Economic and social developments of recent years have also contributed to the changing profile of American consumers. The 1970s witnessed a major recession, widespread unemployment, and other indications that our society may not always offer the endless cornucopia of resources to which consumers have so long been accustomed.

The purpose of this chapter is to present the most important consumer issues that will confront the current generation of marketers. Some specific topics in this realm include:

• What consumers really think about business.

• Who makes up the new consumer coalition and what they are demanding.

• How consumers have actually responded to protective legislation such as that requiring unit pricing, truth-in-labeling, and credit disclosure.

• What buying habits consumers may be willing to change for ecological preservation.

• How consumer behavior fits into demarketing.

As noted throughout the text, marketing will always be an adaptive discipline. And the most successful marketers will continue to be those who recognize changing consumer attitudes and trends as opportunities for innovation rather than threats to traditional practice.

Issues Shaping the Future of Marketing

One fast-growing controversy in the consumer behavior discipline revolves around whether it should serve solely as a tool of marketers or whether research in the field should be skewed toward buyer satisfaction and social goals. A middle-of-the-road position maintains that consumer behavior research should merely supply information about consumers and avoid prescribing what should be done with the findings. Supporting the argument for a consumer and social orientation, two significant issues seem to be shaping the future of marketing and all related disciplines.

The first issue is familiarly termed *consumerism.* Because we are all consumers as well as marketers, we have all encountered products that do not perform to our expectations, service personnel who fail to give service, and other nagging frustrations with the things we buy and use. In recent years, consumers have become increasingly vocal in expressing their dissatisfactions, and consumer legislation has reflected their new militancy.[1]

The second issue is the general area of *social responsibility.* Articulate factions of society are raising questions about what marketers can do to improve the quality of life in America, and they point to such ambitious goals as saving our shrinking environment and reducing social inequality.

Both issues are highly complex and problem-laden, but neither promises to go away until marketers have done something about them. Thus, what appears to be our greatest challenge over the next few years is a *redefinition of the marketing concept* to recognize and repair some of the breakdowns in our marketing system.

This chapter discusses consumerism with an eye toward marketing implications; the advent of a new socially conscious consumer with prescriptions about how he or she may be reached; and a broadening of the marketing concept to include consumer buying strategies. To illustrate the application of social concepts in consumer research, a case study on ecological concern and purchasing is presented.

The Rise of Consumerism

Although consumer advocacy and legislation may be traced back to the turn of the century, the 1960s witnessed the birth of consumerism as we know it today. In 1962, John F. Kennedy offered the first presidential doctrine of consumer protection: the Consumer Bill of Rights. Kennedy defined con-

sumer prerogatives as the right to *safety,* the right to be *informed,* the right to *choose,* and the right to be *heard.*[2] During the same period, consumer scandals such as the thalidomide crisis (caused by a tranquilizer held responsible for grave birth defects) and the controversy over Ralph Nader's *Unsafe at*

Any Speed (concerning automobile safety) erupted and were heavily publicized by the news media.

These developments encouraged the rise of consumer groups, usually made up of upper middle-class, well-educated segments of the population.[3] Through boycotts, media exposure, and exposés of questionable business practices, pressure was brought to bear on lawmakers to define consumer rights through new legislation. A few landmarks of consumer-oriented politics in this decade include:[4]

1. The Kefauver-Harris Drug Amendments (1962), stating that all new drugs must be pretested, registered with the F.D.A. (Food and Drug Administration), and labeled generically.

2. The National Traffic and Motor Vehicle Safety Act (1966), to set safety standards for new and used automobiles.

3. The Cigarette Labeling Act (1966), requiring manufacturers to label each pack "Caution: Cigarette Smoking May Be Hazardous To Your Health."

4. The Truth-in-Lending Act (1968), demanding full disclosure of interest rates and finance charges on loans and credit purchases.

The business section reacted to the new consumerism with considerable nervousness. And typical industry responses to consumer demands during the 1960s ranged from an initial defensive posture to eventual, if sometimes grudging, cooperation.

Consumerism Today

To respond effectively to the demands of the rising movement, it became necessary to know who the consumerists are, what problems have been identified as the prime issues, and how people respond to the outcomes of consumer-oriented policy making. Research in consumer behavior offers some insights, although findings are still subject to questions and controversy.

Who Are the Consumerists?

According to Buskirk and Rothe, consumerists are groups of consumers ". . . seeking redress, restitution and remedy for dissatisfaction they have accumulated in the acquisition of their standard of living."[5] Such a definition accurately describes the consumers who are sufficiently concerned to organize into groups or join existing organizations like Consumers Union or Common Cause. This vanguard is composed of people who are relatively well educated and earn fairly high incomes.[6]

But there are other consumers who have not organized, yet hold views toward business and the marketing system that could be termed "consumerist." And research indicates that these individual consumerists exist in great numbers. In a study of consumers' attitudes toward marketing and consumerism, Barksdale and Darden found that respondents:[7]

1. Disagreed with the idea that manufacturers seldom shirk their responsibility to consumers (55 percent).

2. Agreed that manufacturers often withhold important product improvements from the

market to protect their own interests (37.9 percent).

3. Disagreed with the premise that advertisements usually present a true picture of the products advertised (50.8 percent).

4. Disagreed with the statement that the problems of consumers are less serious now than in the past (54 percent).

5. Agreed that, from the consumer's standpoint, manufacturers' procedures for handling complaints and settling grievances were not satisfactory (53.7 percent).

6. Agreed that the government should set minimum standards of quality for all products sold to consumers (48.6 percent).

The individuals who are most likely to express consumerist views toward marketing are younger and more liberal politically than the average. (But the notion that federal intervention is a remedy for consumer problems seems to be shared by liberals and conservatives alike.)[8] Other researchers conclude that the consumers who most often report deception or misrepresentation of products are high income women, who hold college degrees.[9] It appears that consumerism remains largely an upper middle-class phenomenon, attracting the better educated and better informed. For instance, a recent analysis of people who used a consumer "hot line" telephone number to complain about products and services revealed that 74 percent could be classified as middle-to-upper class in occupational level.[10]

Impact of Consumer Education   Yet this profile will broaden dramatically with the increased emphasis on consumer education in our schools, creating a population of consumers who are far better informed about business and marketing practices than their predecessors.

A typical consumer text for high school students today offers advice on such topics as buying a home, using credit, analyzing advertisements, dealing with salesmen, and relatively sophisticated strategies for getting optimal returns from their purchases.[11] Courses providing such instruction are becoming increasingly popular with educators and students alike, and will probably be standardized in most school systems in the near future. This development has widespread implication for marketers in the advertising we will see, the sales techniques employed by retailers, and the use of consumer credit.

The New Consumerist Coalition   Some consumer analysts point to four groups that will emerge as the new consumerist movement.[12] These include middle-class consumers, the black community and other minority groups, political conservatives, and college students.

Middle-class consumers have already formed the core of the new consumer movement through their concern about poorly manufactured or unsafe products and inefficient services. Blacks and other minority consumers have perhaps suffered the greatest frustrations in paying the highest prices for second-rate goods in ghetto retail outlets. If these consumers achieve a degree of organization—as welfare clients have in New York to demand better services—we might expect some articulate spokesmen and spokeswomen for these groups to emerge. Political conservatives, although the most unlikely consumerist agitators, are reported to be leaning toward more efficient federal controls over business practices. This may be due in part to the fact that many conservatives are found in lower income brackets and suffer the economic pressures of inflationary periods. Also, small retailers are beginning to identify more with their customers than their suppliers, in that they confront the same problems of questionable product quality, misleading advertising, and inadequate manufacturer service. Finally, college students, who were among the first to become involved in consumer activism, have carried the movement to a number of campuses. Some universities have set up their own student-staffed consumer protection agencies, and the first National Conference on Student Consumer Action took place in 1972 at Kansas State University.

It is likely that these four groups will exert the greatest consumerist pressure on business and government over the next decade.

Consumerist Issues

New consumer demands and volatile issues appear almost daily, but contemporary consumerist demands focus upon three main themes: *truth in marketing, product safety and quality,* and *redress of grievances.*

Truth in Marketing Under this heading fall such areas of dissatisfaction as deceptive advertising and fraudulent retail practices. The Federal Trade Commission has recently begun curtailing advertisements consumers believe to be deceptive, yet the advertising industry has always employed "creative license" in making product claims and continues to do so. There is a fine line between "puffery" (exaggerated claims) and actual deceit, and standards are set primarily by the public mood and what other advertisers are saying. Book club ads, for example, have long been a sore point with consumers and must now carry "full disclosure" copy advising

prospects that they will be sent books automatically each month once they join the club.

Mail order fraud is still common, with consumers "taken" to the tune of $500 million each year for worthless health remedies and inferior merchandise. On the retail front, questionable sales techniques such as "bait and switch" (advertising a bargain item that is "sold" just before the consumer enters the showroom) infuriate consumers but are common nonetheless. Retail credit contracts that bind consumers to usurious credit charges are still enforceable in some states, and door-to-door marketing of encyclopedias and other merchandise, though regulated to some degree, continues to employ high pressure sales tactics.

Also at issue here are the packaging and labeling policies of our largest manufacturers. Do the contents of a box of cookies really "settle in handling" so much that we can open a box to find it half full, or is the package deceptively large for the contents? And what does an expensive headache remedy contain that makes it so much better than aspirin? Can we tell by reading the label?

Product Quality and Safety Consumers are dissatisfied when the products and services they use fail to "work" well and when they do not feel they are getting what they paid for. The housewife who has spent $49.95 for a vacuum cleaner may understandably be annoyed when the machine proves to be ridiculously underpowered and picks up only surface dust. In this case, poor product design may be at fault. A few years ago, consumers were rather shocked to find that ready-to-eat breakfast cereals, long touted as energy-packed for growing youngsters, turned out to be of dubious nutritional value. Even the all-American hot dog has been exposed as a product sometimes manufac-

Getting the Product Facts Behind the Baloney

Consumer Union is a nonprofit testing organization that subjects products and services to vigorous tests and publishes the results in its monthly magazine, *Consumer Reports*.

In addition to offering comparative quality ratings of different brands in a product category—such as television sets, small cars, or over-the-counter drugs—*Consumer Reports* points out product deficiencies that are costly or potentially harmful to consumers.

For example, an article entitled "How Good is the Bologna in That Sandwich?" came to some startling conclusions about one of America's favorite lunchtime foods.[14]

First, bologna was compared with other sandwich foods like tuna fish, hamburger, and peanut butter for nutritional quality. The results showed that bologna was rated: (1) highest in cost per ounce of protein, (2) highest in fats and calories, (3) highest in a potentially harmful additive called sodium nitrite. Moreover, bologna was the most expensive, with the highest cost-per-sandwich of all.

Secondly, of the thirty-six brands and varieties bought in food stores and tested for overall quality, nine were either found to be rancid or showed beginning signs of rancidity (which could be detected by a sweet, perfume-like scent).

For these reasons, *Consumer Reports* concluded that bologna was not a very desirable staple for children's diets.

tured under a low level of quality control and often consisting of ingredients that provide little nutritional substance.

Although the United States has been described as moving from a product-oriented to service-based economy, consumers in urban areas have complained about the deteriorating quality of service personnel. They point to instances of surly waitresses, indifferent retail clerks, and the dilapidated state of public transportation in many cities, a service most often controlled by local government rather than business.

Anxiety has also been expressed over the safety of products including children's toys, drugs, automobiles, household appliances, and such seemingly harmless packaged goods as cosmetics. Unfortunately, products that present safety hazards are often not recalled until personal injuries and even deaths have occurred. One recent example was the finding that a woman's contraceptive device caused several deaths during pregnancy before the product was taken off the market. And in a recent poll, Louis Harris reports that:

Majorities of the public express real worry, in health terms, about their soft drinks and the food they eat, the safety of their automobiles (even though a majority still will not wear seat belts), the dangers of taking tranquilizers, sleeping pills, pep-up pills, and a plethora of other instant curatives.[13]

As long as such products continue to be part of the American way of life, marketers will bear the responsibility for ensuring their safety.

Consumer Reports thinks you should know:

How good is the bologna in that sandwich?

Redress of Grievances   Once a consumer has found a product or service unsatisfactory, what can he or she do about it? Barksdale found that a majority of the consumers he surveyed believe that their grievances will not be handled in a satisfactory way by manufacturers.[15] Many products carry warranties, but they usually compensate for product failure with an exchange or "money back" guarantee. Berens points out this may not be satisfactory when an adjustment means the consumer must spend considerable time and energy to get compensation. And replacement of a defective product offers little consolation when a refrigerator breaks down and its expensive food contents spoil or a faulty phonograph needle ruins a record.[16]

Where deception or fraud is involved, the only recourse may be litigation. Yet few consumers have the time or money to become even lightly entangled with a company that maintains its own lawyers. Often deception affects low-income consumers, who are least informed about proper remedial procedures and are not articulate in presenting their case.

Shoddy marketing practices are hardly confined to ghetto neighborhoods; even higher income consumers find difficulty in gaining redress through warranties or litigation. When a large corporation is caught fixing prices or engaging in deceptive promotions, it is merely told by a government regulatory agency to "cease and desist," without making restitution to consumers who have already been exploited.

Behavioral Research and Consumerism

Increasingly, research in consumer behavior has been directed toward uncovering causes of consumer dissatisfaction. Two concepts that have evolved to place consumers' attitudes in a research perspective are *consumer expectancy* and *alienation from the market place*.

Consumer Expectancy   Because consumers are younger, better educated, and more sophisticated today, their expectations about the products and services they buy are higher than ever before. Also, American consumers have become accustomed to an unprecedented level of technology and expect a high level of product performance, quality, and safety. "If we can put a man on the moon," one asks, "why can't they build an electric can opener that works?" Anderson and Jolson view consumer expectations as a major source of irritation when products and services fail to live up to them.[17]

An *expectancy* is a hypothesis formed by a consumer prior to purchase. And a comparison of reality following the purchase with a marketing communication that triggered the purchase will either confirm or reject the hypothesis. Say that a consumer is aroused by an advertisement for a product—an "instant" car wax that promises a perfect shine without any work. "Just spray it on and dry it off," the TV commercial claims, displaying a car that almost blinds the eye with its jewel-like gleam. So the consumer buys the wax and uses it. Unfortunately, the product leaves the car with a dull, streaked appearance rather than a bright shine. An initial hypothesis that the product would "work" is rejected and dissatisfaction results.

Although this is an extreme example, many marketing communications raise consumer expectations beyond a realistic level. Thus a *communications gap* is created. One reason for the gap appears to be that the typical promotional mix is designed as a one-way communication from the marketer to the target markets, with no reverse flow from consumer to marketer. Another is the tendency of advertisers to exaggerate product attributes or benefits to the consumer.

Anderson researched the effects of expectation on consumers' perception of product performance and found that there is a point beyond which they will not accept the difference between product claims and true performance. Upon reaching this point, consumers will perceive the product less favorably than they would have if their expectations had been slightly lower.[18]

Thus marketers might avoid such a communications gap and resulting consumer dissatisfaction by keeping product claims realistic and conducting ongoing surveys of consumer expectations and perceived product performance.[19]

Alienation from the Market Place   Low-income and minority consumers have been described as the group most in need of consumer protection, for they are often the most dissatisfied with the products and services they buy but the least influential in bringing about change. Pruden et al view the condition of minority consumers as one of *alienation* from the market place.[20] Comparing blacks and Mexican Americans with Anglo-Americans, they found that the minority groups experienced sufficiently greater alienation through powerlessness, social isolation, and other handicaps than whites. Minority consumers were also more inclined to favor government intervention in the market place.

From these findings, Pruden et al have devised a measurement technique for alienation from the market place utilizing the concepts outlined in Table 20-1. A brief survey of their test items suggests that alienation may not be limited to low-income consumers.

Consumer Responses to Protective Legislation

Many observers maintain that *voluntary* consumerist action on the part of business often fails through lack of enforcement. Thus *government intervention* in the marketing arena has increased steadily over recent years. To determine how protective legislation has affected consumer attitudes and behavior, Kerin and Harvey have examined consumer responses to three major pieces of legislation: *unit pricing, product labeling,* and *disclosure of interest rate provisions for consumer credit.*[21]

Unit Pricing   This retailing legislation gives consumers two prices for every product item, the price per package and the price per unit measure. With this additional information, consumers should be able to make value comparisons among products and between package sizes.

Awareness   A majority of consumers are found to be familiar with unit pricing after its introduction, although awareness increases with the amount of promotional announcements. Generally, awareness is highest among better educated, middle-income, white, and younger shoppers.

Consumer Usage   All people who are aware of unit pricing do not use it in item selection. About half of those who know about unit pricing actually take advantage of it. Demographically, users tend to fit the profile of affluent, young, white shoppers.

Influence on Purchase Behavior   As expected, unit pricing tends to result in more economical shopping behavior for those consumers who use it. Field studies reported brand, package size and store switching among shoppers after unit pricing.

Table 20-1   Alienation from the Market Place

ALIENATION CONCEPTS	MARKET PLACE ITEMS USED TO MEASURE EACH OF THE CONCEPTS OF ALIENATION
Powerlessness	There is little use in writing complaint letters to company officials because usually they won't do anything to satisfy an individual consumer.
Meaninglessness	There is little that people like myself can do to improve the quality of the products they sell. Any satisfaction I get from trying new products vanishes a short time after they are purchased.
Normlessness	Sometimes, when I look at new products, I wonder if any of them are really worthwhile. Many people with fine homes, new cars and other nice things get them only by going over their heads in debt.
Social Isolation	I sometimes buy products that I really shouldn't buy. The whole idea of fashion and the creation of new styles is not for me.
Self-Estrangement	I really like to own things that have well-known brand names. The products and services I buy and use (for example eating, dressing, entertaining, furnishing my house and so on) allow me to really be myself. The way the world is, I have to buy things that other people expect me to rather than to satisfy myself.

Source: Henry O. Pruden, F. Kelly Shuptrine, and Douglas S. Longman, "A Measure of Alienation from the Marketplace," Journal of The Academy of Marketing Science, *Volume 2, No. 4, (Fall 1974), p 612. Reprinted by permission of the Academy of Marketing Science. Copyright © 1974.*

Consumer Evaluation Shoppers who use unit pricing are favorable to the concept, and no studies have turned up strong negative reactions to it. Both awareness and usage are fairly high and some behavioral changes in shopping have occurred.

Product Labeling Labeling to indicate the nutrient value of a product's ingredients, a date before which the product should be used (open dating), and appropriate warning have all been mandated by federal law. Con-sumer response to open dating appears to be minimal: after extensive promotion of the policy by a food chain, only 20 percent of the consumers interviewed in stores could under-stand the program. Consumers also appear to be generally unaware and apathetic about product caution labels, those who are most sensitive to information on harmful ingre-dients being wealthier and better educated. It is *nutritional* labeling that seems to have evoked the most response from shoppers. *Awareness*   In supermarket tests conducted

by food chains, about 26 percent of the consumers were aware of nutritional labeling and 16 percent understood the labels. Awareness increases with promotion and is, again, positively related to income and education.
Usage Among the customers who understand the nutritional labeling program, 59 percent used the labels in purchasing. Both comprehension and use of nutritional information have been shown to increase with the length of the program.
Nonuse Benefits Many consumers who do not actually use labeling information agree with statements about nonuse benefits such as: (1) Nutritional information for food products will increase consumer confidence in the food industry. (2) More information indicates a greater concern for consumer welfare. (3) Nutritional labels encourage advertising that will promote consumer education. (4) Consumers have the right to know the nutritional value of food products on the market.
Influence on Purchase Behavior FDA studies indicate that consumers are more likely to select packages with nutritional labeling over nonlabeled items. They also concluded that brands with *detailed* nutritional labels are most favored by consumers, and that a label format expressing nutritional values as a percentage of the FDA Recommended Daily Allowance was also preferred.

Disclosure of Interest Rate Provisions The 1968 Truth-in-Lending Act was enacted to give consumers *credit term* information so they might "shop" for the best interest rate. Among other provisions, the law requires that lenders inform consumers of the true annual rate of interest (such as the fact that "1½% percent per month" really means 18 percent per year).
Awareness and Knowledge of Interest Rates Studies report increases in both awareness

of disclosure and knowledge of interest rates after the law was passed. And this was evident across all income groups, although consumers in the higher brackets were best informed. But consumer credit knowledge is still inadequate: almost half the borrowers surveyed in one study either over- or underestimated their interest payments by 50 percent or more. Other research concludes that:

1. Consumers have only a gross awareness of the ranking of different types of lenders according to cost (such as banks versus commercial finance companies).

2. A large proportion of consumers are unaware of current interest rates being charged for home mortgages, automobiles, and department store revolving credit.

3. Consumers tend to be more concerned with the size of the monthly payment than with the interest rate.

Credit Search Behavior Some observers report a significant increase in search behavior after the Truth-in-Lending Act, but more than 75 percent of the consumers contacted still seek credit from only one financing institution. Thus "shopping" behavior remains quite limited. Not surprisingly, interest rate knowledge and search behavior are positively related to education and income. Awareness also increases with the size of the loan in question.

Research into consumer reactions to protective legislation seems to convey two themes:

• Consumers who use the legislation to their purchasing advantage are likely to be white, middle income, and better educated. This tends to support the premise that consumerism is still the province of the upper middle class.

• The consumers who need protective legislation most—lower income and minority consumers—do not appear to be taking advantage of the policies supposedly legislated on their behalf. This development lends credence to Pruden's theory of alienation from the market place found in minority consumers.

Some Prescriptions for Marketers

Consumer activism and legislation have exerted much influence over how marketers can conduct their business in the United States (and increasingly, in other countries as well).[22] In the future, we might reasonably expect more government intervention if voluntary action on the part of business does not appear adequate. What can marketers do on their own? Three items seem to loom above all others.

Reality in Advertising   Of all consumerist complaints about truth in marketing, advertising by far bears the greatest burden of criticism. One advertising agency's own findings point out that roughly 60 percent of Americans believe that critics of advertising are correct and that less than half of the ads they see are informative and honest.[23] Anderson's finding that exaggerated claims in product advertising may increase dissatisfaction with that product underscores the problem. In the era of the consumer, it seems far more productive to base creative strategies on truth and information (perhaps with a touch of humor) than to antagonize consumers further with claims that are perceived as unreal and untrustworthy.

Product Quality Control   Underlying the problem of deceptive advertising in many cases is the problem of little to say in favor of the product. In fact, the most brilliant advertising strategies will tend to kill off low-quality products faster than poor strategies because they will get people to try the merchandise. Thus, the challenge confronting the new generation of marketers is constantly to upgrade the products for which they are responsible.

Two-Way Communication   Consumerists feel they have a right to satisfactory handling of their grievances when products do not live up to their expectations. Where marketers have not responded to this problem, there is usually agitation for laws that would make it easier for consumers to go to court. For example, small claims courts now exist solely for the protection of individual consumers: corporations are now allowed to bring suits under small claims jurisdictions. Some companies have tackled this problem by establishing special channels of communication between themselves and their customers. The "We Listen Better" program, which was heavily promoted by Ford Motor Company, offers an excellent example in an industry that has not always been noted for its responsiveness.

Companies should, in fact, *solicit* complaints from their customers as well as following through effectively on their warranty policies. According to Kendall and Russ, complaints and warranties offer opportunities that can greatly aid marketers:[24]

1. A well-handled complaint has promotional value.

2. A complaint provides useful feedbakc.

3. A good warranty can improve customer attitudes toward a product (that is, it can have promotional value); it can encourage dissatisfied customers to complain; and it can influence the format and content of a complaint letter so that the complaint results in optimal benefits for the consumer and the company.

But along with the responsibilities okf marketers, there is evidence that consumers could accept more responsibility as well. Wood sums up the relationship quite neatly:[25]

Business, to survive, must merit the confidence of its customers. If the consumer activists have done nothing else, they have aroused businessmen and -women all over the country to a greater awareness of their responsibility to eliminate shady practices . . .

But consumers, too, share the responsibility for ethical standards in the market place. Some "perfectly honest" people seem to think it's all right to cheat business. Defraud the telephone company, for instance, by placing long distance calls for fictitious names which, by prearrangement, convey their message. . . . The losses from these petty crimes are necessarily part of the cost of doing business and they add to the price we must all pay for the goods and services we buy.

The Socially Conscious Consumer

To this point we have focused on the consumerist who is principally interested in getting his or her money's worth. But there is another thrust in consumer activism centering around the question of social responsibility. A number of consumers identify themselves with goals such as reducing inequities among rich and poor, cleaning up the environment, asserting the rights of minority groups, and generally effecting progressive social change.

A Question of Segmentation

The emergence of such issues on the consumerist front raises an intriguing question: who are the "socially conscious" consumers and how can they best be reached through conventional segmentation techniques? A number of researchers are addressing themselves to the challenge first identified by Kelly:[26]

With growing consumer sensitivity to social and environmental problems, market segmentation based on consumers' societal orientation is emerging; markets will be evaluated according to the degree to which consumers accept the consumer-citizen concept and buy as individuals concerned not only with their personal satisfactions, but also with societal well-being.

One pioneer study by Anderson and Cunningham concludes that "socially conscious" consumers may be segmented on the basis of demographic and sociopsychological characteristics.[27] These consumers are more likely to belong to higher socioeconomic groups, are inclined to be younger, and score differently than "low social consciousness" consumers on a number of social and psychological items. These findings are summarized in Table 20-2. Other research suggests that the "socially conscious" consumer may best be described as a member of an upper middle-class counterculture—less favorably disposed toward business, more inclined to adopt purchase patterns that reflect his or her own sense of responsibility rather than popularly accepted patterns.[28]

Table 20-2   Relationship Between Selected Variables and Social Consciousness

VARIABLE	HIGH SOCIAL CONSCIOUSNESS	LOW SOCIAL CONSCIOUSNESS
Occupation of the household head	Higher status occupations	Lower status occupations
Annual family income	N.S.*	N.S.*
Education of the household head	N.S.*	N.S.*
Socioeconomic status	Above average socioeconomic status	Average and lower socioeconomic status
Age of the household head	Pre-middle age	Middle age and older
Stage in the family life cycle	N.S.*	N.S.*
Alienation	Less alienated	More alienated
Dogmatism	Less dogmatic	More dogmatic
Conservatism	Less conservative	More conservative
Status Consciousness	Less status conscious	More status conscious
Personal Competence	Less personally competent	More personaly competent
Cosmopolitanism	More cosmopolitan	Less cosmopolitan

*Not significant.

Source: *W. Thomas Anderson, Jr. and William H. Cunningham, "The Socially Conscious Consumer,"* Journal of Marketing, *Vol. 36, No. 3 (July 1972), p. 29. Reprinted by permission of the American Marketing Association.*

The Ecologically Concerned Consumer

Many of the studies directed toward consumer social responsibility deal with questions of the environment—pollution, convenience packaging that winds up as litter, and similar issues.

Ecologically concerned consumers have been better identified through personality variables than socioeconomic characteristics. While there is a slight tendency for these consumers to fall into higher income categories, they are much more predisposed than others to be open to new ideas, interested in satisfying their intellectual curiosity, and

seem relatively high in needs to be assured of personal safety. They are also convinced that individuals can do something about controlling pollution, in contrast to low-concern consumers. Thus, this segment might be reached through advertising appeals that emphasize evidence on the effectiveness of a product in reducing pollution, stressing how one can express social concern through using the product and underscoring the impact that consumers can exert in abating pollution.[29]

Ecological concern has also been shown to affect brand perception of laundry products, with the implication that detergent markets could be segmented on this basis. Buyers who indicate different levels of ecological concern hold different "cognitive maps" for laundry products. The higher a consumer's environmental concern, the more salient his or her ecological consideration becomes in perceiving brands; and also significantly greater is this consumer's perceived similarity of brands that are ecologically nondestructive.[30]

A Case Study: Consumer Ecological Concern and Adaptive Behavior

C. P. Rao notes that there may be considerable divergence between public concern about a social problem and people's willingness to change their behavior as consumers. Where social problems such as ecology are involved, individual adaptive behavior usually means making financial commitments as well as sacrificing convenience. Rao has investigated the relationship between how consumers feel about ecology and how their adaptive consumption behavior (if any) reflects those feelings. His study is summarized in Table 20-3 as an example of research based upon consumerist and social responsibility concepts.[31]

Method Respondents were first divided into two groups on the basis of their level of ecological concern (determined by a preliminary test question about the seriousness of environmental and other social problems).

Table 20-3   Consumer Purchase Intentions of Nonpolluting Products Under Different Conditions of Adaptive Behavior

IF THE NONPOLLUTING		NONPOLLUTING PRODUCT PURCHASE INTENTIONS			
		INTEND TO BUY %	UNCERTAIN	WOULD NOT BUY %	SIGNIFICANCE LEVEL
1. Using poorer quality products than what you are used to	High	17	70.5	12.5	NS
	Low	16.7	61.8	21.5	
2. 10 to 20% extra usage costs (*eg.* automobiles)	High	43.2	48.9	7.9	
	Low	22.6	67.6	9.8	.02
3. Considerably more time in preparing the product for use (*eg.* food items)	High	64.8	30.7	4.5	.15
	Low	50	45.1	4.9	
4. The use of certain products which your friends and neighbors are not presently using	High	73.9	22.7	3.4	
	Low				.20
		60.8	34.3	4.9	
5. The use of containers which need to be taken to the store for refilling from time to time	High	84.1	13.6	2.3	
	Low	68.6	25.5	5.9	.05
6. Giving up the brand of products which you using for a long time and with which you are very satisfied	High	53.4	43.2	3.4	
	Low	26.5	61.8	11.7	NS
7. Visiting several stores because the nonpolluting products are not available in the store in which you usually buy	High	54.5	39.8	5.7	
	Low	35.3	55.9	8.8	.10

High: High Concern Groups (N=88)   Low: Low Concern groups (N=102)   NS: Not significant

Source: C. P. Rao, "Consumer Ecological concern and Adaptive Behavior," Journal of the Academy of Marketing Science, Vol. 2, No. 1 (Winter, 1974), pp. 262–276. Reprinted with permission of the Academy of Marketing Science, Copyright © 1974.

These groups were termed "high concern" and "low concern." Their responses to other questions were then analyzed to determine their attitudes toward pollution control, their purchase intentions about nonpolluting products, and their willingness to make sacrifices to buy such products.

Results

Consumer Attitudes   A large percentage of respondents in both groups do not consider the dangers of pollution exaggerated nor do they think that ecological concern is just a fad. As expected, more high-concern than low-concern respondents disagreed with the notion that industry would clean up pollution if left to its own devices.

Responses to Advertising   In awareness of messages in the media sponsored by corporations as public relations efforts, recollection is actually higher among the low-concern group. But when believability of the messages is the question, the high-concern group is significantly more skeptical.

Purchase Intentions   As had been hypothesized, a higher percentage of the high-concern group expressed their intentions to buy pollution-free products. However, specific kinds of adaptive behavior—using poorer quality products, for example—were not significantly different between the two groups.

Sacrifice of Money and Convenience   Willingness to pay both higher costs in general and to pay extra for a nonpolluting automotive unit were more noticeable in the high-concern group. Thus there appears to be a relationship between concern about ecology and readiness to make monetary sacrifices.

Nonpolluting Purchase Recall   Although the availability and use of nonpolluting products are not very widespread, the high-concern group recalled significantly more purchases in this category than the low-concern group.

Conclusions   Three general implications appear in these findings:

1. Because a large proportion of people in both groups responded that pollution hazards were not exaggerated and interest in the ecology was not a fad, *concern about pollution seems to be enduring and widespread.*

2. More than three-quarters of the respondents in both groups expressed *skepticism about corporate antipollution ads,* suggesting that advertisers might be better off spending their money to promote antipollution products and educating consumers to buy those products.

3. Generally, consumers were more likely to change their behavior where psychological adjustment rather than economic variables or product quality was involved. Many consumers are *uncertain about buying nonpolluting products if they feel quality is sacrificed.*

From these results it appears that the relationship between public concern and private adaptive behavior is by no means firmly established. There are only indications that consumers may be more willing to modify their behavior in some areas than in others.

Ecological Concern and Convenience Packaging

Consumers are increasingly forced to decide between ecology and market choice, and one prominent example is the controversy over convenience packaging. Nonreturnable bottles and cans have achieved great popularity with consumers for their convenience aspect: you simply use one up and throw it away. Unfortunately, many people throw them on highways, streets, and sidewalks, where they become part of the "solid waste" or litter problem. Environmentalists have cited bottles and cans as particularly objectionable because (1) they are highly visible and (2) they are relatively permanent, in that they do not self-destruct as easily as other forms of litter. Thus, a number of states and localities have attempted to ban one-way bottles and cans or tax them out of existence.[32]

This brings up the troublesome question of where marketers' ecological responsibilities end and consumers' begin. Consumers, after all, are the ones who ultimately dispose of packaging once they have used the contents. Is it more realistic to place the burden of correction on manufacturers, under the assumption that people will always litter? Should they be denied access to items they may dispose of improperly? Or is it perhaps better to educate consumers *not* to litter so they may continue to enjoy the convenience of nonreturnable packages? In this area, bottlers and can manufacturers have taken affirmative action by demonstrating that localities can be cleaned up without resorting to restrictive legislation. Their application of behavioral research principles to reducing littering by consumers might serve as an example to other marketers facing similar government intervention.[33]

Redefining the Marketing Concept

The developments outlined in this chapter have convinced many marketers that the *traditional* marketing concept must now be extended to what Kotler calls the *societal* marketing concept:[34]

The dilemma for the marketer . . . is that he cannot go on giving the consumer only what pleases him without considering the effect on the consumer's and society's well-being. On the other hand, he cannot produce salutary products which the consumer will not buy. . . . The societal marketing concept calls for a *customer orientation* backed by *integrated marketing* aimed at generating *customer satisfaction* and long-run *consumer welfare* as the key to attaining long-run profitable volume.

Toward Responsible Consumption

America may have, sadly enough, reached a point at which our environment can no longer sustain our accustomed affluence. This possibility was brought home to many consumers during the environmental shortages of the mid-1970s. For the first time since World War II, people actually spent hours waiting in line at gasoline stations. Hand in hand with our shrinking environment is the enormity of the world's growing crowdedness. By the year 2000, there are indications that the world's current population of 3.5 billion will have swollen to 7 billion.

Fisk points out that rising per capita consumption in advanced nations poses a greater threat to the biological environment than the increasing numbers of people in developing nations. For example, one U.S. consumer wields fifty times the ecological impact of one person in India. What this will probably mean is a movement toward "responsible consumption"—to rational and efficient use of resources with respect to the global population.[35] Margaret Mead views the concept in these terms:[36]

. . . responsibility will include planning for life styles . . . which will contribute to the sense of justice and dignity for all the people of the earth. . . . If the number of cars per capita in an industrialized country is compared with the number of cars in an under-industrialized country, the screaming discrepancy between the rich and the poor countries becomes unbearable. . . . Worldwide television, mass-picture media, and mass travel mean that people all over the world are exposed to the standard of living within the countries and homes of the affluent.

"Demarketing"

The effects of all this upon U.S. marketing has been described by Kotler and Levy as *demarketing* to cope with social issues and shrinking resources.[37] Marketers would turn their attention to *discouraging* people from using certain products and services, such as electricity and other scarce resources. Fisk envisions such developments as the imposition of a luxury goods consumption tax, the use of advertising campaigns to promote frugality, and the organization of postconsumption brigades to collect and recycle trash. He further views responsible consumption in the framework of a "closed" economic system in which the costs and benefits of all consumption activities are carefully weighed by marketers.

While the concept of demarketing is not an appealing one to most marketers, it may be an inevitability where shortages have and will continue to occur.

Buying as Marketing

Kotler and Levy argue that the study of consumer behavior should assist consumers

in *buyer optimization* as well as help sellers in getting consumers to buy. This becomes particularly critical when consumers must deal with *reluctant sellers,* marketers who are confronted with shortages of their product or prefer to sell to a select clientele. Three *buying strategies* are possible in such cases:[38]

1. Inducement—attempting to produce compliance through offering the seller something of value.

2. Persuasion—attempting to influence the seller through identifying his or her natural interests with the transaction.

3. Education—attempting to produce a favorable response by changing the seller's beliefs or values.

This concept is relatively new to marketing, but promises to become established as consumer behavior research grows more consumerist oriented.

Social Marketing

In some instances, the marketing concept has already been broadened to include the marketing of people (political candidates), organizations (fund raising), places, and ideas, as well as products. The marketing of ideas generally refers to promotion of social causes like antismoking and safe-driving messages.

One increasingly popular use of marketing techniques is in the area of family planning. The Louisiana Family Planning Program offers a model example of this approach, as described by El-Ansary and Kramer:[39]

1. The program adopted a *consumer-oriented* philosophy in delivering its services by determining a market target and using segmentation, taking the service directly to the consumer, and emphasizing the idea of "fam-

ily planning" rather than simply a free birth control program.

2. A *marketing mix* was developed, including a product promotion concept offering benefits to the consumers, mass media advertising and personal selling, and continuous market research for information.

3. *Analytical marketing tools* such as break-even and cost-benefit analyses were employed.

Thus social products may be marketed using essentially the same consumer behavioral research techniques as commercial products. This application will probably grow impressively with funding from government agencies and private sources.

The nature of marketing is changing dramatically,[40] due primarily to the issues discussed in this chapter. But no matter how the marketing concept is broadened or our priorities shuffled, there will always be a need for consumer behavioral research. And, because the near future seems to dictate changes in values and life styles, these will probably be the two areas that will receive the most attention.

Summary

Two issues are becoming increasingly important to all marketers—*consumerism* and *social responsibility.*

Consumerism refers to the activism of consumers in seeking redress, restitution, and remedy for dissatisfaction in acquiring the means to maintain their standard of living. In addition to organized groups of consumerists, many individuals appear to hold views about business that could be described as consumerist. Generally, their demands fall into three areas: *truth in marketing, product quality and safety,* and *redress of grievances.* To view consumerism in perspective, consumer behavioral research has developed concepts such as *consumer expectancy* and *alienation from the market place.* Studies have also drawn some conclusions about consumer responses to protective legislation. In addition to the United States, other nations are developing organized consumer movements, suggesting an *international consumerism* paralleling multinational marketing.

In recent years, a new *socially conscious consumer* seems to have emerged. Such a consumer identifies with social problems and may be segmented through traditional market techniques. Most of the research investigating social responsibility of consumers has focused on the environment, and a recurrent problem of ecology versus market choice is said to exist.

Due to the emergence of consumerism and social consciousness, there is pressure to extend our *traditional* marketing concept to a societal marketing concept. This would include such considerations as *responsible consumption, buyer strategies,* and *social marketing.*

NOTES

1. See Norman Kangun et al., "Consumerism and Marketing Management," *Journal of Marketing*, Vol. 39, No. 2 (April 1975); and William H. Cunningham and Isabella C. M. Cunningham, "Consumer Protection: More Information or More Regulation?", *Journal of Marketing*, Vol. 40, No. 2 (April 1976).

2. Arch W. Troelstrup, *The Consumer in American Society* (New York: McGraw-Hill, 1974).

3. Robert O. Hermann, "Consumerism: Its Goals, Organization and Future," *Journal of Marketing*, Vol. 34 (October 1970).

4. Consumerism: *A New and Growing Force in the Marketplace* (Chicago: Burson-Marsteller Public Relations, 1970), pp. 34–36.

5. Richard H. Buskirk and James T. Rothe, "Consumerism—An Interpretation," *Journal of Marketing*, Vol. 34 (October 1970), pp. 61–65.

6. Hermann, "Consumerism."

7. Hiram C. Barksdale and William R. Darden, "Consumer Attitudes Toward Marketing and Consumerism," *Journal of Marketing*, Vol. 36 (October 1972), pp. 28–35.

8. Barksdale and Darden, "Consumer Attitudes."

9. Virginia Knauer, Special Assistant for Consumer Affairs to the President of the United States, in an address to the National Appliance and Radio-TV Dealers Association, Chicago, April 21, 1971, p. 3.

10. Steven L. Diamond, Scott Ward, and Ronald Faber, "Consumer Problems and Consumerism: Analysis of Calls to a Consumer Hot Line," *Journal of Marketing*, Vol. 40, No. 1 (January 1976).

11. Herbert M. Jelley and Robert O. Hermann, *The American Consumer: Issues and Decisions*, rev. ed. (New York: McGraw-Hill, 1973).

12. Troelstrup, *Consumer in American Society.*

13. Louis Harris as cited in Holly MacNamee, "The Socially Conscious Consumer," *Conference Board Record*, May 1970, p. 12.

14. "How Good Is the Bologna in That Sandwich?", *Consumer Reports*, April 1976.

15. Barksdale and Darden, "Consumer Attitudes."

16. John S. Berens, "Consumer Costs in Product Failure," *MSU Business Topics*, Vol. 19 (Spring 1971), p. 28.

17. R. E. Anderson and Marvin A. Jolson, "Consumer Expectations and the Communications Gap," *Business Horizons*, Vol. 16 (April 1973), pp. 11–16.

18. R. E. Anderson, "Consumer Dissatisfaction: The Effect of Disconfirmed Expectancy on Perceived Product Performance," (Ph.D. dissertation, University of Florida, 1971).

19. John E. Swan and Linda Jones Combs, "Product Performance and Consumer Satisfaction: A New Concept," *Journal of Marketing*, Vol. 40, No. 2 (April 1976), p. 25.

20. Henry O. Pruden, F. Kelley Shuptrine, and Douglas S. Longman, "A Measure of Alienation from the Marketplace," *Journal of the Academy of Marketing Science*, Vol. 2, No. 6 (Fall 1974).

21. Roger Kerin and Michael Harvey, "Consumer Legislation: A Proactive or Reactive Response to Consumerism?", *Journal of the Academy of Marketing Science*, Vol. 2, No. 4 (Fall 1974).

22. See Hans B. Thorelli and Sarah V. Thorelli, *Consumer Information Handbook: Europe and North America* (New York: Praeger, 1974).

23. "The Public Is Wary of Ads, Too," *Business Week*, January 29, 1972, p. 69.

24. C. L. Kendall and Frederick A. Russ, "Warranty and Complaint Policies: An Opportunity for Marketing Management," *Journal of Marketing*, Vol. 39, No. 2 (April 1975), p. 36.

25. Mercedes S. Wood, "Business and the Consumer," *The Journal of Business*, Vol. 10 (December 1971), p. 23.

26. Eugene J. Kelley, "Marketing's Changing Social/Environmental Role," *Journal of Marketing*, Vol. 35 (July 1971), p. 1.

27. W. Thomas Anderson, Jr. and William H. Cunningham, "The Socially Conscious Consumer," *Journal of Marketing*, Vol. 36 (July 1972), pp. 23–29.

28. F. E. Webster, Jr., "Determining the Characteristics of the Socially-Conscious Consumer," *Journal of Consumer Research*, Vol. 2, No. 3 (December 1975).

29. Thomas C. Kinnear, James R. Taylor, and Sadrudin A. Ahmed, "Ecologically Concerned Consumers: Who Are They?", *Journal of Marketing*, Vol. 38 (April 1974), pp. 20–24.

30. Thomas C. Kinnear, James R. Taylor, "The Effect of Ecological Concern on Brand Perceptions," *Journal of Marketing Research*, Vol. 10 (May 1973), pp. 191–197.

31. C. P. Rao, "Consumer Ecological Concern and Adaptive Behavior," *Journal of the Academy of Marketing Science*, Vol. 2, No. 1 (Winter 1974), pp. 262–276.

32. Christopher Gilson, "Convenience Package Banning: Economic and Environmental Implications," *Journal of the Academy of Marketing Science*, Vol. 1, No. 1 (Spring 1973).

33. *The Clean Community System* (New York: Keep America Beautiful, Inc., 1977).

34. Philip Kotler, "What Consumerism Means for Marketers," *Harvard Business Review*, Vol. 50 (May–June 1972), p. 54.

35. George Fisk, "Criteria for a Theory of Responsible Consumption," *Journal of Marketing*, Vol. 37 (April 1973), pp. 24–31.

36. Margaret Mead, "Responsible Simplification of Consumption Patterns," *Ekistics*, Vol. 30 (October 1970), pp. 324–326, as cited in Fisk, "Responsible Consumption, p. 25.

37. Philip Kotler and Sidney Levy, "Demarketing, Yes, Demarketing," *Harvard Business Review*, Vol. 49 (November–December 1971), pp. 74–80.

38. Philip Kotler and Sidney Levy, "Buying Is Marketing, Too," *Journal of Marketing*, Vol. 37 (January 1973), pp. 54–59.

39. Adel I. El-Ansary and Oscar E. Kramer, Jr., "Social Marketing: The Family Planning Experience," *Journal of Marketing*, Vol. 37 (July 1973), pp. 1–7.

40. See F. Kelly Shuptrine and Frank A. Osmanski, "Marketing's Changing Role: Expanding or Contracting?", *Journal of Marketing*, Vol. 39, No. 2 (April 1975), p. 58.

MARKETING APPLICATIONS

Conclusion 1 *Where marketers will not, or for some reason cannot, respond positively to consumer grievances, government regulatory agencies may intervene on the disgruntled consumer's behalf.*

Application Assume that, as a consumer, you are "bumped" from an airline flight, even though you hold a perfectly valid reservation, because of an airline's policy of overbooking certain flights to avoid empty seats due to last-minute cancellations. This causes you to miss an important business meeting which may have resulted in a fat contract from a new customer, not to mention your own embarrassment and feeling of lost goodwill. You believe that the airline owes you something over and above a ticket on the next flight, but you receive no satisfaction from management. Now you may appeal (or threaten to appeal) to the complaint division of the Civil Aeronautics Board, which wields regulatory power over the airline. In the past, such action by aware consumers has resulted in personal visits from contrite airline executives, offers of cash settlements, and other substantive attempts on the part of the airlines in question to make amends.

Conclusion 2 *In marketing products designed to avoid harm to our environment, there are often "trade-offs" between what is ecologically desirable and what consumers want for convenience, economy, or other factors. For instance, people don't like smog, but neither do they like auto emission controls which cut fuel economy.*

Application It is apparent that market segmentation can isolate a socially conscious consumer who is more ecologically concerned than most of the market for a given product. Thus, it may be more feasible to introduce products with environmental-protection features to this segment first. Opinion leaders among these consumers are likely to communicate with others and persuade widening groups of people to try the product as well.

Conclusion 3 *A knowledge of consumer behavior is as important to social marketing as it is to the marketing of private goods and services.*

Application The phenomenon of cause marketing—directed to obtaining public support for a controversial group or issue—has attracted some of the brightest talents in the communications field. Usually, cause marketing focuses on organizations which are not "safe" enough for controversial advertising and public relations agencies to handle. Examples are pro- or anti-abortion groups, unusual political organizations, moves to legalize prostitution, and so forth. Consulting marketers study the consumers who are likely to support a cause, then develop ads and obtain the free magazine space and broadcast time to run them. Generally, the "product" is the idea or group, and the objective is to obtain new members or raise money to further some ongoing activity designed to solve a social problem. At present, at least one cause marketing agency exists to perform marketing services for those specialty clients.

542

ASSIGNMENTS

Research Assignment

Background   As a member of the City Council in the town where you live, you face the problem of reducing a steadily growing harvest of litter in your community. Some members of the Council argue forcefully that nonreturnable bottles and cans should be outlawed, since they seem the most visible on streets and sidewalks and will not decompose over time like paper products. But other members lean toward a different view—that littering represents a more basic problem of consumer behavior and that attempting to run a popular form of packaging "out of town" will not solve the problem effectively. You are undecided on this issue as the voting date nears and want more objective information than the local news media (who are probanning) and the local soft-drink distributor (who doesn't want the ban) have offered so far. But while exhausting a catalog of reasons for not wanting his packages outlawed, the distributor has referred to a new program called Clean Community System (CCS) sponsored by the beverage and packaging industries. CCS moves specialists into individual communities with a system for reducing litter up to 90 percent, and keeping the communities clean through local participation, before legislators have to resort to package banning. This idea appeals to you as a sane, positive approach. But you still wonder how adopting a CCS program would affect your voters—both as citizens and consumers, so you attempt to find out.

Methodology   Take the following steps:
   1. Contact Keep America Beautiful, Inc., 99 Park Avenue, New York, N.Y. 10016, for information on establishing a CCS project and a projection of what can be accomplished. Summarize the argument for adopting the CCS approach in fifty words or less.
   2. Contact the Governor's Office, Salem, Oregon 97310 for information on the argument for banning nonreturnable bottles and cans. Summarize this argument in fifty words or less.
   3. Devise a questionnaire of two items: (1) Do you think litter is a problem in this town (city)? a. Yes b. No c. Don't know; and (2) There are two ways that have been proposed to deal with the litter problem. Which do you agree with *more*? Enter both summaries, 1 and 2, under this item.
   4. Administer the questionnaire to a minimum of twenty-five respondents at a shopping center or other heavily trafficked area. Use the following directions:

We'd like to know how you feel about litter in this town. Would you take one minute to read the two questions on this sheet and put a check mark next to the answers you agree with *most.*

Extrapolation   Make a recommendation based on your views toward banning as against

CCS and public attitudes as indicated by your sample. If you would recommend a CCS project, what other community or urban problems could be managed through this system's approach?

Creative Assignment

The Royson Corporation, a large and profitable manufacturer of industrial and consumer goods, has a long-standing reputation for socially responsive management. The current president is interested in giving consumers greater access to business, particularly low-income consumers who have had the least success in that area. As a member of a consulting firm specializing in public communications, you have been hired to develop a program directed to reaching disadvantaged consumers and offering assistance in dealing with their consumer problems—whether with Royson products or other items in the market place. In facing this task, you have familiarized yourself with the "Alienation from the Market Place" concept described on page 529 of this chapter.

Using that concept as a guide, propose a creative strategy that will meet the objective of opening communications with those consumers.

Managerial Assignment

The State Light and Power Company is faced with a continuing dilemma: although consumer demand for its services rises as population within the state grows, the natural resources supplying heat and electricity are not expected to be sufficient to meet that demand. As a Project Director for the utility, you are asked to make recommendations for dealing with this problem within the next few years. There is always the possibility of erecting a nuclear power plant to provide a new energy source, but few residents of the state are interested in finding themselves neighbors to that kind of installation. The alternative is to persuade people to use *less* of the power to which they have become so accustomed.

Research this issue and suggest the best course to take in meeting your customers' future needs.

SELECTED READINGS

Kendall, C. L. and Frederick A. Russ. "Warranty and Complaint Policies: An Opportunity for Marketing Management." *Journal of Marketing Research,* Vol. 39, No. 2 (April 1975), pp. 36–43.

Kerin, Roger and Michael J. Harvey. "Consumer Legislation: A Proactive or Reactive Response to Consumerism?" *Journal of the Academy of Marketing Science,* Vol. 2, No. 4 (Fall 1974), pp. 582–592.

Lipson, Harry A. "Do Corporate Executives Plan for Social Responsibility?" *Business and Society Review* (Winter 1974–1975), pp. 80–81.

McNeil, John. "Federal Programs to Measure Consumer Purchase Expectations, 1946–1973: A Post-Mortem." *Journal of Consumer Research,* Vol. 1, No. 3 (December 1974), pp. 1–10.

Shuptrine, F. Kelly and Frank A. Osmanski. "Marketing's Changing Role: Expanding or Contracting?" *Journal of Marketing Research,* Vol. 39, No. 2 (April 1975), pp. 58–66.

Epilog: The Future of Consumer Behavior Study in Marketing

By the time any textbook on consumer behavior itself becomes available for consumption, some of the material will be dated or subject to reevaluation. This fact may be frustrating for seekers of timeless truths, but it does serve to illustrate one of the few enduring truths—that the nature of marketing changes daily as the society it attempts to serve must change.

What patterns should we look for in the fairly-near future? Some areas seem likeliest to shake the marketer's world (in the planetary as well as personal sense). Here are just a few examples of directions which are apparent now.

New Priorities   Much of our consumption behavior is still based on the premise of boundless natural resources to supply energy for our automobiles, home appliances, and electronic ping-pong games. But our sources of energy are being rapidly depleted. This harsh fact calls for the development of new sources, most notably the controversial harnessing of nuclear energy and the quite promising possibilities for solar heat. Because any widespread use of the sun's benevolent energy now seems a distant goal, consumers may very well be forced to accept nuclear power in the meantime. And since many people tend to associate nuclear manipulation with destructive uses, it will be necessary for policy makers to generate more favorable attitudes toward the prospect of nuclear power plants moving into one's area.

New World Markets   The balance of world influence is shifting from industrialized nations of the West to developing "Third World" nations. This trend is directly related to the resource issue—the concentration of great wealth and power in the Arab nations in exchange for their much-needed oil. And as the once exalted superpowers of Great Britain and Italy suffer economic turmoil, consumers in these "nouveau poor" nations must adjust to lowered product and service expectations, in marked contrast to the spending-spree,

547

nouveau riche behavior of some highly visible Arab oil magnates.

Underdeveloped nations will also pose challenging problems as social marketing efforts are launched to supply food, medical care, and family planning assistance. Will these innovations be readily accepted by the people they are supposed to help? More likely, cultural biases will dictate the need for thorough cross-cultural research before workable systems of product design, promotion, and distribution may be established.

New Life Styles   Most futurists see an "older" American society by the year 2000, when the products of the baby boom of 1945–50 will have reached a stodgier middle age. But complicating this vision are social trends such as the emancipation of women, the greater political and economic influence of subcultural groups, and such possibilities as widespread communal living experiments, a spiraling divorce rate, creating more single parent families, plus whatever lasting benefits may be derived from the current naturalist, spiritualist, and self-actualizing movements.

Increasingly, market segmentation strategies will become more sophisticated as marketers strive to keep pace with the psycho-social composition of target groups. Traditional methods of demographic segmentation, however refined, will probably yield to the more fertile analysis designed to measure life style and psychographic characteristics.

New Media   There are stirrings of revolution in the entertainment industries, and most indicators point to burgeoning growth in the home entertainment field. Consider the probable effects of recent innovations such as the seven-foot color television screen, videotape installations which enable families to create their own TV shows, public access cable-TV stations permitting anyone, for a small fee, to televise whatever they wish in line with FCC "free access" requirements, and services such as Home Box Office which allow viewers the luxury of first-run, uncensored movie-viewing at home . . . with, significantly, no commercial interruptions.

Television programming will be markedly different. Commercials will doubtless remain with us in some form, but not as we see (or suffer through) them today. And the ultimate home viewing development of three-dimensional holograph projection should appear well before the turn of the century.

New Legislation   The disgruntled consumer has found much support in recent legislation regulating products, advertising, and retailing practices. While some observers (mostly marketers) say that the pendulum has swung too far in the regulatory direction, there is little evidence that the current trend will subside. Consumers are more skeptical, more demanding, and more willing to seek redress of their grievances than ever before.

Those who wish to compete for consumer acceptance in the new regulated market place must face certain realities: products must be better designed, honestly portrayed, and backed by meaningful guarantees of expected performance. And with an ever-thickening web of regulations to ensure these lofty standards, consumer research will be directed to very specific goals of consumer need-recognition and satisfaction.

Hopefully, some of the tentative theories and carefully qualified conclusions offered in this text will help a new breed of marketers to meet the demands of a new breed of consumers.

INDEX

ABOUT THE AUTHORS

Harold W. Berkman (Ph.D., St. John's University) is currently Professor of Business Management and Organization and Director of the Executive Master of Business Administration Program at the University of Miami. Prior to his affiliation at Miami he was Professor of Business at C. W. Post Center of Long Island University. Dr. Berkman has published a number of books including: *The Human Relations of Management; Cases and Issues: The Human Relations of Management* (with J Young); *Contemporary and Classical Readings in Human Relations* (Armandi and Barbera, co-editors), *Marketing Update* (Ryans and Vernon, co-editors), and his most current work *Perspectives on International Business* (with Vernon) is scheduled for release in 1978. In addition, he has contributed a number of scholarly articles to various journals. He serves as Director of the Academy of Marketing Science and conference chairman of the annual International Marketing Conference. Dr. Berkman has been involved in various research projects such as airline safety, psychographics, and organizational behavior. He has also served as a consultant to firms in retailing, consumer goods manufacturing, and publishing.

Christopher C. Gilson is Creative Supervisor at Rapp & Collins division of Doyle Dane Bernbach, New York. He has created award-winning advertising campaigns for clients such as Avis Rent-A-Car, Control Data Corporation, Friends of the Earth, GAF, JVC Video Products, Marriott Hotels, Newsweek, Rolling Stone, Save The Children Federation, Scandinavian Airlines, Trinidad-Tobago Tourist Board, and U.S. Industries. Mr. Gilson was graduated magna cum laude from the University of Hartford in 1971, and has studied advertising at New York University and the School of Visual Arts. He has contributed numerous articles to business magazines and journals, and has lectured at Bernard Baruch School of Business, City College of New York and C. W. Post Center of Long Island University.